People and Work in Canada

Industrial and Organizational Psychology

People and Work in Canada

Industrial and Organizational Psychology

E. Kevin Kelloway
SAINT MARY'S UNIVERSITY

Victor M. Catano
SAINT MARY'S UNIVERSITY

Arla L. Day
SAINT MARY'S UNIVERSITY

NELSON / EDUCATION

NELSON EDUCATION

People and Work in Canada:
Industrial and Organizational Psychology

by E. Kevin Kelloway, Victor M. Catano, and Arla L. Day

Vice President, Editorial Director:
Evelyn Veitch

Editor-in-Chief, Higher Education:
Anne Williams

Senior Acquisitions Editor:
Lenore Taylor-Atkins

Marketing Manager:
Ann Byford

Senior Developmental Editor:
Sandy Matos

Photo Researcher:
Jessie Coffey

Permissions Coordinator:
Jessie Coffey

Content Production Manager:
Christine Gilbert

Production Service:
MPS Limited, a Macmillan Company

Copy Editor:
Kelli Howey

Proofreader:
Barbara Storey

Indexer:
David Luljak

Manufacturing Manager—Higher Education
Joanne McNeil

Design Director:
Ken Phipps

Managing Designer:
Franca Amore

Interior Design:
Eugene Lo

Cover Design:
Sharon Lucas

Cover Image:
Lars Thulin/Getty Images

Compositor:
MPS Limited, a Macmillan Company

Printer:
Edwards Brothers Malloy

Library and Archives Canada Cataloguing in Publication

Kelloway, E. Kevin (Edward Kevin), 1959-

People and work in Canada : industrial and organizational psychology / E. Kevin Kelloway, Victor M. Catano, Arla L. Day.

Includes bibliographical references and index.
ISBN 978-0-17-650181-5

1. Psychology, Industrial—Canada—Textbooks.
2. Organizational behavior—Canada—Textbooks. I. Catano, Victor M. (Victor Michael), 1944– II. Day, Arla L. (Arla Lauree), 1968– III. Title.

HF5548.8.K39 2010   158.7
C2010-904693-5

ISBN-10: 0-17-650181-9
ISBN-13: 978-0-17-650181-5

Brief Contents

Contents

Chapter 9 Motivation 253

About the Authors

E. Kevin Kelloway

Dr. Kevin Kelloway is the Canada Research Chair in Occupational Health Psychology at Saint Mary's University, Halifax, Nova Scotia. He received his PhD in Organizational Psychology from Queen's University in 1991 and began his career in the Department of Psychology at the University of Guelph. In 1999 he joined the Faculty of Commerce at Saint Mary's University as Professor of Management and Psychology. In 2006 he was appointed as a Senior Research Fellow at the CN Centre for Occupational Health and Safety. Dr. Kelloway was the founding PhD Program Director for the Saint Mary's Faculty of Commerce (2000–2003), the founding, and current, Director of the CN Centre for Occupational Health and Safety, and a founding principal of the Centre for Leadership Excellence. In 2009 he was appointed as a Tier I Canada Research Chair.

Dr. Kelloway is a prolific researcher, having published over 100 articles, book chapters, and technical reports in addition to 10 authored/edited books. In 2007, Dr. Kelloway received the SMU President's Award for Excellence in Research, and in 2009 he was named a Fellow of both the Society for Industrial and Organizational Psychology and the Association for Psychological Science. In 2010, he was named a Fellow of the Canadian Psychological Association. As a consultant, Dr. Kelloway maintains an active practice consulting to private- and public-sector organizations on issues related to leadership, occupational health psychology, and human resource management.

Victor M. Catano

Dr. Victor M. Catano is Professor and Chairperson of Psychology at Saint Mary's University, Halifax, Nova Scotia. He obtained a B.Sc. in Electrical Engineering from Drexel University in Philadelphia and went on to complete both a master's and a PhD in Psychology at Lehigh University, Bethlehem, Pennsylvania. He is a registered psychologist in Nova Scotia and a member of the Human Resources Association of Nova Scotia (HRANS). Dr. Catano joined the Saint Mary's faculty following completion of his doctoral degree and was instrumental in establishing Saint Mary's master's and doctoral programs in industrial/organizational psychology. He has also served as a special lecturer at the Technical University of Nova Scotia and as a Visiting Research Fellow at the Canadian Forces Personnel Applied Research Unit in Toronto. Dr. Catano has served as President of the Association of Psychologists of Nova Scotia, a member of the Nova Scotia Board of Examiners in Psychology (the body responsible for regulating the profession within Nova Scotia), and President of the Canadian Society of Industrial/Organizational Psychology. He is a past editor of *Canadian Psychology*, and has acted as a reviewer for numerous scholarly journals and granting agencies.

Dr. Catano chairs the Canadian Council of Human Resources Association's (CCHRA) Independent Board of Examiners, the agency responsible for developing and running the examinations and assessments that lead to the CHRP designation. Dr. Catano has extensive consulting experience in personnel selection and assessment, job analysis, utility analysis, occupational families, attitude surveys, productivity issues, statistical analyses and research methodology, and industrial relations. He has served as an expert witness on personnel selection issues before several administrative tribunals. His clients have included NAV CANADA, the Department of National Defence, the Royal Canadian Mounted Police, Asea Brown Bovari, Nova Scotia Government Employees Union, Canadian Society of Association Executives, and the Nova Scotia Nurses Union, among others. He has published over 200 scholarly articles, conference papers, and technical reports. He is the first author of *Recruitment and Selection in Canada*, now in its fourth edition, which is the leading text in this area. His current research interests include personnel psychology, the psychology of labour relations, organizational and environmental constraints on productivity, and the impact of psychological environments on the health, safety, and productivity of workers.

In recognition of his contributions to the science and practice of psychology in Canada, Dr. Catano was elected a Fellow by the Canadian Psychological Association, and an Honorary Member by Canadian Forces Personnel Selection Officers Association. He is the 2003 recipient of the Canadian Psychological Association's Award for Distinguished Contributions to Education and Training and the Canadian Society of Industrial and Organizational Psychology's Distinguished Scientist Award. In 2008, the Human Resources Association of Nova Scotia awarded him an Honorary Membership in recognition of his distinguished contributions to human resources in Canada. In 2009 the Canadian Association of University Teachers presented him with the Donald C. Savage Award in recognition for outstanding achievements in collective bargaining in Canadian universities and colleges.

Arla L. Day

Dr. Arla Day is the Canada Research Chair and Professor in Industrial/Organizational Psychology at Saint Mary's University. She completed her undergraduate degree at the University of Manitoba, and she completed both her master's and PhD degrees at the University of Waterloo. She joined the faculty at Saint Mary's in 1996, and she has worked for the Canadian Forces Leadership Institute as a research consultant. Dr. Day is a founding member of two research and community outreach centres at Saint Mary's: the CN Centre for Occupational Health and Safety and the Centre for Leadership Excellence. She chairs the Nova Scotia Psychological Healthy Workplace Program committee, and she is on the Steering Committee for the American Psychological Association's Business of Practice Network, which oversees state and provincial healthy workplace awards and programs. In 2008, she was named a Fellow of the Canadian Psychological Association.

Dr. Day has authored many articles, book chapters, and conference presentations on her research on healthy workplaces, occupational stress, employee well-being, work–life balance, workplace health interventions, and emotional intelligence. She consults with public and private organizations, and she gives workshops and talks to organizations on issues related to her research expertise.

She tries to put her research into action by balancing her work activities with her non-work activities, which include spending quality time with her friends and family, her husband, her energetic and entertaining daughter, her two overly exuberant dogs, and her one relatively well-behaved horse.

Preface

We had two objectives in writing this text: (1) to present to students and instructors contemporary industrial and organizational research in a Canadian context that is consistent with Canadian legislation and practices, and (2) to celebrate the work of Canadians who have made substantial contributions to I/O psychology. Anyone who has ever taught a course in I/O psychology will appreciate the first objective. Most of the available I/O textbooks are from the United States. Much of the information in those texts is relevant to Canada; however, they also contain information that is irrelevant or inappropriate in a Canadian context (e.g., the two countries have substantially different human rights legislation and traditions that have a dramatic impact on areas in personnel psychology), or omit information that is relevant to Canada (e.g., unions are only rarely discussed in U.S. texts because of the very low unionization rate in that country). Instructors have the choice of either adopting a U.S. text and telling students what parts to disregard, or to cobble together a text, taking chapters from different sources in order to cover the required material. In this text we have tried to be both comprehensive and relevant to the Canadian context.

With regard to the second objective, there is a growing, vibrant, and productive community of I/O psychologists in Canada. Canadians have made a substantial contribution to research in I/O psychology and have advanced our understanding of selection and recruitment, motivation, organizational commitment, unionization, and workplace well-being—to name just a few areas. This research is prominently reported in U.S. textbooks, but in many cases these Canadian contributions are not singled out and recognized as being Canadian (what is more Canadian than not taking credit for your own work?). As instructors we have often challenged our students to "find the hidden Canadian" in these works. In this text we have tried to highlight these "hidden" contributions.

To meet these goals we tried to write a text that incorporated four specific features. First, Canadian content is the hallmark of our text, and the Canadian perspective is particularly critical for issues related to personnel psychology. Many legal issues arise because of the differences in human rights and court decisions. Our book is based on up-to-date legal decisions in Canada and is able to offer insights on recruiting and selection from a Canadian perspective. Second, although most texts offer a review of "stress" at work, we expanded this focus to recognize the newly formed subfield of occupational health psychology. In doing so we consider issues of workplace stress, health and safety in the workplace, and workplace health promotion. Third, the emergence of positive psychology has been seen as a revolution in psychology and has been paralleled by the emergence of positive organizational scholarship. We review the emerging data, suggesting the usefulness of this approach in understanding behaviour in organizations. Finally, throughout the book, we have tried to place special emphasis on areas that, although discussed in the U.S. texts, have a particular relevance for Canada. For example, we devote a chapter to unionization, noting that 30 percent of the Canadian workforce (and more than 85 percent of the public sector) belong to unions—a marked contrast to the U.S. situation, which speaks to the importance of understanding unions and labour relations for Canadian I/O psychology students.

At the same time, we wanted to recognize and celebrate the achievements of Canadian I/O psychologists. The field has a long history in Canada (see Chapter 1) and, as noted throughout the text, we have many accomplishments of which we can be proud. Throughout the text we highlight Canadian research in I/O psychology. In each chapter we include a text box that focuses on the work of one Canadian I/O psychologist who has made a substantial contribution to the subject area of the chapter. As authors, we were impressed by how many times there were multiple candidates that could have been highlighted in a chapter! We could not include everyone—to our colleagues whom we omitted, we beg your understanding.

Structurally, the text is divided into four major sections. The first two chapters provide an introduction to the field of I/O psychology (Chapter 1) and to research methods that provide the basis for much of the work in the field (Chapter 2). The next four chapters focus on issues related to personnel psychology. Job analysis and competency analysis are the focus of Chapter 3, with recruitment and selection being the focus in Chapter 4. Performance management (Chapter 5) and training and development (Chapter 6) round out the focus on personnel issues.

The third major section of the book deals with topics traditional to organizational psychology. Chapter 7 looks at groups and teams. Job attitudes are reviewed in Chapter 8, and motivation is the focus of Chapter 9. Chapter 10 examines issues related to leadership in organizations.

The final section of the book represents emerging areas of enquiry—although some have a long history in I/O psychology, recent developments have led to new ways of thinking about the issues. For example, Chapter 11 deals with counterproductive work behaviours, an area that encompasses traditional areas of enquiry such as absenteeism as well as newer areas of focus (e.g., workplace bullying). Chapter 12 deals with the newly formed subfield of occupational health psychology. In Chapter 13 we address issues related to unionization. Finally, in Chapter 14, we review the most recent development in the field—positive organizational scholarship.

The website (www.iopsych.nelson.com) contains flashcards, the glossary, and other useful resources for students.

Instructors will find the Instructor's Manual a useful supplement in promoting classroom engagement. The Instructor's Manual contains a Test Bank at the end of each chapter. PowerPoint slides are also available on our companion website, www.iopsych.nelson.com. The supplements are available to download only on a password-protected instructor's site or you may contact your Nelson Education Sales Representative for more information.

Acknowledgments

For taking the time to read drafts of the text at every stage, we are grateful to the following reviewers:

Wendi Adair, University of Waterloo

Barbara Bryden, Alberta Health Services at University of Calgary and Yorkville University

Bernadette Campbell, Carleton University

Greg A. Chung-Yan, University of Windsor

Lisa Fiksenbaum, York University

Leah Hamilton, University of Western Ontario

Michael P. Leiter, Acadia University

John Marasigan, Kwantlen Polytechnic University

Sarah Ross, University of Western Ontario

Your advice and comments were especially helpful in shaping the final product.

We also acknowledge with gratitude the efforts of the editorial team at Nelson Education Ltd. Sandy Matos, our Senior Developmental Editor, who encouraged and shepherded the writing of this text; Lenore Taylor-Atkins, our Senior Acquisitions Editor; Ann Byford, our Marketing Manager; Kelli Howey, our Copy Editor; and Barbara Storey, our Proofreader. We appreciate all your support during every stage of this process.

In addition to being incredibly productive, the I/O community in Canada is incredibly supportive, and we are appreciative of our mentors and colleagues who continue to influence our work and the field of I/O psychology. Finally, our enjoyment and understanding of I/O psychology is always shaped by the students enrolled in the SMU graduate programs; we thank you.

E. Kevin Kelloway, PhD
Canada Research Chair in Occupational Health Psychology
Professor of Psychology
Saint Mary's University

Victor M. Catano, PhD
Chair and Professor of Psychology
Saint Mary's University

Arla L. Day, PhD
Canada Research Chair in Industrial/Organizational Psychology
Professor of Psychology
Saint Mary's University

CHAPTER 1

Introduction to Industrial/ Organizational Psychology

This chapter provides an introduction to the field of industrial/organizational (I/O) psychology. After reviewing the definition and scope of I/O psychology, the chapter considers the historical development of the field, the current organization of the field, and current challenges facing I/O psychologists.

Chapter Learning Outcomes

After reading this chapter you should be able to

- Define the field of I/O psychology
- Describe the scientist–practitioner perspective and how it influences I/O psychology
- Recognize the major influences on the development of I/O psychology
- Identify current challenges facing the field

Introduction: History and Development of I/O Psychology

According to the most recent official census, there are just under 32 million people living in Canada (Martel & Caron-Malenfant, 2009).[1] If one excludes the 10 million or so residents who are over the age of 65 (the traditional retirement age), and those under the age of 15, then approximately 74 percent of Canadians (i.e., 17 million people) are employed in the various sectors comprising our economy (see Table 1.1). The vast majority of working Canadians work in service

[1] The 2006 census is the last official count of the population. Statistics Canada also maintains an ongoing estimated population, which is just over 33 million people at the time of this writing (see http://www.statcan.gc.ca/ig-gi/pop-ca-eng.htm).

TABLE 1.1

Canadian Employment by Industry and Sector

Industry	Number of Workers
Good Producing Sector	3,714,600
Agriculture	319,500
Forestry, fishing, mining, oil, and gas	313,500
Utilities	150,300
Construction	1,166,800
Manufacturing	1,765,000
Service Producing Sector	13,123,400
Trade	2,662,900
Transportation and warehousing	797,700
Finance, insurance, real estate, and leasing	1,121,100
Professional, scientific, and technical services	1,199,800
Business, building, and other support services	645,800
Educational services	1,188,400
Health care and social assistance	1,946,800
Information, culture, and recreation	791,500
Accommodation and food services	1,032,000
Other services	805,400
Public administration	932,000

Source: Adapted from Statistics Canada, *Labour Force Information*, 71-001-XWE 2009 September 13 to 19, 2009, Released October 9, 2009.

industries, with a smaller percentage (approximately 23 percent) employed in the goods-producing sector of the economy.

For each of these 17 million individuals, their role as worker will be one of the most important adult roles they will ever experience. Although employment is the primary means through which they will obtain the economic necessities of life, work will also be an important determinant of their health and well-being (see, for example, Kelloway & Day, 2005; Warr, 1987) as well as the quality of their family relationships (Barling, 1990). Each of these workers also has an employer or client—someone who pays the individual for services or goods. Employers (or clients) are interested in ensuring that workers are both efficient and effective.

The Definition of I/O Psychology

Industrial/organizational (I/O) psychology addresses both of these concerns. The Canadian Society for Industrial & Organizational Psychology (CSIOP), for example, defines I/O psychology as follows:

> Industrial-Organizational Psychology is a field of both scientific research and professional practice that aims to further the welfare of people by: understanding the behaviour of individuals and organizations in the work place: helping individuals pursue meaningful and enriching work;

industrial/organizational (I/O) psychology

A field of both scientific research and professional practice that aims to further the welfare of people by understanding the behaviour of individuals and organizations in the workplace, helping individuals pursue meaningful and enriching work, and assisting organizations in the effective management of their human resources

People and Work in Canada

and assisting organizations in the effective management of their human resources. (Kline, 1996, p. 206)

(Source of definition: T.J.B. Kline (1996). Defining the field of industrial-organizational psychology. *Canadian Psychology*, 37 (4): 205-209. Reprinted by permission of the Canadian Psychological Association.)

Note that the definition focuses our attention on both individual (i.e., helping individuals pursue meaningful and enriching work) and organizational (i.e., effective management of human resources) goals. As the statement goes on to point out, these broad objectives mean that the field of I/O psychology overlaps and intersects with many other areas of enquiry.

Within psychology, I/O psychologists often share interests with health psychologists, social psychologists, and counselling psychologists; they also have strong backgrounds in psychometrics, statistics, and research methods. Outside of psychology, I/O psychology overlaps with business topics such as organizational behaviour, human resource management, and industrial relations, as well as with other disciplines such as organizational sociology.

This broad definition also implies that I/O psychologists offer a broad array of services, and Kline (1996, p. 206) offers an illustrative list of the kinds of things I/O psychologists might be called upon to do:

- "carrying out task analyses,
- determining the knowledge, skills, abilities, and personal characteristics needed for certain jobs,
- providing recommendations on how to assess potential employees or actually conducting the assessments,
- providing guidance on how to train employees,
- assessing work performance and the motivation of employees,
- determining group effects on work performance,
- examining communication within and commitment to the organization,
- understanding the human-machine system and the complexities of their interactions,
- assisting in the selection and training of competent leaders,
- assisting in career assessment and career development,
- assisting in changing the organization to become more effective, and
- assisting in managing relationships between employees and managers."

(Source: T.J.B. Kline (1996). Defining the field of industrial-organizational psychology. *Canadian Psychology*, 37 (4): 205-209. Reprinted by permission of the Canadian Psychological Association.)

As Kline points out, this is only a partial list of activities—the role of I/O psychologists is continually expanding in response to demands from organizational and individual clients. For example, the newly emerged subfield of **occupational health psychology** (see Chapter 12) consolidates the interests of many I/O psychologists to focus on issues of individual health and well-being in organizations.

The Scientist-Practitioner Perspective

Aside from the content areas described above, one of the most important aspects of the CSIOP definition is the description of I/O psychology as comprising both scientific research and professional practice. This is an expression of what is more commonly known as the **scientist-practitioner perspective**.

occupational health psychology

A field of research and practice that is based, at least partially, on I/O psychology and is concerned with the health and safety of individuals at work

scientist-practitioner perspective

The view that I/O psychology focuses on both scientific research and applied professional practice

Like most psychologists, I/O psychologists are trained as social scientists. They draw on theories and methods of psychology to understand what is going on in organizations and to improve work practices in organizations. Most I/O psychologists have a thorough grounding in the methods of scientific research and draw on a number of tools including surveys, experiments, and quasi-experiments (see Chapter 2) in order to explain individual and organizational behaviour.

At the same time, I/O psychologists are applied scientists whose scientific work is informed by practice. Many of the research questions addressed by I/O psychologists (e.g., how do we design nondiscriminatory selection procedures, what is the best way to train computer programmers, how can we protect first-line responders from the adverse effects of repeated traumatic exposure) come from day-to-day experience in organizations and are intended to solve common problems.

Considerable variation exists in how individual I/O psychologists enact their dual role as scientists and practitioners. I/O psychologists who work primarily in universities as teachers and researchers may, for example, lean toward the "science" end—focusing their activities on research and publication. I/O psychologists who work primarily in a consulting role may be more attuned to the concerns of practice and less involved with research and publication. Nonetheless, all I/O psychologists share a common body of knowledge that includes both the science and the practitioner perspectives.

Training in I/O Psychology

Like its American counterpart (the Society for Industrial & Organizational Psychology, SIOP), CSIOP has published guidelines for training in I/O psychology (Kline, 1989). These guidelines provide the outlines for graduate-level (i.e., master's and PhD) training in I/O psychology. In essence, the guidelines reinforce the scientist-practitioner model by suggesting that:

a. applicants to graduate school in I/O psychology should have an undergraduate degree in psychology from a recognized institution; and

b. training programs in I/O psychology incorporate applied experiences or internships that are supervised by an I/O psychologist, in order to acquire skills in human resource management and consultation.

Although the training guidelines recognize that not every program can meet the full complement of 22 different areas, they also specify the core areas in which I/O psychologists should be trained. These competency areas include 11 core areas that are central to the field of I/O psychology, and 5 complementary areas that are closely related to the field of I/O psychology in addition to 6 secondary areas that are more distantly related to I/O psychology (see Box 1.1).

As shown in Table 1.2, there are at least 10 graduate programs (7 in English, 3 in French) in I/O psychology in Canada. In addition to these, there are

Box 1.1

Competency Areas in I/O Psychology

Core Areas:

1. Ethical, Legal, and Professional Issues in I-O Psychology
2. Organizational Theory
3. Work Motivation Theory
4. Statistical Methods/Data Analysis
5. Research Methods
6. Personnel Selection, Placement, and Classification
7. Performance Appraisal/Feedback
8. Measurement of Individual Differences
9. Organizational Development Theory
10. Job and Task Analysis
11. Criterion Development Theory

14. Attitude Theory
15. Career Development Theory
16. Human Performance/Human Factors/Ergonomics

Second Areas:

17. Small Group Theory and Processes
18. Decision Theory
19. Program Evaluation
20. Consumer Behaviour
21. Fields of Psychology
22. History and Systems of Psychology

Complementary Areas:

12. Individual Assessment
13. Training: Theory, Program Design, and Evaluation

Source: T.J.B. Kline (1996). Defining the field of industrial-organizational psychology. *Canadian Psychology*, 37 (4): 205–209. Reprinted by permission of the Canadian Psychological Association.

many individuals working in the field of I/O who may be affiliated with graduate programs in other areas. Moreover, a large number of I/O psychologists work in business schools in Canada, and graduate training in organizational behaviour or human resource management often draws heavily on the field of I/O psychology.

Table 1.2

Graduate Training Programs in I/O Psychology

University	PhD	Master's	Url
Saint Mary's University	X	X	http://www.smu.ca/academic/science/psych/PhD_information.doc
Université de Montréal	X	X	http://www.psy.umontreal.ca/
Université de Québec à Montréal	X	X	http://www.psycho.uqam.ca/
Université de Sherbrooke	X	X	http://www.usherbrooke.ca/psychologie/
University of Guelph	X	X	http://www.uoguelph.ca/iopsychology/
University of Waterloo	X	X	http://www.psychology.uwaterloo.ca/gradprog/
University of Western Ontario	X	X	http://psychology.uwo.ca/io.htm
University of Windsor	X	X	http://cronus.uwindsor.ca/units/psychology/applied.nsf/
University of Calgary	X	X	http://www.psych.ucalgary.ca/research/groups/io.htm

Note: Information is based on published program descriptions issued by the respective universities.

The History of I/O Psychology

For the most part, I/O psychology is a creature of the twentieth and twenty-first centuries. As a relatively young field of enquiry, the major developments in I/O psychology have all occurred since the early 1900s. In Canada, I/O psychology was even slower to develop and really has emerged only since World War II. We will begin by considering the development of I/O psychology in the United States, and then consider how Canadian I/O psychology fits into this larger history.

The Early Years

Like any other field, I/O psychology did not appear out of nowhere—rather, it was a natural outgrowth of the times. Many potential influences on the development of I/O can be identified, but historians (e.g., Katzell & Austin, 1992; see also Koppes, 2007) have tended to focus on a handful of the most important. Indeed, one early textbook in I/O psychology (Viteles, 1932) suggested that the major influences were economic, social, and psychological. Economically, there was a boom in industrial activity around the turn of the twentieth century, and as a result a great interest in the notion of efficiency. It is not at all coincidental that the first two books in I/O psychology were entitled *Increasing Human Efficiency in Business* (Scott, 1911) and *Psychology and Industrial Efficiency* (Münsterberg, 1913)—indeed, the notion of efficiency was the hot topic of the day.

At the societal level, there were also great changes. Growing acceptance of the notions of Darwinian evolution was changing the way that individuals thought about communities and society. At the same time, the Protestant work ethic (Weber, 1905/2000) was highly supportive of the goals of capitalism, which became enshrined as the basis of society. Not surprisingly, any field that claimed to advance the interests and tenets of capitalism was widely accepted.

Finally, psychology itself was undergoing a revolutionary change. Growth of the experimental method and a focus on individual differences paved the way for much of what would subsequently be called I/O psychology. Science was increasingly seen as the answer for all problems, and the application of the scientific method to more practical problems was only a matter of time.

One of the great experimentalists was the German psychologist Wilhelm Wundt; although Wundt was not particularly interested in workplace topics himself, his lab was to be the starting point for much of I/O psychology. For example, the German psychiatrist Emil Kraepelin trained under Wundt and in his own research became interested in the study of work performance and fatigue (1896). Wundt also trained two new psychologists who were to provide a seminal influence on I/O psychology: Walter Dill Scott and Hugo Münsterberg.

Walter Dill Scott earned his PhD in the Wundt lab in 1900 and relocated back to the United States, where he became a professor at Northwestern University. He subsequently moved to a position at Carnegie Tech, where he became the first person in North America to receive the title of professor of applied psychology (Vinchur & Koppes, 2007). During his career he became interested in a variety of practical problems related to I/O psychology, including the application of psychological, principles to advertising and personnel selection. Although some have labelled Scott the "first" industrial psychologist, claim to that title is also hotly contested by a fellow graduate of Wundt's lab—Hugo Münsterberg.

Münsterberg was both a psychologist and a physician; he trained in Wundt's experimental psychology lab and subsequently completed his medical training at the University of Heidelberg. After his training he accepted a position at Harvard University. Although he is on record as opposing the application of psychology (Benjamin, 2006), he became the foremost promoter of applied psychology, writing more than 20 books on the topic between 1906 and 1916. In addition to his claim as the first I/O psychologist, Münsterberg also pioneered the fields of educational and forensic psychology. His book *Psychology and Industrial Efficiency* (Münsterberg, 1913) was enormously influential and is often cited as the first text for I/O psychologists. Historians of the field (e.g., Landy, 1997) typically count Münsterberg as *the* founder of I/O psychology.

As Koppes and Pickren (2007) note, Münsterberg is quite properly recognized as the most influential of the early I/O psychologists even if he was not the first. However, many individuals at the same time were becoming interested in problems of industry. In addition to Scott and Münsterberg, notable early contributors to I/O psychology would include Walter Bingham (the founder of the Carnegie Tech applied psychology program), Arthur Kornhauser (a graduate of Carnegie Tech who pioneered the study of job stress and mental health), Louis Leon Thurstone (a pioneer in measurement theory and statistics but who also worked in selection and vocational guidance), and James McKeen Cattell, the founder of The Psychological Corporation, the first I/O consulting firm. Numerous other individuals contributed to the development of the field (see Vinchur & Koppes, 2007), but for the most part the early years of I/O psychology in North America were characterized by individuals working in isolation.

World War I

This situation was to change dramatically as a result of America's entry into World War I. The American military was faced with the problem of selecting and assigning to jobs an unprecedented number of applicants in the most efficient way possible. Robert Yerkes, then president of the American Psychological Association and a professor at Harvard, convinced the military that the newly developed practice of standardized intelligence testing could provide the answer to this problem. He developed a standardized paper-and-pencil test known as **Army Alpha** (Yerkes, 1921), used for the selection and placement of individuals in the U.S. armed forces. Because a large number of candidates had poor literacy skills in English, they also developed a nonverbal equivalent that was known as **Army Beta**.

Although both Army Alpha and Army Beta were abandoned for use after the war, the implementation of this testing program had a marked influence

Army Alpha

A measure of cognitive ability developed for placement of U.S. soldiers during World War I

Army Beta

A nonverbal intelligence test developed for placement of U.S. soldiers during World War I

Chapter 1: Introduction to Industrial/Organizational Psychology on the field. In addition to being the training ground for many who would become well-known I/O psychologists, the success of the program convinced many of the value of selection tests. When military commanders hung up their uniforms and returned to industry they brought their recollection of formal selection testing with them. The new field of I/O psychology was founded largely on this success in selection, and the selection and placement of individuals in organizations continues to be a dominant theme in I/O psychology (see Chapter 4).

Bingham, Thorndike, and Scott also worked with the military in the development of selection tests (Salas, DeRouin, & Gade, 2007). In doing so they pioneered the use of **job analysis** (see Chapter 3) as a means of understanding job requirements. In popularizing the use of these techniques in service of the war effort, these psychologists provided early evidence that the techniques and methods of psychology could be used to answer the problems of industry. In doing so, the field of industrial psychology was born.

job analysis

A way of understanding job tasks and requirements through systematic analysis

Between the Wars: Birth of the Human Relations Movement

Although industrial psychology well established and focused on issues related to selection, training, and job analysis, there was not much interest in issues related to employee morale, group processes, or job attitudes. The seminal event that led industrial psychologists to expand their scope of inquiry to include these new topics was the conduct of the highly influential Hawthorne studies (Highhouse, 2007).

The Hawthorne studies were a series of studies conducted at the Hawthorne Works of the Western Electric Company. As purveyors of electrical devices, the Western Electric Company had a financial interest in demonstrating the value of their lamps that produced more light per watt of electricity than did those of their competitors. Using their own workplace as a lab, they adopted the techniques of applied psychology to study the effects of varying illumination levels on worker productivity. Although the truth of the story is difficult to ascertain (Highhouse, 2007), in essence the researchers found that productivity improved regardless of the change in working conditions. That is, when researchers increased the level of illumination, productivity went up—and when they decreased the level of illumination, productivity also went up!

Hawthorne effect

The suggestion that any intervention will have the desired effect

One explanation of this phenomenon has become known as the **Hawthorne effect**. In essence the Hawthorne effect suggests that any intervention might have the desired effect. That is, simply by paying more attention to the workers, the researchers inadvertently produced an increase in productivity. The merits of this explanation are hotly debated to this day (Adair, 1984). However a more important outcome of the Hawthorne studies is that the researchers were led to think about other aspects of the workplace—including the dynamics of small groups, job attitudes, and even the study of job-related stress and well-being. These content areas became the basis of organizational psychology and would eventually be merged with industrial psychology to form the field we now know as industrial/organizational psychology.

World War II

Both industrial and organizational psychology continued to flourish as fields of enquiry leading up to, and through, World War II. As the Americans considered entry into the Second World War, they recalled the success of psychology in World War I and formed an Emergency Committee in Psychology sponsored by the National Research Council as part of their preparation for war (Salas et al., 2007). The intent of the committee was to link the military system with organized psychology.

As had been done during World War I, psychologists developed selection instruments to screen and place recruits. Perhaps the best known of these was the Army General Classification Test. However, psychologists also became involved in selection for specialized roles, such as the aviation psychology program that focused in part on the selection of fighter pilots. John Flanagan, later to become well-known as the originator of the **critical incident technique** (see Chapter 3), was involved in this effort and subsequently became head of the aviation program. The **assessment centre**, a well-established method of selection (see Chapter 4), was originally developed as a technique for selecting saboteurs and spies (Koppes & Pickren, 2007).

Unlike during World War I, psychologists in World War II became involved in a host of activities expanding beyond selection. The design of training and training techniques, as well as the optimal design of workplaces and equipment, were also foci of enquiry. Just after World War II, Samuel Stouffer (1949) published *The American Soldier*, which included consideration of topics that would be familiar to any modern-day organizational psychologist—job satisfaction, motivation, perceived justice, and group cohesion were all covered in his treatise, showing that organizational psychology also flourished during World War II. Stouffer's (1949) work is still considered an influential landmark and his work on post-traumatic stress reactions continues to be cited in the more recent literature on post-traumatic stress (e.g., Lamerson & Kelloway, 1996).

Post World War II

Again, the cessation of hostilities in World War II meant that many people returned to their civilian jobs with the memory of psychological techniques and interventions that had proven successful in dealing with many human resource issues. The booming economy, with its demands for labour, meant that advances made in personnel selection and other areas of enquiry such as work motivation and leadership became firmly entrenched in the normal operation of organizations. In 1945, Division 14 (Industrial and Business Psychology) of the American Psychological Association was formed, and by 1950, the field of industrial/organizational psychology was firmly established.

Perhaps the single most influential event post World War II was the passage of the Civil Rights Act of 1964 in the United States. Because the Act prohibits discrimination in employment on a number of grounds, there was great impetus for organizations to institute fair and nondiscriminatory hiring practices—a challenge to which industrial/organizational psychologists rushed to respond, furthering work on employment practices and test validation.

critical incident technique

A widely used technique of job analysis developed by Flanagan

assessment centre

A widely used selection technique, originally developed to select potential spies

In the same time frame, a new generation (subsequently to be known as the baby boom generation) began to enter the workforce, and society was undergoing many changes in ideology and attitudes. Greater attention was focused on issues of employee morale, motivation, and job satisfaction. Individuals began to demand more meaningful work, and psychologists such as Frederick Herzberg argued that there was an economic logic to the demand, in that "happy workers were productive workers." Although this hypothesis is still being debated today (Cropanzano & Wright, 2001), it led to an explosion of job satisfaction research. Indeed, by 1976, Locke had identified more than 5,000 empirical articles dealing with the topic of job satisfaction.

In 1965, Kornhauser pioneered the modern study of job stress with his publication *The Mental Health of Industrial Workers*. His book was seminal in that it led researchers to focus on issues such as job pacing and control. The government-sponsored quality-of-employment surveys conducted through the University of Michigan (Quinn & Staines, 1978) extended this analysis, showing the links between work conditions and individual health and safety. These results led the then Secretary of State to commission the widely influential report *Work in America* (1974). Arguably, these key studies led to the formation of the new field of occupational health psychology (Sauter & Hurrell, 1999), in addition to leading organizational psychologists to focus on issues of job stress.

These changes are seen in the evolving name of Division 9 of the American Psychological Association (APA). Originally the Division of Industrial and Business Psychology, in 1962 the name was changed to the Division of Industrial Psychology. In 1973, it became the Division of Industrial and Organizational Psychology, and in 1982 it gained autonomy from APA by incorporating as a separate organization: The Society of Industrial Organizational Psychology. At time of this writing, the society is considering yet another name change. Although the results are as yet unknown, the options being considered all exclude the word "industrial" (i.e., The Society for Organizational Psychology, the Society for Work Psychology, and The Society for Work and Organizational Psychology), reflecting the fact that I/O psychologists are involved in a wide range of organizations beyond the traditional smokestack industries of the early twentieth century.

I/O-eh? Canadian I/O Psychology

The development of industrial/organizational psychology in Canada lagged behind that in the United States. Up until World War II there had been no significant presence of I/O psychology in Canada. Webster (1988) traces I/O in Canada to 1928, when Sun Life hired Gerald P. Cosgrove as personnel supervisor. Prior to the formation of the Canadian Psychological Association in 1938, there were estimated to be only a handful of professional psychologists practising in Canada (Bois, 1949), with an additional 40 psychologists or so working in universities across the country (Wright, 1974).

Just as I/O psychology in the United States was given a "boost" by the two world wars, the story of Canadian psychology really begins with the formation of the Canadian Psychological Association (CPA) just prior to World War II.

In anticipation of the coming hostilities, discussions between government representatives and psychologists were held to discuss the potential contributions of psychologists to the war effort. The psychologists were represented by faculty from the University of Toronto, Queen's University, and McGill University in early meetings in 1939. This was to begin a longstanding and productive collaboration between Canadian I/O psychology and the military (MacMillan, Stevens & Kelloway, 2009), as well as initiating the formation of the Canadian Psychological Association.

The Canadian National Research Council created a War Committee (previously CPA's Test Construction Committee), which was subsequently divided into two separate groups. One was responsible for pilot selection for the Royal Canadian Air Force (RCAF), which operated primarily out of the University of Toronto; the other was responsible for development of the **M test**, which was used for selection and placement of both soldiers and officers in the Army. Interestingly, the development of the highly successful M test was entirely funded by two insurance companies (London Life and Sun Life) with no public money spent on the effort.

M test
A Canadian cognitive ability test developed during World War II

Psychologists were also involved in numerous other activities related to the war effort, for example the establishment of day care centres that allowed women to enter the workforce to replace the male workers who had been called up to active service (Wright, 1974)—perhaps an early sign of psychologists' interest in the balance of work and family concerns (see Chapter 12).

Although psychologists of all specialties participated in the war effort, industrial/organizational psychology in Canada really has its roots in the work of McGill University Professor Ed Webster. A native of Saskatchewan and a graduate of McGill, Webster joined the faculty after a period of service doing morale research during World War II (Rowe, 1990). Although he made many contributions to psychology in Canada, at least three of his contributions substantially advanced the state of I/O psychology.

First, in his scholarly activities, Webster's work on the employment interview was influential in shaping the entire field of personnel selection. His 1964 book *Decision Making in the Employment Interview* is considered a classic in industrial psychology (Rowe, 1990). Gary Latham succinctly described the contributions of Ed Webster:

> While others were content with documenting its lack of reliability and validity, Webster and his students were among the first to conduct systematic experiments to understand what was wrong with the interview and what had to be done to correct it. This work was so heuristic that it has affected over two decades of laboratory and field research on the selection interview. (1988, p. 13)

Second, Webster took an active role in administrative matters. In addition to chairing his own department (Rowe, 1990), Webster wrote the report of the Couchiching conference, which established standards for graduate training in psychology. The guidelines he expressed became the dominant model for training graduate students in Canada. Finally, Webster was a professor who supervised his own graduate students—one of these was Patricia Rowe, who was to make her own substantial and lasting contribution to I/O psychology in Canada.

Patricia (Pat) Rowe went to McGill to study I/O psychology with Ed Webster. She conducted her own influential research on the employment interview, and graduated with her PhD in 1960. Rowe accepted a position at the University of Waterloo, where she founded and singlehandedly ran what is arguably the most long-established I/O graduate program in Canada. Rowe supervised many of the I/O psychologists practising and teaching in Canada today: her name is virtually synonymous with I/O psychology in Canada. In modelling her program after the McGill program, Rowe ensured institutional linkages between her graduate program, consulting firms, and major employers such as the Canadian Forces and the Public Service Commission of Canada. Students in her program frequently did internships in these organizations. Eventually, employees of the organizations would return to her program to complete their graduate education. Pat Rowe's influence as a sustainer and promoter of I/O psychology cannot be overestimated.

By the 1980s several other graduate programs had developed, many of which were based on the Waterloo model. Programs at the University of Calgary, University of Western Ontario, and Queen's University (the I/O program is now defunct) all offered graduate programs leading to a PhD in some area of I/O psychology. Saint Mary's University and the University of Guelph both offered a terminal master's degree, although both now offer PhD programs. Other universities offer graduate education in organizational psychology under the auspices of their programs in applied social psychology.

The Development of CSIOP

Although the formation of the Canadian Psychological Association was prompted by concerns central to I/O psychology, the development of a separate section for I/O would have to wait nearly 40 years. Indeed, it was not until 1972 that CPA had grown sufficiently to warrant the formation of separate sections for subspecialties. To be granted division status, at least 50 members had to sign a petition that included a statement of purpose and the goals of the proposed division (Canadian Psychological Association, 1973). The initial two divisions were experimental psychology and applied psychology, with the latter including many I/O psychologists.

In 1974, prompted by his perception that CPA did not adequately represent I/O psychology, Gary Latham decided to organize a special interest group in I/O psychology within the applied division. The initial meeting of what would become CSIOP was held in the spring of 1975. The initial association boasted 22 members, some of whom (e.g., Robert Haccoun, Lorne Kendall, John Tivendell) would go on to play pivotal roles in the new society.

As CPA and the I/O interest group both grew there were inevitable tensions. Throughout the 1980s CPA considered various organizational structures, eventually abolishing the notion of divisions and establishing sections. The I/O interest group became Section 14 of the newly reorganized CPA. The section was very active in CPA and in promoting guidelines on professional issues (e.g., testing, graduate education, ethics). Today CSIOP (Section 14) boasts

Patricia Rowe

Dr. Patricia Rowe is unequivocally recognized and respected as *the* female pioneer of Canadian I/O psychology. She not only initiated the I/O program at the University of Waterloo but also mentored and supervised more than 75 postgraduate-level students. Dr. Rowe has also extended her expertise in the realms of consulting, cooperative education, and quality assessment of higher education. Dr. Rowe completed her Bachelor of Arts (Honours) at the University of Toronto in 1956, followed by a Master of Arts through Dalhousie University in 1957. Her master's thesis focused on leisure time, studying the flip side of work. Dr. Rowe's interest in this subject stemmed from early employment as a playground supervisor. From 1957–1960, she pursued her doctoral degree at McGill University, studying with Dr. Edward Webster. His interest in selection interviews influenced Dr. Rowe's choice of dissertation, specifically, "Individual Differences in Selection Decisions," which focused on Canadian Forces selection interviews, finding ways to improve selection for military service. During her career, Dr. Rowe published close to 50 studies—including many seminal works, notably Tucker and Rowe (1976)—and she presented at more than 50 symposia and addresses. Dr. Rowe is a fellow of CPA and a member of CSIOP, APA, SIOP, and the World Association of Cooperative Education. She has been the recipient of numerous honours and awards, some of which include the S.H. Janes Silver Medal in psychology from Victoria College, 1956; several awards for her cooperative education research; and an award for distinguished contributions to I/O psychology through CPA in 2000.

Source: Courtesy of Patricia Rowe.

approximately 400 members (see Figure 1.1). The section plays an active role in CPA, offers a very active program of activities at the annual meeting of the CPA, and runs both a newsletter and a listserv for members.

I/O Psychology in Quebec

Membership in CSIOP is open to all Canadian I/O psychologists, and includes many francophones both from Quebec and the rest of Canada. Indeed, as shown in Table 1.3, francophone I/O psychologists have frequently served on the executive of the society. In addition to this involvement, francophone I/O psychologists in Quebec are represented by the Société Québécoise de Psychologie du Travail et des Organisations (SQPTO). Indeed, the membership of SQPTO is comparable to that of CSIOP, indicating that there are many I/O psychologists

FIGURE 1.1

Membership in CSIOP

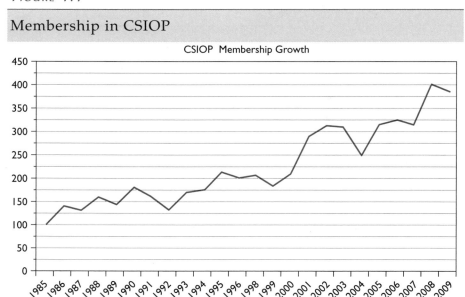

CSIOP Membership Growth

Source: Reprinted by permission of Danielle Durepos.

practising in Quebec and other provinces of Canada. Like CSIOP, the SQPTO has as its mission the promotion of I/O psychology. In addition to hosting an annual conference, the SQPTO hosts regular dinner conferences in each of the four regions (Quebec City, Eastern Townships, Ottawa, and Montreal).

As Forest (2006) points out, English and French I/O psychology continue to exist as the "two solitudes" in many respects. Both CSIOP and

TABLE 1.3

Chairs of CSIOP 1975–2010

Year	Chair	Year	Chair	Year	Chair
1975–1977	Gary Latham	1990–1991	Willi Wiesner	2000–2001	John Meyer
1977–1978	Ken Grant	1991–1992	Suzanne Simpson	2001–2002	Ramona Bobocel
1978–1980	Patricia Rowe	1992–1993	Durhanne Wong–Reiger	2002–2003	Arla Day
1980–1981	Michael McCarrey	1993–1994	Rick Hackett	2003–2004	Patricia Rowe
1981–1982	Robert Haccoun	1994–1995	Terry Prociuk	2004–2005	Natalie Allen
1982–1983	Paul Oeltjen	1995–1996	Theresa Kline	2005–2006	Marjorie Kerr
1983–1984	Tom Janz	1996–1997	Joan Finnegan	2006–2007	Stephane Brutus
1984–1986	Victor Catano	1997–1998	Stephen Harvey	2007–2008	Steve Harvey
1986–1988	Stephen Cronshaw	1997–1998	Brenda Tomini	2008–2009	Kevin Kelloway
1988–1989	Stephen Norman	1998–1999	Lorne Sulsky	2009–2010	Peter Hausdorf
1989–1990	Marc Berwald	1999–2000	Gary Johns	2010–2011	Cheryl Lamerson

Source: Reprinted by permission of Danielle Durepos.

SQPTO have established definitions of I/O psychology and training guidelines, and both conduct regular conferences. However, the two societies work largely independently, with little overlap or consultation (Forest, 2006). For example, in contrast to the definition and competency areas of I/O psychology described earlier, the SQPTO define I/O psychology in terms of five major areas of practice: (a) testing and evaluation, (b) organizational development and diagnosis, (c) training and coaching, (d) career management and reassignment, and (e) employee assistance programs and psychological health (Forest, 2006). Although there is growing recognition of the benefits of the two societies working together, language remains for now a formidable challenge to collaboration. Efforts to overcome this hurdle have been, to date, sporadic and have not resulted in substantial agreement on ways in which the two groups of I/O psychology can work together.

The Contribution of Canadian I/O Psychologists

Compared to our American counterparts, Canadian I/O psychology has always been much smaller organizationally. SIOP, for example, boasts approximately 4,000 members in comparison to only 400 members in CSIOP. Despite our smaller numbers, Canadians have made notable and substantial contributions to the field of I/O psychology. In addition to highlighting the contribution of Ed Webster, Latham (1988) notes that many Canadian I/O psychologists have made substantial contributions to the field. These include the work of Lorne Kendall on performance appraisal, Victor Vroom on the expectancy theory of motivation, Martin Evans and Robert House on the path goal of leadership, and Gary Johns and John Chadwick-Jones's work on absenteeism. To this list might be added Gary Latham's own work on goal setting and performance appraisal, the development of the three-component model of organizational commitment by Natalie Allen and John Meyer, and the contributions to occupational health psychology and leadership by Julian Barling. Arguably the contributions of Canadian I/O psychologists to the field are substantially greater than one might expect given our numbers.

Current and Projected Trends Influencing I/O Psychology

Throughout the history of I/O psychology, the field has been defined by its response to the needs of the time. In both Canada and the U.S., the field of I/O psychology was born out of, or given impetus by, the wartime need for personnel selection on an unprecedented scale. The post-war economic boom and the influx of the post-war baby boomers into the workforce led to concerns tied to employee attitudes, motivation, and retention. The emergence of the civil rights movement in the United States and the promulgation of human rights codes in Canada led I/O psychologists to focus on issues of test bias and fairness in selection systems. As a field, I/O psychology continues to evolve and focus its attention on emerging challenges.

Technology and the Changing Nature of Work

Technology has emerged as a major challenge to our understanding of what constitutes a workplace. Increasingly, employees can work at home, in their cars, or in locations that are remote from a central workplace. Technology poses new challenges and reframes old challenges for the field of I/O psychology. For example, leadership is a topic with an extensive history in I/O psychology (see Chapter 10). However, the challenges of remote or virtual leadership are just now beginning to be understood (e.g., Kelley & Kelloway, 2008; Kelloway et al., 2003). Just how does one "lead" employees whom one never sees in a traditional face-to-face setting? The rapid adoption of technology also leads to the possibility of enhanced stress (e.g., Day, Scott & Kelloway, 2010) as employees are increasingly required to be electronically connected, and responsive, to the workplace at all times. Although aggression and incivility at work is certainly not a new topic (Kelloway, Barling, & Hurrell, 2006), the advent of new technology leads to new ways of expressing aggression, for example **cyberaggression** (Weatherbee & Kelloway, 2006).

cyberaggression

The expression of aggression through computer-mediated communication (e.g., email)

Although technology is a major influence, we are also continually changing our ways of working. For example, most organizations now require and expect individuals to work in teams (Allen & Hecht, 2004), and this has led I/O psychologists to focus more specifically on group dynamics and influences on team performance in organizations.

Our understanding of what is, or is not, expected in the workplace is also changing. For example, absenteeism is one of the most frequently studied topics in I/O psychology (e.g., Darr & Johns, 2008). In recent years, the topic of **presenteeism** (i.e., the notion that individuals show up to work even though they might be sick and not capable of working up to their normal standard) (Johns, 2009) has been recognized. In light of recent potential epidemics such as SARS or H1N1, presenteeism is in some sense a more serious problem—employees who come to work may infect others, and this outweighs any potential cost of absenteeism.

presenteeism

The notion that individuals show up to work even though they might be sick and not capable of working up to their normal standard

Boom, Bust, and Echo

Although there is no debate that work itself has changed as a result of technology and other influences, considerable debate exists over whether the workforce has changed in a fundamental way. The University of Toronto demographer David Foot (2001) popularized the notion of "boom, bust, and echo" as a characterization of the age profile of the workforce. The large post–World War II baby boom was followed by a drop in the birth rate (the bust), and then a subsequent small boom as the baby boomers themselves had children (the echo).

Certainly, workforces are responsive to this changing demographic profile. For example, almost every jurisdiction in Canada has now abandoned mandatory retirement (the requirement that individuals retire at age 65). Although these laws were once commonplace and even hailed as a way of creating new jobs for the incoming baby boomers, the fact that most boomers are now reaching retirement age has raised fears of a massive labour shortage. Simply put, we will not have enough workers to replace the aging baby boomers as they retire. Perhaps not surprisingly, issues of retirement (Warren & Kelloway, 2010), aging workers (Barnes-Farrell, 2006), and post-retirement return to work (Wang, 2007) are becoming more salient for I/O psychologists.

These demographic trends are well established, but debate remains about whether there are real generational differences among the different cohorts of workers. For example, it is now common to distinguish between the Baby Boom (those born between 1945 and 1960), Generation X (those born between 1961 and 1981), and the Ne(x)t Generation (born between 1982 and 2000). There is some suggestion that individuals from these generations may differ in work values and work orientation, although it is difficult to tell whether these are generational differences or cohort differences. For example, in comparison to the career-oriented baby boomers, the members of Generation X are thought to be more family focused and value free time more than career opportunities. However, any such differences might be a function of age— most baby boomers' children are now adults themselves. In contrast, members of Generation X may still have children living at home and may value family time more simply as a function of their current age and life stage. Whether these differences are truly a function of different generations is hard to discern, but it is clear that organizations are tasked with the job of managing a multigenerational workforce with increased diversity in terms of preferences and values. I/O psychologists are involved in helping organizations meet these challenges.

Diversity and Multiculturalism

The workforce in Canada is also becoming more and more ethnically diverse. This is a reflection of a more diverse multicultural population as a whole. For example, about 60.5 percent of the Canadian population are third-generation (or more) Canadians, with immigrants from the United Kingdom accounting for the largest single group among this portion of the population. Another 15.6 percent are second-generation Canadians whose parents immigrated primarily from European nations. Almost 24 percent of the population are first-generation Canadians, the majority of whom come from East and Southeast Asia. These figures tell us that Canada is a nation of immigrants, and the cultural traditions and beliefs of various groups can be expected to exert a powerful influence. This is particularly true given a national policy of multiculturalism that encourages retention of cultural beliefs and traditions. In contrast to the United States, where new immigrants are encouraged to assimilate and adopt American traditions (i.e., "the melting pot"), the Canadian tradition of multiculturalism encourages the retention of ethnic and cultural identity. Second, the figures speak to a dramatic change in immigration patterns, with a majority of new immigrants now coming from Asia rather than from the European countries.

Increased diversity in the workforce creates both challenges and opportunities for Canadian organizations, and I/O psychologists are actively involved in helping organizations manage a workforce that is rapidly changing. See Box 1.2 for more on Canadian culture.

Box 1.2

Canadian Culture

Perhaps the best known approach to understanding the psychology of cultural differences is the work of Geert Hofstede. Hofstede (2001) suggests that countries differ along five salient dimensions. *Power distance* is the extent to which the least powerful members of society accept and expect that power is distributed unequally. *Masculinity* emphasizes competition and assertiveness. *Individualism* is the extent to which people emphasize the role of the individual over the group. *Uncertainty avoidance* reflects a culture's tolerance for uncertainty. *Long-term orientation* is the extent to which members of the society value long-term virtues (e.g., thrift and per-sistence) over short-term virtues (saving face, respect for tradition).

As shown in Figure 1.2, in general Canadians place a great deal of emphasis on individual value—this is very common across the Western world. Note the different scores between Canada, India, and China—what might this imply for a multicultural Canadian workforce? Certainly, one would expect that individuals from China or India would find Canadian values and ways of thinking to

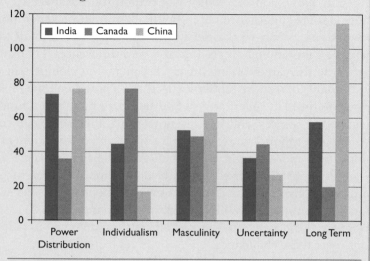

FIGURE 1.2

Hofstede's Classification of Countries According to Cultural Values

Source: Geerte Hofstede, *Culture's Consequences: Comparing Values, Behaviors, Institutions and Organizations Across Nations*, 2nd edition. Thousand Oaks, CA: SAGE Publications, 2001 (ISBN 0-8039-7323-3). Reprinted by permission of Geerte Hofstede B.V.

be very different from the values with which they might be more familiar. (Data are from Hofstede's Web page; refer to the end-of-chapter Internet exercises.)

Summary

Industrial/organizational psychology adopts a scientist-practitioner perspective and focuses on the enhancement of individual well-being and organizational effectiveness in the workplace. I/O psychologists focus on a broad array of issues related to these two primary goals. As a field, I/O psychology has been based on responding to the changing needs of organizations and individuals. Current trends such as technological development and diversity are just the most recent examples of external forces that influence the science and practice of I/O psychology.

Key Terms

Army Alpha 7
Army Beta 7
assessment centre 9

critical incident technique 9
cyberaggression 16
Hawthorne effect 8

Web Links w(w)w

For information on CSIOP, go to: **http://psychology.uwo.ca/csiop**

For information on SIOP, go to: **http://siop.org**

For information on the Société Québécoise de Psychologie du Travail et des Organisations, go to:

http://www.sqpto.ca

For information on careers in I/O psychology, go to:

http://psychology.about.com/od/psychologycareerprofiles/p/ iopsychcareers.htm

For a wide variety of resources in I/O psychology, go to:

http://frank.mtsu.edu/~pmccarth/

Discussion Questions

1. I/O psychologists adhere to a scientist-practitioner model. Should "science" (i.e., research) be influenced by "practice" (e.g., the needs of organizations)? How? What are the pros and cons of basing "practice" (i.e., organizational practices) on research?

2. Early psychologists such as Scott and Münsterberg allied themselves with the goals of industry (i.e., increased efficiency). How might I/O psychology today be different if these early pioneers had adopted the goals of labour organizations?

3. I/O psychologists define themselves as advancing both individual well-being and organizational efficiency. Are these compatible goals?

Using the Internet

1. One of the largest employers of I/O psychologists in Canada is the consulting industry. Firms that specialize in human resource or "talent" management frequently employ I/O psychologists in a variety of capacities. By searching the Web pages of at least five consulting companies, identify the role of I/O psychologists in these firms. What kind of services do I/O psychologists provide as consultants? How do these match with the competency areas presented in this chapter?

2. What might it be like to be a recent immigrant to Canada? Or to be a Canadian working abroad? Use Hofstede's page to explore the differences between your "home" and "host" countries (see http://www.geert-hofstede.com/hofstede_dimensions.php).

Exercises

1. Pat Rowe and her mentor Ed Webster focused much of their research attention on identifying problems with the employment interview. Think of employment interviews you have had. How confident are you that the interviewer got an accurate impression of your skills and abilities? What might have biased the interviewer's decision making?
2. Interview local business people (especially those who work in human resources). Are they aware of I/O psychology as a field and how it might have influenced their work?
3. One of the most common observations is how small the I/O community is in Canada. An easy way to see this is to develop your own "I/O family tree." Who is your professor of I/O psychology, and who was the professor's adviser in graduate school? Who was the adviser of the adviser? In very short order you will often find a host of interconnections with people mentioned in this chapter.

Case

After years of study, Sonya Cannon was now facing the last hurdle of her PhD program in industrial/organizational psychology: the doctoral dissertation (thesis). For her research, Sonya planned to investigate the relationship between the experience of workplace stress and personality characteristics. Based on her reading of the research literature, Sonya hypothesized that some individuals had personality characteristics making them more vulnerable to stress. Others might be more resilient to stress based on their personality profile.

To complete her study Sonya needs to collect data from 300 employees. She has just finished explaining her project to Geoffrey Bains, the vice-president of human resources at IDS Industries. She carefully reviewed the literature that led to her hypothesis, showed him a copy of the questionnaire she hoped to distribute to IDS Industries employees, and assured him that the firm would not incur additional costs by letting her survey its employees.

"That's fine," said Bains. "I can see that your project fits neatly with the scientific literature and is going to make for a very strong piece of research. But, as you might know, our employees already complete an annual morale survey and I am a little worried about giving them a second survey. To be blunt, what's in it for us? How does our company benefit from participating in your research?"

Sonya felt her thesis slipping away from her. She knew that unless she could explain the benefits of her proposed research to Bains, there was no chance of her getting her thesis data. Although she thought she was well-prepared, Bains had asked the one question she didn't have an answer for. He was waiting for her reply....

Discussion Questions

1. How would you answer Bains if you were in Sonya's position?
2. Why should companies participate in research such as described in this case?
3. Should scientists have to "sell" the practical benefits of their research to organizations?

Scientific Methods

This chapter provides a foundation for information presented in the remaining chapters of this text. It takes the position that information obtained through scientific methods is more likely to benefit an organization than decisions based on impressions or intuition. The chapter starts with an introduction to scientific methodology and goes on to examine basic measurement concepts that underlie contemporary research in organizations.

Chapter Learning Outcomes

After reading this chapter you should be able to

- Appreciate the difference between information discovered through scientific and non-scientific ways of knowing
- Understand the scientific method and several different types of research strategies
- Understand the important role that measurement plays in the scientific process and in describing differences between individuals
- Know what a correlation coefficient is, along with a few other basic statistical concepts used in personnel selection
- Recognize the importance and necessity of establishing the reliability and validity of measures used in organizational research
- Appreciate that professionals must adhere to a code of ethics in all of their work

Different Ways of Knowing

There are several ways in which we can acquire information about people, places, things, or events. These different methods fall into four broad categories. While the three non-scientific methods of tenacity, authority, and rationalization provide us with information, the scientific method produces the most accurate information. This is due to the fundamental difference between scientific and non-scientific methods: science is self-correcting. Information that is acquired through a scientific process can be "falsified"; that is, the information, if incorrect, can be disproved through objective, empirical means. If we believe that decisions made by a group are better than those made by individuals, we have to state that relationship in such a way that it can be tested and disproved, if that relationship does not exist. The following sections provide greater detail on these different ways of knowing, including the process of hypothesis testing or "falsification."

Non-Scientific Methods

Method of Tenacity

Often we accept as fact statements that have been made repeatedly over an extended period of time. By continuing to believe that something is true, it becomes true. For example, believing that "women do not have the competence to be corporate executives" may lead to selection policies that exclude women from those positions. This belief may have more to do with stereotypes or traditional roles assigned to women than with their actual ability or skill to do the job. Tenacity produces the poorest quality information. Organizational decisions based on tenacity may lead to serious legal and financial consequences for an organization.

Method of Authority

We often accept as true statements made by people in positions of authority or sources we consider infallible. These may include our own or others' experience, values, and norms derived from a culture or religious system, or statements made by "experts" such as editorial writers or TV commentators. People in organizations frequently seek out authorities for insight into how to manage. The problem here is that truth based on authority is not absolute; it depends on both the authority and the acceptance of the authority by the believer. The authority may change its position on "truth" as easily as changing a pair of socks. Also, not all people accept or recognize the same authority, leading to disagreements over what constitutes the "truth."

Method of Rationalization

This method, also known as the *a priori method*, refers to knowledge developed through the process of reasoning, independent from observation. An individual begins with an initial set of assumptions (which are accepted as true without the benefit of observation or experimentation) and uses these initial assumptions to derive new statements or truths. Mathematicians and philosophers develop a set of initial or *a priori* assumptions and apply the process of logic to deduce new knowledge. Of course, the derived knowledge is true only within the context of the initial, *a priori* assumptions. Different starting assumptions lead to different conclusions. If you believed that (a) women do not have the competence to be corporate executives and (b) good executives are critical to a corporation's success, you could easily reason that women should not be hired for executive positions. If you started with the assumptions that (a) gender is irrelevant to performance in an executive position and (b) good executives are critical to an organization's success, you would come to the conclusion that the best executive should be hired, regardless of gender. Each of these conclusions is correct within the context of its assumptions. The starting assumptions serve as the authority for the new knowledge.

Intuition

Often decisions are made through intuition; a manager hires someone because of a so-called gut feeling about the applicant. Intuition is a form of rationalization based on vague or fuzzy unstated assumptions and a deductive process that may not always be logical. As with other forms of rationalization, once the initial source of knowledge is accepted, so must be the derived information. There is no means to challenge the correctness of decisions based on intuition. Increasingly, today's executives are making decisions through intuition. Managers often feel that their intuition is built upon their accumulated successes and failures in work and in life and use their intuition to make personnel or people-related decisions involving hiring, training, promotion, and performance evaluation (Burke & Miller, 1999).

Scientific Knowledge

Organizational decisions should be as accurate as possible and based on the best information. Science produces the highest quality information; it accepts as true only the information that can withstand continued challenges to its accuracy. Science is self-correcting. Information is checked for accuracy with methods that are objective; this means that scientific methods can be examined, critiqued, and used by others. Conclusions based on badly designed, biased, or flawed experiments become corrected through public examination by other investigators of a study's methods, data, and conclusions. Because of these features, scientific knowledge is constantly undergoing revision. Even in the space of a few years, previously accepted truths may become outmoded through new discoveries.

Characteristics of Science

The quality of scientific knowledge reflects the nature of the scientific process. Science is characterized by several essential features (Whitehead, 1967):

- *Science is concerned with reality*—objects and events exist apart from an observer.
- *Science accepts causality*—the universe, including human behaviour, is based on a set of orderly relations, which can be described, predicted, and explained.
- *Science is empirical*—reliable knowledge about the universe is obtained through observation of objects and events. While reasoning is required as part of the scientific process, it alone does not produce new knowledge; it is used to organize the observed objects and events.
- *Science is public*—observations are subject to error; therefore, scientific knowledge must be made available to others for criticism and review. Approaching all knowledge with a degree of skepticism helps to establish its truthfulness or falsity.

Douglas N. Jackson (1929–2004)

Douglas Jackson was a member of the University of Western Ontario from 1964 until his death in 2004. He was a giant in the area of measurement and psychometrics. Like many psychologists, Jackson's career trajectory was not straightforward. His first degree was in industrial and labour relations, followed by both master's and doctoral degrees in clinical psychology. He believed he was more suited to the study of personality assessment. Over the years he was proved right; he developed more than 20 major psychological instruments, including the Personality Research Form, one of the most frequently used personality measures; the Jackson Vocational Interest Survey, which has influenced the career planning of hundreds of thousands of students; and the Employee Screening Questionnaire, which is used to identify high-risk job applicants from the standpoint of absenteeism and theft. Another important contribution of his was the development of the Multidimensional Aptitude Battery, which has been used extensively in the selection of job applicants, including the selection of astronauts by NASA. Jackson published more than 250 articles, books, and technical reports. His work has been cited in more than 3,000 other publications. His theoretical bases and methods for developing psychological tests have been influential in setting the standard for psychological tests in the latter half of the twentieth century. In recognition of his contributions, Jackson was elected a Fellow of the Royal Society of Canada (1989), as well as the president of various professional associations. He was elected president of the American Psychological Association's Division of Measurement, Evaluation, and Statistics (1989–1990), as well as president of the Society of Multivariate Experimental Research (1975–1976).

Source: Courtesy of Ted Jackson.

- *Science provides method*—science employs specific rules and procedures in the quest for new knowledge. A hallmark is the inclusion of controls built into the procedure, which serve to check or verify the truthfulness of the newly discovered knowledge.

The Scientific Approach

The scientific approach includes a number of methods that can be used to generate knowledge. Regardless of any special features, a scientific method follows a common strategy. Kerlinger (1986) outlined four general steps in this process.

Statement of the Problem

This is often the most difficult yet the most important part of the process. This step involves taking a generally vague idea or feeling and transforming it into a statement that captures the issues at hand. For example, some people may believe that women do not have the competence to be corporate executives. Once the idea is expressed, it can be pursued to the next stage. Simply expressing the idea does not make it true, as may be the case with non-scientific methods. The statement must be capable of being tested and proven false if the idea is incorrect. Do women, in fact, lack competence to be corporate executives?

Hypothesis

A **hypothesis** is a proposition about the relation between two or more events, objects, people, or phenomena. It is an attempt to redefine the problem in terms that are amenable to objective investigation. It is a prediction about relations that can be tested. Believing that women are not suited for executive positions in a corporation might lead you to propose the following hypothesis:

H_1: There is a relationship between gender and corporate earnings

hypothesis

A proposition about the relation between two or more events, objects, people, or phenomena

Reasoning and Deduction

While hypothesis H_1 can be examined empirically, more precision is achieved by deducing the consequences of the hypothesis. Many hypotheses are presented as "If X happens, then Y results" type of statements. The reasoning/deductive process may lead to examination of new or different problems. Based on experience, previous knowledge, or empirical work, we may expect to find that corporations with women in top management positions will have less success than those led by men. This prediction is expressed in a new hypothesis:

H_2: If women are placed in executive positions in corporations, the corporation's success will decrease.

Of course, these hypotheses remain conjecture subject to verification.

Observation/Test/Experiment

Up to this point, the scientific approach is similar to the non-scientific methods of knowing in that all the activity, so far, has emphasized reasoning. Reasoning is only part of the scientific process; it is not the final step. The relationship specified in the hypothesis must be tested empirically. The most critical step is to gather empirical evidence that is relevant to the hypothetical relationship.

Operational Definitions

In science, *empirical* means that an event is capable of being experienced; that it can be observed or measured, either directly or indirectly. Many hypotheses involve relationships between abstract events. While it is fairly easy to categorize humans into groups of males and females, it is more problematic to define *success*. Before any testing can take place, abstract constructs, like success, must be defined in a manner that allows observation and measurement. This is done through use of **operational definitions**, which define an abstract construct in terms of specific procedures and measures. Operational definitions are very specific to the study in which they are used and may differ among studies. Corporate success could be defined as its annual profits, its total annual revenue, bonuses received by executives, or the increase in its stock value over a defined period of time; it could also be defined in many other ways. Operational definitions may differ in the degree to which they represent, or capture the essence of, the abstract construct. Executive bonuses may have little relevance to corporate success (e.g., during the recession of 2009, many executives of bankrupt corporations received multi-million dollar bonuses). In this case the operational definition, based on the size of executive bonus, is affected by processes that are irrelevant to the construct. The degree to which this occurs is called *construct–irrelevant variance*. The increase in stock value may be relevant to the construct but it may not present a complete measure of the corporation's performance. The degree to which the operational definition fails to capture important aspects of the construct is termed *construct underrepresentation*. The validity of operational definitions is an important concern in any scientific investigation. It is also of equal importance when measurements are used to make inferences about constructs such as "success" or "cognitive ability." We often find that two studies using different operational definitions of the same construct come to different conclusions. While this may be disconcerting in the short term, science holds that over the long term a number of studies will converge on the "truth" of the hypothesis.

operational definitions

Define abstract constructs in terms of specific procedures and measures

Variables

The events, objects, people, or phenomena referenced in hypothetical propositions must vary in amount, degree, or kind. Such **variables** must have at least one defined characteristic that has at least two values. The variable of gender has two values—male and female. There must be at least two values associated with the variable of corporate success; the exact number of values depends on how it is operationally defined. It could be defined in terms of dollar-valued earnings, or an expert panel could rate the corporation on a five-point letter grade system of A, B, C, D, or F, a buy or sell statement regarding the company's stock, or one of many others.

variables

Events, objects, people, or phenomena that vary in amount, degree, or kind with respect to certain aspects

Research Plan

Once the variables relevant to the hypothesis are defined, a *research plan* is developed. A research plan, or research design, lays out the framework for making measurements or observations on the variables. The research plan specifies the strategy used in collecting data; it identifies the study participants, the environment in which they will be measured, the frequency with which they will be measured, and any interventions or manipulations that the investigator will introduce into the environment. One way in which research designs vary is the degree of control given to the investigator.

Observational Studies

In *observational studies,* the researcher exercises very little control or manipulation of variables; the investigator records naturally occurring behaviours and establishes patterns of relationships between different aspects of the observed behaviour. A corporation assigns women to executive positions; but corporations still exist in which there are no women at top management levels. Comparing the ratings of success given by experts to these two types of corporations provides a test of H_2. If companies with mixed-gender management teams had lower performance ratings, we might conclude that the hypothesis is correct. Unfortunately, the lack of control allows alternative conclusions to be drawn. The performance of the corporations may have more to do with the market for their products or services than with the gender composition of the management team. The success of the male-managed company may have more to do with demand for its product and services than with the gender composition of the management team. Although there is a relationship between the presence of women in the management team and company performance, the lack of control over other variables makes it very difficult to attribute the lower success rating to the presence of women in the executive positions.

Correlational studies, a class of observational studies, are perhaps the most common design used in organizational research. The goal of this type of study is to understand patterns of relationships among a set of variables. What is the relationship between the presence of women in executive positions and the corporation's performance? One purpose of correlational studies is to predict one variable from another or from a set of several variables. The number of women executives may vary across corporations; so might the corporations' earnings. If the corporations' earnings increase, as does the percentage of women on the team, the two variables are positively correlated, as indicated by a correlation coefficient (see p. 36). We could then use our knowledge of the number of women in top management positions to make a prediction about any corporation's performance by developing a regression equation (see p. 38). To say that two variables are related or that one variable predicts another does not mean, nor does it imply, that the change in the first variable has caused the change in the other. As in any observational study, the lack of control over the variables prevents this type of statement from being made. The corporation's performance may be due to more effective leaders in those corporations that, coincidentally, have more women members.

Experimental Designs

In **experimentation,** the researcher actively manipulates variables and controls different aspects of the environment to exclude alternative explanations for the observed events. To test H_2, an investigator finds two companies that are similar in terms of size, geographic location, product or service produced, and performance

experimentation
Involves active manipulation of variables by a researcher and control of environmental factors to exclude alternate explanations for the observed results

Chapter 2: Scientific Methods

capability. The investigator then assigns women and men to top management positions in each of the corporations in a way that ensures equal ability and experience within each unit. One company is assigned only males, while the second is assigned females. This is the only difference between the two companies. Each corporation is evaluated under identical conditions. If the female-managed company receives lower ratings, there is more justification for attributing the cause of the poor performance to the gender of those in charge. The control procedures lead to greater confidence in making cause and effect statements.

Quasi-Experimental Designs

Unfortunately, many situations do not lend themselves to experimentation either on the grounds of practicality or ethical considerations. In these instances, investigators fall back on less obtrusive strategies. In practice, applied research falls somewhere between the two extremes of pure observation and pure experimentation. In most studies, it is possible to implement some control and to manipulate variables to reduce the number of alternative explanations. In *quasi-experimental* research, we do not have the ability to randomly assign people to the different conditions, or groups. We can, however, manipulate variables that may have an effect on outcomes. What organization would allow a researcher to control the appointment of individuals to top management positions on the basis of gender? The researcher works with management teams that are already in place, similar to those in an observational study. The inability to randomly assign participants to management positions allows for the possibility that the management teams differ on a number of factors, in addition to gender, which might produce differences on the outcome measure. As in experimentation, the researcher manipulates, controls, and measures these conditions as part of comparing the performance of both teams. Both units might undergo a set of standardized exercises (e.g., training on investment strategies). While differences in the performances of the two teams could be due to factors other than the teams' gender composition, the quasi-experimental design reduces the number of alternative explanations. Quasi-experimental research strategies are often used in organizational settings.

See Box 2.1 for a comparison of research designs.

The Null Hypothesis

Testing hypotheses is somewhat more involved than described above. Would any decrease in performance of the female-led management team, no matter how small, be accepted as proof of H_2? Could the difference in company performance be due to chance or to errors in measurement rather than to actual differences in performance? To assess this possibility, researchers actually test a *null hypothesis*, H_0, which proposes that there will be no difference or no relationship in the data collected across different conditions. The null hypothesis that corresponds to H_2 would be:

> H_0: If women are placed in executive positions, the level of success will not decrease.

In other words, the performance of companies with women in top management positions will be the same as companies managed by males, with the exception of slight variation due to chance factors such as measurement error.

Statistical Significance

If the null hypothesis is rejected, the alternative hypothesis, in this case H_2, is assumed to be true. Statistical procedures are used to evaluate the likelihood that a difference across groups occurs by chance. In general, the larger a difference between two groups on some measurement, the less likely that difference is attributable to chance. As part of the research plan, the investigator specifies the size of an empirical difference that is used to reject the null hypothesis and to accept the alternative. If there is only one chance in 20 (a probability of .05) that a difference of such size could have occurred by chance, the difference is said to be *statistically significant*; that is, the difference is probably NOT due to chance. A statistically significant

Box 2.1

Comparison of Research Designs

Research Design	Advantages	Disadvantages
Observational/Correlational Designs—Provide researchers with little, if any, control or manipulation of variables; the investigator records naturally occurring behaviours and establishes patterns of relationships between different variables.	Research takes place in a natural setting; results are applicable to other environments and populations.	No manipulation of variables; no control of the research environment; no random assignment of people to conditions or groups; design does not eliminate possibility of alternate explanations for results; does not allow researcher to draw cause and effect conclusions from the results.
Quasi-Experimental Designs—Allow researchers to manipulate and control variables in applied research settings where random assignment of people to different conditions or groups is not possible.	Allow manipulation and control of variables in an applied setting; allow study of behaviour in naturally occurring groups; research takes place in a natural setting; results are applicable to other environments and populations.	No random assignment of people to conditions or groups; in most cases, design does not eliminate possibility of alternate explanations for results; normally do not allow researchers to draw cause and effect conclusions from the results.
Experimental Designs—Allow researchers to manipulate and control variables as well as the environment in which the research takes place. These designs provide for the random assignment of people to different conditions or groups.	Allow manipulation and control of variables normally in a laboratory setting; allow the random assignment of people to conditions or groups; design eliminates possibility of alternative explanations for results; allow researcher to make cause and effect conclusions from the results.	Research normally takes place in an artificial environment; results may not be applicable to other environments or populations.

result does not automatically mean that the research hypothesis is accepted. The researcher must also show that alternative explanations for the results are unlikely, a task that is more easily accomplished with a well-designed experiment.

Drawing Conclusions

The results of a study, whether positive or negative with respect to the research hypothesis, have implications for both theory and application. In either case, we draw conclusions, based on the empirical evidence, about the initial problem. While there is an end to any one study, the research process is ongoing. The results and conclusions from one study are integrated into a larger body of knowledge. There is always a probability that a research hypothesis should NOT have been accepted. With repeated research over time, evidence accumulates on the appropriateness of the findings from any one study. Similarly, theories and proposed solutions to problems evolve with the knowledge obtained from new studies.

The Nature of Measurement

Measurement plays an important role in the scientific process. Hypothesizing that higher levels of cognitive ability are related to higher levels of job performance implies that both cognitive ability and job performance can be measured. **Measurement** is the assignment of numbers to *aspects* of objects or events according to a set of rules or conventions. The fundamental assumption in measurement is that relations among numbers assigned to the aspects convey information about relations among the objects themselves. The starting point in measurement is to define the construct that is to be measured. What do cognitive ability and job performance mean? Defining *cognitive ability* as "knowing how to use words and numbers" might produce a different set of measurements than defining it as "knowing how to get things done." Both of these definitions are legitimate ways of defining cognitive ability, yet each emphasizes different *aspects* of the cognitive ability concept. Similarly, *job performance* could be defined to emphasize either quality or quantity aspects. Job performance could be based on a supervisor's assessment or it might reflect the number of units a worker produced in a given time period. The next step is to select or to develop a set of operations or measurement procedures that will define the abstract constructs and then assign numbers to the different objects to reflect the degree of the aspect inherent in the object. That is, we develop an operational definition of our abstract constructs by defining them in terms of specific procedures and measures. As we noted in our discussion of operational definitions, how we define the construct may lead to specific results that would not occur if a different operational definition had been used. In examining research, it is always necessary to keep in mind the way a construct had been operationalized in the study.

measurement

The assignment of numbers to aspects of events, objects, people, or phenomena according to a set of rules or conventions

Measuring Individual Differences

For industrial/organizational psychology, the purpose of measurement is to describe differences among individuals, teams, groups, or organizations with respect to those constructs that are important to the task at hand. Defining cognitive ability as a score on an assessment instrument such as the Wonderlic

Personnel Test (WPT) implies that some people have more cognitive ability than others and that numbers can be systematically assigned to represent each person's degree of cognitive ability. Measurement quantifies characteristics of individuals who belong to a specific group or population. We may, for example, seek to quantify differences between individual job applicants on the basis of their cognitive ability, skill level, or personality; we may also wish to characterize different work groups in terms of their organizational commitment, job satisfaction, and nature of the group leadership. We assume that for the most part these variables, or characteristics, remain stable over time unless there are significant interventions that may lead to changes. In fact, organizational research often examines how characteristics change following a planned intervention.

Methods of Measurement

Several methods can be used to assess differences in work settings (Sackett & Larson, 1990). The most prominent include the following techniques.

Self-report measures involve individuals responding to a series of questions, or items, which require them to report on their own characteristics. In the above example we used a person's score on the WPT to indicate the degree of cognitive ability. Surveys, interviews, and questionnaires constitute self-report measures. Self-reports may serve as (1) substitutes for factual information that can be verified (e.g., asking an individual to report their age); (2) a means to assess constructs that may not be easily observed (e.g., having an individual answer a series of questions related to attitudes, values, intentions, and beliefs); or (3) ways in which to measure an individual's perception of events or other people (e.g., asking an employee to rate the abilities required to perform a given task). Self-reports may consist of responses to single items or to a series of related items, in which case an individual's score is derived from the set of items.

Behavioural observation occurs when someone measures behaviours that are produced by someone else. Behavioural observation may be either direct or indirect. In the first case, an individual is observed and the quality, frequency, or intensity of some aspect of overt behaviour is recorded. For example, the researcher might count the number of times a participant pauses in mid-sentence during an interview. Indirect observation focuses on the products of the behaviour rather than on the behaviour itself. Applicants for a secretarial position might be asked to type a sample document; the number of errors made or the number of words typed per minute by each applicant is an indirect measure of one aspect of their typing skills.

Reports about others involve an individual describing the characteristics of another person. For example, employees may complete a survey that asks them to rate how well a series of items describes their supervisor. In another instance, a group of workers might be asked to describe the personality of their supervisor.

Unobtrusive measures involve the analysis of archives, records, documents, or other physical evidence to make inferences about characteristics of interest. These physical traces are used as proxies for actual behaviour or for internal states of individuals. For example, increase in employee absenteeism following the hiring of a new supervisor might indicate that problems exist between the supervisor and employees.

Each of these different types of measures has strengths and weaknesses. There is no such thing as a perfect measure. However, it is important that the measure being used captures the essence of the characteristic or aspect under consideration. The measure must also assign values to the different characteristics in a fairly consistent manner.

The Nature of Observed Scores

Many characteristics and attitudes that play an important role in industrial/organizational psychology remain stable over time. Therefore, when that attribute is measured on two different occasions we should expect that the same score should result. However, this does not generally happen because the two measurements reflect not only the characteristic being measured but also error. The difference in the two scores is attributed to error that varies randomly over time. For example, if a job interview takes place in a noisy environment, the score assigned to the candidate may be different than if the interview were conducted in a quiet room. The noise may have caused the interviewer to miss vital information and give a lower score than deserved. Hardly any human characteristic is measured without error. Measurement models deal with errors in different ways. The classical measurement model (Nunnally & Bernstein, 1994) assumes that any **observed score**, X, is a combination of a **true score**, T, and an **error score**, e, such that:

$$X = T + e$$

This model assumes that the characteristic being measured is stable and that the only reason an observed score changes from one measurement to another is due to **random errors**. Error scores are independent of the characteristic being measured; errors are attributable to the measurement process, not the individual. That is, the magnitude of error scores is unrelated to the magnitude of the characteristic being measured. The error score for an applicant with a very high level cognitive ability could be very large, or very small; that same situation would hold for any level of cognitive ability. The model also assumes that true scores and error scores combine in a simple additive manner. We will return to this point a bit later after a brief introduction to some statistical concepts that will aid that discussion. If you are familiar with basic statistical concepts you may want to skip ahead to the section on Reliability.

Correlation and Regression

Basic Statistics

If only a few job applicants were interviewed, it is possible to directly compare the applicants on the basis of their interview scores. What if there were a very large number of applicants? How would you keep track of all the scores? One way is to use statistical procedures to describe important information contained in the set of applicant scores (Kerlinger, 1986). The manager could compute the *mean* or average score. The mean represents the most typical or "average" score that might be expected within a group of scores; it is the one score that best represents the set of scores. Not every applicant has a score that is similar to the

---

observed score

Any score assigned to an attribute or characteristic of an individual through a measurement process; thought to be a combination of true scores and measurement error

true score

The average score that an individual would earn on an infinite number of administrations of the same test or parallel versions of the same test

error score or measurement error

The hypothetical difference between an observed score and a true score

random errors

Errors that vary in unpredictable ways upon repeated measurement mean score. It is also useful to know how different, on average, any one score is from the mean score and from any other score. The *variance* gives this information. The more the observed scores differ from one another and from the mean, the higher the variance; scores that are tightly clustered around a mean score will have a smaller variance. Often in reporting scores the *standard deviation* is used rather than the variance. The standard deviation is the square root of the variance; it is more convenient to use since it presents information in terms of the actual **measurement scale**. Knowing both the mean and the variance allows the interviewer to know the score that an average applicant should attain, and how much variability to expect in interview scores. If most applicant scores fall within one standard deviation on either side of the mean, then someone with a score that exceeds +3.00 standard deviations might be considered an exceptional applicant, whereas someone whose score was −3.00 would be considered an exceptionally poor applicant. Figure 2.1 presents a standard normal curve where the mean is set to 0.00 and each standard deviation is 1.00 units from the mean in either direction.

In reality we rarely measure in units of 1.00 as represented on the curve. Whatever scale of measurement we are using we can transform it into a normal curve as long as we know the mean and standard deviation. For example, if the mean interview score were 50 (0.00 on the curve) and the size of the standard deviation were 10 (1.0 standard unit), most applicant scores normally would fall between 40 (−1.00) and 60 (+1.00). Scores greater than 80 (+3.00) would be exceptional and indicate that an applicant received a very high rating compared to the average applicant; on the other hand, scores less than 20 (−3.00) would indicate that the applicant fared poorly.

measurement scale

A set of rules by which numbers may be assigned to aspects of events, objects, people, or phenomena

Correlation

Measures of central tendency and variability are quite useful in summarizing a large set of observations. However, the relationship between two variables

Figure 2.1

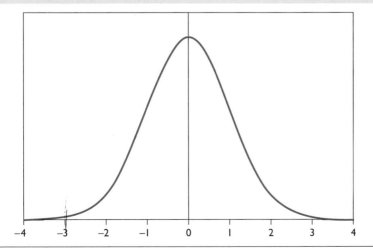

Standard Normal Curve

Chapter 2: Scientific Methods

may also be of considerable interest—for example, the relationship between cognitive ability and job performance in selecting job applicants. A valid measure of cognitive ability may be used to predict job performance if the degree of variation in cognitive ability is associated with the degree of variation in job performance. If that relationship exists, then giving job candidates a pre-employment cognitive ability test would allow the employer to predict how successful a performer that job candidate might become if they were hired. The alternative, at the expense of both the candidate and the company, would be to hire the candidates and then to discharge them if they did not meet performance standards. A *correlation coefficient* is a statistic that presents information on the extent of the relationship between two variables. To establish this correlation, there must be two measurements taken from the same source. In the example above, both the measure of cognitive ability and the measure of job performance must come from the same employee.

In Figure 2.2, each data point in the ellipse represents a score from a measure of cognitive ability and a score related to the employee's job performance. In this case the ellipse tends to tilt upward as both the cognitive ability and job performance scores tend to increase together. This orientation of the ellipse suggests a linear, positive relationship between cognitive ability scores and job performance scores. High cognitive ability scores are associated with high job performance scores. If the ellipse had tilted downward at the high end of the job performance axis and upward at the low end, it would have suggested a linear, negative relationship, one where high cognitive ability scores are associated with low job performance scores.

Figure 2.2

Scatterplot of Cognitive Ability and Job Performance Scores

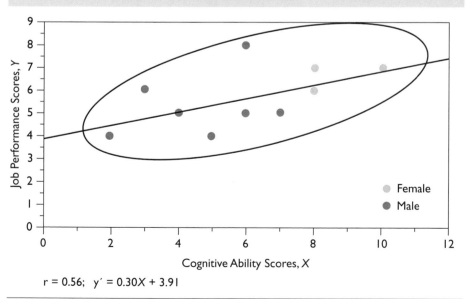

$r = 0.56$; $y' = 0.30X + 3.91$

People and Work in Canada

Correlation Coefficients

While Figure 2.2 gives a good visual indication of the relationship between the two variables, its usefulness becomes limited as the size of the data set increases. The information contained in Figure 2.2 is summarized through an index, r, the correlation coefficient. A correlation coefficient indicates both the *size* and *direction* of a linear relationship between two variables. A correlation coefficient is represented by the symbol r, and the sign attached to it represents the direction of the relationship. For the data represented in Figure 2.2, $r = 0.56$ and indicates a positive, linear relationship between the two variables. Negative or indirect relationships are indicated by minus signs; for example, $r = -.56$ indicates a situation where high cognitive ability scores predicted low job performance scores. The strength or size of the relationship is indicated by the value of the correlation coefficient. A correlation of $r = 1.00$ indicates a perfect positive, linear relationship between two variables, while $r = -1.00$ indicates a perfect negative, linear relationship. Correlations of $r = 0.00$ signify that there is no linear relationship between the two variables. With correlations approaching $r = 0.00$, one variable cannot be used to predict the score on the second variable; knowing the status of the first variable or characteristic does not help you to know anything about the status of the second. The more closely the correlation coefficient approaches a value of either plus or minus 1.00, the more accurately one variable predicts the other. A value of $r = 0.00$ does not necessarily mean that there is no relationship between the two variables. It means that there is no linear relationship. You may get a zero correlation when the nature of the relationship is quite complex; for example a U-shaped relationship where both high and low cognitive ability scores were related to job performance would likely lead to a zero linear correlation. Such complex relationships often prove of little value in predicting relationships in areas related to I/O psychology. For more on correlation, see Box 2.2.

Coefficient of Determination

Another index that gives an indication of the strength of a relationship between two variables is r^2, the *coefficient of determination*. This value represents the proportion of variability in one variable that is associated with variability in another. It is the proportion of variability that can be accounted for in one variable by knowing something about a different variable. For data presented in Figure 2.2, about 31 percent (i.e., $r^2 = .56 \times .56 = .31$) of the variance in job performance ratings can be accounted for by knowing the applicants' cognitive ability scores. Looking at this from a different direction, about 69 percent of the variability in job performance ratings is not related to cognitive ability scores. Both r and r^2 give an indication of the size of a relationship.

Simple Regression

The relationship between two variables can also be expressed in terms of a straight line. Remember that a correlation expresses the degree and direction of a linear relationship between two variables. The correlation coefficient is used to derive an equation for a straight line that best fits the data points

Box 2.2

Controversy: Correlation and Cause and Effect

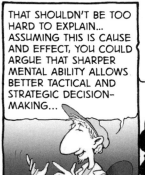

I'VE BEEN ANALYZING BIOGRAPHIC DATA FOR POLITICIANS OVER THE LAST CENTURY, AND DISCOVERED THAT A HIGHLY SIGNIFICANT CORRELATION EXISTS BETWEEN THEIR MENTAL ABILITY AND THE ULTIMATE LEVEL THEY ATTAIN IN PUBLIC OFFICE...

THAT SHOULDN'T BE TOO HARD TO EXPLAIN... ASSUMING THIS IS CAUSE AND EFFECT, YOU COULD ARGUE THAT SHARPER MENTAL ABILITY ALLOWS BETTER TACTICAL AND STRATEGIC DECISION-MAKING...

MMM....THERE'S ONLY ONE MINOR PROBLEM THAT I CAN SEE WITH THAT PARTICULAR INTERPRETATION...

YEAH?

IT'S A **NEGATIVE** CORRELATION...

nick@lab-initio.com

In the above cartoon, the young woman is asserting that a correlation exists between mental (cognitive) ability and attaining political office (job performance), much like we do in this chapter. The young man assumes, however, that the correlation is evidence of cause and effect; that is, that higher levels of mental ability cause attainment of high political office. Regardless of what we may think about politicians, the young man is making a fundamental mistake, much like most people unfamiliar with statistics: that the correlation has proven a causal relationship. As we noted in this chapter, much of the research in I/O psychology is correlational and not based on true experiments. Ethically, we cannot do the type of experiments that would prove cause and effect; we cannot manipulate variables or control different aspects of the environment. How can we accumulate correlational data to the point where we can make causal statements? There is an advanced statistical technique called *structural equation modelling* that is used with correlational data to make causal statements. The researcher hypothesizes a model or a set of relationships between several variables. If the correlational data "fit" the model, the model is accepted, including the directional or causal relationships underlying the model. The problem is that many other models that have not been tested may fit the data equally well. The key to accepting the model lies in the thoroughness and correctness of the theoretical basis of the proposed model. Correlation does not prove causation, but many researchers accumulate correlational data to argue for causal relationships.

Source: Courtesy of Nick Kim.

contained in the scatterplot. This is a *regression line.* The diagonal line in Figure 2.2's scatterplot is the regression line that provides the best fit to the data contained in the ellipse. In regression, one variable is used to predict another. The independent or *predictor variable* is plotted along the *X*-axis of the scatterplot with the dependent or *criterion variable* plotted along the *Y*-axis. The equation used to generate the straight line is:

$$Y' = bX + c$$

This equation states that a predicted job performance score, Y', is equal to an individual's cognitive ability score, X, multiplied by b, the regression coefficient, plus c, a constant. The regression coefficient, b, represents the slope of the straight line and the constant, c, represents the intercept, where the line crosses the *Y*-axis. For the regression line presented in Figure 2.2, $b = .30$, and

$c = 3.91$; these values are used to generate a predicted job performance score, Y', for each applicant. The predicted values will differ from the actual values; the magnitude of the difference is variable from one case to another. The most typical method used to generate a regression line produces the smallest error between predicted and actual values of the criterion variable.

Multiple Regression

Many practical situations involve more than two variables. In assessing job applicants, you may have not only information about cognitive ability but also other information obtained from an interview and an application form. Each one of these sources of information, on its own, may predict job performance scores to some degree. The set of predictors can be combined into one equation to indicate the extent to which the set, taken as a whole, is related to the criterion variable. The mathematical procedure to compute this equation, while more complicated than the case of two variables, follows the same logic as that for simple regression. The following equation represents a multiple regression based on cognitive ability (X_1), an interview (X_2), and an application form (X_3). The values of b_1, b_2, and b_3 represent the relative contribution that each of the predictors, respectively, provides to the equation, which is still a straight line.

$$Y' = b_1X_1 + b_2X_2 + b_3X_3 + c$$

Both simple and multiple regression techniques are used to combine information to make predictions and decisions in personnel selection.

Reliability

Hardly any human characteristic is measured in an error-free manner. The act of measuring produces a score that measures both the true score and an error component. **Reliability** is the degree to which observed scores are free from random measurement errors. Reliability is an indication of the stability or dependability of a set of measurements (Kerlinger, 1986). Reliability refers to the consistency of a set of measurements when a testing procedure is repeated on a population of individuals or groups (American Educational Research Association (AERA), American Psychological Association (APA), & National Council on Measurement in Education (NCME), 1999). Think of an employer who requires each employee to punch a time clock upon arrival at work. Mr. X, Ms. Y, and Mr. Z, without fail, arrive at work each morning at 8:55 a.m., 8:56 a.m., and 8:57 a.m., respectively. If, on each day, the time clock stamped these same times, exactly, on each employee's time card, the time clock would be considered extremely reliable. The observed score, the time stamped on the time card, is the same as the true score, the time the employees arrived at work; no degree of error has been added to the measurement. On the other hand, if the clock stamped times of 9:03 a.m., 9:00 a.m., and 9:00 a.m. for Mr. X, Ms. Y, and Mr. Z, the measurement would include an error component. Mr. X's time is off by eight minutes, Ms. Y's by four minutes, and Mr. Z's by three minutes. The time clock is not accurate, or reliable, in reporting the time people arrived for work. In this case, the error appears to be random or unsystematic; the occurrence or degree of the

reliability

The degree to which observed scores are free from random measurement errors; an indication of the stability or dependability of a set of measurements over repeated applications of the measurement procedure error does not appear to be predictable. Errors may also be systematic; that is, the errors may be made in a consistent, or predictable, fashion. If the time clock were five minutes fast, it would report the three arrival times as 9:00 a.m., 9:01 a.m., and 9:02 a.m. The clock is still reliable in reporting the arrival times of the three employees, but it is systematically adding five minutes to each worker's time. The observed scores are reliable, but they do not represent the true arrival times. In other words, while the observed scores are accurate, they are not a valid indication of whether the employees started work on time. **Systematic errors** do not affect the accuracy of the measurements but rather the meaning, or interpretation, of those measurements.

Interpreting Reliability Coefficients

Another way to think of reliability is in terms of the variability of a set of scores. If the measuring instrument is not very accurate, that is, if it adds large random error components to true scores, then the variance of the measured scores should be much larger than the variance of the true scores. Reliability can be thought of as the ratio of true score variance, $\text{Var}(T)$, to observed score variance, $\text{Var}(X)$ (AERA et al., 1999); this can be expressed as the following equation:

$$r_{xx} = \frac{\text{Var}(T)}{\text{Var}(X)}$$

where r_{xx} is the reliability coefficient, the degree that observed scores, which are made on the same stable characteristic, correlate with one another. In this case, r^2 represents the proportion of variance in the observed scores that is attributed to true differences on the measured characteristic. For the arrival times in our example, $\text{Var}(T) = 1.0$; for the reported times, $\text{Var}(X) = 3.0$, with $r_{xx} = 0.33$. Only 10 percent of the variability in the reported arrival times $(r_{xx})^2$, is attributable to the true arrival time; the remaining 90 percent of the variability is attributable to the inaccuracy of the time clock. When the time clock is systematically fast by five minutes, $\text{Var}(X) = 1.0$, giving an $r_{xx} = 1.00$, the systematic error did not affect the reliability coefficient; the scores are very reliable, but they do not tell anything about the time people actually arrived at work.

Measurement Error

Measurement error can be thought of as the hypothetical difference between an individual's observed score on any particular measurement and the individual's true score. Measurement error, whether systematic or random, reduces the usefulness of any set of measures or the results from any test. It reduces the confidence that we can place in the score the measure assigns to any particular individual. Does the score accurately represent the individual's knowledge or ability, or is it so fraught with error that we cannot use it to make meaningful decisions? Information on the degree of error present in any set of measurements must be considered when using the measurements to make decisions. The *standard error of measurement* is a statistical index that summarizes information related to measurement error. This index is estimated from observed scores obtained over a group of individuals. It reflects how an individual's score would vary, on average, over repeated observations that were made under identical conditions.

Factors Affecting Reliability

The factors that introduce error into any set of measurements can be organized into three broad categories.

Temporary Individual Characteristics

If a job candidate were ill when undergoing a job interview, his/her score might be low reflecting a larger than normal error component arising from the illness. If the applicant asked for, and was given, a second interview, the new score might be higher because of a lower error component. The difference in the two scores is attributed to the difference in the applicant's state of well-being. The applicant's ill health negatively affected performance during the initial interview, leading to a lower score. Factors such as health, motivation, fatigue, and emotional state introduce temporary, unsystematic errors into the measurement process.

Lack of Standardization

Changing the conditions under which measurements are made introduces error into the measurement process. Mr. X, Ms. Y, and Mr. Z are asked different questions during their interviews. Mr. X is interviewed over lunch in a very comfortable restaurant while the other candidates are interviewed in a very austere conference room. Ms. Y is given a few minutes to answer each question, but others are given as long as they need. The interviewer displays a lack of interest in Mr. Z during the interview, but reacts very positively to Ms. Y. These changing conditions produce random error in the scores assigned to the candidates. On the other hand, if all female candidates were interviewed in a restaurant and all male candidates in an office, then the errors introduced into the measurement process would be systematic and the measurements would be biased. These are just a few of the ways that lack of standardization can enter into the measurement process and lead to measurement error.

Chance

Factors unique to a specific procedure introduce error into the set of measurements. Luck of the draw may have done in Mr. Z during his interview. His score is based on how he answered a specific set of questions. Mr. Z did poorly on the questions he was asked, but he might have done extremely well on any others. Mr. X had no prior experience with interviews, while Ms. Y knew what to expect from previous experience but was distracted and did not understand a critical question. Chance factors produce unsystematic or random measurement errors.

Methods of Estimating Reliability

To measure reliability, we have to estimate the degree of variability in a set of scores that is caused by measurement error. We can obtain this estimate by using two different, but parallel, measures of the characteristic or attribute. Over the same set of people, both measures should report the same score for each individual. This score will represent the true score plus measurement error. Both measures reflect the same true score; discrepancies between the two sets of scores suggest the presence of measurement error. The correlation coefficient based on the scores from both measures gives an estimate of r_{xx}, the reliability coefficient. It is extremely difficult, if not impossible, to obtain two parallel measures of the same characteristic; therefore, several strategies have been developed as approximations of parallel measures.

Test and Retest

The identical measurement procedure is used to assess the same characteristic over the same group of people on two different occasions. Job applicants are invited back for a second interview. They are asked the same questions in the same order. The correlation of their first and second interview scores estimates the reliability of the interview. High correlations suggest high levels of reliability.

Alternate Forms

Having a person take the same interview twice may lead to a false estimate of the reliability of the interview process. The candidates may recall their original answers to the interview questions; they also may think of better answers after the first interview and give the improved answers on the second opportunity. To prevent the intrusion of effects from the first interview, the applicants are asked alternate questions during the second interview. The correlation between both sets of scores again estimates reliability, with high correlations once more indicating strong reliability.

Internal Consistency

Both test-retest and alternate forms procedures require two sets of measurements made on different occasions. In the case of interviews, it is quite costly in time and money to put all the candidates through a second interview procedure. Besides, isn't each question in the interview directed at measuring the underlying construct being measured? Why not consider any two questions in the interview to be an example of a test-retest situation, and determine the correlation between scores given to each item in that pair? This is the logic behind establishing reliability through internal consistency. Rather than select any particular pair of items, the correlations between the scores of all possible pairs of items are calculated and then averaged. This average estimates the internal consistency, the degree to which all the questions in the set are measuring the same construct. These estimates are called *alpha* coefficients, or *Cronbach's alpha,* after the formula used to produce the estimate. *Split-half reliability* is a special case of internal consistency where all the items are first divided into two arbitrary groups. For example, all the even-numbered items may form one group with the odd-numbered items placed into the second, or scores to questions on the first half of the interview are correlated with scores from the second half of the interview. The correlation over each person's average scores in the two groups is used as the reliability estimate. The major assumption here is that all the items are measuring the same underlying construct and that they are not measuring multiple constructs. If the one set of questions measured interpersonal behaviour and the second set assessed motivation, then the internal consistency for the total set of questions would be low.

Inter-Rater Reliability

Measurement in industrial/organizational psychology is often based on the subjective assessment, or rating, of one individual by another. How likely is it that the rating assigned by one judge would also be assigned by other judges? The correlation between these two judgments estimates the reliability of their assessments. Two managers independently rate each job applicant's interview; a high correlation between their assigned scores to each candidate suggests that the interview is reliable. Sometimes, this index is referred to as *classification consistency* or *inter-rater agreement*.

Choosing an Index of Reliability

Measures of test-retest reliability, alternate forms reliability, and internal consistency are special cases of a more general type of index called a generalizability coefficient. These three measures, however, provide slightly different views of a measure's reliability. Each is limited and does not convey all the relevant information that might be needed in making a decision on whether to use the measuring device. The specific requirements of a situation may dictate which index is chosen. As well, it remains within the professional judgment of the psychologist to choose an appropriate index of reliability and to determine the acceptable level of reliability as part of using a specific measure. Before using any measurement to make decisions about employees, the psychologist must consider the consequences of the decisions based on the measure. The need for accuracy increases with the seriousness of the consequences for the employee (AERA et al., 1999).

Validity

It is important and necessary to demonstrate that a measure is reliable; it is also necessary to show that the measure captures the essence of the characteristic or attribute being measured. Often, validity is incorrectly thought of as indicating the worth or goodness of a test or other measurement procedure. **Validity** simply refers to the legitimacy or correctness of the inferences that are drawn from a set of measurements or other specified procedures (Cronbach, 1971). During an employment interview, a psychologist measures the height of each applicant with a metal measuring tape. These height measurements are likely to be very reliable. What if the psychologist assumes that taller applicants have more cognitive ability and hires the tallest people? Are the inferences drawn from the physical height measures valid statements of cognitive ability? In other words, can the psychologist make a legitimate inference about cognitive ability from the height data?

Before using any set of measurements, it is essential to demonstrate that the measurements lead to valid inferences about the characteristic or construct under study. It is relatively easy to demonstrate that the metal tape provides valid measures of physical height. The metal tape measure can be scaled to an actual physical standard that is used to define a unit of length. The standard exists apart from the measurement process. In the case of length, the standard is a bar of plutonium maintained under specific atmospheric conditions in government laboratories. It is more difficult to demonstrate the validity of inferences made from many psychological measurements because they deal

validity
The degree to which accumulated evidence and theory support specific interpretations of test scores in the context of the test's proposed use

Chapter 2: Scientific Methods

more with abstract constructs, such as cognitive ability. As discussed earlier in this chapter, the measures may not represent important aspects of a construct (construct underrepresentation), or they may be influenced by aspects of the process that are unrelated to the construct (construct-irrelevant variance). In most of these cases, independent physical standards for the construct do not exist, making validation more difficult, but not impossible. Validation rests upon evidence accumulated through a variety of sources and a theoretical foundation that supports specific interpretations of the measurements.

Validation Strategies

Validity is a unitary concept (AERA et al., 1999; Binning & Barrett, 1989). Different but interrelated strategies are commonly used to assess the accuracy of inferences based on measurements or tests used in the workplace. Sometimes the traditional forms of validation strategies—content validity, construct validity, and criterion-related validity—are mistakenly viewed as representing different types of validity. The *Standards for Educational and Psychological Testing* (AERA et al., 1999) classifies these validation strategies into two categories: (1) *Evidence Based on Test Content,* which includes content and construct validation strategies, and (2) *Evidence Based on Relations to Other Variables,* which includes criterion-related validity. One major document that I/O psychologists rely on is *Principles for the Validation and Use of Personnel Selection Procedures,* 4th ed. (Society for Industrial and Organizational Psychology Inc., 2003). The *Canadian Society of Industrial and Organizational Psychology* has endorsed both the *Standards* and *Principles,* and Canadian I/O psychologists are ethically responsible for their implementation in their work.

Evidence Based on Test Content

This type of validity evidence comes from analyzing the relationship between a test's content and the construct the test is intended to measure. Each construct has a set of associated behaviours or events; these include not only test questions but also tasks, themes, and procedures for administering and scoring the test, among others. In any measurement situation, only a relatively small handful of these behaviours are measured. Evidence of validity based on test content can consist of either empirical or logical analyses of how well the contents of the test, and the interpretation of the test scores, represent the construct. For example, 10 questions are used to test your knowledge of the content of this chapter. Based on the number of correct answers, your professor makes an inference about your *knowledge of scientific methods*. Is the inference justified; that is, do the 10 questions measure knowledge of scientific methods and does the score based on those questions represent your degree of knowledge of scientific methods? Evidence for the validity of your professor's test may be based on the consensus of a group of experts that the behaviours being measured do, in fact, fairly represent the behaviours associated with the construct. It is a judgmental process. Evidence of the validity of the 10 questions used to measure knowledge of scientific methods could be established by a review of those questions by several experts on scientific methods. The agreement of these subject-matter experts (SMEs) that the questions fairly represented the information contained in this chapter constitutes evidence of validity based on the test contents.

Job performance may represent a large number of tasks that have been identified through one of the job analysis procedures we discuss in Chapter 3. SMEs next identify those tasks that are the most important, the most frequently performed, or the most critical to successful job performance. An I/O psychologist can take that information and turn it into a test that samples critical job tasks. The issue here is the degree to which valid inferences can be made about the job performance of an employee from the measure used to assess job performance. Keep in mind that any one of several measures could have been chosen to assess job performance; for example, we could use a supervisor's assessment of the employee, the number of units produced by the employee, the number of days absent, and so on. We will discuss these measures in our chapter on performance management. Similarly, we could have chosen one of many psychological tests to assess cognitive ability. Which one best matches "cognitive ability" as we have defined it and allows us to make the best inferences about that construct? In other words, do our measures of cognitive ability and job performance measure the two constructs that they purport to measure? Answers to these questions are based on logical analysis, expert opinion, and the convergence of the measures with other accepted measures of the construct.

Evidence Based on Relations to Other Variables

This type of evidence is based on an analysis of the relationship between test scores and other variables that are external to the test. For example, a relatively high correlation between a new test of cognitive ability that we created and the Wonderlic Personnel Test, a measure of cognitive ability, and a relatively low correlation between our new cognitive ability test and the NEO-FF, a measure of personality, would be evidence for its validity. In personnel selection, a test score is usually correlated with a score from a performance criterion, an outcome measure, rather than one from another test.

Job applicants are selected for employment; over time, some of the applicants perform at a higher level than do others. Measures of job performance are criterion measures. In selecting job applicants, one goal is to hire only those applicants who will perform at very high levels. But, the applicants have to be hired before job performance can be measured. Is there another variable that is correlated with job performance that can be measured prior to hiring the applicant? Can we use information from this pre-employment measure to make valid inferences about how an individual will perform once in the job? How accurately do test scores predict criterion performance? The goal of establishing *test-criterion relationships* is to address questions like these. The usefulness of test-criterion relationship data rests on the reliability of the measures of the test and of the criterion and on the validity of the inferences drawn from those measures about their respective constructs.

Predictive Evidence for Test-Criterion Relationships

Predictive and *concurrent* validation strategies are popular methods used to provide evidence for test-criterion relationships. Predictive evidence is obtained through research designs that establish a correlation between predictor scores (e.g., cognitive ability scores) obtained before an applicant is hired and the criteria (performance scores) obtained at a later time, usually after an applicant is employed. If all those who apply are hired, both variables can be measured, but at a substantial cost. If all the applicants are hired, some will likely fail on the job. This not only is expensive for the organization but also causes a great deal of emotional distress for those applicants who fail. This procedure also raises serious legal and ethical considerations about the rights of job applicants and the obligations of people who make hiring decisions. To circumvent these problems, a variation on this procedure requires that hiring decisions are made without using information from the predictor measure; the hiring decisions are made according to existing procedures while the validity of the new predictor is established. All the applicants are interviewed and complete a cognitive ability test, but the hiring decision is based solely on their performance on the interview. Job performance information is subsequently collected from the group of hired applicants and correlated with their cognitive ability scores. If the correlation is high, the cognitive ability test may be used to select future job applicants. The high correlation is evidence in support of the position that accurate inferences can be made about job performance from cognitive ability. But there is a problem with this strategy as well. Validity concerns the correctness of inferences made from a set of measurements. Does the validity coefficient, which is based on only those applicants who were hired, apply to all applicants? This will be the case only if the hired applicants fairly represent the total pool of applicants; the only way this can happen is if those hired were randomly selected from the larger pool. Therefore, those who are hired on the basis of the interview will likely differ from those not hired on at least one characteristic, whether or not that characteristic is related to job success.

Concurrent Evidence for Test-Criterion Relationships

Concurrent evidence is obtained through research designs that establish a correlation between predictor and criteria scores from information that is collected at approximately the same time from a specific group of workers. Current employees are asked to take the cognitive ability test; their scores are then correlated with existing measures of their job performance. While concurrent evidence may be easier to collect, these strategies, too, are problematic. The group of existing workers used to develop the validity evidence is likely to be older, more experienced, and certainly more successful than those who apply for jobs. Unsuccessful or unproductive workers most likely are not part of the validation study, as they probably were let go or transferred to other positions. The primary concern here is whether a validity coefficient based on only successful employees can be used as evidence to validate decisions based on predictor scores from a pool of job candidates. Does the validity coefficient computed on one group of workers apply to the pool of applicants? The current workers, who are asked to complete a selection test, may approach the whole exercise with a different attitude and level of motivation than job applicants. These differences may affect selection instruments, particularly those like personality and integrity tests that rely on the test-taker's cooperation in responding truthfully. Statistically, validity coefficients based on concurrent evidence will likely

Box 2.3

Evidence-Based Practice: Validity

Validation studies require relatively large numbers of hires. This is a challenge for many Canadian organizations, particularly small businesses that do not hire many people. Several validation techniques are suited for use with small samples (Sackett & Arvey, 1993):

- Build a database by combining *similar* jobs *across* organizations or companies, with special care taken to ensure comparability of performance measures.
- Accumulate selection scores and performance measures *over time*, as workers leave and are replaced.

- Generalize to your particular case the mean (average) predictive validity for a test as found for jobs similar to the one to which you wish to generalize (i.e., *validity generalization*).
- Generalize to your case the *specific* validity of the test as previously established for a similar job in another setting (i.e., *validity transportability*).

Source: Reprinted by permission of the Society for Industrial and Organizational Psychology.

underestimate the true validity of using the predictor to make decisions within the pool of applicants. For more on validation techniques, see Box 2.3.

Validity Generalization

Suppose that, in attempting to establish the validity of cognitive ability as a predictor of job performance, the I/O psychologist discovered there were many other studies that also investigated the validity of cognitive ability as a predictor of job performance. Could the I/O psychologist combine all the information provided by these other correlation coefficients to obtain an estimate of the true validity of cognitive ability as a predictor of job performance in the new employment setting? These other validity coefficients were obtained under vastly different measurement conditions and from employees who differ dramatically across these studies on a number of characteristics. Most likely the value of the individual validity coefficients will be very inconsistent. In other words, can one estimate the validity of cognitive ability as a predictor of job performance in a specific work setting from the validity coefficients based on other measures of cognitive ability found in other work settings with other groups of workers?

Schmidt and Hunter (1977), in conjunction with several colleagues, challenged the idea that a validity coefficient was specific to the context or environment in which it was measured. They used a procedure known as *meta-analysis* to combine validity coefficients for similar predictor and criterion measures reported by different validity studies. Schmidt and Hunter argued that the relative inconsistency in validity coefficients across studies could be attributed to statistical artifacts such as the range of scores in each study, the reliability of the criterion measures, and sample size (i.e., the number of people in the validity study). In combining the data, meta-analysis weights the results from each separate validity study according to its sample. On the whole, the smaller the study size, the less accurate the results. Validity

validity generalization

The application of validity evidence, obtained through meta analysis of data obtained from many situations, to other situations, which are similar to those on which the meta analysis is based

Chapter 2: Scientific Methods

studies usually involve relatively small study sizes since most organizations do not hire large numbers of people. Schmidt and Hunter demonstrated that, once the effects associated with study size and the other artifacts were removed, the validity between a predictor and a criterion remained relatively stable within similar occupations. For example, the I/O psychologist could use the cognitive ability scores to make predictions about job performance if other validity studies had linked cognitive ability to job performance for similar jobs and if the cognitive ability test being used was a valid measure of cognitive ability.

Factors Affecting Validity Coefficients

Range Restriction

When measurements are made on a subgroup that is more homogeneous than the larger group from which it is selected, validity coefficients obtained on the subgroup are likely to be smaller than those obtained from the larger group. This reduction in the size of the validity coefficient due to the selection process is called *range restriction*. Selection results in a more homogeneous group. Review Figure 2.2 and assume that the 10 data points are from new employees who have been hired on the basis of an interview and file review. The company is now considering using a cognitive ability test as part of its selection program. The most recent new hires are given the cognitive ability test, and their performance is measured one month later. On the basis of these data the company decides to use the cognitive ability test to select new employees; applicants must now score above a 7.0 on cognitive ability to receive a job offer. As shown in Figure 2.2, the cognitive ability scores for the pool of employees range from a low score of 2.0 to a high score of 10.0. The employees who would have been hired had the cognitive ability test been used in selection fall in the upper range of cognitive ability. The range of cognitive ability scores for the hired workers will be narrower or more restricted than the scores of all the applicants. In the case of our example, the cognitive ability scores for the three employees who would have been hired had the test been used ranges from 8.0 to 10.0. Statistically, the magnitude of correlation coefficients, including validity coefficients, decreases as the similarity or homogeneity of characteristics being measured increases. In our example, the correlation between cognitive ability and job performance for the entire pool of employees is $r = 0.56$; for the three who would have been hired with the test, the correlation is smaller, $r = 0.50$. In most cases the size of the reduction in the correlation is much greater than what is shown here with a limited data set. Several statistical procedures correct for range restriction and provide an estimate of what the validity coefficient is likely to be in the larger, unrestricted group.

Measurement Error

The reliability of a measure places an upper limit on validity. Mathematically, the size of a validity coefficient cannot exceed the reliability of the measures used to obtain the data. Validity coefficients obtained from perfectly reliable measures of the predictor and criterion will be higher than those obtained with less than perfect measures. The decrease in magnitude of the validity coefficient associated with measurement error of the predictor, the criterion, or both is called *attenuation*. As with range restriction, statistical procedures provide an estimate of what the validity coefficient would be had it been obtained by using measures that were perfectly reliable (i.e., $r_{xx} = 1.00$).

Sampling Error

Criterion-related validity coefficients are obtained from people who have been hired and are used to assess the accuracy of inferences that are made about individual applicants. The validity coefficient based on a sample is an estimate of what the coefficient is in the entire population; usually, it is impractical or impossible to measure the validity coefficient directly in the population. Estimates of the validity within a population may vary considerably between samples; estimates from small samples are likely to be quite variable.

The statistical procedures that are used to compensate for range restriction, attenuation, and problems related to sampling will almost always produce higher estimates of validity than the uncorrected coefficients. When correction procedures are used, both the corrected and uncorrected validity coefficients should be reported along with a justification for the use of the correction.

Bias and Fairness

Bias

In discussing reliability, we noted that measurement errors could be made in a consistent, or predictable, fashion. In the time clock example, five minutes were added to each worker's arrival time. What if the clock had added five minutes only to the arrival times of female employees? The observed scores are still reliable; however, now they validly represent the true arrival times for male employees but not females. The clock is biased in measuring the arrival times of female employees. This is an example of measurement bias. **Bias** refers to systematic errors in measurement, or inferences made from measurements, that are related to different identifiable group membership characteristics such as age, sex, or race (AERA et al., 1999). An example of bias would be females always scoring higher than males on the cognitive ability measure being used to select employees, when in fact there are no differences in cognitive ability between men and women. Inferences, or predictions, drawn from the biased measurements are themselves biased. Figure 2.2 illustrates a hypothetical situation where the cognitive ability scores of females are higher, on average, than those for the males, reflecting some type of systematic error. In most cases of measurement bias the members of different subgroups perform differently on test items. Items that function differently for subgroups can be identified through statistical procedures and removed from the test, thus reducing the bias.

Predictive bias occurs when errors in prediction are made for members of a subgroup. Consider the regression line in Figure 2.2, which is based on data from both men and women. If regressions were computed for men and

bias

Systematic errors in measurement, or inferences made from measurements, that are related to different identifiable group membership characteristics such as age, sex, or race women separately, it is likely in this case that the two resulting regressions would be different either in terms of their slope, where they cross the *Y*-axis (the intercept), or both. Intercept differences between subgroups tend to be more common than differences in regression slopes. If the regression line in Figure 2.2 were used to make hiring decisions for the company (e.g., "We want employees who will be very good performers, those with performance scores of 6 or better, so hire only applicants with cognitive ability scores of 8 or higher"), the predictions of successful job performance would be biased in favour of the female applicants. This type of bias is known as differential prediction; that is, the predicted, average performance score of a subgroup, in this case males or females, is systematically higher or lower than the average score predicted for the group as a whole. This situation results in a larger proportion of the lower scoring group being rejected on the basis of their test scores even though they would have performed successfully had they been hired. One way to overcome this type of bias is to generate separate regression lines (that is, separate prediction formulas) for males and females (AERA et al., 1999). In Canadian federal organizations, separate prediction formulas are often used in selecting job applicants from anglophone and francophone linguistic groups. In U.S. federal organizations, the use of different selection rules for different identifiable subgroups (often referred to as subgroup norming) is prohibited by U.S. federal law.

Other, more complicated types of bias might occur in a set of measurements (Sackett & Wilk, 1994). Items on a test may elicit a variety of responses other than what was intended, or some items on a test may have different meanings for members of different subgroups. For example, the Bennett Test of Mechanical Comprehension contains pictures related to the use of different tools and machines that tend to be used mostly by males. Males are more likely to recognize these tools and their proper use and perform well on the test. On the other hand, females with good mechanical comprehension may not do as well on the test because of their lack of familiarity with specific tools pictured on the Bennett test. The result is that the test may underestimate the true mechanical ability of female job applicants. This is another example of measurement bias. The statistical procedures needed to establish bias are often complicated and difficult to carry out. Nonetheless, the question of bias can be answered through empirical and objective procedures.

Fairness

fairness

The principle that every test taker should be assessed in an equitable manner

The concept of **fairness** in measurement refers to the value judgments people make about the decisions or outcomes that are based on measurements. An unbiased measure or test may still be viewed as being unfair either by society as a whole or by different groups within it. Canada is a bilingual country composed of French and English language groups. Suppose a completely unbiased cognitive ability test were used to select people for the Canadian civil service, and that all the francophone applicants scored well above the highest scoring anglophone. Such cognitive ability scores would predict that francophones do better on the job than anglophones; only francophones would be hired for the civil service. This outcome would very likely be judged as unfair by

English-speaking Canadians even though it would be the empirically correct decision. Canadians might expect their civil service to represent both official language groups. In fact, political considerations might require that the civil service be proportional to the two linguistic groups. Issues of fairness cannot be determined statistically or empirically. Fairness involves perceptions. An organization may believe it is fair to select qualified females in place of higher-ranking males in order to increase the number of women in the organization; on the other hand, the higher-ranking males who were passed over might not agree. The *Principles for the Validation and Use of Personnel Selection Procedures* (SIOP, 2003) states this about fairness:

> Fairness is a social rather than a psychometric concept. Its definition depends on what one considers to be fair. Fairness has no single meaning, and, therefore, no single definition, whether statistical, psychometric, or social.

(Source: Reprinted by permission of the Society for Industrial and Organizational Psychology.)

Fairness is an even more complex topic issue than bias. Achieving fairness often requires compromise between conflicting interests (Gottfredson, 1994; Sackett & Wilk, 1994). This is particularly so in the case where, for whatever reason, there may be persistent differences in average test scores between different groups in the population but those differences do not necessarily indicate test bias. A test score predicts the same level of performance for members of all groups, but the average test score for one group is lower than another group's, leading to the exclusion of a larger proportion of the group with the lower average score. Lowering the selection standards to include more applicants from this subgroup in order to make the workforce more representative of the general population may come at the cost of reduced productivity. Does an organization have an obligation to make the enterprise as profitable as possible on behalf of its owners, or does it have an obligation to meet the objectives of society by providing equal employment opportunities for members from different population groups? There are no easy answers to this question. In cases such as this, one resolution is to compare the fairness of the test in question to the fairness of an alternative that might be used in place of the test (AERA et al., 1999).

An Introduction to Ethical Issues

Ethics is the means by which we distinguish what is right from what is wrong, what is moral from what is immoral, what may be done from what may not be done. Of course, the laws of our country also tell us what is or is not permissible by imposing penalties, such as fines or imprisonment, on violators. Ethics is a difficult subject because it deals with the large grey area between those behaviours that society punishes as illegal and those that everyone readily agrees are noble and upright. A careful consideration of ethics is important because I/O psychology requires the balancing of the rights and interests of organizations with those of workers, as well as the rights and interests of the I/O psychologist with those of the larger society.

ethics

The determination of right and wrong; the standards of appropriate conduct or behaviour for members of a profession (i.e., what those members may or may not do)

The CPA Code is based on the following four ethical principles, which provide a guide for individual ethical decision making: (1) respect for the dignity of persons, (2) responsible caring, (3) integrity in relationships, and (4) responsibility to society. These principles apply to the research, teaching, and practice carried out by a psychologist. The Code governs the psychologist's relations with other individuals, organizations, and with society in general. The Code requires members of the CPA to obey the laws of the country, avoid conflicts of interest, and remain current in their fields of expertise. Ethical codes place constraints on what those individuals bound by the Code may or may not do as psychologists. However, ethical decision making is not always clear-cut; often decisions must be made in the grey areas of ethics where reasonable people differ in what they consider to be right and wrong. Consider the following two ethical dilemmas.

> As an I/O psychologist you have been directed by your organizational client to find a way to reduce employee theft. You believe that this can be accomplished by screening out people who fail a commercially available "honesty" or "integrity" test. You purchase the test and administer it to all current employees and new applicants and reject or dismiss those who fail the test. Should you be concerned that the test is screening out honest people? Should you be concerned about the reliability and validity of the test and whether it is appropriate to use in your situation? Should you be concerned about wrongful dismissal lawsuits on the part of employees, or human rights actions on the part of applicants? Can you defend your actions if you are charged with violating your code of ethics?

Consider this second ethical dilemma:

> You are a consulting I/O psychologist who is asked by a large employer to design and implement a system to select workers for a manufacturing plant. The plant is unionized, and there is a history of poor union–management relations. Management informs you that it intends to break the union and, as a part of this effort, you are to come up with a selection system that will screen out all new job applicants having pro-union attitudes. The idea is to skew the workforce toward management so that the union can be broken in a future decertification vote. What's more, you are to keep the purpose of the selection system a secret and are asked by management to sign a contract in which you promise not to reveal its intentions to the union, the labour board, or any other outsiders. Where do your loyalties lie? Whose interests should you serve? Is it wrong for you, as an I/O psychologist, to accept a fee to do what management is asking? Does this request violate the CPA Code of Ethics?

Ethical dilemmas raise difficult questions that cut to the very core of ethics. But such questions are unavoidable, because ethics are central to the work of an I/O psychologist. The codes and standards noted in this chapter provide guidance on ethical matters. Violations of these codes and standards may result in professional censure, embarrassment, and, in the most serious cases, removal from the profession. Membership in the profession is based on adherence to its ethics and professional standards. Membership in the professional association is a public guarantee that the member operates in accordance with accepted principles.

Research in Organizational Settings

In this chapter we have discussed research methods from a generic perspective; that is, research methods that apply to all research. Doing research in organizations brings with it some unique problems. In closing, we will highlight briefly some of the additional problems and challenges faced by organizational researchers (Rogelberg & Brooks-Laber, 2002).

Need for New Measures

Researchers often use ad hoc measures that may not adequately address the construct being measured. Researchers often over-rely on retrospective surveys and ignore the potential for other methodologies. New computer technologies allow measuring constructs in real time and across time without geographical constraints. New technologies make physiological measurements affordable and practical in assessing work-related constructs such as affect and emotion.

Participant Burnout

A frequent complaint heard by organizational researchers is "Oh no! Not another survey!" Employees are asked to participate in too many surveys and feel burned out from answering too many questions about their work. The ease of doing Internet surveys has compounded this problem. This is evident in the declining response rates to surveys. As researchers we would like to see response rates to surveys of more than 50 percent of the people we sample; we are very glad, however, when we get a response rate of 30 percent or higher. A related issue is lack of motivation to do the survey. Or, if employees feel obligated to participate, they may sabotage the survey by skipping large sections or responding haphazardly. To encourage participation, researchers often send out several notices or email solicitations, which may backfire and instead discourage participation. Employees often feel "used" and don't see any value in participating. These feelings can be overcome by providing the participants with meaningful feedback through a debriefing that is both informative and educational. Participants should be told what actions have stemmed from the research in which they participated. If there is no action, they should be told why that has happened.

Employee Mistrust

Most employees view the entry of organizational researchers into a company with a high degree of suspicion. In many cases the suspicion is well earned. The researcher is often viewed as a management spy. Researchers have to be completely honest about whom they are working for, who will see the data, and whether the responses will be confidential and anonymous.

Lack of clarity in answering these questions breeds mistrust. In cases such as personnel selection, the I/O psychologist must make it absolutely clear who they are working for; that is, who is the client—the employee or the company, or both?

Overreliance on Correlational Methods

As we noted previously in this chapter, it is difficult to do true experimental studies within organizations for a variety of reasons. A result of this is the use of surveys. In addition to participant burnout, we then have a database created through only one methodology. Different methodologies should be used to examine an issue, as each provides a different perspective on what may be the true state of affairs. Different methods may be costly to implement, but the payoff in new knowledge is worth it. Organizational researchers need to develop valid, appropriate methodologies to examine organizational issues.

What We Can Learn from Others

As I/O psychologists, researchers have been trained with a set of specific research methods that we present in this chapter; however, there may be much to learn from other disciplines. We tend to ignore qualitative methods but they may provide valuable insights. We can draw on the methods used by sociologists, anthropologists, and cognitive psychologists to examine organizational issues.

Demonstrating Value

Research can be initiated by an organization, or an organization may allow a researcher to collect data within the company. Often young researchers or students approach a company and ask if they can use its employees as study participants because they need data to complete a thesis. More often than not, the researcher or student is told no. Organizations need to see both the relevance and value of the research, and it is up to the researcher to make these connections. The questions that researchers ask and wish to study must be meaningful to the organization.

Summary

Science produces information that is based on accepting as true only that objective information that can withstand continued attempts to cast doubt on its accuracy. The accuracy of scientific statements is examined empirically through methods that can be observed, critiqued, and used by others. Scientific information is dynamic and constantly evolving. Scientific procedures allow for the measurement of important human characteristics that are related to industrial and organizational psychology. The reliability and validity of the information used as part of I/O psychology procedures must be established empirically. The methods used to establish reliability and validity can be quite complex and require a good statistical background. The measures used by I/O psychologists to make inferences about people and organizations must be able to withstand attempts to cast doubt on their correctness. In all of their work, I/O psychologists are obligated to follow the codes of ethics endorsed by their profession.

Key Terms

bias 49

error score or measurement error 34

ethics 51

experimentation 29

fairness 50

hypothesis 27

measurement 32

measurement scale 35

observed score 34

operational definitions 28

random errors 34

reliability 39

systematic errors 40

true score 34

validity 43

validity generalization 47

variables 28

Web Links

Athabasca University lists an extensive list of links to resources on research methods and statistics; go to:

http://psych.athabascau.ca/html/aupr/tools.shtml

For more information on psychological research methods, go to:

http://psychology.about.com/od/researchmethods/Psychology_Research_Methods.htm

For more information on basic statistical procedures, go to:

http://wise.cgu.edu

Test reliability and validity information is provided at:

http://www.socialresearchmethods.net/kb/relandval.php

The Principles for the Validation and Use of Personnel Selection Procedures, 4th ed., may be viewed online at:

http://www.siop.org/_Principles/principlesdefault.aspx

The Code of Ethics of the Canadian Psychological Society can be found at:

http://www.cpa.ca/cpasite/userfiles/Documents/Canadian%20Code%20of%20Ethics%20for%20Psycho.pdf

Discussion Questions

1. Does an organization have an obligation to make the enterprise as profitable as possible on behalf of its owners, or does it have an obligation to meet the objectives of society by providing equal employment opportunities for members from different population groups?

2. This chapter lays the groundwork for scientific selection of personnel. Reviewing the chapter suggests that implementation of scientific procedures may be a cost to the employer. Why is this better than going with a "gut feeling" about an appropriate applicant to hire?

3. If a selection test is given only once to an applicant, how can the employer assess its reliability and validity?

4. Considerable correlational evidence shows that smokers are less productive than nonsmokers. Costs to organizations, besides those related to medical care and health and life insurance, include absenteeism and loss of on-the-job time. Estimates place time loss per day due to smoking at 35 minutes a day, or 18.2 lost days per year per employee who smokes. In addition, smokers are absent three more days per year than other employees. These correlational data suggest that it is in an employer's best interests to hire only nonsmokers, or to fire smokers who cannot overcome their addiction. Would such policies—hiring only nonsmokers and firing smokers—be acceptable? How would you defend these policies if you are challenged by a group of smokers' rights advocates?

Using the Internet

(Instructors may wish to assign this exercise a week ahead of class time.)
A significant portion of this chapter has dealt with tests and testing procedures. In a later chapter we will explore the use of different types of employment tests that have very good reputations for reliability and validity. Access to these tests is restricted for obvious reasons. They can be administered only by qualified examiners, unlike the "IQ" and "personality" tests you may come across in newspapers or magazines. While these tests are fun to take, they may have questionable reliability and validity.

There are many sites on the Internet devoted to tests, some serious and some for fun. One of the better sites is Queendom Mind and Body, at http://www.queendom.com.

This site offers an array of tests, including IQ, personality, and emotional intelligence. All of the tests are free, can be taken online, and are immediately scored. Unlike some of the other sites it offers statistical information on the reliability of almost all of its tests and on the validity of some. Most of the reliability data are based on measures of internal consistency.

As part of this exercise we will ask you to take the Classical IQ Test, the Emotional IQ Test, and the Extroversion/Introversion Inventory. Queendom.com will provide you with a report containing your scores and inferences from your scores about how you fare on the three constructs. Please download copies of each report as well as the statistical data provided for each test. Your instructor will arrange for you to anonymously record your scores from these tests so that data may be accumulated over the whole class for the following exercises. We will also ask you to record your sex and your cumulative grade point average or percentage (if you don't know this last item, an estimate will do).

a. Test-Retest Reliability. Wait at least one week after taking the three tests and then retake all three. Once all the data from the class are compiled, your instructor will compute the correlation between the first and second administration of the three tests.

- Is each test reliable (tests with reliability coefficients greater than .70 are generally considered to have acceptable reliability)?
- How does the test-retest reliability compare with the reliability values presented online?
- What do you think the reasons may be for any differences?
- What factors may have led you to perform differently on each of the two testing occasions?

b. Validity. Examine the content of each test; that is, examine the nature of the test questions (you are allowed to download a copy of each test).

- Do you think that the contents of each test reflect the essential nature of the construct it attempts to measure?
- Based on other empirical and theoretical evidence, we would not expect there to be a strong relationship between classical IQ (a measure of cognitive ability) and extroversion/introversion (a measure of personality). Emotional intelligence has been presented as a construct, which is different from both cognitive ability and personality. There should be very low correlations among the test scores from these three tests. A high correlation between emotional intelligence and extroversion/introversion might suggest that both tests are measures of the same construct. Your instructor will correlate the three test scores for the class using data from the first test administration. What is the relationship among the three test scores?
- Cognitive ability is associated with academic performance. The Classical IQ test measures cognitive ability and your cumulative grade point average (GPA) is an estimate of your academic performance. GPA is a criterion. What is the correlation between Classical IQ and GPA for your class, as reported by your instructor? Does this correlation indicate that you may make accurate inferences about academic performance from your IQ test scores? Is there a strong correlation between the Emotional IQ scores and GPA? Between Extroversion/Introversion? If so, what do you think these correlations suggest?

c. Bias. You or your instructor will have to analyze the class data separately for males and females. Compare the mean score for each group across the three tests. Compute the correlations among the three tests for men and women.

- Do you obtain similar results for males and females?
- Are any of the three tests biased?

d. Fairness. Do you believe that each of these three tests is fair? How would you react if you were given any of these three tests when you applied for your next job?

Exercises

1. Measure the length of your classroom without using a measuring tape or ruler. Describe the standard of measurement you chose to use. What are the difficulties inherent in using a standard such as the one you chose?
2. Have at least three different people measure the length of the room using your standard of measurement. How similar are their measurements? What does this imply about the accuracy of your measure? What does this imply about the accuracy of the observers?
3. We presented two ethical dilemmas in the text, but intentionally did not provide any guidance on a resolution of those issues. In this exercise, obtain and read a copy of the CPA Code of Ethics from the CPA website at www.cpa.ca. Form small groups and prepare a resolution to the two dilemmas.

Case

A growing number of Canadian companies are using measures of emotional intelligence (EQ) as part of the screening devices administered to job applicants. These companies are looking for a measure to tap into emotions. They are seeking candidates who have the ability to inspire colleagues, to handle customers, and to be a positive influence in the office. One of the more popular measures of emotional intelligence is the Bar-On Emotional Quotient Inventory (EQ-i), which is distributed by Multi-Health Systems of Toronto. Proponents of EQ-i argue that cognitive ability has to do with solving math problems and verbal ability has its place, but emotional skills are much more valuable to being successful in the workplace. Can a measure of emotional intelligence predict job success? Some industrial-organizational psychologists are skeptical because the concept is too fuzzy and EQ tests are too imprecise to be reliable. They ask, "Why should there be a relationship between job performance and EQ?"

Discussion Questions

1. What do you think? Do the data that you collected in the Internet exercise help you to answer this question?
2. Should there be a relationship between job performance and EQ? Can you support your answer with any empirical data?
3. How can the construct of EQ be improved? Is it too broad? Is EQ simply another aspect of personality?
4. If you were going to use EQ as part of your selection system, discuss the steps that you would take to ensure you were able to make reliable and accurate inferences about job performance in your work situation.

CHAPTER 3

Job Analysis and Competency Models

This chapter is divided into two parts. The first part begins with a discussion of job analysis and its relevance to human resources development, and continues with a discussion of several job analysis techniques. Then the chapter concludes with a presentation on competency models as an alternative procedure to job analysis.

Chapter Learning Outcomes

After reading this chapter you should be able to

- Understand the importance of job analysis and the role it plays in human resource functions
- Recognize processes for identifying job descriptions and job specifications used in human resources
- Recognize some of the common job analysis methods
- Appreciate the relation of job analysis to legal requirements
- Understand the factors to consider in choosing among different job analysis procedures
- Understand what competencies are
- Distinguish competency-based human resources models from those based on job analysis

Job Analysis

The passage in Box 3.1 is taken from the Supreme Court of Canada decision— now commonly referred to as the *Meiorin* decision—that set new legal standards in Canada for the use of tests in personnel selection. For the moment, our interest in the case pertains to the importance of doing a proper job analysis prior to establishing criteria for hiring job applicants. In the *Meiorin* case, the British Columbia government undertook a job analysis of the position of firefighter to determine the essential components of firefighting and then to create a series of tests to measure those components among firefighters. In terms of a selection process, the researchers did not show that "the prescribed aerobic capacity was necessary for either men or women to perform the work of a forest firefighter satisfactorily." In the Court's opinion, the research failed to establish a linkage between the test and firefighter performance, and also failed to take into account physiological differences between men and women. In Chapter 2 we reviewed several measurement and validity issues with which every I/O psychologist must be familiar; some of these issues surfaced in this case. In this chapter we extend our discussion to the concept of job analysis itself.

Box 3.1

The *Meiorin* Case

Ms. Meiorin was employed for three years by the British Columbia Ministry of Forests as a member of a three-person Initial Attack Forest Firefighting Crew in the Golden Forest District. The crew's job was to attack and suppress forest fires while they were small and could be contained. Ms. Meiorin's supervisors found her work to be satisfactory.

Ms. Meiorin was not asked to take a physical fitness test until 1994, when she was required to pass the Government's "Bona Fide Occupational Fitness Tests and Standards for B.C. Forest Service Wildland Firefighters" (the "Tests"). The Tests required that the forest firefighters weigh less than 200 lbs. (with their equipment) and complete a shuttle run, an upright rowing exercise, and a pump carrying/hose dragging exercise within stipulated times. The running test was designed to test the forest firefighters' aerobic fitness and was based on the view that forest firefighters must have a minimum "VO$_2$ max" of 50 ml·kg^{-1}·min^{-1} (the "aerobic standard"). "VO$_2$ max" measures "maximal oxygen uptake," or the rate at which the body can take in oxygen, transport it to the muscles, and use it to produce energy.

The Tests were developed in response to a 1991 Coroner's Inquest Report that recommended that only physically fit employees be assigned as front-line forest firefighters for safety reasons. The Government commissioned a team of researchers from the University of Victoria to undertake a review of its existing fitness standards with a view to protecting the safety of firefighters while meeting human rights norms. The researchers developed the Tests by identifying the essential components of forest firefighting, measuring the physiological demands of

those components, selecting fitness tests to measure those demands, and, finally, assessing the validity of those tests.

The researchers studied various sample groups. The specific tasks performed by forest firefighters were identified by reviewing amalgamated data collected by the British Columbia Forest Service. The physiological demands of those tasks were then measured by observing test subjects as they performed them in the field. One simulation involved 18 firefighters, another involved 10 firefighters, but it is unclear from the researchers' report whether the subjects at this stage were male or female. The researchers asked a pilot group of 10 university student volunteers (6 females and 4 males) to perform a series of proposed fitness tests and field exercises. After refining the preferred tests, the researchers observed them being performed by a larger sample group composed of 31 forest firefighter trainees and 15 university student volunteers (31 males and 15 females), and correlated their results with the group's performance in the field. Having concluded that the preferred tests were accurate predictors of actual forest firefighting performance—including the running test designed to gauge whether the subject met the aerobic standard—the researchers presented their report to the Government in 1992.

A follow-up study in 1994 of 77 male forest firefighters and 2 female forest firefighters used the same methodology. However, the researchers this time recommended that the Government initiate another study to examine the impact of the Tests on women, but there is no evidence that the Government responded to this recommendation.

Two aspects of the researchers' methodology are critical to this case. First, it was primarily descriptive, based on measuring the average performance levels of the test subjects and converting these data into minimum performance standards. Second, it did not seem to distinguish between the male and female test subjects.

After four attempts, Ms. Meiorin failed to meet the aerobic standard, running the distance in 11 minutes and 49.4 seconds instead of the required 11 minutes. As a result, she was laid off. Her union subsequently brought a grievance on her behalf. The arbitrator designated to hear the grievance was required to determine whether she had been improperly dismissed.

Evidence accepted by the arbitrator demonstrated that, owing to physiological differences, most women have lower aerobic capacity than most men. Even with training, most women cannot increase their aerobic capacity to the level required by the aerobic standard, although training can allow most men to meet it. The arbitrator also heard evidence that 65% to 70% of male applicants pass the Tests on their initial attempts, while only 35% of female applicants have similar success. Of the 800 to 900 Initial Attack Crew members employed by the Government in 1995, only 100 to 150 were female.

There was no credible evidence showing that the prescribed aerobic capacity was necessary for either men or women to perform the work of a forest firefighter satisfactorily. On the contrary, Ms. Meiorin had in the past performed her work well, without apparent risk to herself, her colleagues, or the public.

Source: From CATANO/WIESNER/HACKETT. *Recruitment and Selection in Canada*, 4E. © 2010 Nelson Education Ltd. Reproduced by permission. www.cengage.com/permissions.

The *Meiorin* case illustrates the need to do a proper and valid job analysis before setting out to establish employment standards. In most employment situations, there are many applicants for each available job. The employer's goal is to hire an applicant who possesses the knowledge, skills, abilities, or other attributes (KSAOs) required to successfully perform the job being filled. A properly conducted job analysis helps the employer identify the KSAOs that are related to successful job performance. The job analysis also helps to identify both the duties that will be performed as part of the job and the level of performance required for job success. Hiring someone through an assessment of job-related attributes is based on an assumption that higher levels of attributes are linked to higher levels of job performance. Next we proceed to discuss job analysis in more detail, followed by an overview of some of the more popular methods used in conducting job analyses.

What Is Job Analysis?

Job analysis is the process of collecting information about jobs "by any method for any purpose" (Ash, 1988). In its simplest terms, a job analysis is a systematic process for gathering, documenting, and analyzing data about the work required for a job. Job analysis data include a description of the context and principal duties of the job, including job responsibilities and working conditions, and information about the knowledge, skills, abilities, and other characteristics required in its performance. In short, it is a method that provides a description of the job and profiles the characteristics or competencies people need to have in order to be successful in the job. There are three key points to remember about job analysis:

1. A job analysis does not refer to a single methodology but rather to a range of techniques.

2. A job analysis is a formal, structured process carried out under a set of guidelines established in advance.
3. A job analysis breaks down a job into its constituent parts, rather than looking at the job as a whole

Figure 3.1 presents an overview of our discussion on job analysis; it starts with the sources of information and the methods used to obtain data for a job analysis and concludes with the two products of a job analysis—a job description and a job specification—that are then used in different human resource functions. As presented in Figure 3.1, job analysis data support several organizational activities including recruitment and selection, training and development, performance appraisal, compensation or job evaluation, and health and safety in the workplace (Levine, Ash, & Bennett, 1980). These activities, which focus on identifying a match between a person and a job, rely on accurate information produced by a job analysis. Job analysis helps to ensure that decisions made with respect to these activities are good decisions (i.e., fair and accurate), and that these employee-related decisions can be defended in courts and legal tribunals when necessary. Job analysis is a procedure to assess the goodness of fit between people and jobs in a specific environment. Job analysis provides information about both the duties and tasks that form part of the job (job description) as well as the knowledge, skills, abilities, and other characteristics (**KSAOs**; see Box 3.2 for definitions) that are needed to perform those duties and tasks successfully (job specification).

KSAOs

The knowledge, skills, abilities, and other attributes necessary for a new employee to do well on the job; also referred to as *job, employment, or worker specifications*

job description

A written description of what job occupants are required to do, how they are supposed to do it, and the rationale for any required job procedures.

FIGURE 3.1

Overview of Job Analysis Process and Outcomes

Data Sources
Supervisors
Employees
Job Analyst
O*NET
NOC

Types of Data
Tasks
Duties
Responsibilities
Standards
Knowledge
Skills
Abilities
Other Characteristics
People
Things
Information

Job Description
Tasks
Duties
Responsibilities

Human Resource Functions
Recruitment
Selection
Training and Development
Performance Appraisal
Health and Safety
Compensation

JA Methods
Interviews
Questionnaires
Observation
PAQ
FJA
FJAS
Critical Incidents
Other Methods

Job Specification
Knowledge
Skills
Abilities
Other Characteristics
Physical Demands
Work Environment

A job analysis identifies the job tasks and duties or responsibilities and the related KSAOs; these are the two basic products of a job analysis. The first is formally referred to as a **job description**, a written description of what the people in the job are required to do, how they are supposed to do it, and the rationale for any required job procedures. A job description contains a summary of job analysis data. The second product is a **job specification**, which states the KSAOs that are required to perform the job successfully.

An advertisement for a job generally includes elements of both the job description and the job requirements, although they may not necessarily be labelled as such. Box 3.3 presents a possible job ad for the position of company recruiter. Both the job description and job requirements may be much more detailed and specific than what is presented in the job ad. The advertisement generally concentrates on the most important aspects of the position.

Job Analysis and the Law

In today's society, many employers often find themselves having to defend employment decisions before courts or administrative tribunals such as arbitration boards. One of the best defences against such lawsuits is to demonstrate that the decisions were based on sound, job-related information (Sparks, 1988). Job analysis is a legally acceptable way of determining job-relatedness. In Canada any job requirements that have the potential to discriminate against individuals with respect to a "prohibited ground of discrimination" (see Box 3.4) must meet the standards set by the Supreme Court of Canada in *British Columbia (Public Service Employee Relations Comm.) v. BCGSEU* (also known as the *Meiorin* decision) for being bona fide occupational requirements. A bona fide occupational requirement (BFOR) is a

job specification

The knowledge, skills, abilities, and other attributes that are needed by a job incumbent to perform well on the job.

Box 3.3

Example Job Description for a Company Recruiter

The recruiter is responsible for all organizational recruiting of new personnel. The major goal of this position is to bring into the company the best new talent available. The recruiter will develop recruiting plans that employ both traditional and innovative recruiting strategies, including approaches such as Internet-based recruitment. The primary job duties for the recruiter are to:

- Develop and execute recruiting plans
- Network through industry and business contacts, trade groups, and related business associations
- Develop a pool of qualified candidates for available positions
- Staff vacant positions
- Proactively search for the best available talent
- Use appropriate sources, including the Internet, to locate talent
- Coordinate and implement all recruiting initiatives
- Review applicant files to determine fit with position
- Conduct preliminary screening interviews
- Maintain and manage applicant files and databases

The successful candidate must demonstrate proficiency with respect to the following requirements:

- Previous recruiting experience of three to five years in a corporate environment
- A bachelor's degree
- Excellent interpersonal skills
- Excellent computer skills, including database management
- Knowledge of effective interviewing techniques
- Excellent oral and written communication skills
- Knowledge of recruiting sources
- Ability to work as part of a team
- Free to travel for recruitment-related purposes
- A certified human resources professional (CHRP) is preferred

Applicants are invited to submit a cover letter, a résumé, and the names of three references by email to Jane Doe, WXYZ Co., by August 31. The WXYZ Co. is committed to Employment Equity. Reasonable accommodations will be made for applicants with disabilities to enable them to perform essential job functions.

procedure used to defend a discriminatory employment practice or policy on the grounds that the policy or practice is job-related and was adopted in an honest and good-faith belief that it was reasonably necessary to ensure the efficient and economical performance of the job without endangering employees or the general public. The BFOR must be reasonably related to the accomplishment of legitimate work-related purposes. Finally, an employer must show that it is impossible to accommodate individuals sharing the characteristic on which the discrimination is based without imposing undue hardship upon the employer (Catano et al., 2009).

A good job analysis ensures that accurate information on skill, effort, responsibility, and working conditions is specified, reducing the likelihood of impediments to equitable employment access for all Canadians. A job analysis provides objective evidence of the skills and abilities required for effective performance in the job, which can then be used to provide evidence of the relevance of the selection procedures measuring those abilities. It is essential to establishing a BFOR defence with respect to alleged discriminatory practices. In practice, if not in law, the starting point for defensible employment decisions is a job analysis.

Box 3.4

Prohibited Grounds of Employment Under the *Canadian Human Rights Act*

Section 8 of the *Canadian Human Rights Act* refers to "a prohibited ground of discrimination." Under this Act, the following are grounds on which discrimination is prohibited:

- Race
- National or ethnic origin
- Colour
- Religion
- Age
- Sex (including pregnancy and childbirth)
- Marital status

- Family status
- Mental or physical disability (including previous or present drug or alcohol dependence)
- Pardoned conviction
- Sexual orientation

The prohibited grounds of discrimination vary somewhat among the provinces and territories. There are six prohibited grounds of employment discrimination on which all jurisdictions agree: race or colour, religion or creed, age, sex, marital status, and physical/mental handicap or disability.

Work- and Worker-Oriented Job Analysis

With one or two exceptions, all job analysis methods fall into one of two categories (Peterson & Jeanneret, 2007). In **work-oriented job analysis,** the emphasis is on work outcomes and description of the various tasks performed to accomplish those outcomes. These methods produce "descriptions of job content that have a dominant association with, and typically characterize, the *technological* aspects of jobs and commonly reflect what is achieved by the worker" (McCormick, Jeanneret, & Mecham, 1972). The descriptions of tasks or job duties generated via work-oriented methods are typically characterized by their frequency of occurrence or the amount of time spent on them, the importance to the job outcome, and the difficulty inherent in executing them (Gael, 1983; Ghorpade, 1988). Because task inventories generated via work-oriented techniques are developed for specific jobs, or occupational areas, the results are highly specific and may have little or no relationship to the content of jobs in other fields (McCormick & Jeanneret, 1991).

work-oriented job analysis
Job analysis techniques that emphasize work outcomes and descriptions of the various tasks performed to accomplish those outcomes

Alternatively, **worker-oriented job analysis** methods focus on general aspects of jobs that describe perceptual, interpersonal, sensory, cognitive, and physical activities. Worker-oriented methods generate descriptions "that tend more to characterize the generalized human behaviours involved; if not directly, then by strong inference" (McCormick, Jeanneret, & Mecham, 1972). These techniques are not limited to describing specific jobs; they are generic in nature and the results can be applied to a wide spectrum of task-dissimilar jobs (McCormick & Jeanneret, 1991).

worker-oriented job analysis
Job analysis techniques that emphasize general aspects of jobs that describe perceptual, interpersonal, sensory, cognitive, and physical activities

Getting Started: Gathering Job-Related Information

In preparing for a job analysis, the first step should be to collect existing information describing the target job from sources such as organizational charts, legal requirements, job descriptions, union regulations, and previous data from related jobs. In addition, job-related information can be found in two excellent occupational databases, the National Occupational Classification and the Occupational Information Network.

The National Occupational Classification (NOC) systematically describes occupations in the Canadian labour market based on extensive occupational research. It is available online at http://www5.hrsdc.gc.ca/NOC-CNP/app/index.aspx. NOC profiles present both a description and a specification of the job or occupation. Each job or occupation is given a four-digit code that provides a more extensive description related to the KSAOs associated with the job.

Figure 3.2 presents a synopsis of the descriptors used in the NOC, along with scales used to rate each job. For example, a rating of 3 on the "Vision" subscale in the "Physical Activities" section means that the job in question requires both near and far vision for successful completion. Full descriptions of all the scales can be found in the *Career Handbook* that is available on the NOC website. Such information, when gathered and studied in advance, will prove invaluable for organizing and conducting the ensuing analysis.

The Occupational Information Network (O*NET) is an electronic database developed by the U.S. Department of Labor. O*NET was first released for public use in the fall of 1998, and is available online at http://www.doleta.gov/programs/onet/. Figure 3.3 presents the conceptual foundation of the O*NET model, which provides a framework that identifies the most important types of information about work and integrates them into a theoretically and empirically sound system.

In addition to occupational databases, attention should be given to determining which techniques will be employed for gathering additional information related to the job in question. The two major databases are good starting places, but each job may have unique characteristics that require further analysis within the local context. Depending on the objective of the job analysis, some techniques are better suited than others for providing job information (Gael, 1988). Job analysis typically involves a series of steps, often beginning with interviews or observations that provide the information to construct a task inventory or to complete a structured questionnaire. Ideally, a combination of strategies is used to arrive at a comprehensive and accurate description of the job (Cascio, 1998; Harvey, 1991), although each job analysis method contributes slightly different information.

Job Analysis Methods

The following section presents an overview of some of the more popular job analysis methods, including comments on their major strengths and weaknesses. People who carry out the job analysis are called *job analysts*. Those who are most knowledgeable about a job and how it is currently performed are called **subject-matter experts (SMEs)**. Generally, SMEs are job incumbents—the employees currently in the job, and their supervisors. SMEs may also be trained job analysts or consultants who are familiar with the job analysis method being used.

subject-matter experts (SMEs)

Those who are most knowledgeable about a job and how it is currently performed

FIGURE 3.2

A Synopsis of Descriptors and Labels

APTITUDES

One of five levels assigned for each factor, with levels representing normal curve distribution of the labour force:

G	General Learning Ability	**Q**	Clerical Perception
V	Verbal Ability	**K**	Motor Coordination
N	Numerical Ability	**F**	Finger Dexterity
S	Spatial Perception	**M**	Manual Dexterity
P	Form Perception		

INTERESTS

Three of five descriptive factors, assigned in order of predominance and lower case rating indicating weaker representation:

D	Directive
I	Innovative
M	Methodical
O	Objective
S	Social

DATA/INFORMATION, PEOPLE, THINGS

D – Data/Information

0	Synthesizing
1	Coordinating
2	Analyzing
3	Compiling
4	Computing
5	Copying
6	Comparing
7	—
8	Not significant

P – People

0	Mentoring
1	Negotiating
2	Instructing – Consulting
3	Supervising
4	Diverting
5	Persuading
6	Speaking – Signalling
7	Serving – Assisting
8	Not significant

T – Things

0	Setting up
1	Precision working
2	Controlling
3	Driving – Operating
4	Operating – Manipulating
5	Tending
6	Feeding – Offbearing
7	Handling
8	Not significant

PHYSICAL ACTIVITIES

One of several levels assigned for each factor:

Vision

1	Close visual acuity
2	Near vision
3	Near and far vision
4	Total visual field

Colour Discrimination

0	Not relevant
1	Relevant

Hearing

1	Limited
2	Verbal interaction
3	Other sound discrimination

Body Position

1	Sitting
2	Standing and/or walking
3	Sitting, standing, walking
4	Other body positions

Limb Coordination

0	Not relevant
1	Upper limb coordination
2	Multiple limb coordination

Strength

1	Limited
2	Light
3	Medium
4	Heavy

ENVIRONMENTAL CONDITIONS

Location

L1	Regulated inside climate
L2	Unregulated inside climate
L3	Outside
L4	In a vehicle or cab

Hazards

H1	Dangerous chemical substances
H2	Biological agents
H3	Equipment, machinery, tools
H4	Electricity
H5	Radiation
H6	Flying particles, falling objects
H7	Fire, steam, hot surfaces
H8	Dangerous locations

Discomforts

D1	Noise
D2	Vibration
D3	Odours
D4	Non-toxic dusts
D5	Wetness

EMPLOYMENT REQUIREMENTS

Education/Training Indicators

1	No formal education or training requirements
2	Some high school education and/or on-the-job training or experience
3	Completion of high school
4	Completion of course work, training, workshops and/or experience related to the occupation
5	Apprenticeship, specialized training, vocational school training
6	College, technical school (certificate, diploma)
7	Undergraduate degree
8	Postgraduate or professional degree
+	Indicating an additional requirement beyond education/training (e.g., extensive experience, demonstrated or creative ability, appointments, etc.)
R	Regulated requirements exist for this group

Source: *National Occupation Classification Career Handbook* (Table 11), Human Resources Skills and Development Canada, 2003. Reproduced with the permission of the Minister of Public Works and Government Services Canada, 2010.

FIGURE 3.3

The O*NET Content Model

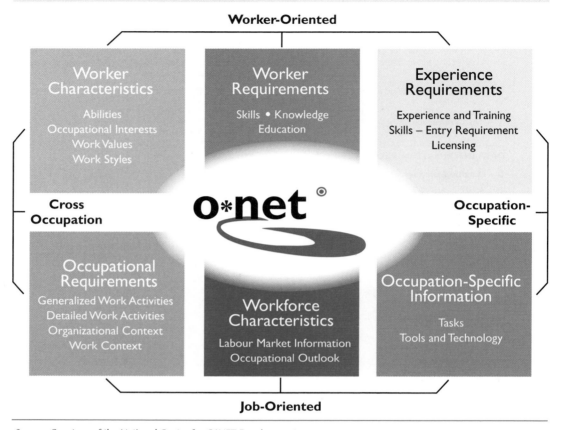

Worker-Oriented

Worker Characteristics

Abilities
Occupational Interests
Work Values
Work Styles

Worker Requirements

Skills • Knowledge
Education

Experience Requirements

Experience and Training
Skills – Entry Requirement
Licensing

Cross Occupation

O*net

Occupation-Specific

Occupational Requirements

Generalized Work Activities
Detailed Work Activities
Organizational Context
Work Context

Workforce Characteristics

Labour Market Information
Occupational Outlook

Occupation-Specific Information

Tasks
Tools and Technology

Job-Oriented

Source: Courtesy of the National Center for O*NET Development.

Interviews

The interview is perhaps the most commonly used technique for gathering job facts and establishing the tasks and behaviours that define a job. This method involves questioning individuals or small groups of current employees and supervisors about the work that gets done. The people who are interviewed should include those who have a good working knowledge of the job. The interview may be structured or unstructured, although for job analysis purposes a structured format produces better information. The results of a job analysis interview may stand on their own, as in a formal integrated report, when there are few incumbents working within a small geographical area. Or, they may provide the necessary information for completing a task inventory, structured questionnaire, or other job analysis procedure (Gael, 1983, 1988). The structured interview method is designed so that all interviewees are asked the same job-related questions.

An interview outline prompts the interviewer to ask important questions about the job to all interviewees. The intent is to identify the tasks that make up each job. The result of the interview should be a clear description of the job and its requirements. Interview outlines can vary from presenting a few informal prompts to listing very structured questions to be addressed in a specific order. In general, the more specific the interview outline is, the more reliable the information obtained from interviewees will be.

Although interviews should be well structured, they also allow interviewees to contribute information that may be overlooked by other analysis techniques. There are, however, certain disadvantages to job analysis interviews. First, they can be expensive and time consuming and may be impractical for jobs with a large number of incumbents. Interviews take a great deal of time to conduct and may require a substantial number of interviewees to be truly representative of the job incumbent pool. See Box 3.5 for job analysis interview guidelines.

Box 3.5

Guidelines for a Job Analysis Interview

1. **Announce the job analysis well ahead of the interview date.** The impending job analysis and its purpose should be well known among employees and management. The job analysis process should be positioned as a collaborative effort with all job incumbents and their supervisors holding valid information about the job and invited to contribute to the process.

2. **Participation in interviews should be voluntary, and job incumbents should be interviewed only with the permission of their supervisors.** The job analyst avoids creating friction within the organization and is sensitive to the use of coercion in obtaining information. In general, when analysis interviews are free from organizational politics they can be completed in a timely manner with valid, uncontaminated results.

3. **Interviews should be conducted in a private location free from status earmarks.** It would be unwise, for example, to conduct interviews with hourly workers in the company president's office. The job analyst is a nonpartisan party whose primary objective is to accurately describe the content of jobs; interviewees should feel comfortable and able to provide truthful information about their work and the conditions under which it is done.

4. **Open the interview by establishing rapport with the employee and explaining the purpose of the interview.** Interviews are often associated with anxiety-provoking events such as job and promotion applications and even disciplinary action. The experienced interviewer takes time at the outset to create a non-threatening environment and alleviate any fears that interviewees might have.

5. **Ask open-ended questions, using language that is easy to understand, and allow ample time for the employee's responses.** Most people, given the opportunity, will talk in great detail about the work they do. The good analyst avoids rushing or intimidating people, does not talk down to them, and takes a genuine interest in the interviewee's responses.

6. **Guide the session without being authoritative or overbearing.** Keep the interview on topic and avoid discussions concerning worker–management relations and other unrelated topics. When discussions become tangential, the analyst can bring them back on track by summarizing relevant details and referring to the interview outline.

7. **Explain to the employees that records of the interviews will identify them only by confidential codes.** The names of interviewees and other personal information should be protected. When confidentiality is ensured, more accurate information will be obtained. The limits of confidentiality should be explained to all interviewees before they agree to participate. For example, data on age, sex, and ethnic background may have to be recorded in order to demonstrate in any subsequent court challenges that the data are based on a representative sample of the workforce.

Source: From CATANO/WIESNER/HACKETT. *Recruitment and Selection in Canada*, 4E. © 2010 Nelson Education Ltd. Reproduced by permission. www.cengage.com/permissions.

Direct Observation

One of the most effective ways to determine what effective employees do on the job is to observe their behaviour as they carry out their jobs (Martinko, 1988), sometimes called *job shadowing*. This method allows the job analyst to come into direct contact with the job; thus, the data are obtained firsthand, rather than obtained indirectly through questionnaires and surveys (Martinko, 1988). Direct observation is most useful when the job analysis involves easily observable activities (Cascio, 1998). Analyzing the job of "poet" through direct observation would likely produce little of value, whereas the job of "landscaper" lends itself more readily to direct observation.

Job analysts conducting direct observation sessions should be aware that their presence may change the behaviour of the employees. Imagine yourself at work, and a strange individual with a clipboard begins to write down everything you do, or to video record your efforts. Knowing you are being watched, you may respond by doing your work according to what you think the observer is looking for rather than doing it as you would in your normal day-to-day routine. This effect can be minimized when the observer blends into the surroundings (e.g., by choosing an unobtrusive observation position) and when employees have been informed of the purpose of the observations and are observed only with their explicit permission.

The interview or observational data are next used by the job analyst to identify critical task statements, which are used to generate employee specifications. The critical components of the job are described in terms of (1) the actions performed, (2) the people, data, or things affected by the actions, (3) the intended outcome or product of the action, and (4) the materials, tools, and procedures used in performing the action. Once the task statements are identified, they are further described in terms of the KSAOs that are required to perform the job successfully. Identification of the KSAOs is not automatic; it depends on the expertise and knowledge of the job analyst to understand what KSAOs are needed to perform a task. Direct observation and interview methods are generally used in conjunction with other job analysis methods.

Rating Task Statements and KSAOs

Tasks are examples of the work that employees perform as part of their job. In a job analysis specific tasks are written in the form of task statements, which have a specific format that lends them to further analysis. Task statements should provide a clear picture of what is being done, how it is being done, and why it is being done. A task statement should include information that answers four questions:

1. What action is being performed?
2. Whom or what is the object of the action?
3. What is the outcome of the action?
4. What tools or equipment are used, if any?

An example of a good task statement for an airport security officer might be: "Pats down traveller by hand following x-ray screen to find prohibited material."

All tasks are not equal. Some are performed more frequently than others, some are more important, and some require a degree of difficulty to perform. A task may be performed frequently but has little importance and does not require a great deal of skill; another may be performed rarely but has extreme importance attached to it. Thus, the job analyst asks the SMEs to rate the importance of the final set of task statements and their associated KSAOs. Generally, the SMEs rate each task with respect to frequency, importance, and difficulty. Evaluation of the ratings obtained from all the SMEs helps the job analyst identify the most important tasks and the KSAOs that are needed to perform those tasks to fully understand what goes on in the job.

Structured Job Analysis Questionnaires and Inventories

Structured job analysis questionnaires and inventories require workers and other subject-matter experts to respond to written questions about their jobs. Respondents are asked to make judgments about activities and tasks, tools and equipment, and working conditions involved in the job. These can be off-the-shelf questionnaires and inventories that are amenable for use in a variety of jobs, such as the worker-oriented Position Analysis Questionnaire (PAQ) (McCormick, Jeanneret, & Mecham, 1989), or they can be developed by the analyst for the specific job and organization, such as a task inventory developed for a specific job. We present examples of both worker-oriented and work-oriented job analysis methods.

POSITION ANALYSIS QUESTIONNAIRE (PAQ) The PAQ is a worker-oriented, structured job analysis questionnaire that focuses on the general behaviours that make up a job. It assumes that all jobs can be characterized in terms of a limited number of human abilities. The PAQ includes 195 items, called job elements, that are organized into six dimensions:

1. *Information input* assesses the sources of information a worker uses on the job;
2. *Mental processes* statements refer to the types of reasoning, decision-making, planning, and information-processing behaviours used by the employee;
3. *Work output* items relate to the physical activities engaged in and the tools used by the worker;
4. *Relationships* with other persons measure the types of interpersonal relationships inherent in the job;
5. *Job context* elements measure the physical and social environment in which the work takes place; and
6. *Other job characteristics* measure conditions of work not falling into the other five categories (McCormick, Jeanneret, & Mecham, 1989).

(Source: Reprinted by permission of PAQ Services, Inc.)

Each of the six dimensions is subdivided into sections made up of items related to particular job facets (i.e., components of job dimensions). Facets of information input include visual and non-visual sources of job information, and sensory and perceptual processes. Items used to assess visual sources of job information ask respondents to rate the extent to which they use written, quantitative, and pictorial materials, visual displays, mechanical devices, and so on. With this method, the job analyst reviews background job information, conducts extensive interviews with incumbents, observes the job, and rates the extent to which each item of the questionnaire applies to the target job (McPhail et al., 1991). Each item is rated using an appropriate response scale.

There are several advantages to using the PAQ. First, it can be used with a small number of incumbents yet generates valid results, and it is standardized, thereby permitting easy comparisons between jobs. Second, it is a straightforward process to get from PAQ results to selection procedures. Finally, the PAQ has been rated as one of the most cost-efficient job analysis methods (Levine, Ash, & Bennett, 1980). The primary disadvantages are that (1) because it is a worker-oriented technique, the PAQ does not quantify what work actually gets done on the job (Gatewood, Feild, & Barrick, 2008; McCormick, 1979), that is, even though there are numerical scales, these cannot be used to compare different jobs or aspects of jobs; and (2) the reading level of the PAQ is too difficult for many lower-level workers. Important task differences between jobs may not be picked up because of the PAQ's focus on behaviours and the emphasis on overlooking the context within which the work occurs.

The PAQ does not generate task statements; instead SMEs note whether a PAQ attribute is essential for new hires to possess at the time of their hiring. If so, the attribute is included as a KSAO to be used in employee selection. More information on the PAQ can be found on the PAQ website at http://www.paq.com.

COMMON METRIC QUESTIONNAIRE   The common metric questionnaire (CMQ) (Harvey, 1993; Personnel Systems and Technologies Corporation (PSTC), 2000) is a structured, off-the-shelf job analysis questionnaire that captures important context variables. It promises up-to-date job analysis information corresponding to what people actually do at work, and a database describing jobs in terms of observable aspects of the work rather than subjective ratings systems (PSTC, 2000). The reading level is appropriate for lower-level jobs, and the content appears to be appropriate for both lower- and higher-level jobs. The CMQ asks questions in five sections pertaining to background information, contacts with people, decision making, physical and mechanical activities, and work setting (HR-Guide.com, 2000). More information on the CMQ can be found at http://cmqonline.com.

WORK PROFILING SYSTEM   The work profiling system (WPS) is a worker-oriented job analysis method that consists of three versions applicable to managerial, service, and technical occupations. The WPS is a computer-administered structured questionnaire that can be completed and scored online in the workplace. It measures ability and personality attributes including hearing skills, sight, taste, smell, touch, body coordination, verbal skills, number skills, complex management skills, personality, and team role (Harvey, 1991). WPS defines the KSAOs required for effective performance and generates employment specifications based on the highest-ranking survey items across respondents. Another advantage to using the WPS is that according to its developers it builds an organizational map of related jobs and job families, providing critical information for selecting jobs for rotation, cross-training, and teams.

TASK INVENTORIES Task inventories are work-oriented surveys that break down jobs into their component tasks. A well-constructed survey permits workers to define their jobs in relation to a subset of tasks appearing on the inventory (Christal & Weissmuller, 1988). Task inventories should assess (1) the duties performed, (2) the level of difficulty of job duties, (3) the job context, and (4) criticality of duties to the job. The task statements that form the task inventory are objectively based descriptions of what gets done on a job. Tasks are worker activities that result in an outcome that serves some specified purpose (Levine et al., 1983; McCormick & Jeanneret, 1991). These inventories are typically developed for specific jobs or occupations in contrast to worker-oriented methods that permit application of instruments to a wide variety of unrelated jobs.

task inventories
Methods used to infer employee specifications from job analysis data; commonly included in the job analysis literature

FUNCTIONAL JOB ANALYSIS Fine and Cronshaw (1999) distinguish between what a worker does and what is accomplished in the functional job analysis (FJA) method. They define task statements as "verbal formulations of activities that make it possible to describe what workers do *and* what gets done so that recruitment, selection and payment can be efficiently and equitably carried out."

In FJA, well-written task statements clearly describe what an employee does so that an individual unfamiliar with the job should be able to read and understand each task statement. Task statements are based on the four elements discussed above (Fine & Cronshaw, 1999; Levine, 1983). Taken together, task statements describe all the essential components of the job. Task statements that define a job may vary from as few as six (Gatewood et al., 2008) to more than 100 (Levine, 1983). The task statements should be specific enough to be useful in pinpointing job specifications, but not so specific as to be cumbersome. Once the inventory is completed, SMEs rate the tasks on several scales. Primarily, the scales rate each task with respect to the degree that it involves data, people, and things (Fine, 1989; Fine & Cronshaw, 1999; Gatewood et al., 2008). Workers then rate each task according to how frequently they perform the task, the task's criticality (i.e., the consequences of errors), and its importance to the job.

Fine (1988) argues that, "the most important issue is whether the task needs to be performed to get the work done. If it is necessary, then it is important and critical, and frequency does not matter." A worker in a nuclear power facility may, for example, be required to enter and conduct rescues in radiologically contaminated spaces. While the rescue operation is rarely, if ever, necessary in the life of a job, it is essential that certain workers be able to perform to stringent standards at any given time and is thus a critical component of the job.

Task inventories are advantageous in that they are efficient to use with large numbers of employees and are easily translated to quantifiable measures. On the other hand, they can be time consuming to develop and thus can be expensive (Cascio, 1998). Motivating incumbents to participate in the rating process may also be a problem with long inventories. When the task inventory

Steven F. Cronshaw

Steven Cronshaw is a professor in the School of Business at the University of Northern British Columbia. He holds a BA in psychology and a BComm degree in accounting from the University of Saskatchewan. He completed his graduate work at the University of Akron, where he obtained both an MA and a PhD in industrial/organizational psychology. He is a fellow of the Canadian Psychological Association. Prior to moving to UNBC, Dr. Cronshaw was a professor at the University of Guelph in Ontario, where he was one of the leaders in developing that school's doctoral program in I/O psychology. Dr. Cronshaw is author and co-author of

books, book chapters, and journal articles on human resources management and consulting psychology. He has consulted widely to Canadian organizations on job analysis, recruitment and selection, and human rights in the workplace. He has worked extensively with Dr. Sidney Fine, the father of functional job analysis, and in 1999 co-authored with him *Functional Job Analysis: A Foundation for Human Resources Management*, published by Lawrence Erlbaum as part of its applied psychology series. Edward Fleishman, another leading authority on job analysis, made these remarks in the preface to that text:

> Fine and Cronshaw go well beyond the conventional description of HR techniques. They capture the excitement and vitality—the spirit—of JA and JR activities as diverse as recruitment and selection, job design, career development, and individual accommodations for disabled workers. Fine and Cronshaw feel deeply that this spirit, which reflects the wholeness of the individual in trusting and healthy organizations, represents a better future for Americans at work. Their hope is that FJA will have a role to play in bringing about that better future.

Source: Courtesy of Steven Cronshaw.

procedure and analysis are well planned, the results can be extremely valuable in developing recruitment and selection programs.

CRITICAL INCIDENT TECHNIQUE   Critical incidents are examples of effective and ineffective work behaviours that are related to superior or inferior performance. The critical incident technique generates behaviourally focused descriptions of work activities (Bownas & Bernardin, 1988). It provides important, contextually rich examples of job behaviours.

The first step in this method is to gather a panel of job experts, usually consisting of people with several years' experience, who have had the opportunity to observe both poor and exemplary workers on the job. The job of the panel is to write critical incidents based on their work experience. A critical incident is an observable human activity that is sufficiently complete to facilitate inferences and predictions about the person performing the act (Flanagan, 1954). Panel members describe incidents, including the antecedents to the activity, a complete description of the behaviour, the results of the behaviour, and whether the results were within the control of the worker. Incidents are also rated in terms of whether they represent effective or ineffective behaviour on the part of the employee. The incidents are gathered by asking the panellists to address three points:

1. The situation leading up to the incident.
2. The actions or behaviours of the main person involved in the incident.
3. The results or outcomes of the actions or behaviours.

After the incidents are gathered, they are edited into narratives. Box 3.6 provides examples of effective and ineffective critical incidents. Once all of the critical incidents are in hand, SMEs sort the incidents into categories that reflect underlying performance dimensions that can be used to identify important KSAOs that are related to the job.

FLEISHMAN JOB ANALYSIS SURVEY The Fleishman Job Analysis Survey (F-JAS) (Fleishman, 1992) was developed as a system for identifying employee characteristics that influence job performance. The F-JAS is an example of a **worker trait inventory** method that makes inferences about the KSAOs needed for a job without first defining the tasks required by the job. It assumes that job tasks differ with respect to the abilities required to perform them successfully, and that all jobs can be classified according to ability requirements. Fleishman

worker trait inventories
Methods used to infer employee specifications from job analysis data; commonly included in the job analysis literature

---

Box 3.6

Examples of Edited Critical Incidents

An incident illustrating effective behaviour on the part of a dentist:

As a child, regular visits to the dentist were always somewhat perilous. The [child] patient was never very enthusiastic. The dentist was very friendly, and after every session—whether treatment or checkup—she would give the child a gift such as a toothbrush, eraser, or toy. The result was that the child was not as anxious about going to the dentist and in fact looked forward to the visit.

An incident illustrating ineffective behaviour on the part of a dentist:

A child was visiting the dentist for the first time and he was scared. The child finally stopped crying and allowed the dentist to check his teeth. When the dentist was feeling inside the mouth, the child bit down on the dentist's fingers as hard as he could. The dentist excused himself and went to the staff room where he punched a hole through the wall and cursed loudly. The mother, who had heard the dentist, grabbed the child and stated that she would never return.

---

and his colleagues identified 52 ability categories that included oral comprehension to multi-limb coordination to night vision, among others. SMEs are presented with a job description or task list that has been developed through other methods. The experts rate the extent to which each ability is required for the job as a whole or for each task. Ratings on the ability scales are then averaged to identify the overall ability requirements essential to the job (Fleishman & Mumford, 1988). The F-JAS is relatively simple to administer and cost-efficient, but its biggest limitation is that it provides information only on the 52 abilities. Fleishman and Reilly (1992) have produced a companion handbook that provides examples of tasks and jobs that require the specific ability, as well as listing examples of tests designed to measure the ability. The F-JAS, however, does not identify knowledge, skills, or other attributes that may also be required to perform a job.

Choosing a Job Analysis Method

Levine et al. (1983) developed a set of questions that can be used to help decide among various job analysis techniques.

- *Operational status:* Has the method been tested and refined sufficiently?
- *Availability:* Is it available off the shelf?
- *Occupational versatility:* Is it suitable for analyzing a variety of jobs?
- *Standardization:* Is it possible to compare your results with others that have been found elsewhere?
- *User acceptability:* Is the method acceptable to the client and the employees who will have to provide the information?
- *Training requirements:* How much training is needed and available to use the method; must one receive special certification in the procedure to use it? Can it be done in-house?
- *Sample size:* From how many employees must data be collected for the method to provide reliable results?
- *Reliability:* Will the method give results that are replicable?
- *Cost:* What are the costs of a method in materials, consultant fees, training, and person-hours?
- *Quality of outcome:* Will the method yield high-quality results (e.g., legally defensible)?
- *Time to completion:* How many calendar days will the data collection and analysis take?

(Source: Duane Thompson and Toni Thompson (1982). Court standards for job analysis in test validation. *Personnel Psychology*, 24(4): 865–874. Copyright © 1982, John Wiley and Sons.)

Furthermore, the job analyst must determine whether the job analysis procedure will meet legal standards. Thompson and Thompson (1982) developed a set of guidelines to help answer this question. The guidelines are based on U.S. court decisions but represent what might also be expected from Canadian courts and tribunals when they evaluate the information produced by a job analysis.

- A job analysis must be performed according to a set of formal procedures. It is not acceptable to rely on what "everyone" knows about a job, since that knowledge may be based on inaccurate, stereotyped notions of the job demands.
- The job analysis must be well documented; it is not enough to simply carry around job information in the analyst's head.
- The job analysis should collect data from several up-to-date sources. This suggests using several different methods of job analysis.
- The sample of people interviewed should be sufficient in number to capture accurately the job information. The sample should also represent the full diversity of job incumbents (e.g., ethnic and gender groups, people with and without formal qualifications) to ensure the validity of the data.
- The job analysts should be properly trained in the different techniques to ensure they collect objective information and are as free from bias as possible.
- The job analysis should determine the most important and critical aspects of the job, and it is upon these that the key attributes and selection and evaluation for the job should be based.

There is no guarantee that any job analysis method will find acceptance before the courts. The best that can be said is that having done a formal job analysis, regardless of method, is better than not having done one, and having carried it out properly will increase the probability that the courts will accept its results. Given the limitations of different methods and their suitability to different HR management functions, it is not unusual for an organization to use several job analysis techniques. Often, such multi-method approaches are needed to understand the complexity of today's jobs where the dividing lines between job, worker, and job-related behaviours become blurred. Using a variety of approaches is a form of "triangulation" and provides different

Box 3.7

Job Analysis Resources on the Internet

The Web addresses listed at the end of this chapter under Web Links provide useful resources to help students and professionals learn about and conduct job analyses. The sites provide information on job analysis methods, their uses, and links to other relevant sites. The most comprehensive site, HR-Guide.com, also provides links for users to research legal issues, tips for conducting job analyses, and FAQs, along with up-to-date descriptions of commonly used interview, observation, and structured questionnaire methods. Official websites for the NOC and O*NET are sources of standard occupational dictionaries and employment specifications. The NOC site, for example, contains a search engine enabling the user to retrieve information by searching job titles, aptitudes, interests, and other work characteristics. Sites for specific job analysis tools enable users to review the tools and learn about their application, scoring, and commercially available services.

Source: From CATANO/WIESNER/HACKETT. *Recruitment and Selection in Canada*, 4E. © 2010 Nelson Education Ltd. Reproduced by permission. www.cengage.com/permissions.

perspectives on the job that, when synthesized, produces the best information for matching people to jobs. Ultimately, what the HR practitioner must decide is: (1) Which job analysis method best serves the intended purpose of the job analysis (i.e., will the data be used for selection, performance appraisal, job evaluation, etc.); (2) Can the job analysis be carried out reliably given the number of positions to be assessed, the availability of SMEs, the time allowed to complete the project, and the cooperation of job incumbents; and (3) Which job analysis method has the best track record with respect to technical adequacy and legal defensibility (Peterson & Jeanneret, 2007)? See Box 3.7 for information on online job analysis resources.

The Role of Competencies in Recruitment and Selection

Today's workplace is in the midst of unprecedented change as it struggles to adapt to increasing global competition, rapid advances in information technology, multitasking, and changing workforce demographics. Emerging from this turbulence are worker requirements unlike any we have seen in the past. With many of the routine aspects of work now done by machines, jobs have been redefined, with a greater emphasis given to the management of technology. In this post-industrial information era, workers are required to apply a wider range of skills to an ever-changing series of tasks. Individuals just entering the workforce will face at least three to four career changes in their lifetime. Workers will be expected to possess the skills and knowledge of two or three traditional employees (Greenbaum, 1996). On the factory floor, jobs change rapidly, and workers constantly rotate among positions, acquiring multiple and generic skills. Today's workplace poses special challenges when trying to match people to jobs.

For many workers, these changes mean that the tasks performed today may be radically different from those required a few months from today. Skill requirements for employees may be increased or decreased depending on the type of technology employed (Methot & Phillips-Grant, 1998). Task and job instability create a growing need for hiring people with an already-learned set of skills and the ability to make decisions and adapt to changing organizational demands. The results of a job analysis may hold for only as long as the job remains configured the way it was at the time of the job analysis (Cascio, 1998). With decreasing specialization and shifting of shared work assignments typical of today's work, traditional methods of job analysis may not be appropriate. That is, they are simply inconsistent with the new management practices of cross-training assignments, self-managed teams, and increased responsibility at all organizational levels.

The evolution toward rapidly changing jobs and organizations that demand flexibility of their workers has led to a search for alternatives to traditional job analysis techniques. In order to recruit, select, and promote flexible workers who are able to make their own rules and adjust to the changing demands of work, there is an ever-increasing need to adjust methods to ensure that people are hired based on the needs of the organization while remaining within legal boundaries. One approach being used in rapidly changing environments is to select employees based on **competencies** that are thought to be related to successful job performance. A growing number of Canadian organizations have implemented competency-based management strategies.

competencies

Groups of related behaviours that are needed for successful job performance in an organization

What Is a Competency?

Boyatzis (1982) popularized the term "competency" in *The Competent Manager* and defined it as a combination of a motive, trait, skill, aspect of one's self-image or social role, or body of relevant knowledge. This definition left much room for debate and has been followed since by a plethora of definitions that tend to reflect either individual or specific organizational concerns. While various definitions of competency may differ, they generally contain three elements. First, most suggest that competencies are the KSAOs that underlie effective or successful job performance; second, the KSAOs must be observable or measurable; and third, the KSAOs must distinguish among superior and other performers (Catano, 2002). Competencies, then, are measurable attributes that distinguish outstanding performers from others in a defined job context.

Competencies have also been defined as groups of related behaviours, rather than the KSAOs, that are needed for successful job performance in an organization. Similarly, they have been defined as the behaviours that superior performers in an organization exhibit more consistently than others do, although in practice competencies at times have been based on "average" performance. In both cases, we are concerned with identifying and measuring the KSAOs that underlie what the organization considers to be successful job performance, whether that performance is recognized as average or superior.

Competency-based management systems take the view that employees must be capable of moving between jobs and carrying out the associated tasks for different positions (Reitsma, 1993). In the competency-based approach, organizations attempt to identify those KSAOs that distinguish superior performers from others and that will allow an organization to achieve its strategic goals. By selecting people who possess KSAOs that lead to superior performance, organizations are attempting to establish a closer connection between organizational success and individual performance. Recall that worker trait systems identify KSAOs for specific jobs; competency-based approaches initially sought to identify KSAOs that applied to all employees *regardless* of the job they held. However, this has changed and many competency-based systems now identify job-level KSAOs as well as those that apply at the organizational level.

Competency Framework or "Architecture"

Competency models identify a common set of generic competencies that apply to a broad range of jobs (Mansfield, 1996). In this way, the KSAOs for a specific job are de-emphasized. While identifying only broad-based organizational competencies had value for certain human resource functions, it had limited

Chapter 3: Job Analysis and Competency Models

value for others, such as selection. Would you want to fly in an airplane where an airline selected both pilots and flight attendants using only the competencies of leadership, motivation, trust, problem solving, interpersonal skills, and communication, and ignored the specific skills and abilities required for either position? More recently, organizations that use competency models have recognized that they must include the competencies required at the specific job level. Today, organizations that use competency models mostly develop a three-tiered framework or architecture. They identify competencies that apply across all jobs in the organization (core competencies), those that apply to a group of similar jobs (functional competencies), and those that apply to a single class of jobs (job-specific competencies).

Competency Categories

core competencies

Characteristics that every member of an organization, regardless of position, function, job, or level of responsibility within the organization, is expected to possess

Core competencies are those characteristics that apply to every member of the organization regardless of their position, function, or level of responsibility within the organization. Core competencies hold for every position in the organization. Core competencies support the organization's mission, vision, and values. They are organizational KSAOs that are required for organizational success (Prahalad & Hamel, 1990). Core competencies are what an organization or individual does or should do best; they are key strengths that organizations and individuals posses and demonstrate (Lahti, 1999). An airline could require that all employees from the chief executive officer down to pilots and flight attendants and on to the lowest-level employee exhibit the common core competencies of leadership, motivation, trust, problem solving, interpersonal skills, and communication.

functional competencies

Characteristics shared by different positions within an organization (i.e., a group of related or similar jobs); only those members of an organization in these positions are expected to possess these competencies

Functional competencies are characteristics shared by different positions within an organization that belong to a common job group or occupational family or by employees performing a common function. They are the common characteristics shared by different positions within the job group. They describe the KSAOs that are required for any job within the job group. For example, pilots and navigators may share the same KSAOs of map reading and developing flight plans, while flight attendants and ticket agents must both exhibit courtesy and a service orientation.

job–specific competencies

Characteristics that apply only to specific positions within the organization; only those people in the position are expected to possess these competencies

Job-specific competencies are characteristics that apply only to specific positions within the organization. These are competencies that are associated with a position in addition to core and role competencies. A pilot needs a wide range of skills to fly a plane; a navigator does not have to have those skills even though they may be part of the same occupational family. Similarly, a ticket agent needs to operate the computerized reservation system; the flight attendant does not need those skills. Employees need to know the competencies that are required for them to do their own job successfully.

Core, functional, and job-specific competencies comprise the architecture of a company's competency model. Core competencies are the foundation on which to build functional competencies, which in turn serve as the base for job-specific competencies. In practice, the architecture may vary across organizations, with some companies increasing or decreasing the number of layers.

As well, organizations may choose to use different names for the layers in the competency model; for example, referring to "organizational" competencies in place of "core" competencies, "group" in place of "functional," and "task" in place of "job-specific."

Competency Dictionaries

A **competency dictionary** lists all the competencies that are required by an organization to achieve its mandate. It would include the core and all functional and job-specific competencies identified throughout the organization. It defines each competency in terms of the behaviours and KSAOs related to each competency. As part of developing a competency framework, an organization must develop a competency dictionary. Figure 3.4 presents a sample page from a competency dictionary for the core competency of Communication.

competency dictionary
A listing of all of the competencies required by an organization to achieve its mandate, along with the proficiency level required to perform successfully in different functional groups or positions

FIGURE 3.4

A Sample Competency Dictionary Entry and Its Associated Proficiency Scale

Communication proficiency levels required for different positions within a company

Communication involves communicating ideas and information orally and/or in writing in a way that ensures the messages are easily understood by others; listening to and understanding the comments and questions of others; marketing key points effectively to a target audience; and speaking and writing in a logical, well-ordered way.

Proficiency Level			
Basic 1	Proficient 2	Very proficient 3	Mastery 4
Using basic communication skills	*Using effective communication skills*	*Using effective presentation skills*	*Using strategic communication skills*
• Writes and speaks meaningful language	• Delivers information in a timely manner to ensure that others have needed facts	• Structures communication to meet the needs of the audience	• Represents the organization with tact and diplomacy both internally and externally
• Comprehends written and verbal instructions	• Communicates effectively with other work units	• Presents complex information in a clear, concise, and credible manner	• Articulates and promotes the interests of the organization

Level 1: Data entry clerk
Level 2: Sales associate
Level 3: General manager
Level 4: Corporate vice-president

Source: From CATANO/WIESNER/HACKETT. *Recruitment and Selection in Canada*, 4E. © 2010 Nelson Education Ltd. Reproduced by permission. www.cengage.com/permissions.

proficiency level

The level at which a competency must be performed to ensure success in a given functional group or position

A competency dictionary also includes information on the **proficiency level** needed to successfully perform each competency for each position in the organization. All organization members are expected to exhibit all of the core competencies; however, they are not expected to do so to the same degree. For example, the behavioural expectations for communication may vary across positions in the organization (see Figure 3.4) for Communication. The level of proficiency increases with organizational level. A corporate vice-president would be expected to have a greater proficiency in communication than a sales representative. Those at the higher levels are expected to be capable of expressing the behavioural demands at one level before moving on to a higher-ranking position. Organizations using a competency model identify the proficiency levels on the required competencies for each position in the organization. The organization assesses each employee or potential employee with respect to the required proficiency levels and then uses these for selection, development and training, and promotion purposes.

proficiency scale

A series of behavioural indicators expected at specific levels of a competency

Proficiency scales, like that represented in Figure 3.4, are included as part of a competency dictionary. The proficiency scale is independent of any position. The levels in a proficiency scale reflect real, observable differences from one organizational level to another. The proficiency scale is not a tool to assess employees; it presents a series of behaviours that are expected at specific levels of a competency. The behavioural indicators listed on the scale in Figure 3.4 are there simply to illustrate the concept. An actual scale might have considerably more indicators at each proficiency level as well as having more rating levels. The proficiency scale would be developed to meet the needs of the organization.

competency profile

A set of proficiency ratings related to a function, job, or employee

A **competency profile** is a set of proficiency ratings related to a function, job, or employee. Since core competencies apply to all functions and jobs, they are included as part of functional and job-specific profiles. The proficiency level required on the core competencies, however, would vary across functions and positions. A functional competency profile would include the proficiency levels for all the core and functional competencies related to the occupational family that form the functional group. A job-specific profile adds the proficiency levels required for a specific position within the functional group. Figure 3.5 presents a competency profile developed by Human Resources and Skills Development Canada (HRSDC) for the position of Citizen Service Agent (Bonder, 2003). The number in parentheses following each competency represents the proficiency level required for that competency for successful job performance. An organization that decides to use competency models must have the capability to identify the required competencies and then to assess accurately the competency level of each employee with respect to the competency and match the employee's competency profile to that required by a position.

Competency Modelling versus Job Analysis

A recent task force composed of advocates of both traditional job analysis and competency-based procedures reviewed both methodologies using technical and non-technical criteria for evaluation. Job analysis was judged superior on

FIGURE 3.5

A Competency Profile for an HRSDC Citizen Service Agent

Citizen Service Agent (PM–01)

Group Competencies (Primary)
- Applying Principles and Procedures (4)
- Diagnostic Information Gathering (4)
- Verification and Accuracy (4)
- Interpersonal Awareness (4)

competency profile

Core Competencies
- Communication (4)
- Thinking Skills (4)
- Using Technology (3)
- Changing and Learning (3)
- Client Focus (4)
- Initiative (3)
- Positive Attitude (4)
- Working with Others (3)
- Knowing Our Business (3)

Task Competencies
- Knowledge of Service Canada Programs and Services (3)

Source: Courtesy of Arieh Bonder.

nine of ten criteria. The only criterion where competency modelling was seen to have an edge was with respect to a more transparent linkage between business goals or strategies and the information provided by the competency-based approach. In all other instances, both proponents of job analysis and competency modelling rated the traditional job analysis methods as more rigorous, particularly in providing more reliable information (Shippmann et al., 2000).

The task force also identified other, less technical criteria and concluded that competency approaches were more likely to focus on generic personal characteristics that are common across a broad range of jobs. It viewed competency approaches as being closely aligned with worker-oriented job analyses. The emphasis on these types of characteristics gave competency modelling higher levels of "face validity" with organizational decision makers. Executives typically commented that competencies provided them with a common language. As organizations continue to "de-complicate" business processes, the increased face validity of competency modelling procedures and their focus on core competencies holds wide appeal. However, these factors have resulted in decreased quality of the technical information needed for legal defensibility purposes (Shippmann et al., 2000).

A Generic Competency Framework

Competency management frameworks are increasingly used by Canadian organizations. They are used by the federal government's Organizational

Readiness Office and Personnel Psychology Centre, the Royal Canadian Mounted Police, the Canadian Society of Association Executives, and the Police Sector Council, among others. The competency models used in these organizations vary, but there are some commonalities with respect to the competencies they value.

Bartram (2005) analyzed 29 competency studies through a meta-analysis. He presented a model of performance that was based on eight broad competency factors. The eight factors were based upon analyses of self- and manager ratings of workplace performance. The eight "great" factors aggregate 112 sub-competencies. These eight generic factors and their definitions are presented in Table 3.1, along with likely predictors of those competencies.

TABLE 3.1

Eight "Great" Competencies

Factor	Competency	Competency definition	Predictor
1	Leading and Deciding	Takes control and exercises leadership. Initiates action, gives direction, and takes responsibility.	Need for power and control, extraversion
2	Supporting and Cooperating	Supports others and shows respect and positive regard for them in social situations. Puts people first, working effectively with individuals and teams, clients, and staff. Behaves consistently with clear personal values that complement those of the organization.	Agreeableness
3	Interacting and Presenting	Communicates and networks effectively. Successfully persuades and influences others. Relates to others in a confident, relaxed manner.	Extraversion, general mental ability
4	Analyzing and Interpreting	Shows evidence of clear analytical thinking. Gets to the heart of complex problems and issues. Applies own expertise effectively. Quickly takes on new technology. Communicates well in writing.	General mental ability, openness to new experience
5	Creating and Conceptualizing	Works well in situations requiring openness to new ideas and experiences. Seeks out learning opportunities. Handles situations and problems with innovation and creativity. Thinks broadly and strategically. Supports and drives organizational change.	Openness to new experience, general mental ability
6	Organizing and Executing	Plans ahead and works in a systematic and organized way. Follows directions and procedures. Focuses on customer satisfaction and delivers a quality service or product to the agreed standards.	Conscientiousness, general mental ability
7	Adapting and Coping	Adapts and responds well to change. Manages pressure effectively and copes well with setbacks.	Emotional stability
8	Enterprising and Performing	Focuses on results and achieving personal work objectives. Works best when work is related closely to results and the impact of personal efforts is obvious. Shows an understanding of business, commerce, and finance. Seeks opportunities for self-development and career advancement.	Need for achievement, negative agreeableness

Source: Bartram, D. 2005. The great eight competencies: A criterion-centric approach to validation. *Journal of Applied Psychology* 90: 1185–1203. Copyright © 2005 by the American Psychological Association. Reproduced with permission.

People and Work in Canada

Summary

This chapter began with a discussion of job analysis and its relevance to human resource functions, continued with a discussion of several job analysis methodologies, and ended with an introduction to competency-based models as alternatives to job analysis. As the workplace rapidly changes with the introduction of new technologies and global competition, human resources practitioners will need to combine organizational and job analysis techniques to hire the best job candidates.

Job analysis is a process of collecting information about jobs and encompasses many methods, which fall into two broad categories: work-oriented and worker-oriented methods. Work-oriented methods result in specific descriptions of work outcomes and tasks performed to accomplish them. Worker-oriented methods produce descriptions of worker traits and characteristics necessary for successful performance. There is no one right way of conducting a job analysis; all methods follow a logical process for defining employment or worker specifications (KSAOs). While job analysis is not a legal requirement for determining KSAOs and selecting employees, the employer must demonstrate job-relatedness of selection criteria if challenged in court.

Regardless of the method used, a good job analysis begins with the collection of background information. Gathering job descriptions defined in the NOC or O*NET is a recommended first step. It is also good practice for the analyst to employ a combination of methods, typically beginning with interviews or observations of employees on the job. The resulting information can then be used to construct a task inventory or provide a backdrop for completing structured questionnaires. Employment specifications are generated by identifying the most frequently occurring activities or requirements in interviews and observations or by identifying those items in an inventory or questionnaire receiving the highest ratings of criticality. A wide variety of techniques are available for analyzing jobs. While some focus primarily on the work that gets done, others focus on generic human behaviours that are relevant to all work. Deciding which of these techniques to use is based on the goal of the analysis, the resources available to the analyst, and the needs of the organization. No one method will be completely acceptable for all selection needs in an organization. Job analysts must themselves be adaptable in the methods they apply.

Organizations that compete in a global environment that is often unpredictable and unstable have to change quickly in order to survive. To meet these demands, some organizations are placing more emphasis on the competencies of individual workers rather than on the specific tasks that those workers will perform. They expect all employees to possess core competencies that are related to the organization's mission or goals, as well as functional and job-specific competencies that are related to successful performance in a position or job. This emphasis on competencies has taken place in the absence of an agreed-upon definition of what constitutes a "competency" and of an agreed-upon methodology for identifying competencies. In several respects, competency-based systems are similar to worker-trait job analysis methods in providing information about the KSAOs and behaviours needed for successful job performance but without identifying the tasks that workers are required to do in their jobs.

Competency-based systems, just as more traditional job analysis methods, must provide information that is valid and meets legal requirements. In deciding between both approaches, competency-based models may "speak the language of business" but they provide technically inferior information. I/O psychologists must decide which of these factors is most relevant to their situation.

Key Terms

competencies 79

competency dictionary 81

competency profile 82

core competencies 80

functional competencies 80

job description 62

job specification 63

job-specific competencies 80

KSAOs 62

proficiency level 82

proficiency scale 82

subject-matter experts (SMEs) 66

task inventories 73

work-oriented job analysis 65

worker trait inventories 75

worker-oriented job analysis 65

Web Links w(w)w

General Information Sites

HR-Guide.com contains links to Web-based resources for HR professionals and students:

http://www.hr-guide.com/jobanalysis.htm

Harvey's Job Analysis & Personality Research Site:

http://harvey.psyc.vt.edu/

Job Analysis Internet Guide:

http://www.job-analysis.net/

Sites for Job Classification Systems

NOC:

http://www5.hrsdc.gc.ca/NOC-CNP/app/index.aspx

O*NET:

http://online.onetcenter.org/

Sites for Job Analysis Tools

PAQ:

http://www.paq.com/

CODAP:

http://www.icodap.org/

CMQ:

http://cmqonline.com

WPS:

http://www.shl.com

F-JAS:

http://www.managementresearchinstitute.com/

Discussion Questions

1. Why is a job analysis essential to the defence of any selection process or selection system?
2. What are the major differences between worker-oriented and work-oriented job analyses?
3. Identify and briefly describe three different types of job analysis techniques.
4. What are the major differences between a competency-based selection system and one developed through job analysis?
5. What is a competency? Defend your answer.
6. Discuss why you might not wish to fly in an airplane whose pilot was selected only on the basis of core competencies.
7. What is the difference, or similarity, between a proficiency level and a skill?

Using the Internet

1. Using the NOC and O*NET websites, compare the occupational descriptions, main duties or tasks, and employment requirements listed for "Psychologist."

   a. Provide a one-page summary describing the similarities and differences you found between the information contained in the two databases for these jobs.
   b. Provide a brief critique regarding the ease or difficulty of retrieving information from each system.
   c. Write a job description for an I/O psychologist. Do you get different descriptions based on which source you used?

2. Job analysis is useful for describing many job types, even those you know well and can describe objectively.

   a. Identify a job that you are familiar with and list the tasks associated with it. Now, using the O*NET website, search the job title and compare the task inventory listed there to the one that you wrote down.

b. How does O*NET function as an SME?

c. What are the benefits to using the O*NET database as opposed to conducting a full-scale job analysis? What are the costs?

3. Look up the HR-Guide.com site found at http://www.hr-guide.com/jobanalysis.htm and the Job Analysis Internet Guide found at http://www.job-analysis.net. What resources are available on both sites? Briefly summarize what you found at these sites.

Exercises

1. Observe someone at work or monitor your own work for a short time period (e.g., 30 minutes). Record the conditions and activities that the worker engages in over that period: describe the activities and tasks the worker engages in, the tools used, and the amount of time spent on each activity. Do not choose a job that does not lend itself to direct observation. If you are observing another person at work, get permission before doing so. Identify the tasks engaged in. What KSAOs are related to those tasks? Ask the worker to rate the frequency, importance, and criticality of both the tasks and KSAOs.

2. Develop an interview that can be used to conduct a job analysis. Select a job for which you can find three or more incumbents willing to provide job analysis data. These may be jobs held by family, friends, or classmates. Conduct the analysis and provide a summary report that includes a list of task statements and describes the requisite abilities for your chosen job.

3. Determine the competencies related to being an excellent student. Act as your own subject-matter experts. Do this exercise in groups of five and compare the competencies identified by the different groups. (*Note:* This exercise can be carried out for any occupation, but use an occupation with which all students will have some familiarity. Occupations such as doctor or dentist may be substituted.)

a. Are the groups using different labels for the same set of behaviours?

b. Specify the KSAOs that are critical to successful learning performance.

c. Develop a competency profile for a superior student.

Case

JoJo's is a restaurant chain with several locations across Canada. Each location has 24 employees to cover bar and food service and the kitchen. The company has experienced a recent drop in revenues and profits, which the owners attribute to competition from a new chain. Their number one concern is customer satisfaction; their slogan is "You get more than you pay for." Complimentary wine is available for those who have a reservation and have to wait. The employee motto is "We aim to please."

You have been hired to find out why JoJo's revenue and profits are dropping. You discover that patrons have been satisfied with the food but not the service. Data show waiting time to get a table is, on average, 20 minutes, even for patrons with reservations. Comments often state that no complimentary glass of wine has been offered. Additionally, once patrons are finally seated, comments show that it is often another five minutes before menus are delivered, and even then there is a considerable delay until a server returns to take orders. Comments note that staff are typically unable to describe specials and that meals can take up to 20 minutes to arrive after ordering. The good news is that once the food arrives, it is well presented and people love it.

You decide to make sample observations from four of the restaurant locations. Initial observation data tell you that there is a great deal of laughing and talking a bit too loudly by employees while restaurant patrons attempt to get the attention of their servers. Food is commonly placed on a counter from the kitchen and left sitting under the heat lamps for five minutes or more before it is picked up. Patrons have to request beverage refills and tables are cleared only as they are needed, not as customers leave.

There is a high turnover in wait staff and JoJo's hire a lot of students, especially in peak seasons. They do have a training program where established staff train the new staff during their first two or three shifts. The behaviours they want to see employees display are summarized as: "Greet every customer within 10 seconds of entering the restaurant. Those who have reservations and have to wait should be offered free drinks. When the servers are busy, the shift manager will provide drink refills, menus, and any other assistance. The people who bus the tables can also fill in to assist the servers. Here we all work together to make this a great chain of eateries." The company believes that since employee performance is specified, everyone knows what to do and they do it reliably.

Discussion Questions

1. Describe which job analysis technique you would use to determine the job requirements that JoJo's should use to recruit and select employees. Provide a rationale for your selection based on the size and type of the organization and the usefulness of the data produced by your chosen technique.

2. If you had chosen the critical incident technique for your job analysis method, write a possible critical incident based on the information presented in the case.

3. Based on the information in this case, identify the competencies that you would expect to find in wait staff. What is your definition of a competency? Describe the architecture you would use for this position.

Recruitment, Selection, and Decision Making

This chapter reviews the role played by recruitment in human resources planning. We present this topic from the perspective of recruitment as the first step in selection. This chapter reviews factors that may attract job applicants and influence them to apply for jobs with an organization as well as the different recruitment methods and their overall effectiveness. This chapter introduces procedures that are commonly used in applicant *screening*—the early stages of a sequential selection process in which applicants meeting critical minimal qualifications or selection criteria are selected for further consideration involving more resource-intense assessments, while those without these requirements are "screened out." The chapter reviews some of the more commonly used screening procedures and then introduces the use of testing in personnel selection and reviews some of the more popular testing procedures. It also reviews the use of the employment interview in selection. This chapter considers ways of reducing subjectivity and error in making selection decisions by using scientific methods that maximize selection effectiveness and efficiency. It concludes with a discussion of utility analysis, decision-making procedures that may be used to evaluate the overall performance of selection systems.

Chapter Learning Outcomes

After reading this chapter you should be able to

- Understand the link between recruitment and selection
- Recognize the internal and external factors that influence an organization's recruitment strategy
- Discuss why a realistic job preview may benefit both the job seeker and the organization
- Differentiate between employee screening and employee selection
- Understand the advantages and disadvantages of using common screening devices, including biographical data, application forms, résumés, interviews, and work experience and reference checks
- Understand psychological tests and their use in selection

- Recognize the advantages and disadvantages of using some of the more popular selection testing procedures, including personality and ability testing
- Understand the five-factor model of personality and its relation to employment testing
- Appreciate the potential of work samples, simulations, and assessment centres as selection procedures
- Understand the purposes and uses of employment interviews
- Appreciate the selection errors associated with traditional approaches to employment interviewing
- Understand different structured interviewing techniques and their relative advantages and disadvantages
- Understand the legal and psychometric status of different screening and selection procedures
- Recognize common decision-making errors in employee selection
- Understand the distinction between judgmental and statistical approaches to the collection and combination of applicant information
- Understand the advantages and disadvantages of various decision-making models
- Be familiar with utility analysis as a way to evaluate personnel selection systems
- Discuss the benefits of using best practices in recruitment and selection

Figure 4.1 presents a simplified view of the human resources management system, which serves as the framework for our discussion of recruitment and selection. Recruitment is an outcome of human resources planning. The decision to recruit candidates for jobs in an organization is based on (1) an assessment of the internal and external factors affecting the organization; (2) human resources planning based on those factors; and (3) a job analysis that identifies worker behaviours and characteristics required by the position. The ultimate goal of a job-related selection system is to bring people into the organization who will perform at above-average levels and who will increase the productivity of the organization. The goal of recruitment is to bring to the organization a large pool of qualified candidates from whom the organization can select the best-qualified people for the position. The goal of selection is to find the most qualified applicants who are likely to be successful in the job.

External Factors

Labour Markets and Recruiting

The overall nature of the economy may influence an organization's decision to hire or not to hire, but once a decision to hire is made, the nature of the labour market determines how extensively the organization will have to search to fill the job with a qualified candidate. When qualified labour is scarce, the organization must broaden its recruiting to attract applicants it might not seek in more favourable times. The organization may also recruit outside its normal

FIGURE 4.1

Recruitment and Selection as Part of the HR Planning Process

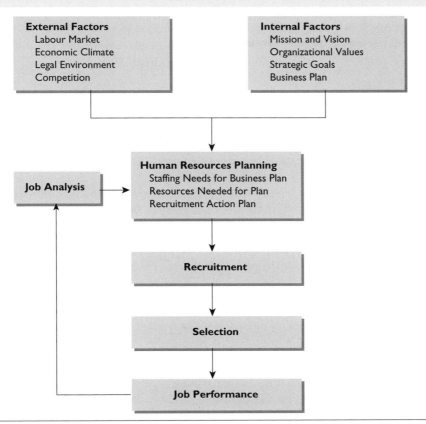

Source: From CATANO/WIESNER/HACKETT. *Recruitment and Selection in Canada*, 4E. © 2010 Nelson Education Ltd. Reproduced by permission. www.cengage.com/permissions.

territory, emphasizing those geographic regions with high unemployment rates or low economic growth. In favourable labour markets, the organization may only advertise in local media. In a scarce labour market, it may use a variety of media to attract as many qualified applicants as possible; it may also make the job more attractive by improving salary and benefits, training and educational opportunities, and working conditions to increase the attractiveness of the organization as a place of employment.

The Legal Environment

Any recruitment program must comply with legal and regulatory requirements. The most important considerations are **employment equity** and pay equity legislation. In employment, the intentional or unintentional exclusion of members of groups that are protected under human rights legislation through recruiting, selection, or other personnel practices or policies constitutes discrimination. In Canada, employment equity legislation seeks to eliminate discrimination in the workplace for women, people with disabilities, Aboriginal people, and visible minorities. Good-faith recruitment efforts mean that the

employment equity

Policies and practices designed to increase the presence of qualified women, visible minorities, Aboriginal people, and people with disabilities in the workforce organization must use a variety of communication channels to get its message to members of different groups. The recruitment effort must make members from these groups feel welcome within the organization. Organizations perceived as hostile to workplace diversity will see the effectiveness of their recruitment efforts significantly compromised, and the quality of their overall applicant pool adversely affected. Box 4.1 summarizes the major legal sources that have an impact on recruitment and selection procedures.

Box 4.1

Legal Sources Affecting Recruitment and Selection

Constitutional law, which has its origins in the *British North America Act of 1867*, spells out the division of powers between the federal and provincial/territorial governments, as well as the rights and freedoms that Canadians enjoy under governments at all levels. All citizens are stakeholders under constitutional law, and its provisions directly or indirectly affect all of us. *The Canadian Charter of Rights and Freedoms*, which forms part of the *Constitution Act of 1982*, addresses human rights issues and guarantees equality, reflects a commitment to provide fair workplace opportunities, and is an acknowledgment that equal opportunity in employment has not always been the case in Canada. The *Charter* is significant because it takes primacy over all other laws except the Constitution. The *Charter* also permits any law, program, or activity designed to improve the conditions of disadvantaged individuals or groups. The *Canadian Charter of Rights and Freedoms* makes clear that it is the result of employment practices and not their intent that determines whether discrimination has occurred. Even if you can show that a policy or practice intended no discrimination, you have violated the law if its effect was discriminatory.

Human rights legislation (federal and provincial/ territorial) exists in Canada partly in response to international conventions declared by the United Nations and partly because of domestic pressure to eliminate discrimination in the workplace and in other areas such as housing and provision of services. The *Canadian Human Rights Act* prohibits discrimination on basis of race, colour, national or ethnic origin, religion, age, sex (including pregnancy and childbirth), sexual orientation, family status, marital status, physical and mental disability (including dependence on

alcohol and drugs), and criminal conviction for which a pardon has been granted. Employment decisions influenced by these "prohibited grounds" are discriminatory and unlawful. Employers, however, are allowed to hire and select individuals based on attributes that would be considered discriminatory if they can establish that these are bona fide occupational requirements (BFORs), which a person must possess to perform the essential components of a job in a safe, efficient, and reliable manner.

Employment equity legislation, policies, and programs have evolved in Canada as a response both to affirmative action programs in the United States and to pressures within our own country to increase workforce diversity. Employment equity law in Canada addresses the concerns of four designated groups (visible minorities, women, Aboriginal peoples, and people with disabilities) and has no force or effect beyond these stakeholder groups in organizations that are federally regulated.

Labour laws in the federal and provincial/territorial jurisdictions across Canada are a response to a long history of labour union activity undertaken to improve workers' job security, wages, hours, working conditions, and benefits (see Chapter 13). These laws provide mechanisms for collective bargaining and union certification and rules for a "fair fight" between management and unions, as well as protecting the public interest (Carter et al., 2002). Of course, the stakeholders under this legislation are unionized workers covered by collective agreements and managers in unionized workplaces.

Employment standards, both federal and provincial, trace their origins back to the *British North America Act* and reflect societal norms about the respective rights and responsibilities of employers and their employees, whether or not these employees are unionized. Employment standards covered in legislation across Canada include statutory school-leaving age, minimum age for employment, minimum wages, vacations and leave, holidays with pay, and termination of employment. All workers in Canada, and their managers, are stakeholders in this legislation.

Other related legislation, including regulation of federal government workers, results from unique conditions in specific sectors and is restricted to addressing the needs of those stakeholders. As a general rule, human rights and employment equity address the problem of discrimination, whereas the remainder of the legal means (labour law, employment standards, and related legislation) provide mechanisms to resolve procedural or contractual disagreements between specific stakeholders named in the legislation. (Examples of the latter would be promotion based on the merit principle for federal government employees under the *Public Service Employment Act* passed by Parliament, seniority rights in collective agreements for employees of Crown corporations, and other types of contractual and legal obligations between employer and employee in either the private or public sectors.) However, even this basic distinction between antidiscrimination legislation and procedural/contract enforcement legislation can blur in practice. For example, equal pay for men and women for work of equal value, which is a discrimination issue, comes under human rights acts in some provinces/territories and employment standards legislation in others.

Source: Carter, England, Etherington, & Trudeau (2002).

Internal Factors

An organization's business plan includes a statement of its mission and philosophy, a recognition of its strengths and weaknesses, and a statement of its goals and objectives for competing in its economic environment. An organization's business plan influences the degree to which the organization fills vacancies with internal or external applicants (Rynes, 1991), or with the best candidate regardless of whether that person is an internal or external applicant. Both the type of occupation and the nature of the industry in which it is involved influence an organization's recruiting strategy (Rynes, 1991). In some industries or occupations people are recruited in a particular way, not so much because that method is very effective, but because it is the norm. It is how recruiting is done for that type of work, and how it is expected to be done.

Human Resources Planning

Human resources planning is a process that organizations undertake to ensure that the right number and type of individuals are available at the right time and place to fill their needs (Dolan & Schuler, 1994). This planning process is based on analysis of the organization's business plan, resulting in a forecast of the number and type of employees required to meet the plan's objectives. The planning process identifies the human resources needed to carry out the business plan, both those resources that exist within the organization and those that must be secured through a recruiting program. Human resources planning develops an action plan to meet the recruiting objectives.

Applicant Pool

applicant pool

The set of potential candidates who may be interested in, and who are likely to apply for, a specific job

An effective action plan targets recruiting efforts on a specific pool of job applicants who are believed to have the appropriate knowledge, skills, abilities, competencies, and other talents needed to perform the job. This **applicant pool** may be concentrated in one geographic area or spread widely throughout the country. The human resources team must know where to find the appropriate applicant pool. Targeting a specific applicant pool allows the organization to tailor its message to that group, to understand where that applicant pool is likely to be located, and to attract applications from that pool.

Timing of recruitment initiatives is another factor to be considered in developing an action plan. In many organizations, recruiting occurs in response to need. An employee leaves for one reason or another and, if the position is retained, must be replaced either through internal or external hiring. In other organizations, where there is a systematic turnover of employees, recruiting may follow a well-defined pattern. This pattern occurs most often in large organizations, which recruit heavily from among college and university graduates (Barber & Wesson, 1999).

Job Description

One of the most important pieces of information candidates rely on throughout the recruiting process is a description of the job and worker requirements. Human recruiting information should give applicants a clear idea of the duties and tasks that form part of the job and the resources that they will need to do the job. It is very difficult to recruit job applicants without knowing the essential characteristics of the position or the requirements of the workers. Job descriptions that are up-to-date and based on a job analysis lead to accurate expectations on the part of the job candidate. Both applicants and recruiters should have a clear idea of the qualifications needed by people in the position.

Recruitment Sources

Once the target applicant pool has been identified and located, the human resources team must choose the most appropriate recruitment sources for reaching all members of internal and external applicant pools, including members of protected groups. Some of the more popular recruiting sources that have been used to contact members of different applicant pools are presented in Table 4.1, which presents data from Statistics Canada's Workplace and Employee Survey (WES) that were gathered in 1999, 2001, and 2003 (Catano & Bissonnette, 2009; see Catano et al., 2009, for additional information on the sources listed in Table 4.1, along with information on their effectiveness as recruiting media). The data were obtained in each cycle from approximately 5,400 for-profit organizations and 25,000 employees. The organizations and employees were a representative sample of Canadian business and industry and their employees. Table 4.1 presents data from those employees who were hired within a year of completing the survey. Family and friends were the most frequently used recruitment source used by job seekers. While only

Table 4.1

Percentage of Canadian Employees Finding a Job through Different Recruitment Methods, Change Over Time

Recruitment Source	1999	2001	2003
Family or friend	37.3 %	42.6 %	37.5 %
Personal initiative	21.2 %	17.7 %	22.9 %
Help wanted ad	20.3 %	16.6 %	14.6 %
Directly recruited by the employer	9.5 %	7.9 %	10.3 %
Canada Employment Centre	2.7 %	2.3 %	3.2 %
Recruitment firm	3.0 %	4.1 %	3.7 %
On-campus recruitment	2.4 %	1.8 %	2.0 %
Union posting	0.5 %	0.3 %	0.7 %
Job fair	0.3 %	0.6 %	0.3 %
News story	0.1 %	1.3 %	1.1 %
Internet	0.6 %	2.5 %	5.1 %

a small proportion of new hires, 0.6 percent, found a job through **Internet recruiting** in 1999, that percentage had grown to 2.5 percent in 2001 and then 5.1 percent in 2003. Catano and Bissonnette's Canadian data reflect findings from previous American research (Zottoli & Wanous, 2000).

Internet recruiting

The use of the Internet and the World Wide Web to match candidates to jobs through electronic databases that store information on jobs and job candidates

Recruitment

In the past, the availability of a job and the need for money were assumed to be motivation enough to attract job candidates. Hardly any consideration was given to the possibility that candidates were using the recruiting process to select the organization. During the recruitment and selection process, applicants form opinions about the organization, the selection process, the people they meet, and the desirability of working in the organization.

Because of their experience, many candidates conclude that they do not want to work in a particular organization, or that they will not fit in; they may also form other attitudes, which last through their early work experience (Rynes, 1993). Organizational characteristics such as location, size of the enterprise, and type of industry may steer individuals away from applying for jobs no matter how attractive the job or how qualified they are to do it (Turban, Campion, & Eyrung, 1995). In the long run, **self-selecting out** may be in the interests of both the applicant and the organization, if that decision is based on accurate information and a realistic perception of the job and the organization. Ultimately, the *interests and values* of the job applicant influence the relative importance of different organizational attributes and whether an individual will apply for a specific job. Interests and values do not indicate whether a person is qualified for a job. Interests and values only suggest the type of work a person may find satisfying.

self-selecting out

Occurs during the recruitment and selection process when candidates form an opinion that they do not want to work in the organization for which they are being recruited

person–job fit

A process through which an organization reaches a decision that a job candidate has the knowledge, skills, abilities, or competencies required by the job in question

person–organization fit

A process through which an organization reaches a decision that a job candidate fits the organization's values and culture and has the contextual attributes desired by the organization

No matter how desirable or compatible a job and organization appear to the candidate, it is all for naught unless the candidate receives an offer of employment. During the recruitment process, the organization, through its representatives, is seeking to learn as much as it can about the candidate. Recruiters assess potential employees in terms of their fit with both the job and the organization. **Person–job fit** concerns whether the job applicant has the knowledge, skills, abilities, or competencies required by the job, while **person–organization fit** is the recruiter's belief that the candidate fits the organization's values and culture; that is, the candidate has the contextual attributes that the company is looking for. Recruiters distinguish between these two types of "fit" and tend to make decisions early on in their interview with a candidate on whether the candidate matches what the organization is looking for (Kristof-Brown, 2000). The recruiter's perception that the applicant fits the job appears to be based mainly on an assessment of the candidate's skill and experience derived from information gathered during the recruiting process. These sources are likely to include a review of the candidate's résumé and a brief screening interview. In some cases, candidates may also be asked to take employment tests at this stage. These screening and selection procedures are discussed in detail later in this chapter. The recruiter's perception of a person–organization fit is mostly based on an assessment of the candidate's personality and values. Both the perception of person–job fit and of person–organization fit predict whether the company will make a job offer. The perception of a poor person–organization fit, however, will reduce the likelihood that a person with a good job fit will receive a job offer. Recruiters form and use perceptions of a candidate's organizational fit as part of the hiring process just as applicants form their opinion of the organization (Kristof-Brown, 2000).

The perception of fit and the decision of the company to make an offer—and of the candidate to accept the offer, based on the candidate's perception of the company—are based on the exchange of information that takes place over the recruitment process. If the job candidate does not make an adequate investigation of the job or organization, or if the organization does not represent itself accurately through the people involved in recruiting and selection, the probability of a person–organization mismatch increases. Mismatches can be quite costly in terms of absenteeism, low productivity, and turnover. A major goal of any recruitment campaign should be to improve the chance of making a good fit between candidates and the organization.

Accurate Expectations

Courts in both Canada and the United States have held employers accountable for the accuracy of information they present to job candidates as part of the recruiting process. False promises and misrepresentations made in recruiting candidates to work for a company may result in a damage award. Employees who believe that they were misled about the nature of their working conditions or their working environment are likely to take legal action against their employers to the extent that they are injured through reliance on the false or misleading statements (Buckley, Fedor,

& Marvin, 1994). As part of orienting newcomers into an organization, a company may wish to initiate a set of procedures that are designed to lower the expectations of the new hire to more realistic and accurate perceptions of the organization, apart from that individual's specific job (Buckley et al., 1998).

Realistic Job Previews

Recruitment programs can be designed to increase the accuracy of the expectations that job candidates hold about the job and the organization. One such program, **realistic job previews** (RJPs), is intended to improve the fit between the job candidate and the organization. The primary goal of RJPs is to reduce turnover among newcomers to an organization by providing job candidates with accurate information about the job and the organization (Wanous, 1980). Other hoped-for outcomes of the RJP are (1) that the job candidates will develop realistic perceptions of what it is like to work in the organization; (2) that they will view the organization in a more credible light; and (3) that, if they accept the job offer, they will be more satisfied with their job and committed to the organization. Extensive research shows that while RJPs accomplish their goals, they do so at a modest level (Phillips, 1998).

realistic job preview
A procedure designed to reduce turnover and increase satisfaction among newcomers to an organization by providing job candidates with accurate information about the job and the organization

Rather than have a candidate accept a job on the basis of unrealistic expectations only to quit after discovering a mismatch with the organization, RJPs give the candidate an accurate preview of the job before the job offer is accepted (e.g., weekend work is required; there are limited opportunities for promotion). In this way, candidates who discover a mismatch self-select out, or remove themselves from the competition, saving themselves the aggravation of having made a bad decision and the organization the cost of hiring and training them. There are some concerns that the realism also discourages very qualified candidates from accepting job offers from the organization (Rynes, 1991); however, the number of withdrawals from the applicant pool after an RJP is not great (Phillips, 1998).

The more exposure a job applicant has to a job, the more likely it is that the applicant may overemphasize the negative aspects of the job and refuse a job offer; this aspect of RJPs may prove problematic in extremely competitive job markets (Meglino, Ravlin, & DeNisi, 1997). The negative information in the RJP appears to influence the job applicant's decision and may have a greater adverse impact on the best-qualified applicants (Bretz & Judge, 1998), requiring greater compensation to attract them to the position (Saks, Wiesner, & Summers, 1996). On the other hand, presenting negative information as part of the RJP may have positive effects. In addition to lowering job candidates' expectations and attraction to the organization, RJPs may increase perceptions of trustworthiness of the organization and facilitate a person–organization match more so than a traditional job preview (Travagline, 2002). Similarly, RJPs enhance a job candidate's perception that the organization is a caring one that is concerned for its employees (Meglino, DeNisi, & Ravlin, 1993). There is some evidence that RJPs lead to increased commitment and reduced turnover through perceptions of employer concern and honesty (Hom et al., 1999).

RJPs remain one of the most intriguing aspects of the recruiting process. Notwithstanding the methodological flaws in RJP research (Rynes, 1991), RJPs lead to accurate expectations on the part of job candidates, to reductions in turnover, and to improvements in job satisfaction (Phillips, 1998); however, the magnitude of these significant effects are small, raising questions about whether the costs and time needed to develop an RJP are balanced or offset by its benefits. Rynes and Cable (2003) do not expect RJPs to remain a major priority for recruitment research, given the modest effects found by Phillips (1998). Nonetheless, when prospective employees know more about an organization, whether through an RJP or other means, there appears to be more positive outcomes for the employees with respect to their job satisfaction and organizational commitment.

Employment Equity

Any recruiting program must consider whether it has produced an increased presence of qualified women, visible minorities, Aboriginal people, and people with disabilities in its workforce. In the context of Canadian employment equity legislation, recruiting efforts must be judged on this basis as well as having filled vacancies. In this regard, organizations must make an effort to reach out to these groups. Table 4.1 indicates that most job seekers learn about a job from family and friends. While this may be a very inexpensive form of recruiting, particularly for entry-level positions, it has a disadvantage of possibly leading to **systemic discrimination**. If most of the workers are, for example, white males, they may tell their friends and relatives, who are white, about the vacancy—resulting in a workforce for the organization that continues to be predominantly white. Despite the popularity of this recruiting source, organizations have an obligation under employment equity legislation to reach out into the broader community to find qualified employees.

Selection

The following sections in this chapter discuss the different tools that have been used in the screening and selection of job applicants. Our recruitment efforts have resulted in a large pool of applicants; now, how do we proceed to identify those who will turn out to be the best employees? In making hiring decisions we have to use selection tools that will allow us to make valid inferences about future job performance and will not run afoul of applicable legislation and human rights consideration. Figure 4.2 provides a simplified model of the selection process. Let's assume that an employer has used one of the job analysis methods presented in Chapter 3 to update the job description for the position of "Recruiter." The analysis identifies a large number of tasks associated with job performance to the extent that we can develop an idea of the job performance domain (we will discuss job performance in more detail in Chapter 5). From our knowledge of similar jobs and our understanding of job performance, we assume that **cognitive ability** will be a major predictor of job performance (Line A). Figure 4.2 represents this thinking in the form of the

systemic discrimination

In employment, the intentional or unintentional exclusion of members of groups that are protected under human rights legislation through recruiting, selection, or other personnel practices or policies

cognitive ability

Refers to intelligence, general mental ability, or intellectual ability

FIGURE 4.2

A Simplified Model of the Selection Process

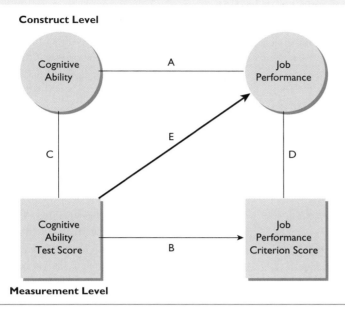

Source: From CATANO/WIESNER/HACKETT. *Recruitment and Selection in Canada*, 4E. © 2010 Nelson Education Ltd. Reproduced by permission. www.cengage.com/permissions.

two ovals representing cognitive ability and job performance. These represent constructs or ideas we have formed to help us understand the situation and which in general are not observed. Next we have to identify a valid measure of cognitive ability (Line C) and a valid criterion measure (Line D) of job performance. The measures are concrete and observable. In personnel selection we wish to make an inference about the applicant's job performance from the applicant's score on the cognitive ability measure (Line E). That is, we use a score on the predictor measure to make an inference about how the applicant will perform overall on the job. We test the validity of our inference by establishing a relationship between the cognitive ability measure and the criterion measure of performance (Line B).

In applicant selection, whether to identify those who meet our minimal qualifications (screening) or those who are the best candidate (selection), we assume that applicants who score higher on the predictor measure will perform better on the job than applicants who score lower. In the following sections we will review both screening and selection procedures and the predictors used in making those decisions. An underlying assumption is that we must be capable of making valid inferences that are within the limits imposed by applicable legislation. Box 4.2 presents some legal terms and concepts that apply to selection following significant Canadian court cases. Compliance with employment legislation results in unbiased selection systems that are fair to all job candidates. An effective selection system begins with a job analysis that clearly defines the KSAOs needed to carry out the job tasks, and the use of selection tools that are reliable, valid, and related to the relevant KSAOs.

Box 4.2

Legal Terms and Concepts that Apply to Selection

We present some legal terms and concepts that follow from the Canadian law and legislation we presented in Box 4.1.

Discrimination In employment, discrimination refers to any refusal to employ or to continue to employ any person, or to adversely affect any current employee, on the basis of that individual's membership in a protected group. All Canadian jurisdictions prohibit discrimination at least on the basis of race or colour, religion or creed, age, sex, marital status, and physical or mental disability.

Direct discrimination Occurs where an employer adopts a practice or rule which on its face discriminates on a prohibited ground.

Indirect discrimination Occurs when an employer, in good faith, adopts a policy or practice for sound economic or business reasons, but when it is applied to all employees it has an unintended, negative impact on members of a protected group.

Protected groups Protected groups are those who have attributes that are defined as "prohibited grounds" for discrimination under the human rights act that applies to the employing organization.

Designated groups The *Employment Equity Act* defines designated groups as women, Aboriginal peoples, persons with disabilities, and visible minorities.

Employment equity Refers to the elimination of discriminatory practices that prevent the entry or retention of members from designated groups in the workplace, and to the elimination of unequal treatment in the workplace related to membership in a designated group.

Adverse impact Occurs when the selection rate for a protected group is lower than that for the relevant comparison group. U.S. courts consider adverse impact to occur when the number of members selected from a protected group is less than 80 percent of the number of majority-group members selected.

Bona fide occupational requirement (BFOR) Bona fide occupational requirements are those that a person must possess to perform the essential components of a job in a safe, efficient, and reliable manner. To defend employment practice or policy on the grounds that the policy or practice may be perceived as discriminatory, the employer must show that the practice or policy was adopted in an honest and good-faith belief that it was reasonably necessary to ensure the efficient and economical performance of the job without endangering employees or the general public.

Accommodation Refers to the duty of an employer to put in place modifications to discriminatory employment practices or procedures to meet the needs of members of a protected group being affected by the employment practice or procedure. As part of a BFOR defence, an employer must demonstrate that such accommodation is impossible to achieve without incurring undue hardship in terms of the organization's expense or operations.

Sufficient risk As part of a BFOR defence, an employer may argue that an occupational requirement that discriminates against a protected group is reasonably necessary to ensure that work will be performed successfully and in a manner that will not pose harm or danger to employees or the public.

Undue hardship Undue hardship describes the limit beyond which employers and service providers are not expected to accommodate a member of a protected group. Undue hardship usually occurs when an employer cannot bear the costs of the accommodation.

Selection I: Applicant Screening

Screening refers to the early stages of a sequential selection process, in which applicants meeting critical minimal qualifications or selection criteria are selected for further consideration involving more resource-intense assessments, while those without these requirements are "screened out." Screening might also refer to any rough and quick selection process even when not followed by further selection assessments (Anastasi, 1988). Screening takes on increasing importance the larger the ratio of applicants to positions (or, conversely, the fewer selected for hire as a percentage of the total applicant pool—the **selection ratio**). Because the more resource-intense assessments are reserved for the most promising candidates, well-developed and well-implemented screening programs result in efficiency in applicant processing, and savings in cost and time for both the job seeker and the employer. Savings will be greater the more the supply of talent exceeds demand. What follows is a review of some of the more commonly used screening procedures, including biographical data, application forms, résumés, and reference checks.

Screening is the first phase of selection, which performs the "rough cut" of the larger applicant pool. Typically, it involves identifying those candidates who meet the **minimum qualifications (MQs)** established for a position. MQs are often listed as statements of education, experience, and closely related personal attributes required to perform a job satisfactorily that are used as standards to screen applicants (Levine et al., 1997). Screening procedures are designed to cut down the number of job applicants by eliminating at this point those candidates who fall short of the minimum standards. Accordingly, MQs critically affect the entire selection process, and are often closely scrutinized for possible adverse impact against **designated targeted groups**.

Recruitment, Screening, and Selection

Recruitment seeks to find a sufficient number of qualified applicants; *screening* identifies whether those candidates who applied meet minimum require-ments; and *selection* reviews each qualified candidate to find those who will be most successful in the job.

The screening devices are designed to quickly and inexpensively sort applicants into acceptable and unacceptable categories. Usually, the criteria on which these decisions are made are subjective; the decision maker often has to interpret what an applicant meant upon writing a specific statement, or what a person's job experience and training actually are. Screening proce-dures are open to errors, both **false positives** and **false negatives**. Over the complete selection process, applicants who pass through the initial screening as false positives are likely to be eliminated through more extensive testing. The false negatives, those who met the qualifications but were eliminated, are gone forever. Applicants who find themselves in this position may turn to the courts if they believe the initial screening procedures discriminated on grounds that were unrelated to job performance. Screening instruments that are used without consideration of their psychometric properties and without regard for the legal environment leave employers open to litigation.

Screening Methods

Application forms, résumés, interviews, and reference checks are most com-monly used in screening. These procedures all seek to predict job performance

selection ratio

The proportion of applicants for one or more positions who are hired.

screening

Involves identifying individuals from the applicant pool who have the minimum qualifications for the target position(s); candidates "passing" this first hurdle are referred for more extensive assessments

minimum qualifications (MQs)

Knowledge, skills, abilities, experiences, and other attributes deemed necessary for minimally acceptable performance in one or more positions; designed for making the "first cut" in screening job applicants and sometimes referred to as *selection criteria*

designated targeted groups

The four groups designated in the federal government's *Employment Equity Act* that receive legal protection in employment policies and practices because of their under-representation in the workplace: women, Aboriginal people, visible minorities, and people with disabilities

recruitment

The generation of an applicant pool for a position or job in order to provide the required number of qualified candidates for a subsequent selection or promotion process

false positives

Individuals who are predicted to perform successfully for a given position (based on pre-selection assessment scores), but who do not perform at satisfactory levels when placed on the job

false negatives

Individuals who are predicted to perform unsuccessfully for a given position (based on pre-selection assessment scores), but who would perform at satisfactory levels if hired

from past life or work events. If the screening procedures are properly developed, they will identify individuals who meet minimum qualifications. Box 4.3 presents questions that should be avoided either in application forms or as part of interviews. These questions relate to subjects that are protected by human rights legislation. Box 4.3 also shows how these subjects could be addressed in a nondiscriminatory manner. The following sections examine these screening tools in more detail.

Box 4.3

Guidelines for Screening and Selection Questions

Subject	Avoid Asking	Comments
Name	About name change: whether it was changed by court order, marriage, or other reason for maiden name	Ask after selection if needed to check on previously held jobs or educational credentials
Address	For addresses outside Canada	Ask place and duration of current or recent address
Age	For birth certificates, baptismal records, or about age in general	Ask applicants if they are eligible to work under Canadian laws regarding age restrictions
Sex	Males or females to fill in different applications; about pregnancy, child-bearing plans, or childcare arrangements	During the interview or after selection, the applicant, for purposes of courtesy, may be asked which of Dr., Mr., Mrs., Miss, or Ms. is preferred
Marital Status	Whether the applicant is single, married, divorced, engaged, separated, widowed, or living common-law; whether the applicant's spouse may be transferred; about the spouse's employment	If transfer or travel is part of the job, the applicant can be asked whether he or she can meet these requirements; ask whether there are any circumstances that might prevent completion of a minimum service commitment
Family Status	About number of children or dependants; about childcare arrangements	Contacts for emergencies and/or details on dependants can be determined after selection
National or Ethnic Origin	About birthplace, nationality of ancestors, spouse, or other relatives; whether born in Canada; for proof of citizenship	Since those who are entitled to work in Canada must be citizens, permanent residents, or holders of valid work permits, applicants can be asked whether they are legally entitled to work in Canada. Documentation of eligibility to work (papers, visas, etc.) can be requested after selection

Subject	Avoid Asking	Comments
Military Service	About military service in other countries	Inquire about Canadian military service where employment preference is given to veterans by law
Language	About mother tongue; where language skills were obtained	Ask if applicant understands, reads, writes, or speaks languages required for the job. Testing or scoring applicants for language proficiency is not permitted unless job-related.
Race or Colour	Any question related to race or colour, including colour of eyes, skin, or hair	
Photographs	For photo to be attached to applications or sent to interviewer before interview	Photos for security passes or company files can be taken after selection
Religion	Whether the applicant will work a specific religious holiday; about religious affiliation, church membership, frequency of church attendance; for references from clergy or religious leader	Explain the required work shift, asking whether such a schedule poses problems for the applicant. Reasonable accommodation of an employee's religious beliefs is the employer's duty
Height and Weight		No inquiry unless there is evidence they are genuine occupational requirements
Disability	For a list of all disabilities, limitations, or health problems; whether the applicant drinks or uses drugs; whether the applicant has ever received psychiatric care or been hospitalized for emotional problems; whether the applicant has received worker's compensation	The employer should: disclose any information on medically related requirements or standards early in the application process; then ask whether the applicant has any condition that could affect his or her ability to do the job, preferably during a pre-employment medical examination. A disability is relevant to job ability only if it: threatens the safety or property of others, prevents the applicant from safe and adequate job performance even when reasonable efforts are made to accommodate the disability.
Medical Information	Whether the applicant is currently under a physician's care; name of family doctor; whether the applicant is receiving counselling or therapy	Medical exams should be conducted after selection and only if an employee's condition is related to job duties. Offers of employment can be made conditional on successful completion of a medical exam.

(*Continued*)

Box 4.3 (continued)

Subject	Avoid Asking	Comments
Pardoned Conviction	Whether the applicant has ever been convicted; whether the applicant has ever been arrested; whether the applicant has a criminal record	If bonding is a job requirement, ask whether the applicant is eligible. Inquiries about criminal record or convictions are discouraged unless related to job duties
Sexual Orientation	About the applicant's sexual orientation	Contacts for emergencies and/or details on dependants can be determined after selection
References		The same restrictions that apply to questions asked of applicants apply when asking for employment references

Source: *Guide to Screening and Selection in Employment*. http://www.chrc-ccdp.ca/pdf/screen.pdf. Canadian Human Rights Commission. Reproduced with the permission of the Ministry of Public Works and Government Services, 2010.

Application Blanks or Forms

application blank or form

A form used by job candidates to provide an employer with basic information about their knowledge, skills, education, or other job-related information

When individuals apply for a job with an employer, they are frequently asked to complete an employment **application form** (sometimes referred to as an **application blank**). Practically all organizations use employment application forms to collect information that will allow them to assess whether the candidate is minimally suitable for the job in question. Application forms consist of a series of questions aimed at securing information on the general suitability of the applicants for the target position. Questions often ask about the applicant's educational background, job experience, special training, and other areas deemed relevant to performance of the job. For example, applicants for a security dispatcher position may be required to have passed a course on CPR (cardiopulmonary resuscitation). Applicants who do not have such training can be identified through a question on the application form and screened out of the competition.

Employers often overlook the fact that, outside of basic demographic data, information requested by an application form should be job-related and established through a job analysis. For example, in a court challenge it must be shown that CPR training is related to the work of a security dispatcher. It is not sufficient to believe that applicants "ought" to have a particular level of education, or to have graduated from a specific type of training program. Where there is adverse impact against members of a designated minority group, whether intentional or otherwise, the standard used to screen applicants must be demonstrably job-related. Because information collected at this stage may be used to restrict or deny employment to women and members of minority groups, the human rights issues must be considered during the development and use of application forms. Guidelines on what is legally inappropriate to ask on application forms are provided by the Canadian Human

Rights Commission (http://www.chrc-ccdp.ca) and by other jurisdictions throughout Canada. The Canadian Human Rights Reporter (http://www.cdn-hr-reporter.ca) is a useful source of information for human rights cases and legal guidelines for recruitment, screening, and assessment.

Weighted Application Blanks (WABs)

Each item on an application form provides information about the candidate. Only rarely is any one item sufficient to screen out a candidate. How can information obtained from an application form be objectively combined to make a decision when there is no single item that screens out candidates? Can information from the application form be used to make a prediction about job success or failure? In many cases, the person responsible for making the decision examines the application and makes a subjective decision. Much like a clinical psychologist making a diagnosis, the recruiter examines all the information and comes to a conclusion about a particular applicant based on personal experience and knowledge. There is an alternative to this subjective procedure: develop a scoring key for applicant responses to items on the application form. For example, a weight of 1 might be assigned to job applicants who are bilingual and 0 to those who are not. Similarly, weights would be assigned to the responses given to other items; adding all of the assigned weights together produces a total score on the application form for each job candidate. The weights are not assigned arbitrarily; they reflect the difference between successful and unsuccessful workers on some criterion measure of performance that is usually determined empirically for current or previous employees. This alternative is called a **weighted application blank (WAB) or form**.

Performance measures such as turnover, absenteeism, and accident rates are typically used to validate WABs. As we will discuss in Chapters 5 and 11, these behaviours are examples of counterproductive work behaviours that do not provide information on an applicant's ability to perform the tasks required by the job. WAB scoring keys are derived to predict one specific, often narrow, criterion such as absenteeism. While WABs provide the basis for good empirical predictions (Mitchell & Klimoski, 1982), they do not offer any *understanding* of why those relationships exist (Guion, 1967, 1998).

weighted application blank (WAB) or form

Method for quantitatively combining information from application blank items by assigning weights that reflect each item's value in predicting job success

Biographical Data

Application forms require job candidates to make a report about their past experiences and accomplishments. A typical application form addresses a very narrow range of job-related items. Owens (1976; Owens & Schoenfeldt, 1979) extended this approach to include a much broader range of biographical topics in the **biographical information blank (BIB)**. The BIB typically covers a variety of areas, including educational experiences, hobbies, family relations, leisure-time pursuits, personal accomplishments, and early work experiences. Whereas a WAB focuses on more limited, factual, and verifiable information on educational background, training, and work experience, a BIB covers an array of less verifiable information, such as personal interests, attitudes, and values (Gatewood, Feild, & Barrick, 2008). Some content areas of BIBs may run afoul of privacy and human rights legislation.

biographical information blank (BIB)

A pre-selection questionnaire in which applicants are asked to provide job-related information on their personal background and life experiences

Chapter 4: Recruitment, Selection, and Decision Making

On a BIB, applicants answer a series of multiple-choice or short-answer questions. The information obtained from the BIB is scored to produce either a total overall score, or scores for specific sets of items or factors. Compared with the WAB, the BIB provides greater insights into the type of individuals who experience job success, given the content and higher contextual richness of the items.

The BIB, which is also known as a life history or personal history inventory, is based on the view that past behaviour is the best predictor of future behaviour. Understanding how a job applicant behaved in the past through examination of related BIB items allows one to predict that applicant's future interests and capabilities. Despite the impressive predictive validity of biodata, concern remains over its use for selection purposes. Many items on a BIB raise issues of privacy. For example, job applicants may feel that it is inappropriate to share with any prospective employer information pertaining to their financial status or the number of credit cards they carry. If a BIB includes items that give the appearance of unfair discrimination or invasion of privacy, it may have the unintended effect of turning away highly qualified candidates. In one study, potential job applicants who completed application forms with discriminatory items reacted more negatively to the organization than those potential applicants who completed forms with the discriminatory items removed (Saks, Leck, & Saunders, 1995).

Overall, carefully developed and validated BIBs can be a very effective and defensible means of screening job applicants, particularly for counterproductive work behaviours (see Chapter 11, where we review the use of BIBs in this regard). Moreover, recent research shows that BIBs can have similar levels of predictive validity for similar jobs across organizations. Validation research on biodata produces results similar to that for the WAB. Biodata predicts quite well certain types of job behaviours (e.g., absenteeism, turnover, job proficiency, supervisory effectiveness, and job training) in a wide range of occupations (Asher, 1972; Ghiselli, 1966; Hunter & Hunter, 1984; Maertz, 1999; Rothstein et al., 1990; Vinchur et al., 1998). Rothstein et al. (1990) place biodata second only to cognitive ability as a valid predictor of job proficiency. On average, corrected correlations between scores on biodata instruments and job-relevant criteria range from .30 to .40 (Hunter & Hunter, 1984; Reilly & Chao, 1982; Schmitt et al., 1984). Asher and Sciarrino (1974) reported that the validity coefficients for biodata exceeded .50 in six of the 11 studies they reviewed. Hunter and Hunter reported the mean correlation between biodata and job proficiency as .37 (Hunter & Hunter, 1984). Moreover, we know that biodata, when used with other predictors such as personality assessments or cognitive ability test scores, increases the accuracy of our predictions of job performance (Mael & Hirsch, 1993; McManus & Kelly, 1999; Mount, Witt, & Barrick, 2000).

Résumés

A résumé is another source of biographical information produced by job applicants. The intent of the résumé is to introduce the job applicant to the organization through a brief, accurate, written self-description. The information contained on most résumés overlaps with the information requested by the employer through application blanks or biographical inventories. One difference is that on the résumé applicants voluntarily provide biographical information about themselves. They believe this information is job-related and that it will lead a potential employer to decide that they meet the minimum job requirements and are worthy of further consideration. A second difference is that job applicants may include information on the résumé that the employer might rather not see. Although it is not as common as it was a few years ago, some job applicants still list information about their citizenship or national origin, height, weight, marital status, or other characteristics that, if used as part of selection, run afoul of employment legislation. It might be extremely difficult for an employer to prove that such prohibited information did not influence an employment decision. Another important difference is that résumés are not standardized. The uniqueness of each applicant's résumé makes the use of standardized scoring techniques difficult, if not impossible. Nonetheless, all of the psychometric and legal considerations that apply to application forms and biodata apply equally to the use of résumés in selection. Information obtained from the résumé must be job-related and not discriminate against designated minority groups.

Honesty and the Résumé

In an increasingly competitive labour market, job candidates may be more prone to fudging the truth about their credentials. There is often a fine line between presenting yourself in the best possible light and intentionally misrepresenting your background. A Toronto-based reference-checking firm, Infocheck Ltd., reported in 1999 that its second annual résumé fraud study showed 33 percent of final candidates lied, compared with 24 percent the previous year (Resume inflation, 1999). The study included 1,000 short-listed candidates who already had been through successful interviews or had been referred to prospective employers by search firms. The candidates were applying for jobs ranging from general office help to senior executive positions. As examples of the sort of problems that can occur when employers neglect to verify information presented in résumés, Infocheck described an incident in which a customer service representative at a call centre "hacked his way" into the employer's computer system and crashed it for five hours, at great cost and disruption to client service. Another incident involved an autoworker who assaulted a coworker, resulting in production-line shutdown, again at great expense to the employer. In each of these cases, the individual said he had resigned from his previous job, when in fact he had been fired (Hamilton, 2000).

Few validation studies have been done directly on the résumé itself. Rather, studies report the validity of inferences based on information typically found on a résumé. Hunter and Hunter's (1984) meta-analysis showed that information of the type included on a résumé had relatively low validity in predicting future job success. Experience had the highest validity ($r = .18$), followed by academic achievement ($r = .11$) and education ($r = .10$). Nonetheless, a résumé and its accompanying cover letter remain the primary means by which many job applicants introduce themselves to an organization and create an impression of their fit to the job and to the company.

Screening Interviews

In North America, the interview is the most popular selection device; it is used nearly universally (Catano & Bissonnette, 2003; Rowe, Williams, & Day, 1994). The interview, a face-to-face interaction between two people, is designed to allow one of the parties to obtain information about the other. In employment, the employer's representative is called the interviewer, while the job applicant is called the interviewee or applicant. This traditional terminology does not convey the complex, dynamic, interactive nature of the interview. It is used only as a matter of convenience to identify each of the parties involved in the interview, since both attempt to obtain information about the other through the interview process. Each, at times, is both an interviewer and an interviewee.

In a screening interview, the interviewer takes the opportunity to find out information about the applicant that is not apparent from an application form or résumé. The interview has considerable value as a recruiting device and as a means of initiating a social relationship between a job applicant and an organization (Rowe et al., 1994). The interview is used to present information, mostly favourable, about the organization as an employer, with the hope of increasing the odds that an applicant will accept a forthcoming job offer. The job applicant uses the occasion of the interview to learn more about the company as an employer and to make inferences about its values and philosophy in deciding whether there is a fit (Gati, 1989). Interviewing that is done as part of the recruitment process serves as a screening mechanism. Job applicants who do not meet the recruiter's and the organization's standards, including values believed necessary to achieving the company's strategic goals, do not proceed further.

Screening interviews typically consist of a series of freewheeling, unstructured questions that are designed to fill in the gaps left on the candidate's application form and résumé. Such traditional interviews take on the qualities of a conversation and often revolve around a set of common questions, like "What is your greatest accomplishment?" These questions cover the applicant's personal history, attitudes and expectations, and skills and abilities. The information obtained by many of these questions probably would be better left to a well-constructed application form. Skilful interviewees often have learned how to give socially desirable answers to many of these frequently asked questions. While some distortion is to be expected in the answers an applicant makes during an interview, there is no reason to believe that those inaccuracies, intentional or otherwise, occur with greater frequency than inaccuracies in biodata and résumé information. There is very little direct evidence on the rate or percentage of misinformation that takes place over the course of an interview. As with application forms and biodata, when interview questions focus on verifiable events related to past work or educational experiences, accuracy will likely increase.

Interviewers use both the verbal and nonverbal behaviour displayed by job applicants in forming an impression of the applicant (Dreher & Sackett, 1983; Webster, 1982). Similarly, the applicant uses the interviewer's verbal and nonverbal behaviours in forming an impression of the interviewer and the organization, in judging the probability of receiving a job offer, and in considering the desirability of accepting it and working for the organization. Box 4.4 lists common behaviours displayed by applicants during an interview that lead to either positive or negative impressions on the part of the interviewer.

Box 4.4

Interviewee Behaviours that Influence Interviewer Impressions

Applicant Behaviours that Make a Favourable Impression

- Being on time for the interview.
- Being prepared for the interview by having done homework on the company and anticipating common interview questions.
- Making direct eye contact with the interviewer.
- Remaining confident and determined throughout the interview, regardless of how the interviewer's cues suggest the interview is going.
- Providing positive information about oneself when answering questions.
- Answering questions quickly and intelligently.
- Demonstrating interest in the position and organization.

Applicant Behaviours That Make a Negative Impression

- Presenting a poor personal appearance or grooming.
- Displaying an overly aggressive, know-it-all attitude.
- Failing to communicate clearly (e.g., mumbling, poor grammar, use of slang).
- Lacking career goals or career planning.
- Overemphasizing monetary issues.
- Evasiveness or not answering questions completely.
- Lacking maturity, tact, courtesy, or social skills.

Source: From CATANO/WIESNER/HACKETT. *Recruitment and Selection in Canada*, 4E. © 2010 Nelson Education Ltd. Reproduced by permission. www.cengage.com/permissions.

Value of the Screening Interview

Considerable time and energy have been spent on investigating the effectiveness of the interview. In recent years, however, the selection interview has received much more attention than the screening interview. Past reviews of the employment interview (Harris, 1989; Webster, 1982) suggest that it is a useful screening device. Interviewers who screen for production or clerical workers generally develop a stereotype of an acceptable applicant and quickly decide whether the applicant fits that mould. In the remainder of the interview, the interviewer seeks information from the applicant either to confirm or to contradict the interviewer's impression. Negative information, particularly when it occurs early in the interview, is difficult to ignore and tends to influence the outcome more than positive information. Training for interviewers may reduce some types of errors that can be made in rating applicants, but there is no evidence that this reduction affects the quality of the overall judgments made by the interviewer.

Predictive Validity of Screening Interviews

There is considerable research on the validity of interviews in employee selection. Meta-analyses report the validity for unstructured employment interviews, the type mostly used in screening, as ranging from .14 to .20 (Hunter & Hunter, 1984; Wiesner & Cronshaw, 1988). Even at .20, the validity of the screening interview is still substantially low in comparison with other types of selection procedures. It is likely that an interview will always play a role in hiring regardless of its validity. Employers will always want to meet the prospective employee face-to-face before making a job offer. Later in this chapter, in discussing the use of the interview in selection, we present ways of substantially improving the interview by asking questions based on job analysis information. Properly developed interview questions have the potential for being excellent screening devices. The reality is that, as currently done, most unstructured screening interviews cannot be justified in terms of their predictive validity.

Reference Checks

Job applicants are often asked to provide the names of personal references as well as the names of their supervisors from previous jobs. It is understood that these individuals will be contacted and asked for their views on the applicant. These people may be asked to verify information presented by the applicant or to make judgments about the traits, characteristics, and behaviours of the applicant. Consequently, the term **reference check** may be applied to vastly different procedures, with different levels of reliability and validity.

reference check

Information gathered about a job candidate from that applicant's supervisors, coworkers, clients, or other "referees"; usually collected from the referees through telephone interviews

In assessing the worth of reference checks, it is necessary to keep in mind the specific procedure that was actually used. Reference checks normally take place *last* in the screening process; references are sought only for those applicants who have survived the previous screens. Reference checking is typically done last to protect the confidentiality of the candidates (who may not have informed their current employers that they are seeking alternative employment), and because it can be labour-intensive when done properly. There are implicit assumptions made when a former supervisor or a personal reference is called upon for information about a job candidate; namely, that the referees themselves are competent to make the assessment and are sufficiently knowledgeable about the candidate to provide accurate information. These are not always well-founded assumptions. A former supervisor may not have been in a position long enough to learn much about the employee's behaviour; there is also no guarantee that the supervisor is capable of discriminating poor job behaviour from excellent. When these assumptions are met, the reference information is likely to have a higher degree of accuracy. In effect, the reference checker must also know something about the referees to establish the credibility of their references. This is why greater value is placed on references from people who are known to the reference checker.

Chapter 11 presents additional information on the use of reference checking as part of predicting counterproductive work behaviours. Chapter 11 also presents the use of background checks and field investigations, which are much more elaborate and expensive ways of assessing whether an individual is prone to certain counterproductive or deviant behaviours. Because of the time and costs involved in undertaking such types of investigations, they are generally reserved for applicants for high-level positions or those within security-related services.

Work Experience

Application blanks, résumés, preliminary interviews, and reference checking provide information on a candidate's formal training and work experiences. This information is used to predict how the individual will perform on the job. Work experience involves both quantitative aspects, such as length of time on the job, and qualitative aspects, such as the level and complexity of the candidate's work experience. Qualitative assessments of work experience are generally done during the screening interview but can also be inferred to a certain extent through the résumé.

Several studies have shown a significant and positive relationship between work experience and work performance. Job tenure—the most widely used measure of experience—relates positively to job performance because it increases job knowledge and skill competencies (Borman, Hanson, Oppler, Pulakos, & Whilte, 1991; Schmidt, Hunter, & Outerbridge, 1986). For example, Vance, Coovert, MacCallum, and Hedge (1989) reported that the length of time spent as an engine mechanic predicted performance on three different sets of tasks. Three meta-analyses (quantitative reviews) of the relationship between work experience and job performance show mean correlations ranging from .18 to .32, with work experience defined in terms of job tenure (Hunter & Hunter, 1984; McDaniel, Schmidt, & Hunter, 1988; Quinones, Ford, & Teachout, 1995). These mean correlations were considerably higher, $r = .41$, when work experience was defined in terms such as "number of times performing a task" or "level of task difficulty." Finally, work experience has higher correlations with hard (e.g., work samples) as opposed to soft (e.g., ratings) measures of performance: mean $r = .39$ versus mean $r = .24$ (Quinones et al., 1995). This suggests that careful consideration should be given to work experience when making screening or selection decisions. Specifically, the kind (quantitative and qualitative) of work experience that is most relevant to the work to be performed in the new job should be identified, and then the screening and selection process should be fine-tuned to ensure that those aspects of work experience are adequately assessed.

Selection II: Employment Testing

In most hiring situations, there are more applicants than there are positions to be filled. The employer's goal is to select those candidates who best possess the knowledge, skills, abilities, or other attributes and competencies (KSAOs) that lead to successful job performance. The employer believes that applicants differ with respect to essential KSAOs and wishes to measure these individual differences to meet the goal of hiring the best-qualified people for the job. The central requirement for any selection tests or assessment procedures is that they accurately assess the individual's performance or capacity to perform the essential components of the job in question safely, efficiently, and reliably without discriminating against protected group members except where the KSAO can be established as a *bona fide occupational requirement* (Canadian Human Rights Commission, 2007). Any test that is used must meet professional standards for reliability and validity. We also expect tests to allow us to make decisions in a fair and unbiased manner.

Ability Tests

Abilities are attributes that an applicant brings to the employment situation. **Abilities** are enduring, general traits or characteristics on which people differ. It is of no importance whether an ability has been acquired through experience or inheritance. Abilities are simply general traits that people possess and bring

ability

An enduring, general trait or characteristic on which people differ and which they bring to a work situation with them to the new work situation. Finger dexterity, for example, is the ability to carry out quick, coordinated movements of fingers on one or both hands and to grasp, place, or move very small objects (Fleishman & Reilly, 1992).

An ability can underlie performance on a number of specific tasks; finger dexterity might be required to operate a computer keyboard and to assemble electronic components. One keyboard operator may have taken several months of practice to develop the finger dexterity needed to type 100 words per minute; another may have come by that ability naturally. Both have the same ability, regardless of how it was acquired. An ability exists in individuals at the time they first begin to perform a task, whether that task is operating a keyboard or assembling electronic components.

skill
Refers to an individual's degree of proficiency or competency on a given task that develops through performing the task

Skill, on the other hand, refers to an individual's degree of proficiency or competency on a given task, based on both ability and practice, that has developed through performing the task. Two keyboard operators may have the same level of finger dexterity; however, one may have learned to type with hands raised at an inappropriate angle in relation to the keyboard. As a result, the two have different skill levels, or proficiencies, in using a keyboard despite having the same ability. Similarly, a keyboard operator and an electronics assembler might have the same level of finger dexterity but the keyboard operator might be more skilled at word processing than the assembler is at wiring circuit boards. An **aptitude** can be thought of as a specific, narrow ability or skill. Measures or tests of different aptitudes are used to predict whether an individual will do well in future job-related performance that requires the ability or skill being measured.

aptitude
A specific, narrow ability or skill that may be used to predict job performance

Based on a test of finger dexterity, an I/O psychologist might predict that a job applicant has an aptitude for operating a keyboard, or for assembling electronic components. Over the years, Fleishman and his associates (Fleishman & Quaintance, 1984) have identified 52 distinct human abilities, which can be grouped into four broad categories: cognitive, psychomotor, physical, and sensory/perceptual abilities. Over time, many psychometrically sound tests have been developed to assess these different abilities.

Cognitive Ability Tests

Cognitive abilities are related to intelligence or intellectual ability. These abilities include verbal and numerical ability, reasoning, memory, problem solving, and processing information, among others. The first wide-scale, systematic use of cognitive ability testing took place during World War I, when a group of industrial psychologists developed the U.S. Army Alpha test. This was a paper-and-pencil test that could be efficiently administered to groups of army recruits to determine how those recruits could best be employed. The Army Alpha test sought to measure intellectual or basic mental abilities that were thought to be essential to performing military duties. Today, an extensive array of paper-and-pencil tests are available to measure specific cognitive abilities. The Public Service Commission's Personnel Psychology Centre uses many different types of tests to evaluate applicants and employees. These include "general competency tests," which are a form of general cognitive ability testing that assesses verbal and quantitative abilities. Sample test questions from the General Competency Test 1 are available online (http://www.psc-cfp.gc.ca/ppc-cpp/psc-tests-cfp/gct1-ecg1-eng.htm), and are reprinted in Box 4.5.

Box 4.5

GCT 1 Sample Questions

The General Competency Test: Level 1 (GCT1) contains 3 types of questions: understanding written material, solving numerical problems, and drawing logical conclusions.

A sample question of each type is provided below.

Type I – Understanding Written Material

This type of question involves reading a short passage, which is usually in memorandum format, and answering a question about the information in the text.

QUESTION 1

Government of Canada	Gouvernement du Canada
MEMORANDUM	NOTE DE SERVICE

___

TO: All employees

FROM: Manager

Please note that the answer sheets currently being used will be replaced with new ones next year. The existing supply of answer sheets should be used from now until the end of the year. It is important that the new sheets are used next year because they will enable the collection of additional information that will be required at this time.

    The main purpose of this memorandum is to:

1. Indicate the need for new answer sheets.
2. Notify employees that new answer sheets will replace the existing ones.
3. Notify employees that the current answer sheets are inadequate.
4. Indicate the need for additional information.

Type II – Solving Numerical Problems

This type of question involves choosing the correct answer to a practical numerical problem.

QUESTION 2

You are in charge of financial services and must calculate overtime pay for employees in your division. Due to a heavy workload, an employee had to work 35 hours of overtime in two weeks. For 28 of these hours, the employee was paid at one and one half times the hourly rate. For the remaining hours, the employee was paid at twice the usual hourly pay. The employee's hourly pay is $10. How much overtime money should the employee be paid for the two week period?

1. $340   3. $560

2. $420   4. $760

Type III – Drawing Logical Conclusions

In this type of question, the task is to choose the correct answer to a practical problem.

(Continued)

Box 4.5 (continued)

QUESTION 3

One of your duties is the selection and disposal of boxes of obsolete files. According to regulations, ordinary files become obsolete after 24 months, protected files after 36 months, and classified files after 48 months. Which of the following boxes of files can be discarded?

A.   A box containing ordinary files dated 26 months ago and classified files dated 34 months ago.

B.   A box containing ordinary files dated 38 months ago and protected files dated 28 months ago.

1. A only
2. B only
3. Both A and B
4. Neither A nor B

Answers
2.
3.
4.

Source: *General Competency Test: Level 1 (GCT1) Instructions and Sample Questions 2009*, Personnel Psychology Centre, Public Service Commission, 2009. Reproduced with the permission of the Minister of Public Works and Government Services, 2010.

emotional intelligence
The ability to perceive accurately, appraise, and express emotion; the ability to access and/or generate feelings when they facilitate thought; the ability to understand emotions and emotional knowledge; and the ability to regulate emotions to promote emotional and intellectual growth

General cognitive ability, or general mental ability (abbreviated *g*, GCA, or GMA), is thought to be the primary ability among those that make up intellectual capacity. General cognitive ability is believed to promote effective learning, efficient and accurate problem solving, and clear communications. General cognitive ability can be thought of as a manager of other, specific cognitive abilities, similar to a computer's operating system managing other software programs. It is, essentially, the ability to learn (Schmidt, 2002). General cognitive ability has been related to successful job performance in many different types of occupations (Ree & Carretta, 1998). It is related to how easily people may be trained to perform job tasks, how well they can adjust and solve problems on the job, and how well-satisfied they are likely to be with the demands of the job (Gottfredson, 1986). Measures of general cognitive ability, which have an average validity coefficient of .50, are among the most powerful predictors of success in training and job performance for a variety of occupational groups ranging from retail clerks to skilled workers to managers and executives (Gottfredson, 1997; Ree & Carretta, 1998). There is one concern with the use of cognitive ability tests in that they may have an adverse impact on blacks and other minority groups.

Emotional intelligence (EI) is a concept that has become quite popular through its discovery by the media and business press. While there are several definitions of EI, the one which has generated the most research is based on

(Source of definition: Copyright © 1997 Peter Salovey. Reprinted by permission of Basic Books, a member of the Perseus Books Group.)

the work of Salovey and Mayer (1990), who proposed that emotional intelligence represents a group of abilities that are distinct from the traditional verbal-propositional/spatial-performance dimensions of intelligence. Mayer, Salovey, and Caruso (2000) later defined EI as the "ability to recognize the meanings of emotions and their relationships, and to reason and problem solve on the basis of them." That is, EI is "the capacity to perceive emotions, assimilate emotion-related feelings, understand the information of the emotions, and manage them" (p. 267).

On the whole, there is inadequate evidence to support the use of EI as part of a selection system, despite the claims of the popular press and test publishers, who advocate the use of EI tests for personnel selection on the grounds that research shows a strong correlation between EI and job performance (Multi-Health Systems, 2001). There is little, if any, published evidence that supports using EI as a decision-making tool in organizational settings. Additional research needs to be done on the EI construct before it can be used to make reliable and valid selection decisions. EI, as an ability-based concept, remains promising, as emotions and moods may be better predictors of specific, short-term workplace behaviours than more stable personality traits (Arvey, Renz, & Watson, 1998).

Psychomotor Ability Tests

Psychomotor abilities involve controlled muscle movements that are necessary to complete a task. Examples of psychomotor abilities include finger dexterity, multi-limb coordination, reaction time, arm–hand steadiness, and manual dexterity. Many tasks, from simple to complex, require coordinated movements for their success. Psychomotor abilities are often overlooked in selecting people for jobs. Consider a drummer who must independently move all four limbs and exercise hand–wrist coordination, all in a controlled and coordinated fashion; imagine an orchestra whose drummer had an extensive knowledge of music theory but very little psychomotor ability. While a test of cognitive ability might predict ability to learn to read and understand music, it would not predict the level of motor coordination.

psychomotor abilities
Traits or characteristics that involve the control of muscle movements

Tests of psychomotor ability tend to be very different from cognitive ability tests. They generally require the applicant to perform some standardized task on a testing apparatus that involves the psychomotor ability in question. The Purdue Pegboard Test, which is a measure of finger dexterity, requires applicants to insert as many pegs as possible into a pegboard in a given time. This test has good predictive validity for many industrial jobs, including watch-making and electronics assembly. Canadian dental schools also use tests of finger and manual dexterity as part of their selection process; all applicants are required to carve a tooth from a block of soap, which is subsequently judged by a panel of dentists. The General Aptitude Test Battery (GATB) also includes tests that involve apparatus that validly measure psychomotor ability in addition to cognitive and perceptual aptitudes. The Manual Dexterity and Finger Dexterity scales of the GATB are among those that Fleishman and Reilly (1992) list as suitable measures of those abilities.

Physical and Sensory/Perceptual Ability Tests

physical abilities

Characteristics involved in the physical performance of a job or task that involve the use or application of muscle force over varying periods of time either alone or in conjunction with an ability to maintain balance or gross body coordination

sensory/perceptual abilities

Traits or characteristics that involve different aspects of vision and audition, as well as the other senses

Physical abilities are those characteristics involved in the physical performance of a job or task. These abilities generally involve the use or application of muscle force over varying periods of time, either alone or in conjunction with an ability to maintain balance or gross body coordination. Physical abilities include both static and dynamic strength, body flexibility, balance, and stamina. Physical requirements for occupational tasks generally fall into three broad physical ability categories: strength, endurance, and quality of movement (Hogan, 1991).

Sensory/perceptual abilities involve different aspects of vision and audition. These abilities include near and far vision, colour discrimination, sound localization, and speech recognition, among others (Fleishman & Reilly, 1992). Although they focus on different sets of abilities, physical abilities and sensory/perceptual abilities are very similar in their relation to job performance and in how they are assessed

The performance of many jobs or tasks may require the worker to possess one or more physical or sensory/perceptual abilities. A firefighter may need the strength to carry a body out of a burning building; a pilot may need adequate near and far vision to fly a plane; a soldier may need the strength and stamina to carry 100 kg of equipment for a long period of time and still be ready for combat; a construction worker may need strength to lift material and balance to keep from falling off a roof. These ability tests predict performance in jobs that are physically demanding or require sensory or perceptual skills. People who possess greater amounts of these abilities perform better in jobs where such abilities play an important role (Campion, 1983). Physical tests of strength and endurance are routinely used in selecting police officer applicants and other protective services personnel such as firefighters (Arvey, Landon, Nutting, & Maxwell, 1992).

Tests of sensory/perceptual abilities generally require the use of specialized tests or equipment that have been designed to assess each sensory or perceptual ability. Almost everyone has had his or her vision examined through the use of a Snellen chart, which contains letters of various sizes. This test assesses an individual's far vision ability. Similarly, many people have experienced a test of their hearing sensitivity when they are asked to recognize a series of tones, which are presented at different levels of intensity and pitches to either or both ears through a headset.

Tests of physical ability are quite varied but involve physical activity on the part of the applicant. Only a few physical ability tests require equipment. For example, a hand dynamometer is used to measure static strength. The hand dynamometer resembles the handgrips used in most gyms. The applicant squeezes the grips with full strength and the resultant force is measured by an attached scale. Pull-ups or push-ups are used to measure dynamic strength, sit-ups are used to assess body trunk strength, while 1,500-metre runs, step tests, and treadmill tests are used to measure stamina and endurance.

Personality Tests

personality

A set of characteristics or properties that influence, or help to explain, an individual's behaviour

One of the major difficulties in using personality for selection purposes is the lack of agreement about its definition. **Personality** is generally defined as a set of characteristics or properties that influence, or help to explain, an individual's behaviour (Hall & Lindzey, 1970). Differences in ways in which people vary (e.g., aggressiveness, pleasantness) are called **personality traits**, which are thought to be stable over time and measurable. Traits can be distinguished from *personality states*, which are more transitory or temporary characteristics. Generally, personality is measured through paper-and-pencil tests that ask the applicant to make a self-report of their feelings or attitudes to a number of items.

personality traits
Stable, measurable characteristics that help explain ways in which people vary.

Personality Tests as a Predictor of Job Performance

Historically, personality tests were not thought to be good predictors of job performance. Guion (1965; Guion & Gottier, 1965) reviewed the technical and ethical problems associated with personality testing and concluded that there was insufficient evidence to justify the use of personality tests in most situations as a basis for making employment decisions about people. This view prevailed until the 1990s, when both meta-analytic and new empirical studies suggested that personality testing could predict certain aspects of job performance. These studies grouped related personality characteristics into a smaller number of personality dimensions and then linked those broader dimensions to job performance (Barrick & Mount, 1991, 1998; Hough, Eaton, Dunnette, Kamp, & McCloy, 1990; McHenry, Hough, Toquam, Hanson, & Ashworth, 1990; Salgado, 1997; Tett, Jackson, & Rothstein, 1991). This body of research (Hough & Furnham, 2003) demonstrates convincingly that personality characteristics can be used successfully as part of a personnel selection system, provided that the personality measure meets acceptable standards and the personality dimensions are linked to job performance through a job analysis. Personality is one of the "other" attributes often identified as a KSAO and included in competency dictionaries.

The "Big Five" Dimensions

These more recent studies, which led to the change in views on the usefulness of personality in selection, have been heavily influenced by the argument that the many hundreds of different personality traits could be summarized under five categories or dimensions (Digman, 1990). These "Big Five" dimensions are conscientiousness, emotional stability (also known as neuroticism), openness to experience, agreeableness, and extroversion. Box 4.6 presents definitions for each of these dimensions and examples of the traits associated with them. While not everyone agrees with the Big Five model as the best way to categorize personality, it has become an important classification scheme in summarizing relationships between personality and job-performance variables (Hough & Furnham, 2003).

Barrick and Mount found that each of the Big Five dimensions could predict at least one aspect of job performance with some degree of accuracy, while conscientiousness predicted several different aspects of job or training performance at moderate levels. Of all the Big Five dimensions, conscientiousness correlates most strongly with job performance, $r = .31$ (Mount & Barrick, 1995). The other four Big Five personality dimensions vary in ability to predict job success by occupational group. For example, extroversion predicts performance in occupations involving social interaction, such as sales occupations (McManus & Kelly, 1999), while openness to experience and extroversion predict training readiness and training success (Barrick & Mount, 1991). Moreover, conscientiousness and extroversion together predict job performance for managers in highly autonomous positions (Barrick & Mount, 1991). Agreeableness and emotional stability, in addition to conscientiousness, play an important role in predicting performance in jobs that involve interpersonal interactions (Mount, Barrick & Stewart, 1998).

Integrity or Honesty Testing

In Chapter 11 we discuss counterproductive work behaviours, which are voluntary behaviours that violate significant organizational norms and in so doing threaten the well-being of an organization, its members, or both. A wide range of work behaviours are considered to be counterproductive. One of the primary concerns

---

Box 4.6

The Big Five Personality Dimensions

Conscientiousness A general tendency to work hard and to be loyal; to give a full day's work each day and to do one's best to perform well—following instructions and accepting organization goals, policies, and rules—even with little or no supervision. It is an approach to work characterized by industriousness, purposiveness, persistence, consistency, and punctuality. It also includes paying attention to every aspect of a task, including attention to details that might be easily overlooked.

Emotional stability Reflects a calm, relaxed approach to situations, events, or people. It includes an emotionally controlled response to changes in the work environment or to emergency situations. It is an emotionally mature approach to potentially stressful situations reflecting tolerance, optimism, and a general sense of challenge rather than of crisis, and maturity in considering advice or criticism from others. (*Note:* "Emotional stability" is used in place of the older term "neuroticism" to describe this factor.)

Openness to experience Reflects a preference for situations in which one can develop new things, ideas, or solutions to problems through creativity or insight. It includes trying new or innovative approaches to tasks or situations. It is a preference for original or

unique ways of thinking about things. It is concerned with newness, originality, or creativity.

Agreeableness Reflects a desire or willingness to work with others to achieve a common purpose and to be part of a group. It also includes a tendency to be a caring person in relation to other people, to be considerate and understanding, and to have genuine concern for the well-being of others; it is an awareness of the feelings and interests of others. It is the ability to work cooperatively and collaboratively either as part of a group or in the service of others. It is involved in assisting clients and customers as a regular function of one's work, or assisting coworkers to meet deadlines or to achieve work goals.

Extroversion Reflects a tendency to be outgoing in association with other people, to seek and enjoy the company of others, to be gregarious, to interact easily and well with others, and to be likable and warmly approachable. It involves enjoying the company of others and a concern for their interests; it implies sociableness whether work is involved or not. Extroversion refers to being comfortable and friendly in virtually any sort of situation involving others.

Source: Barrick & Mount (1991) and Digman (1990).

of employers is employee theft and property damage. One strategy organizations have adopted to reduce employee theft is to screen out potential employees who may be dishonest. As a result, organizations have increased their reliance on *honesty* or *integrity tests*. These tests are personality-based measures (Sackett, Burris, & Callahan, 1989). Unlike other selection tests discussed in this chapter, where the intent of the test is to screen in those applicants with the appropriate KSAOs needed for the job, the intent of honesty or integrity tests is to screen out potentially dishonest employees. Honesty or integrity testing is controversial. You may wish to read the section in Chapter 11 on honesty and integrity testing for a complete discussion of this topic within the broader context of counterproductive work behaviours.

Faking and Social Desirability

One criticism of personality inventories is that they are prone to faking and social desirability. Unlike cognitive ability measures, there are no right or wrong answers on a personality inventory. Faking occurs when individuals respond to inventory questions with answers that do not reflect their true beliefs or feelings. Social desirability is a form of faking where individuals choose responses they believe will present them in a socially desirable way or in a positive light. For example, a woman may believe that men and women are equally aggressive but states that men are more aggressive than females because she believes that this is what she is expected to say, and not saying it may create a negative impression. There is no doubt that individuals can distort their responses on self-report inventories in desired directions (Hough, 1998; Ones & Viswesvaran, 1998a). What is less clear is the impact of such distortions on employment decisions based on personality inventories. The major concern in using self-report inventories as part of personnel selection is that job applicants who do distort their responses in a socially desirable manner will improve their chances of being hired (Ellington, Sackett, & Hough, 1999; Hough, 1998; Rosse, Steecher, Miller, & Levin, 1998). Response distortion may cause a change in the rank ordering of applicants at the upper end of a distribution of personality scores, leading to a loss of the best-qualified candidates (Zickar & Drasgow, 1996).

There is no doubt that people can distort their responses on self-report measures in laboratory settings when instructed to do so. It is less certain what impact intentional distortion or faking may have in real-life settings where most of the evidence, based on change in validity coefficients, suggests that faking takes place but its impact is not as serious as shown in laboratory studies, particularly when applicants are warned that faking can be detected and that it will have negative consequences for them (Hough & Furnham, 2003). Recently, Hogan, Barrett, and Hogan (2007) examined personality test data taken from more than 5,000 applicants who had been rejected for customer-service positions with a large, national U.S. company. The applicants had reapplied for the position and were required to retake the selection tests. Hogan et al. concluded that the applicants' scores did not significantly change on the retest. Hogan et al. argued that it is reasonable to assume that the applicants would have tried to improve their performance on the second attempt and were unable to do

Richard Goffin

Dr. Richard Goffin received his master's degree in I/O psychology from the University of Guelph and went on to complete a doctoral degree at the University of Western Ontario, where he worked with Dr. Doug Jackson (see his biography in Chapter 2). Dr. Goffin exemplifies the scientist-practitioner model; prior to taking up a position in the psychology department at Western, Dr. Goffin worked as a personnel psychologist at the Personnel Psychology Centre of the Public Service Commission of Canada and at the Human Resources Branch of Revenue Canada. His duties in those positions included the investigation of diversity issues in personnel selection, development and validation of various personnel selection devices, and the design and management of job analysis projects. He consults with private and public-sector organizations and has published peer-reviewed journal articles based on data collected from his consulting work. His research is primarily concerned with job performance measurement and personnel selection. With respect to job performance measurement, he is particularly interested in exploring the validity of comparative (e.g., ranking-based) approaches, and the intersection of performance appraisal with social comparison theory. Regarding personnel selection, much of his current research focuses on the use of personality testing as a means of hiring the most promising employees, and the problem of faking as it relates to personality testing within this context. He has published a substantial body of work on these topics.

Source: Courtesy of Richard Goffin.

so substantially. Unfortunately, we know very little about the processes that underlie an applicant's willingness to fake on a personality test, except that faking does have an effect on the usefulness of personality testing in selection (Goffin & Boyd, 2009). Perhaps the best way to deal with faking is to warn job applicants that faking can be detected and that it will be taken into consideration when making hiring decisions about the applicants. In addition, the results from a self-report inventory should be viewed not in isolation but in conjunction with a careful review of a candidate's complete file for evidence of distortion (Rosse, Steecher, Miller, & Levin, 1998).

Interviews

unstructured interview

A traditional method of interviewing that involves no constraints on the questions asked, no requirements for standardization, and a subjective assessment of the candidate

Although interviews, as discussed previously, are often used as preliminary screening devices, they are most frequently used as one of the last stages in the selection process. The traditional approach to employment interviewing, including screening interviews, is one that has become known as an **unstructured interview**. In such interviews, the interviewer typically engages in an open-ended conversation with the interviewee. There are few constraints on the kinds of questions that may be asked, and, furthermore, many of the questions used in the interview may not occur to the interviewer until partway through the interview. Most interviewers, however, appear to rely on a common set of questions, often ones that they have heard others use. Box 4.7 presents a list of questions often used by interviewers. Many interviewees have learned to respond to such questions with standard answers. For example, common responses to the question, "What are your weaknesses?" include "I get too involved in my work" and "I'm too much of a perfectionist." Answers to such questions reveal very little useful information about the applicant.

Another characteristic typical of unstructured interviews is that no systematic scoring procedure is used. Interviewers are free to interpret interviewee responses in any manner they choose. Rather than evaluating responses or answers to interview questions, the interviewer, in fact, uses the interview to get a "feeling" or a "hunch" about the applicant. The interviewer emerges from the interview with a global, subjective evaluation of the applicant, which is biased by personal views and preferences and likely to be inaccurate. In fact, many interviewers report that they rely on such "gut feelings" in making their hiring decisions. Worse yet, some writers are still recommending such practices (Buhler, 2007).

Webster (1964, 1982) and his colleagues at McGill University, Dipboye (1992), Jelf (1999), Posthuma (Posthuma, Morgeson, & Campion, 2002), and others, have documented the numerous biases and perceptual and information-processing errors that have plagued the unstructured employment interview. For example, interviewers rate applicants more favourably if the applicants are perceived as being similar to themselves (Garcia, Posthuma, & Colella, 2008). Moreover, interview ratings are susceptible to first impressions (Dougherty, Turban, & Callender, 1994; Macan & Dipboye, 1990). That is, an interviewer's initial impression of an applicant, such as might be formed upon

---

Box 4.7

Commonly Used Unstructured Interview Questions

1. Why did you leave your last job? (Why do you want to leave your current job?)
2. What do you consider to be your strengths? What are your weaknesses?
3. What were your strongest/weakest subjects at school? (What did you learn in school that you could use in this job?)
4. How would someone who knows you or has worked with you describe you as an individual?
5. What is your greatest accomplishment (or most meaningful work experience)?

6. What were the most enjoyable aspects of your last job? What were the least enjoyable aspects?
7. Why do you want this job? What are you looking for from this job (or from us)?
8. Why should we hire you? (What can you do for us? or Why are you the best candidate for this position?)
9. What are your long-range plans or goals? (Where do you plan to be five years from now?)
10. Tell me about yourself.

Source: From CATANO/WIESNER/HACKETT. *Recruitment and Selection in Canada*, 4E. © 2010 Nelson Education Ltd. Reproduced by permission. www.cengage.com/permissions.

reading the résumé, affects the way the interview is conducted, the questions asked, and the evaluation of the candidate's answers. In addition, interview ratings are influenced by visual cues such as physical attractiveness of the applicant, eye contact, body orientation, smiling, and hand gestures, as well as vocal cues such as rate of speaking, number and duration of pauses, variability in loudness, and pitch; for example, lower voices tend to be rated more positively than higher voices for management positions (DeGroot & Motowidlo, 1999). Unstructured interviews have poor validity, as noted in our discussion of screening interviews. Nonetheless, the interview remains an extremely popular method of selecting employees (refer to Table 4.2 on page 132).

In the early 1980s a number of researchers began working on new approaches to employment interviewing, which have become known as **structured interviews** (Janz, 1982; Latham & Saari, 1984; Latham, Saari, Pursell, & Campion, 1980). Structuring factors include standardized interviews, job-relatedness of interview questions, and standardized scoring systems. Structured interviews are based on a job analysis—usually a critical incident technique—so that they assess only job-relevant attributes. Appropriate scoring guides and interviewer training are essential features of the structured interview. Structured interviews have significantly greater reliability and predictive validity than traditional, unstructured interviews—validity of approximately .50 versus .20 (Conway, Jako, & Goodman, 1995; Huffcutt & Arthur, 1994; McDaniel, Whetzel, Schmidt, & Maurer, 1994; Wiesner & Cronshaw, 1988). The two predominant structured interview formats are *situational interviews and behavioural description interviews.*

The Situational Interview

In the **situational interview (SI)** (Latham et al., 1980; Latham & Saari, 1984), the interviewer describes hypothetical situations that are likely to be encountered on the job and asks the applicants what they would do in the situations. The interviewer then uses a **scoring guide** consisting of sample answers to each question to evaluate and score the applicant's answers. The scoring guide is designed using the critical incident technique (see Chapter 3; Flanagan, 1954), in which examples of actual job-related behaviours that varied in effectiveness in particular situations are collected and refined to serve as sample answers. Thus, numerical values on the scale are illustrated with examples of answers that would be worth a 1 or a 3 or a 5. An example of an SI question is provided in Box 4.8. The assumption underlying the SI approach is that intentions are related to subsequent behaviours (Fishbein & Ajzen, 1975).

The Behaviour Description Interview

In **behaviour description interviews (BDIs)** job applicants' descriptions of their past behaviour are used to predict how they will behave in similar jobs (Janz, 1982, 1989). Box 4.9 provides an example of a BDI question based on the same critical incidents used in the development of the SI question in Box 4.8. Because BDI questions are concerned with past behaviours in a potentially wide variety of settings, they tend to be more general. BDI questions are likely to generate responses with considerably broader scope than similar SI questions.

structured interview

An interview consisting of a standardized set of job-relevant questions, and a scoring guide

situational interview (SI)

A highly structured interview in which hypothetical situations are described and applicants are asked what they would do

scoring guide

A behavioural rating scale consisting of sample answers to each question used by the interviewer to evaluate and score the applicant's answers

behaviour description interview

A structured interview in which the applicant is asked to describe what he or she did in given situations in the past

Box 4.8

Example of a Situational Interview Question and Scoring Guide

You have just been hired as the manager of our purchasing department and it's your first day on the job. After carefully reviewing product and price information, you make a decision to purchase parts from a particular supplier. Your immediate subordinate, an experienced supervisor who is considerably older than you, questions your judgment in front of other employees and seems quite convinced that you are making a mistake. The employees look to you for a response, some of them smirking. What would you do?

Scoring Guide

1—I would tell the supervisor that I'm in charge and I am going with my initial decision.

3—I would do what the supervisor suggests as he knows the suppliers and materials better than I do *or* I would openly discuss the merits of his suggestion versus my own judgment.

5—I would take the supervisor to a private place, thank him for the information, and instruct him never to question me in front of the employees again. Then, after asking him for information on the best supplier and dismissing him, I would think about the options again. After a brief period I would announce *my* decision to go with the supplier suggested in our private conversation.

Source: From CATANO/WIESNER/HACKETT. *Recruitment and Selection in Canada*, 4E. © 2010 Nelson Education Ltd. Reproduced by permission. www.cengage.com/permissions

---

The broad nature of BDI questions and probable responses makes it likely that the interviewer will need to clarify the applicant's answers in order to allow them to be scored accurately. Follow-up questions or **probes** are used to guide the applicant's descriptions of situations or events until

probes
Follow-up questions or prompts used by the interviewer to guide the applicant's descriptions of situations or events or to provide elaboration of answers

Box 4.9

Example of a Patterned Behaviour Description Interview Question

We all encounter situations in which our judgment is challenged. Tell me about a time when you were not certain you had made the right decision and then someone openly challenged your decision. What did you do?

Probes

- What aspect of your decision were you uncertain about?
- Did the person who challenged you have essential information that you did not possess?
- Could anyone overhear the person's challenge?
- What issues and possible consequences did you consider in responding to this person's challenge?
- What was your final decision and what was the outcome?

Scoring Guide

1—I told the person that I was in charge and I was sticking with my decision.

3—I changed my mind and did what the person suggested *or* I openly discussed the merits of the person's suggestion (in front of others).

5—I took the person to a private place, thanked the person for the advice, and asked not to be questioned in front of other people. Then, after asking the person for suggestions, I took some time to reconsider the options and consequences. I made the decision that had the greatest probability of success, regardless of where the ideas came from, but made it clear it was *my* decision.

IKEA job interview

MAKE A CHAIR AND TAKE A SEAT

CANARY PETE

www.CartoonStock.com

sufficient information is obtained to permit scoring. Some probes are written in advance in anticipation of probable responses and with consideration of the information that will be required for scoring; however, the interviewer is permitted to supplement the list of probes with others during the interview if the information obtained is insufficient to make a rating. Probing to obtain required information without giving away the content of the ideal answer requires considerable skill on the part of the interviewer.

Summary

Structured interviews provide improved reliability and predictive validity and are more legally defensible than unstructured interviews. However, interviewers should be trained on the proper administration and scoring of the interview. Validity coefficients for the SI and BDI types of structured interviews appear to be reasonably similar. Research does not suggest that either approach has an advantage in terms of predictive validity (Taylor & Small, 2002).

Work Samples and Simulation Tests

work samples and simulations

Testing procedures that require job candidates to produce behaviours related to job performance under controlled conditions that approximate those found in the job; provide a closer approximation to the actual job and work environment

Work samples and simulations require the job candidate to produce behaviours related to job performance under controlled conditions that approximate those found in the real job. The candidate is not asked to perform the real job for several reasons. Actual job performance may be affected by many factors other than the applicant's proficiency or aptitude for the job; these factors could affect candidates differentially so that two applicants with the same proficiency might perform differently. Placing the applicant in the job may also be extremely disruptive, costly, and time-consuming, if not outright dangerous in some situations. The major difference between work samples and simulations is the degree of their approximation of the real work situation. The major difference between both of these tests and a job knowledge test is that work samples and simulations rely on the reproduction of job-related behaviours, whereas written responses to a job knowledge test are used to make inferences about the applicant's potential to perform required job behaviours.

Work sample tests include major tasks taken from the job under consideration; these tasks are organized into an assignment that the applicant is asked to complete. The work sample and the scoring of an applicant's performance are standardized, allowing for comparisons of skill or aptitude across candidates. Work samples include both motor and verbal behaviours. Motor work samples require the applicant to physically manipulate some machinery or tools; verbal work samples require the applicant to solve problems that involve communication or interpersonal skills. For example, a secretary's job might include using a computer and related software to type letters and reports, to manage the office budget, to track purchases, to send data files electronically to other people, together with operating the phone and voicemail systems, scheduling appointments, and receiving people into the office.

A work sample test given to applicants for this position might include both a *motor work sample*, using a computer to type and to electronically transmit a standardized letter, and a *verbal work sample*, dealing with a message from the boss that asks the secretary to reschedule several important appointments to allow the boss to keep a dental appointment. The work sample test would not seek to include every aspect of the job but only those deemed to be the most important. The work sample test could be given to the candidate in the actual place of employment or in an off-work setting. Regardless of where the testing takes place, it would be carried out using standardized instructions, conditions, and equipment. The results of the work sample test tell how well the applicant performed on the work sample tasks. Work sample performance is only an estimate, or prediction, of actual job performance. Work sample tests, if developed properly, will predict job performance in a reliable and valid manner. Because they incorporate aspects of the job into selection, work samples have the potential to attain relatively high levels of validity.

Simulations, like work sample tests, attempt to duplicate salient features of the job under consideration. Candidates perform the set of designated tasks and are given an objective score based on their performance. The score is used to predict aptitude or proficiency for job performance. Unlike work samples, the tasks and the setting in which they are carried out represent less of an approximation of the actual job. That is, the simulation asks the candidate to carry out critical job tasks in a more artificial environment than work sample testing.

The most distinguishing feature of a simulation is its fidelity, the degree to which it represents the real environment. Simulations can range from those with lower fidelity (e.g., a computer flight simulator where the applicant controls the aircraft through the computer) to those with higher fidelity (e.g., a stand-alone flight simulator that highly resembles an aircraft cockpit that the applicant enters and then "flies" the plane) (See Figure 5.5 on page 175 in Chapter 5.). High-fidelity simulations can be quite expensive, but in some cases there may be no alternative. The simulation allows a type of hands-on performance in an environment that provides substantial safety and cost benefits compared with allowing the applicant to perform in the actual job. While a flight simulator may cost several million dollars to develop and construct, it is far preferable to having prospective pilots demonstrate their flying proficiency in an actual aircraft where a mistake can be deadly, as well as much more costly.

Situational Exercises

Situational exercises are a form of work sample testing used in selecting managers or professionals. They attempt to assess aptitude or proficiency in performing important job tasks, but do so by using tasks that are more abstract and less realistic than those performed on the job. To a large extent, situational exercises are really a form of low-fidelity simulation. The situational exercise involves the types of skills that a manager or professional may be called on to use in the actual job, such as problem-solving ability, leadership potential, and communication skills. *Leaderless group discussions* and *in-basket tests* are two frequently used situational exercises.

situational exercises
Assess aptitude or proficiency in performing important job tasks by using tasks that are abstract and less realistic than those performed on the actual job

A simulation exercise
designed to assess
leadership, organizational,
and communication skills.

in-basket test

A simulation exercise
designed to assess
organizational and problem-
solving skills

situational judgment test
(SJTs)

Type of situational exercise
designed to measure an
applicant's judgment in
workplace or professional
situations

A **leaderless group discussion** is a situational exercise in which a group of candidates for a managerial position might be asked to talk about or develop a position or statement on a job-related topic. The group is not provided with any rules to conduct the discussion, nor is any structure imposed on the group. The primary purpose of the exercise is to see which of the candidates emerges as a leader by influencing other members of the group. Each candidate is assessed on a number of factors by a panel of judges; these factors might include communication and organizational skills, interpersonal skills, and leadership behaviour.

The **in-basket test** seeks to assess the applicant's organizational and problem-solving skills. As part of an in-basket test, each candidate is given a standardized set of short reports, notes, telephone messages, and memos of the type that most managers would have to deal with on a daily basis. The applicants must set priorities for the various tasks, determine which can be deferred or delegated, and which must be dealt with immediately. They must also indicate how they would approach the different problems the material suggests they will encounter as a manager. Each candidate's performance on the in-basket test is scored by a panel of judges. The Public Service Commission of Canada uses an in-basket test in selecting applicants for certain managerial and professional positions in the federal civil service (http://www.psc-cfp.gc.ca/ppc-cpp/psc-tests-cfp/in-basket-810-eng.htm).

The in-basket has great intuitive appeal as a selection test for managers because it resembles what managers actually do; unfortunately, empirical evidence suggests that it does not have high validity as a selection instrument (Schippman, Prien, & Katz, 1990). In part, this may be due to the lack of agreed-on scoring procedures for the in-basket test; successful managers who complete the in-basket do not always arrive at the same conclusions. Additionally, those judging the in-basket performance often fail to distinguish among various target abilities that are supposed to be measured by the in-basket exercise, calling into question the accuracy of inferences made about potential managerial performance that are based on in-basket scores (Rolland, 1999).

Situational judgment tests (SJTs) are a special type of situational exercise designed to measure an applicant's judgment in workplace or professional situations. They are normally paper-and-pencil tests that ask job candidates how they would respond in different workplace situations (Weekley & Ployhart, 2006). Each situational question includes several response alternatives from which an applicant is asked to identify the "best" response that should be made in the situation. Box 4.10 presents an example of an SJT item.

On the whole, SJTs are very good predictors of job performance. McDaniel, Morgeson, Finnegan, Campion, and Braverman (2001) reported results from a meta-analysis that placed their validity coefficient in the population at .34 for predicting job performance. SJTs' correlation with cognitive ability, $r = .36$, suggests that they are tapping into some aspect of general mental ability, which one would expect to see in a test of judgment. However, as Chan and Schmitt (2002) showed when working with 164 civil service employees, SJTs measure a stable individual difference attribute that is distinct from cognitive ability and personality.

A Sample Situational Judgment Test Item

You are the new supervisor of a 22-member department. The department is organized into two working groups of ten members, plus a group leader. You have been on the job for less than a month, but members from one working group have been dropping by your office to complain about their leader, Jane. They claim that she has been absent, on average, almost two days a week for the last three months and is not there to provide advice and help when they need it. Even when she is physically present, they claim that she is "not there." As a result, they believe that their own work is suffering. They demand that you take action to ensure their group leader is performing her job.

Of the following options, which is the best course of action to take?

a. Inform Jane of the complaints made against her and encourage her to meet with her work group to resolve the problems between them.

b. Call Jane to a meeting and inform her that you have reviewed her absence record and that she has been missing two days a week for the last three months. Tell her that this must stop immediately and that any further missed time must be accompanied by a medical doctor's note or she will be suspended.

c. Consult with your boss on how to handle the problem. Find out whether Jane is "well-connected" to minimize any problems for you in case you have to take action against Jane.

d. Review Jane's absence record to verify her work group's claims. Review her absence and performance record prior to the recent poor record of absence. Once you have completed the information, call Jane to a meeting, lay out your concerns, and try to determine the causes for her poor attendance. Help formulate a plan for Jane to overcome the obstacles to her attendance.

Source: From CATANO/WIESNER/HACKETT. *Recruitment and Selection in Canada*, 4E. © 2010 Nelson Education Ltd. Reproduced by permission. www.cengage.com/permissions.

Assessment Centres

Although situational exercises can be used as stand-alone selection tests, they generally play a prominent role in testing carried out as part of an **assessment centre**. The term "assessment centre" is somewhat misleading. It does not refer to a physical place but rather to a standardized assessment procedure that involves the use of multiple measurement techniques to evaluate candidates for selection, classification, and promotion purposes. Assessment centres had their origin in World War II, when they were used by both Germany and Britain to assess the military leadership potential of recruits. Following the war, the procedure was adapted by AT&T in the United States to assess managerial potential. Today, the procedure is mostly used to assess applicants for managerial or administrative positions. The candidates are evaluated in groups by a panel of trained assessors that includes managers, psychologists, and other human resources professionals who are familiar with the job for which the candidates are being selected (Finkle, 1976).

Assessment centres generally include ability and aptitude tests, personality tests, situational exercises, and interviews. Following completion of all the assessment centre components, the team of assessors reviews each individual's performance on a number of variables such as administrative skills, cognitive

assessment centre

A standardized procedure that involves the use of multiple measurement techniques to evaluate candidates for selection, classification, and promotion skills, human relations skills, decision-making ability, problem-solving skills, leadership potential, motivation, resistance to stress, and degree of flexibility (Bray, Campbell, & Grant, 1974). Based on the ratings and observations made over the period of the assessment, the team prepares a report summarizing the information obtained through the various techniques. Candidates are provided with feedback on their performance at the assessment centre.

Do assessment centres improve on other selection techniques? Are they worth the cost? Both organizations and candidates who have gone through an assessment centre attest to their satisfaction with the procedure. The objective data supporting their effectiveness, however, are equivocal. While many research studies have confirmed the validity of the procedure, a troubling number have not shown any improvement in validity that can be attributed to the assessment centre, or have reported low validities. A meta-analytic evaluation of 50 assessment centres reported a validity coefficient of .37 (Gaugler, Rosenthal, Thornton, & Bentson, 1987), while a study of one assessment centre evaluated across 16 sites found a much lower validity of .08 to .16, depending on the criterion measure (Schmitt, Schneider, & Cohen, 1990). A more recent meta-analysis (Hermelin, Lievens, & Robertson, 2007) that looked only at the ability of assessment centres to predict supervisory performance ratings found a corrected validity coefficient of .28. Nonetheless, assessment centres are likely to increase in popularity as a procedure for assessing potential for managerial or professional careers. The procedure produces a wealth of information, which is useful throughout the candidate's career within the organization. It provides a comprehensive assessment of an individual and identifies strengths and weaknesses that form the basis of future development programs. Organizations have started to use assessment centres as a means of providing realistic job previews to job applicants and as a source of organizational and employee development (Howard, 1997). Additional information on assessment centres can be found at the Web site of the International Congress on Assessment Center Methods (http://www.assessmentcenters.org).

Physical Fitness and Medical Examinations

Many employers routinely administer physical fitness tests as part of the hiring process. The intent of these physical fitness tests is not to identify job-related physical abilities, but rather to screen out unhealthy or unfit employees who may pose a liability to the employer. The employer is concerned that placing physically unfit employees in jobs that require some degree of physical effort may lead to injury or illness, or that the work will be carried out in an unsafe manner. From the employer's view, hiring physically unfit workers means lost productivity, replacement costs, and legal damages from fellow workers and customers who have been injured through their actions. Fitness testing or physical or medical examinations should be administered only after the applicant has been given an offer of employment, which is made conditional on the applicant's passing the test or exam. The physical or medical exam is generally the last step in the selection process. The employer must demonstrate that the health or fitness requirement is related to carrying out the job in question safely, reliably, and efficiently. Physical fitness testing is no different from any other assessment procedure and must meet the same technical standards. In Canada, various human rights acts require that medical or physical examinations of job candidates be job-related as established through a job analysis.

Requiring physical examinations before any offer of employment is made raises issues of privacy and also leaves the prospective employer open to charges of discrimination. This last concern is a major issue in hiring people who may have a disability. Canada was the first country to include equality rights for persons with mental or physical disabilities within its constitution. Section 15.1 of the *Canadian Charter of Rights and Freedoms* provides for equal protection and equal benefit of the law without discrimination based on mental or physical disability. Every human rights act in Canada now includes protection against discrimination on the grounds of disability or handicap. Canadian employers cannot discriminate on the basis of a medical, genetic, or physical condition unless that condition poses a serious and demonstrable impediment to the conduct of the work or poses serious threats to the health and safety of people. Employers have an obligation to accommodate workers with medical or physical conditions on an *individual* basis. An employer could not refuse to hire an applicant who was the best computer programmer simply because the programmer used a wheelchair and the employer had no provision for such disabilities in the workplace. The employer would be required to make suitable accommodations. The only exception would be if the employer could establish that the mobility of the employee was a bona fide occupational requirement under the stringent test laid out in the *Meiorin* decision. The Treasury Board Secretariat, which is the employer for the federal government, has policies on the accommodation of persons with disabilities that can be found at http://www.tbs-sct.gc.ca/pol/doc-eng.aspx?id=12541.

Drug and Alcohol Testing

Employers are increasing the use of drug and alcohol testing. Mostly these tests are used with existing employees and not as part of pre-employment selection programs. Like honesty and integrity testing, they are use to select out rather than to select in employees. We deal with drug and alcohol testing in Chapter 11 on counterproductive work behaviours.

Use of Selection Predictors in Canada

Rynes, Colbert, & Brown (2003) noted that many U.S. organizations have not made use of the best human resources practices. The same can be said for Canadian companies with respect to the use of selection tests. Table 4.2 presents data on use of selection tools from Statistics Canada's Workplace and Employee Survey (WES), which was discussed earlier in this chapter. In 1999, 19 percent of employees hired within the last year reported not receiving any type of pre-hiring assessment; however, this decreased to 13 percent by 2003. A selection interview (83 percent in 2003) was the most commonly used method in each of the three years the survey was administered. A notable change is the significant increase in the use of pre-hire security checks, increasing from 9 percent in 1999 to 13 percent in 2003 (Catano & Bissonnette, 2009). This increase probably

TABLE 4.2

Reported Use of Pre-Employment Assessment Procedures by Newly Hired Canadian Employees Hired in the Last Year Reporting Use of Pre-Selection Assessment

SELECTION TOOLS	1999	2001	2003
Personal interview	77.9 %	80.0 %	82.6 %
Medical examination	10.8 %	8.6 %	9.3 %
Skills test	10.2 %	9.4 %	11.2 %
Security check	9.1 %	8.8 %	14.1 %
Aptitude or personality test	7.6 %	6.4 %	9.2 %
Test of job knowledge	6.2 %	5.2 %	8.4 %
Recruitment agency test	0.5 %	0.6 %	1.7 %
Test on general knowledge or literacy skills	0.7 %	0.8 %	1.8 %
Drug test	1.6 %	1.7 %	2 %
Other test	1.5 %	1.5 %	2.6 %
No selection tools selected	19.3 %	18 %	13.4 %
Using one selection tool	52.0 %	56.9 %	56.5 %
Using two or more selection tools	29.1 %	25.4 %	30.1 %

Source: Catano & Bissonnette, 2009.

criterion measures

Measures of job performance or productivity that attempt to capture individual differences among employees; these performance measures, such as supervisory ratings or absenteeism rates, are used in establishing the validity of screening or selection instruments

reflects increased concerns with security issues following the terrorist attacks of 9/11.

Table 4.3 summarizes the average validity of the predictors we have discussed in this chapter (data are corrected for range restriction and unreliability in the **criterion measures**). It is fairly clear that most Canadian employers are not using the best selection tools. As we will see in the section on utility analysis beginning on page 136, validity has a major influence on utility, or the gain that accrues to an organization from using the best selection tools. A well-developed selection system has the potential to return significant economic gains to an organization through the selection of the best qualified workers.

Decision Making

As we saw in Table 4.2, about 57 percent of Canadian employees were selected with one type of pre-employment selection procedure and 30 percent with more than one procedure. Once an employer has obtained all of this information, how do they make a decision to hire or not to hire? Sometimes all information is in agreement and the decision can be straightforward. Other times the information is contradictory and the decision is more difficult. For example, if one applicant looks very good "on paper" (i.e., the résumé), has a high score on a cognitive ability test, and receives glowing recommendations from references but does poorly in the interview, while another applicant does well on everything except the cognitive ability test, what is the appropriate decision? The employer must find some way of making sense of this information so that the best possible selection decision can be made.

TABLE 4.3

Mean Validities for Predictors Used in Selection with Overall Job Performance as the Criterion[1]

PREDICTOR	MEAN VALIDITY WHEN USED BY ITSELF	MEAN VALIDITY WHEN USED TO SUPPLEMENT COGNITIVE ABILITY TEST*
Cognitive ability*	.51	—
Work samples/SJTs*	.54	.63
Interview—structured*	.51	.63
Job knowledge tests*	.48	.58
Integrity tests*	.41	.65
Interview—unstructured*	.38	.55
Assessment centre*	.37	.53
Biographical data*	.35	.52
Psychomotor ability**	.35	—
Perceptual ability**	.34	—
Physical ability***	.32	—
Conscientiousness*	.31	.60
Reference checks*	.26	.57
Emotional stability#	.12	—
Extraversion#	.12	—
Agreeableness#	.10	—
Openness to experience#	.05	—
Résumé components		
Grade Point Average***	.32	—
Job Experience*	.18	—
Years of Education*	.10	.52
Graphology*	.02	.51

[1] The validity coefficients have been corrected for range restriction and unreliability in the criterion measures.

Sources: * Schmidt & Hunter (1998); **Hunter & Hunter (1984); ***Schmitt, Gooding, Noe, & Kirsch (1984); #Barrick & Mount (1991).

Information collected from some sources, such as test scores, tends to be more objective. A good test provides a reliable and valid measure of some attribute, which can be readily used to compare applicants on a numerical or statistical basis. That is, no (or very little) human judgment is involved in collecting this score. Applicants with the higher score are assumed to do better on the job. Information collected from more subjective sources, such as unstructured interviews or résumés, relies much more on human judgment. Can we combine the data from these two types of information? We can combine the data in several ways, but the primary means are judgmental and statistical composite methods.

The *judgmental composite* involves collecting both judgmental and statistical data and then combining them judgmentally. A decision maker might conduct unstructured interviews and reference checks (judgmental data) and have access to test scores (statistical data). The decision maker then examines the test scores and considers the impressions of the applicants gained from the interviews and reference checks in order to form an overall impression and make a decision concerning who should be hired. This is probably the most common method used by employers to make selection decisions.

The *statistical composite* also involves collecting both judgmental and statistical data, but the data are combined statistically. Ratings or scores are given or obtained from each component, such as an interview, a reference check, a personality test, and a mental ability test. The ratings or scores are combined in a formula or regression equation to produce an overall score for each applicant. Selection decisions are thus based on the applicants' scores.

Statistical methods provide much better decisions than judgmental methods of combining information (Kleinmuntz, 1990). First, in judgmental methods irrelevant factors such as the applicant's appearance or mannerisms are likely to unduly influence the decision. Second, judgmental methods often fail to take into account the complexity of all the information available; decision makers often simplify or summarize the data. Third, it is virtually impossible to assign appropriate weights to all the selection instruments when judgmental procedures are used. How important should reference checks be in comparison to ability tests or interviews? It is difficult to give equal weighting to all selection information in a subjective manner. Sometimes particular applicant data, such as test scores, are largely ignored in favour of impressions based on other sources, such as the interview. Statistical approaches are likely to provide better decisions, even when scores from all the selection instruments are weighted equally, because all applicant information is taken into consideration in a systematic manner (Kleinmuntz, 1990).

Cut-off scores serve as criteria or thresholds in selection decisions. Applicants who score below the cut-off on a given predictor (e.g., test, interview) are rejected. Thus, cut-off scores ensure that applicants meet some minimum level of ability or qualification to be considered for a job. In college or university, a grade of 50 percent often serves as a cut-off. A student whose grade is lower than 50 percent fails the course. This cut-off has been established by convention. In most organizations, cut-offs are established based on the predictor scores from successful employees, or based on expert judgments concerning the difficulty of the predictor items (Saks, Schmitt, & Klimoski, 2000). In this latter case, the expert judges, usually people who have held the position under consideration, estimate the score that a minimally competent individual should receive on the test or interview.

Top-Down Selection When only one predictor is used in selection, the applicants are ranked in terms of their scores. Job offers are made to the highest ranked applicant and proceed down the merit list until the desired number of positions is filled. If a top ranked applicant rejects an offer, the offer is then made to the next highest ranked candidate. In no case are offers made to applicants who fall below the cut-off score, as those applicants are deemed to be unqualified for the position. This approach is based on the assumption that individuals scoring higher on the predictor will be better performers on the job than individuals scoring lower on the predictor (i.e., there is a linear relationship between predictor scores and job performance). As long as this assumption is not violated, top-down selection is considered the best approach for maximizing organizational performance (Gatewood et al., 2008). Only those who are likely to be the top performers are hired. When multiple predictors are involved, top-down selection can still be used as long as one of the decision-making procedures attaches a score to each candidate.

Decision-Making Models

Decision making becomes more complex when several selection tools are used to hire employees. Several models may be used to combine applicant information statistically. These models are *multiple regression, multiple cut-off, multiple hurdle,* and *combination* (Gatewood et al., 2008). We will briefly consider these models.

Multiple Regression

In the multiple regression model, the applicant's scores on each predictor (e.g., tests, interviews, reference checks) are weighted through a multiple regression equation and summed to yield a total score that is used to predict job performance. Candidates are ranked based on their regression score and selected in a top-down fashion. The multiple regression model assumes that a high score on one predictor can compensate a low score on another predictor. An applicant could do very poorly in the interview and still do well if the applicant received high scores on the tests and a reference check. However, this assumption may not be warranted. A minimum level of competence might be required on each of the predictors for successful job performance. The multiple regression approach also has the disadvantage of being expensive, particularly for large applicant pools, because all applicants must be assessed on all predictors.

Multiple Cut-Off

Multiple cut-off is straightforward in that a cut-off score is established for each of the predictors and an applicant is required to take all of the selection tests or procedures. Candidates are ejected if they fall below the cut-off score on any one of the predictors. The model assumes that each predictor is equally important in predicting job success and that applicants must be at least minimally competent on each predictor. It has, however, the same disadvantage as multiple regression when dealing with large applicant pools. It is expensive, as all the applicants must be tested on all the predictors.

Multiple Hurdle

The multiple hurdle approach is similar to a multiple cut-off in that the candidate must pass the cut-off on each predictor; however, applicants are screened out as soon as they fail to meet the cut-off score on any one predictor. That is, if they fail the first test, they never move on to the second test. In this method, the most valid or least expensive tests are placed first in the sequence; e.g., only those applicants who passed a cognitive ability test would be invited for an interview. This model is less expensive than the multiple cut-off model; its major disadvantage is one of time. All applicants must be evaluated at each stage before the next stage can be initiated. Also, if the applicant pool is small, it may remove too many applicants in the early rounds, leaving the decision makers with very few applicants to choose from. While a composite score can be developed for the survivors, generally offers are made through judgmental procedures since the outcome identifies those who are minimally competent on each predictor but not the degree to which they are competent.

Combination Model

In the combination model, all applicants are measured on all predictors and those falling below the cut-off on any of the predictors are rejected, just as in the multiple cut-off model. Then, multiple regression is used to calculate the total scores of those applicants who pass the cut-offs. The applicants are ranked by total score and selected on a top-down basis, as in the multiple regression method. The combination model is therefore a mixture of the multiple cut-off and multiple regression approaches. Like the multiple cut-off model, the combination model assumes that a minimum level of each predictor is required for effective job performance. A further assumption is that, once minimum levels have been reached, high scores on one predictor can compensate for low scores on another predictor. The combination model has the same advantages as the multiple cut-off model but has the additional advantage of providing a means of selecting from among those candidates who pass all the cut-offs. The combination approach is just as expensive as the multiple cut-off approach because all applicants are assessed on all predictors.

Utility Analysis

Decisions based on a selection system have important implications for both applicants and the company. The selection system must produce benefits or advantages that exceed the cost of developing and operating the selection system, or that lead to benefits that exceed those produced by the old system. **Utility analysis** is a decision-making procedure that is used to evaluate selection systems by determining the net gains that accrue to the organization from their use.

Taylor and Russell (1939) developed a procedure to demonstrate the practical effectiveness of selection systems. The procedure relied not only on the validity coefficient but also on two other conditions that influenced the worth of the system: the selection ratio and base rate. The *selection ratio* is the proportion of job applicants selected for positions in the company. The **base rate** is the proportion of applicants who would be successful had all the applicants been hired without any type of selection, or who had been hired through the existing system. The base rate is estimated from available employee performance data. Figure 4.3 shows that an organization considers employees who achieve a score of six or greater on its performance appraisal to be successful performers. If half of the workers hired through the organization's selection system achieved a performance score of six or higher, then, the base rate is 50 percent. Figure 4.3 presents the scores of ten applicants on a cognitive ability test. Let's assume that an applicant must achieve a score of seven on the test to be considered for one of four vacant positions with the company, and that the four applicants with a score of seven or greater are hired. The selection ratio, in this

utility analysis

A decision-making procedure used to evaluate selection systems

base rate

The proportion of applicants who would be successful had all the applicants for a position been hired

FIGURE 4.3

Outcomes of a Selection System

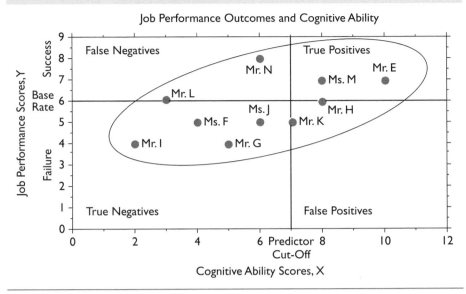

Source: From CATANO/WIESNER/HACKETT. *Recruitment and Selection in Canada*, 4E. © 2010 Nelson Education Ltd. Reproduced by permission. www.cengage.com/permissions.

case, would be .40 (i.e., 4 out of 10 applicants are hired). These four new hires are predicted to obtain performance scores that are equal to or greater than 6 on the performance evaluation needed to be considered successful. Selecting the four applicants with the highest cognitive ability scores above a score of seven would lead to the employment of Mr. E, Ms. M, Mr. H, and Mr. K.

The intersection of the lines representing the base rate and selection ratio divide the scatterplot into four quadrants, representing four different outcomes of the selection process described in Figure 4.3. Mr. E, Ms. M, and Mr. H represent applicants who are true positives (those predicted to be successful and who turn out to be successful). Mr. K. is an example of a false positive (predicted to be successful but would fail if hired). Mr. L and Mr. N are false negatives (predicted to be unsatisfactory but would be successful if hired). Ms. F, Mr. G, Mr. I, and Ms. J. are true negatives (those predicted to be unsatisfactory and would be so if hired). Of course, we could not have obtained performance data from the six applicants who were not hired, but we could have current employees take the cognitive ability test and then link their scores to their performance data to estimate the likelihood that cognitive ability test scores predict performance and to establish the cut-off score on the test (see the discussion of concurrent validation in Chapter 2).

Taylor and Russell defined the **success rate** as the proportion of applicants hired through the selection system who are judged satisfactory. In our example, three of the four people who had a test score of seven or greater and were hired fall into this category, producing a success rate = .75. If the success rate is greater than the base rate, as it is here (.75 versus .50), the selection system is considered to be useful since it leads to a greater proportion of successful hires than would otherwise be the case.

success rate

The proportion of applicants hired through the selection system who are judged satisfactory

The success rate is determined by the specific base rate, selection ratio, and validity that apply in any given situation. Changing the selection ratio (effectively moving the cut-off line to the left or right in Figure 4.3) or the base rate (moving the base rate line up or down to reflect the level of performance the organization considers to represent successful performance) would alter the number of people falling in each quadrant and would have an impact on the success rate. A different validity, changing the orientation or shape of the oval, would also affect the success rate. Taylor and Russell produced a series of tables that estimate the success rate for any given combination of validity, base rate, and selection ratio.

The Taylor-Russell model evaluates the worth of a selection system in terms of an increase in the percentage of successful workers who are hired through the system. It assumes that workers fall into only two categories: successful or unsuccessful. However, most workers vary in the degree of success they exhibit in doing their jobs. Those who are more successful are more valuable employees because they increase the overall productivity of an organization. Can this overall increase in productivity, or utility, be established for selection systems? If so, then comparison of the utility figures reflects the relative worth of different selection systems. Higher utility values indicate that the selection process has added well-qualified, more productive workers to the organization.

Over the years several researchers have developed a formula for calculating the utility of a selection test or system (Brogden, 1949; Cronbach & Gleser, 1965). The formula, known as the Brogden-Cronbach-Gleser utility model, shows that the benefit that accrues from each person hired through the selection system is related not only to the size of the validity coefficient but also to the standard deviation of job performance of the employees and the average predictor score of the hired employees. A large standard deviation suggests that there is great variability in job performance among the workers. A selection system, for any validity coefficient, will be more valuable in this situation, since the outcome of the selection process may result in hiring someone who is either exceptionally good or exceptionally bad. If all the workers, once hired, perform at relatively the same level, the selection system will have less impact on productivity. The model also takes into account the selection ratio and the costs of developing and operating the selection system. Costs can be quite variable, ranging from a few dollars to administer a paper-and-pencil test to several million to develop a system to select jet pilots.

Evaluating testing programs through the Brogden-Cronbach-Gleser utility model is complicated. Often, many assumptions have to be made about the appropriate way to calculate costs and to estimate the other parameters needed by the models. Utility analyses provide a means of comparing different selection systems and can provide quite useful information. Utility models can demonstrate, in quite convincing fashion, whether the implementation of personnel testing programs will produce productivity gains for the organization. Some variations on the Brogden-Cronbach-Gleser model, however, can result in utility gains of millions of dollars, which raise concerns about the credibility of such analyses with managers, and may lead to less support for valid selection procedures (Whyte & Latham, 1997). Utility analysis, when carried out properly, can provide the kind of information that managers want when making decisions about selection systems (Macan & Foster, 2004).

Summary

Recruitment is the first step in the hiring or staffing process, but, unlike other aspects of this process, the actions and decisions of the job seeker play a major role. The recruitment process must take into account the strategies that job seekers use to investigate jobs and organizations. The process should provide job candidates with information they need to make appropriate job choices. Recruitment campaigns should be based on the principle of improving the fit between job candidates and the organization. Organizations can help to achieve this by presenting an accurate image of both the job and the organization to job seekers. The organization should use communications in a way that develops accurate expectations and perceptions on the part of job applicants. One method that appears capable of doing this is a realistic job preview. All recruitment is influenced by external factors over which the organization has little control (e.g., the labour market and the legal environment), as well as internal factors that it can influence (e.g., its compensation strategy, business plan, and values). Every recruitment strategy must contain an action plan, which schedules recruiting initiatives and provides a means of identifying and locating the target applicant pool. The action plan must also identify the appropriate methods for contacting the target applicant pool. The action plan should also include a method for evaluating the effectiveness of the recruitment campaign.

Organizations must be staffed with people capable not only of doing the work required, but also of doing that work well. Though the role of recruiting is primarily to secure an adequate supply of qualified job applicants, the role of screening is typically to identify those individuals within the applicant pool possessing the basic required qualifications for the position. Individuals so identified are then referred for further assessment using more resource-intense selection procedures. If screening is to be successful, it must be based on a job analysis, predict relevant job performance criteria, be legally defensible, and be perceived as "acceptable" (fair) to job candidates.

Screening categorizes job applicants as either acceptable or unacceptable with respect to job requirements. Selection gives greater emphasis to identifying the *degree* to which applicants will be successful. In screening, organizations commonly rely on the application form or biodata, the résumé, the preliminary screening interview, and reference checks. Candidates who pass these screening assessments go on for further, more in-depth assessments. As part of the selection process, these screening devices must meet the same psychometric and legal standards required of other more extensive and expensive selection procedures.

Employment testing must meet acceptable professional and legal standards and should be carried out by professionals who are knowledgeable about tests and testing procedures. Only those tests that are psychometrically sound should be used for employment purposes. The rights of job applicants asked to take employment tests, including the right to privacy, must be respected at all times and balanced against the needs of the organization. A fundamental issue is whether the test provides information that is job-related as identified through job analysis.

Ability tests, both general cognitive ability and more specialized tests, consistently provide highly valid information about future job performance for a broad class of occupations. Cognitive ability tests are the primary predictor for almost every job. Work samples and simulations, particularly situational judgment tests, attempt to base selection on the ability of job applicants to perform actual job components either directly or in some abstract form. Work samples have validity coefficients in the same range as cognitive ability tests and may be very appropriate to use in cases where cognitive ability testing might provoke a negative reaction. Adding personality measures to a selection system can improve overall validity and reduce adverse impact from testing for cognitive ability. Assessment centres appear to be well suited for the selection of managers and professionals and provide a wealth of information. Employers are increasingly seeking information on applicant physical fitness and medical condition. Collection of this type of information may pose a threat to the applicant's privacy and their use must conform to appropriate human rights guidelines and professional and ethical standards.

Employment interviews are the most popular selection procedure among employers and employees. Many employers continue to use unstructured interviews that are plagued by poor reliability and validity and that place employers in a legally vulnerable position. Structured approaches to employment interviewing are based on standardization of questions, job-relatedness of interview questions, and standardized scoring systems. Structured interviews provide improved reliability and predictive validity and are more legally defensible than unstructured interviews.

On the whole, the use of selection tools other than the employment interview is not extensive in Canada. Most Canadian organizations continue to use selection procedures that have low validity and result in less productive employees and organizations than would be the case if they had adopted selection tools with higher validities for predicting job performance. Hopefully, HR professionals who are exposed to the benefits of using valid selection tests will have an impact on their company's future bottom line.

Employers face a difficult task in trying to combine and make sense of complex applicant information in order to make selection decisions. They are vulnerable to numerous biases and errors and they often oversimplify information because their information processing abilities are overloaded. Unfortunately, many employers prefer to rely on their "gut instincts" rather than on more objective sources of information. Although several approaches to making selection decisions can be used, methods that involve combining applicant information in a statistical manner are generally superior to other methods in reducing errors and predicting job performance. Various decision-making models, such as multiple regression, multiple cut-off, multiple hurdle, and combination, can help in making effective selection decisions. Generally, the models produce a total score, which can be used to rank candidates and select them from the top down until the desired number of candidates has been selected. Finally, utility analysis is a means to evaluate the effectiveness of selection systems.

Key Terms

Web Links

To view updated news releases and list of publications of the Canadian Human Rights Commission, visit:

http://www.chrc-ccdp.ca

A useful source of information for human rights cases and legal guidelines for recruitment, screening, and assessment is the *Canadian Human Rights Reporter*:

http://www.cdn-hr-reporter.ca/

To view examples of job-posting websites, visit:

http://www.monster.ca

http://www.workopolis.ca

http://www.thingamajob.com

http://www.careerbuilder.ca

http://hotjobs.yahoo.com

To view an Internet-based recruitment and applicant screening service provider, visit:

http://www.workstreaminc.com

To view examples of firms that provide for applicant background checks, visit:

http://www.axiom-int.com

To view examples of sites for posting and/or viewing video résumés, visit:

http://www.vidres.net

http://www.resumetube.com

www.interviewstudio.com

Principles for the Validation and Use of Personnel Selection Procedures, 4th ed., is available at:

http://www.siop.org/_Principles/principlesdefault.aspx

The U.S. government's Uniform Guidelines on Employee Selection Procedures can be found at:

http://www.dol.gov/dol/allcfr/Title_41/Part_60-3/toc.htm

The Personnel Psychology Centre's Testing Information and Sample Tests can be found at:

http://www.psc-cfp.gc.ca/ppc-cpp/index-eng.htm

The Treasury Board Secretariat's guidelines on the duty to accommodate persons with disabilities can be found at:

http://www.tbs-sct.gc.ca/pol/doc-eng.aspx?id=12541

A computer simulation of an air traffic controller's function can be found at:

http://www.atc-sim.com/

The International Congress on Assessment Center Methods is located at:

http://www.assessmentcenters.org

For interviewing tips for applicants, visit:

http://www.careercc.com/interv3.shtml

http://www.ctdol.state.ct.us/progsupt/jobsrvce/intervie.htm

http://www.quintcareers.com/intvres.html

For a summary of biases in the unstructured interview, visit:

http://www.indiana.edu/~uhrs/employment/best.html

For more information on situational interviews, visit:

http://www.theiia.org/download.cfm?file=81429

For more information on behavioural interviews, visit:

http://careerplanning.about.com/library/weekly/aa080900a.htm and http://www.brockport.edu/career/behave.htm

For more information on situational, comprehensive, and behaviour description interviews, visit:

http://www.mmsearch.com/html/interview_prep.html

For sites devoted to the development of structured interview questions and scoring guides, visit:

http://www.spb.ca.gov/WorkArea/showcontent.aspx?id=1208

For more information on employment interviewing and human rights in Canada, visit:

http://www.chrc-ccdp.ca/pdf/screen.pdf

An example of a multiple hurdle approach can be found at:

http://winnipeg.ca/policerecruiting/constable/process.aspx

More information on the multiple hurdle approach, as well as other methods for integrating selection data, can be found at:

http://www.hr-guide.com/data/G366.htm

Information on setting cut-off scores for tests, as developed by the Public Service Commission of Canada, can be found at:

http://www.psc-cfp.gc.ca/ppc-cpp/index-eng.htm

A more detailed presentation of the Brogden-Cronbach-Gleser utility model is available online at:

http://www.dgps.de/fachgruppen/methoden/mpr-online/issue4/art2/holling.pdf

Discussion Questions

1. Discuss the relationship between recruitment and selection.
2. Why does a realistic job preview benefit both the job seeker and the organization?
3. What are the internal and external factors that influence an organization's recruitment strategy?
4. What are the differences between employee screening and employee selection?
5. What are the advantages and disadvantages of using the following screening devices?

    a. biographical data
    b. application forms
    c. résumés
    d. reference checks

6. What is the purpose of a screening interview? Does it differ from a selection interview? If so, how?
7. Are screening procedures exempt from legal challenges? If not, how would you defend them?
8. What are the limitations of cognitive ability testing? Do these limitations outweigh the advantages of selecting employees based on cognitive ability?
9. What is the Big Five model of personality and what is its relationship to employment testing?

10. Is an employer free to test for physical fitness or require a medical assessment before making a job offer? Explain your answer.
11. What is an assessment centre?
12. What are the different errors or biases that commonly occur as part of a traditional employment interview?
13. What is a situational interview? What role does a critical incident play in formulating situational questions?
14. What is a behaviour description interview? What does it have in common with a situational interview? How does it differ?
15. How do structured interviews compare to traditional interviews in terms of reliability and validity?
16. Which is more effective, a situational interview or a behaviour description interview?
17. What are the common decision-making errors made in employee selection? Can these be eliminated? Can they be reduced?
18. What is the difference between judgmental and statistical approaches to decision making in selection?
19. What are the advantages and disadvantages of the following decision-making models?

    a. Regression
    b. Multiple hurdle
    c. Multiple cut-off

20. What is meant by top-down selection?
21. Discuss how utility analysis can be used to evaluate personnel selection systems.

Using the Internet

1. The interactive Government of Canada website (https://www.jobsetc.gc.ca/home.jsp) contains exercises that help you assess the degree of fit between yourself and a specific job or organization. These exercises illustrate many of the issues presented in this chapter. Visit the site and complete the interactive exercises. Print out your summaries from these quizzes. Do they provide an accurate picture of you? What do they suggest in terms of your "fit" to an organization, career, or job? Is this an accurate picture of your abilities and interests?
2. Identify three Canadian employers that have Web-based application systems. If possible, download copies of the application forms. Summarize the biodata items and discuss the potential usefulness of these biodata items given the nature of the job(s) for which the application is intended. Discuss whether the items on the application blank conform to the applicable federal or provincial legislation. Do you consider the items an invasion of your privacy? How do you feel about applying to an employer that collects data which you consider to be private?

3. The Canadian Forces (www.forces.ca), Shell Canada (www.shell .com), and Bruce Power (www.brucepower.com) all use realistic job previews as part of their recruiting efforts. Go to each of the websites and review the types of RJPs that the companies use. The Canadian Forces is perhaps the most elaborate, with videos available for all entry-level jobs in the CF (see the Job Explorer) in addition to written descriptions. Shell Canada (see the "Students and Graduates" link) uses "a series of scenarios, questions and multiple answers, …[to let you] explore exactly what we're after, how suitable you are, and may actually give you an idea of what sort of employee you could be." Bruce Power uses a detailed brochure to describe the job of Nuclear Operator (see the "Staff and Careers" link). These examples demonstrate the variety of RJPs used by Canadian organizations. Use Google to find others. What type of RJP provides you with the best information? Which one lets you determine whether there is a fit between you and the job or occupation?

Exercises

1. Examine an organization's recruiting program from a job candidate's perspective. Locate a recently hired employee who was an external applicant for a position in the organization. Interview that employee with respect to job search strategy, perceptions of the organization, compensation strategy and the job, the recruiting process, what influenced that person's decision to take the job, and whether his or her views have changed after being in the organization for a period of time. Prepare a report summarizing this interview.

2. Suppose you are managing a Swiss Chalet franchise and are looking to recruit table servers for your restaurant. List in priority order the three things you would be most inclined to screen for. Explain how you would do the screening, and provide a rationale for each item.

3. Develop a screening interview using the items you identified in Discussion Question 3.

4. Think of the key activities of a job that you have held (part-time or full-time). From these key activities, list biodata items that could be helpful in predicting success in this job. A brief rationale should accompany each item. Develop a one-page biodata questionnaire by phrasing each item in question format.

5. Survey ten companies or organizations in your community to determine whether they use selection tests as part of their hiring procedures. List the tests that are used. If the company did not use any type of testing, report the procedures it used and its reasons, if any, for not using selection tests.

6. Employees are being hired less for specific job skills and more for their abilities to fit themselves to the needs of the organization. Organizations are looking for employees who are innovative,

flexible, willing to learn, conscientious, and fit into the organizational culture.

   a. Can the employment interview be used to assess such personality characteristics effectively? How?

   b. Are there better selection tools than the interview for assessing these characteristics? If so, what are they and why are they superior? If not, why not?

   c. Does the assessment of organizational fit and relevant personality attributes pose a danger to human rights? If so, how? If not, why not? How might you reduce the dangers of human rights violations while still pursuing employees who fit into the organizational culture?

7. You are trying to improve selection procedures in your organization. Under the current system, application forms are screened by relevant department managers to determine who should be interviewed. References are also collected. The managers do their own interviewing using individual, unstructured interviews and base their selection decisions almost exclusively on these interviews. They tend to have a lot of confidence in their gut feelings about candidates and believe they've been doing a pretty good job of selecting the right applicants.

   a. How would you go about trying to convince them that they should adopt a more structured, objective (i.e., statistical) decision-making system?

   b. What objections to your suggestion do you anticipate would be raised by the managers?

   c. How would you address these objections?

Case 1

When qualified applicants are scarce, recruiting becomes extremely competitive, particularly when two companies go after the same candidate, as often happens in the case of searching for professionals. After interviewing three short-listed candidates, a high-tech company, Company X, made an offer to one candidate and advised the other two that they were unsuccessful. The successful candidate was given one week to consider the offer. The candidate asked for a week's extension to consider the offer but was granted only an additional three days. At the end of the time period the candidate verbally accepted the offer and was sent a contract to sign. Rather than returning the signed contract, the candidate informed Company X that he had accepted a position at Company Y. He had received the second offer after verbally accepting the first position at Company X. The second company knew that the candidate had verbally accepted Company X's offer. Before accepting Company Y's offer, the candidate had consulted a respected mentor who advised him to ignore his verbal commitment and to accept Company Y's offer. There were no substantial differences in the salaries being offered by each company or in the work that each would expect the candidate to perform. The candidate saw Company Y as the more prestigious of the two employers.

Discussion Questions

1. Did the candidate act in an appropriate manner?
2. What should the candidate have done?
3. What would you have done if you had been in the candidate's position?
4. Did Company Y act ethically, knowing that the candidate had verbally accepted an offer?
5. Does a verbal acceptance constitute a legal and binding contract?
6. What should the candidate's mentor have advised him to do?
7. Should Company X take any action to enforce the verbal commitment? Should it take any legal action against the candidate or Company Y? Why or why not?
8. How can situations like this be avoided?

Case 2

Steelmaking has become an increasingly sophisticated activity and, as a result, the levels of skill required have been rising. Not surprisingly, training and development have become vital elements of success. One of the ways in which a steel producer motivates employees is through its "promote-from-within" policy. As a result, when the company hires employees from the outside it not only is concerned with their ability to do entry-level jobs, but also is looking for evidence of promotion potential (e.g., leadership potential) and organizational fit.

Given the company's commitment to employee relations and development, it has one of the lowest turnover rates in the manufacturing sector. In fact, the extremely low turnover rate has created a bit of a problem. Over the next ten years about one-half of the company's workforce (including management) will be retiring. The challenge will be to fill the many vacated entry-level positions with employees who have the potential to quickly acquire the skills necessary to be promoted into the various technical and leadership positions that also will need to be filled. In particular, the company will need new team leaders for work teams and project teams, new supervisors, and new managers.

Historically, such leaders have been drawn from employee ranks and have been promoted on the basis of job performance and demonstration of leadership attributes such as initiative, decision-making ability, ability to communicate, ability to influence and motivate others, and conscientiousness. These attributes become apparent over a period of time and are developed through training, special assignments, and other developmental opportunities. However, as the company faces the need to fill leadership positions quickly, the amount of time employees spend in entry-level positions will likely be greatly reduced and many will find themselves in leadership positions shortly after joining the company. Thus, the company will need to identify leadership potential at the selection stage and fast-track individuals identified as potential leaders through special training and developmental initiatives. An alternative would be to abandon the promote-from-within policy and hire experienced leaders, supervisors, and managers from outside the organization.

Discussion Questions

You have been put in charge of staffing for the company. Your job is to plan and execute a selection strategy for the next ten years. Assume that the rate of retirements will be fairly evenly distributed over the next ten years.

1. What steps can you take now in preparation for the large-scale selection task that lies ahead? What information will you need to collect? How can this information be used? What strategy will you put in place to deal with the large number of employees that will need to be hired each year? Will you maintain a promote-from-within policy? If so, how? If not, what consequences do you anticipate and how will you deal with them?

2. What selection tools might be appropriate to assess the potential of applicants to acquire knowledge and skills quickly? How might you assess leadership potential? How about organizational fit? Justify your choices.

3. Design a selection system for entry-level employees, specifying the various selection tools you will use (e.g., structured interviews, personality tests, reference checks, etc.), the order in which you will apply them, and the weight you will assign to each of the selection tools. What decision-making model will you use? How will you determine whether your selection system is working (i.e., selecting the best possible employees)? Should you find your system is not working as well as it should, how might you go about improving it? How will you determine whether your selection system has adverse impact on minority applicants? Should you discover your system does adversely affect minorities, what steps will you take to address the problem? Provide a detailed rationale for your design.

CHAPTER 5

Performance Management

This chapter provides the foundation for the measurement of job-related performance. Job performance is a multidimensional construct that is composed of task, contextual, and counterproductive behaviours. This chapter discusses measures of job performance that may be used as criteria in evaluating employees.

Chapter Learning Outcomes

After reading this chapter you should be able to

- Describe the importance of developing and using scientifically sound measures of job performance in evaluating employees
- Understand the relationship between individual performance measures, criteria, and performance dimensions related to a job
- Appreciate the importance of measuring job performance
- Discuss the strengths and weaknesses of different types of performance rating systems
- Define the characteristics that a performance appraisal system should have in place to satisfy human rights and legal concerns

Performance management or performance appraisal allows an organization to monitor the quality of its employees (refer to Figure 3.1 on page 62). Job performance and performance management are complex topics. Performance management refers to the system of measuring employee performance, while performance appraisal is often used to refer to the measurement of one employee's performance using specific performance-measurement techniques. In common usage, performance management and performance appraisal are often used interchangeably. Our goal in this chapter is to introduce the current thinking on performance management and to consider some of the more common performance measurement techniques.

To manage performance, organizations and companies must take job performance and its measurement seriously. Performance measurement is a means to emphasize and reinforce an organization's core values in addition to identifying performance differences between employees. Performance measurement is used to transform companies into results-oriented organizations. It provides a means of identifying employees who need improvement and development (Best Practices, 2000). In this regard there are three major purposes in doing performance appraisals.

- *Administrative decisions* Every organization needs systematic procedures in making decisions that affect the life of both employees and the organization. How does an organization know that an employee deserves a promotion or an increase in pay? How does it know that an employee is not performing up to capabilities and should be dismissed or reassigned to a different job? In Canada, about 40 percent of all employees or professionals work in a unionized environment—where collective agreements generally regulate whether performance appraisals may be carried out, and if so what the nature of those appraisals can be. Performance appraisal data are often the basis for dismissing underperforming employees. Even in non-unionized environments, it is difficult to fire an employee without evidence of their poor performance. Lack of evidence may lead to civil action of wrongful dismissal.

- *Formative decisions* In every organization, supervisors provide feedback to their employees on their work performance, whether they are performing to expectations, and if they need to develop additional skills or to take more training to meet their job demands. These are normal situations where employees need help in developing into good performers. The performance appraisals are used to determine which areas require development and training. Appraisals used for formative purposes tend to meet with less resistance by both supervisors and employees and are not normally used for administrative decisions.

- *Validation research* The third major reason for performance appraisals is to obtain the data needed to validate employee selection procedures. Organizations want to select the best employees for any given job. To do this, they use a variety of selection instruments including ability tests, interviews, or personality assessments. Selection tools must be capable of predicting job performance. The job performance data serve as the work standards against which the selection tests are measured. Does the tool predict job applicants who will perform at an acceptable level once they are hired? In addition to validation research, the performance data can also be used for a number of other research purposes; for example, do employees who have been on the new training program show improved performance compared to their pre-training performance?

Defining Job Performance

job performance
Behaviour (the observable things people do) that is relevant to accomplishing the goals of an organization

Measuring performance is easier said than done. The organization must decide what performance to measure and the level of performance needed to attain organizational excellence. **Job performance** is behaviour—the observable things people do—that is relevant to accomplishing the goals of an organization. Rarely if ever do jobs involve the performance of only one specific behaviour. Also, individuals may perform at different levels of proficiency across job-related tasks or competencies.

Job performance is complex and multidimensional (Borman & Motowidlo, 1993; Campbell, Gasser, & Oswald, 1996). One model of job performance, which forms the basis of this chapter, breaks job behaviour into three subcategories: task performance, **contextual performance**, and **counterproductive performance** (Rotundo & Sackett, 2002). Task performance includes the direct production of goods and services and direct contribution to the efficient functioning of the organization and is, perhaps, closest to traditional definitions of "job performance" (Motowidlo, Borman, & Schmit, 1997). Task performance behaviours contribute to the core activities of an organization and include producing goods, selling merchandise, acquiring inventory, and managing and administering the enterprise (Motowidlo & Schmit, 1999). Contextual performance is closely related to the notion of organizational citizenship behaviour (Coleman & Borman, 2000). Generally, contextual performance has included both interpersonal job performance and job dedication (Conway, 1999; VanScotter & Motowidlo, 1996). Contextual performance contributes to the culture and climate of the organization; it is the context in which the organization's core activities take place (Motowidlo & Schmit, 1999). For example, an employee who is respectful of other employees and cooperates with them to make sure all of their work gets done on time is being a good organizational citizen. That behaviour may not be directly related to the tasks they must perform, but it is nonetheless important to their job performance. Counterproductive behaviour is the opposite of task and contextual performance; while these two types of performance positively promote the organization's goals and values, counterproductive work behaviour works against them. Counterproductive behaviours include both deviance and aggression (Robinson & Bennett, 1995). Counterproductive behaviours range from taking time off to sabotaging equipment to employee theft.

Measures of job performance that attempt to capture differences in these different types of job performance are called **criteria** (Austin & Villanova, 1992). They are the performance standards for judging success or failure on the job. Criteria also provide guidance on the standards that must be met by someone placed into a job.

contextual performance

The activities or behaviours that are not part of a worker's formal job description but that remain important for organizational effectiveness

counterproductive behaviours

Voluntary behaviours that violate significant organizational norms and in so doing threaten the well-being of an organization, its members, or both

criteria

Measures of job performance that attempt to capture individual differences among employees with respect to job-related behaviours

Measuring Performance

Choosing a criterion or performance measure may be rather complex. Suppose you are a personnel selection officer in the Canadian Forces and are placed in charge of selecting military engineering officers. You are responsible for recruiting and selecting men and women who will perform successfully in places such as Afghanistan, Rwanda, Bosnia, and Somalia. Do you recruit and select people on the basis of their job-related technical skills, or do you also consider core competencies such as leadership, courage, loyalty, selflessness, and self-discipline? What, then, constitutes successful performance by a military engineer? What if someone is judged to be a success as a leader but a failure in the technical aspects of engineering, or vice versa? Are any of the competencies on which we select people more important than others? And what about self-discipline—how does that enter into the equation?

What performance should we measure? The answer to this question depends on how we define performance and those aspects of performance that we believe are most important. In reality, we cannot measure every aspect of job performance, so we have to concentrate on those we feel contribute the most to job success. Without a clear understanding of what constitutes job performance in a specific organizational position (i.e., task, contextual, or counterproductive behaviour), we will never be able to effectively measure performance at work. We need first to define job performance before we can attempt to assess it (Sulsky & Keown, 1998). One implication of a multidimensional conception of job performance is that any performance management system should include measures of task, contextual, and counterproductive behaviours.

Effective Performance Measures

Once we have identified the major performance dimensions, the next step is to measure employee performance on those dimensions. Before we can measure performance on any job dimension, we have to define that dimension in terms of specific, measurable activities or behaviours. For example, the job dimension of supervision might include giving orders to subordinates, accomplishing organizational goals, and teaching employees the proper way to do a job, among many other things. One person may be better at "giving orders to subordinates" than "teaching subordinates"; our view on that person's supervisory performance will depend on which of these behaviours we include in our measure of supervisory performance. Smith (1976) established general guidelines to help identify effective and appropriate performance measures. She identified relevancy, reliability, and practicality as key components of any performance measure or criterion.

Relevancy, Deficiency, and Contamination

Relevancy requires that a criterion measure be a valid measure of the performance dimension in question. Suppose we develop a measure of a sales associate's performance based on an overall rating assigned by a supervisor. This measure might be relevant to sales performance in that it captures behaviours related to the job-related competencies of service orientation, communication, and interpersonal relations. The measure may be deficient in not measuring competencies such as achievement, business orientation, self-discipline, and organizing, which may also be related to success in sales. Additionally, the measure may be influenced by problem solving, learning, and management competencies that are not critical for success in this particular job. As a criterion measure, a supervisor's rating may be contaminated in that it is measuring things other than the sales associate's performance. **Criterion relevancy** is the degree to which the criterion measure captures behaviours or competencies that constitute job performance. **Criterion deficiency** refers to those important

criterion relevancy
The degree to which the criterion measure captures behaviours or competencies that constitute job performance

criterion deficiency
Refers to those job performance behaviours or competencies that are not measured by the criterion

job performance behaviours or competencies that are not measured by the criterion. **Criterion contamination** is the degree to which the criterion measure is influenced by, or measures, behaviours or competencies that are not part of job performance. These three aspects of criterion measurement are illustrated in Box 5.1.

Reliability

Reliability involves agreement between different evaluations or appraisals, at different periods of time, and with different, although apparently similar, measures; that is, the criterion measure must meet scientific and professional standards of reliability as discussed in Chapter 2. Reliability is the degree to which observed scores are free from random measurement errors (i.e., the dependability or stability of the measure). Criterion or performance measures are subject to the same errors as any other kind of measurement. There is no such thing as error-free criterion measurement; some criteria, however, are more reliable than others. Reliable criterion measures will tend to produce similar scores when the same behaviour is measured on more than one occasion.

criterion contamination

The degree to which the criterion measure is influenced by, or measures, behaviours or competencies that are not part of job performance

reliability

The degree to which observed scores are free from random measurement errors; an indication of the stability or dependability of a set of measurements over repeated applications of the measurement procedure.

Box 5.1

Illustration of Criterion Relevancy for Performance in a Sales Associate Position

Unmeasured Competencies	**Relevant to Sales Performance**	**Criterion Deficiency** Achievement Business Orientation Self-Management Organizing
Measured Competencies	**Relevant to Sales Performance**	**Criterion Relevance** Service Orientation Communication Interpersonal Relations
	Not Relevant to Sales Performance	**Criterion Contamination** Problem Solving Learning Management

Source: From CATANO/WIESNER/HACKETT. *Recruitment and Selection in Canada*, 4E. © 2010 Nelson Education Ltd. Reproduced by permission. www.cengage.com/permissions.

Chapter 5: Performance Management

Practicality

Practicality means that the criterion measure must be available, plausible, and acceptable to organizational decision makers. The supervisor's rating of the sales associate's performance must mean something to those responsible for evaluating the sales associate. It must also be a number that can be readily obtained from the supervisor with little cost in time or money. It should also be a plausible indicator of individual performance. That is, the criterion measure must have meaning and credibility for those who will use the measurements in making decisions. There is a danger of being seduced by practicality and choosing criteria that, while readily available, do not meet standards of validity and reliability. These two requirements cannot be traded off in favour of practicality. For example, the supervisor may be tempted to use the number of units sold in a month to evaluate the sales associate's performance. This is a very practical measure; however, it may be neither reliable nor valid. The sales volume may be affected by a number of factors outside the sales associate's control, such as the state of the economy, sales campaigns by the competition, and so forth. As well, the records of the number of sales attributed to the associate may not be accurate or entered consistently into a database. That is, while the monthly sales volume may be an easy-to-use, practical measure, it may not meet acceptable standards for reliability and validity. Criteria must be practical as well as being reliable and valid measures of job performance.

Developing Criterion Measures

Several issues must be considered as part of the process of developing a criterion or a set of criteria. Criteria are "dynamic, multidimensional, situation-specific, and serve multiple functions" (Austin & Villanova, 1992). The resolution of these issues influences which measures are selected as criteria and when measurements are made.

Multiple, Global, or Composite Criteria

It is unlikely that you will ever find one measure that will tell you everything about performance in a specific job, considering the complexity of measuring task, contextual, and counterproductive behaviours. The multidimensionality of job performance argues for the use of multiple, independent criteria to measure the independent performance dimensions. Smith believes that the independent criteria should not be combined into an overall composite measure of job performance. In an attempt to measure the performance of an aircraft pilot, combining the job dimensions of *navigational skills, managing air crew,* and *self-discipline* would be, to use Smith's (1976) analogy, like adding toothpicks to olives to understand a martini. Furthermore, others would not believe it was appropriate to obtain a separate, overall measure of performance because such a global criterion measure would lose the rich information contained in the multiple performance dimensions. Our discussion of task, contextual, and counterproductive job performance supports this position. Nonetheless, there is still support for use of a global criterion measure, particularly if there is a need to make a global, overall assessment: "If you need to solve a very specific problem (e.g., too many customer complaints about product quality), then a more specific criterion is needed. If there is more than one specific problem, then more than one specific criterion is called for. But in most situations, a global measure will serve quite well" (Guion, 1987). The difficulty is in identifying those situations where the global measure is best suited. In practice, the best strategy will be to collect multiple criteria data to measure important, diverse dimensions.

Multiple data can always be combined into a composite measure where the different components are weighted according to their importance. Since performance measures will be used for a variety of purposes, it makes sense to collect each criterion measure separately. That information can be combined to compute a composite criterion as needed for different administrative decisions. The weights assigned to the separate performance measures in creating a composite measure should reflect the priority of the different performance dimensions as set by the organization's goals. Implicit in this position is a recognition that the priority of organizational goals may change over time. If separate performance measures have been maintained, it is a relatively straightforward exercise to re-compute the composite to reflect the new organizational, and economic, realities. Caution should be taken in creating a composite performance measure. Performance on one dimension may be so critical that deficiencies cannot be made up by excellent performance on other dimensions. In this case, a composite criterion would be inappropriate.

Consistency of Job Performance

Dynamic Criteria

In discussing reliability as a requirement for criterion measurement, we assumed that the employee's behaviour was more or less consistent at the time the observations were made and remained at that level over time. Not everyone agrees with that position. Employee performance appears to decrease over time regardless of the employee's experience or ability. These changes may reflect the effects of many personal, situational, and temporal factors. Early job performance may be limited only by ability and experience, since every new employee is motivated to do well, while later job performance may be influenced more by motivation (Austin & Villanova, 1972; Deadrick & Madigan, 1990). This is a substantially different issue from the random, daily fluctuations in performance. Changing performance levels may affect criterion measurements. This issue of changing performance levels is called the dynamic criterion problem—a bit of a misnomer, as it is the performance that is changing and not the criterion measure.

Training versus Job Proficiency Criteria

Do you obtain the same results if you measure performance very soon after a person is placed in a job as opposed to several months or years later? Generally, early performance in a job involves informal learning or systematic training. Workers are continually evaluated during training or probationary periods. Performance measures taken during early training will be very different from those taken later, when workers are more proficient. Criterion measurements taken during training periods may produce validity coefficients that overestimate the selection system's ability to predict later job proficiency (Ghiselli, 1966).

Nonetheless, the convenience of short-term performance measures, rather than their relevance to long-term performance, dictates their use in many situations as criteria. Training criteria remain very popular performance measures.

Typical versus Maximum Job Performance

Maximum performance occurs in situations where individuals are aware that they are being observed or evaluated, such as a training situation, or where they are under instructions to do their best. Their performance is measured over a short time period when their attention remains focused on performing at their highest level. Typical performance is the opposite of maximum performance; in typical performance individuals are not aware that their performance is being observed and evaluated, are not consciously attempting to perform to the best of their ability, and are monitored over an extended period of time. There is very little relationship between performance under typical and maximum performance situations, for either inexperienced or experienced workers. In maximum performance, motivation is probably at high levels for everyone; in typical performance situations in the actual work setting, motivation is likely to differ among individuals (Sackett, 2007; Sackett, Zedeck, & Fogli, 1988).

Job Performance Criteria and Performance Appraisal

It is very unlikely that any two workers doing the same job will perform at exactly the same level. Factors such as knowledge, skill, and motivation are likely to cause variation in job performance within and between workers. As we saw in our discussion of competencies, the essence of a competency profile is the specification of the proficiency level required on each competency to successfully perform a job and then being able to assess those employee proficiencies in a reliable and valid manner. Two employees doing exactly the same job, although they meet the minimum proficiency required for a job, may not perform at the same level. Every employee has strengths and weaknesses. How do we actually measure these differences in performance between employees on the relevant job dimensions? How do we determine that they meet the performance requirements for a position? How do we determine areas in which an employee needs training and development? What do we actually use as the criterion data necessary for validating selection systems? The remainder of this chapter reviews some of the more common ways of measuring job-related performance.

Performance Appraisals

Despite their importance, performance appraisals tend to be resisted by both employees and their supervisors. Many managers responsible for completing annual performance evaluations express considerable discomfort with the

Relying on his vast CD collection, manager Walt Friboski liked to provide an appropriate soundtrack when he gave performance reviews.

process and as a result may give uniformly high ratings to all employees that they are evaluating (Bowman, 1999). Employees, who are on the receiving end of the appraisal, express dissatisfaction with both the decisions made as a result of performance assessment and the process of performance assessment (Milliman et al., 2002). Bowman (1999) offered the somewhat tongue-in-cheek definition of performance appraisal as something "given by someone who does not want to give it to someone who does not want to get it." One reason that performance evaluation is stressful for both employees and their supervisors is that most performance measures are based on a judgmental process subject to many sources of error and bias. Even some performance measures that are thought to be more objective are influenced by factors that are not under the employee's control. Some performance measures are better than others and have a better chance of being accepted by workers and their supervisors as well as legal tribunals. Performance appraisals, and the perceived fairness of performance appraisal systems, are playing a greater role in legal challenges to human resources decisions (Martin, Bartol, & Kehoe, 2000). Performance evaluations that are perceived by employees as unfair are more likely to be challenged before a tribunal or a court. Employees may view negative performance evaluations as unfair if they perceive them to be nothing more than the opinion of their boss. Performance appraisals that are formed through a methodology that is perceived as fair, or represent the ratings from several sources, may be more acceptable to employees.

In an attempt to produce a more favourable attitude toward the use of performance appraisals, many organizations limit the use of appraisals to developmental or formative uses and prevent their use in administrative situations such as promotions or pay increases. That is, they are intended to help the employee grow as an employee. The reasoning behind this is that raters, when they know that the appraisals will be used only for feedback to the employee, will be more honest in their evaluations. Research, however, shows otherwise. The different uses of performance appraisals does not improve rating accuracy. In fact, limiting their use may lead the rater to believe that the organization does not take the appraisal system seriously and may not be motivated to take the appraisal process seriously (Tziner, Murphy, & Cleveland, 2005).

Objective Measures: Production, Sales, and Personnel Data

Objective production, sales, and personnel data, also known as *hard criteria* or ancillary measures, are often used as performance measures. These data are produced by the workers in doing their jobs, or are related to observable characteristics or behaviours of the workers. They are called **objective performance measures** because they represent the actual number of things produced or number of sales made. The assigned number does not depend on the subjective judgment of another person. The number of error-free audits completed by an accountant is known for any given period. In this case, the number of error-free audits is an objective measure related to the actual job performance of the accountant. If the quality of the audit rested on the judgment or perception of the accountant's supervisor that the audits met acceptable professional standards, quality would then constitute a subjective measure. Production or sales measures generally involve quantity, quality, and trainability (which is the amount of time needed to reach a specific performance level).

objective performance measures

Production, sales, and personnel data used in assessing individual job performance

Personnel data are objective measures that are not directly related to actual production or sales but convey information about workplace behaviour. Criteria derived from personnel data may tell more about contextual and counterproductive work performance than they do about actual job performance. Personnel data may be better measures of organizational behaviours than of job performance. Absence data are routinely collected and stored in each worker's file and are often used as criteria. Absence measures likely tell more about employee rule-following behaviour than how well employees perform their jobs; however, absence or tardiness data may be criteria that managers value highly when rating employees. Criteria should be selected because they are reliable, relevant, and practical. While most objective measures may meet the test of practicality, they may not necessarily be reliable or relevant. Table 5.1

TABLE 5.1

Examples of Objective Measures of Job Performance

PRODUCTION OR SALES MEASURES	PERSONNEL DATA
Quantity	**Absenteeism**
• Number of items produced	• Number of sick days used
• Volume of sales	• Number of unscheduled days off work
• Time to completion	• Number of times late for work
• Number of calls processed each day	
• Average size of sales orders	
• Words typed per minute	
• Speed of production	
Quality	**Tenure**
• Number of errors	• Length of time in job
• Dollar cost of errors	• Voluntary turnover rate
• Number of customer complaints	• Involuntary turnover rate
• Number of spelling and grammatical mistakes	
• Degree of deviation from a standard	
• Number of cancelled contracts	
Trainability	**Rate of Advancement**
• Time to reach standard	• Number of promotions
• Rate of increase in production	• Percent increase in salary
• Rate of sales growth	• Length of time to first promotion
	Accidents
	• Number of accidents
	• Cost of accidents
	• Number of days lost to accidents
	• Number of safety violations

Source: From CATANO/WIESNER/HACKETT. *Recruitment and Selection in Canada*, 4E. © 2010 Nelson Education Ltd. Reproduced by permission. www.cengage.com/permissions.

presents examples of commonly used objective criteria that have been used in evaluating employees.

Objective performance measures are often deficient criteria. While they focus on the most measurable part of a job because of the ease of doing so, they may not measure other important aspects. For example, concentrating only on the number of words per minute a secretary can type may miss the important component of interpersonal relations with other staff. Using the number of units produced may fail to recognize that others are responsible for feeding the employee parts to assemble and that their work speed limits that of the employee being assessed. Using personnel data—absenteeism, turnover, rate of advancement, salary history, accidents—as criteria leaves an organization open to criticism of criterion deficiency or contamination with respect to task performance. Some of these measures, however, may be good indicators of counterproductive behaviours that we will discuss in more detail later in this book. It is important to understand what job behaviour a criterion measures and the factors that may influence that criterion besides the employee's performance. Box 5.2 illustrates some potential organizational constraints on individual performance. The practicality and convenience of objective data do not justify their use if the measure is not related to critical aspects of the employee's behaviour over which the employee has control. Before objective data can be used as criteria, their reliability and validity must also be established.

Subjective Measures: Rating Systems

It is relatively easier to find objective measures for jobs that involve people in the actual production of goods and services. As a person's job becomes removed from actual production or sales work, it becomes more difficult to associate objective measures to the employee's performance. Upper-level jobs in an organization may involve more administration, leadership, team building, and decision making—dimensions that are not easily measured in objective terms. The

---

Box 5.2

Some Potential Organizational Constraints on Individual Performance

Lack of supplies/materials	Change in policies, procedures, and/or regulations
Lack of needed staff	Peer pressure to limit production
Absenteeism of critical personnel	Poor communication of goals and objectives
Failure to receive material/assemblies from other units	Lack of necessary equipment
Poor working conditions	Inadequate training of new hires
Inadequate physical facilities	Too many inexperienced staff in unit
Poor leadership	Lack of support staff
Excessive bureaucracy	Budget restrictions/cost-saving measures
Unpredictable workloads	
Overextended staff	
High stress levels in workplace	

Source: From CATANO/WIESNER/HACKETT. *Recruitment and Selection in Canada*, 4E. © 2010 Nelson Education Ltd. Reproduced by permission. www.cengage.com/permissions.

issues of criterion relevance, deficiency, and contamination become even more serious. How should an organization evaluate the performance of an accountant's supervisor? Most likely, the supervisor's own manager, peers, and perhaps even subordinates will be asked to rate, or judge, the supervisor's performance on relevant job dimensions. Without a doubt, performance ratings are the most frequently used criterion measure. Ratings do represent the subjective opinions of those making the ratings, and as we noted above may lead to perceptions of bias and unfairness when the employee does not agree with the rating. In the next section we describe some commonly used subjective rating systems. We will identify those **subjective performance measures** that are based on a sound methodology—for example behaviourally anchored rating scales and behavioural observation scales—that bases ratings on behaviour rather than typical graphic rating scales that represent one person's unsubstantiated opinion. Figures 5.1 and 5.2 present examples of these types of rating scales.

Relative Rating Systems

Relative rating systems compare the overall performance of one employee with that of others to establish a rank order of performance. With the exception of the relative percentile method, these techniques provide global assessments as the rater compares overall performance of one employee to another rather than performance on each job dimension. Global criteria may not always be the most appropriate to use, since they provide no information on how the employee performs on different job dimensions and cannot be used for developmental or training purposes. There are three traditional relative rating systems—rank order, paired comparisons, and forced distribution—as well as the more recent relative percentile method.

Rank Order

The rater ranks the employees in order of their perceived overall performance level. For a group of 10 workers, the best performer would be assigned rank 1; the worst, rank 10. There are two problems with this procedure. Raters may have a good idea of who are the best and worst performers but often have difficulty discriminating—that is, assigning ranks—among the remaining employees. Second, because the system is relative, it does not tell whether any or all of the workers are performing above or below acceptable levels. In other words, an employee may be rated the third-best accountant but, in absolute terms, may not meet acceptable performance standards.

Paired Comparisons

The rater compares the overall performance of each worker with that of every other worker who must be evaluated. In rating four employees, their supervisor compares every possible pair of workers: Employee 1 versus Employee 2, Employee 1 versus Employee 3, and so on. The workers are then ranked on the basis of the number of times they were selected as the top-rated performer over all the comparisons. One problem with the procedure is the large number of comparisons that often have to be made. With four workers, a supervisor

---

subjective performance measures

Ratings or rankings made by supervisors, peers, or others that are used in assessing individual job performance

relative rating systems

Compare the overall performance of one employee with that of others to establish a rank order of employee performance must make six comparisons; for 10 workers, the number of paired comparisons increases to 45. Making a large number of paired comparisons becomes tedious, leaving some raters to rush through the procedure. While this technique does guarantee that all employees being rated are given due consideration, it still does not provide information on absolute performance levels.

Forced Distribution

Rather than rank workers from top to bottom, this system sets up a limited number of categories that are tied to performance standards. For example, the rater may be given a scale with the categories excellent, above average, average, below average, and poor to evaluate each worker overall or on specific job dimensions. The rater is forced to place a predetermined number or percentage of workers into each of the rating categories. For example, the procedures may require that only 15 percent of employees be placed in the excellent category, another 15 percent in the poor category, and the remaining 70 percent judged to be average. Often raters oppose labelling a given percentage of their subordinates into extreme categories on the grounds that this distorts the true state of affairs. They may feel that the number of poor or excellent performers working for them does not match the quota the system has allocated to those categories.

Relative Percentile Method

The relative percentile method (RPM) is a new and improved comparative rating system (Goffin et al., 1996). The system overcomes one of the major shortcomings of other comparative rating systems by allowing raters to compare individuals on job performance dimensions that have been derived through job analytic procedures. The system can also be used to make overall performance ratings. The RPM requires raters to use a 101-point scale (0 to 100), with a score of 50 representing *average* performance. For each performance dimension, or for the global comparison, a rater uses the 101-point scale to assess each ratee relative to one another. The rating scale anchors each rater's comparisons to an absolute standard, and thus allows meaningful comparisons among ratings obtained from different raters. The RPM produces validity estimates and levels of accuracy that surpass those obtained with some absolute rating scales (Goffin et al., 1996; Goffin et al., 2009; Wagner & Goffin, 1997). By far, it is the best relative rating method.

Absolute Rating Systems

Absolute rating systems compare the performance of one worker with an absolute standard of performance. Rating scales are developed to provide either an overall assessment of performance or assessments on specific job dimensions. A review of several of the more popular rating formats follows.

absolute rating systems
Compare the performance of one worker with an absolute standard of performance; they can be used to assess performance on one dimension or to provide an overall assessment

Graphic Rating Scales

Graphic rating scales, the most popular subjective rating scale, usually consist of the name of the job component or dimension, a brief definition of the dimension, a scale with equal intervals between the numbers placed on the scale, verbal labels or anchors attached to the numerical scale, and instructions for making a response. Figure 5.1 presents samples of graphic rating scales that have been designed to rate effort. The presence or absence of elements such as a definition, instructions on how to make a response, and the subjectivity of labels attached to different numerical values on the scale help to distinguish between the relative goodness of the scales. The poor rating scale presented in Figure 5.1(a) does not provide the rater with a definition of effort. Each rater may define this term in a different way or have a different understanding of the characteristic, leaving open the possibility that different raters are not assessing the same thing. The better example in Figure 5.1(b) provides a definition of the performance dimension and instructions on how to make a response. There is no guarantee that the raters will not use other interpretations of effort in making their ratings, but at least they have had to consider the standardized definition. The poor example contains very general anchors at each end of the scale but provides no information on what constitutes high or low effort. Again each rater may use a different reference point to characterize the effort of the person being rated. The anchors

FIGURE 5.1

Examples of Graphic Rating Scales

a) A Poor Rating Scale: The scale does not provide a definition of the trait or characteristic being measured, and it provides little if any instruction on how to make a response. The labels for values "1" and "5" are subjective and open to interpretation by different raters. Does the "X" represent a value of "2," "3," or somewhere in between?

Effort

Low   High

| 1 | 2 | X | 3 | 4 | 5 |

b) A Better Rating Scale: The scale offers a definition of "Effort" and provides instructions on how to rate, but the value labels are still subjective and open to different interpretations by different raters.

EFFORT – Consider the amount of energy brought to the job. Personal convenience is secondary to completing work in a professional manner. Circle the number that best reflects the employee's effort on the job.

1	2	(3)	4	5
Poor	Below Average	Average	Above Average	Excellent

Source: From CATANO/WIESNER/HACKETT. *Recruitment and Selection in Canada*, 4E. © 2010 Nelson Education Ltd. Reproduced by permission. www.cengage.com/permissions.

in the better example provide benchmarks to help understand the differences between various degrees of effort; however, different raters may still have different understanding of what constitutes "average" behaviour, or any of the other types specified on the scale. Finally, the poor example allows the rater such latitude in making a response that the person in charge of reviewing the completed assessments may have difficulty knowing what rating was given. In the poor example, does the X indicate a rating of 2 or 3? In the better example, there is no doubt about which response was intended. The legal defensibility of appraisals made with graphic rating scales is very questionable.

Trait-Based Rating Scales

Trait-based rating scales are graphic rating scales that ask the rater to focus on specific characteristics of the person being reviewed. The rater judges the extent to which a worker possesses traits such as dependability, leadership, friendliness, and so on. In most cases the traits are either very poorly defined or extremely vague. Furthermore, the traits under assessment are rarely chosen because they are job-related. The same set of traits tends to be used across all jobs that are being evaluated. The failure to demonstrate the relevance of the chosen traits to job dimensions is a fatal flaw, which makes such appraisal systems next to worthless. Nonetheless, trait-based performance measurement systems continue to be used due to the ease with which such scales can be designed, and the apparent cost savings of using one general performance measure across all jobs that are being evaluated. Organizations that use such systems in decision making run the risk of justifying the validity of such performance ratings in costly litigation before various tribunals.

Checklists

Checklists present the rater with a list of statements that may describe either work behaviours or personality traits. Sometimes the list is restricted to behavioural statements only. The rater goes through the list and identifies those statements that apply to the employee being evaluated. With behavioural checklists, the rater is describing what the worker does. Since some behaviours may be more valuable to an organization, weights can be assigned to the different statements. Generally, the weights are developed through a job analysis or by people who are very familiar with the job. The rating for an individual is obtained by adding the weights of those statements that have been identified for that person. This approach is known as the method of summated ratings.

Behaviourally Anchored Rating Scales

Behaviourally anchored rating scales (BARS) use job behaviours derived through a critical incident job analysis to anchor the values placed on a rating scale. Although this procedure sounds simple, it is actually quite complex and time-consuming. To construct a BARS, a group of workers most familiar with the job use a critical incident procedure to identify specific job dimensions. Other independent groups generate behavioural examples of excellent, average, and poor performance on each dimension and then develop a measurement scale for the behavioural examples. The resultant scale is tested and refined before being adopted for general use (Smith & Kendall, 1963).

FIGURE 5.2

Behavioural Anchors Used to Access Communication Competency

Communication involves communicating ideas and information orally and/or in writing in a way that ensures the messages are easily understood by others; listening to and understanding the comments and questions of others; marketing key points effectively to a target audience; and speaking and writing in a logical, well-ordered way. Circle the rating that best represents the degree of communication exhibited by the employee you are rating.

5 — Excellent

Makes interesting and informative presentations; explains complicated points in different ways to ensure understanding; written reports are concise, understandable, and lead to defendable and convincing conclusions; uses e-mail effectively and replies in a timely fashion; actively listens to others to ensure understanding of what they said; uses humour to capture and maintain attention of audience; makes effective use of nonverbal communication; provides feedback to ensure comprehension of messages that are received.

4 — Above Average

Written and oral communication exhibit excellent grammar and vocabulary; maintains eye contact with audience during oral presentations; speaks with confidence and authority; written and oral presentations are well organized; gets to the point in oral presentations; accurately summarizes positions taken during group discussions; listens carefully to opinions and concerns of others.

③ — Average

Performs well in a structured setting; actively participates in group discussions; presents unpopular positions in a nonthreatening manner and acknowledges opposing points of view; asks for feedback from audience; makes presentations in a clear and concise manner.

2 — Below Average

Oral presentations are factual and accurate but lose the attention of the audience; presentations are overly long; leaves out important points in both oral and written reports; e-mail messages are confusing; performs other tasks while listening to people and does not hear what was said; needs to repeat points to get them across to an audience; does not make an effort to obtain feedback from audience.

1 — Unsatisfactory

Has difficulty establishing a relationship with the audience; uses inappropriate grammar and vocabulary; responds inappropriately to what has been said; does not make an effort to ensure that presentation was understood; ideas are presented in a disorganized manner; written communication and e-mails are brief and incomplete.

Source: From CATANO/WIESNER/HACKETT. *Recruitment and Selection in Canada*, 4E. © 2010 Nelson Education Ltd. Reproduced by permission. www.cengage.com/permissions.

Figure 5.2 shows the resulting behaviourally anchored rating scale developed for the competency of communication. In Figure 5.2, statements such as, "Makes interesting and informative presentations," "Uses email effectively and replies in a timely fashion," and "Explains complicated points in different ways to ensure understanding" would have been assigned similarly high ratings. Compare the richness of information provided by the scale in Figure 5.2 to those in Figure 5.1. The behavioural anchors provide greater guidance to raters and help to ensure greater consistency in ratings by providing raters with detailed behavioural descriptions of what is meant by "average" or "excellent" behaviour. BARS is the Rolls-Royce of rating scales (and perhaps as costly). It integrates job analytic information directly to the performance appraisal measure. It also involves a large number of people in the development of the measure. Generally, these people—supervisors and workers—support the process and become committed to its success.

Behaviour Observation Scales

Behaviour observation scales (BOS) are very similar to BARS in that the starting point is an analysis of critical job incidents by those knowledgeable about the job to establish performance dimensions (Latham & Wexley, 1981). Once the list of behaviours that represent different job dimensions is constructed, supervisors are asked to monitor the frequency with which employees exhibit each behaviour over a standardized time period. Next, the frequency data are turned into a performance score that is obtained by summing all the behavioural items that belong to a particular dimension.

Table 5.2 presents an example of a BOS scale used to evaluate the performance of a security dispatcher. In a BOS, the rater judges the frequency with which each employee displays the critical behaviours. Latham and Wexley (1981) recommend using a five-point scale where the numbers are defined in terms of

TABLE 5.2

Behavioural Observation Scale Used to Evaluate a Security Dispatcher

JOB-SPECIFIC TASK PROFICIENCY

Properly secures lost and found articles	Almost Never	1 2 3 4 5	Almost Always
Controls visitor access to buildings	Almost Never	1 2 3 4 5	Almost Always
Monitors multiple surveillance devices	Almost Never	1 2 3 4 5	Almost Always
Ensures confidentiality and security of information	Almost Never	1 2 3 4 5	Almost Always
Activates appropriate emergency response teams as needed	Almost Never	1 2 3 4 5	Almost Always

Total Score_____

6–16	17–19	20–21	22–23	24–25*
Very Poor	Unsatisfactory	Satisfactory	Excellent	Superior

*Management sets performance standards

Source: From CATANO/WIESNER/HACKETT. *Recruitment and Selection in Canada*, 4E. © 2010 Nelson Education Ltd. Reproduced by permission. www.cengage.com/permissions.

frequencies; for example, they would assign the value 1 if the worker displayed the critical behaviour 0–64 percent of the time, 2 for 65–74 percent, 3 for 75–84 percent, 4 for 85–94 percent, and 5 for 95–100 percent. In this way, the rater assesses the frequency of engaging in actual critical behaviours as opposed to rating the employee in terms of a behavioural expectation that the worker might not have had an opportunity to perform. BOS generally take less time and money to develop than BARS. The BOS development procedure requires participation of supervisors and workers, leading to their greater acceptance of the system.

Perceived Fairness and Satisfaction of Rating Systems

An important consideration in the choice of a rating system is not only the validity and reliability of the system, but also its acceptance by those it will be used to evaluate. Acceptance of the rating system by those subject to evaluation by the system is critical to the system's successful implementation and continued use (Hedge & Teachout, 2000). The perceived fairness and perceived justice of the performance appraisal process plays a central role in determining employee reactions. Rating systems that are perceived to be fair and those that produce a high degree of satisfaction among the ratees are more likely to find acceptance (Smither, 1998). Both the BOS and BARS produce greater degrees of satisfaction by focusing on the employee's behaviours. Most employees, when shown the results of a BOS or BARS appraisal, tend to accept the accuracy of the behavioural statements as being compatible with their self-perceptions of their performance. Both BARS and BOS are also perceived as being fairer than trait or graphic scales. The BOS also reflects a greater degree of procedural justice. Managers do not view trait scales as an acceptable measurement instrument, particularly when they are used to assess their own performance by other managers (Latham & Seijts, 1997). Most importantly, organizations are more likely to win cases involving performance evaluation when they can show a court or tribunal that the performance appraisals were fair and carried out with due process (Werner & Bolino, 1997).

What influences perceptions of fairness? Participation in the performance appraisal process is strongly correlated with positive reactions on the part of employees, particularly if the employees have an opportunity to express their opinions as part of the process (Cawley, Keeping, & Levy, 1998). Fairness perceptions also increase when both managers and employees have an opportunity to participate in the development of performance standards and the rating forms that will be used to assess performance on those standards (Roberts, 2002). Also, following the work of Rotundo and Sackett (2002), rating forms that address all relevant aspects of job performance are more likely to receive both managerial and employee support and lead to employee acceptance and satisfaction with the system.

Rating Errors

Distributional Errors

A rating system is simply a procedure that is used to quantify an opinion or judgment. As with any measurement system, ratings are open to error. Leniency, central tendency, and severity errors are types of distributional errors made by

Gary Latham

Dr. Gary Latham is the Secretary of State Professor of Organizational Effectiveness and Professor of Organizational Behaviour at the Rotman School of Management, University of Toronto. Dr. Latham has played an important and significant role in the development of I/O psychology in both Canada and the United States. He was one of the founders of the Canadian Society of Industrial and Organizational Psychology and served as its Chair. He has also served as the president of the Society of Industrial and Organizational Psychology as well as president of the Canadian Psychological Association. He has received more than 30 honours and awards in recognition of his distinguished scientific contributions to industrial and organizational psychology and for his contributions to consulting psychology as a practitioner. Dr. Latham has made significant contributions to many areas of I/O psychology, including performance appraisal, selection interviews, employee motivation, and training. He has also researched the use of goal-setting theory as a basis for enhancing transfer of training, and ways of increasing organizational justice and organizational citizenship in the workplace. He and his doctoral students have worked on ways to help Aboriginal individuals develop career exploration, job search, and interview skills.

Source: Courtesy of Gary Latham.

judges who restrict their ratings to only one part of the rating scale. Some raters may assign only extreme ratings; some may give only very positive ratings **(leniency errors)** (like a teacher who gives only As and Bs), while others give only very negative ones **(severity errors)** (like a teacher who gives only Ds and Fs). Others may judge all performance to be average and not assign extreme ratings in either direction **(central tendency errors)** (like a teacher who gives only Cs).

Halo Errors

These types of errors occur when the rating a judge first assigned to a particularly important dimension influences or biases the judge's ratings over several other job dimensions. For example, after assigning a very high rating on "leadership," a rater may feel that the same score is warranted for "effort," particularly since the judge may have little experience with the employee on this dimension. **Halo errors** are often the result of the following type of thinking: "If I rated her excellent on leadership, she must be excellent on effort as well. Besides, if I give her a low rating on effort, or say I have no basis for judging her effort, my boss,

leniency errors

Rating errors in which a rater tends to assign only positive ratings regardless of the true level of performance

severity errors

Rating errors in which a rater tends to make only negative ratings regardless of the true level of performance

central tendency errors

Rating errors in which a rater tends to assign only average ratings regardless of the true level of performance

halo errors

Occur when a rater uses a rating assigned to one job dimension to rate several other dimensions regardless of the true level of performance on those dimensions who will review this assessment, may think I'm not doing my job. So, I know she's excellent on leadership; she's probably excellent on effort. I'll give her an excellent rating on effort." A similar effect can occur when a manager's negative perception or observation of the employee on one job dimension or competency spills over to another dimension. That is, the "black mark" on one dimension colours the whole appraisal. These types of rating errors introduce the personal biases of the raters into the measurement process and reduce the likelihood that the assigned ratings are appropriate measures of the performance under review.

Impact of Rating Errors

What impact do rating errors have on the accuracy of a performance rating? Surprisingly, the answer may be "Not much." Rating errors are largely unrelated to direct measures of the accuracy of the ratings. Murphy and Balzer (1989) computed accuracy scores and measures of the common rating errors. There was little, if any, correlation between the two sets of measures. The relationships that did emerge, particularly for halo errors, were paradoxical in that rater errors appeared to contribute to rating accuracy! These results started a discussion of halo that represents true error or true halo, which means that the employee has performed similarly on all dimensions and the supervisor rated that behaviour accordingly. That is, the employee performed at an excellent level on all dimensions and was rated excellent on all dimensions. How then does one separate "true error" from "true halo"? Murphy and Cleveland (1995) make the point that raters may have goals that influence the ratings they assign to employees. A supervisor who comes to a conclusion about an employee's performance may assign a value to represent that belief regardless of the job dimension or competency being rated. The rater's own personality and attitudes about both the organization and the performance appraisal system are related to rating behaviour. These factors may influence tendencies to give inappropriately high or low ratings (Tziner et al., 2005).

Reducing Rating Errors

Over the years many different aspects of both raters and rating systems have been examined in an attempt to reduce rating errors. While rating errors can never be eliminated, they can be reduced by (1) defining the performance domain more clearly; (2) adopting a well-constructed rating system; and (3) training the raters in using the rating system. Reducing rating errors may have unintended effects. The procedures used to reduce rating errors may also reduce rating accuracy. Trained raters appear to be so focused on avoiding rating errors that they stop using whatever strategy they were using before training. Rather than devising strategies to reduce rating errors, a better approach may be to develop programs to increase rating accuracy (Murphy & Cleveland, 1995).

Improving Ratings through Training and Accountability

Rater Training

Training raters in the use of the rating system helps to reduce rating errors and to increase the reliability of the measurements (Day & Sulsky, 1995). A training program for raters ensures that all the raters are operating from a common frame of reference. One criticism of performance appraisal systems is that they often measure the wrong things (Latham & Mann, 2006). **Frame-of-reference (FOR) training** seeks to ensure that raters have the same understanding of the rating system's instructions; that they have the same interpretation of the performance dimensions that are to be evaluated; and that they know how to use the rating system's measurement scale.

Uggerslev and Sulsky (2008) provided insight into FORs impact on raters' use of performance dimensions. They had undergraduate students rate instructors based on videotaped lectures and identify the performance dimensions the students were using as part of those ratings. Before FOR training, the researchers measured the degree of rater idiosyncrasy; that is, the degree to which the raters used different performance dimensions than those specified by the researchers to rate the instructor's videotaped performance. In comparison to a group that had just been given the appraisal forms, those raters who had been given the FOR training showed increased accuracy in their ratings, with those who were more idiosyncratic showing the largest increases in accuracy. Uggerslev and Sulsky make the point that all raters are idiosyncratic to some degree and that FOR training therefore improves the accuracy of all raters.

Training programs can also include information on the types of rating errors that occur and how to avoid them. Some programs include information on how to improve observation of work behaviour. Although training programs can become quite elaborate, involving role-playing and use of demonstration videotapes, many rater-training sessions consist of workshops built around explanation of the rating system, accompanied by practice rating sessions.

Rater Accountability

Apart from training, the factor that has the most impact on rating accuracy is rater accountability. Feelings of accountability on the part of a rater have an impact on the ratings they assign to those being evaluated (Roch & McNall, 2007). Rating accuracy increases when raters are called on to explain or to justify the ratings they make. Accountability can be built into a system by requiring the rater to provide the employee who is being rated with feedback from the appraisal. Many supervisors are uncomfortable doing this, particularly when the feedback is negative. However, if feedback is not given, the employee can neither benefit from the appraisal by improving performance nor challenge evaluations that are suspect.

Most organizations that undertake performance appraisals require both the rater and the employee to review, and to sign, the completed rating form. Employees, however, cannot be forced to sign rating forms with which they disagree. Accountability is also established by building into the rating system a mechanism for the formal review of all performance appraisals. When raters are required to account for their ratings in person as opposed to in writing, their ratings become more accurate, particularly when they have to account for those ratings to those with higher status (Mero, Guidice, & Brownie, 2007).

frame-of-reference (FOR) training

A procedure used to "calibrate" raters by ensuring that they have the same understanding of a rating system's instructions; that they have the same interpretation of the performance dimensions that are to be evaluated; and that they know how to use the rating system's measurement scale

Who Does the Rating?

Supervisor Ratings

Most workplace assessments are traditionally carried out by an immediate supervisor or manager. In recent years, organizations have started to recognize that this may not be the best practice. They have started to obtain ratings from other coworkers and subordinates. Some organizations also ask workers to perform an appraisal of their own performance. Each of these groups provides information about the employee's performance from a different perspective and some may not see the total scope of the employee's job performance (Murphy & Cleveland, 1995).

Peer Ratings

Coworkers tend to provide more lenient reviews than supervisors. As part of a class project, suppose the professor requires members of the group to evaluate each other with respect to certain criteria related to the project. Would you assign a very lenient grade in the expectation that the other students will evaluate you similarly, or would you assign a grade that reflects your honest judgment of how others contributed to the project? If you knew your grade was based on this peer evaluation, would group performance be enhanced or hindered? Self-comparisons with other members of a work group do have an impact on peer performance evaluations and may lead to tensions within the work group and ultimately affect both individual and group performance (Saavedra & Kwin, 1993). Most organizations avoid involving coworkers in the assessment process out of this fear that doing so will lead to hostility between coworkers, increased competitiveness among coworkers, and a breakdown in team functioning. Nonetheless, evaluations from coworkers or peers can be quite reliable and valid sources of information about an employee's job performance (Borman, 1991). In fact, peer feedback is among the best predictors of job performance since peers may have access to relevant job performance data that are not available to other raters. This information may be related to peers placing more consideration on aspects of contextual performance that may have been overlooked by other raters (Zazanis, Zaccaro, & Kilcullen, 2001).

Subordinate Ratings

Ratings by subordinates of their supervisor are relatively rare, although some large companies do obtain such ratings as part of reviewing managerial performance. Subordinate ratings, however, are very common in universities, where a professor's teaching performance is evaluated through student evaluations, and where faculty routinely evaluate the performance of their supervisors (department heads, deans, presidents). Student evaluations of teaching performance are used by a professor's peers in evaluating that professor for promotion or tenure. While the students would be in a good position to observe teaching effectiveness, they might not be the best people to evaluate the professor's research productivity or administrative work on committees. There are two related concerns about subordinate ratings: that either the subordinates will give lenient ratings to influence their own treatment ("If I rate my professor highly, I'm more likely to get a good grade"), or the supervisor will attempt to manipulate the subordinate ratings through altering performance expectations ("I'll give them an easy test so they all pass, and perhaps they'll remember this gift when they evaluate my teaching").

Self-Ratings

What if your professor asked you to evaluate your own performance on the group project? How would your evaluation compare with those of other students in your group and of your professor? Generally, self-appraisals are the most lenient of all. That is, while people tend to give ratings that accurately reflect differences in their performance on different job dimensions, the ratings they give themselves tend to be higher than ratings given to them by others. More and more companies, including most of the Fortune 500 firms, are including self-assessments as part of their performance appraisal systems. These self-ratings are typically used along with ratings obtained from other sources as part of a 360-degree feedback process. Self-ratings, however, have the least agreement with ratings from other sources. They also are not very good predictors of actual job performance (Beehr et al., 2000).

Self-ratings and those made by an employee's manager will disagree substantially. The extent of the disagreement extends not only to the appropriate rating that should be applied but also to fundamental differences in how the employee and supervisor view the job dimensions underlying the rating scales (Cheung, 1999). That is, if both were evaluating the competency of communication, the employee and supervisor would most likely have different views of what that competency included. Employees and managers have different perceptions of whether job factors are under the control of the employee. When employees perform less than their best, they tend to attribute this to external factors beyond their control. On the other hand, their supervisor tends to attribute the less-than-stellar performance to internal factors under the employee's control. These differences in perception are another factor in the discrepancy between self- and supervisory ratings (Bernardin, 1992).

Client or Customer Ratings

An increasing number of organizations ask customers or clients to rate the performance of employees with whom they have interacted. For example, Sun Life of Canada asks customers to rate the performance of salespeople in terms of the service they provided to the customer. Other companies, such as Ford and Honda's Acura division, also obtain information from an employee's internal clients. Internal clients include anyone who is dependent on the employee's work output. For example, the manager of an engineering division might be asked to evaluate the human resources manager in charge of recruiting engineers for the division. Both internal and external customers can provide very useful information about the effectiveness of an employee or a team of employees (Belcourt et al., 1996). This information provides a unique view of the employee's performance from individuals who are directly involved with the employee, but who at the same time are neither subordinate nor superior to the employee.

360-Degree Feedback or Multisource Feedback

360-degree feedback or multisource feedback

The use of information obtained from supervisors, peers, subordinates, self-ratings, and clients or customers to provide the employee with feedback for development and training purposes

The **360-degree feedback or multisource feedback** procedure uses information obtained from supervisors, peers, subordinates, self-ratings, and clients or customers to provide the employee with feedback for development and training purposes (see Figure 5.3). To a lesser extent, such feedback also has been used for administrative purposes such as promotion or pay increases. The intent of the process is to provide employees with feedback about their performance from numerous independent sources to give the employees as complete a picture as possible about their performance (Sulsky & Keown, 1998). This method of multisource feedback is an increasingly popular performance appraisal process (Ghorpade, 2000). Brutus and Derayeh (2002) reported that 43 percent of their sample of Canadian organizations obtained appraisals from multiple sources, and that the use of multisource feedback was more likely to occur in larger organizations. The 360-degree feedback procedure is largely limited to managerial-level employees (Ghorpade, 2000). The majority of companies that use multisource feedback did so solely for the purposes of employee development (Brutus & Derayeh, 2002).

As noted above, the information provided by these different sources is likely to disagree to some extent. Self-ratings tend to be higher than those provided by others and show less congruence with others' ratings. There is a relatively high correlation between peer and supervisor ratings, but only modest

FIGURE 5.3

Illustration of 360-Degree Performance Feedback Elements

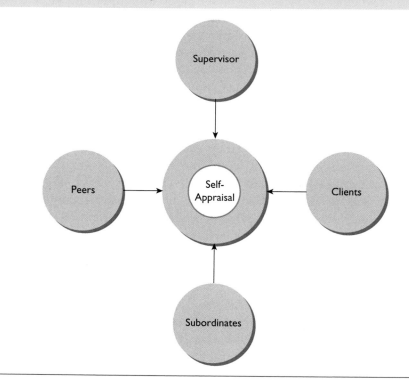

correlations between self–peer and self–supervisor ratings (Beehr et al., 2000; Harris & Schaubroeck, 1988). That is, supervisors and peers are more likely to agree on a rating they apply to someone else than that person is likely to agree with either of them (Furnham & Stringfield, 1998). Over time, however, some ratings may converge. Bailey and Fletcher (2002) found this happening with respect to a subordinate's rating of a manager and the manager's self-rating. The difference in information from different sources may suggest that no one evaluation is the right one. Given conflicting feedback from the different sources, which ones should the ratee follow? Darr and Catano (2008) linked feedback on eight competencies used to develop police officers for promotion to executive-level positions. A critical aspect of the promotion was performance on a structured interview that was based on the same eight dimensions that were used as part of the 360-degree evaluation. Supervisor and peer ratings predicted performance on the interview. As well, peer, subordinate, and subordinate ratings did not improve upon the supervisors' predictions (Darr & Catano, 2008).

During the mid-1990s many companies embraced 360-degree feedback and saw it as an essential tool in developing managers. Many organizations that adopted this procedure had no clear idea of what they wanted to achieve through its use or which competencies they wished to evaluate. Experience suggests that the success of this procedure depends on the organizational culture in which it is embedded. It does not do well in a "command and control" environment (McCurry, 1999). Because 360-degree feedback includes peer appraisals, it is also prone to all the disadvantages associated with peer ratings.

The Future: Non-Traditional Methods for Measuring Performance

Balanced Scorecard

A balanced scorecard links higher-level strategic goals to individual performance. It provides feedback around both internal business processes and external outcomes in order to continuously improve strategic performance and results. The balanced scorecard approach is an approach to describing and communicating strategy and selecting performance measures linked to strategic outcomes (Kaplan & Norton, 1996). The balanced scorecard approach provides a measurement system for evaluating organizational effectiveness as well as providing a management framework for aligning activities with an organization's mission, vision, and strategy. The basic premise of the balanced scorecard system is that organizational effectiveness is a multidimensional concept and that the major elements of the system, including individual performance, must be in alignment with accepted organizational objectives. The balanced scorecard incorporates performance feedback around internal business process outputs and business strategy outcomes. It assesses performance from four perspectives: financial, customer, internal business processes, and learning and growth, as shown in Figure 5.4.

The balanced scorecard approach is a useful method for clarifying the multiple performance dimensions of a job that should be the basis of evaluation. It also establishes the linkages of any one job or position to other

FIGURE 5.4

A Balanced Scorecard

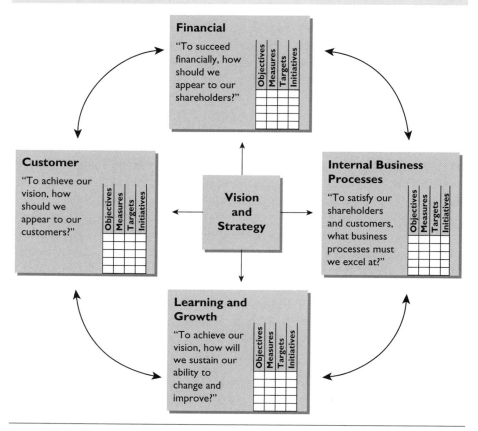

Source: Adapted from Robert S. Kaplan and David P. Norton, "Using the Balanced Scorecard as a Strategic Management System," *Harvard Business Review* (January–February 1996): 76.

components of the organization. In the case of teams, the balanced scorecard can be used to track and evaluate team performance with respect to key objectives or activities. Actions or processes that are under the control of individual team members can be tracked and can help the team to take corrective action in support of individual members. The approach can help the team to identify ongoing problems and to address those issues to avoid further complications (Meyer, 1998).

Job Knowledge/Skill Testing

job knowledge/skill testing

In performance appraisal, a procedure that is based on an assessment of an employee's knowledge or skills required to achieve a desired outcome

Job knowledge or skill testing procedures include paper-and-pencil tests as well as "walk-through" procedures, which require an individual to demonstrate knowledge or general skills such as manipulating controls or equipment to achieve a desired outcome. These types of measures reflect a worker's requisite skill or knowledge to perform a task; they do not indicate the worker's proficiency or what the worker will or can do. Since these measures are "tests," the same issues arise as when they are used as predictors; particularly, they must not lead to adverse impact against subgroups.

Hands-On Testing and Simulation

Hands-on testing and simulation contain related techniques but differ in the degree to which they attempt to reproduce actual critical work behaviours. In **hands-on testing**, workers perform one or more tasks associated with their job. The testing may take place either through formal observation of normal job tasks or off-site, where the worker is asked to perform using normal job equipment and techniques. This latter case is really a type of work samples test where the employee is asked to produce a sample of job-related behaviour. Similarly, **simulations** attempt to duplicate salient features of the work site and to measure job proficiency under realistic conditions (Murphy, 1989). Simulations can range from those which are "low fidelity" to those which are "high fidelity." As part of the RCMP's promotion procedures, constables must successfully complete a paper-and-pencil, job-situation exercise that simulates conditions they might encounter on the job (Catano, Darr, & Campbell, 2007). This is a type of low-fidelity simulation (see Box 4.10 in Chapter 4 for an example). Airline pilots have to undergo periodic recertification in computer-based simulators that realistically represent the cockpit of an airplane and the

hands-on testing

In performance appraisal, a procedure in which raters assess workers as they perform one or more tasks associated with their job

simulations

In performance appraisal, a procedure in which raters assess workers as they perform one or more tasks associated with their job in a setting that emulates salient features of the job and the work environment

FIGURE 5.5

A Twin-Jet Flight Simulator

 NASA Dryden Flight Research Center Photo Collection
http://www.dfrc.nasa.gov/Gallery/Photo/index.html
NASA Photo: EC04–0288–4   Date: October 4, 2004   Photo By: Tom Tschida

The C–17 simulator at NASA's Dryden Flight Research Center, Edwards, California.

Source: NASA.

conditions that the pilot might encounter (see Figure 5.5). This is an example of a high-fidelity simulation.

When used to measure performance, hands-on methods appear to produce reliable scores on critical job-related tasks. These new evaluation procedures are generally complex, expensive to develop, and demanding to administer, raising the issue of their practicality in most situations. Nonetheless, they may have immense potential for use in validation research.

Human Rights and Performance Appraisal

Ever since *Griggs v. Duke Power Co.* (1971), personnel practices in the United States and Canada have been increasingly subject to review by judiciary or human rights tribunals. Although the Canadian legal precedents have occurred more recently, they have been influenced by U.S. case law (Cronshaw, 1986, 1988). Reviews of U.S. decisions related to criterion-related validity studies and performance measurement systems emphasize that the defensibility of performance measures rests on the ability to demonstrate that they are job-related (Barrett & Kernan, 1987). This point was emphasized in the Supreme Court of Canada's *Meiorin* decision (*British Columbia*, 1999; see Box 3.1 in Chapter 3). The court ruled that a standard—that is, a criterion—must be reasonably related to the accomplishment of work-related purposes.

The absence of a job analysis as part of criterion development will likely cast suspicion on any performance measurement system subject to judicial review (Landy, 1989). In *B.L. Mears v. Ontario Hydro* (1983), a tribunal under the Ontario Human Rights Commission decided that black employees were unfairly ranked for layoffs, compared with white employees, through the use of vague and undefined criteria (e.g., productivity, safety, quality of work, attendance, and seniority). Additionally, the ranking system was informal, as no written records of productivity or quality of work were kept. In reviewing U.S. court decisions involving performance appraisal systems, Barrett and Kernan (1987) also note the requirement for written documentation regarding performance measurements. They go on to advise employers to maintain a review mechanism through which employees can appeal performance assessments they believe to be unfair or discriminatory.

Increased critical examination of performance measurement practices by Canadian human rights commissions and courts will mean strict adherence to accepted professional standards of criterion development (Cronshaw, 1988). These standards will include those that apply in the United States unless it can be shown that professional standards in Canada seriously deviate from those in the United States, or that Canadian legislation or case law has established practices that vary from U.S. standards. At present neither of these conditions hold. A performance measurement system must meet both legal and professional practice standards to satisfy human rights requirements.

Summary

This chapter illustrates the important role that job performance plays in the life of an organization. One useful approach to understanding job performance is to recognize that job performance is a multidimensional construct composed of task, contextual, and counterproductive behaviours. Understanding the factors that underlie job performance is necessary to its measurement. The usefulness of any personnel selection system is determined by how well it predicts job performance as measured by job-related criteria. Any criteria chosen as a measure of job performance must be valid, reliable, practical, and capable of withstanding legal challenge. Once job-related performance dimensions or competencies have been identified, the type of criterion measure that most validly represents each performance dimension or competency should be selected. Most likely there will be different measures for different performance dimensions or competencies.

The chapter reviews different factors that affect criteria and the pros and cons of combining different criterion measures to form composites. It also assesses the stability of performance measures over time. Current research suggests that training criteria are acceptable performance measures for estimating maximum performance. However, to obtain a better understanding of possible changes in validities over time, repeated measures of performance should be taken over time. Data from the various criterion measures should be collected in an uncollapsed form and formed into composites when necessary. The weighting of composites should reflect the priority assigned by the organization to the different goal-related behaviours. All the procedures used in establishing the performance dimensions or competencies, their measures, and data collection and analysis should be documented.

There are many ways to measure performance; these fall into two main groups: objective and subjective measures. Objective measures are constrained by other employee and organizational constraints, but some types (e.g., absenteeism measures) may serve as indicators of counterproductive behaviour. Subjective measures, mostly performance appraisals carried out by employee supervisors, are the predominant method of evaluation. There are many different types of performance appraisal/rating systems. All rating systems are subject to rating errors; however, these can be reduced through appropriate training of the raters. While there is no evidence to suggest that any one type of measure is inherently more sound than any other, BARS and BOS methods appear to produce better rater and ratee satisfaction. The perceived fairness of an appraisal system is key to its acceptance as well as its legal defensibility. Performance appraisal systems, if properly developed, will provide data that are as reliable as systems based on objective measures.

Recently, 360-degree feedback systems that acquire performance information from an employee's peers, subordinates, supervisors, and clients have become very popular. The 360-degree process illustrates the different views that these sources have on someone's performance. Mostly, these views reflect concern with different aspects of performance that are not normally seen by only a supervisor. Peers are more likely to attend to contextual performance than to task performance. Supervisors are more likely to focus on task behaviour.

Although performance appraisals may be problematic, most organizations will continue to use them to assess employee job behaviours. More consideration is being given to performance measurement that is not based on performance ratings but direct observation of the employee in actual or simulated work environments. While many technological improvements can be made with respect to performance appraisal instruments, they will continue to be problematic unless they are placed into the broader context of an organizational performance management system. Performance appraisals must be used to integrate and align individual and organizational objectives.

Key Terms

absolute rating systems 161	job knowledge/skill testing 174
central tendency errors 167	job performance 150
contextual performance 151	leniency errors 167
counterproductive behaviours 151	objective performance measures 157
criteria 151	practicality 154
criterion contamination 153	relative rating systems 160
criterion deficiency 152	reliability 153
criterion relevancy 152	severity errors 167
frame-of-reference (FOR) training 169	simulations 175
halo errors 167	subjective performance measures 160
hands-on testing 175	360-degree feedback 172

Web Links w w w

The Performance Management & Appraisal Help Centre provides a wealth of information on performance management including appraisal tools and access to expert articles on performance management and appraisal. The Centre can be found at:

http://performance-appraisals.org/

An example Performance Appraisal Handbook that is used by the U.S. Department of the Interior to appraise performance of its employees is available at:

http://www.doi.gov/hrm/guidance/370dm430hndbk.pdf

Information on workplace violence, one form of counterproductive work behaviour, from the Workplace Violence Research Institute can be found at:

http://www.workviolence.com

Examples of 360-degree performance software and other appraisal forms can be found at three companies:

Cognology: http://www.cognology.com.au/

Halogen Software: http://www.halogensoftware.com/

SumTotal: http://www.sumtotalsystems.com/

More information on the balanced scorecard approach can be found at:

http://www.balancedscorecard.org/

Discussion Questions

1. What is the difference between performance management and performance appraisal?
2. In this chapter we discuss task performance, contextual performance, and counterproductive behaviour. Discuss the role that each of these plays in developing a performance management system.
3. If you were limited in selecting on the basis of only one of the three types of performance discussed in this chapter, which one would you choose? Why?
4. What are the advantages of using a global measure of performance? What are the advantages of using multiple measures?
5. Discuss the distinction between criterion relevance, criterion contamination, and criterion deficiency.
6. What are the characteristics of a good criterion measure?
7. Discuss the problems in using "objective" measures of performance to assess job performance.
8. Discuss the characteristics of a good rating scale.
9. Do you think that rating errors can be reduced? How?
10. Do you think that the newer forms of performance evaluation capture all the important aspects of an employee's job performance? If not, what is missing?
11. What characteristics should a performance appraisal system have to satisfy legal and human rights concerns?

Using the Internet

1. Many online consulting companies offer services in the area of performance appraisal and 360-degree feedback. These companies generally offer software packages that assist in both types of appraisals. Three companies that do so are Cognology (http://www.cognology. com.au/), Halogen Software (http://www. halogensoftware.com/), and SumTotal (http://www.sumtotalsystems.com/). All these companies offer free demonstrations of their software. Choose any two companies and evaluate their 360-degree software packages against the standards we have discussed in this chapter. First, you may want to review their mission statements, hiring policies, and procedures if these are available online.

    a. Does the software allow assessment of task, contextual, and counterproductive behaviours?
    b. Does the software allow appraisals from self, peers, subordinates, supervisors, and clients?
    c. Is the software interactive?
    d. Can the software be modified to suit the needs of a client?
    e. Which of the approaches are likely to be perceived as fair?
    f. Which of the two do you prefer? Why?

Exercises

Many of the forms used by colleges and universities to assess teaching performance suffer from all the defects of graphic rating scales. For this exercise:

1. Obtain a copy of the teaching assessment form used by your institution and critique it using the information presented in this chapter. If a teacher were dismissed solely on information obtained from this instrument (i.e., comments that the person was a poor teacher), would the decision stand up before a court or labour arbitration board?

2. Assume that teaching involves the following major activities: lecture preparation and organization; communication skills; use of examples and exercises; use of audiovisual materials/PowerPoint/Internet; grading; course-related advising and feedback; interaction with students; and maintaining class and office hours.

   a. Place these activities into the job performance dimensions or competencies. More than one activity may be placed in a dimension or competency.
   b. Identify the major behaviours and/or KSAOs for each dimension.

3. For each job dimension or competency, construct a behaviourally anchored rating scale of the type shown in Figure 5.2. You do not have to follow all the steps required to construct a BARS. Generate behavioural statements that reflect different levels of performance on the job dimension or competency. Your classmates should give you an estimate of the value of each behavioural statement. (This exercise should be done as a group exercise.)

4. Compare your scale with the one used in your institution. Which one would you prefer to use? Which does your professor prefer? Why?

5. What are your views on performance appraisal? Do you believe that individual performance feedback has an impact on improving team or organizational performance?

Case

As part of restructuring, a television network decided to close one of its local stations in Cape Breton. Several different unions represented the employees at the station. Employees were given severance packages or opportunities to transfer to the network's Halifax station if they were qualified for any available positions. Two electronic news-gathering (ENG) camera operators received layoff notices and requested transfer to Halifax, where two ENG positions were open. Two ENG operators, two ENG positions to fill. No problem? Not quite. A recent hire at the Halifax station also applied for one of the two positions. Under the terms of the ENG operators' collective agreement, during any restructuring the employer had the right to fill positions with employees deemed to be the best performers.

The network had never employed any type of performance assessments with its unionized employees and was at a loss as to how to determine which two of the three were the best, other than through their supervisors' opinions. The collective agreement, however, called for an "objective" assessment. The network's HR director recalled that a few years previously their Toronto station had to prepare for compliance with pay equity legislation and had developed a rating system to evaluate all their Toronto employees, from secretaries to on-air news anchors. The survey was a graphic rating scale very similar to the type shown in Figure 5.1(b) on page 162. It listed 12 traits or characteristics, including "effort," as shown in Figure 5.1(b). The 12 traits were very general characteristics, such as "knowledge," "willingness to learn," and so on. The HR director asked two different managers who had worked with the three employees to use the form to rate the employees' performance. The new hire received the highest rating and was offered a position. The two potential transfers received low ratings and neither was offered a position.

Under the terms of the collective agreement, the two laid-off employees had the right to grieve the decision and their union carried the case to arbitration. The arbitration panel was composed of a neutral chairperson, who was mutually selected by the other two members of the panel, one of whom was appointed by the employer and the other by the union. In presenting its case to the arbitration panel, the union's lawyer decided to call in an expert in human resources to comment on the performance measure that had been used to assess the employees. After hearing the expert's opinion, which was not challenged by the employer, the arbitration panel threw out the decision based on the performance measure and declared that the two laid-off employees must be offered the two vacant positions.

Discussion Questions

1. What did the expert most likely tell the arbitration panel?
2. If you were that expert, what would you tell the arbitration panel? Be as detailed as possible and call upon all the material that has been covered in previous chapters.
3. Do you think an "off-the-shelf" measure that was designed for one purpose can be used to assess performance in another context?
4. After rejecting the performance measure, the arbitration panel itself was charged with assessing which of the three employees were the best performers. What would you advise the panel to do in this situation? How should they evaluate the employees' performance?

CHAPTER 6

Training

Training and development activities represent a substantial investment by organizations in enhancing organizational performance by improving the skills and abilities of employees. A common distinction is made between education and training. Although both activities may occur in organizations, education is typically thought of as imparting knowledge and general principles whereas training is focused on the development of specific skills. Moreover, it is clear that the opportunity to learn new skills and to develop is highly prized by organizations. The available data do support the effectiveness of well-designed and well-conducted training in improving individual performance and attitudes. In this chapter, we consider what the phrase "well designed and well conducted" means in the context of organizational training and development.

Chapter Learning Outcomes

After reading this chapter you should be able to

- Discuss the importance of training in organizations
- Identify the components of a training program
- Explain the role of a needs assessment when designing a training program
- Discuss issues that arise in training design and delivery
- Discuss the role of evaluation in any training program
- Describe some common training initiatives in organizations

According to the Conference Board of Canada, Canadian organizations spend an average of $787 per employee (about 1.5 percent of payroll) on training and development. Canadian workers, on average, receive approximately 20 hours each year of training (Newswire.ca, 2009). Although these estimates show a decline in training expenditures from previous years, they still indicate that training is a substantial investment for Canadian industry.

For the most part, discussions of training expenditures include only "formal" training such as classroom training or organized courses. However, this may be misleading in that a focus on formal training costs may underestimate training expenditures. A recent survey by the Canadian Federation of Independent Business suggested that small and medium-sized enterprises spend an average of $746 per employee on formal training initiatives, with a further $1,958 spent on informal training. In total, CFIB estimates that small and medium-sized enterprises spend approximately $18 billion each year on employee training and development.

These costs are not distributed equally. Although almost all businesses do some form of training, employees in large businesses are more likely to receive training than those in small businesses (http://www.cfib-fcei.ca/cfib-documents/rr3083.pdf). Moreover, the incidence of training varies across the geographic regions of Canada (see Figure 6.1).

Why Training and Development?

Why do organizations spend so much on training and development? Although the answer to this question might seem self-evident (i.e., so that employees acquire skills and improve performance), there are actually a wide variety of reasons for organizations to invest in training and development activities (see Box 6.1).

First, training might be legislatively mandated. For example, employers are required to provide health and safety training, such as WHMIS (Workplace Hazardous Materials Information System) training. Training may also be a means of achieving other goals, such as employment equity (i.e., training is used as a means of ensuring qualified applicants from a variety of identified groups). Implementation of human rights legislation has frequently resulted in the need for organizational training in topics such as diversity, gender awareness, or sexual harassment in order to ensure compliance. In Ontario,

FIGURE 6.1

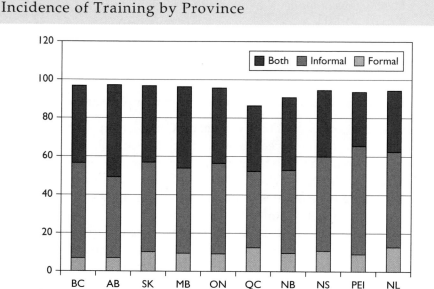

Source: Reprinted by permission of the Canadian Federation of Independent Business.

Box 6.1

The Learning Organization

In his book *The Fifth Discipline*, MIT professor Peter Senge (1990) popularized the notion of the "learning organization." A learning organization is one that invests heavily in the learning of its members—enabling employees to continually acquire new skills. As a result, learning organizations are always transforming themselves as they adapt to this new knowledge and to the changing conditions around them. Senge argued that learning organizations would be more successful in a rapidly changing environment. In his view, the five disciplines necessary to building a learning organization are personal mastery, shared vision, mental models, team learning, and systems thinking. Canadian organizations such as Fairmont Hotels (see http://www.fairmontcareers.com/learning/) have embraced this model of organizational learning.

the recent enactment of the Customer Care Standards under the Accessibility for Ontarians with Disabilities Act means that organizations must establish policies to ensure equal access to individuals with disabilities. Moreover, they must train staff, volunteers, and others in the application of those policies.

Second, and related to the previous point, training may be a means of screening employees for promotions or higher positions in the organization. In the Canadian Forces, for example, all recruits undergo an initial period of "basic training" to teach essential military skills. Those who pass this training then progress to "trades," or occupationally specific training to learn basic technical skills. Further promotions and advancement require further training to acquire more advanced technical skills, leadership skills, and, perhaps, second-language skills. Promotion is often dependent on successful completion of the training requirements for each rank.

Third, training may be "remedial" in the sense that training is offered to individuals in order to correct perceived performance deficits. A manager who does not get along well with others, for example, may be sent on some form of leadership or human relations training.

Finally, and paradoxically, training may also be used as a reward in which successful employees are offered training as a perk. Indeed, in surveys of employees, the desire to learn new things, acquire skills, and develop is most frequently identified as one of the top "things" that employees want from their jobs (e.g., *BusinessWeek*, 2006). Ensuring that employees get the training they desire may result in improved job satisfaction and decreased turnover in organizations.

The Effectiveness of Training and Development

Perhaps one of the most fundamental questions about training in organizations is whether or not it "works." In some circles there is a great of deal of skepticism about how much skill learning or behavioural change can take place as a result of a two- to three-day course or workshop (a frequently used training design). Arthur et al. (2003) explored this question in their meta-analysis of training interventions in organizations. Although the magnitude varied by the type of criterion (see the section on evaluation), overall results of this study supported a medium to large effect from organizational training. Training appears to be particularly effective when evaluated with learning criteria (e.g., knowledge tests), but is less effective in terms of changing behaviour in the workforce. As we shall discuss, this is known as the "transfer" problem in training—skills/knowledge acquired during the training course sometimes do not transfer into changes in on-the-job behaviour.

As Arthur et al. (2003) note, the effectiveness of training also varied considerably with the design of training. Training appears to be most effective when there is a match between the type of skill or knowledge being trained and the method of training. Overall the results from Arthur et al. suggest that (a) training is one of the most effective organizational interventions and (b) training is most effective when it is designed and administered according to a formal means of training design. One of the most well accepted of these means is discussed in Box 6.2.

Toward a Model of Training

As our starting point we take the **instructional systems design (ISD) model of training**. The ISD model incorporates a three-part process: needs analysis, training design and delivery, and training evaluation. The model is depicted in Figure 6.2. Each stage of the model is detailed in the sections that follow.

Needs Analysis

The training and development process begins when some form of need or concern arises. Often that need may come about as a result of a regulatory or legislative change (e.g., the passage of new legislation), a perception that performance is lacking in some area, or the acquisition of new technology. Following such incidents, company officials may be concerned about the availability of employees and wish to develop a training program. Whatever the case, a training development process begins with a **needs analysis**.

---

instructional systems design (ISD) model of training

A general model of the training process that incorporates needs analysis, training design and delivery, and training evaluation and notes the interdependencies among the three major components of the training process

needs analysis

An initial stage of the training development process intended to identify employee and organizational deficiencies that can be addressed with training and recognize potential obstacles to success of a training program

---

Box 6.2

Training Certification

Training and development specialists in Canada are frequently members of the Canadian Society for Training and Development (CSTD; www.cstd.ca). The Society offers two levels of certification–the Certified Training Practitioner (CTP), and the Certified Training and Development Professional (CTDP). Both certifications require applicants to (1) have completed a diploma or degree in adult learning, (2) pass a knowledge exam, and (3) pass a skill competency demonstration. The CTP is intended for individuals with two or more years of part-time instruction or facilitation, while the CTDP is intended for professionals with four or more years of experience in one of the five designated competency categories (facilitating training, evaluating training, assessing training needs, coaching, and designing training).

A 17-minute webinar describing the certification process is available on the CSTD Web page.

FIGURE 6.2

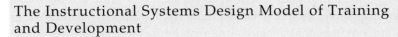

The Instructional Systems Design Model of Training and Development

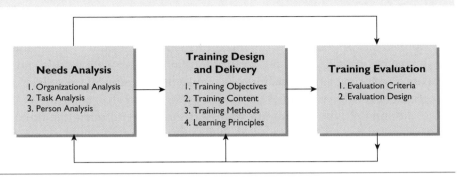

Source: From SAKS/HACCOUN. *Managing Performance Through Training & Development*, 5E. © 2010 Nelson Education Ltd. Reproduced by permission. www.cengage.com/permissions.

Certainly, needs analysis is the recommended starting point in many models of organizational training. A needs analysis helps determine the nature of the problem at hand. Needs analysis is a way to determine the gap between the way things are and the way things should be. It can also be used to identify potential obstacles to the effectiveness of a training program so that they can be dealt with early in the training and development process. Although most authors accept that needs analysis is required for effective training design, Arthur et al. (2004) were unable to substantiate this view because so very few studies report the results of a needs analysis.

Such an analysis ideally includes an assessment of the organization, the task or job at hand, and the employee(s) in question. The inclusion of all three levels in the initial analysis will help answer questions pertaining to what groundwork must be done before training begins, what the content of the training program should be, who should receive training, and how the program should be delivered. These considerations comprise the organizational, job/task, and individual (person) levels of analysis.

Organizational Analysis

A needs analysis at the organizational level should be the starting point in any training intervention. The **organizational analysis** should involve a study of the whole organization, considering such areas as its resources and strategy and the industry in which it operates. The organizational analysis can identify the areas that are in need of improvement and may be targets for a training program. This analysis should also highlight any constraints that may limit the success of a training program prior to the design and delivery of the training.

Successful training initiatives tend to be those that are in line with the organization's overall strategy. Similarly, it is important to consider the resources that the organization can dedicate to the training process. The extent of the available resources can influence the nature of the training program. For example, if the organization has training facilities onsite, this may influence

organizational analysis

An analysis of the entire organization designed to examine its resources, strategy, and environment in order to assess the organization's support for training decisions about the delivery of the training. One would also consider the budget available for training, as financial constraints will influence decisions later in the training development process. Similarly, it is important to consider the industry and environmental factors that may impact the training program. For instance, if the organization is unionized, one should consider the role of the union in training program development.

Another major goal of the organizational analysis should be to establish the degree of organizational support for a training intervention. This can be done by developing a relationship with management. Support from the organization is vital to the success of any training program. If an organization truly values training, it will provide the necessary resources to make the training program a success. For instance, an organization that supports a training intervention is more likely to encourage its employees to actively take part in the program than is an organization that is merely going through the motions of implementing some form of training.

One aspect of an organizational analysis that should not be overlooked is the results of previous training interventions. In particular, the results of training evaluation should feed back into the needs analysis process to ensure that training in the organization continues to build on previous success and rectifies any problems noted in previous training programs.

Job/Task Analysis

job/task analysis

A component of the training needs analysis process during which the jobs and specific job tasks that are in need of training are identified and studied

Following the organizational analysis, the second step in the training needs analysis is to conduct a **job/task analysis**. The first critical step is to identify the jobs that are targeted for training. Some forms of training, like an orientation or a seminar on the role of a health and safety committee, will apply to employees in many positions within the organization. Other types of training will be far more specific in their target jobs. For example, implementation of new accounting software may require training that is relevant only for those employees who will be responsible for using the software.

Once the target job has been identified, one should obtain a detailed job description that outlines the tasks, duties, and responsibilities for individuals who hold that position (see Chapter 3). Working with a group of job incumbents and subject-matter experts, the required tasks can be rated on their importance and frequency in the job. The person developing the training program might also wish to observe a number of people performing the tasks to identify concerns or issues that were not mentioned by the subject-matter experts. From here, the information can be analyzed and interpreted.

The evaluation of the job and the inclusion of people with experience performing the job can greatly inform the training program that will ultimately be offered. The task analysis can help determine the exact nature and scope of the problem to be solved. To consider a health and safety example, the survey component of the task analysis might reveal that, although employees are vigilant about wearing their protective equipment, they tend to use it incorrectly. In that case, the training program should focus more on instruction in the proper use of the equipment rather than on convincing people to wear the equipment. This point might have been missed if it were not for the completion of a task analysis.

Person Analysis

The final assessment to be carried out in the training needs analysis is to investigate the training needs of individual employees. Individual employees' behaviour is considered to see whether performance meets desired standards. The ultimate goal in the **person analysis** is to determine who needs training. Such a decision can be made by comparing a person's current performance to a desired standard or level of performance. Which individuals will be included at this stage of the analysis will be largely determined by the needs of the organization. In some cases the consultant or training director may be asked to assess those individuals who have demonstrated poor or unsafe performance in the past. In other organizations, employees included in the person analysis may be chosen randomly.

A particular concern of the person level of analysis may be to assess the "trainability" (Cheng & Ho, 2001) of the individual. Trainability refers to the degree to which training participants are able to learn and apply the material emphasized in the training program, and is generally thought to be a function of trainees' ability and motivation (Goldstein, 1993). Researchers note that the *motivation* variable is often neglected in training research (e.g., Clarke, Dobbins, & Ladd, 1993; Noe, 1986), with trainee ability levels (e.g., cognitive ability) and backgrounds (e.g., educational levels) emerging as the main variables of focus. Despite this focus on ability, motivation has emerged as an important consideration in assessing individual readiness for training.

Training motivation refers to the trainees' intended effort toward mastering the content of a training program (Noe, 1986). Evidence shows that trainees who enter a training program with high levels of motivation actually learn more in the training, perform better in training, and are more likely to complete the training than those with lower levels of pre-training motivation (Baldwin, Magjuka, & Loher, 1991). Indeed, the results of a meta-analysis by Colquitt, LePine, and Noe (2000) suggest that training motivation predicted training outcomes over and above the effect of cognitive ability.

In addition to motivation to learn in training, pre-training motivation is also related to post-training outcomes. Tannenbaum, Matthieu, Salas, and Cannon-Bowers (1991), for instance, found pre-training motivation to be related to trainee attitudes *after* training. Furthermore, they found pre-training motivation to account for additional variance in post-training commitment. Tannenbaum et al. (1991) suggest that entering training with high levels of motivation may enhance the likelihood of developing other positive attitudes during training, and thus is likely related to motivation to transfer. Taken together, the research suggests that pre-training motivation prepares trainees to receive the maximum benefits from the training, and thus should be viewed as an important consideration in conducting needs assessment at the person level of analysis.

person analysis

A component of the training needs analysis process during which individual employees' behaviour is studied to identify gaps in performance

Training Design and Delivery

Following the needs analysis process, an informed decision can be made about the potential effectiveness of training as an option to address identified needs. A number of decisions are possible at this point. These decisions involve translating what was learned from the needs assessment into the actual training initiative. Some of the pertinent decisions include:

training objective

A statement regarding the knowledge, skill, and behavioural changes that trainees should acquire in the training program

- What are the **training objectives**?
- Will the training program be designed or purchased?
- What is the appropriate content for the training?
- Who will receive the training?
- Who will deliver the training?
- Where will the training take place?

The first pressing question involves the objectives for training. In other words, what do you hope the trainees will take away from the training program? In general, the objectives will involve the knowledge, skill, and behavioural changes that will be acquired through training. Objectives serve a number of important functions including setting the groundwork for the needed training content and providing a starting point for tools to evaluate the effectiveness of the training program.

A second question in the development of a training program is whether an existing training package can be purchased or an original program needs to be designed. In many cases the purchase of an existing prepackaged program is more economical and fully meets the needs of the organization. The organization may not possess the expertise necessary to conduct the training, or it may be too costly to develop the training program from existing organizational resources.

For example, most companies are required to have a certain percentage of employees trained in First Aid. Institutions such as St. John Ambulance specialize in First Aid and CPR training. In fact, St. John Ambulance offers readily available generic and custom First Aid and CPR programs. In the case of an organization wanting to institute a First Aid training program for individuals involved in particular high-risk jobs, it would make sense to choose a proven, prepackaged program from a reputable provider. The time and cost of developing a First Aid course, paying a qualified trainer, and purchasing the necessary tools would be both unnecessary and prohibitive given the quality and accessibility of existing programs.

In other cases, the final decision reached by an organization will be to design a custom training program from scratch either in-house or via the services of a consultant. In what situations might an organization decide that a customized program is needed? We suggest that in cases where the content of the program is highly specific to the organization, the custom design of a program may be necessary. For instance, a company that wants to offer an orientation for its new hires would need to incorporate information that is unique to the company and as such would be difficult to purchase in a prepackaged form. Additionally, training in the use of particular equipment or the performance of particular tasks may require a training program that is not readily available for purchase; a customized program may be the only option.

It is important that the content of the training program matches the needs identified in the needs analysis and allows trainees to achieve the training objectives. Even if the training program is purchased, there is likely some flexibility in the material that will be presented. One way to ensure the training content is appropriate is to consult subject-matter experts.

Who will receive the training is also an important question at this phase of the curriculum development. In some cases, the answer will be obvious. If law mandates that all operators of a particular type of machinery must have training in the operation of that equipment, then all operators must be trained. In this situation, the job of selecting who receives training is as simple as identifying the operators. In other cases, the decision of who receives training will not be as obvious.

A related issue is that of how many people will be trained at the same time. The accumulated research on training in general and that pertaining to health and safety training in particular shows that smaller groups make for more effective learning environments. Individuals within the training groups should also have similar jobs characterized by common risk exposure. This combination of people will contribute to the maximal success of training initiatives.

Another issue to consider when designing training programs is who will deliver the training. An effective trainer is a vital aspect of a successful training program. Of course, the trainer should be both knowledgeable about the material and an effective communicator. In some cases the trainer will require certification in a particular area; for example, the person who delivers First Aid training will need to be certified as an instructor.

Another approach to finding effective trainers who are both subject-matter experts and effective educators is to use a **train the trainer** program. In train the trainer initiatives, a subject-matter expert with the appropriate content skills is given coaching in areas such as program delivery and communication. An effective train the trainer program can allow organizations to use in-house individuals to deliver training programs.

train the trainer
Programs designed to offer subject matter experts in various content areas skills in program delivery and communication

The final training delivery question that we will consider involves where the training will take place. Traditionally, this has been a question of on-the-job or off-the-job training. On-the-job training takes place while individuals are at work, performing their regular job tasks. In other words, the training is incorporated while the task is being conducted. For example, on-the-job training in the safe operation of a particular tool may have subject-matter experts demonstrate the use of the tool while a new hire observes the process. The new hire may then have the opportunity to use the tool under the guidance of the subject-matter expert.

Off-the-job training is training that takes place away from the area where the work is conducted. It may be in a room on-site or in a different facility. The nature of the room will depend on the nature of the training. Some forms of training may require little more than a boardroom and some PowerPoint slides. Other forms of training may require simulators or particular equipment.

Learning Theory and Training Design

How information is presented is a vital decision in the design of any training effort. The ultimate goal is that the knowledge and skills gained in the training environment are transferred to the workplace. Principles determined from extensive psychological research on learning can help create such a training environment. Two major approaches to the study of learning are the

Chapter 6: Training

behaviourist perspective and the *cognitive perspective*. How might these learning theories from the behaviourist and cognitive approaches influence the design of health and safety training programs?

Behaviourist Theory

The behaviourist approach characterizes learning in terms of observable stimuli and responses without reference to any activity that occurs inside the individual. Behaviourists state that a person's behaviour is a product of the person's past experience in an environment. Certainly, this notion applies to the training context; the experience gained during training should influence later job performance.

A number of behaviourist principles have been used to inform the design of training programs. A substantial concern for training designers is transfer of training. Transfer of training refers to the degree to which the knowledge, skills, and abilities gained in the training environment are then applied in the job environment. Four basic learning principles have been used extensively in an attempt to maximize transfer of training (Baldwin & Ford, 1988). These are reviewed below.

- *Identical Elements:* According to this principle, transfer of training is maximized to the extent that the stimuli in the training environment are identical to those in the transfer environment. Therefore, the training environment should be as similar as possible to the job environment. For instance, in a safety training program on the proper use of protective equipment, the same brand and type of safety gear that is used on the job site should also be used in the training program.

- *General Principles:* Learning theory suggests that transfer of training is improved when trainees are taught not only applicable skills, but also general rules that underlie the training content. For example, a training program on the safe operation of a piece of heavy equipment should also stress underlying principles regarding the widespread importance of safe behaviour in the workplace and the basic workings of the machinery itself.

- *Stimulus Variability:* Multiple examples of a concept should be provided for trainees. Having access to multiple examples allows trainees to see the applicability of the training content in their job environment and thus enhances transfer of training. To apply this notion to safety training, consider an emergency preparedness training program. The trainers should be sure to provide examples from several types of emergency scenarios.

- *Conditions of Practice:* Conditions of practice refers to the manner in which the trainee is exposed to the content of the training program.

  a. *Whole versus part learning* addresses whether the knowledge, skills, and abilities being covered in the training program should be introduced to trainees as the whole task or as separate task elements. Whole learning involves practising an entire duty, whereas part learning asks participants to practise pieces of a larger task separately. The general finding is that for tasks that have highly interdependent parts, whole learning is preferred. However, tasks that have largely independent elements should be trained using part learning.

b. *Spaced versus massed practice* concerns the dispersion of practice sessions. With spaced trials, a rest period is allowed between practice sessions, whereas with massed practice, the trainee practises the task continually until mastery. It is generally accepted that spaced trials are preferable. This conclusion is generally applicable in safety training as well. However, massed practice may be used in a case where errors are critical and learning from errors is important.

c. *Overlearning* implies that a task should be practised until it can be performed with few attentional resources (i.e., automatically). Overlearning is invaluable in health and safety–related training programs, specifically those involving safety procedures in an emergency situation where actions must be performed under pressure and quickly.

Cognitive Learning Theories

The increasingly complex nature of many jobs requires that workers have complex cognitive skills. One popular cognitive approach to learning is social learning theory, which posits that people observe others to learn. Observing others can help us learn various motor skills or styles of behaving. For instance, observing more experienced others can help a new employee learn how to properly use safety equipment at work. The people we observe during social learning are called models. The psychologist most often associated with social learning theory is Canadian Albert Bandura. Bandura (1986) proposed that four mental processes facilitate social learning:

- *Attention:* The learner must notice the behavioural models and find them interesting. For instance, new employees who are looking for models will likely look to experienced employees who attract their attention and seem willing to help.
- *Memory:* The learner must be able to remember the information obtained by observation to use at a later time. New employees who are observing more senior employees operate a particular piece of machinery must remember all of the actions taken by the senior employees as they complete the task at hand.
- *Motor Control:* Learners must be able to use the information obtained from observation to guide their own actions. With respect to safe behaviour in the workplace, new employees who have been observing others must be able to reproduce the behaviour. If a particular work task involves heavy lifting, the new employees must be capable of lifting that weight themselves.
- *Motivation:* The learner must have some reason to perform the modelled actions. In the case of occupational health and safety, the learner must be motivated to perform the job in a safe manner.

Chapter 6: Training

It is clear that the four components of Bandura's social learning theory can be useful in the training environment. The trainer assumes the role of the model. The trainer must capture the attention of the trainee and appear interesting. Thus the trainer should be perceived as an expert in the relevant field, as well as be credible and appealing to the trainees. The information should be presented in such a manner that the trainees store it in memory and draw on this information.

Training Methods

Given the widespread use of technology in Canada (a recent report indicated that 80 percent of Canadians used the Internet), it may surprise you to learn that traditional classroom-based instruction is the predominant method of training in Canadian organizations. Hughes and Grant (2007) reported that classroom instruction accounted for 75 percent of training time in organizations, with the use of learning technologies (i.e., computer-based or computer-assisted training) accounting for only 16 percent of training time. Furthermore, they suggested that the use of learning technologies is growing but at a very slow rate. These figures may reflect the observation that managerial and leadership training remain the most frequent topic for organizational training (Hughes & Grant, 2007), and that this requires (or is thought to require) face-to-face interaction.

So what goes on in traditional classroom-based training? One can think of training methods as ranging along a continuum of trainee involvement ranging from very passive (the trainee is not actively participating in the training) to very active (trainees are highly involved in training activities).

At the passive end of the continuum is the traditional classroom lecture, where an instructor delivers content to a group of trainees. Trainees are not actively engaged with the material, and as a result might get bored and "tune out," especially as the lecture increases in length. These problems are compounded when lectures are pre-recorded and administered online or as a podcast—trainees often find it hard to sustain attention to the content being delivered. Of course, skilled lecturers try to engage trainees in the lecture by asking questions, soliciting input, and in general trying to increase interaction. Mixing up the presentation (e.g., with videos, lectures, and visual aids) also helps to sustain attention.

Rather than simply receiving information, as in the case of a lecture, more active forms of training require trainees to engage with the material to process and use information. Problem-solving exercises, discussion groups, debates, and case studies (which require the application of information to solve organizational problems) are examples of training techniques that focus on the application or processing of information.

Acquiring behavioural skills requires a different type of training that allows participants to actually practise the skills. It is only through such practice that behavioural skills can be developed. You would not, for example, expect to learn how to play the piano by listening to a lecture or engaging in a discussion about piano-playing techniques. More typically, you would expect to be shown how to play a scale (for example), and then have the opportunity to practise this skill. A variety of training exercises allow the development and rehearsal of actual skills. Role-playing exercises allow trainees to practise interpersonal skills, and a variety of games and simulations allow trainees to practise skills in a controlled environment.

Air Canada, for example, trains pilots through the use of simulators. You would not want to fly with a pilot who is in the cockpit for the first time—or with one who learned to fly by listening to a lecture. The simulators are designed to look and feel like the actual cockpit of the aircraft and allow pilots to practise under a variety of conditions. They replicate not only the "feel" of the aircraft but also the psychological experience of flying. The degree to which simulations are able to reflect the real experience is known as the *fidelity of the simulation*. Training transfer is thought to be enhanced by high-fidelity simulations that mimic the actual workplace wherein the newly learned skills will be used.

Training Evaluation

Evaluation efforts following training programs consider the extent to which the program has added value to the organization and the individual employees. Information gathered during **training evaluation** may be useful for identifying strengths and weakness in the training program and thus guide further curriculum development. Evaluation results may also be used to estimate the economic value of a training program. In a safety training endeavour, an economic factor that may be evaluated is the number of accidents or injuries. If a training program designed to improve safety in the workplace actually reduces injury, it will save the company money in days lost and compensation claims.

training evaluation
A component of the ISD training model, designed to assess the value added for individuals and organizations following the implementation of a training program

What type of information should be considered in the evaluation of a training program? Kirkpatrick's (1967) Hierarchical Model, a frequently used training evaluation model, suggests that four important levels of training outcomes provide insight into the effectiveness of a training program. Kirkpatrick suggests that a training evaluation effort should ask the following four questions:

- Did the trainees have positive *reactions* to the training?
- Did the trainees *learn* the material covered in the training?
- Did the trainees apply what they learned in training and realize a change in their work *behaviour*?
- Did the organization see positive *organizational results* following training?

(Source: Adapted from R.L. Craig (1967). "Evaluation of training," *Training and Development Handbook*. Copyright © 1967 The McGraw-Hill Companies, Inc. Reprinted by permission.)

According to Kirkpatrick, these levels of evaluation outcomes form a hierarchy—with succeeding levels providing increasingly important information regarding the value of the training program. Training programs in which trainees report positive reactions, successfully learn the material, apply that learning to their workplace behaviour, and contribute to positive organizational outcomes (e.g., increased productivity, fewer lost-time injuries) are considered effective.

A study by the Conference Board of Canada (Hughes & Grant, 2007) suggests that reaction criteria are evaluated far more often than other levels of evaluation. In a 2006 survey of Canadian organizations, it reported

Chapter 6: Training

that 74 percent of surveyed firms assessed reaction criteria in evaluating training. Only 33 percent of the surveyed firms used learning criteria, and only 15 percent assessed behavioural criteria. Results criteria were used by only 7 percent of the surveyed firms.

In many cases, training evaluation simply consists of handing out a survey at the conclusion of a course, much like is done in university or college courses. Most typically, these surveys focus on reaction criteria, such as "Did you enjoy the training," or "Did you find the training useful." Trainers often refer to these reaction measures as "smile sheets" (Brown, 2005) and point to data that show reaction criteria to be virtually unrelated to learning or subsequent behaviour (Alliger et al., 1997). Certainly, it is hard to justify evaluating training purely in terms of trainee reactions. However, these data may be useful as means of feedback on which to improve training and as a means of marketing training (i.e., encouraging others to take a specific training course). They may also provide some indication of courses that need to be discontinued or instructors who should be replaced. Given that most individuals enjoy training and rate it highly (hence the use of the term "smile sheets"), a training course that gets uniformly bad ratings from participants should be reviewed carefully to identify and correct the source of the problem.

Efforts to measure learning must assess mastery of the information presented in the training session. Evaluators are generally interested in how well trainees recall information and the extent to which they are able to incorporate the information into actions. There are a number of ways to assess this knowledge. An evaluation may measure a trainee's ability to recognize the material covered in training using multiple-choice tests. The mastery of skills introduced in the training program can also be assessed using longer, written test formats. To continue the example given above, a trainee may be asked to list all of the steps included in the safety inspection for a particular piece of equipment. Obviously, a successful training program is one that results in considerable knowledge and skill acquisition on the part of trainees.

Behavioural outcomes following training are assessed in the workplace. On-the-job behaviour may be assessed using self-report inventories, where trainees rate their own behaviour, or by having supervisors complete a report on a trainee's actions when performing the task. Similarly, the training evaluator may observe the employee's on-the-job performance. For example, following the training program on the safe operation of heavy machinery, a supervisor may observe an employee performing a safety inspection on the piece of equipment and rate their performance. The evaluator may also be able to use objective indices of performance to assess behavioural change. For instance, following a training program on the importance and use of safety equipment such as ear plugs for loud environments, a behavioural assessment may include observing employees at work to see whether they have a high rate of compliance in using their ear plugs and other safety equipment.

Organizational results following training initiatives can also be assessed. Usually, the assessment of outcomes involves the analysis of organizational records. The training evaluator will want to compare the organization's performance after the training program is complete to its performance prior to training. Having both pre- and post-training information will allow the evaluator to reach a conclusion about any improvements in organizational outcomes that are a result of training.

The Transfer Problem

As previously mentioned, "transfer" refers to the application of knowledge, skills, and attitudes learned from training on the job, and their subsequent maintenance (Baldwin & Ford, 1988). In many cases the results of training

evaluation suggest that the skills/knowledge were acquired by the participants but did not result in behaviour change in the workplace—the classic example of a transfer problem.

Fitzpatrick (2001) reported that only 10 percent of learning transfers to the job. Although some researchers have since reported somewhat more positive transfer rates (e.g., Saks & Belcourt, 2006), designing training that transfers to the workplace remains an ongoing problem. Transfer failures mean that individuals are not improving their behaviour on the job, and consequently organizational performance will not be affected as a result of training (Gaudine & Saks, 2004). Indeed, transfer of training is considered to be the critical process through which training affects organizational outcomes (Kozlowski, Brown, Weissbein, Cannon-Bowers, & Salas, 2000). Baldwin and Ford (1988) identified three broad factors that have been shown to have an influence on transfer of training: training design, trainee characteristics, and the work environment. The role of trainee characteristics (e.g., motivation and trainability) has been discussed previously; here, we focus on the role of training design and conditions of the work environment required to enhance training transfer.

Training design that closely simulates the workplace (i.e., the actual environment in which the skills are to be used) is thought to enhance transfer from the training environment back to the workplace. Indeed, the popularity of on-the-job training techniques is at least partially based on the observation that such training allows trainees to learn skills in the "real" workplace. When training takes place off-site, the use of practice sessions back at the workplace or a supervised period of practice may enhance transfer. Most training in trades in Canada takes this approach. Students first learn the basic skills of the trade in a classroom setting and then are required to complete a period of supervised practice under the supervision of a qualified tradesperson. Students then return to the classroom for a period to solidify the learning and acquire more skills, at which point they again go out into the workplace for supervised practice. The goal of this sequencing is to ensure that students have both the theoretical knowledge and the practical experience required to effectively work in the trade.

Various characteristics of the work environment also facilitate or inhibit training transfer; the characteristics that do so have been defined as the "transfer climate" of the organization (Burke & Hutchins, 2007). Transfer climate has been found in several studies to influence transfer outcomes (e.g., Lim & Morris, 2006). Furthermore, researchers have suggested that efforts to enhance the transfer environment by targeting team leaders and immediate supervisors may provide the greatest outcomes in terms of transfer (e.g., Smith-Jentsch, Salas, & Brannick, 2001). That is, transfer is more likely when supervisors and managers are supportive of the newly acquired skills and knowledge.

Types of Training in Organizations

Given the variety of occupations and industries in Canada, it is safe to say that organizational training and development covers a large number of topics. For the most part the model of training discussed thus far has been designed with the intent of teaching specific job skills. In this section we consider other types of training and development commonly offered in organizations.

Safety Training

Safety training is common in Canadian organizations, and indeed some forms of training are mandated by law for certain workers. This includes general training that is required for all workers (e.g., hazardous materials); training aimed at specific groups (e.g., safety awareness for young workers); and training in specific safety-related tasks (e.g., confined space entry). All these forms of training are intended to educate employees on safe working practices in order to influence their behaviours (Burke & Sarpy, 2003). Most of these programs emphasize the development of both declarative knowledge (e.g., knowledge of various emergency procedures), and procedural knowledge (e.g., proper use of tools or equipment) (Burke & Sarpy, 2003).

A wide range of successful safety training interventions are included in the literature, from programs on personal protective equipment (e.g., masks and respirators) (Komaki, Heinzmann, & Lawson, 1980) to operating machines (e.g., truck lifts) (Cohen & Jenson, 1984). Reviews of well-designed safety interventions are strongly supportive of the effectiveness of safety training (e.g., Colligan & Cohen, 2004).

Interpersonal Skills Training

The vast majority of training expenditures in organizations are targeted toward some form of interpersonal skills training (Gist & Stevens, 1998), including instruction in topics such as leadership, communication, teamwork, feedback, and active listening. Such interpersonal and intrapersonal "soft skills" allow people to make better use of the technical skills required for their work (Kantrowitz, 2005). In some ways this type of training departs significantly from the model of training design discussed earlier in this chapter. Rather than beginning with a needs analysis to determine the training "content," interpersonal skills training is most frequently rooted in a theoretical model (e.g., a model of communication or teamwork). Thus the task of training is to teach individuals the principles of the model and allow them to develop and practise the skills advocated.

Cameron and Whetten (1995) have suggested that this form of training is based on four essential elements: (1) Trainees are presented with the behavioural principles (e.g., the model) that are to be learned; (2) The behavioural principles are modelled (most frequently using role plays or videos) so that trainees can see the principles in action; (3) Trainees are given the opportunity to practise the principles (again, most typically through role plays and exercises); and (4) Trainees are given feedback on their performance.

Leadership Training

One form of interpersonal skills training, leadership training, deserves separate mention because it is one of the most widely used forms of training. Although considerable skepticism exists about the effectiveness of leadership training in organizations (Kelloway & Barling, 2000), there is clear evidence that leadership development works. That is, the available data support the suggestion that activities designed to enhance leadership in organizations do in fact result in improved perceptions of leadership (see, for example, Barling et al., 1996;

Kelloway et al., 2000; Mullen & Kelloway, 2009). Such activities have typically involved training in the form of workshops (Dvir, Eden, Avolio, & Shamir, 2002), participation in coaching (Kombarakaran, Yang, Baker, & Fernandes, 2008), or combinations of both approaches (e.g., Barling et al., 1996; Kelloway et al., 2000).

In their recent meta-analysis, Avolio, Reichard, Hannah, Walumbwa, and Chan (2009) provided a comprehensive review of the effectiveness of leadership interventions. Drawing on data from over 200 studies over a period of more than 50 years based on a variety of leadership theories, Avolio et al. (2009) reported evidence that leadership interventions do in fact work. In 62 of the studies considered, the intervention in question was the development or training of a leader (as opposed to the assignment of a leader or an actor portraying a particular leadership style). The data supported a slightly stronger effect for developmental, as opposed to training, activities but overall resulted in the conclusion that leadership development was an effective intervention.

Coaching

Although coaching is not the same as training, it is a widely used method of employee development. Executive coaching in particular has been widely implemented in both the public and private sector (Kilburg, 2001), and has become one of the fastest-growing executive development options within global companies (Goldsmith, Lyons, & Feras, 2000). One primary dimension along which coaching interventions differ is whether the coach is external to the organization or part of the same organization as the executive being developed.

The use of external executive coaches to work with organizational leaders on their performance and development has significantly increased in recent years (Kilburg, 1996; Smither & Reilly, 2001; Tyler, 2000). In Kilburg's (1996, p. 144) conceptual framework, executive coaching is defined as

> a helping relationship formed between a client who has managerial authority and responsibility in an organization and a consultant who uses a wide variety of behavioral techniques and methods to help the client achieve a mutually identified set of goals to improve his or her professional performance and personal satisfaction and, consequently, to improve the effectiveness of the client's organization.

There are several advantages to using an external coach. First, external coaching does not require the use of in-house resources or additional employees. Second, it appears that external coaches are perceived by executives as being highly credible and objective (Hall, 1999) due to their extensive experience and credentials (Tobias, 1990). Perceptions of credibility and objectivity are critical in situations where executives feel hesitant or defensive about the coaching process (Frisch, 2001). In fact, executives reported that the process of choosing an external coach depended primarily on whether coaches had graduate training, business experience, and an established reputation (Wasylyshyn, 2003). Finally, external coaches are perceived by executives as posing less of a confidentiality risk. In fact, Wasylyshyn (2003) reported that trust and confidentiality were the major factors that explained executives' preference for an external coach. Of course, using an external coach also has disadvantages—the primary one being the cost of retaining a suitably qualified coach (Tobias, 1996).

Perhaps in recognition of the cost factor, organizations are increasingly choosing to use internal coaches (Tyler, 2000) to increase performance/productivity. The emerging role of an internal coach is deemed appropriate given that coaching requires a base knowledge of the organizational context and functioning as well as the individual's specific performance requirements (Frisch, 2001). Internal coaching is defined as "a one-on-one developmental intervention supported by the organization and provided by a colleague of those coached who is trusted to shape and deliver a program yielding individual professional growth" (Frisch, 2001, p. 242). Internal coaching has been derived from external coaching; thus, the overarching goal of each process is to improve individual and organizational functioning.

Whether coaching is internal or external, there are common features to most methods. Anderson (2009) has suggested that these commonalities lie in the "canon" of psychological skills for enhancing performance. Coaching relationships often begin with some form of assessment that identifies areas in which to focus attention (in executive development this often takes the form of a 360-degree performance review; see Chapter 5). Goal setting is the "workhorse" of the relationship, as individuals are encouraged to set and work toward specific goals that will result in improved performance. Coaches may also use a variety of techniques such as relaxation training, self-talk, and imagery to help individuals overcome barriers to performance. Coaches may also help individuals identify necessary training (e.g., in leadership, teamwork, time management) that will help their performance. Coaching relationships typically occur over a lengthy time period, and ongoing feedback and problem solving is an integral part of the process. Coaches regularly meet with individuals to assess goal progress, work on problem areas, and recalibrate goals as necessary. See Box 6.3 for further insight into professional development plans.

Until fairly recently, it was fair to claim that little progress had been made in empirically demonstrating the effectiveness of executive coaching (Hall, Otazo, & Hollenbeck, 1999; Kilburg, 2001). However, several recent quasi-experimental investigations have begun to rectify this omission and provide evidence for the effectiveness of coaching interventions. Evers, Brouwers, and Tomic (2006) compared managers participating in a coaching program with a control group and found that, relative to a pre-test, the coached group reported greater self-efficacy and enhanced outcome expectancies over a four-month period. Luthans and Peterson (2003) reported positive results from an intervention combining 360-degree feedback and coaching. In this case, the coaching focused on discrepancies between self and other ratings of managers' performance, and managers were assisted in developing plans to reduce those discrepancies. Finally, Kombarakaran et al. (2008) reported that a coaching initiative resulted in improved managerial performance in five areas (people management, relationships with other managers, goal setting and prioritization, engagement and productivity, and dialogue and communication). Although not conclusive, these three studies suggest that coaching may be an effective way to develop managers' skills.

Summary

Training and development activities represent a substantial investment by organizations in enhancing organizational performance by improving the skills and abilities of employees. In this chapter we discussed the reasons why organizations and employees value training (e.g., performance improvement, compliance with legislation, career advancement) and reviewed the evidence supporting the effectiveness of training in organizations.

We then presented the instructional systems design model as a comprehensive approach to training design that moves from needs analysis, through the development of training goals/outcomes, to the design and delivery of training. Training evaluation was then discussed—the results of the evaluation of the course then feed back into the needs analysis for the next round of training.

Finally, we reviewed some common types of training in organizations (e.g., safety training, interpersonal skills training, leadership training, coaching). Although certainly not exhaustive, this list illustrates some common training applications.

Key Terms

instructional systems design (ISD) model of training 186
job/task analysis 188
needs analysis 186
organizational analysis 187

person analysis 189
train the trainer 191
training evaluation 195
training objective 190

Web Links

The Canadian Society for Training and Development can be found at:

www.cstd.ca

Human Resources and Skills Development Canada can be found at:

http://www.hrsdc.gc.ca/eng/home.shtml

Templates for one approach to training needs analysis can be accessed at:

http://www.nwlink.com/~Donclark/hrd/templates/analysis.rtf

Information on Air Canada's use of flight simulators can be found at:

http://www.aircanada.com/en/training/training.html

Discussion Questions

1. As a student you are involved in acquiring new skills and knowledge. How closely does the training process described in this chapter match your experience? Why might university or college courses not follow a training model? How might they benefit from the instructional development model described in this chapter?
2. Although companies often are willing to pay for professional training, they are very reluctant to pay for rigorous evaluation of training outcomes. They prefer to evaluate training simply through "smile sheets" that assess only reaction criteria. Why do companies not want to evaluate training more rigorously?
3. Consultants often sell "canned" training programs—pre-developed programs designed to teach a particular skill or body of knowledge that are implemented with little or no needs analysis or customization to the organization. Is this a useful approach to training in organizations? Why or why not?
4. Although the literature suggests that trainee motivation is an important requirement for effective learning, we frequently require people to take training (e.g., in safety, diversity, etc.) regardless of their motivation. Is this an effective approach? Why or why not?

Using the Internet

Many organizations have posted templates for needs analysis, training evaluation, or training design on the Web. Using a search engine, find examples, and compile your own training manual from the materials you find. The manual should cover each of the major phases of the instructional development model discussed in this chapter.

Exercises

1. Working in groups, develop short training exercises designed to teach others (a) a set of facts or theory and (b) a particular skill. After delivering the training, discuss how knowledge learning and skill learning differ.
2. Interview employed people about the training they receive at work. How much training have they received through their job? Is this training formal (i.e., courses) or informal (on-the-job training)? Would they like more or less training?
3. Interview people in different courses. From the standpoint of the participants, what makes for a good course? A bad course?
4. Most educational institutions offer some form of continuing education/professional development through which people can obtain additional training after leaving school. What is available through your school?
5. Professionals often have a requirement for continuous learning throughout their careers. Identify a profession that has a regulatory body and determine what the continuing education requirements are for that profession.

Case

Sabine is the new HR manager at A1 Manufacturing. In her first week on the job she received very clear instructions from the CEO, Karin Henderson. "I want you to roll out safety training for all our employees," Karin said. "Our accident rate is through the roof and the Department of Labour is always on my back about safety issues. I want to see a plan that will address these issues in the next six months. We can do a lot of training in-house using our own people, so costs should be minimal."

Sabine is overwhelmed with the scope of this assignment. A1 Manufacturing has more than 500 employees working in production, research and development, shipping and receiving, and administration, and the safety issues are different for each group of employees. As far as she can determine, most employees received safety training in their orientation, and both the production and shipping/receiving departments conduct regular safety briefings. Sabine is not sure that additional training is required, or would address the problems identified by Karin. Nonetheless, she knows that she needs to put a concrete plan on Karin's desk in the near future and has turned to you for advice.

Discussion Question

What steps should Sabine take to develop the training plan? What issues does she need to consider?

CHAPTER 7

Groups and Teams in Organizations

Have you ever worked in a team at work or at school? Were you assigned to a team, or did you get to choose your own team members? Did the team members have control over the work, or did an external person supervise your work? What was your experience with the team? Did you find it energizing, such that the output was greater than the total of what each individual alone could produce? Or was the group plagued with decision-making and interpersonal problems, making it difficult to get any work done?

Increasingly, businesses are organizing their work around teams. Organizations seem to love teams: they have project teams, "virtual" teams, team-building sessions, and goals and rewards based on team performance. If you check the Web, you will be flooded with employee team-building exercises, consulting groups, job postings involving teams, and overall suggestions to improve team performance. But how much do we actually know about the effectiveness of teams? Do teams enhance performance, or do they create more challenges for their members? Are there benefits to organizing our work using teams? If yes, what can we do to create high-performance teams? What are the implications for organizations? How does having a team structure influence individual performance and motivation?

Chapter Learning Outcomes

After reading this chapter you should be able to

- Distinguish between groups and teams
- Identify the different types of teams
- Recognize the challenges associated with teams
- Understand the situations in which teams are most effective
- Identify the components of teams
- Explain why some teams may fail
- Describe the components of effective teams
- Identify some of the problems of group decision making and identify the solutions

Groups and Teams

TEAMS = <u>T</u>ogether <u>E</u>veryone <u>A</u>chieves <u>M</u>ore

Since the 1990s, organizations have been shifting their focus of work from individuals to teams (Kozlowski & Ilgen, 2006). This shift may be due to increased pressure for skill diversity, rapid response, and adaptability caused by greater competition and innovation (Kozlowski & Ilgen, 2006). Whatever the reason, teams are very popular in organizations. See Box 7.1 for a relatable example of a team problem-solving situation.

Defining Teams

team

Two or more people working interdependently toward the achievement of a common goal

What exactly makes up a **team**? Is it simply a group of individuals working together, or is there more involved? Teams have been defined as complex, dynamic, and adaptive systems (Ilgen, Hollenbeck, Johnson, & Jundt, 2005) that "exist in a context, develop as members interact over time, and evolve and adapt as situational demands unfold" (Kozlowski & Ilgen, 2006, p. 78). Allen and Hecht (2004) succinctly defined teams as "two or more people working interdependently toward the achievement of a common goal" (p. 441).

More specifically, a work team can be defined as two or more people who (1) interact and share a common goal, such that their tasks are interdependent; (2) are brought together to perform tasks relevant to the organization; (3) have different roles and responsibilities (which, however, may be interchangeable); and (4) are rooted in an overall organizational system that sets constraints on, and provides context for, the team (Kozlowski & Bell, 2003; Kozlowski & Ilgen, 2006).

Are teams different from groups? What about a work unit or work crew? Some researchers have distinguished between teams and groups, such that groups are made up of individuals working on interdependent tasks but not necessarily requiring interdependent work, whereas teams are "more" than a group in that they have a shared goal and vision and great interdependence. Although these precise differences may be important in specific research

Box 7.1

Effective Team Problem Solving for *Apollo 13*

"Houston, we've had a problem."

These often misquoted words bring back memories of the near-disastrous *Apollo 13* flight (or at least of the movie of the same name), when a technical malfunction forced the *Apollo* crew to abandon its lunar mission. One of its two oxygen tanks exploded due to a fault in the electrical system, which created a loss of power and failure of both oxygen tanks.

A team of NASA engineers were brought together to try to problem solve from a distance. They had the

Herculean task of trying to adapt the components of the spaceship to bring the crew home safely. They problem solved, worked with the crew, and adapted components so that the crew returned safely to Earth, and the mission was termed a "successful failure."

The engineering team worked together efficiently to solve a problem that probably no one would have been able to solve individually, and thus has become an example of an effective team in action.

purposes, many of them are less critical when looking at the overall team literature. Moreover, many researchers do not make a distinction between the two terms, and instead acknowledge that many different types of teams exist (e.g., Allen & Hecht, 2004; Guzzo & Dickson, 1996; Kozlowski & Bell, 2003).

Therefore, in this chapter we will use "teams" and "groups" interchangeably, but begin by looking at the specific *types* of teams.

Types of Work Groups and Teams

Are all teams the same? We can use sports teams as an analogy to answer this question. Obviously, all sports teams typically have the goal to win or perform at their best, and differ on the content of their activities (e.g., basketball vs. softball vs. racing). But do they actually differ on their format? Even though swim teams, soccer teams, and volleyball teams are all "teams," variations exist in how they are organized: (1) the extent to which the members *interact* with each other on their individual tasks; (2) the *interdependence* of the tasks; (3) the extent to which the roles and tasks are *well defined* and formalized; and (4) the extent to which the members are *interchangeable*. These factors may be internally driven within the group or externally derived based on restraints put on them by the organization or regulating body.

Team Member Interaction and Task Interdependence

For some sports teams (e.g., bowling, diving, running), total team performance is simply the additive function of individual members' performance; that is, the *interdependence* of the tasks that the members perform (i.e., **task interdependence**)—the *interaction* among members performing the tasks (i.e., **team member interaction**)—is nominal or nonexistent. For example, a synchronized swimming team is highly interactive, such that the actions of one member can influence the performance of all team members; these teams involve *high interaction and interdependence.* Conversely, a diving team's score is the sum of all the individual scores, and the performance of one diver doesn't directly impact the performance of another diver. This example would parallel a work group in which the tasks are independent and divided up among the members. Members work on their own, and the final product is simply the sum of each individual effort.

Role Definition and Interchangeability

We look at various types of sports teams to illustrate how the roles of their members can vary in the extent to which they are well-defined (i.e., **role definition**) and the degree to which the members can play any position and do any task (i.e., **interchangeability**).

In some sports teams, such as synchronized swimming, there are no specified roles. There is *low role definition*, such that all members perform the same general tasks (although we do recognize that members will still have specific strengths and weaknesses, and may therefore fall into specific tasks more frequently). Moreover, team members perform essentially the same tasks; they are *interchangeable,* because all members can typically perform the same movements.

task interdependence
The extent to which performance on team-based tasks are dependent on other members' performance

team member interaction
The extent to which members interact with each other while completing their job tasks

role definition
The extent to which members have highly defined (and sometimes regulated) roles within the group, such that they are differentiated from other specific roles within the group

interchangeability
The extent to which members can fulfill any of several roles on the team.

Chapter 7: Groups and Teams in Organizations

Likewise, sports teams such as tennis and badminton doubles involve specific tasks that are shared by all members. This type of team involves players who are totally *interchangeable* and must do all tasks (e.g., serve, play the net, etc.). We may see this format in a small consulting firm in which all members are somewhat interchangeable; they must have the knowledge, skills, and abilities to do all tasks (e.g., conducting surveys, completing individual assessments, providing training to clients), but not necessarily at the same time. That is, at some point they may take a lead role on a project (i.e., be the "server" in tennis), or play a more secondary role. They may work on certain tasks at various stages of a project. Similarly, our "textbook team"—Drs Kelloway, Catano, and Day—don't have specific roles: we all write chapters, and edit them. Moreover, we are interchangeable: although we have specific research expertise (to focus on specific topics and chapters), we each have the necessary knowledge and skills to write on any of the topics in this book.

Conversely, in some sports teams the roles and tasks are very *well defined,* and are assigned to specific members based on the players' individual strengths. For example, guards in basketball try to defend their net, quarterbacks in football try to move the ball forward through passing or running plays, and goalies in soccer try to stop the ball from entering their net! Each position is fairly well defined.

The degree to which these positions are *interchangeable* varies somewhat. For example, the forwards in hockey try to stay in the offensive zone to be in position to score goals. However, they may have to fall back to cover defence if a team member is not in position, and even cover for a goalie who is pulled out of the net. We would say that the tasks of the members are highly *interdependent* and have high *role definition,* but that there is some ability to switch roles (i.e., *interchangeable*). The members' positions and tasks are well defined, but they are more fluid within each shift change, and players decide how best to use their talents (with the exception of the goalie, who is less interchangeable with other team members). We may see this format in a dynamic computer programming environment where members are highly interdependent and must interact to produce the final product, but each have well defined, specialized roles. Although they each have specific, expert skills and tasks, they have the general knowledge and ability to cover for each other when required.

Some sports not only have high role definition for each position, but also have very *specific rules* about positions. Certain players can perform only certain tasks, and the players can not change their tasks and positions; that is, they are *non-interchangeable*. For example, in football only designated people can throw the ball, catch the ball, and block; if players perform "non-designated" tasks (e.g., an offensive lineman catches a pass), the team is penalized. Some work teams may have such specialized roles; for example, in a construction team, only certified electricians can work on the electrical, and only certified plumbers can work on the plumbing. They each have *high role definition,* with specific, regulated, and non-interchangeable tasks, but their performance is dependent on each other's work (*interdependence*).

These examples highlight how several defining factors of a team (the interdependence of tasks, and structural controls such as formal rules and regulations) may all impact on team processes and team functioning so that teams

People and Work in Canada

can look very different from each other. That is, although we define teams as groups of two or more people working together on a common goal, there can be a variety of groups that take different forms.

Categories of Teams

We can differentiate among six broadly defined categories of teams (Cohen & Bailey, 1997; Kozlowski & Bell, 2003; Sundstrom et al., 1990, 2000): (1) *production teams*, whose members manufacture tangible products on a cyclical basis (e.g., assembly-line teams); (2) *service teams*, whose members interact with and assist clients on a regular basis (e.g., sales teams); (3) *project teams*, whose members temporarily come together for a specific purpose and tasks (e.g., computer software development); (4) *management teams*, whose members work together to provide leadership and support for subordinate employees and work units; (5) *action and performance teams*, whose members are interdependent specialists working on a time-constrained task (e.g., surgical teams); and (6) *advisory teams*, whose members are experts and have been brought together for a specified period (usually in the short term) to advise and assist on a specific task or project.

These categories are based on the products or services offered by each team. However, we can also differentiate among groups based on other characteristics as to how they are formed, how they operate and make decisions, and the geographic location of members. We will review the specific examples of work crews, autonomous work teams, and virtual work groups.

Work Crews

We can distinguish crews from teams in that crews band together quickly to perform a specific task and do not undergo a specific developmental process (Arrow, 1998). Examples include surgical teams and military combat units. **Crews** are typically made up of experts who are highly trained and who follow specific, standardized performance guidelines. Although crews typically form, disband, and reform with new members, they usually have strict performance standards. These standards are a substitute for the lack of developmental process and socialization among group members, and they allow the group to function effectively (Kozlowski & Bell, 2003).

crews

Groups of two of more people who come together quickly to perform a specific task and do not undergo a specific developmental process

Autonomous Work Teams

Autonomous work teams (sometimes referred to as *self-managing teams*) are teams in which members typically have highly interdependent tasks and are given a substantial amount of control over their work in terms of decision making, scheduling, and planning (Dobbelaere & Goeppinger 1993; Guzzo & Dickson, 1996). In autonomous work groups, members are responsible for many tasks that are often reserved for management roles (e.g., delegating tasks, problem solving, and holding team meetings) (Guzzo & Dickson, 1996; Hackman, 1986; Lawler, 1986; Manz, 1992).

Benefits of autonomous work groups include increased productivity and quality of work and decreased absenteeism and turnover (Cohen & Ledford,

autonomous work teams

Teams in which the interdependent members are given a substantial amount of control over their work and who are assigned whole tasks

1994; Lawler, 1986; Manz & Sims, 1987). However, some research has shown that self-managed teams may not create a good environment because team members create increased constraints for themselves, which limits productivity (Sewell, 1998).

Virtual Work Groups

virtual work groups

Groups involving two or more interdependent team members who are separated geographically and/or by time differences, and who typically use information and communication technologies (ICTs) to help the flow of their work and interactions with each other

With the increased use and abilities of technology, "virtual" work groups are becoming more common (Hertel, Konradt, & Orlikowski, 2004; Kozlowski & Ilgen, 2006). **Virtual work groups** can be defined as groups involving two or more interdependent team members who are separated geographically and/or by time differences, and who typically use information and communication technologies to help the flow of their work and interactions with each other (Bell & Kozlowski, 2002; Thompson & Coovert, 2003).

That is, members of virtual groups may use technology to coordinate their activities. Virtual teams may be used to bring together employees in multinational firms who work across the globe (Kozlowski & Bell, 2003), or they may simply be used in organizations whose employees telecommute or have offices in different locations within the same city or country. Because virtual teams can bring together experts from different parts of the world, they are also responsible for increasing the presence of multicultural teams (Kozlowski & Ilgen, 2006).

In their qualitative study of student virtual teams, Johnson, Suriya, Won Yoon, Berrett, and La Fleur (2002) concluded that virtual teams can collaborate and effectively complete their tasks. But how do people feel about working with virtual team members? People who are part of teams that use computer-mediated technology to communicate much of the time tend to report less positive mood and be less committed to their teams (Johnson, Bettenhausen, & Gibbons, 2009).

One of the key aspects in the effectiveness of virtual teams may be the extent of trust among the members. In their study of 200 team members from 33 virtual teams, Peters and Karren (2009) found that the more team members trusted each other, the higher they rated their own team performance, even after controlling for the effects of the project and team (size, project length) and individual (age, gender) characteristics. However, this trust was not related to managers' ratings of the team's performance. Kuo and Yu (2009) found that when trust developed in virtual teams during the early weeks there was more communication and cohesiveness in the team at later stages. However, other research has indicated that although trust is associated with team communication, it tends to be unrelated to the quality of task performance (Jarvenpaa, Shaw, & Staples, 2004). Interestingly, teams with more functional diversity (in terms of team members' areas of expertise) also rated their own team performance higher (Peters & Karren, 2009).

How Do Teams Develop?

In 1965, Tuckman published his now seminal model of group development. He proposed that groups went through four different phases of growth: forming, storming, norming, and performing. That is, the first step that new groups take involves the introductions and socialization of bringing people together; that is, **forming**. The next stage, **storming**, involves working out the interpersonal and work demands of the group. **Norming** occurs when the group develops its own norms for behaving in the group environment and imposes its own rewards and sanctions to reinforce these behaviours. Finally, **performing** occurs when the group finally gets down to productively working on the task (Tuckman, 1965).

Despite the influence of this model on early work on groups, Kozlowski and Bell (2003) argued that most of this research does not apply to organizational work groups for several reasons: First, the area of "development" assumes that the group members have no prior history, which may not accurately reflect work groups. Second, most research ignores the "broader organizational context, work roles, or prescribed interactions" (p. 341), which again are not accurate depictions of work groups. Kozlowski and Bell (2003) argued that this model, and its focus on interpersonal challenges, is helpful for simple non-work teams, but not for work teams that have a common goal and are subject to organizational rules and constraints, such that "interpersonal issues are relevant, but they do not dominate the developmental process" (p. 341). Surprisingly, few models and theories focus on the development of *work* teams specifically (Kozlowski & Bell, 2003).

According to Kozlowski et al.'s (1991) multilevel theory of compilation and performance across levels and time, teams progress through four phases: (1) Phase 1 involves the *formation* of the group (similar to Tuckman's theory); (2) Phase 2 involves *task compilation,* in which members primarily focus on demonstrating competence in their own tasks; (3) Phase 3 involves a switch of focus to other team members (and *developing dyadic relationships*); and (4) Phase 4 involves *team compilation,* with a switch in focus to the entire network of relationships within the team.

These two theories have slightly different perspectives; however, they both highlight the importance of viewing teams as changing entities. Moreover, they both may be helpful in thinking about how teams develop, as well as what issues may be salient to them at different times in their development. These issues not only should influence how organizations and leaders view and interact with teams, but also should help them to understand how teams can be managed more effectively (Williams & Allen, 2008). Williams and Allen (2008) argued that more research is required to understand how teams can be developed.

Group Norms

Let's take a minute to review Tuckman's third stage, *norming,* in more detail. Group norms are defined as legitimate, socially shared standards (Birenbaum & Sagarin, 1976) that may influence how group members interact and work together (Chatman & Flynn, 2001). Group norms are established through the socialization and interaction of members of the work group (Kozlowski & Bell, 2003). As we discussed above, Tuckman (1965) referred to "norming" as a stage in the group developmental process where the group establishes ground rules, roles, and common goals. Conflict decreases during this stage, and the group becomes more cooperative and cohesive. Norms reduce ambiguity

forming
The first step of new groups, which involves bringing members together, introducing them, and socializing them into the team

storming
The second stage of group development, which involves working out the interpersonal and work demands of the group

norming
The third stage of group development, which involves the group developing its own norms for behaving in the group environment, and imposing its own rewards and sanctions to reinforce these behaviours

performing
The fourth stage of group development, which involves the group finally getting down to productively working on the task

Chapter 7: Groups and Teams in Organizations

within the group, because they guide behaviour and interactions among team members (Kozlowski & Bell, 2003).

So what is the impact of norms on teams? Norms may affect individual members' behaviours and team performance. However, the exact impact may depend on two factors; that is, part of the answer may lie in the characteristics of the individual *team members*. For example, Bamberger and Biron (2007) examined employees and their informal "referent group" (i.e., the coworkers to whom they compared themselves). In general, referent group norms about work absences were associated with actual absence behaviour of the employee, even after taking into account the norms of the overall organization units. Moreover, members who had a greater tendency to conform and who had a permissive referent group (i.e., groups with a higher number of absences) tended to have excessive absences (Bamberger & Biron, 2007).

Another part of the answer may depend on the *type* of norm established in the group. As noted above, permissive referent group absence norms may lead to excessive absenteeism (Bamberger & Biron, 2007). Chatman and Flynn (2001) examined cooperative norms in the context of team diversity. Perceptions of cooperative norms in student teams were significantly related both to judges' ratings of members' satisfaction and to peer ratings of members' contributions (Chatman & Flynn, 2001). More importantly, compared to teams with uncooperative norms, teams characterized by cooperative norms were rated by independent judges as being more effective and efficient (Chatman & Flynn, 2001). When examining financial officers in a business unit, respondents who perceived more cooperative norms were more satisfied, performed better, and received higher compensation increases.

How can we incorporate positive norms into teams? Taggar and Ellis (2007) examined norm development (in terms of collaborative problem solving) in 56 student groups. High expectations from the team leader and staff both significantly influenced the teams' collaborative problem-solving norms. Interestingly, when members initially had low expectations of problem-solving behaviours for their team, leaders were able to significantly increase these team norms by having high expectations for these behaviours. Most importantly, the problem-solving norms of the team significantly influenced individual team members' problem-solving behaviours.

Challenges with Groups

Groups and their members face some unique work challenges that may not be applicable to individuals when working alone. We will explore a decision-making problem (groupthink) and two social-interaction and motivational issues (team conflict and social loafing).

Groupthink

groupthink

A psychological phenomenon in which there is a tendency for highly cohesive groups to press for consensus and conformity, such that the group members' strivings for unanimity override their motivation to realistically appraise alternative courses of action

Groupthink is a psychological phenomenon in which there is a tendency for highly cohesive groups to press for consensus and conformity (Janis, 1972), such that the group "members' strivings for unanimity override their motivation to realistically appraise alternative courses of action" (Janis, 1982, p. 9).

Typically, groupthink may develop in situations in which people assume consensus exists among the other team members, and where they fear being the dissenting view. Therefore, concerns are not expressed, leaving the false impression of agreement among all members.

Ironically, this phenomenon tends to take place in high-functioning, highly cohesive groups; that is, in groups where people get along and like each other. No one wants to "rock the boat" and provide criticism or differing opinions, in case they are viewed negatively or perceived as detracting from the unity of the group. See Box 7.2 for an example of the ramifications of groupthink.

Team Conflict

Team conflict is the tension created among team members resulting from perceived differences (De Dreu, Harinck, & Van Vianen, 1999). This conflict can be divided into two types: relationship conflict and task conflict. **Relationship conflict** involves interpersonal conflicts based on differing values, personalities, and personal preferences (De Dreu & Weingart, 2003). **Task conflict** involves conflicts based on job-related aspects—allocation of resources, differing procedures, and differing perceptions of the task and decisions (De Dreu & Weingart, 2003).

Although most researchers have always agreed that relationship conflict has a negative impact on team efficiency, productivity, and satisfaction, there has been some question about the impact of task conflict on these outcomes (see, for example, Jehn, 1994, 1995, 1997). De Dreu and Weingart (2003) argued that during the 1990s there was a shift toward "a more optimistic view of conflict as possibly functional and stimulating because it surfaces issues that otherwise might not be considered" (p. 746). For example, perhaps team conflict encourages members to review their perspectives and decisions more carefully, thus leading to more innovation and higher performance (De Dreu & West, 2001). That is, if there was absolutely no conflict within the team, the team might not recognize inefficiencies and might make poor decisions (De Dreu & Weingart, 2003).

team conflict
The tension created among team members resulting from perceived differences

relationship conflict
Interpersonal conflicts based on differing values, personalities, and personal preferences

task conflict
Conflicts based on job-related aspects, such as allocation of resources, differing procedures, and differing perceptions of the task and decisions

Box 7.2

Groupthink and the Space Shuttle *Challenger* Disaster

Several well-publicized examples show the potentially devastating effects of groupthink in action. One of the best known examples is the Space Shuttle *Challenger* disaster. On January 28, 1986, *Challenger* broke apart 73 seconds into its flight, leading to the deaths of its seven crew members. The technical cause of the disaster was the failure of an O-ring seal in its right solid rocket booster at liftoff. One organizational/psychosocial factor attributed as a precursor to the disaster is groupthink. NASA knew about the problem with the O-ring, and the scientists had indicated they did not know how it would react in cold weather. NASA was impatient with previous delays in launching and pressured them to make a decision to launch. The scientists felt this pressure, and although they individually had strong feelings about NOT going forward, they eventually went along with the requests and agreed to the launch.

Research has shown that when differences exist among members prior to any discussion, or when there is a "devil's advocate" (a proponent of alternative ideas and perspectives), the quality of decisions tends to be higher (Schulz-Hardt, Jochims, & Frey, 2002; Schwenk, 1990). However, although differences in opinion may increase the quality of decisions, high levels of conflict tend to be damaging (De Dreu & Weingart, 2003).

In their meta-analysis of 30 studies that had examined team conflict and outcomes (i.e., performance and/or satisfaction), De Dreu and Weingart (2003) concluded that both relationship conflict and task conflict were negatively related to team performance and to team member satisfaction. That is, there were no benefits to either performance or satisfaction in having increased task conflict (and, in fact, the conflict was associated with lower satisfaction and performance). Moreover, the negative effects of conflict tend to be greater in teams doing ambiguous and complex tasks.

What happens when slight conflicts or disagreements escalate to rude interpersonal interactions, or to more serious incidents of bullying, harassment, or aggression? Sometimes the norms of the group implicitly or explicitly reward these dysfunctional interactions. Can these behaviours and norms undermine the functioning of the team?

The negative costs of such behaviours, not only on individual well-being and productivity but also on overall team and organizational performance, are well-documented. For more information, see Chapter 11, which explores counterproductive behaviours across a range of organizational scenarios.

Social Loafing and Perceived Loafing

Have you ever been involved in a team project in which you thought you did a lot more of the work than your teammates? Have you ever been on a team when you didn't put in as much effort as you would have had you worked on your own? Social loafing and perceived loafing are related constructs pertaining to the real and perceived contributions of other individuals.

social loafing

Situations in which individuals put forth less effort when working in a group than when working alone

perceived loafing

One's perception that one or more other group members are not contributing as much to the team as they should be

Social loafing describes situations in which "individuals put forth less effort working in a group than when working alone" (Mulvey & Klein, 1998, p. 63). In contrast, **perceived loafing** is one's perception that one or more other group members are not contributing as much to the team as they should be (Comer, 1995; Mulvey & Klein, 1998). Both of these phenomena come into play when examining work groups, and can impact group functioning.

Perceived loafing tends to be negatively related to group cohesion and team efficacy (Mulvey & Klein, 1998). Mulvey and Klein (1998) also found that it was related to setting easier goals, and having less commitment to those goals. Finally, they found that perceived loafing was related to decreased group performance.

Team Performance and Outcomes

Allen and Hecht (2004) argued that although organizations are enamoured with the concept of teams, we have very little evidence of their effectiveness. However, we do have some knowledge of the factors that may influence performance. That is, if we put five people in a team, would that team have better performance than the total of each of the five individuals' work? As with many questions in field of psychology, the answer is "It depends."

We have to look at this answer from two perspectives: (1) in terms of our definition of effectiveness; and (2) in terms of the team processes and characteristics.

Definition of Performance

First, how do we actually define performance, or "productive" and "effective" behaviours? We use previous conceptualizations of effectiveness and organize measures of effectiveness in terms of group outputs related to quantity and quality of work, speed, and so on; benefits for its members in terms of the social benefits of teams; and future functioning and productivity (Guzzo & Dickson, 1996; Hackman, 1987). As argued by Hackman (1987), team effectiveness should encapsulate both internal outcomes (e.g., team member satisfaction) and external outcomes (e.g., organizational performance outcomes).

Group Outputs

Although it is intuitive that teams must perform more than the combination of individual work, there has been much research to the contrary. Several studies have shown that groups actually generate fewer ideas (or, in the case scenarios, the same number of ideas) than the collective works of individuals (see Mullen et al., 1991, for a meta-analysis using many group performance studies). For example, McGrath (1984) found that individuals working alone produced the same number of ideas with the same quality as groups working together to generate ideas. See Box 7.3 for a comparison of the effectiveness of individuals and groups.

The implementation of autonomous work teams has been associated with increased productivity and decreased withdrawal (although the effects were small for both outcomes (Beekun, 1989), and with improvements in the financial outcomes of the organization (Macy & Izumi, 1993).

Benefits for Members

Regardless of the direct impact of teams on performance, it makes sense that perhaps teams satisfy some social or emotional needs of workers (Allen & Hecht, 2004). In fact, in some situations working in teams may be related to members' increased sense of belongingness (Godard, 2001) and job satisfaction (Godard, 2001; Harley, 2001).

It is argued that these positive social relationships and attitudes may then help the work in other ways (e.g., reduced absenteeism and turnover). In fact, some studies have shown that working in teams has been associated with improved mental well-being (e.g., Wallin & Wright, 1986), and lower stress and fatigue (Godard, 2001). These findings, however, are not conclusive (see Harley, 2001; Wall et al., 1986).

Box 7.3

Individuals vs. Groups: Which Is More Effective?

Round 1: The Case for Individuals

Although lab-based research has demonstrated that individuals tend to produce more creative ideas than do groups, several researchers have said the comparison is unfair. We need to compare oranges to oranges. That is, we need to compare two types of groups: *interacting groups* (whose members are working together on the task) and *nominal groups* (i.e., whose members are together but who are working by themselves). Given this more "fair" comparison, which group would you guess performs better?

The interacting groups that have the members work together tend to have substantially fewer ideas (and lower quality of ideas) than the groups with members who worked alone (Ziegler, Diehl, & Zijlstra, 2000; Mullen et al., 1991; see Allen & Hecht, 2004, for an overview).

Why would groups be less productive than individuals? Deihl and Stroebe (1987) suggested that during face-to-face brainstorming only one person can speak at a time, and members may forget their idea when they have to wait their turn to speak. Also note, however, that many of these studies are lab-based and may not apply in the real world.

Round 2: The Case for Groups

Despite the research showing the superiority of individuals over groups, several studies have shown that groups can be—and are—as effective or more effective.

Laughlin, Bonner, and Miner (2002) conducted a study in which 82 four-person groups and 328 independent individuals both performed a random letters-to-numbers coding problem of the letters A–J on the numbers 0–9. The objective was to determine how the numbers mapped onto the letters in as few trials as possible. The researchers found that the four-person groups needed fewer trials to solve the problem than did the individuals. These findings support previous research that groups perform better than individuals on highly intellective tasks that require recognition of correct answers, rejection of erroneous answers, and collective information-processing strategies. The researchers also argue that groups perform better than the highest-performing individuals would perform alone.

Allen and Hecht (2004) concluded that although teams are appropriate in many situations and can be associated with high performance, teams don't "consistently, or robustly, produce the gains in productivity that are reported" (p. 444).

Future Functioning and Productivity

Finally, it has been suggested that to have a complete overview of the value of teams we need to look at future productivity. That is, teams may not have the same immediate productivity as do individuals. However, if organizations take a longer-term perspective of productivity, teams may easily meet and surpass individuals' goals and performance.

Team Processes, Composition, and Characteristics

So, what factors influence team performance? The second perspective in our answer of "It depends" pertains to the characteristics of the team. That is, as we know, not all teams are the same, and many factors can impact on team effectiveness, functioning, and performance. Therefore, some of the differences we see in the research literature regarding the effectiveness of teams may lie in the differences among the teams themselves. We will focus on four of the more salient characteristics of teams: the extent to which the members are familiar with each other and like each other; the attitudes of the team members in terms of their efficacy beliefs; their size; and the diversity of the team members—not only in their demographic characteristics but also in other ways, such as their work roles and expertise.

Team Familiarity and Cohesion

Familiarity is the extent to which team members have interacted and are well-known to each other. Several studies have shown that the effectiveness of teams increases over time, and increased familiarity is credited with at least some of this improvement.

There are two cautions, however. Newer teams sometimes may have more energy and enthusiasm than older teams (Dubnicki & Limburg, 1991). Also, there may be a limit in terms of team life: after longer periods of time (perhaps two to three years), familiarity may be a detriment to performance (Guzzo & Dickson, 1996; Katz, 1982).

Festinger (1950) defined **cohesion** as the result of "all the forces acting on the members to remain in the group" (p. 274), and suggested that cohesion is made up of three components: member attraction, the nature of group activities, and group pride. Group cohesion may be related to the composition of the group in terms of personality characteristics. Barrick et al. (1998) found that groups with members high in agreeableness, extraversion, and emotional stability had higher group cohesion.

In general, research has indicated that team cohesion is positively related to team performance (Kozlowski & Ilgen, 2006). For example, several studies found that cohesion in top-management teams was related to improved sales and return on investment (Hambrick, 1995; Katzenbach & Smith, 1993; Smith et al., 1994). Moreover, a few meta-analyses have shown that group cohesion tended to be related to improved group performance (e.g., Beal, Cohen, Burke, & McLendon, 2003; Evans & Dion, 1991; Gully et al., 1995; Mullen & Cooper, 1994). However, varying degrees of relationships existed across studies in these meta-analyses, such that the relationships were somewhat equivocal in some cases.

Beal et al. (2003) tried to address criticisms of previous meta-analyses on cohesion and performance by clarifying the criteria. For example, they argued that when studying team cohesion and performance it may make more sense to focus on behaviours rather than team outputs, to examine both efficiency and effectiveness as criteria. *Efficiency* takes both input and output into account (such that a smaller organization may be just as efficient as a larger organization). Conversely, *effectiveness* typically considers only output. They also suggested that the interdependence of team members (i.e., workflow) would affect results. As hypothesized, cohesion and performance were more strongly correlated when the criteria focused on behaviours (versus outcomes) and on efficiency (versus effectiveness), and when there were more intensive patterns of workflow (i.e., higher interaction and interdependency).

Team Efficacy

Team efficacy is the team members' beliefs that the team has the ability to successfully perform the job tasks (Bandura, 1997; Lindsley, Brass, & Thomas, 1995). It has been argued that perceived competence of team members may be associated with individual and group performance outcomes.

Teamwork self-efficacy and collective efficacy have been found to be related to individual teamwork behaviour, and collective efficacy was related to team performance of business students (Tasa, Taggar, & Seijts, 2007). Collective efficacy was related to team adaptive performance of undergraduates learning a flight-simulation task (Chen, Thomas, & Wallace, 2005).

In addition to its relationship to performance, the perceived competence of one's team members may be associated with decreased burnout. For example, Zeller and colleagues (1999) found a significant negative correlation between collective efficacy beliefs and reported levels of burnout in nurses. Efficacy also may moderate the relationship between stressors and individual outcomes (Bandura, 1997; Grau, Salanova, & Peiro, 2001). Jex and Bliese (1999) found that collective efficacy moderated the relationship between some work stressors and outcomes in one of two ways: High collective efficacy was associated with higher satisfaction, regardless of the level of the work overload, whereas respondents with low collective efficacy had lower satisfaction especially when experiencing high overload. Conversely, collective efficacy was positively related to higher commitment regardless of the level of the task significance, with the relationship being stronger at high levels of efficacy.

High efficacy was associated with lower cynicism regardless of the level of role conflict. In both of these studies, however, self- and collective efficacy moderated only some of the relationships. Thus, efficacy's ability to moderate the relationships between stressors and strains is contingent upon the specific stressors and outcomes (Jex & Bliese, 1999).

Therefore, some evidence exists that team efficacy is an important factor not only because of its direct relationship to team performance, but also because of its relationship to the individual health of team members, as well as its ability to buffer the negative impact of stress on members' levels of job satisfaction and commitment.

Team Size

Much discussion has focused on the "optimal" size of a team. Some experts maintain that seven members is ideal (e.g., Scharf, 1989); some argue that 12 is ideal (e.g., Katzenbach, & Smith, 1993), and some contend that team size is unrelated to performance (see, for example, Martz, Vogel, & Nunamaker, 1992). Campion et al. (1993) found that team size was related to effectiveness, with larger teams being more effective.

Kozlowski and Bell (2003) argued that optimal team size depends on the task and environment in which the team functions. Wheelan (2009) found that groups with three to eight members were significantly more productive and developmentally advanced (according to the integrated model of group development outlined below) than groups with nine members or more. These discrepant findings suggest that both large and small groups can experience unique challenges.

Team Diversity (Homogeneous vs. Heterogeneous Work Teams)

With increasing diversity in workplaces, more heterogeneous groups have arisen. However, findings are conflicting in terms of whether diverse teams are more effective than more homogeneous teams (for overviews, see Guzzo & Dickson, 1996; Mannix & Neale, 2005). For example, although some research has found that groups of similar members perform better than groups of diverse members (e.g., Bettenhausen, 1991), other research has found that diversity in work groups is unrelated or negatively related to performance (e.g., Campion et al., 1993). Milliken & Martins (1996) labelled work group diversity as a "double-edged sword" in that increased diversity may result in lower group cohesion, but may increase performance and innovation. That is, it is often believed that team diversity in the workplace will allow various strengths to be brought in and utilized for more productive work (Mannix & Neale, 2005). More pessimistically, however, others believe that workplace team diversity creates divisions among colleagues, leading to poor integration and outcomes (Mannix & Neale, 2005). Which is the correct view?

Before addressing this question, we need to determine exactly what we mean by diversity. When we talk about diversity, we must remember that not all diversity is the same (Argote & McGrath, 1993; Mannix & Neale, 2005). The effects of diversity really depend on the *type* of diversity: We can mean diverse skill sets and expertise, or diverse ethnic backgrounds, or diverse geographical locations, or diverse personalities. Obviously, we wouldn't expect identical results for all these types of "diversity." For example, perhaps having diverse expertise and complementary skills may be an asset for a group, whereas having diverse personalities (which may conflict) would be a drawback. Therefore, Pelled (1996) argued that we need to differentiate among types of diversity to better understand the relationship of team diversity and organizational outcomes.

Harrison, Price, and Bell (1998) differentiated between surface-level diversity (i.e., differences based on demographics such as race, age, or gender) and deep-level diversity (differences based on work attitudes). They found that, over time, surface-level diversity between colleagues became less important for group dynamics, whereas deep-level diversity became more important.

In their meta-analysis of 24 studies on diversity, cohesion, and performance, Webber and Donahue (2001) differentiated between *job-related diversity*, such as educational and occupational background, and *non–job related diversity*, such as age, gender, and race. They found that, overall, neither type of work group diversity tends to be related to cohesion and group performance. Similarly, in their review of the literature on diverse teams, Mannix and Neale (2005) concluded that, although many people believe workplace diversity can increase levels of performance and expertise due to differences in educational backgrounds and information, no consistent evidence exists in the literature to support this belief.

Given the discrepancies in previous findings, several factors may affect whether diversity is beneficial to a team:

1. *Type of task:* The task the team must perform will affect how diversity affects performance (Argote & McGrath, 1993). For example, as we read in the team conflict section above, perhaps diversity in a team may be beneficial for more creative or innovative tasks. However, if the group must reach a consensus decision, diversity may be a hindrance.
2. *Criteria:* Whether diversity is beneficial or effective really depends on how we define these outcomes. That is, what do we mean by effectiveness? Diversity tends to be positively related to creativity

(see Jackson et al., 1995, for an overview), but it is also positively related to turnover (Jackson et al., 1991; Wiersma & Bird, 1993).

3. *Timing and stage of group:* The impact of diversity may change over time and at different stages of the group process (Argote & McGrath, 1993). That is, diversity may impede effectiveness in the short run, but may have beneficial effects as familiarity increases in the long term.

The discussion around diverse teams may be even more complex than a comparison of homogeneous and heterogeneous groups' direct relationship with performance; that is, it may be important to understand diversity because the *pattern of relationship* between team characteristics and performance outcomes may be dependent on the type of team—for example, homogeneous versus heterogeneous. For example, Van der Vegt and Janssen (2003) found that task interdependence and goal dependence were not associated with increased innovative behaviour when cognitive and demographic group diversity was low (i.e., homogeneous groups). However, task interdependence was associated with increased innovative behaviour for team members who had high goal dependence and when diversity was high (i.e., heterogeneous groups). That is, the level of diversity of the team affected the extent to which interdependence was related to innovation. Therefore, we need to have a better understanding of diverse teams to help us understand the complex pattern of relationships that may exist in them.

Finally, how does diversity impact on group norms? Chatman and Flynn (2001) expected that any negative effects of diversity on norms would dissipate over time. Their hypothesis was supported: they found that the negative impact of team demographic heterogeneity on cooperative norms decreased over time. That is, team heterogeneity was negatively associated with cooperative norms at time 1, but was unrelated to cooperative norms at time 2 of their study.

Improving Team Performance

Despite the mixed evidence regarding the effectiveness of teams, developing team effectiveness is important: Kozlowski and Ilgen (2006) concluded that "team effectiveness matters to individuals, to organizations, and to societies" (p. 111). Therefore, what can we do to improve team performance?

Three levels of interventions influence team processes: (1) *team design,* such that the team is aligned with the organizational goals, has sufficient resources to attain its goals, and has the knowledge, skills, and abilities balanced across members to be successful (see Hackman, 1992; Kozlowski & Ilgen, 2006; Kozlowski & Klein, 2000); (2) *training and development,* such that individual training focuses on developing individual skills and team training focuses on the teamwork skills required to develop integrated behaviours and tasks (Cannon-Bowers & Salas, 1998; Dyer, 1984; Kozlowski & Ilgen, 2006) and informal development processes help to align social interactions and work processes (Kozlowski & Ilgen, 2006); and (3) *leadership,* such that positive leadership may have indirect effects on team performance through individual perceptions of effectiveness (Kozlowski & Ilgen, 2006). We know that leadership can directly impact team processes (Hambley, O'Neill, & Kline, 2007; Zaccaro, Ardison, & Orvis, 2004). Therefore, it would seem wise to direct organizational resources toward training and developing leaders in general, and more specifically, training them on how to lead teams.

Leading and Managing Teams

Given all the information you have read in this chapter, what will you do when you are in a position of leading and managing teams? Kline (1999) identified the tasks of a team leader. Team leaders should:

1. Communicate a clear purpose to the team members. Leaders can provide the "big picture knowledge" (p. 40) from the organization to ensure the team's and organization's goals are the same.

2. Identify the available resources (in terms of physical, financial, human, or time-based resources) and provide the required resources to help the team successfully attain its goals.

3. Develop team members' talents in terms of their knowledge, skills, and abilities to help increase individual performance and overall team effectiveness.

4. Run interference and protect the team from outside requests and criticism when required. The leader may not always need to be the liaison between the group and the outside world, but should step in to help buffer external comments or requests, or act as an advocate to ensure the group gets the required resources.

5. Deal with team conflict. Leaders do not need to step in at lower levels of conflict (e.g., disagreements about a course of action to take); however, when "a team member or members are disruptive and hinder the team from moving forward in its work" (p. 43), a leader can help the team work through the conflict and move forward.

6. Understand constraints, problems, and resources. In communicating the goals (#1), the leader also must see the big picture of the scope and limitations of the team working within a specific organizational context. The role of the leader is to problem solve not only for current issues, but also for potential issues that may arise in the future.

7. Plan and organize tasks and coordinate work activities. Some teams prefer more autonomy and may not want this type of "hands-on" leadership approach. Good leaders can recognize if and when they need to be more involved in day-to-day tasks, and how to make the transition back and forth from being more or less involved in specific tasks.

(Source: Theresa Kline, *Remaking Teams: The Revolutionary Research-based Guide that Puts Theory into Practice.* Copyright © 1999 Jossey Bass. Reproduced with permission of John Wiley & Sons, Inc.)

Given these tasks, where does team leadership go wrong? Hackman (1998) identified six mistakes that managers make when creating and leading teams:

1. *Using a team to complete work that would be better completed by an individual.* Not all work is best completed by a group. Therefore, it is important to differentiate among tasks that are best done by groups or by individuals.

2. *Labelling the group as a team but managing each person individually.* If you want a team, treat employees as team members (including team goals, feedback, and performance reviews).

Chapter 7: Groups and Teams in Organizations

3. *Giving up all authority to team members when attempting to delegate work.* Hackman (1998) argued that teams are most effective when managers still retain some authority in dictating the goals and focus but allow autonomy in how the team does its work.
4. *Bypassing organizational structures so that teams will have more freedom.* A lack of structure may lead to ambiguity and confusion on how to interact.
5. *Creating specific goals without providing any organizational supports.* The leader and manager needs to provide all the relevant organizational supports to ensure team success.
6. *Assuming that the members already possess all the skills required to work well as a team.* Just because the members are great performers individually doesn't mean they have the necessary skills to be great team members. It is incumbent upon managers to provide coaching to team members on a variety of task- and team-related skills.

Therefore, a successful leader would (1) ensure the task is suited to be completed by a team; (2) lead and manage the members as a team; (3) retain authority while allowing the team autonomy in getting tasks completed; (4) retain the organizational structures to help the team attain its goals; (5) provide organizational supports to help the team attain its goals; and (6) provide training for members (in terms of team-relevant skills as well as task-relevant skills; Hackman, 1998).

See Box 7.4 for an illustration of the functioning of teams.

Box 7.4

Teams on the Sea

Imagine you work for Secunda Marine Services. You wake up in the morning, get dressed, eat breakfast, walk up the stairs, and are met with freezing temperatures and the spray of the sea stinging your face. You are now at work!

Secunda Marine Services owns and operates a technologically advanced fleet of offshore support vessels servicing oil and gas companies nationally and internationally. Secunda was founded in Nova Scotia and has grown its fleet to 14 vessels and one training vessel, working on a solid foundation of highly experienced sailors, maritime work ethic, and a philosophy of providing superior service to its customers.

Most of Secunda's employees work on their ships for 30 days at a time, sometimes in very adverse weather. They live together, eat together, and work together during those times. Although many challenges accompany this working environment, it also provides many opportunities for strong teams.

What Are They Doing?

Secunda uses team-building exercises to decrease stress and improve morale. For example, Health and Wellness Day combines team building with physical exercise and socialization. They also use teams for fun activities, like onshore/offshore dragon boating. Employees practise as a team and participate in charity boat races. In these and other initiatives, the crew gets to dictate the issues, prioritize, and come up with practical solutions.

How Are These Initiatives Working?

Secunda has been recognized by the Nova Scotia Psychologically Healthy Workplace Program, and its "Ship Shape at Secunda" program (involving an initial health check, health and wellness training, and new fitness equipment) was recognized with an International Best Practice Award through the American Psychological Association's Psychologically Healthy Workplaces program.

Theresa Kline

Theresa J.B. Kline is a professor in the Department of Psychology at the University of Calgary. She has an active research program in the area of team performance, and her other research interests include psychometrics, organizational effectiveness, and work attitudes. Theresa has published two books on teams, *Teams That Lead* (2003) and *Remaking Teams* (1999), and one on psychometrics, *Psychological Testing* (2005). She also has more than 70 peer-reviewed articles. Dr. Kline teaches statistics/methods and organizational psychology at both the undergraduate and graduate levels. She has an active organizational consulting practice, with projects ranging from individual and organizational assessment to strategic alignment.

Source: Courtesy of Theresa Kline.

Summary

Work teams comprise two or more individuals working toward a common goal. Not all teams are created equal: they may differ in a number of important ways in terms of their composition, size, commitment to the goal, geographic dispersion, and cohesion.

The most contentious issue that surrounds teams is whether they actually are more effective than working individually. Some argue that team performance is the same as or worse than the sum of individuals working alone, whereas other research has suggested teams may be more effective in certain situations. One thing that is agreed upon is that teams are not effective for every situation, and not everyone is suited for teamwork.

However, even though performance may not be enhanced by working in a group, teams may have other important functions: Group members feel more satisfied, and they perceive that the group has higher performance. Given that it is unlikely organizations will eliminate the use of teams, our primary goal as work specialists may be to identify the situations in which teams are most effective and identify the factors that can improve the functioning of existing teams. Several interventions toward improving teams can focus on team design, training and development, and providing good leadership.

Kozlowski and Ilgen (2006) nicely summarize the role that teams play: "[T]eams are central and vital to everything we do in modern life" (p. 78). Organizations are increasingly incorporating team models into their work systems. Work teams are ubiquitous and probably here to stay.

Key Terms

autonomous work teams 209

cohesion 217

crews 209

familiarity 217

forming 211

groupthink 212

interchangeability 207

norming 211

perceived loafing 214

performing 211

relationship conflict 213

role definition 207

social loafing 214

storming 211

task conflict 213

task interdependence 207

team 206

team conflict 213

team efficacy 217

team member interaction 207

virtual work groups 210

Web Links w(w)w

For "Group Dynamics: Basic Nature of Groups and How They Develop," go to:

http://managementhelp.org/grp_skll/theory/theory.htm

For "A Business Case for Diversity," by Dr. Jeffrey Gandz (an article that describes some cases of heterogeneous teams in Canadian and U.S. business), go to:

http://www.hrsdc.gc.ca/eng/labour/equality/racism/racism_free_init/summary_business.shtml

Discussion Questions

1. Why is it important to study group processes in organizations?
2. Describe the four stages of the integrated model of group development. Think of a work group you have recently been a member of, perhaps for a class project. Describe whether your group followed this sequence of stages, and what stage your group reached when the project was done.
3. Compare and contrast homogeneous and heterogeneous work groups. What factors influence diversity as beneficial to group performance?
4. Describe the benefits of a cohesive group and outline the factors that can promote cohesiveness within a group.
5. What is an autonomous work group, and what are its benefits?

Using the Internet

You are the owner of JT McScott Consulting Firm, which helps companies and universities host conferences. In the past, you would get one of your consultants to be the liaison with the client company, and that consultant would ask colleagues for help in organizing the conference as needed.

However, there have been problems with this process in the past (lack of coordination, failing to meet deadlines, duplication of effort, etc.), and you realize that you need to organize the work around teams. Each team could be asked to do a variety of tasks for each conference (e.g., choosing the venue, helping select and coordinate speakers, ordering food, getting organizational sponsors, etc.).

You have no idea how to start the process of creating teams, so you decide to go on the Internet and research tips for forming teams.

1. What tips and strategies can you find on forming teams?
2. Which of these strategies would you implement for your team? Why?
3. Once you have created a process for your team formation, think about the impact on your team. Based on what you've learned in this chapter, do you believe that your teams would be effective? Why or why not?
4. What factors will influence their effectiveness?

Exercises

1. Baillie Inc. is a Canadian business company looking to expand to other countries. It is a small company, and therefore does not have the resources to send employees abroad to help train the new employees. Baillie Inc. has the technology and resources to create a virtual team but lacks expertise in this area. Management has asked your advice because of your expertise in teams.

   a. What challenges would the company face with the new virtual team compared to its work teams that interact in person?
   b. What are the pros and cons of having a virtual team?
   c. What are some strategies the company can use to ensure the virtual team will run effectively?
   d. How would you help Baillie Inc. set up a virtual team?

2. Review the following different teams. What types do they represent? What factors (e.g., dependency among members) may exist within each example?

   a. An independent lawyer who sometimes brings in a team to assist on a large case.
   b. Workers who jointly inspect defects on children's toys on an assembly line.
   c. Flight attendants for WestJet.
   d. A representative council for a teachers' union.
   e. Firefighters who deal with the specific task of fire control within a larger firefighting unit.

3. Think about a time when you worked on a team. Did everyone contribute equally? Have you ever experienced a time in which not every member contributed equally?

   a. Describe a time when you believe social loafing took place. What objective evidence can you point to in order to rule out that this was not *perceived* loafing?

b. How does either social loafing or perceived loafing affect your team?

c. Based on everything you have learned about teams, what strategies could you implement to ensure this situation does not occur again?

4. Think back to a time when you were part of a successful team. What did the team look like, and what were its tasks? How was performance measured?

a. Did you have any group norms that contributed to your success?

b. How did group cohesion play a role in your team?

c. Based on what you have learned, explain which strategies your team leader used that were beneficial, and which may have hindered the group performance.

d. Describe your group dynamics. (e.g., team efficacy, size, diversity). How did these factors affect your team performance?

e. In what ways could the team have improved its overall performance? Knowing what you now know about teams, would you have done anything differently?

Case

Catwill Lighting Inc. has asked you, an organizational consultant, to help the company put together a team of its most innovative employees to design a new type of track lighting system for office settings. The team will be required to research the needs of the market, design a new lighting system in response to those needs, and develop a marketing strategy for the system. As their consultant, you will be responsible for deciding how employees will be selected to be a part of this team and choosing employees for the team.

Discussion Questions

1. What strategies would you use to assemble an effective and innovative team? How would you select individuals for the team? What size should the team be? What type of people should be included on the team in order to facilitate group cohesion?

2. What advice would you give Catwill Lighting about how to facilitate the team development process?

3. What kind of control should the team have over their project? What are the benefits of autonomous work groups?

CHAPTER 8

Job and Organizational Attitudes, Affect, and Behaviours

Think about a job you have or one you held in the past. How do you feel about your job? Would you recommend working at that organization to someone else? In considering your answers, think about the physical aspects of the workplace, the type of work you performed, how much you were paid, and how you were treated by your supervisor, coworkers, and customers. Have you ever quit a job because you didn't like it?

We have a range of feelings about our job that can affect not only our own work behaviours and health, but also organizational outcomes. This chapter provides an overview of workers' behaviour at work, as well as their attitudes and feelings toward their organization, work, colleagues, supervisors, subordinates, and customers.

Chapter Learning Outcomes

After reading this chapter you should be able to

- Define the term "attitudes"
- Identify reasons why studying attitudes is important
- Define job satisfaction
- Identify the antecedents and outcomes of job satisfaction
- Define involvement
- Identify the antecedents and outcomes of involvement
- Define organizational commitment
- Identify the antecedents and outcomes of organizational commitment
- Define organizational justice
- Identify the antecedents and outcomes of organizational justice
- Recognize the predictors of injustice perceptions

Job Attitudes and Affect

job attitude

A relatively stable *view or opinion* of a specific person, group, organization, job, or situation

job affect

One's *feelings* about work

What do you *think* about your work? What are your attitudes about your job? Your organization? Your supervisor and coworkers? When we talk about **job attitudes**, we mean relatively stable views or opinions of a specific person, group, organization, job, or situation.

Now … how do you *feel* about your job? Affect involves both moods and emotions (Weiss & Brief, 2001). **Job affect** refers to one's *feelings* about work (Lee & Allen, 2002), such that it is a "generalized overall feeling state" (Mitchell & Daniels, 2003, p. 236).

See Box 8.1 for a discussion of job satisfaction at a leading Canadian company.

Why Do We Care about Attitudes?

We care about attitudes toward jobs and at work for two main reasons. The first reason is because research has shown that our attitudes strongly influence our behaviours. For example, if you like your job, you'll be more likely to stay in your job. If you feel your organization treats you unfairly, you may be more likely to leave your job or engage in counterproductive work behaviours (see Chapter 11).

The second reason is because these attitudes are important for their own sake. For example, Warr (1987) argued that it is important to study job satisfaction not only because it may influence turnover and absences, but because having happy workers is important in and of itself.

Box 8.1

Job Satisfaction at RIM

Research In Motion (RIM), located in Waterloo, Ontario, is a leading manufacturer of wireless communication products and services, including the BlackBerry smart phone. RIM was recently named one of Canada's top 100 employers of 2010, one of Waterloo's top 15 employers, and one of the *Financial Post*'s 10 best companies to work for (Yerema & Caballero, 2009).

Job satisfaction is a priority at RIM. In fact, an employee satisfaction survey is conducted every 12 months to stay in touch with employees and keep on top of the issue. Elizabeth Pfiefer, RIM's vice-president of organizational development, says that the company's perks are essential for maintaining high employee satisfaction (McGinn, 2008).

Among other perks, all 8,576 of RIM's full-time employees receive a free BlackBerry with paid usage and services, a profit-sharing plan, year-end bonuses, and on-site massage services and discounted gym memberships through the "Healthy @ RIM" program (Lopez, 2009). RIM also provides tuition subsidies to employees, and is only a short walk away from both the University of Waterloo and Wilfrid Laurier University (Yerema & Caballero, 2009). Employees at RIM enjoy casual dress daily, employee sports teams, and "RIM Rocks" concerts— with previous performances by Aerosmith, the Barenaked Ladies, and U2—to celebrate organizational milestones (Yerema & Caballero, 2009). In the workplace, employees benefit from on-site shower facilities for bicycle commuters, a religious observance room, organized car pools, escorted walking service to cars after dark, a walking trail, and an on-site cafeteria with subsidized meals (Yerema & Caballero, 2009).

So, do all of the perks impact satisfaction and organizational outcomes? As a result of these organizational programs, RIM has a low voluntary turnover rate of 7 percent and receives a large number of applications every year due to its popularity as an employer (Yerema & Caballero, 2009).

Job Satisfaction

Job satisfaction is one of the most studied constructs in the work domain. Typically, we have simply measured job satisfaction as synonymous with job affect, although Kemery, Bedeian, & Rawson Zacur (1996) noted that *job affect* is only the feeling component of job satisfaction, and that satisfaction may also involve cognitions (i.e., thoughts and attitudes) about the job. Interestingly, other researchers argued that job satisfaction is only one small aspect of job affect, and we need to study the "feeling component" of work more broadly.

Therefore, we will first look at job satisfaction and then more broadly at other types of work-related affect.

Definition and Theories of Job Satisfaction

Locke (1976) defined job satisfaction as "a pleasurable or positive emotional state resulting from appraisal of one's job or job experiences" (Locke, 1976, p. 1300). In other words, job satisfaction is the extent to which people enjoy their job and may include all aspects surrounding their work (e.g., pay, supervisor, coworkers).

We can distinguish among three aspects of job satisfaction: (1) *Cognition* involves your *thoughts and beliefs* about your job (e.g., "I have a good job"); (2) *Affect* involves your *feelings* about your job ("I like my job"); and (3) *Behaviours* involve how you behave at work (e.g., "I will go above and beyond what is expected of me in my job" (Ajzen, 1989; Kemery, Bedeian, & Rawson Zacur, 1996; Locke, 1976; Weiss, Nicholas, & Daus, 1999).

As we noted in the opening paragraph, when thinking about your own job satisfaction you may have asked yourself questions about various aspects of your job pertaining to the type of work you do, your salary and benefits, your supervisor and colleagues, and even the physical work environment and the location of the workplace.

What if you are satisfied with your pay, but not with your supervisor? Are you still satisfied with your job? So what exactly is job satisfaction? Is it a global feeling of how much you like your job overall, or is it a combination of how you feel about all of the individual aspects of your job?

One issue around the measurement of job satisfaction involves whether it is better to measure global work satisfaction or to measure the specific "facets," or components, of satisfaction. For example, we could ask you, "Taking everything about your job into consideration, how satisfied are you with your job?" (i.e., one item: global satisfaction). Conversely, we could ask you "How satisfied are you with your pay; your supervisor; your coworkers; the type of work you do," and so on.

Most measures ask about the components of the job, but some combine them into a global score. Conversely, other measures create separate scores for each aspect of the job (e.g., satisfaction with your pay and benefits, satisfaction with the type of work you are doing) (Smith, Kendall, & Hulin, 1969). These researchers argue that it is better to use measures that look at various facets of the job to obtain more detailed information on job satisfaction. These researchers also argue that these different factors may have different relationships with

job satisfaction

The extent to which people enjoy their job; may include all aspects surrounding their work (e.g., pay, supervisor, coworkers) outcomes, and therefore need to be studied individually (Edwards, Bell, Arthur, & Decuir, 2008). Although both global and facet scales are used, global satisfaction is not simply the sum of facet scales (Ironson, Smith, Brannick, Gibson, & Paul, 1989): General scales tend to be more highly correlated with the "work" subscales than any of the facet scales (Ironson et al., 1989).

Do we need a lot of items to measure job satisfaction? Interestingly, Wanous, Reichers, and Hudy (1997) argued that using a one-item overall measure of job satisfaction may be almost as effective as using a more complicated scale. They found that a one-item measure of job satisfaction was correlated .67 with longer measures of job satisfaction that included facets of the job. That is, simply asking people how satisfied they are with their job gets almost the same results as asking a lot of different questions about the job. In general, people can accurately report their own level of satisfaction.

Measures of Job Satisfaction

The Job Descriptive Index

Job Descriptive Index (JDI)

One of the most widely used job satisfaction measures, measuring five facets of job satisfaction: satisfaction with work, pay, promotion, supervision, and coworkers.

The **Job Descriptive Index (JDI)** is one of the most widely used job satisfaction measures, translated into at least nine languages and administered in at least 17 different countries as of 2005 (Wang & Russell, 2005). The JDI was developed by Smith et al. (1969) and was most recently revised in 1997 (Balzer et al., 1997). The JDI contains five facet scales describing satisfaction with one's work, pay, promotion, supervision, and coworkers (Wang & Russell, 2005). Respondents are asked to respond with "yes," "no," or "?" to indicate whether certain phrases describe each aspect of their work. A sample of some items from the JDI is provided in Box 8.2. Boxes 8.3 and 8.4 examine the topic of job satisfaction in Canada.

Box 8.2

Measuring Job Satisfaction: Using One-Item Tests vs. Multiple-Item Tests

Sample Items from the Job Descriptive Index (JDI) including the Job in General (JIG) scale

In the blank beside each word or phrase below, write
1 for "Yes"
2 for "No"
3 for "?"

WORK ON PRESENT JOB

How well does each of the following describe your work?

___ Fascinating
___ Routine
___ Satisfying
___ Boring

OPPORTUNITIES FOR PROMOTION

How well does each of the following describe your opportunities for promotion?

___ Good opportunities for promotion
___ Opportunities somewhat limited
___ Promotion on ability
___ Dead-end job

PRESENT PAY

How well does each of the following describe your present pay?

___ Income adequate for normal expenses
___ Fair
___ Comfortable
___ Bad

CO-WORKERS

How well does each of the following describe the people you work with?

___ Stimulating
___ Boring
___ Slow
___ Helpful

How well does each of the following describe your supervision?

___ Supportive
___ Hard to please
___ Impolite
___ Praises good work

JOB IN GENERAL

How well does each of the following describe your job most of the time?

___ Pleasant
___ Bad
___ Great
___ Worthwhile

Source: Bowling Green State University (1975–2009).

Box 8.3

Job Satisfaction in Canada

How happy are you with your job? According to a 2002 Canadian Community Health Survey of approximately 21 000 employed Canadians aged 18 to 75, Shields (2006) found that most Canadians were satisfied with their jobs, with approximately 6 percent of respondents reporting that they were "not too satisfied" and 2 percent of respondents reporting that they were "not at all satisfied."

What work-related factors tend to be associated with decreased satisfaction for Canadian workers? Shift workers tended to be more dissatisfied than workers in a regular day shift. Younger workers and workers with lower incomes were more likely to be dissatisfied with their jobs than were older workers and workers with higher incomes, respectively. Employees in processing/manufacturing/utilities jobs, in sales and service jobs, and in administrative/financial/clerical jobs tended to be more dissatisfied than workers in other occupations. Conversely, employees in management and professional jobs tended to report lower levels of dissatisfaction. "Not surprisingly, few self-employed men and women were dissatisfied with their jobs" (p. 34).

Also, workers who reported high job stress also tended to report higher job dissatisfaction. That is, "among workers who reported that most of their days were extremely stressful, 1 in 4 were dissatisfied with their jobs. By contrast, among those for whom stress was not really an issue, only 1 in 15 was dissatisfied."

What outcomes were related to job satisfaction? Workers who were dissatisfied with their jobs tended to report lower physical and mental health, and they tended to take more disability days.

Source: Shields, M. (October, 2006) Unhappy on the job. *Health Reports*, 17(4), Statistics Canada, Catalogue 82–003.

The Jobs in General Scale

The **Jobs in General Scale** (Ironson et al., 1989) is a global measure of job satisfaction. It was developed to be compatible with the JDI but to be more global, more evaluative, and to consider a longer time period at work (Ironson et al., 1989). Employees are asked to rate their jobs on several characteristics—pleasant,

Jobs in General Scale

A global measure of job satisfaction in which a total score is created based on ratings of several general characteristics

Box 8.4

Job Satisfaction of Canadian Workers

Refer to Figure 8.1. How do employees compare in their levels of job satisfaction across Canada? Are there differences across provinces? Are employees generally satisfied or dissatisfied? What province has the highest job satisfaction? Which one has the least satisfied workers?

Would it surprise you to learn that employees in Newfoundland and Labrador (followed closely by PEI and New Brunswick) report the highest levels of satisfaction? British Columbia employees reported the lowest levels of satisfaction.

FIGURE 8.1

Job Satisfaction in Canada

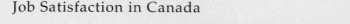

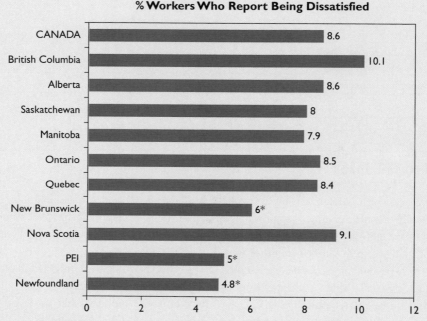

Percentage reporting job dissatisfaction by province (excluding territories), employment population aged 18–75

NOTE: Dissatisfied = respondents indicating "not too satisfied" or "not at all satisfied"

* significantly different from estimate for Canada ($p < .05$)

Source: Adapted from Statistics Canada, Health Reports 82-003-XIE2005004 vol. 17 no. 4, Released October 17, 2006.

Minnesota Satisfaction Questionnaire (MSQ)

A measure of job satisfaction that measures overall intrinsic and extrinsic satisfaction, as well as 21 specific aspects (e.g., pay, flexibility, coworkers)

worse than most (reverse scored), enjoyable, waste of time (reverse scored)—using the same scale as the JDI (i.e., "yes," "no," or "?"). Ratings of these characteristics are combined to create a total job satisfaction score.

The Minnesota Satisfaction Questionnaire

The **Minnesota Satisfaction Questionnaire (MSQ)** was developed by Weiss et al. (1967); it was revised in 1977 and 1985. The measure can be administered in a long form, with 21 different scales, or in a short form measuring two scales: intrinsic and extrinsic satisfaction (Mardanov, Heischmidt, & Henson, 2008). Examples of extrinsic satisfaction items include, "The way my coworkers get along with each other," and "My pay and the amount of work I do." Examples of intrinsic satisfaction items include, "The chance to do things for other people," and "The freedom to use my own judgment." Responses are typically scored on a five-point Likert-type scale, from 1 "strongly disagree" to 5 "strongly agree" (Weiss et al., 1967).

Antecedents of Job Satisfaction

What job, organizational, and individual factors are related to job satisfaction?

Job and Organizational Factors and Job Satisfaction

How can organizations promote job satisfaction? Many organizations hope to improve job satisfaction and morale, but is it even possible to increase satisfaction? Many studies have shown how job and organizational factors can influence satisfaction. These antecedents of job satisfaction provide a starting point for suggestions for promoting employee satisfaction.

Improve Person–Job Fit and Training

Have you ever tried to do a job for which you weren't qualified and didn't have the training? It was probably quite frustrating, and you may not have enjoyed it. Alternatively, have you ever done a job for which you were overqualified, or a job you didn't find challenging? You may have been bored and disengaged. If employees are well-equipped to do their job, there is a greater likelihood they will be satisfied with it. That is, organizations must ensure that employees have the skills to do their jobs first by selecting the right employees into the right jobs, and then by training them properly. In general, job satisfaction is best when workers have the required skills, some autonomy, and challenging (engaging) work.

As we noted in Chapter 4, *person–job fit* is the extent to which there is a match between employees' abilities and job demands (Cable & DeRue, 2002). Similarly, *person–organization fit* refers to a match between employee and organization values (Kristoff, 1996; O'Reilly, Chatman, & Caldwell, 1991).

Having a good fit between an employee and the job is related to higher job satisfaction (Tinsley, 2000), although person–organization fit seems to be an even better predictor of job satisfaction than person–job fit (Cable & DeRue, 2002; Hinkle & Choi, 2009). Similarly, Amos and Weathington (2008) looked at the relationship between congruence of employee and organizational values and job satisfaction and found that perceived congruence was positively related to job satisfaction. Having a fit between your values and the values of the organization is related to improved communication, mutual liking, friendship, and trust among colleagues, which in turn are related to higher job satisfaction (Edwards & Cable, 2009).

Treat Employees Fairly

Once we have selected the right people and trained them, we must ensure we treat them well. This fair treatment includes having fair procedures in place, providing fair outcomes (including pay) to them, and ensuring fair treatment by supervisors. It is important that all these factors are in place:

Simply providing fair pay to employees will not guarantee their satisfaction. Organizations must consider other employee needs, such as work–family balance, employee health benefits plans, and a comfortable work environment (we provide more information on *organizational justice* later in this chapter).

Ensure Good Leadership

One of the biggest stressors at work is poor supervision (Dale & Fox, 2008). Having high-quality, supportive, and knowledgeable managers and supervisors is related to higher job satisfaction.

Encourage Employee Involvement

Have you had a job or worked in a group where no one cared about your ideas and suggestions? In general, employees want to be involved and have their opinions heard by the organization. Autonomy and a chance to have input into decisions is associated with higher satisfaction (De Cuyper & De Witte, 2006).

Provide a Healthy Workplace

Healthy workplaces can foster respectful interactions with colleagues, which in turn can improve job satisfaction. Supportive organization initiatives and good work–life balance also have been associated with job satisfaction. (For more, see Box 8.5.)

Have a Supportive Organization and Colleagues

Even if the work—or the workload—is getting you down, having support from your organization and your coworkers can help your level of satisfaction. For example, good communication, liking your colleagues, and trust in the organization all are related to higher job satisfaction (Edwards & Cable, 2009).

Individual Factors and Job Satisfaction

Your level of satisfaction is not solely affected by work factors: individual characteristics also play an important part. That is, some people may be predisposed to being happy in general and to being happy with their jobs.

Personality

Agreeableness and conscientiousness tend to be related to job satisfaction (Judge, Heller, & Mount, 2002). Similarly Ilies, Spitzmuller, Fulmer, & Johnson (2009) found that highly conscientious people tended to have higher job satisfaction. Why would there be a relationship between conscientiousness and

Box 8.5

Healthy Workplaces and Job Satisfaction

Did you know? According to the American Psychological Association, organizations that have implemented psychologically healthy workplace practices tend to have higher rates of job satisfaction than the general organizational population. Read more about it in Chapter 12, which examines occupational health and healthy workplaces.

satisfaction? Ilies suggested that agreeable and conscientious employees are diligent, reliable, and engage in behaviours that are often recognized and rewarded by the organization, which may increase employees' job satisfaction.

Workers with high self-esteem also may be more satisfied. In fact, LeRouge, Nelson, and Blanton (2006) found that employees with high self-esteem reported higher job satisfaction than employees with low self-esteem, regardless of the stressfulness of the work.

Demographic Characteristics

Li and Lambert (2008) found that years of experience in nursing was a significant predictor of job satisfaction in hospital nurses. As employees work longer, they become more confident in doing the job, and their pay, benefits, and rewards may improve as well, leading to greater job satisfaction.

Outcomes of Job Satisfaction

Job Satisfaction and Performance

Many managers and CEOs would agree that having happy workers is an important organizational goal in and of itself. However, other less altruistic individuals may argue that having happy workers is important only when it impacts the bottom line. Is job satisfaction associated with increased performance?

The Happy vs. Productive Worker

Do happy workers demonstrate higher levels of job performance than unhappy workers? Decades of study have produced inconsistent findings regarding this hypothesis, perhaps because of differences in the way happiness has been operationally defined. Wright, Cropanzano, Denney, & Moline (2002) two-year longitudinal study examined the effect of psychological well-being, job satisfaction, and dispositional affect on job performance. They found that although psychological well-being (i.e., general happiness) predicted job performance, neither job satisfaction nor dispositional affect (i.e., a tendency to be positive and happy) significantly predicted job performance. Similarly, in their meta-analysis Iaffaldano and Muchinsky (1985) found that job satisfaction was only weakly related to performance.

However, Judge, Thoresen, Bono, and Patton (2001) argued that some of these weak or null relationships between satisfaction and performance may be due to limitations in analyses and/or misinterpretation of findings. In their meta-analysis, Judge et al. found a moderate correlation between job satisfaction and job performance.

Another reason why the relationship between satisfaction and performance isn't stronger may be that performance is a function of other important individual factors (e.g., motivation, ability) and organizational constraints (e.g., lack of access to information and money; interdependence of workers). Therefore, we can argue that there is a low to moderate relationship between job satisfaction and performance.

So, should we just forget about job satisfaction as an important organizational variable? Some researchers have argued that "productivity" and "performance" have been too narrowly defined and that we should look at other

Chapter 8: Job and Organizational Attitudes, Affect, and Behaviours important organizational outcomes. For example, job satisfaction is associated with "helping behaviours" such as organizational citizenship behaviours (Ilies et al., 2009; Organ & Ryan, 1995; see below for more discussion on OCBs), which may benefit other workers and the organization. Also, satisfaction is significantly related to other organizational outcomes, such as absenteeism and turnover (Edwards & Cable, 2009; Hausknecht, Hiller, & Vance, 2008), which have huge associated costs. Employees with low job satisfaction are also more inclined to behave aggressively toward the organization (Hershcovis et al., 2007). Finally, high satisfaction is also associated with individual health outcomes, which has important implications for absenteeism and organizational healthcare costs.

Thus, having satisfied employees may improve their behaviours toward coworkers and the organization, and may reduce absenteeism and turnover—all which are important to organizations. So, maybe organizations should still be concerned about making workers happy ☺! (For more about the benefits of happy workers, refer to Box 8.6.)

Box 8.6

In the Media: A Happy Worker Is a Cheaper Worker

Happier workers tend to be more productive, take fewer sick days and cost employers less in disability expenses, a survey to be released Wednesday suggests.

Stress tends to affect about 28 per cent of highly engaged employees compared with 39 per cent of disgruntled workers, according to consultancy Hewitt Associates' annual survey of 115,000 Canadian employees.

The survey asked how many days employees missed in the past six months due to emotional, physical, or mental fatigue, and found organizations with low engagement scores recorded more than twice as many days off on average than high-engagement employers.

This difference can cost a large organization, with at least a thousand employees, about $1 million a year in disability costs and lost productivity, the report said.

"Better health, lower job stress and a manageable workload translate into tangible benefits for employers, particularly in terms of lower absenteeism," said Rochelle Morandini, Hewitt's senior organizational health consultant.

Engaged workers tend to be in better physical health. More than half, or 56 per cent, of people at high-engagement places reported being in good health, versus about 41 per cent who said so in low-engagement organizations.

Workloads also tend to differ. Disengaged workers tend to have heavier work overloads while those at engaged organizations reported fewer workload problems.

"High engagement goes hand-in-hand with better health and well-being," said Neil Crawford, leader of Hewitt's Best Employers in Canada study. "Employees at organizations with high engagement reported better physical health, lower job stress and work overload, and greater financial security."

The research was carried out in conjunction with Hewitt's 2009 best employers in Canada study (see http://www.hewittassociates.com/Intl/NA/en-CA/AboutHewitt/Newsroom/PressReleaseDetail.aspx?cid=6350 for more information).

Source: Tavia Grant, "A happy worker is a cheaper worker," *The Globe and Mail*, February 18, 2009. © CTVglobemedia Publishing Inc. All Rights Reserved.

Absenteeism and Turnover

Despite the debate over whether happy workers are more productive, less controversy exists surrounding the relationship of satisfaction with absenteeism and turnover. In general, higher job satisfaction is associated with lower absenteeism (Hausknecht et al., 2008). However, other factors (e.g., organizational policies about sick leave, organizational culture) can influence the extent to which employees use their leave absences.

Similarly, workers who are satisfied with their job tend to be more likely to report that they will stay in their job (i.e., intent to stay) (Edwards & Cable, 2009), and less likely to actually leave their job (i.e., turnover) (Shore, Newton, & Thornton, 1990). Conversely, employees who are dissatisfied with the job tend to leave the job (Li & Lambert, 2008).

Organizational Citizenship Behaviours

Job satisfaction has been consistently related to contextual performance in the form of organizational citizenship behaviours (OCBs; Brief, 1998; Le Pine, Erez, & Johnson, 2002). OCBs, or contextual behaviours, are work behaviours—such as helping colleagues or helping the organization—that don't directly support the core job tasks but that support the broader social and psychological context at work (Borman & Motowidlo, 1993; Organ, 1997). In fact, research suggests that job satisfaction is the best predictor of organizational citizenship behaviours (for reviews, see Ilies et al., 2009; Organ & Ryan, 1994; Schnake, 1991). It stands to reason that if employees are not satisfied they may be less likely to choose to engage in these types of behaviours. Conversely, if they are satisfied, they may be happy to take on extra work that will benefit either other employees or the organization as a whole. Ilies et al. (2009) argued that employees who benefit from satisfying work environments should be more likely to reciprocate favourable treatment back to the organization by engaging in OCBs. Indeed, in their large meta-analysis using 123 studies, they found that employees with higher job satisfaction tended to demonstrate higher levels of OCBs.

You may think that one's inclination to behave positively toward the organization may simply be a function of their personality. However, in the same meta-analysis, Ilies et al. (2009) found that job satisfaction mediated the relationship between personality and OCBs. That is, the effect of personality on OCBs was explained through the job satisfaction (see Figure 8.2). For a further note on job satisfaction, see Box 8.7.

FIGURE 8.2

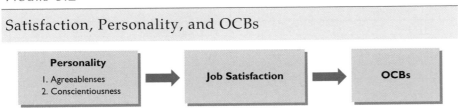

Satisfaction, Personality, and OCBs

| Personality
1. Agreeablenses
2. Conscientiousness | → | Job Satisfaction | → | OCBs |

Source: Ilies, R., et al. 2009. Personality and citizenship behavior: The mediating role of job satisfaction. *Journal of Applied Psychology* 94(4): 945-959. Copyright © 2009 by the American Psychological Association. Adapted with permission.

Box 8.7

Looking Beyond Job Satisfaction

Some researchers have argued that we need to go beyond job satisfaction when we measure job affect. That is, we really don't want our workers to be simply "satisfied" with their jobs. We want them to be engaged and love their jobs! Do you think this difference is important? If not, think about the following example: Imagine coming home to your spouse one day, who greets you with an "I love you." What would happen if you responded to your spouse, "I'm very satisfied with you as well." We suspect you may end up sleeping on the couch for the night (or for the entire week!).

Job Affective Well-Being Scale (JAWS)

Measures the full range of job-specific affect that isn't contaminated by beliefs or complex attitudes

The construct of "satisfaction" may not adequately describe all the emotions we feel about our jobs. Therefore, Van Katwyk, Fox, Spector, and Kelloway (2000) developed the **Job Affective Well-Being Scale (JAWS)** to measure this range of emotions. They wanted to create a measure of job-related affect that was "pure" (i.e., not contaminated by beliefs or complex attitudes). To contrast their scale with general measures of affect (e.g., "I feel angry"), they wanted to create a context-specific

FIGURE 8.3

Job Affective Well-Being Scale: How Do You Feel about Your Job?

Below are a number of statements that describe different emotions that a job can make a person feel. Please indicate the amount to which any part of your job (e.g., the work, coworkers, supervisors, clients, pay) has made you feel that emotion in the past 30 days. Base your answers on the following scale:

1	2	3	4	5
Never	Rarely	Sometimes	Quite Often	Extremely Often or Always

My job made me feel...

1. ...at ease	2. ...angry
3. ...annoyed	4. ...anxious
5. ...bored	6. ...cheerful
7. ...calm	8. ...confused
9. ...content	10. ...depressed
11. ...disgusted	12. ...discouraged
13. ...elated	14. ...energetic
15. ...excited	16. ...ecstatic
17. ...enthusiastic	18. ...frightened
19. ...frustrated	20. ...furious
21. ...gloomy	22. ...fatigued
23. ...happy	24. ...intimidated
25. ...inspired	26. ...miserable
27. ...pleased	28. ...proud
29. ...satisfied	30. ...relaxed

Source: Table 1 (adapted), p. 225, from Van Katwyk, P.R., Fox, S., Spector, P.E., & Kelloway, E.K. (2000). Using the Job-Related Affective Well-Being Scale (JAWS) to investigate affective responses to work stressors. *Journal of Occupational Health Psychology*, 5(2), 219–230. doi: 10.1037/1076-8998.5.2.219. Copyright © 2000 by the American Psychological Association. Adapted with permission.

measure that was also job-specific ("My work makes me feel angry"). Finally, they wanted to ensure they measured the full spectrum of affective states that could possibly be associated with one's job (Van Katwyk et al., 2000). Therefore, **job affective well-being** involves your entire range of feelings—or *affect*—about your job. Try it out: How do you measure on the JAWS (see Figure 8.3)?

Van Katwyk et al. (2000) developed their scale based on Warr's (1987) work on affective well-being and Russell's (1980) general affect model outlining the two dimensions of pleasure and arousal (see Figure 8.4). That is, thinking about your job may bring pleasure or misery to you, or an array of emotions in between these two extremes. Similarly, you may experience high arousal or low arousal (sleepiness), or an array of arousal levels in between these two extremes. For example, excitement would be classified as high pleasure and moderate to high arousal.

When using this general affect model in a work context, Van Katwyk et al. (2000) found that job-related affect was structured into four categories based on Russell's two dimensions of high vs. low arousal and high vs. low pleasure. That is, there are four quadrants of affect: (1) high-pleasurable and low-arousal emotions (HPLA; e.g., content, relaxed); (2) high-pleasurable and high-arousal emotions (e.g., ecstatic); (3) low-pleasurable and low-arousal emotions (LPLA; e.g., indifferent, bored); and (4) low-pleasurable and high-arousal emotions (e.g., hostile, angry); see Figure 8.5.

job affective well-being
Your entire range of feelings or "affect" about how your job makes you feel

FIGURE 8.4

Russell's (1980) Two-Dimensional Model of Affect

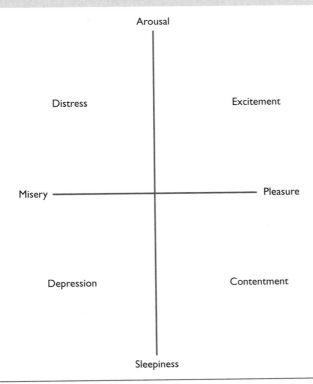

Source: Russell, J.A. 1980. A circumplex model of affect. *Journal of Personality and Social Psychology* 39(6): 1161–1178. Copyright © 1980 by the American Psychological Association. Reproduced with permission.

FIGURE 8.5

Van Katwyk's (2000) Two-Dimensional Model of Job-Related Affective Well-Being (JAWS)

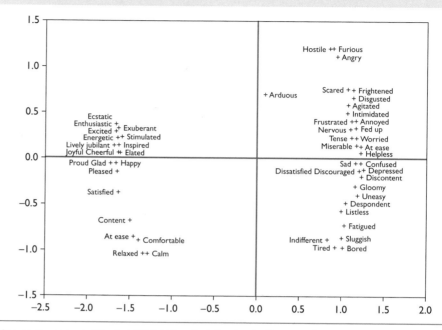

Source: Van Katwyk, P.T., et al. 2000. Using the Job-related Affective Well-being Scale (JAWS) to investigate affective responses to work stressors. *Journal of Occupational Health Psychology* 52(2): 219–230. Copyright © 2000 by the American Psychological Association. Reproduced with permission.

Job affective well-being tends to be related to job satisfaction and job stressors and strain (Van Katwyk et al., 2000). For example, regardless of the arousal level, a high-pleasure affect was related to lower turnover intentions, whereas low pleasure was related to higher intentions to quit. Interestingly, having lower workload, fewer organizational constraints, and interpersonal conflict was associated with high pleasure and low arousal but unrelated to high pleasure and *high* arousal. As expected, these negative work demands also were associated with low pleasure (regardless of arousal level; Van Katwyk et al., 2000).

Unlike the vast amount of research on job satisfaction, as well as the large number of studies looking at affect in general, there has been comparatively little research on context-specific, broad-base affect (i.e., job affect). However, the few studies on the topic tend to be relatively consistent.

Antecedents and Outcomes of Job Affect

In terms of antecedents of job affect, it is probably not surprising that job stressors, such as workplace conflict, tend to be related to negative job affect (Fox, Spector, & Miles, 2001).

Positive affect may be related to performance variables. People who have high positive job affect will be more likely to initiate change at work because they are more emotionally connected to their job. Also, employees with positive job affect are more likely to take more risks and to be more creative in their jobs (Staw & Barsade, 1993). Finally, negative job affect has been shown to be related to increased counterproductive workplace behaviours (both personal and organizational; Fox et al., 2001). Counterproductive work behaviours (CWBs) are behaviours that are intended to hurt either the organization (organizational CWBs) or other employees (personal CWBs). Given the relationships between negative job affect and CWBs, Spector and Fox (2002) proposed that negative job affect will promote CWBs and that positive job affect will promote OCBs. (See Chapter 11 for more on CWBs.)

Job Involvement

Again, think about a job you currently hold or held in the past. Why were you working in this job? Was it a summer job to earn money for your tuition? Was it an internship in which you were learning on-the-job skills that would help you in your career? How much did you care about the work you were doing? How "involved" were you in your job?

Job involvement is the extent to which individuals identify with their work and the importance of work in their self-image (Lodahl & Kejner, 1965). It "implies a positive and relatively complete state of engagement of core aspects of the self in the job" (Brown 1996, p. 235). That is, it is the extent to which you define yourself in terms of your work. For example, imagine introducing yourself at a party. Do you introduce yourself as "John, the accountant" or "Lisa, the lawyer"? Does your job help to define you or is it not really an integral part of who you are?

job involvement
Job involvement is the extent to which you identify with your job and the value you place on it

Antecedents and Outcomes of Job Involvement

Involvement has been associated with several antecedents and outcome variables. In a large meta-analysis on job involvement, Brown (1996) found that ratings of job involvement tended to be related to personality and situational variables. Moreover, involvement was strongly related to job and work attitudes.

The extent to which employees are involved in their jobs tends to be associated with both turnover intentions and actual turnover (Sjoberg & Sverke, 2000). Similarly, Wegge, Schmidt, Parkes, & van Dick (2007) found that low job involvement was associated with total number of days absent from work.

Finally, employees with higher levels of job involvement tend to have higher job performance. For example, Cohen, Ledford, and Spreitzer (1996) found that higher job involvement predicted higher performance in self-managing teams. Moreover, job involvement is even associated with overall firm performance (Gibson, Porath, Benson, & Lawler, 2007).

Recently, we have moved away from the construct of "job involvement" and have looked more into "engagement" (see Chapter 14). However, the research on involvement really helps to bring meaning to the area of job attitudes. Because it is quite broad, the construct of job involvement (Lodahl & Kejner, 1965) may add to our knowledge of employee perceptions of themselves and their work (Kahn, 1990), but may be too general to be of practical use (Harter, Schmidt, & Hayes, 2002).

Organizational Commitment

We've talked about how people may feel about their job and their colleagues. But what about how employees feel about the organization as an entity on its own? Do our views toward our organization affect how we work and how we feel?

Another well-studied area at work is the extent to which workers are committed to their organization (Mowday, Porter, & Steers, 1982). Organizational commitment is the "strength of an individual's identification with and involvement in a particular organization" (Mowday et al., 1979, p. 226). That is, it is the extent to which you are committed to your organization and either want or need to stay with it. Meyer, Allen, and Smith (1993) described organizational commitment as "a psychological state that (a) characterizes the employee's relationship with the organization and (b) has implications for the decision to continue or discontinue membership in the organization" (p. 539).

The construct of commitment may have different components. That is, we may feel committed to an organization for different reasons. For example, have you worked at an organization where you felt "part of the family" and never wanted to leave? Have you had to stay with a company simply because you simply had no other options? In both situations, we say that you are "committed" to the organization, but for different reasons.

affective commitment

Employees' emotional attachment to, identification with, and involvement in the organization

continuance commitment

Commitment based on the costs that employees associate with leaving the organization

normative commitment

Employees' feelings of obligation to remain with the organization

Allen and Meyer (1990) identified and measured three *components* of commitment. **Affective commitment** refers to "employees' emotional attachment to, identification with, and involvement in, the organization" (Allen & Meyer, 1990, p. 1). It involves remaining in the organization because one feels attached to the organization and enjoys membership in it (i.e., you like the organization and you *want to* stay in it). **Continuance commitment** "refers to commitment based on the costs that employees associate with leaving the organization" (Allen & Meyer, 1990, p. 1). It involves staying because there is a perceived cost associated with leaving the organization (i.e., you may not have other employment opportunities, so you feel you *have to* stay with the organization). **Normative commitment** "refers to employees' feelings of obligation to remain with the organization" (Allen & Meyer, 1990, p. 1). It involves staying because one feels an obligation to remain in the organization (i.e., you feel that you *should* stay with the organization because it is the right thing to do). For more on these three dimensions, consult Box 8.8.

Research supports this model of commitment. Some research has shown that affective and normative commitment tend to be highly correlated, such that they are not independent (Hackett, Bycio, & Hausdorf, 1994; Meyer, 1991). For a perspective on developing commitment, see Box 8.9.

Box 8.8

Assessing Affective, Continuance, and Normative Organizational Commitment

Think about the organization in which you work. Using the following scale, indicate the extent to which you agree or disagree with the following statements.

1	2	3	4	5	6	7
STRONGLY DISAGREE	DISAGREE	SLIGHTLY DISAGREE	NEITHER AGREE NOR DISAGREE	SLIGHTLY AGREE	AGREE	STRONGLY AGREE

Affective Commitment	I would be very happy to spend the rest of my career with this organization.
Affective Commitment	I do not feel emotionally attached to this organization.
Affective Commitment	This organization has a great deal of personal meaning for me.
Continuance Commitment	Right now, staying with my organization is a matter of necessity as much as desire.
Continuance Commitment	It would be very hard for me to leave my organization right now, even if I wanted to.
Continuance Commitment	I feel that I have too few options to consider leaving this organization.
Normative Commitment	I would feel guilty if I left my organization right now.
Normative Commitment	This organization deserves my loyalty.
Normative Commitment	I would not leave my organization right now because I have a sense of obligation to the people in it.

Source: Reproduced with permission from the *Journal of Occupational and Organizational Psychology*. © The British Psychological Society.

Box 8.9

Developing Commitment

Given the importance of commitment to reducing absenteeism and turnover, how can organizations increase the commitment of their employees? Obviously, not all commitment components are equally positive. Intuitively, we would like to have employees who *want* to stay with the organization (and not stay simply because they don't have a better offer). Therefore, how do we increase *affective* commitment in organizations? Meyer (1997) identified five mechanisms to help develop affective commitment:

1. *Improved person–environment fit:* Person–environment fit is defined as the match between the characteristics of an individual and an organization (Kristof-Brown, Zimmerman, & Johnson, 2005), and can be broken down into person–job fit and person–organization fit.

Person–job fit can refer to either the match between employees' abilities and the job requirements or the match between what the individual needs and what the job provides (Carless, 2005; Edwards, 1991; Kristof-Brown et al., 2005). *Person–organization fit* refers to the compatibility or match between employee and organizational values (Kristoff, 1996; O'Reilly et al., 1991). When there is a good match between the individual and the job or organization, individuals tend to report higher organizational commitment (O'Reilly et al., 1991).

2. *Met expectations and positive work experiences.* "Met expectations" occur when employees' on-the-job experiences match their pre-entry expectations (Wanous, 1980). Although some research has shown that met

(Continued)

Box 8.9 (continued)

expectations are correlated with increased commitment (Wanous, Poland, Premack, & Davis, 1992), other research found only modest support for this relationship (Irving & Meyer, 1994). Instead, Irving and Meyer (1994) found that commitment was higher among employees who had positive work experiences during the first few months of work, regardless of their expectations.

3. *Attributions about the organization.* These attributions are the extent to which employees feel that the organization is responsible for their positive experiences at work (Meyer & Allen, 1991). That is, positive experiences at work are associated with increased organizational commitment only when employees believe that the organization is actually responsible for those positive experiences (Meyer & Allen, 1991).

4. *Organizational justice and support:* As we saw with the relationship between justice and job satisfaction, when employees feel that the organization treats them fairly and shows concern for their general well-being, they tend to feel greater commitment to the organization (Folger & Konovsky, 1989; Konovsky & Cropanzano, 1991; Meyer, 1997; Sweeney & McFarlin, 1993).

5. *Retrospective rationalization:* Commitment develops based on employees' evaluations of what benefits they will derive from being associated with the organization (Meyer, 1997). If employees determine that they benefit from working for the organization, they will feel more committed.

Source: Reproduced with permission from the *Journal of Occupational and Organizational Psychology.* © The British Psychological Society.

Antecedents and Outcomes of Organizational Commitment

There are a variety of antecedents of affective commitment, including personal characteristics of the employee, job-related characteristics, structural characteristics, and employees' work experiences (Mowday et al., 1982). Similarly, Mathieu and Zajac (1990) proposed several factors that may impact organizational commitment: personal characteristics, job characteristics, group-leader relations, organizational characteristics, and role states.

Interestingly, Meyer (1997) has argued that commitment tends to be "more strongly related to characteristics of the job and work situation than to personal or structural characteristics" (p. 179). That is, commitment doesn't simply measure individual personality traits; instead, it tends to be associated with aspects of one's organization and working conditions. In fact, extensive evidence demonstrates that commitment is associated with important individual and organizational outcomes. However, the pattern of results is different depending on the component of commitment. Therefore, we need to look carefully at the type of commitment.

Absenteeism and Turnover

Of all three components of commitment (i.e., affective, continuance, normative), affective commitment is most highly related to voluntary absence (Hackett, Bycio, & Hausdorf, 1994; Somers, 1995), and the link between affective commitment and absenteeism is stronger when continuance commitment is low (Somers, 1995). That is, if you stay with your organization primarily because you love it (and not because you feel that you "have to" stay because you have no other options), you will be more likely to have a high attendance rate. Interestingly, the highest rates of absenteeism tend to occur with employees who have both low affective commitment (don't want to stay) and low continuance commitment (has other options) (Somers, 1995).

Both affective and normative commitment have been found to be significantly negatively related to turnover and turnover intentions (Chang, Chi, & Miao, 2007; Meyer, Allen, & Smith, 1993; Vandenberghe & Tremblay, 2008; Wagner, 2007). Committed employees tend to have high overall job satisfaction and low intentions to quit (Meyer, Allen, & Smith, 1993). Although some research has found that continuance commitment is negatively related with turnover intentions and turnover (Hackett, Bycio, & Hausdorf, 1994), the evidence is less consistent with this form of commitment (e.g., Somers, 1995). This finding may be due to the nature of continuance commitment, which is that employees feel like they have to stay with the organization. In some cases, organizational commitment has been found to be even a better predictor of turnover than job satisfaction (Shore et al., 1990).

In fact, Meyer (1997) argued that commitment correlates more strongly with turnover than with other consequences of commitment (i.e., job performance, intention to search, intention to leave, attendance, lateness). However, the effect may be stronger with affective and normative commitment. One study found that continuance commitment didn't predict turnover after controlling for the other types of commitment, but it reduced the intensity of the relationship between affective commitment and intent to leave the organization (Somers, 1995).

Individual Well-Being

The extent to which one is committed to the organization may also be related to their personal health. For example, Ostroff and Kozlowski (1992) found a significant negative correlation between commitment and self-reported psychological and physical stress in recent university graduates in their first few months of employment. They also found a significant positive correlation with commitment and adjustment to the work situation. Wittig-Berman and Lang (1990) found a significant negative relationship between commitment and self and other reports of stress and commitment and alienation in a sample of employed MBA students.

Job Performance and OCBs

Mathieu and Zajac (1990) found that intention to search, intention to leave, attendance, lateness, and turnover were consequences of low organizational commitment. Interestingly, job performance had a very weak relationship with organizational commitment, suggesting that despite its significant relationships with other important organizational outcomes, commitment may not influence performance directly.

Commitment is more strongly linked to OCBs (i.e., "extra-role" behaviours) than to job performance (i.e., "in-role" behaviours) because OCBs are discretionary (Meyer, 1997). That is, employees have much more control over whether they engage in OCBs because they aren't part of their formal job descriptions (i.e., the tasks they *have* to do). That is, regardless of their level of commitment, employees still have to do their job task (or risk being fired). However, highly committed individuals may go the extra step by engaging in OCBs.

Meyer, Allen, and Smith (1993) found that affective commitment was related to nurses' self-reports of helping others as well as making effective use of time, and normative commitment was positively related to making effective use of time. However, continuance commitment was not related to either measure of these behaviours.

Commitment to Other Groups and Domains

Although the original focus of organizational commitment was the extent to which employees were committed to their *organization* (Allen & Meyer, 1990; Meyer, Allen, & Smith, 1993), research also has examined commitment to other domains, including one's profession (Blau & Lunz, 1998; Meyer et al., 1993); one's job (Rusbult & Farrell, 1983); one's work group or unit; and organizational change (Herscovich & Meyer, 2002). That is, employees may demonstrate different types of commitment toward different groups.

Becker and Billings (1993) identified four different patterns of commitment toward different groups within the organization. That is, employees can be attached to their supervisor and work group only (local commitment), to top management and the organization (global commitment), or to both local and global groups. Conversely, uncommitted employees are not attached to either local *or* global groups.

Organizational Justice

Have you ever worked in a job in which you thought you were treated poorly? Perhaps you felt that the organization's procedures for figuring out raises were unfair. Perhaps you felt that your supervisor treated you and your coworkers inconsistently, and favoured some subordinates over others. Perhaps you felt that you didn't receive the pay and benefits you really deserved. Basically, you felt that employees were treated unfairly; that is, there was not a lot of organizational justice.

Organizational justice is defined as our perceptions of fairness in the workplace (Greenberg, 1990). How employees are treated within an organization, and how employees perceive how they are treated, have important implications for organizations. Typically, we can talk about three different types of justice: (1) procedural justice; (2) distributive justice; and (3) interactional justice (Cropanzano, Byrne, Bobocel, & Rupp, 2001; Konovsky, 2000).

procedural justice

The perceived fairness of the means by which organizational decisions are made

Procedural justice is the perceived fairness of the means by which organizational decisions are made (Cropanzano & Ambrose, 2001; Leventhal, 1980; Thibaut & Walker, 1975). Leventhal (1980) identified six rules for creating fair procedures. That is, organizations can create fair procedures by ensuring that procedures are (a) consistent; (b) accurate; (c) free from bias; (d) representative of employees' needs (i.e., providing a "voice" to employees by allowing them to express personal opinions and offer input into decisions); (e) correctable; and (f) based on established ethical standards.

Conversely, **distributive justice** involves the perceived fairness of the distribution of economic or socioemotional outcomes (Cropanzano & Ambrose, 2001). That is, employees may view the organizational outcomes as being fair if they are distributed on the basis of one of three rules: (a) equality, (b) equity, and (c) need (Deutsch, 1975, 1985; Kabanoff, 1991):

distributive justice
The perceived fairness of the distribution of outcomes

- *Distribution based on equality* is the belief that all employees should have an equal opportunity to receive rewards regardless of their ability, contributions, tenure, or other job-related factors. That is, everyone should receive the same outcomes (Cropanzano & Ambrose, 2001).
- *Distribution based on equity* is the belief that rewards are distributed equitably when individuals receive outputs that are consistent with the contributions they make to their job (Cropanzano & Ambrose, 2001). Note that equity is not the same as equality, because everyone doesn't receive the same outcome. For example, according to equity theory, employees who work harder or longer hours or are more productive should receive higher salaries. This equity-based distribution has received the most attention in the literature (Cropanzano & Ambrose, 2001; Greenberg, 1982).
- *Distribution based on need* is the belief that rewards should be distributed based on need. That is, employees who have greater needs should receive the most outcomes or compensation (Cropanzano & Ambrose, 2001). Typically, this type of distribution is not prevalent in organizations in Western countries. Distribution based on need is more common in collectivist cultures than individualistic societies.

Obviously, each individual is going to have a different view of what is considered a fair outcome. Their perceptions of fairness will influence how they view the organization.

Finally, **interactional justice** involves the extent to which individuals are treated fairly within an organization (Cropanzano & Ambrose, 2001). Interactional justice can involve two components: (a) interpersonal justice and (b) informational justice:

interactional justice
The extent to which individuals are treated fairly within an organization

- *Interpersonal justice* pertains to interpersonal interactions involving a person in power (typically a supervisor) and subordinates. Employees will perceive higher interpersonal justice when they are treated with respect, dignity, and sincerity and when they are shown concern for their well-being.
- *Informational justice* pertains to the quality and quantity of information employees receive regarding a workplace decision.

Employees will perceive higher informational justice when they receive valid and timely information about their work and the organization. That is, the more information given to employees (and the more accurate the information), the higher their sense of fairness.

For an illustration of organizational justice in practice, refer to Box 8.10.

Antecedents and Outcomes of Organizational Justice

Beyond the moral imperative of treating employees fairly because it is "the right thing to do," why should we be concerned with organizational justice? What is the impact of treating employees fairly?

Treating employees in a fair manner is associated with several positive outcomes, such as increased job satisfaction, performance, organizational commitment, and organizational citizenship behaviour (Fischer & Smith, 2006; Kamdar, McAllister, & Turban, 2006; Weiner, Hobgood, & Lewis, 2008) and lower absenteeism and turnover rates (Dailey & Kirk, 1992). Conversely, if employees feel that they have been treated unfairly, there can be an increase in counterproductive behaviour and aggression (Bechtoldt, Welk, Hartig, & Zapf, 2007; Beugré, 2005).

Treating employees fairly also can benefit employees' health symptoms. For example, Greenberg (2006) examined insomnia among nurses who had received pay cuts. He found that the level of insomnia was significantly lower among nurses whose supervisors had received training in interactional justice, even six months later.

Can we train people to be more "fair"? In two studies, Skarlicki and Latham (1996, 1997) examined whether training leaders and union officers on the skills required to increase organizational justice could improve employees' perceptions of fairness and their level of OCBs. They found that their training did increase employees' perceptions of their leader's fairness as well as OCBs directed toward the organization and toward their coworkers.

Box 8.10

Organizational Justice in Practice

How can we implement what we have just learned about justice into a real organization?

In a classic study on organizational justice, Greenberg (1994) examined the impact of procedural justice on employee acceptance of a smoking ban at work. The more information that employees were given and the more sensitivity that was shown by the organization, the more accepting employees were of the ban. Even when it came to heavy smokers (the group one might expect to be most resistant to such a ban), the more sensitivity shown and information shared, the more they accepted the ban.

People and Work in Canada

Courtesy of Natalie Allen

Courtesy of John Meyer

Natalie Allen and John Meyer

Natalie J. Allen, PhD, is a professor in the Department of Psychology at the University of Western Ontario in London, Ontario, and Director of the TeamWork Lab at Western. Her research interests include the psychology of teams, methodological issues in team research, and the psychology and management of employee commitment. She is a fellow of the Society for Industrial & Organizational Psychology and of the Canadian Psychological Association, and a former associate editor of the *Journal of Occupational and Organizational Psychology*. Dr. Allen's work appears in numerous academic and practitioner journals and she is the co-author, with John Meyer, of *Commitment in the Workplace: Theory, Research and Application* (Sage, 1997).

Dr. John Meyer received his PhD from the University of Western Ontario in 1978. After spending three years at St. Thomas University in Fredericton, New Brunswick, he returned to Western, where he is now a professor and chair of the graduate program in industrial and organizational psychology and director of the Research Unit for Work and Productivity. His research interests include employee commitment, work motivation, leadership, and organizational change. His work has been published in leading journals in the field of I/O psychology (e.g., *Journal of Applied Psychology, Personnel Psychology*) and management (e.g., *Academy of Management Journal, Journal of Management*). He is also co-author of *Commitment in the Workplace: Theory, Research and Application* (Sage Publications, 1997) and *Best Practices: Employee Retention* (Carswell, 2000), and co-editor of *Commitment in Organizations: Accumulated Wisdom and New Directions* (Routledge, 2009). He has consulted with private and public organizations in Canada on issues related to his research, and has been invited to conduct seminars and workshops in Europe, Asia, and Australia. Dr. Meyer is a fellow of the Canadian Psychological Association, the American Psychological Association, and the Society for Industrial and Organizational Psychology, and a member of the Academy of Management. He is a former chair of the Canadian Society for Industrial and Organizational Psychology and co-editor of the OB/HRM section of the *Canadian Journal of Administrative Sciences*.

Summary

Job attitudes are important to study and understand for several reasons. First, many of these attitudes are important in and of themselves; that is, it is important to understand satisfaction and perceived fairness, because we should be concerned about our employees. Second, our attitudes and perceptions influence how we behave at work.

Job satisfaction at work is a well-studied phenomenon, and has been shown to be related to numerous work-related factors and organizationally relevant outcomes. Despite its ubiquity, some researchers have challenged organizations and other researchers to look beyond job satisfaction to more varied job affect. Measures of general job affect (such as the JAWS) assess employees' entire range of feelings or "affect" about how their job makes them feel.

Two other well-studied job attitudes are job involvement and job commitment. Finally, fairness perceptions about the outcomes employees receive, the processes and practices used by the organization, and the treatment received from supervisors and other organizational personnel all influence employees' well-being, their views toward the organization, and their behaviours.

Key Terms

affective commitment 242
continuance commitment 242
distributive justice 247
interactional justice 247
job affect 228
job affective well-being 239
Job Affective Well-Being Scale (JAWS) 238
job attitude 228

Job Descriptive Index (JDI) 230
job involvement 241
job satisfaction 229
Jobs in General Scale 231
Minnesota Satisfaction Questionnaire (MSQ) 232
normative commitment 242
procedural justice 246

Web Links

Many examples of job satisfaction scales are available online. Check out information on the Job Descriptive Index at:

http://www.bgsu.edu/departments/psych/io/jdi/index.html

You also can see an example of the Minnesota Satisfaction Questionnaire at:

http://www.psych.umn.edu/psylabs/vpr/pdf_files/MSQ%201977%20 Long%20form.pdf

The Job Satisfaction Scale, created by Paul Spector at the University of Florida, (includes scoring and norm information) can be found at:

http://shell.cas.usf.edu/~pspector/scales/jsspag.html

Discussion Questions

1. Why are I/O psychologists interested in studying attitudes at work?
2. How does job satisfaction relate to an organization's bottom line through variables such as absenteeism, turnover, and productivity?
3. Job satisfaction can be assessed in many different ways. Describe some of the measures of job satisfaction and their differences from one another.
4. Compare and contrast job satisfaction and job affect. How are these two constructs similar to and different from one another?
5. Consider your last job. Did you experience organizational commitment? If yes, which of the three components of commitments did you experience (i.e., affective, continuance, normative)? Describe how your feelings of commitment affected your decision to remain or not to remain working with that organization.
6. Describe how commitment to one's organization can be related to one's individual well-being and personal health.

Using the Internet

Do organizations care about employees' job satisfaction? If yes, what are they doing to increase satisfaction? Search the Internet to gauge the extent to which job satisfaction is being addressed in organizations.

Consult the APA link to psychological workplace issues for discussions of work attitudes: http://www.apa.org/topics/workplace/index.aspx. Then go to http://www.phwa.org and search for job satisfaction, citizenship behaviours, and involvement for abstracts of research articles on this topic.

Exercises

1. You work as the manager of organizational health for a large national grocery-store chain. In one of your annual employee surveys, you notice that employees are experiencing lower job satisfaction than you have seen in the past. What do you do? Describe some strategies that you could apply to promote job satisfaction among employees. Plan and describe a program of action for the organization.
2. You have been hired as a consultant for an oil company in Alberta to "do something" to improve morale. You have conducted a short survey and have identified that one of the major issues facing employees is that they feel the organization treats them unfairly. Think about the three types of organizational justice (procedural, distributive, and interactional) and create a plan for the organization to improve in this area.

Case

Fast Action Storage & Transfer Company (FAST) is a medium-sized courier company in need of help, and fast. A year ago, management tried to address problems with employee dissatisfaction, low organizational commitment, and high absenteeism and turnover—employees were missing work regularly, and many were quitting their jobs. Management assumed that employees weren't happy in their jobs because their tasks were unclear. In response, they increased the number of managers (assigning one manager to every three employees, up from one to every ten employees). They gave each employee very specific tasks, instead of tasks where they had to problem-solve their own solutions. They also changed the pay system so that instead of being paid an hourly wage based on seniority, employees were paid for their productivity. These changes only seemed to make matters worse: turnover is now up to 23 percent, and no one appears to be happy. Productivity has also decreased by nearly 20 percent.

Discussion Questions

1. Why do the employees seem to be so unhappy, and why are they behaving the way that they are?
2. What did the managers at FAST do wrong, and what can they do to fix their problem?

CHAPTER 9

Motivation

I can get a job, I can pay the phone bills
I can cut the lawn, cut my hair, cut out my cholesterol
I can work overtime, I can work in a mine
I can do it all for you
But I don't want to.

("Enid" by the Barenaked Ladies)

Think about what you are doing at this moment. Why are you reading this textbook? Perhaps a professor has assigned it for you to read for class and will be testing you on the material, so you want to read it for the exam. Is that the only reason? Are you reading it because your professor assigned it? Are you reading it because you want to do well on the exam? Are you reading it because you want to learn the material? Are you reading it because you enjoy it? All these reasons may be different *motivators* for you.

These same types of motivators apply to work. Do you work hard because you need the money? Do you work hard because you love your job? Do you work hard because you don't want to disappoint your boss and team? For example, suppose you work for a management consulting firm. Your boss asks you to stay late to finish a project because the client wants it early. What is your motivation for staying? Do you finish the project because you want to earn extra money? Do you do it because you want to impress the boss (or you don't want to disappoint her)? Do you stay late because you love the project and want to ensure it is perfect?

We also have to differentiate between ability and motivation. Just as is shown in the Barenaked Ladies lyrics above, there is a difference between what we *can* do (i.e., ability) and what we are *motivated* to do or *want* to do (i.e., motivation). This chapter focuses on the motivation aspect of behaviour. See Box 9.1 for an illustration of one company's experience with motivation.

Chapter Learning Outcomes

After reading this chapter you should be able to

- Define the term "work motivation"
- Identify facets of need theories of work motivation

(Source: *Enid*. Words and Music by STEVEN PAGE and ED ROBERTSON © 1994 WB MUSIC CORP. (ASCAP) and TREAT BAKER MUSIC INC. (SOCAN). All Rights Administered by WB MUSIC CORP. All Rights Reserved. Used by permission of ALFRED MUSIC PUBLISHING CO., INC.)

- Define expectancy theory and equity theory
- Understand reinforcement at work
- Differentiate between intrinsic and extrinsic motivation
- Identify the types of motivation in self-determination theory
- Understand the basics of motivational programs
- Apply motivation theories to your own work behaviour

Box 9.1

Motivation and Recognition at Scotiabank's Atlantic Customer Contact Centre

What types of things at work motivate you? What would you like to see as recognition for your hard work? What if you worked at a call centre? Call centres are notorious for being challenging places to work. You are on the phone most of the day, sometimes dealing with upset or irate customers.

Keeping employees healthy and happy may seem to be a daunting task, but Scotiabank's Atlantic Customer Contact Centre, located in Halifax, embraces it. Recognizing its employees is at the core of Scotiabank's values. The company has developed and implemented numerous types of recognition programs to reward and motivate employees.

In fact, the company surveys its employees regularly about the initiatives that motivate them. The Atlantic Customer Contact Centre had been working hard at providing public recognition for its employees, and provided a variety of awards and gift certificates to acknowledge their accomplishments. It even provided catered events for employees to demonstrate how much their efforts were appreciated. Imagine the company's surprise when the 2009 feedback results showed that these types of activities were valued but weren't at the top of the list of what employees wanted! As shown in Table 9.1, employees rated promotions, time off, and money as the top three

TABLE 9.1

What Management Uses and What Employees Rate as Important

Recognition Practice	Employee Rankings of Importance	Practices That Management Use the Most	Gap between Employee Ratings & Management Usage
Job Promotions	1	4	−3
Paid Time Off	2	6	−4
Cash	3	5	−2
Gift Certificates	4	1	3
Additional Training	5	11	−6
Awards/Certificates	6	8	2
Gifts/Merchandise	7	10	−3
Contests	8	3	5
Meeting Senior Management	9	7	2
Public Recognition	10	9	1
Notes/Cards	11	2	9

Source: Reprinted by permission of Mike Desmarais.

important recognition initiatives. However, the Atlantic Customer Contact Centre had these initiatives ranked as numbers 4, 6, and 5, respectively, in terms of frequency of use. The largest gap between what management uses and what employees prefer is notes and cards: Although employees ranked notes and cards as their *least preferred* recognition incentive, managers ranked this initiative as their *second highest used* recognition incentive. Conversely, employees ranked receiving additional training as being important (i.e., their fifth choice), whereas managers ranked this initiative as last on the list.

So, what did Atlantic Customer Contact Centre do? It listened to its people and worked at providing the things that actually motivated employees—additional training and job promotion opportunities, formal recognition initiatives, and increased focus on work–life balance.

That type of responsiveness is why the Atlantic Customer Contact Centre has been recognized as one of Canada's top 50 employers, and consistently (in 2007, 2008, and 2009) achieves highest employee satisfaction among financial institutions as measured by Service Quality Measurement Group. Employees at the Atlantic Customer Contact Centre were extremely proud to receive recognition from the American Psychological Association and the Nova Scotia Psychologically Healthy Workplace Program for their initiatives in creating a healthy workplace.

What Is Work Motivation?

Why do people behave the way they do at work? What motivates them? We always talk about being motivated (or *un*motivated) to do a good job, but what exactly do we mean by "motivation"?

Simply put, "To be motivated means *to be moved* to do something" (Ryan & Deci, 2000, p. 54). **Motivation** involves the energy that an individual applies to work (Pinder, 1998). We can define motivation as an internal set of discretionary, psychological processes that (1) arouse, (2) direct, and (3) maintain attention and behaviour toward attaining a goal (Mitchell & Daniels, 2003).

Mitchell and Daniels (2003) highlighted how these three psychological processes operate:

1. **Arousal** may be brought about by an unfilled need or some discrepancy between your current and desired or expected state.
2. **Direction** is the focus of the arousal, creating a goal, and the resulting behaviour.
3. **Intensity** depends on the importance and attainability of the goal.

These three processes then impact our behaviour (and, ultimately, our performance) in four ways: They focus our *attention* on a particular task, goal, or behaviour. They define the amount of *effort* we put into a task, and how long we *persist* at the task. Finally, they define our *task strategies*, which affect the way we do the task or behaviour (Mitchell & Daniels, 2003).

It is also important to note that motivational levels and motivators vary not only across individuals, but also within individuals (Mitchell & Daniels, 2003). For example, Alec may (in general) have higher levels of motivation than does Tina. However, within their own levels of motivation, Alec may be highly motivated to do parts of his job, but not others. Similarly, Tina may usually have lower levels of motivation, but respond well to the pressure of deadlines to get her work completed. Motivation levels differ not only between these two employees, but also within each person at different times.

motivation

An internal set of discretionary, psychological processes that arouse, direct, and maintain attention and behaviour toward attaining a goal

arousal

Brought about by an unfilled need or some discrepancy between your current and desired or expected state

direction

The focus of arousal, creating a goal, and the resulting behaviour

intensity

The maintenance of attention and behaviour towards attaining a goal; depends on the importance and attainability of the goal

Target Behaviour of Motivation

When we first think about motivating employees, we may typically think in terms of improving productivity or increasing performance in some manner. However, recall from Chapter 8 that we have talked about an expanded view of "outcomes" to include organizational citizenship behaviours (OCBs), which are work behaviours that don't directly support the core job tasks but that support the broader social and psychological context at work (Borman & Motowidlo, 1993; Organ, 1997). In addition to traditional "performance" measures, organizations may be interested in understanding how to motivate these types of behaviours. In fact, Grant (2009) noted that finding ways of motivating employees to be "more helpful and giving—to care about contributing to other people and the organization," or *prosocial motivation*, is one of the primary concerns of many managers (p. 94). Thus, in reading the theories about work motivation, it is important to keep in mind that the target behaviour (or "task" or "activity") may be work-task related, or more broadly defined as prosocial behaviour.

Theories of Motivation

There is "no agreed-upon integrative theory of motivation" (Mitchell & Daniels, 2003, p. 227). Indeed, there are a plethora of theories about what motivates us, and how these motivation processes work. We will explore the more popular ones, using Kanfer et al.'s organizational framework for motivation (Kanfer, 2009b; Kanfer et al., 2008). They identified the three "C's" of work motivation: (1) content; (2) context; and (3) change. That is, the motivation process is affected by the "content (person) and context (situation) domains" as well as by time (i.e., change) (Kanfer, 2009, p. 79). We examine theories that focus on one's underlying, driving needs (i.e., need theories) as well as the more cognitive-based theories (e.g., expectancy theory, goal-setting theory, and self-determination theory). We will also look at how personality is linked to motivation and performance, and we will examine theories that are "external" to the individual (e.g., reinforcement theory).

Need Theories

Need theories are based on the notion that people are striving to fulfill their needs, and this striving involves directed attention, effort, and persistence (Mitchell & Daniels, 2003).

Maslow's (1943) Hierarchy of Needs Theory

Maslow's hierarchy of needs

Five categories of human need arranged in order of importance, such that when basic-level (lower-level) needs are met, higher-level needs emerge and drive behaviour

One of the first theories of general motivation arose almost 70 years ago. **Maslow's hierarchy of needs** theory (1943) outlines five categories of human need, which he arranged in what he considered to be their order of importance. Maslow argued that when basic (i.e., lower-level) needs are met, higher-level needs emerge and drive behaviour (see Figure 9.1). That is, if lower-level needs are not met, according to Maslow the person is dominated by thoughts of meeting these needs (e.g., for a person who is extremely hungry, food is the biggest motivator).

FIGURE 9.1

Maslow's (1943) Hierarchy of Needs

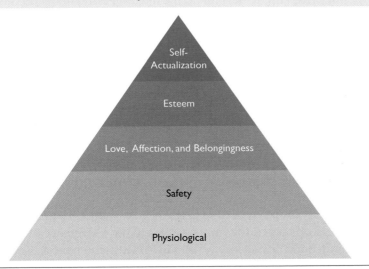

1. *Physiological needs:* Physiological needs include the basic elements of human survival: appetite, thirst, maintaining homeostasis within the body.
2. *Safety needs:* Safety needs involve the need for a safe, orderly, and predictable world and environment, such that the person is motivated to avoid danger, pain, and the unexpected.
3. *Love, affection, and belongingness needs:* These needs involve a need for affectionate relationships with others, both giving and receiving love, and a sense of belonging.
4. *Esteem needs:* Esteem needs entail a need for a stable and high evaluation of oneself, including: (a) *self-esteem* (the desire for strength, achievement, adequacy, confidence, independence, freedom) and (b) *esteem from others* through prestige and gaining respect, recognition, and appreciation from other individuals.
5. *Self-actualization needs:* Finally, the need for self-actualization is the highest category of needs, and it involves the desire to grow and develop in order to become everything one is capable of becoming.

According to Maslow, when all needs are satisfied one can become creative and healthy, but reaching self-actualization is uncommon in society.

Despite the allure of Maslow's theory and the appeal of the need hierarchy, there is very little research to support his theory. This lack of research may be because the early research on his model (conducted in the 1950s and 1960s) failed to find a link between individuals' levels of these needs and their behaviour (Mitchell & Daniels, 2003). Moreover, the "hierarchy" has been criticized because lower-level needs may be "surpassed" in favour of higher-order needs; that is, people may neglect their lower-level needs in order to pursue the higher-level needs. Although it isn't supported by research, Maslow's work provided an interesting foundation from which other need theories, and other areas of motivation, arose.

McClelland's (1961) Need Theory

Two decades after Maslow's theory, McClelland (1961) focused on three specific needs: the need for achievement, the need for affiliation, and the need for power.

need for achievement

The need to be successful and to avoid failure

1. The **need for achievement** involves the need to be successful and to avoid failure; people with a high need for achievement tend to select tasks with a moderate level of difficulty. Conversely, people with a low need for achievement tend to select easy tasks or avoid tasks because of their fear of failure (Mitchell & Daniels, 2003).

need for affiliation

The tendency to want to be liked or accepted by others and to strive for friendship

2. The **need for affiliation** refers to the tendency to want to be liked or accepted by others and to strive for friendship. Employees who have a high need for affiliation tend to avoid competition and to prefer cooperative work environments (McClelland & Watson, 1973).

need for power

The need to stand out publicly in some way, to do something important, or to have influence over others

3. The **need for power** refers to the need to stand out publicly in some way, to do something important, or to have influence over others (McClelland & Watson, 1973). Employees who have a high need for power are more likely to pursue their own goals than to work cooperatively with others.

McClelland's need theory

Three needs (i.e., need for achievement, affiliation, and power) motivate behaviour and performance by directing attention, increasing effort, and increasing persistence

According to **McClelland's need theory**, these three needs can impact behaviour and performance by directing attention, increasing effort, and increasing persistence. For example, McClelland and Boyatzis (1982) found that having a *high* need for achievement, a *high* need for power, and a *low* need for affiliation was predictive of success in a managerial role. They argued that these characteristics allow managers to have an influence over other individuals and to make decisions without worrying about whether subordinates will like them or not.

Baruch, Fenton, Hind, & Vigoda-Gadot (2004) found that need for achievement was associated with increased prosocial behaviour and organizational commitment. They also found a relationship between need for achievement and job performance, but not between need for control and job performance.

Putting McClelland's Need Theory into Action

So how would McClelland's need for achievement, need for affiliation, and need for power actually motivate employees? According to this theory, you would have to know an individual's level of each need to provide appropriate motivators for them. His theory also may suggest that certain people (who have specific needs) may be better suited to particular jobs and job requirements. For example, an employee who has high power needs (and, thus, who may be more competitive) may not be best suited for collaborative teamwork. Employees who are high in need for affiliation may not enjoy being in positions in which they must provide critical reviews of their colleagues' or subordinates' performance. Finally, employees who are high in need for achievement may have higher performance, commitment to the organization, and prosocial behaviours (or citizenship behaviours) toward their colleagues and the organization.

Job Characteristics Theory (JCT) of Motivation

Hackman and Oldham (1976) proposed a model of work motivation that identifies the work conditions "under which individuals will become internally motivated to perform effectively on their jobs" (p. 250). This model was developed to identify means of redesigning jobs to improve motivation, and Hackman and Oldham proposed that employee motivation is a function of the interaction among job characteristics, employee characteristics, and employee's psychological states.

According to this model, job characteristics (in terms of skill variety, task identity, task significance, autonomy, and feedback) create three psychological states (i.e., experienced meaningfulness of the work, experienced responsibility for the outcomes of the work, and knowledge of the actual results of the work activities). These psychological states then lead to several beneficial personal and work outcomes, including work motivation, performance, as well as job satisfaction, and reduced absenteeism and turnover. They argued that intrinsic motivation should be highest when the psychological states are all high (i.e., the employee experiences high responsibility for a meaningful and valuable task and has knowledge of the work results and his or her own effectiveness; Oldham & Hackman, 2010). These relationships are moderated by employee growth and need strength. Moreover, "motivating potential scores" (MPS) can be created for each job to determine the extent to which it can motivate employees. It is a function of the five job components, such that:

$$\text{MPS} = \left(\frac{\text{Skill variety} + \text{Task identity} + \text{Task significance}}{3}\right) \times \text{Autonomy} \times \text{Feedback}$$

This formula allows employers to determine where changes need to be made in order to increase motivation in employees (Hackman & Oldham, 1976). As noted almost 35 years later by Oldham and Hackman (2010), because of the changing nature of work, job characteristics theory's (JCT) focus on job factors may be perceived as a limitation. Moreover, JCT doesn't focus on social factors, which "have become increasingly pervasive in contemporary organizations" (p. 469). However, in their meta-analysis, Fried and Ferris (1987) concluded that the JCT was "reasonably valid" (p. 287), and Oldham and Hackman (2010) argued that the original JCT job factors are still relevant, especially when the focus is on work motivation.

Putting Job Characteristics Theory into Action

Because the focus of JCT is on changing the environment, it has many practical applications for increasing motivation. According to Hackman and Oldham (1976), employers can identify what factors need to be changed, and redesign the jobs accordingly to make the jobs more "motivating." However, there is an underlying assumption that all employees value the same job characteristics to the same degree. To address employee differences in these values, we now turn to Expectancy Theory.

Expectancy Theory

expectancy theory

Posits that people will decide whether to exert effort based on whether they think they are able to perform at a required level, believe their performance will result in the outcome, and value the outcome

valence

How much one *values the secondary outcome* of effort, such as increased pay, or promotion (i.e., "Do I value the outcome of a pay raise?")

instrumentality

How much one believes that a given performance level will initiate secondary outcomes such as increased pay or promotion (i.e., "Will I actually get a pay raise if I finish the project early?")

expectancy

How much one believes that a given level of effort will produce a certain level of performance (primary outcome; i.e., "Even if I try, am I able to complete the project early and to the standards expected of me?")

Expectancy theory was proposed by Victor Vroom (1964), who argued that people will decide whether to exert effort based on how valuable they think the outcomes of such action will be to them. Expectancy theory is sometimes called *VIE theory*, which stands for valence, instrumentality, and expectancy (Vroom, 1964).

According to Vroom, **valence** describes how much one *values the secondary outcome* of effort, such as increased pay or promotion (i.e., "Do I value the outcome of a pay raise?"). **Instrumentality** describes how much one believes that a given performance level will initiate secondary outcomes such as increased pay or promotion (i.e., "Will I actually get a pay raise if I finish the project early?"). **Expectancy** describes how much one believes that a given level of effort will produce a certain level of performance (primary outcome; i.e., "Even if I try, am I able to complete the project early and to the standards expected of me?").

Motivation force arises when deciding whether to exert effort. When making such a decision, individuals consider all three processes: valence, instrumentality, and expectancy. For example, suppose your boss asks you to stay late to create a new ad campaign for one of your most valued clients. You may be more likely to engage in this behaviour if you *value* the outcome of staying late (you may be promoted; i.e., valence); if you believe that staying late and creating a new ad campaign will actually *result* in a promotion (i.e., instrumentality); and if you believe that you have the *ability* to create this new program (i.e., expectancy).

Putting Expectancy Theory into Action

According to expectancy theory, employees will exert effort toward a goal if they believe they have the ability to complete the activity, if they value the reward or outcomes associated with the activity, and if they are confident that they will obtain the reward/outcomes if they successfully complete the activity.

Therefore, managers must first ensure that their employees have the ability to complete the tasks. This means that managers are responsible for selecting the employees with the correct skill set or training employees to ensure they gain the requisite skills. Managers also need to identify what factors are truly motivating for employees. That is, the reward or outcomes must be *valued* by the employees. If managers are offering extra money for working overtime when their employees really want to bank that time to take off later, it will be much more difficult to motivate them to work overtime.

Finally, managers must ensure that the rewards and outcomes always follow the behaviour. If rewards or outcomes are given irregularly (or, worse, promised but never delivered), employees not only will not be motivated to complete the activity, but also may actually have negative views toward the organization and/or manager (see Chapter 8 for more on organizational attitudes). However, expectancy theory deals with employee reactions only to externally driven motivators. Other theories that follow also address the value of increasing internal (or intrinsic) motivation.

Equity Theory

According to **equity theory,** people evaluate the fairness of their situation by comparing the ratio of their own effort and rewards to that of other employees. If the comparison is not equal, people will be motivated to change their behaviour by changing their level of effort and/or outcomes and rewards, changing the comparison other, changing their perceptions, or quitting (Adams, 1965).

For example, imagine you are working at a retail clothing store. You arrive on time every day, work hard throughout the day, and even cover for your coworkers if they aren't doing their jobs. You never complain, and you receive high sales records and commendations from your customers. You are happy with your job. However, one day you find out that all your other coworkers earn $2 an hour more than you do. How does that make you feel? What would you do? According to equity theory, you have several options: (1) You could simply not work as hard (i.e., decrease your level of effort); (2) You could talk to your supervisor about getting a raise (i.e., increase your rewards); (3) You could compare your pay to that of another store, where everyone is paid less than you are (i.e., change your comparison other); (4) You could tell yourself that pay is not really that important to you, and you do the job because you love the work (i.e., change your perceptions); or (5) You could quit.

So, does everyone perceive the same situation in the same manner? That is, if two people are underpaid in the above example, would they both feel the same level of unfairness and be motivated to act in the same way?

People do differ in the extent to which they perceive a situation to be fair or unfair: the difference appears to be due to their level of equity sensitivity (Huseman, Hatfield, & Miles, 1987). Individuals can be categorized along a continuum of benevolents, equity sensitives, and entitleds (King, Miles, & Day, 1993). *Benevolents* tend to be satisfied regardless of reward condition and can tolerate high levels of inequity. *Equity sensitives* tend to respond to underreward negatively and respond to overreward positively, as typically predicted by inequity theory. *Entitleds* prefer to be overrewarded and are likely to value extrinsic reward more highly than intrinsic reward.

Based on these perceptual differences, we would expect that being underpaid may not create the same type of inequity in everyone, and thus not have the same arousal, direction, and intensity to motivate one's behaviour.

Putting Equity Theory into Action

So what are the implications of equity theory to motivating employees? Organizational policies that reward all people equally regardless of their input (i.e., productivity and performance) may have a detrimental effect on motivation (and, ultimately, performance). However, providing rewards based on performance has many challenges. For example, sometimes some aspects of performance are out of the control of the individual (e.g., your sales territory is larger but with fewer customers than your colleague's sales territory, so you must work much harder just to have an equal number of sales). Also, "equity" depends on individual perceptions. That is, you may

equity theory
Posits that people will evaluate the fairness of their situation by comparing the ratio of their own effort and rewards to those of other employees. If the comparison is not equal, people will be motivated to change their behaviour by either changing their level of effort and/or outcomes and rewards, changing the comparison other, changing their perceptions, or quitting

perceive that you worked twice as hard as your colleague (and therefore deserve twice the money), whereas your colleague thinks that the two of you worked equally hard.

Nonetheless, equity theory has important implications for how rewards are allocated, how they are perceived by employees, and the employees' views of the organization (see more on organizational justice in Chapter 8).

Goal-Setting Theory

goal

A level of performance that one wishes to achieve within a certain amount of time

goal-setting theory

A motivation theory based on the idea that most behaviour is the result of people's conscious decisions and intentions

A **goal** is a level of performance that one wishes to achieve within a certain amount of time (Latham & Locke, 2006). Within the motivation literature, we can look specifically at how employees achieve goals. That is, what factors motivate an individual to complete a specific goal? **Goal-setting theory** (Locke & Latham, 1990, 2002; Latham & Locke, 2006) has been very popular with organizations, and it has received a lot of research attention. It is based on the idea that most behaviour is the result of people's conscious decisions and intentions (Mitchell & Daniels, 2003).

Research has shown that when setting goals to achieve at work, difficult and specific goals tend to be associated with better performance than moderately difficult or easy goals, or vague goals such as telling employees to "do your best" (Latham & Locke, 2006; Mitchell & Daniels, 2003). Vague goals allow people to give themselves the benefit of the doubt when judging performance, whereas a clear goal provides a specific measure with which to judge one's effectiveness (Latham & Locke, 2006). Higher performance is typically associated with more difficult goals, as long as goal commitment remains high (Locke, 1997). Refer to Box 9.2 for further insight into goal setting.

However, several conditions are essential for goal setting to be effective: (1) Employees need to receive *feedback* so that they can measure their progress in reaching the goal (Erez, 1977); (2) Employees must be *committed* to the goal (Tubbs, 1994); and (3) Employees must have the required *knowledge and abilities* to achieve the goal (Mitchell & Daniels, 2003).

Box 9.2

How Does Goal-Setting Work in Real Organizations?

In a classic goal-setting study, Latham and Yukl (1975) examine what influenced the performance of logging crews when different goal-setting instructions were used. Of the sample, 24 were educationally disadvantaged crews who hadn't set any specific performance goals in the past, and who had been described as "marginal workers … in that their productivity, absenteeism and turnover are considered by the wood products industry in general to be unsatisfactory" (Latham & Yukl, 1975, pp. 300–301). For these crews, participating in setting goals (i.e., setting them jointly with workers and management) led to higher performance than when they were simply told to do their best. They achieved their goals more frequently and achieved more difficult goals when the goals were set participatively than when they were assigned goals.

So, why does goal setting increase performance? Locke, Shaw, Saari, and Latham (1981) suggest three processes to explain it: (1) Setting goals focuses employees' attention on the accomplishment of the goal, thus increasing the likelihood of goal attainment. (2) Employees who have goals tend to exert more effort, and persist in their tasks and goals despite failures. Again, these actions are more likely to lead to goal attainment. (3) Finally, employees who have set goals tend to develop strategies to achieve these goals, and ultimately improve performance.

(Source: Locke, E., et al. 1981. Goal setting and task performance: 1969–1980. *Psychological Bulletin* 90: 125–152. Copyright © 1981 by the American Psychological Association. Reproduced by permission.)

Box 9.3

Canadian Influence on Motivation Theories

What Motivates These Researchers?

The following people all have three things in common: they are successful researchers, they were born in Canada, and they have made significant contributions to the area of motivation.

Victor Vroom was born in 1932 in Montreal, and currently is at Yale University. In addition to his work on decision making, his research primarily focuses on his expectancy theory (1964). As we noted above, expectancy theory outlines how people will decide whether to exert effort based on (1) whether they think they are able to perform at a required level, (2) whether they believe their performance will result in the outcome, and (3) whether they value the outcome. Vroom has written many articles and several books on motivation, leadership, and decision making. Check out his website at http://www.mba.yale.edu/faculty/profiles/vroom.shtml.

Albert Bandura was born in 1925 in the small northern town of Mundare, Alberta, and worked in the Psychology Department at Stanford University for most of his career. Although Bandura isn't an I/O psychologist, he is well-known for many theories and research areas, two of which are most relevant to our discussion of motivation at work: social learning theory and self-efficacy. His social learning theory—you may recall from your intro psychology class that Bandura conducted the classic Bobo doll study, in which children mimicked acts of violence on an inflatable Bobo doll—had substantial implications for all areas of learning, including how people "learn" at work and how these social factors influence performance.

Bandura's work also has shown the impact of goal setting and self-efficacy on motivation and performance (Bandura & Locke, 2003). For example, individuals with higher levels of self-efficacy show increased perseverance when trying to solve a difficult problem. Moreover, when people achieve a difficult goal, they tend to set subsequent goals that are even more difficult (Bandura & Locke, 2003).

How well-known is Bandura? He has been ranked as the fourth most-frequently cited psychologist of all time (behind B.F. Skinner, Sigmund Freud, and Jean Piaget) (Haggbloom, 2002), and the highest ranked *Canadian* psychologist. You can Google his name to find numerous websites about Bandura and his work.

Gary Latham is the Secretary of State Professor of Organizational Effectiveness and Professor of Organizational Behaviour in the Rotman School of Management at the University of Toronto. He spent his early years conducting research around goal-setting theory. Latham co-authored a book with Edwin A. Locke, entitled *A Theory of Goal Setting and Task Performance*, and was a co-author with Locke and Miriam Erez on a seminal article on understanding the intricacies of goal setting. Find out more about Latham at www.rotman.utoronto.ca/facbios.

Craig Pinder is the Distinguished Professor of Organizational Behaviour at the University of Victoria. He has spent his career studying why people work, as well as the problems and encouragements they face at work. To date, he has written two books on motivation, and he has written many articles on work motivation and human resources management. Find out more at www.business.uvic.ca.

Research has also shown that making a public commitment to a goal is more effective than making a private commitment (Hollenbeck, Williams, & Klein, 1989). Assigned goals can be just as effective as self-set or participatively set goals because they often are assigned by authority figures, who can have an influence on the subordinate's own personal goals and their compliance with assigned goals (Locke & Latham, 1990). (See Box 9.3 for an introduction to Gary Latham and some other prominent Canadian researchers who work in the field of motivation.)

Putting Goal-Setting Theory into Action

Goal-setting theory has several practical suggestions for managers who are looking to increase motivation, goal attainment, and performance:

1. Try to avoid vague goals or simply telling employees to "do their best."
2. Use difficult, but achievable, goals to achieve high commitment.
3. Use specific goals for higher performance.
4. Ensure you provide feedback to employees to help them attain their goal.
5. Try to increase employee commitment to the goal.
6. Understand that goals set jointly by the manager and employee are effective (although assigned goals can be as effective as well).
7. Provide training to employees to ensure they have the requisite knowledge, skills, and abilities to successfully attain the goal.

Reinforcement Theory

One of the basic theories of motivation comes from B.F. Skinner's (1969) work on operant conditioning. We are motivated to engage in behaviours that are reinforced, and to avoid behaviours that are not extrinsically or intrinsically rewarded (or behaviours that are punished).

reinforcement theory

A motivation theory that states we are motivated by the outcomes of behaviour; reinforcers will increase the likelihood of displaying the same behaviour again, while punishment will decrease the likelihood of the behaviour

Komaki, Coombs, and Schepman (1991) described **reinforcement theory** as a motivation theory that emphasizes the outcomes of behaviour; that is, whereas some behavioural consequences will increase the likelihood of displaying the same behaviour again, other consequences will decrease this likelihood.

For example, if you show up late for work, you may be docked pay. The negative consequence (i.e., docking pay) should decrease your behaviour of showing up late for work. Conversely, if you make a successful presentation to your work group, the work group (and hopefully your boss) may praise you and the work you did. This reinforcer (i.e., praise) should increase the likelihood that you engage in those same behaviours again.

reinforcer

Increases the frequency of a desired behaviour; should be presented consistently and frequently in order to be effective

A **reinforcer** (e.g., pay, praise) increases the frequency of a desired behaviour and should be presented consistently and frequently in order to be effective (Mitchell & Daniels, 2003). Organizations typically use two categories of reinforcers: pay or other financial incentives, and feedback and other formal recognition initiatives (Luthans & Stajkovic, 1999). Both financial and non-financial incentives can be equally motivating and have similar effects on performance (Luthans & Stajkovic, 1999). Conversely, a **punishment** (e.g.,

punishment

Decreases the frequency of a undesired behaviour (i.e., arriving late) docking pay) decreases the frequency of an undesired behaviour (i.e., arriving late). However, the problems associated with punishment are well documented: Punishment only decreases a specific behaviour, and it doesn't identify the behaviour you want to occur. Punishment may decrease a behaviour only temporarily when employees think they will be monitored. Finally, punishment can create negative feelings toward the punisher (i.e., both the manager and, by extension, the organization).

The process for rewarding the behaviours that we want and trying to eliminate the behaviours we don't want (i.e., by not reinforcing them, or by punishing them) seems very straightforward. Although reinforcement may appear to be a simple method of increasing behaviour, many times leaders mistakenly reward bad behaviour.

FRANKLY, I WAS EXPECTING SOMETHING A BIT MORE SOPHISTICATED...

Courtesy of Jim Barker, www.jimbarker.net.

Putting Reinforcement Theory into Action

Reinforcement theory has been used in many settings to help increase performance. Managers can use reinforcement theory to understand what motivates employees and how to implement reinforcers into the job and avoid punishment. Managers must first understand what behaviours they want to reward and ensure they aren't inadvertently rewarding the wrong behaviour (see Box 9.4, "Reward Systems at Work," to see how this may happen). Similar to the

Box 9.4

Reward Systems at Work

In his classic article, Kerr (1975; reprinted 1995) argued that many times the reward systems at work (and in government and universities) get "fouled up in that the types of behaviour rewarded are those which the rewarder is trying to discourage, while the behaviour desired is not being rewarded at all" (p. 7).

Kerr provided an example of an insurance company that rewarded "outstanding" employees with a 5 percent raise. Only two employees in each work section could receive this rating. The company also provided "above average" employees with a 4 percent raise. Typically, all workers who were not considered "outstanding" fell into this group. Finally, all employees who "committed gross acts of negligence and irresponsibility for which he or she might be discharged in many other companies" (p. 11) received a 3 percent raise.

If you are interested in improving performance, this method is not particularly successful. The small difference between the 4 percent and 5 percent raise was so negligible (especially compared to the effort required to be one of the chosen two "outstanding" employees per section) that few employees viewed it as a motivator.

In contrast, the organization had a very strict attendance policy such that employees who had three or more incidents of absence or lateness in a six-month period would lose their entire raise. Based on their actions, Kerr argued that it was obvious the company was not rewarding performance (as it had hoped, and indeed assumed, it had been doing). Instead, the company was rewarding attendance only. The reward system was terribly flawed and ineffective.

expectancy theory, managers must ensure that the reinforcer is really viewed as rewarding by employees (e.g., are "Employee of the Month" awards seen as a benefit, or simply as a silly non-achievement that anybody can win). The reinforcer must be applied consistently and fairly so that employees understand that certain behaviours are always rewarded.

Self-Determination Theory

Currently, one of the more popular motivation theories at work is **self-determination theory (SDT)** (Ryan & Deci, 2000). This model builds on the work of Vroom's (1964) expectancy theory and Porter and Lawler's (1968) work on intrinsic and extrinsic work motivation.

Intrinsic motivation involves doing an activity because you find it enjoyable (Gagné & Deci, 2005; Ryan & Deci, 2000). For example, you may cook a gourmet meal not because you "have to" do it, but because you find the actual activity of cooking to be enjoyable. Intrinsic motivation is viewed positively in work situations because the activity is sustained by the individual in the absence of direct, external rewards.

Conversely, **extrinsic motivation** involves doing an activity because some tangible rewards arise from that activity (Gagné & Deci, 2005; Ryan & Deci, 2000). For example, you may not enjoy the actual cooking, but you look forward to the rewards associated with it (i.e., perhaps the respect and praise of your friends and family enjoying the meal, or simply being able to eat good food!). Extrinsic motivation is not necessarily a "bad" thing, it just is more challenging to sustain motivation using extrinsic motivators than when using intrinsic motivators. That is, externally motivated employees need to be externally rewarded before continuing with a task, whereas internally motivated employees will continue the task because they enjoy it.

Research on intrinsic and extrinsic motivation shows that employees may exert more effort over a longer period of time on a task when that task is intrinsically satisfying (Mitchell & Daniels, 2003). Interestingly, providing some types of extrinsic rewards, such as monetary incentives, or extrinsic punishment, such as threats, can actually *decrease* levels of intrinsic motivation (Deci, 1975; Gagné & Deci, 2005). However, extrinsic rewards, such as verbal feedback or praise, tend to increase levels of intrinsic motivation (Deci, Koestner, & Ryan, 1999, 2001), but only if they are given in a supportive manner. That is, positive feedback that is given in a controlling way can decrease motivation (Ryan, 1982; Van den Broeck, Vansteenkiste, & De Witte, 2008).

Other theories, such as self-determination theory (SDT) (Deci & Ryan, 1985, 2000), expand on the intrinsic and extrinsic motivation framework. According to Deci and Ryan (2000), motivation varies not only in intensity, but also in terms of the level of perceived autonomy. That is, people need to feel competent and autonomous to maintain their intrinsic motivation (Gagné & Deci, 2005). **Autonomy** refers to the extent to which individuals freely choose to pursue a specific course of action and "take ownership" of the behaviour.

Therefore, instead of having just two types of motivation (i.e., intrinsic and extrinsic), Deci and Ryan (2000) proposed a range of motivation levels based on the extent to which the motivation is *controlled* or *autonomous*.

FIGURE 9.2

Model of Self-Determination Theory

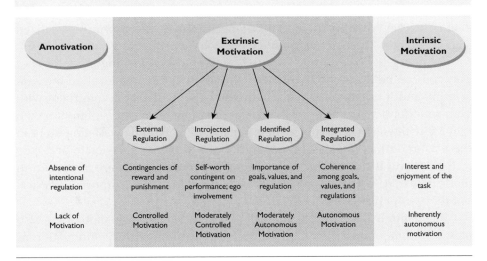

Source: Ryan, R., and Deci, E. 1985. Intrinsic and extrinsic motivations: Classic definitions and new directions. *Contemporary Educational Psychology* 25: 54–67. Copyright © 2000 Elsevier. Reprinted with permission of Elsevier.

As shown in the model (see Figure 9.2), motivation can range from **amotivation** (i.e., the lack of intention or motivation; Deci & Ryan, 2008; Gagné & Deci, 2005) to intrinsic motivation (in terms of **autonomous motivation**), which involves engaging in activities that are integrated into one's identity and sense of self (Deci & Ryan, 2000). When "people engage [in] an activity because they find it interesting, they are doing the activity wholly volitional" (Gagné & Deci, 2005, p. 334). That is, they are *choosing* to do it—not because someone is telling them to, but because they want to. For example, autonomous motivation may involve choosing to stay late to run more analyses on the data, not because someone told you to or because you feel you "should," but because you love conducting statistical analyses.

Extrinsic motivation falls in between the two ends of the continuum. The model makes an important contribution by including a variety of levels of extrinsic motivation in terms of the extent to which it is controlled or autonomous. In contrast to both amotivation and autonomous motivation, **controlled motivation**, or feeling that you are being controlled, is the perception that you "have to" engage in a specific action because of external pressures (Gagné & Deci, 2005).

At one end of the extrinsic levels is **external regulation** (also identified as *controlled motivation*), which refers to motivation that is controlled either by external reward or punishment or by avoidance of shame, contingent self-esteem, or seeking approval such that the individuals feel they have to engage in the activity (Deci & Ryan, 2000; Gagné & Deci, 2005). That is, individuals are motivated to engage in behaviours that would gain external rewards or that would avoid external punishments. For example, you may be motivated to

amotivation

The lack of intention or motivation

autonomous motivation

Engaging in activities that are integrated into one's identity and sense of self

controlled motivation

Feeling that you are *being controlled* and that you "have to" engage in a specific action because of external pressures

external regulation

Motivation that is controlled either by external reward or punishment, by avoidance of shame, or by seeking approval, such that individuals feel that they have to engage in the activity

introjected regulation

Employees internalizing the external controls and evaluating their own worth in terms of their ability to meet some internalized standard; individuals feel pride for completing a task, and guilt for not doing it

identified regulation

Motivation toward behaviour that it is congruent with your self-identity

integrated regulation

Engaging in an activity because the activity is consistent with deeply held values and is seen as a reflection of one's self

study for your exam not because you love the material, but because you want to get an "A+" (and avoid an "F").

The next type of extrinsic motivation along the continuum is **introjected regulation**, which involves employees internalizing the external controls and evaluating their own worth in terms of their ability to meet some internalized standard. That is, individuals would feel pride for completing a task, and guilt for not doing it. For example, you feel pressured into writing a good paper that you can be proud of. **Identified regulation** is the next level on the continuum, and it refers to motivation toward behaviour that is congruent with your self-identity. Gagné and Deci (2005) provided an example of nurses who may view the tasks they do for their patients (e.g., bathing, assisting them in the washroom) as unpleasant, but important to the overall health and care of the patient. If these values (providing high-quality care) are important to them, they may feel that it is their choice to provide such an important service, but they won't necessarily enjoy it.

Interestingly, Deci and Ryan (2000) argued that extrinsic motivation also may be autonomous. They labelled this next level of extrinsic motivation as **integrated regulation**, which involves engaging in an activity because the activity is consistent with deeply held values and is seen as a reflection of one's self. Similar to identified regulation, integrated regulation would involve a value being held closely to one's sense of self, but to a greater degree such that it is "an integral part of who they are, that it emanates from their sense of self and is thus self determined" (Gagné & Deci, 2005, p. 335). Integrated regulation is the most autonomous of the types of extrinsic motivation but there is still a lack of enjoyment of the task, which is the key factor associated with intrinsic motivation.

To summarize, Deci and Ryan's (2000) SDT model outlines a continuum of motivation based on the extent to which behaviour is internalized and is "chosen" by the employee. According to the self-determination continuum, levels of motivation can range from no motivation (i.e., amotivation) to four different levels of extrinsic motivation, and finally to intrinsic motivation (i.e., autonomous motivation).

Amotivation involves no motivation or intent to do the behaviour. *Extrinsic motivation* involves intending to do the behaviour either because (a) you are being rewarded for doing it or punished for not doing it (*external regulation*); (b) you feel pressured to do it so that you feel good about yourself (*introjected regulation*); (c) you choose to do so not because you like the behaviour, but because it is compatible with your values and goals (*identified regulation*); or (d) you choose to do it because you internalize the behaviour such that it is congruent with your self-identity and "who you are" (*integrated regulation*). Finally, *intrinsic (autonomous) motivation* involves intending to do the behaviour because you truly enjoy it (Deci & Ryan, 2000; Gagné & Deci, 2005).

Autonomous Motivation and Outcomes

Several studies have shown that autonomous orientation is related to positive psychological outcomes and effective behavioural outcomes, whereas the controlled orientations have been related to poor psychological well-being and poor functioning. For example, compared to controlled motivation, autonomous motivation tends to lead to higher performance, increased persistence in tasks, and greater psychological health (Deci & Ryan, 2008). Work-related self-determined behaviour (characterized by intrinsic motivation, integrated regulation, and identified regulation) tends to be related to organizational citizenship behaviours, organizational commitment, and organizational involvement and negatively related to deviant behaviours (Trembley, Blanchard, Taylor, Pelletier, & Villeneuve, 2008). Conversely, work-related non-self-determined behaviours (characterized by introjected regulation, extrinsic motivation, and amotivation) tend to be negatively related to citizenship behaviours and positively related to deviant behaviours. All in all, SDT (and specifically autonomous motivation) appears to be useful to predict optimal functioning in terms of employee engagement, high job performance, subjective well-being, and retention (Gagné & Forest, 2008).

Putting Self-Determination Theory into Action

So how can SDT help managers improve motivation and performance? According to the research, managers would probably want employees who are intrinsically motivated (i.e., inherently autonomous motivation)—those employees who are interested in their work tasks and love what they are doing. Obviously, matching employees' skills, interests, and values with work that matches these attributes would increase the likelihood of employees enjoying their work. Managers may also be able to conduct job redesign to provide more meaningful work (and, sometimes, more inherently interesting work). In some cases, the work may have greater meaning and interest, and it is simply a case of making the connections to the end product. In other cases, the role may need to be expanded to provide more potential for meaning and enjoyment.

See Table 9.2 for a summary of the motivation theories discussed in this chapter.

Motivation, Emotion, and Personal Characteristics

One of the fastest-growing areas in the motivation literature involves the role that personality plays in the motivational process (Mitchell & Daniels, 2003). That is, we know that competence in a given area and other situational constraints impact performance. However, even after taking these factors into consideration, personality can influence performance through motivational processes.

For example, conscientiousness has been shown to be related to training performance (Martocchio & Judge, 1997), sales levels (Barrick, Stewart, & Piortowski, 2000), and group performance (Neuman & Wright, 1999). Both extraversion (Barrick et al., 2000) and agreeableness (Neuman & Wright, 1999) have been shown to be related to performance.

Similarly, research has shown that self-efficacy and performance tend to be positively related (Stajkovic & Luthans, 1998). If we evaluate ourselves positively, we tend to have higher performance. This relationship may be because these positive evaluations result in motivational factors such as increased

TABLE 9.2

Overview of Motivation Theories

Theory	Main Components	Critique
Maslow's Hierarchy of Needs Theory	Involves a proposed hierarchy of five categories of human needs: physiological, safety, belonging, esteem, and self-actualization, arranged in what Maslow considered to be their order of importance. He argued that when basic-level (lower-level) needs are met, higher-level needs emerge and drive behaviour.	Despite the popular appeal, there is very little empirical research to support this theory. In some cases, lower level needs may be "surpassed" in favour of higher-order needs
McClelland's Need Theory	Focuses on three needs—need for achievement, affiliation, and power—that McClelland argued direct attention, increase effort, and increase persistence. The implications are that leaders should know followers' level of each need to provide appropriate motivators for them, and that certain people (who have specific needs) may be better suited to particular job tasks.	Again, this theory has a wide intuitive appeal, but there is a lack of empirical support. It may be beneficial in that it highlights the importance of individual differences in needs and motivation. Another limitation is that it may apply only to certain jobs.
Job Characteristics Theory	Identifies the job characteristics that are necessary to help individuals become internally motivated. Focuses on how to redesign jobs to increase motivation.	Doesn't identify social factors that influence motivation. Because of the changing nature of work, the focus on one's "job" may be a limitation.
Expectancy Theory	Posits that people will decide whether to exert effort based on whether they (1) think they are able to perform at a required level, (2) believe their performance will result in the outcome, and (3) value the outcome.	Expectancy theory tends to be very complex and hasn't received a lot of empirical support; "newer" theories have taken precedence. (However, there is more support for reduced conceptualizations of the theory.)
Equity Theory	States that employees evaluate the fairness of situations by comparing the ratio of their own effort and rewards to those of others. If the comparison is not equitable, they will seek to change their level of effort, outcomes, and rewards, their comparison other, their perceptions, or simply will quit in order to restore equity.	Equity theory has received differential support depending on whether the inequitable situation involves underpayment or overpayment.
Goal-setting theory	Based on the idea that most behaviour results from people's conscious decisions and intentions. Specific goals are better than vague goals. Difficult goals lead to higher performance as long as the goal is attainable. Employees need to receive feedback, be committed to the goal, and have the required knowledge and abilities to achieve it.	Although goal setting has been described more as a technique than a theory of motivation, it has received a lot of attention. It may be difficult to maintain over time, and it may lead to competition or to a person focusing on "quantity" over "quality" (although quality can be part of the goals).
Reinforcement Theory	Based on basic learning principles involving reward and punishment: Behaviour that is rewarded tends to increase; conversely, behaviour that is punished (either directly or by withholding reinforcers) tends to decrease (although there are problems with using punishment).	There is a lot of research and support for reinforcement theory. However, it doesn't fully take into account the impact of individual differences (although some argue it is implicit in the definition of reinforcers and punishment), and it may ignore the impact of freedom of choice.
Self-Determination Theory	Differentiates types of work motivation on a continuum of amotivation, extrinsic, introjected, regulated, integrated, and intrinsic (autonomous) motivation.	SDT has become quite popular and it has received a lot of attention recently. However, research has had a difficult time differentiating among the three types of extrinsic motivation, leading to the question of whether it is unduly complicated.

activity level, goal setting, and goal commitment (Erez & Judge, 2001). That is, this relationship may be attributed to increased motivational processes: Compared to individuals with low self-efficacy, individuals with high self-efficacy tend to work harder and longer on tasks (Bandura, 1997). Also, people with high self-efficacy are more likely to set more challenging goals, and to commit to those goals, than people with low self-efficacy (Locke & Latham, 1990).

Self-efficacy and motivation can be influenced by how other people perceive us; that is, we may increase or decrease our motivation to perform a task, and ultimately our performance, based on how others perceive and interact with us. The **Pygmalion effect** refers to a situation in which high expectations are communicated to the employee (typically by a supervisor), which in turn leads to improved self-efficacy and improved performance. Conversely, the **Golem effect** refers to a situation in which low expectations are communicated to the employee (typically by a supervisor), which in turn leads to decreased self-efficacy and performance (Eden, 1992; Mitchell & Daniels, 2003).

Pygmalion effect

May occur when high expectations are communicated to the employee, which leads to improved self-efficacy and improved performance

Golem effect

May occur when low expectations are communicated to the employee, which leads to decreased self-efficacy and performance

Using Personal Constructs in Motivation

In the preceding sections in this chapter, we have highlighted how you can apply the motivational theories to work situations. At first glance, it may seem impossible to have any practical application for personal characteristics and work motivation beyond selecting individuals who have the "right" personalities to be motivated at work. That is, it is unlikely that we would be able to change employees' personalities in order to create higher levels of performance. One area of personal characteristics, however, is particularly useful for managers: improving self-efficacy. As shown

"Mr Frimley, sir, can I have a word about the motivational artwork..."

www.CartoonStock.com

above, self-efficacy is related to a wide range of motivational factors. We also know that how employees are treated in organizations is related to their levels of self-efficacy. Therefore, by improving the self-efficacy of employees, managers may be able to improve activity level, goal setting and commitment, attention to task, and duration focused on task. As shown by the Pygmalian and Golem effects, how managers perceive and treat their employees can translate into real differences in employees' self-efficacy and performance.

Summary

Motivation is a psychological process that involves energy or arousal, a focus of that energy, and the maintenance of one's attention and behaviour toward attaining a goal (Mitchell & Daniels, 2003). That is, motivation is to be *moved* to do some specific behaviour. We can differentiate it from ability, such that ability is what one "can" do, and motivation is what one "wants" to do (or is motivated to do). In this chapter, we explored various theories of motivation to explain how the motivational process works and the factors that may influence motivation. We explored motivation both toward a task and toward more general prosocial behaviour. We also examined each theory in action in terms of how managers would use the components of the theory to motivate employees and increase performance.

Key Terms

amotivation 267
arousal 255
autonomous motivation 267
autonomy 266
controlled motivation 267
direction 255
equity theory 261
expectancy 260
expectancy theory 260
external regulation 267
extrinsic motivation 266
goal 262
goal-setting theory 262
Golem effect 271
identified regulation 268
instrumentality 260

integrated regulation 268
intensity 255
intrinsic motivation 266
introjected regulation 268
Maslow's hierarchy of needs 256
McClelland's need theory 258
motivation 255
need for achievement 258
need for affiliation 258
need for power 258
punishment 264
Pygmalion effect 271
reinforcement theory 264
reinforcer 264
self-determination theory (SDT) 266
valence 260

Web Links

The Daily Motivator:

http://www.greatday.com/

MotivateUs.com:

http://www.motivateus.com/

365 Days of Coaching:

http://www.365daysofcoaching.com/

Top Achievement Steps for Successful Goal-Setting and Achievement:

http://www.selfgrowth.com/articles/Christenbury1.html

How to Set and Achieve your Personal Goals:

http://www.make-your-goals-happen.com/

Discussion Questions

1. Apply each of the motivation theories to your own motivation at school or at work. Which theory do you think best explains your own motivation?
2. What individual or personal characteristics are related to employee motivation and performance in organizations?
3. Assume that a friend has approached you for help with low motivation in school work. Using one or more of the motivational theories described in the chapter, what strategies would you provide to help increase your friend's motivation?
4. Compare and contrast extrinsic and intrinsic motivation. Give examples of times when you have felt either intrinsically or extrinsically motivated in your life.

Using the Internet

Visit http://www.canadastop100.com and look up your region's winners. Who are they? Select three of these organizations. For each organization, answer the following questions:

1. What theories of motivation is each organization using?
2. Why do you believe these strategies are effective?
3. What are some other motivational strategies the organization could incorporate into its business?

Exercises

1. Think back to the insurance organization from Kerr's (1995) article: the company was rewarding attendance, but not performance. (See Box 9.4 for an overview.) What advice would you give this organization as to how to change its reward systems in order to improve motivation and, ultimately, performance?

2. You have been hired as a consultant to help a company with high levels of absenteeism and lateness. You have determined that the problem is likely related to low levels of motivation among employees. What strategies could you implement to motivate employees to arrive to work on time and to avoid absenteeism?

Case

Vancouver contact lens online retailer Coastal Contacts Inc. uses several strategies to motivate its employees. CEO Roger Hardy aims to make the organization's values, such as teamwork and innovation, prevalent throughout the company and adopts a "work hard, play hard" perspective (Spence, 2007). The organization has more than 175 employees worldwide, with the head office in Vancouver and other offices in Singapore, Sweden, and the Netherlands (Coastal Contacts Inc., n.d.). Last year, the company organized a quarterly contest where employees compete to win the right to drive a company-branded Mini Cooper for three months, including gas and parking (Spence, 2007). In addition to this program, employees receive stars or stickers from managers for acts that represent the organization's values, such as generating an innovative idea or exhibiting strong teamwork. Employees who receive five stars within one quarter win an iPod (Spence, 2007). Coastal Contacts Inc. was number 18 on the 2007 Profit 100 list by *Profit* magazine.

Source: Coastal Contacts Inc. (n.d.). The media kit. Retrieved January 26, 2010, from http://www.coastalcontacts.com/about-us.ep; Spence, R. (2007, June). Bright ideas! Electrify your employees and supercharge your sales with the management tactics of Canada's fasted growing companies. Profit. Retrieved on January 26, 2010 from http://www.canadianbusiness.com/entrepreneur/managing/article.jsp?content=20070601_102910_5560&page=1

Discussion Questions

1. What type of motivators is Coastal Contacts using? What motivational theory described in the text is Coastal Contacts applying to motivate its employees?
2. To what extent would Coastal Contacts' motivational strategies motivate you to work harder for the organization?
3. Would you suggest other types of motivators? Why or why not? What further motivational strategies would you suggest to CEO Roger Hardy?

CHAPTER 10

Leadership

This chapter reviews theory and research in I/O psychology related to leadership in organizations. We begin by considering the effects of organizational leadership, and go on to review the development of leadership theories in I/O psychology. We end the chapter by considering some important questions related to leadership in organizations: are leaders born or made, and does leadership vary across culture or gender?

Chapter Learning Outcomes

After reading this chapter you should be able to

- Describe the effects of leadership on a range of organizational and individual outcomes
- Identify the major theories of leadership and their current status
- Answer the question "are leaders born or made?"
- Discuss the effect of gender and culture on leadership style

What Is Leadership?

Although the book stores are filled with books on leadership and prescriptions for how to become a better leader, we rarely think about exactly what "leadership" actually means. Barling, Christie, and Hoption (2010) point to two ways in which we use the term leadership. First, leadership is sometimes used to refer to the emergence of leaders. Who will become the leader of the group or rise to power in an organization? Second, and perhaps more commonly in I/O research, leadership is sometimes used to refer to the relative effectiveness of leadership. Is a particular individual a "good" leader or a "bad" leader? It is this latter definition that has been the focus of most research attention in I/O psychology.

Why Leadership?

Why have organizational researchers been so interested in leadership? Perhaps the simplest answer to this question is that most believe leadership is related to other outcomes we are interested in. Thus, we believe that effective leadership can enhance group processes or job performance and, ultimately, organizational productivity and profitability. Although this belief is widespread, it is useful to take a minute to question whether or not leadership actually affects organizational outcomes.

One problem with studying leadership effectiveness is that we tend to judge whether a leader is effective or not based on the success of the organization he or she leads. Jack Welch, the former CEO of GE Corporation, is widely viewed as a successful leader—based, at least partially, on the fact that GE delivered consistent and positive financial results over a period of 17 years while Welch was at the helm (Byrne, 1998). Yet we often fail to recognize that the success of organizations is most likely due to a multitude of factors. In one longitudinal study, for example, the **charisma** of leaders (CEOs) did not predict organizational financial performance. However, leaders were seen as being more charismatic if the organization they led delivered positive financial returns (Agle, Nagarajan, Sonnenfeld, & Srinivasan, 2008). The tendency to attribute organizational success to the actions of one particular leader has been termed the "romance of leadership" phenomenon (e.g., Meindl, 1995). The success of an organization may have multiple determinants.

Although we should be cautious about attributing too much of organizational success to leadership, there are data linking organizational leadership to a wide range of attitudinal, behavioural, and performance outcomes, and several meta-analyses are available that summarize this information (e.g., Judge & Piccolo, 2004; Lowe, Kroeck, & Sivasubramaniam, 1996).

With regard to employee attitudes, leadership in organizations has been associated with increased trust in the leader (Burke, Sims, Lazzara, & Salas, 2007), satisfaction with the leader (Judge & Piccolo, 2004), commitment to the organization (Barling, Weber, & Kelloway, 1996), turnover intent (Bycio, Hackett, & Allen, 1995), and a wide range of other attitudinal variables. In terms of behavioural outcomes, organizational citizenship behaviours (OCBs) are more likely when the formal supervisor is also a good leader (e.g., Piccolo & Colquitt, 2006). Leadership is also associated with motivation (Dvir, Eden, & Shamir, 2002) and creativity (Shin & Zhou, 2003). Data also consistently link leadership to performance at the individual (e.g., Kirkpatrick & Locke, 1996), group or team (Bass, Avolio, Jung, & Berson, 2003; Lim & Ployhart, 2004; Srivastava, Bartol, & Locke, 2006), and organizational (Barling, Weber, & Kelloway, 1996) levels.

A more recent line of research has begun to document the effects of leadership on individual well-being (for a review, see Mullen & Kelloway, 2010). In summarizing this literature, Kelloway and Barling (2010) recently concluded, "In short, virtually every outcome variable in the field of occupational health psychology is empirically related to organizational leadership." Examples of such outcomes have included psychological (e.g., Arnold, Turner, Barling, Kelloway, & McKee, 2007; Offerman & Hellman, 1996) and physical (e.g. Kivimaki, Ferie, Brunner, Head, Shipley, Vahtera, & Marmot, 2005; Wager, Feldman, & Hussey, 2005) in addition to outcomes related to occupational health and safety (e.g., Barling, Loughlin, & Kelloway, 2002; Kelloway, Mullen, & Francis, 2006; Mullen & Kelloway, 2009; Zohar 2002a, 2002b) and health-related behaviours such as alcohol use (e.g., Bamberger & Bacharach, 2006).

Read Box 10.1 for an analysis of how a serious problem was recently handled by one Canadian leader.

charisma

The ability to influence others simply by strength of character; typically refers to being popular and influential and is often thought of as a personality trait

Box 10.1

A Leader Says, "I'm Sorry"

We often think of leaders as "take charge" people who rarely explain, or apologize for, their actions. In fact, both research and practice suggest that knowing how and when to apologize can be a critical skill for leaders.

Take, for example, the case of Maple Leaf Foods. In June 2008, public health officials in Ontario noticed that more cases of listeria had been reported than usual. In late August, tests conducted by public health officials definitely linked the listeriosis outbreak with meat products produced at a Maple Leaf plant. Later that day, Maple Leaf CEO Michael McCain issued a public apology, accepting full responsibility for the outbreak and announcing the recall of all 220 products produced at the Toronto plant where the contamination originated. At this point, eight people had already died as a result of the listeria infection. Because listeria takes time to manifest itself in its victims, the fallout from the contamination continued to come to light for weeks following the initial recall. In all, at least 22 people lost their lives due to the listeriosis outbreak.

Michael McCain, CEO of Maple Leaf, played a critical role in managing this crisis. Through his apologies and public statements, he became the face of Maple Leaf. Although he delivered the apology personally, he represented the source of Maple Leaf's direction and symbolized the conduct of the organization as a whole. He appeared alone in video announcements to apologize to the Canadian public and accept responsibility for the organization's shortcomings. Because most Canadians did not know who McCain was prior to these events, their perception of him—as a person and, more particularly, as a leader—stem in large part from the behaviour they observed during the recall.

Cannon and Kelloway (2009) had participants view McCain's apologies on YouTube and make ratings of both McCain and Maple Leaf Foods. They found that perceptions of McCain as being sorry (contrition) and taking appropriate action (restitution) were linked to both the perception that McCain was a transformational leader and individual willingness to forgive Maple Leaf and resume buying the company's products. In this case, McCain's apology and leadership may have saved the company and allowed it to return to "normal" operations.

A Brief History of Leadership Theories

Great Man Theories

Perhaps the very earliest approach to understanding leadership was an approach known as the **great man theory** of leadership. In essence, this theory suggested that leaders are born, not made, and that leaders will emerge to suit the needs of the day. According to this view we can best learn about leadership by studying the lives of "great men." Gender issues were not well-recognized, and it is doubtful whether proponents of the approach would have recognized the possibility or existence of "great women." Studying leadership in this approach meant studying the lives of these great men by reading biographies or first-person accounts of their careers. Although this theory is no longer a mainstream approach to leadership, the popularity of biographies of highly successful businesspeople (Welch & Byrne, 2003) suggests its enduring popularity.

great man theory

An early approach to understanding leadership by studying the lives and careers of "great men"

Trait Theories

A natural outgrowth of the great man theories was to focus on the physical or psychological characteristics that differentiated leaders from non-leaders— or good leaders from poor leaders (House & Aditya, 1997). **Trait theories**

trait theories

Leadership theories that focused on the identification of enduring characteristics of leaders (traits) that predicted effectiveness in a leadership role dominated leadership research in the mid-twentieth century, and there is a degree of empirical support for this approach. For example, leadership is positively associated with both height (Judge & Cable, 2004) and intelligence (Judge, Colbert, & Ilies, 2004). Despite these relatively consistent findings, by the 1950s there was general agreement among leadership researchers that there was very little evidence for universal traits that could predict leadership (Barling et al., 2010).

Although the trait approach to leadership was effectively abandoned by 1950, it re-emerged with a resurgence of interest in personality traits (Barling et al., 2010). In general, this research suggests that the "Big Five" model of personality (i.e., agreeableness, conscientiousness, extraversion, neuroticism, and openness to experience) is associated with leadership (Judge et al., 2002). The consistency of these findings suggests that there are individual characteristics, such as personality and intelligence, that predict both leadership emergence and leadership effectiveness.

The emergence of trait theories of leadership was an important evolution, as it suggested that organizations had some control over leadership emergence and effectiveness. That is, if one could identify the "traits" of effective leaders then one could simply select new leaders who had the same traits, and presumably they would also be effective leaders.

Behavioural Theories

The idea that one could identify universal characteristics of leaders that predicted effective leadership eventually gave rise to the **behavioural theories** of leadership. Rather than focusing on personality or physical characteristics, the intent was to identify the specific behaviours that characterized effective leaders. If this attempt was successful, then presumably organizations could not only select leaders who displayed these behaviours, but also train leaders in effective leadership techniques.

A series of studies that became known as the Ohio State studies identified two primary dimensions of leadership behaviour. **Initiating structure** comprised behaviours that resulted in the creation of clear guidelines and procedures. Setting clear goals, scheduling, and defining standards of performance are all examples of initiating structure (e.g., Kerr, Schriesheim, Murphy, & Stogdill, 1974). **Consideration** referred to behaviours that were more focused on people than on task. Showing concern for the welfare of others and acting so as to build respect and trust would be examples of consideration behaviours (Kerr et al., 1974).

Both of these leadership styles were measured by the **Leader Behaviour Description Questionnaire (LBDQ)**. Respondents are asked to rate the frequency with which their leader displayed each of a list of 40 behaviours. Fifteen of the items relate to initiating structure (e.g., "He schedules the work to be done"), with another 15 items referencing consideration (e.g., "He finds time to listen to group members"). Ten of the items comprising the original scale were not scored. Versions of the LBDQ allowed individuals to rate (a) a specific leader (i.e., a supervisor or manager), (b) their ideal leader, or (c) themselves as a leader. The initial hypothesis

behavioural theories

Leadership theories emerging from the Ohio State studies that identified two dimensions (initiating structure and consideration) of effective leadership behaviour

initiating structure

Behaviours that result in the creation of clear guidelines and procedures; setting clear goals, scheduling, and defining standards of performance are all examples of initiating structure

consideration

Behaviours that are more focused on people than on task; showing concern for the welfare of others and acting to build respect and trust would be examples

Leader Behaviour Description Questionnaire (LBDQ)

The measure developed at Ohio State to assess initiating structure and consideration regarding these two types of leadership behaviour was that (a) initiating structure would predict task performance while consideration would predict employee attitudes and satisfaction, and (b) the most effective leadership style would involve high levels of both initiating structure and consideration.

Several problems emerged with the behavioural approach. First, the correlation between initiating structure and consideration was generally quite modest (i.e., $r = .17$; Judge et al., 2004), and indeed sometimes the two dimensions are negatively associated. This would suggest that optimal leadership (high levels of both initiating structure and consideration) rarely occurred in organizations. Moreover, although the Ohio State studies resulted in a great deal of research, the results were not very consistent and often contradicted the hypotheses (e.g., consideration would be negatively correlated with job satisfaction). Eventually, the lack of consistency across studies led to researchers abandoning the search for universal predictors of leadership in favour of contingency theories.

To some extent this decision would now seem to be premature. In their meta-analysis of behavioural leadership research, Judge et al. (2004) present compelling evidence for the validity of the behavioural approach. In particular, they show that previous inconsistencies in findings were a result of methodological problems with the research and that there was quite substantial evidence for the propositions of the behavioural theory. In particular, the available evidence suggests that consideration behaviours are moderately to strongly correlated with attitudinal and morale variables, while initiating structure was associated with task and group performance. In short, the propositions of the behavioural theory of leadership seem to be quite well supported by the empirical data.

Contingency Theories

Partially as a result of results that were seen as lacking in consistency, researchers moved away from universalistic behavioural theories and toward the notion that different leadership styles might be more effective under different conditions. These were known as the contingency or situational theories of leadership, and the two most well-researched theories were Fiedler's contingency theory and the path–goal theory of leadership.

Fiedler's Contingency Theory

Fiedler's (1967) theory is frequently identified as the first true contingency theory of leadership (e.g., Barling et al., 2010). Similar to the behavioural theories, **contingency theory** speaks of leaders who are task-motivated or relationship-motivated. This categorization is determined from an instrument called the **least-preferred coworker scale**, in which leaders are asked to rate the coworker who they like least. Individuals are asked to think about all the people they have worked with and to focus on the one individual with whom they have worked least well. They are asked to rate their least preferred coworker on a series of bipolar items (e.g., Unfriendly 1 2 3 4 5 6 7 8 Friendly). Relationship-motivated individuals are thought to describe their least-preferred coworker

contingency theory

Theory that categorizes leaders into task-motivated or relationship-motivated

least-preferred coworker scale

A measure used in Fiedler's contingency theory. Users were asked to rate the characteristics of the coworker that they like least in more positive terms (and thus score high on the LPC), while task-motivated individuals use more harsh descriptors (and thus score low on the LPC).

However, contingency theory also goes beyond this initial classification to consider three aspects of the situation that Fiedler thought were particularly important: the quality of leader–follower relationships, the clarity of performance goals, and the formal authority or power relationships in the workplace. Fiedler proposed that these three characteristics can be used to rate the situation along a dimension of favourableness. Task-motivated leaders were predicted to be most effective in the extreme situations (i.e., very unfavourable, or very favourable), whereas relationship-motivated leaders were expected to be most effective in the moderately favourable situations. For example, in a crisis or natural disaster leaders might be working with people they do not know, in a situation that is chaotic with little structure (i.e., formal power relationships), and at a time when nobody knows what is going on or what the correct solution is. Fiedler would suggest that in this very unfavourable situation a task-motivated supervisor—someone who focuses on identifying and assigning the most immediate and pressing tasks—would be most effective.

There is fairly good empirical evidence supporting Fiedler's basic proposition. Meta-analyses generally offer support for the notion that different leadership styles are more or less effective in different situations (e.g., Peters, Hartke, & Pohlmann, 1985; Schriesheim, Tepper, & Tetrault, 1994). However, the data are most clearly supportive in laboratory, rather than field, settings (Ayman, McChemers, & Fiedler, 1995), and the lack of consistency has led researchers to look for other explanations of leadership in organizations.

Path–Goal Theory

Path–goal theory (House, 1971) also emerged as a response to the perception that universal behavioural theories were not doing an adequate job of explaining leadership. In essence, **path–goal theory** was based on the premise that the leader's role is (a) to align the goals of the organization and the followers, and (b) to help followers achieve those goals. Leaders could help followers by clarifying the means or path to goal achievement (hence the label path–goal theory), raising followers' sense that they could accomplish the goals and ensuring that followers valued the goals. In articulating these mechanisms, path–goal theory drew directly on the expectancy theories of motivation (see Chapter 9).

Path–goal theory suggested that four leadership styles or categories of leadership behaviour could be used to motivate followers (House & Mitchell, 1974). The four styles were

a. **Participative leadership**: engaging followers in decision making and inviting feedback;

b. **Supportive leadership**: demonstrating concern for the needs of followers

c. **Directive leadership**: providing task structure, clear goals, and contingent feedback, and

path–goal theory

Theory based on the premise that the leader's role is (a) to align the goals of the organization and the followers, and (b) to help followers achieve those goals

participative leadership

One of the four leadership styles identified in path–goal theory; focused on engaging followers in decision making and inviting feedback

supportive leadership

One of the four leadership styles identified in path–goal theory; focused on demonstrating concern for the needs of followers

directive leadership

One of the four styles identified in path–goal theory; focused on providing task structure, clear goals, and contingent feedback

People and Work in Canada

d. **Achievement-oriented leadership**: setting high standards for performance and challenging followers to achieve these standards

(Source: From R.J. House, "A Path Goal Theory of Leadership Effectiveness," *Administrative Science Quarterly*, Vol. XVI (1971): 321–38.)

As a contingency theory, path–goal theory suggests that the effectiveness of these leadership styles varies according to environmental, job, and follower characteristics. This results in a very complex theory that is difficult to test in practice. In their meta-analysis, Wofford and Liska (1993) found support for 6 of the 16 interactions hypothesized in path–goal theory—suggesting, at best, mixed support for the theory. As Barling et al. (2010) note, the very complexity of the theory may make it difficult to adequately test the path–goal theory of leadership.

Substitutes for Leadership Theory

Kerr and Jermier (1978) proposed an additional contingency theory of leadership known as **substitutes for leadership theory** based on the notion that two types of situational variables affect the relationship between leadership and outcomes. **Neutralizers** block the effects of leadership, rendering leadership inconsequential. Substitutes for leadership, on the other hand, make leadership a moot point by "substituting" for any potential effects of leadership. If, for example, an individual is interested in a task and has the ability, training, and experience to perform that task well, then that individual does not need "leadership" to be satisfied and motivated.

As Barling et al. (2010) note, this theory makes intuitive sense and it is therefore surprising that there is a general lack of evidence supporting its propositions (Dionne, Yammarinio, Atwater, & James, 2002). Rather than substituting for leadership, factors such as task motivation and ability seem to have an additive effect—they influence outcomes without diminishing the effect of leadership (Keller, 2006).

Leader–Member Exchange (LMX) Theory

Again, the lack of consistent support for contingency theories of leadership led researchers to consider alternate frameworks. One of the most influential of these is known as leader–member exchange theory, or LMX (Dansereau, Graen, & Haga, 1975; Gerstner & Day, 1997). As implied by the name, LMX focuses on the relationship between the leader and the follower rather than solely on the leaders' behaviour. The quality of leader–member relationships has been assessed by a large number of instruments over the years. Currently the most used measure appears to be a short (six or seven items depending on the version) measure known as the LMX.

An explicit premise of LMX is that leaders and followers influence each other and that it is the quality of leader–member relationships (i.e., mutual liking, loyalty, support, and trust) that is important in predicting outcomes. There is support for this notion. High-quality leader–member relationships are associated with positive outcomes such as employee commitment, satisfaction, and performance (see Gerstner & Day, 1997). Moreover, recent evidence suggests that low-quality relations may lead to retaliation against

achievement-oriented leadership

One of the four leadership styles identified in path–goal theory; focused on setting high standards for performance and challenging followers to achieve these standards

substitutes for leadership theory

Makes leadership a moot point by "substituting" for any potential effects of leadership

neutralizers

Block the effects of leadership, rendering leadership inconsequential

Chapter 10: Leadership

the leaders (Townsend, Phillips, & Elkins, 2000). However, LMX theory also has its difficulties. Leaders and followers, for example, often disagree on the quality of their relationships (Gerstner & Day, 1997)—a particular problem given that it is the quality of the relationship that is most important in LMX. In focusing on the quality of relationship, LMX provides little guidance as to what leaders could, or should, do to enhance the relationship (Barling et al., 2010).

Charismatic Leadership Theory

The sociologist Max Weber (1947) introduced the term *charisma* to refer to the belief among followers that their leaders had exceptional and unusual qualities that set them apart as a leader. Theorists have taken different approaches to understanding charismatic leadership, with some emphasizing the actual behaviours of the leaders (House, 1977) and others emphasizing attributions that followers make about their leaders (Conger & Kanungo, 1998). Charismatic and transformational leadership theories emerged at about the same time and have much in common. Indeed, most commentators have noted that there are only modest differences between the two theories (e.g., Conger & Kanungo, 1998; House and Podsakoff, 1994). Judge and Bono (2000) noted that charismatic and transformational leadership theories were the focus of more leadership research in the 1990s than all other leadership theory combined. See Box 10.2 for perspectives from history on charismatic leadership.

Box 10.2

Was Hitler a Leader?

The vast majority of organizational research assumes that leadership is a "good" thing and that by enhancing organizational leadership we will achieve better outcomes for people and organizations. The often unstated assumption of this view is that leaders will do good things.

Although this is a popular view, we can also think of many counterexamples—that is, leaders who inspire their followers to do things that most of us would find abhorrent. Certainly, Hitler is one of the first names that one thinks of as exemplifying the dark side of charismatic leadership. Jim Jones, founder of the Peoples Temple who in 1978 led 900 people in a mass suicide in Jonestown, Guyana—the largest civilian loss of life in the U.S. prior to Sept. 11, 2001—is another person frequently identified as a charismatic but ultimately evil leader.

In an organizational context the examples are less extreme, but we can think of leaders such as Kenneth Lay, the former CEO of Enron who was convicted of 10 counts of securities fraud and whose name became synonymous with accounting fraud. More recently, financial leaders and investment bankers who continued to receive large bonuses despite driving their firms into near bankruptcy and receiving large financial bailouts from government have been seen as exemplars of corporate greed and unethical behaviour.

How do such people rise to positions of leadership? In their popular book *Snakes in Suits*, Babiak and Hare (2006) argue that psychopathic personalities—individuals essentially without a context—not only are likely to rise through the leadership ranks but also may be particularly successful in organizations precisely because they can seem charming, personable, and charismatic.

Julian Barling

Dr. Julian Barling received his PhD in 1979 from the University of the Witwatersrand, in Johannesburg, South Africa, where he subsequently taught industrial psychology. In 1982, he joined the State University of New York at Stony Brook as a visiting professor of psychology. He joined Queen's University in 1984, initially teaching in the Department of Psychology and moving to the School of Business in 1994, where he is professor of organizational behaviour and psychology. Formerly one of the directors of the executive MBA program, Dr. Barling is currently the associate dean with responsibility for the PhD, MSc, and research programs in the School of Business.

A prolific researcher, Dr. Barling is the author/editor of numerous books and well over 150 articles and book chapters. He is most noted for his contributions to research in unionization, work–family relationships, occupational health psychology, leadership, and workplace aggression. He is the former editor of the *Journal of Occupational Health Psychology*.

Dr. Barling's awards and honours include two "excellence in research" awards, the first from Queen's School of Business in 1995, the second from Queen's University in 1997. A 1996 *Maclean's* magazine survey of Canadian universities named Dr. Barling as one of the most popular professors at Queen's. In 2001, Dr. Barling received the *National Post*'s Leaders in Business Education award. In 2002, the Royal Society of Canada's Canadian Academy of the Sciences and Humanities and Queen's University recognized Dr. Barling's achievements and academic excellence: Dr. Barling was elected to the Royal Society in June and was inducted into the Society in a ceremony at Rideau Hall in November 2002. In the same month, Principal William C. Leggett announced that Dr. Barling had been awarded one of the inaugural Queen's Research Chairs in recognition of his distinguished accomplishments in research and scholarship. In 2008, Dr. Barling was elected a fellow for the Society of Industrial and Organizational Psychology, as well as the European Academy of Occupational Health Psychology, and received Queen's University's award for excellence in graduate student supervision. In 2009, Dr. Barling was elected a fellow of the Association for Psychological Science.

Source: Courtesy of Julian Barling.

Transformational Leadership Theory

Barling et al. (2010) extended this analysis by looking at all leadership research conducted between 1980 and 2007. They found that transformational, LMX, and charismatic (in order of popularity) theories accounted for 63 percent of all leadership research in that period, with transformational leadership theory generating the most research. Initially developed by Burns (1978) and elaborated on by Bass (1985), transformational leadership theory has a great deal of empirical support.

transactional leadership

Based on the notion of an exchange (i.e., a transaction); the focus is on what the leader does in response to followers' behaviour

transformational leadership

Leadership behaviours that go beyond the level of transactions to result in higher levels of performance

laissez-faire leadership

Occurs when the leader has no response to the behaviour of followers

management by exception

A form of transactional leadership that occurs when leaders only take action to correct employee mistakes and failure to meet standards

contingent reward

Setting clear goals for followers and providing immediate and contingent feedback based on follower behaviour. A form of transactional leadership

Transformational leadership theory begins by making a distinction between "transactional" and "transformational" leadership behaviours. **Transactional leadership** behaviours are based on the notion of an exchange (i.e., a transaction)—that is, the focus is on what the leader does in response to followers' behaviour. **Transformational leadership** behaviours are leadership behaviours that go beyond the level of transactions to result in higher levels of performance.

Transactional Leadership

Three forms of transactional leadership behaviours are typically considered. First, **laissez-faire leadership** occurs when the leader has no response to the behaviour of followers. A laissez-faire leader avoids or denies responsibility and refuses to take any action in the workplace. In a very real sense, laissez-faire is "non-leadership."

Management by exception occurs when leaders take action only to correct employee mistakes and failure to meet standards. Management by exception can be either active or passive. In the active form, leaders are actively looking for employee mistakes—engaging in micro-management and constantly checking up on employees to ensure that tasks are performed properly. When mistakes are detected, the management-by-exception leader takes steps to punish followers, which may lead to employees experiencing this form of leadership as abusive (Kelloway et al., 2005). Passive management by exception combines both laissez-faire and management-by-exception behaviours. Leaders engaging in this style do not actively monitor followers or look for mistakes. Rather, they essentially ignore followers until mistakes or errors are so serious that they can no longer be ignored.

Laissez-faire and management by exception are examples of negative transactions. However, transactional leadership can also involve a more positive form of transactions known as **contingent reward** behaviours. Leaders engaging in contingent reward are practising good management in that they set clear goals for followers and provide immediate and contingent feedback based on follower behaviour. They do not ignore mistakes, but neither do they focus solely on the failure to meet standards—rather, they provide both positive and negative feedback as appropriate, based on follower behaviour.

As one might expect, the overall association between laissez-faire and passive management by exception and follower outcomes is negative. Judge and Piccolo's (2004) meta-analytic review found that the more leaders engaged in these behaviours, the less satisfied followers were with both their jobs and their leaders and the less effective the leaders were rated. Kelloway, Mullen, and Francis (2006) extended this observation in their study of workplace safety. They expected to find that leaders who ignored safety concerns (a combination of laissez-faire and passive management by exception they labelled *passive leadership*) would have a neutral effect (i.e., neither good nor bad) on safety outcomes. However, their data showed that passive leadership actually detracted from the safety of the workplace. They speculated that by ignoring safety issues and behaviours, leaders sent the message that safety doesn't matter, and this influenced how followers thought and behaved with regard to workplace safety.

In contrast to these negative associations, contingent reward behaviours were positively associated with follower satisfaction, follower motivation, and both individual and organizational performance (Judge & Piccolo, 2004). Indeed, although contingent reward is classed as a "transactional" leadership behaviour, it is seen by employees as a very positive form of leadership that is closely associated with transformational leadership (Bycio et al., 1995).

Transformational Leadership

Transformational leadership is based on four forms of behaviour (Bass & Riggio, 2006). First, leaders who are concerned with what is best for followers and the organization (i.e., doing the "right" thing rather than taking the easiest course of action) and who create a sense of shared mission are engaging in **idealized influence**. Leaders who act this way build trust and respect among their followers because they can be counted on to go beyond self-interest to do what is right. As Barling et al. (2010) note, a hallmark of idealized influence leadership behaviours is that the leader acts, and is seen as acting, with integrity.

Second, leaders who set high but achievable standards and who encourage followers to achieve more than they thought possible are evidencing **inspirational motivation**. Such leaders encourage followers by telling stories (e.g., about how others have overcome similar obstacles) or by using symbols (think of the rubber "live strong" bracelet worn by Tour de France champion Lance Armstrong). In essence, the use of inspirational motivation enhances followers' sense of self-efficacy and motivation.

Third, leaders who encourage employees to think for themselves, challenge existing beliefs and stereotypes, and try to generate new solutions for longstanding problems are engaging in **intellectual stimulation**. Such leaders encourage creativity and independent thought, thereby facilitating problem solving and enhancing self-confidence among their followers.

Finally, **individualized consideration** is displayed by the leader who pays attention to followers as individuals—recognizing their individual strengths, weaknesses, and needs. These leaders are supportive, have a great deal of empathy for followers, and spend time coaching and assisting followers. In doing so, they enhance the interpersonal relationship with followers.

In one sense there is a great deal of empirical support for transformational leadership theory. Leaders who are rated as being transformational (i.e., displaying the behaviours described above) are seen as more productive, elicit better performance from their followers at the individual, team, and organizational levels, and have followers who are more satisfied with their jobs and their leaders (Judge & Piccolo, 2004). Despite this support, the theory is not without its difficulties.

Perhaps most importantly, transformational leadership theory is typically operationalized using a measure known as the **Multifactor Leadership Questionnaire (MLQ)**. Several meta-analyses have found that the four styles comprising transformational leadership are not easily distinguishable in practice (Bycio, Hackett, & Allen, 1995; Tepper & Percy, 1994). The scales representing these constructs are highly intercorrelated, and in practice researchers

idealized influence

A dimension of transformational leadership; leaders are concerned with what is best for followers and the organization (i.e., doing the "right" thing rather than taking the easiest course of action) and create a sense of shared mission

inspirational motivation

A dimension of transformational leadership; leaders set high but achievable standards and encourage followers to achieve more than they thought possible

intellectual stimulation

A dimension of transformational leadership; leaders encourage employees to think for themselves, challenge existing beliefs and stereotypes, and try to generate new solutions for long-standing problems

individualized consideration

A dimension of transformational leadership; leaders pay attention to followers as individuals, recognizing their individual strengths, weaknesses, and needs

Multifactor Leadership Questionnaire (MLQ)

The most widely used measure of transformational leadership

often combine the four dimensions into one overall measure of transformational leadership.

It is not clear how serious a problem this is for the theory as a whole. Although it has not generally been possible to isolate specific effects for each of the four dimensions of transformational leadership, the theory does seem to identify behaviours that are predictive of desired outcomes. It is possible that the four transformational leadership behaviours naturally occur together. For example, when researchers have experimentally manipulated leadership styles, the scales of the MLQ "pick up" the appropriate distinctions (Kelloway, Barling, & Helleur, 2000).

Nonetheless, ongoing concerns with the inability of the MLQ to separate the dimensions of transformational leadership have led researchers to develop alternative measures (e.g., Alimo-Metcalfe & Alban-Metcalfe, 2001; Carless, 2000; Herold, Fedor, Caldwell, & Liu, 2008; Rafferty & Griffin, 2004). Hopefully the development of new measures will result in more refined testing and understanding of the effects of transformational leadership theory.

Summary of Leadership Theories

Before moving to other questions, it is useful to try to reach some general conclusions about the progress of leadership theory. At first consideration it may seem as if researchers have been going in circles. Early notions that defined leadership in terms of traits or behaviours were abandoned in favour of contingency theories. It now seems clear that both trait and behavioural theories have some validity, whereas in many respects contingency theories did not live up to their initial promise. We suggest that researchers have been moving in a spiral rather than a circle—although we return to similar themes over and over again, each time our knowledge of what constitutes effective leadership is a little more refined and our understanding a little more nuanced.

Although theorists differ in the details, it does seem clear that there are some universal behaviours associated with leadership. Certainly effective leadership involves being concerned with both task performance and relational or "people" issues. It also seems clear that effective leaders may need to shift their focus depending on some characteristics of the situation, although we have not reached the point where we can offer leaders the perfect recipe for when to show concern for tasks versus people. The wealth of available evidence in support of transformational leadership theory speaks to the fact that leadership involves more than simply the ability to manage task performance or relationships. Although these are important skills to master, when we think about what constitutes "leadership" we often find ourselves using the language of transformational leadership theory—speaking of leaders who "inspire," "have vision," and motivate exceptional performance (Kelloway et al., 2000). These behaviours seem central to what it means to be an effective leader.

Negative Leadership

With the exception of management by exception and laissez-faire or passive leadership, most leadership theory has focused on the identification of

People and Work in Canada

effective styles of leadership behaviour. More recently, however, researchers have begun to consider the effects of negative styles of leadership (see, for example, Kelloway et al., 2005; Kelloway, Teed, & Prosser, 2007).

Abusive Leadership

Abusive leadership occurs when individuals in a formal leadership role engage in aggressive or punitive behaviours toward their employees (Tepper, 2000, 2007). These behaviours can vary widely, from leaders degrading their employees by yelling, ridiculing, and name-calling to terrorizing employees by withholding information or threatening employees with job loss and pay cuts.

Such leadership also has been associated with increased levels of employee stress (Offerman & Hellman, 1996) and retaliation (Townsend, Phillips, & Elkins, 2000). Ashforth (1997) found that when abusive supervisors used non-contingent punishment, employees felt a sense of helplessness and alienation from work. Furthermore, Atwater, Dionne, Camobreco, Avolio, and Lau (1998) reported that leadership effectiveness of supervisors in the military is negatively impacted when supervisors resort to non-contingent punishment. Richman, Flaherty, Rospenda, and Christensen (1992) found heightened levels of psychological distress among medical residents who reported to abusive supervisors.

More generally, employees who perceive their supervisors to be abusive experience low levels of job and life satisfaction, lower levels of affective commitment, increased work–family conflict, and psychological distress (Tepper, 2000), as well as psychosomatic symptoms, anxiety, and depression (Hoel, Rayner, & Cooper, 1999). Additionally, Dupre, Inness, Connelly, Barling, and Hoption (2003) found a relationship between teenagers' experience of abusive supervision and their own aggression directed toward their supervisors.

Followers of abusive supervisors are likely to feel unfairly treated, and a great deal of recent data have emerged showing that leaders' unfair treatment of employees is associated with adverse outcomes for employees. In their meta-analysis, Colquitt et al. (2000) reported moderately strong relationships between perceptions of organizational justice and measures of mental health such as job satisfaction and organizational commitment. In a series of prospective studies, Kivimaki and his colleagues (Kivimaki, Elovainio, Vahtera, & Ferrie, 2003; Kivimaki et al., 2007) have identified procedural (organizational) and relational (supervisory) injustice as predictors of minor psychiatric morbidity as well as sick absence. In the well-known Whitehall II studies (e.g., Stansfeld, Fuhrer, Shipley, & Marmot, 2009), data have also emerged suggesting the importance of supervisory injustice as a predictor of psychiatric illness (Ferrie et al., 2009).

The effects of supervisory injustice on well-being are not limited to psychological outcomes. Rather, a growing body of literature points to empirical links between supervisory injustice and a wide range of health-related outcomes including heavy drinking (Kuovonen et al., 2008), impaired cardiac regulation (Elovainio, Leino-Arjas, Vahtera, & Kivimaki, 2006), and use of sick time (Kivimaki et al., 2003). Studies have consistently documented an association

abusive leadership

Occurs when individuals in a formal leadership role engage in aggressive or punitive behaviours toward their employees between supervisory injustice and death from cardiovascular disease (see, for example, Kivimaki et al., 2003, 2005). In one prospective cohort study, employees reporting more favourable experiences of justice at work had a 45 percent lower risk of cardiac death than respondents reporting lower levels of justice (Elovainio et al., 2006). These data are consistent with a growing literature showing the positive effect of supportive and fair social interactions on the cardiovascular system (see Heaphy & Dutton, 2008, for a review), including effects on both systolic and diastolic blood pressure (Brondolo, Rieppi, Erickson, Bagiella, Shapiro, McKinley, & Sloan, 2003; Wager et al., 2003), and strengthened immune systems (Kiecolt-Glaser, McGuire, Robles, & Glaser, 2002).

Unethical Leadership

In the wake of recent corporate scandals, a great deal of interest has been paid to the topic of unethical leadership in organizations. Brown et al. (2005) define ethical leadership as "the demonstration of normatively appropriate conduct through personal actions and interpersonal relationships, and the promotion of such conduct to followers through two-way communication, reinforcement, and decision-making" (p. 120). Unethical leaders would be those who do not adhere to this standard.

Unfortunately, being unethical does not mean that these leaders are ineffective. Rather, researchers have identified a leadership style called **pseudo-transformational leadership** (Hooijberg & Choi, 2000). These are leaders who place their own self-interest above the good of the group. Although they have a powerful ability to motivate and inspire others, they do not care about the welfare of followers and, therefore, may induce them to act against their own best interests.

In their popular book, *Snakes in Suits,* Babiak and Hare (2006) suggest that some leaders may even demonstrate psychopathic tendencies. Such leaders are thought to be incapable of empathy or loyalty to others and are solely focused on achieving their own goals at the expense of others.

pseudo-transformational leadership

When leaders place their own self-interest above the good of the group

Are Leaders Born or Made?

One of the most common questions about leadership is whether leaders are "born," or "made" (Barling et al., 2010). This question involves two separate although related questions. The first relates to how leadership develops or originates in an individual. Is leadership a function of genetic endowment? Acquired through experience? Both? Second, setting aside the question of whether leadership is a function of nature and nurture, the most practical question is whether leadership can be taught. We will address both questions in turn.

Nature versus Nurture

Although most people would probably scoff at the notion that one is, literally, born a leader, there is empirical support for the suggestion that leadership is at least partially a function of genetics. This evidence derives primarily from the Minnesota Twin studies (see Bouchard et al., 1990), and has focused largely on whether genetic heritage can explain whether an individual holds a leadership position in an organization. In the Minnesota Twin studies, researchers compare the characteristics of twins (both identical and non-identical) who were either raised in the same household or raised in different environments (e.g. as a result of adoption). Because we know that twins share the same genetics, comparing the characteristic of twins raised apart and raised separately allows us to determine how much of any similarity is due to genetic or environmental factors.

Arvey et al. (2006) published the first such study based on analysis of 100 identical and 94 non-identical twin pairs taken from the Minnesota Twin Registry. They measured both the hierarchical level of each participant's leadership level in the organization (e.g., executive, senior manager, supervisor) as well as the number of leadership positions each participant held in work-related professional associations. Their analysis showed that (a) twins were very similar in role occupancy. If one held leadership positions in professional associations, the other was likely to also hold similar positions; and (b) approximately 30 percent of the variance in leadership roles was explained by genetic factors even after controlling for personality traits thought to be related to holding a leadership role. These results are striking in suggesting that there is a substantial genetic component to leadership.

The original Arvey et al. (2006) study was based on male twins. However, a subsequent study (Arvey, Zhang, Avolio, & Krueger, 2007) was based on 214 identical and 178 non-identical female twins from the Minnesota Twin Registry and substantially replicated the initial findings. Again twins were similar in their leadership roles, and genetic factors explained a substantial (i.e., 32 percent) amount of variance in the leadership experiences. Strikingly, the amount of variance explained by genetic factors was almost twice the amount explained by work experience (17 percent).

Although these findings suggest a substantial genetic influence on leadership, they also leave lots of room for environmental influences to play a role. One of the most potent sources of environmental influence is one's own family experience. Cox and Cooper (1989) examined the life experiences of successful British CEOs. They showed that more CEOs than one would expect by chance had experienced either separation from a parent or loss of a parent at a very early age. They suggested that individuals who had experienced these losses learned at an early age to take care of themselves and assume responsibility and that these characteristics translated into subsequent success as leaders.

There is more empirical evidence to support the role of family influences on leadership. Hartman and Harris (1992) reported that leaders modelled their behaviour after salient role models and, in particular, their parents. Early family dynamics may also play a role, with parental warmth being positively associated and parental control negatively associated with leadership among young people (Barling et al., 2010). In a direct test of family influences on transformational leadership theory, Zacharatos, Barling, and Kelloway (2000) showed that young athletes who saw their parents displaying transformational leadership behaviours were themselves rated as transformational leaders by others. Taken together, these findings suggest that both genetic and environmental influences play a role in the development of leadership.

Chapter 10: Leadership

Can Leadership Be Taught?

Although the question of how leadership develops is an important one from a scientific standpoint, the more pragmatic question for organizations is whether leadership can be taught. Valid answers to this question can be obtained only from research that is conducted with a high level of methodological rigour. Four fairly recent field experiments have been reported, and in each case the authors report evidence that leadership development activities can result in significant changes in both leadership behaviour and the outcomes associated with leadership.

Barling, Weber, and Kelloway (1996) randomly assigned nine branch managers from a regional bank to the experimental group, and 11 managers to a wait-list control group. Managers all worked within the same geographic area but each worked in a separate branch of the bank. Managers assigned to the experimental group participated in a one-day workshop on transformational leadership. A day after the training, the leaders met with a coach who provided individual feedback based on a 360-degree assessment. During the sessions, the emphasis was placed on the development of specific goals to improve the manager's transformational leadership. Subsequently, the managers met with the coach for three follow-up sessions (one each month for three months), during which goals and progress were reviewed. Managers assigned to the control group received neither the training nor the workshop.

In evaluating the intervention, the authors implemented a comprehensive assessment (Kelloway & Barling, 2000) based on comparison of pre-test and post-test (i.e., three months following training) measures. Barling et al. (1996) demonstrated that (a) subordinate perceptions of managers' transformational leadership increased in the experimental but not the control group, (b) employee attitudes (i.e., affective commitment to the organization) were enhanced in the experimental group but not the control group, and (c) measures of financial performance were enhanced in the experimental but not the control group.

In a subsequent study, Kelloway, Barling, & Helleur (2000) attempted to disentangle the effects of workshop participation and feedback/coaching on the effectiveness of leadership development. Again using a pre-test, post-test design, 40 health care managers were randomly assigned to either a workshop or a training condition in a 2 x 2 factorial design. Results showed that either training or feedback/coaching was an effective means of enhancing subordinate perceptions of transformational leadership but that the interaction of training and feedback did not increase scores above the main effects attributable to the intervention.

In their study of infantry soldiers, Dvir, Eden, Avolio, and Shamir (2002) also focused on the development of transformational leadership. They had seven individuals who were randomly assigned to the transformational leadership condition, which included five days of training, including role-playing exercises, simulations, video presentations, and group, peer, and trainer feedback. Participants in the experimental group also participated in a three-hour booster session after assignment to a leadership position. Comparison with data from a control group suggested that training participants increased both their knowledge of transformational leadership theory constructs and their transformational leadership behaviours as rated by subordinates.

Mullen and Kelloway (2009) further adapted the training program developed by Barling and colleagues (Barling et al., 1996; Kelloway et al., 2000) in their evaluation of a safety-specific management training intervention. They randomly assigned 54 health care managers from 21 organizations to one of three training interventions (general vs. safety-specific) or control group (no training). The general transformational leadership training intervention consisted of a half-day workshop for the managers (Barling, 1996; Kelloway et al., 2000) designed to familiarize managers with the theory of transformational leadership and goal setting. Mullen and Kelloway began by having managers identify the behaviour of the best and worst leaders they encountered. These characteristics were categorized by the training facilitator as being transformational, transactional, or passive leadership behaviours. Managers were provided with an overview of transformational leadership and facilitators worked with participants to develop specific behavioural goals (Locke & Latham, 1984) related to transformational leadership.

The safety-specific training followed a similar format but the focus was on safety issues throughout the training program. Both the general and safety-specific transformational leadership training interventions were standardized in format, length, and method of delivery. The only difference between the two types of training was the experimental manipulation (general vs. safety-specific content). The control group was a wait-list control, the members of which received the safety-specific training at the conclusion of the study.

Mullen and Kelloway (2009) examined data from both the 54 participant leaders and 115 matched respondents in order to assess the effectiveness of the training. They found that participation in training resulted in improvements in leaders' own safety attitudes, intent to promote safety in the workplace, and safety-related self-efficacy. Data from employees also showed that the employees of leaders in the safety-specific transformational leadership group reported (a) enhanced perceptions of their leaders' safety-specific transformational leadership; (b) enhanced perceptions of safety climate and safety participation; and (c) fewer safety-related events and injuries.

Each of these intervention studies was conducted within the framework of transformational leadership. However, in their recent meta-analysis, Avolio, Reichard, Hanna, Walumba, and Chan (2009) provided a more comprehensive review of the effectiveness of leadership interventions. Drawing on data from over 200 studies over a period of more than 50 years based on a variety of leadership theories, Avolio et al. (2009) reported evidence that leadership interventions do in fact work. In 62 of the studies considered, the intervention in question was the development or training of a leader (as opposed to the assignment of a leader or an actor portraying a particular leadership style). The data supported a slightly stronger effect for developmental, as opposed to training, activities, but overall resulted in the conclusion that leadership development was an effective intervention.

Diversity in Leadership

Do Men and Women Lead Differently?

As it relates to leadership, the question of gender is often phrased as whether men and women are equally effective in leadership roles. In general, the data seem to suggest that men and women are equally effective as leaders, although

Chapter 10: Leadership

each is more effective when performing in a gender-typed role. Thus men are more successful when they are in a "masculine role" and women were more successful as leaders in a "feminine" role (Eagly, Karau, & Makhijani, 1995). Although they are equally effective, there may be differences in how men and women lead in organizations. Women leaders tend to be less autocratic and more participative—as a result, they are seen as slightly more transformational than are male leaders (Eagly & Johnson, 1990; Eagly, Johannesen-Schmidt, & van Engen, 2003).

There are clearer differences between men and women when one considers who becomes a leader in organizations. Despite a changing society, men remain far likelier than women to be in leadership roles and the stereotype of women as ineffective leaders persists despite a lack of supporting evidence (Ryan & Haslam, 2007). A number of reasons contribute to this disparity. First, women may hit "glass ceilings" in organizations that prevent their advancement into more senior management positions (Maume, 1999). Second, Ryan and Haslam (2007) proposed that women are now more likely to fall over the "glass cliff." That is, women are more likely to be selected to lead high-risk projects that may be doomed to failure. When the project does fail, it becomes a self-fulfilling prophecy. Third, women may also be less motivated to pursue advancement into senior leadership positions either because they continue to bear a disproportionate amount of family responsibilities or because they are aware of the stereotypes about women as leaders (Davies, Spencer, & Steele, 2005).

Cultural Diversity

With the exception of the contingency theories, most theories about leadership implicitly assume that leadership is universal—what constitutes effective leadership in one culture will also be considered effective in another culture. In its strongest form, this view was expressed by Bass (1997), who wrote "in whatever the country, when people think about leadership, their prototypes and ideals are transformational" (p. 135). See Box 10.3 for a project that focuses on understanding the interplay of leadership and culture.

In contrast to this perspective, several authors have questioned the universality of transformational leadership theory. Shao and Webber (2006) suggested that intellectual stimulation may not be an effective leadership behaviour in China because it clashes with the dominant culture of uncertainty avoidance. Japanese workers have been shown to prefer contingent reward behaviours over transformational leadership (Fukushige & Spicer, 2007). Other researchers have documented substantial differences in preferences for different styles of leadership across cultures (Gerstner & Day, 1994), and even across cultural groups within a country (Ah Chong & Thomas, 1997). For example, contemporary leadership theories emphasize the democratic and participative side of leadership—and encourage leaders to be "collaborators" with their followers. However, in societies with a preference for clearly defined power relationships (e.g., what Hofstede (2001) would call a high "power distance"), this may be seen as weak leadership, and followers might expect their leaders to "take charge" in a more authoritarian way.

Box 10.3

The GLOBE Project

The GLOBE (Global Leadership and Organizational Behaviour Effectiveness) project has a focus on understanding the interplay of leadership and cultures. Researchers from all over the world participated in the project, which was conducted over a 10-year period and involved the collection of data from 17,000 managers in 951 organizations across 62 different societies (House, 2004). With this kind of data, researchers are able to ask questions about the universality of leadership—precisely the question addressed by Den Hartog et al. (1990). These researchers used the GLOBE data to determine whether there are universally endorsed characteristics of leadership. In fact, they identified five such characteristics that seem to be central to the definition of leadership across all cultures: *trustworthiness, justice, honesty, encouraging,* and *positive* are traits that seem to be characteristic of leaders in many cultures. Note that these characteristics are also core descriptors used in transformational leadership theory.

Summary

Leadership is one of the most intensely studied topics in I/O psychology and has been an important area of inquiry for many years. It is also an important area of practice, and many I/O psychologists provide leadership development and coaching services as part of their consulting practice. Our understanding of what constitutes effective leadership has progressed from the "trait" view of the great man theories, through the identification of effective leadership behaviours, the suggestion that leadership may vary by situation, and the development of theories of transformational and charismatic leadership. Currently, issues of gender and cultural diversity are challenging our understanding of what constitutes effective leadership and this is likely to result in an even more refined understanding of leadership dynamics. There is little doubt that leadership research and practice will continue to constitute a focus of I/O psychologists.

Key Terms

abusive leadership 287
achievement-oriented leadership 281
behavioural theories 278
charisma 276
consideration 278
contingency theory 279
contingent reward 284
directive leadership 280
great man theory 277
idealized influence 285
individualized consideration 285
initiating structure 278
inspirational motivation 285
intellectual stimulation 285
laissez-faire leadership 284

Leader Behaviour Description Questionnaire (LBDQ) 278
least-preferred coworker scale 279
management by exception 284
Multifactor Leadership Questionnaire (MLQ) 285
neutralizers 281
participative leadership 280
path–goal theory 280
pseudo-transformational leadership 288
substitutes for leadership theory 281
supportive leadership 280
trait theories 277
transactional leadership 284
transformational leadership 284

Web Links

The Center for Creative Leadership is a non-profit leadership organization and a source of numerous resources related to organizational leadership. They are found at:

http://www.ccl.org/leadership/index.aspx

The Niagara Institute (the Canadian Equivalent of the CCL) can be found at:

http://www.niagarainstitute.com/

Dr. Bruce Avolio, a leading expert in transformational leadership theory, talks about the effects of leadership at:

http://www.foster.washington.edu/centers/leadership/Pages/leadership-footprint-bruce-avolio.aspx

Dr. Kevin Kelloway talks about the potential for leadership development as a means to improve health and safety here:

http://mediasite.colostate.edu/Mediasite/Viewer/?peid=40c8e4c349b849bfbc678b7c6a217cff

Information on the Globe Leadership project can be found at;

http://www.thunderbird.edu/sites/globe/

Discussion Questions

1. Most of the behavioural theories of leadership suggest that the optimal style of leadership combines both initiating structure and consideration (i.e., both task and people orientation). Do you think this is true? Can you think of instances in your own work history when you would have preferred a different type of leader (e.g., one who only demonstrated initiation structure, or only demonstrated consideration)?

2. Some contingency theories of leadership suggested that leaders needed to change their style to suit different circumstances. Fiedler, on the other hand, said that it was very difficult for leaders to change their style and a more effective approach would be to change (e.g., replace) the leader or change the situation. Which do you think is the right approach? Can leaders change their style from situation to situation?

3. One recent trend in organizations is to have "leaderless teams"—groups that work together without any one individual being assigned to the leader role. Do you think it is possible to have a leaderless team? Or will someone always emerge as a leader?

4. A topic of increasing concern of late has been the spiralling rates of executive compensation. The concern is that leaders at the top of large publicly traded companies have been compensated far in excess of their value to the organization. What is "leadership" worth? Should we pay leaders more or less based on their leadership style? Their individual performance? Organizational results?

Using the Internet

Although many of the measures of leadership mentioned in this chapter are copyrighted and cannot be reproduced, some are available on the Web. Search for copies of the LBDQ (behavioural leadership styles) and the LPC (from Fiedler's contingency theory) scales. Complete and score the surveys according to instructions. Do the answers agree? (i.e., if you score high on consideration on the LBDQ, do you also score as relationship motivated on the LPC? Does your initiating structure score on the LBDQ correspond to your level of task motivation on the LPC?)

Repeating the format of the exercise presented in Chapter 2, record your scores and complete both instruments again in a week or two. Have your scores changed, or are the measures consistent over time?

Exercises

1. One of the greatest leaders in recent memory was the American civil rights leader Dr. Martin Luther King, Jr. His most famous speech was the "I have a dream" speech, delivered on August 28, 1963 at the Lincoln Memorial. A recording and transcript of the speech are found at http://www.americanrhetoric.com/speeches/mlkihaveadream.htm. Listen to and read this speech, which is considered one of the most transformational leadership addresses of all time. Can you identify the four elements of transformational leadership in the speech?

2. It seems that every day a new leadership style is identified and the popular management literature describes styles such as "servant leadership," "authentic leadership," and "value-centred leadership." Look up these leadership styles and see how they correspond to the theories of leadership discussed in this chapter. Are these "new" styles of leadership or restatements of what is captured in the academic treatment of leadership?

3. As a class exercise, divide into groups of three or four individuals. Each group is to prepare a speech introducing an individual who is to receive the "leader of the year" award. In your speech you should identify the characteristics or behaviours that led to this person's nomination as leader of the year. How closely do your speeches correspond to the leadership theories discussed in this book?

4. Interview individuals who occupy leadership positions in local organizations (e.g., managers, executives). How did they "learn" to be a leader or develop their leadership style?

Case

Sunjeev Das is an industrial/organizational psychologist employed with CDC Corporation. CDC focuses on leadership issues and, more specifically, executive coaching and assessment. Sunjeev has just spent the day with a new client.

So far he is puzzled. His client, Bob Ramsey, was a very successful CEO. The company he led was outperforming the market and profits were well above the industry average ever since he had taken over. Sunjeev's experience was that Bob was a pleasant, well-spoken, and thoughtful leader. He seemed to be familiar with the major theories of leadership, and he and Sunjeev had spent some time discussing the application of transformational leadership to Bob's initiation of a new division of their company. Bob and Sunjeev were at the airport preparing to fly to the company's head office in another city. The day had gone well, and as they waited for their flight to be called, Sunjeev was reviewing the terms of his assignment.

When Sunjeev had been hired, the Board had mentioned some interpersonal difficulties Bob had experienced. Although they were pleased with the success of the firm, there had been rumblings of discontent from staff and several senior executives had left the firm in recent months. So far, Sunjeev had seen nothing that would lead him to suspect that Bob was anything but a highly effective leader.

Things changed when the airline clerk came over the PA system to announce that their flight had been cancelled due to poor weather. Before the announcement was even finished, Bob was at the counter, visibly enraged. "Are you out of your mind?" he shouted at the clerk. "I don't have all day to fool around with you people, I'll have your job for this. I can't believe that you people are this incompetent." As he continued to berate the stunned clerk, he kicked his suitcase across the floor. Sunjeev watched in shock—suddenly he saw where some of the complaints were coming from. If this was the way Bob handled a minor setback, how would he handle real difficulties at work when they occurred?

Discussion Questions

1. If you are Sunjeev, what do you recommend to the Board?
2. Can and should the organization tolerate Bob's "short fuse" in light of his remarkable success in creating a successful business?
3. What is the likelihood that Bob can learn more effective coping skills to deal with frustrations at work?
4. Will changing this behaviour reduce his effectiveness as a leader?

CHAPTER 11

Counterproductive Work Behaviour

This chapter builds upon previous chapters in this book, which took the position that job performance is a multidimensional construct that is composed of task, contextual, and counterproductive behaviours. The first two aspects of job performance are usually associated with productive employees while the last encompasses those negative behaviours that operate against productivity. Counterproductive work behaviours (CWBs) are voluntary behaviours that violate significant organizational norms and in so doing threaten the well-being of an organization, its members, or both. CWBs range from tardiness and absenteeism through property damage to violence and aggression toward others. This chapter reviews the incidence rates of these behaviours and their costs to organizations, and examines the known causes for such workplace deviance. Finally, it asses the methods used to predict counterproductive workplace behaviours.

Chapter Learning Outcomes

After reading this chapter you should be able to

- Understand the differences and relationships among task performance, contextual performance, and counterproductive work behaviour
- Recognize counterproductive work behaviours as acts designed to intentionally hurt the employing organization or coworkers
- Understand the types of behaviours that comprise counterproductive work behaviours, and the frequency with which they are likely to occur in the workplace
- Distinguish between withdrawal behaviours and those leading to violence
- Recognize workplace bullying as a form of workplace aggression
- Understand the tools used to predict deviant workplace behaviour and their limitations

In Chapter 5 we presented job performance as being complex and multidimensional in character and said it could be broken into three subcategories: task performance, contextual performance, and counterproductive performance. Our discussion focused primarily on task and contextual performance—behaviours

counterproductive work behaviours

Voluntary behaviours that violate significant organizational norms and in so doing threaten the well-being of an organization, its members, or both

that lead to productivity for the organization—and how to measure that performance. A complete discussion of performance must also include behaviours that have negative impacts on organizational effectiveness. Robinson and Bennett (1995) define **counterproductive work behaviours** as "voluntary behaviours that violate significant organizational norms and in so doing threaten the well being of an organization, its members or both" (p. 556).

Examples of CWBs include lying, theft, property damage, violence, engaging in risky behaviours, harassment of coworkers, and sabotage, among others (Gialacone & Greenberg, 1997). Perhaps the most negative work behaviour is withdrawal from the job. This may take the form of complete withdrawal through resignation but also includes partial withdrawal through tardiness,

Profile in I/O Psychology

Gary Johns

Gary Johns (PhD, Wayne State University) is Professor of Management and the Concordia University Research Chair in Management in the John Molson School of Business, Concordia University, Montreal. His research has contributed significantly to our understanding of absenteeism from work. He also has research interests related to presenteeism, personality, job design, self-serving behaviour, research methodology, and the impact of context on organizational behaviour. He has published in all of the top journals in industrial and organizational psychology and is the co-author of *Organizational Behavior: Understanding and Managing Life at Work* (8th edition, Pearson Prentice Hall). He is the recipient of the Academy of Management Organizational Behavior Division's New Concept Award, Society for Industrial and Organizational Psychology's Edwin E. Ghiselli Research

Design Award, the Concordia University Research Award, and the award for the best article published in *Human Relations* in 2007. He is a fellow of SIOP, the American Psychological Association, and the Canadian Psychological Association. He is a former Chair of the Canadian Society for Industrial and Organizational Psychology. He has served on the editorial boards of the *Journal of Organizational Behavior, Journal of Applied Psychology, Organizational Behavior and Human Decision Processes, Journal of Occupational Health Psychology, Human Relations, International Journal of Selection and Assessment,* and *Applied Psychology: An International Review, Academy of Management Journal, Journal of Management, Personnel Psychology, Canadian Journal of Administrative Sciences,* and *Journal of Occupational and Organizational Psychology.* He has held visiting positions at University of Sheffield, University of Oregon, Queensland University of Technology, Australian Graduate School of Management (University of New South Wales), and Hong Kong University of Science and Technology.

Source: Courtesy of Christian Fleury, Van Schmôck et Gros Moineau.

absenteeism, leaving work early, and taking extended breaks. Hanish (1995, 1998) proposed that frustrated employees who cannot engage in withdrawal behaviours may lash out at their employer through counterproductive behaviours such as theft, sabotage, or violence. Regrettably, violence in the workplace has given rise to the term "going postal" after an incident where a U.S. Postal Service worker opened fire on his coworkers, killing one and himself. These workplace incidents are not limited to the postal service or the United States. A number of "going postal" incidents have occurred in Canada, including one at OC Transpo in Ottawa. The causes for these different types of counterproductive behaviours vary. Violence, abuse, and sabotage appear to be most strongly related to anger and stress, while withdrawal appears to be associated with boredom and being upset (Spector, Fox, Penney, Bruursema, Goh, & Kessler, 2006).

Counterproductive work behaviours are intentional acts by employees intended to harm their organization or the people in it. CWBs include acts of both physical and psychological violence (Spector, Fox, & Domagalski, 2006). Estimates of the prevalence of physical and psychological violence in the workplace vary dramatically. A survey of 455 U.S. companies by the Mercer consulting organization in 2008 placed the cost of unscheduled absences at 9 percent of a company's payroll; for a mid-size organization with 1,000 employees whose salaries average $50,000, the cost of unscheduled absences for that company amounts to $4,500,000 per year (Mercer Consulting, 2008). This cost does not include the impact of absence on team performance and coworker morale. Even more dramatic is the cost of workplace violence. A survey of 2,508 representative wage and salary workers in the U.S. workforce found that 6 percent, or nearly 7 million workers in the U.S., had experienced nonfatal physical violence in the workplace, with 41 percent reporting that they had experienced psychological harassment (Schat, Frone, & Kelloway, 2006). In the U.S., Bureau of Labor Statistics data showed that workplace homicides accounted for 631 deaths in 2003 (Schat, Frone, & Kelloway, 2006). Counterproductive behaviours lead, ultimately, to decreases in productivity through loss of efficiency and effectiveness. In the U.S., workplace violence is estimated to cost around US$35 billion per year by the Workplace Violence Research Institute (http://www.workviolence.com).

Productivity is the end result of a complex interaction of task, contextual, and counterproductive behaviours. For example, in highly technical and complex occupations (e.g., air traffic controller), the role of contextual performance to the organizational effectiveness may be less critical than task performance (Griffin, Neal, & Neal, 2000), but counterproductive behaviours on the part of the controller could have devastating consequences. In most cases, contextual behaviours should lead to increases in productivity that are primarily influenced by task behaviour, while counterproductive behaviours detract from it. How individuals differ in terms of knowledge, skill, motivation, and other factors such as personality may determine how they ultimately perform in the workplace. In the remainder of this chapter we will first take a closer look at the different types of CWBs and then follow with a discussion of whether we can predict counterproductive work behaviours and the types of tools that have attempted to do so.

productivity
The end result of a complex interaction of task, contextual, and counterproductive behaviours

Types of Counterproductive Work Behaviours

tardiness
Being late for work

Counterproductive work behaviours include withdrawal behaviours such as **tardiness** (i.e., being late for work); absence (i.e., not showing up for scheduled work) (Johns, 2002); and voluntary turnover (i.e., quitting the job permanently). Withdrawal also includes psychological withdrawal, where employees show up for work on time, do not miss a day of work, and have no intention of quitting, but withhold effort and do not perform to their fullest capabilities. Psychological withdrawal may also take the form of drug and alcohol use in the workplace during working hours. CWBs also include different forms of **workplace deviance** including both psychological aggression and physical violence.

workplace deviance
The voluntary violation of significant organizational norms in a way that threatens the well-being of the organization, coworkers, or both

Withdrawal Behaviours

Tardiness

Tardiness, or being late for work, is more prevalent than previously thought. A survey of 8,000 Canadian workers by CareerBuilder.com (Zupek, 2009) reported that 20 percent said they were late one day per week, with 12 percent late two days a week. The excuses they gave for their lateness were traffic (33 percent), lack of sleep (24 percent), children's school or daycare issues (10 percent), and to a lesser extent lateness was blamed on public transportation, wardrobe issues, or dealing with pets. We present some of the more outrageous excuses offered for lateness in Box 11.1 for your amusement. Laughing aside, time is money and many organizations undertake programs to manage attendance, particularly lateness.

Lateness, or tardiness, is no laughing matter. DeLonzor (2005) estimated lateness costs U.S. businesses more than $3 billion per year in lost productivity, and has a negative impact on those employees who have to pick up the late employee's work. While individual attitudes toward lateness are

---

Box 11.1

Outrageous Excuses for Being Late for Work

If you've decided honesty is not the best policy for you, don't try using any of the following excuses as the reason why you're late—they've been heard before.

1. My heat was shut off so I had to stay home to keep my snake warm.
2. My husband thinks it's funny to hide my car keys before he goes to work.
3. I walked into a spider web on the way out the door and couldn't find the spider, so I had to go inside and shower again.
4. I got locked in my trunk by my son.
5. My left turn signal was out so I had to make all right turns to get to work.
6. A gurney fell out of an ambulance and delayed traffic.
7. I was attacked by a raccoon and had to stop by the hospital to make sure it wasn't rabid.
8. I feel like I'm in everyone's way if I show up on time.
9. My father didn't wake me up.
10. A groundhog bit my bike tire and made it flat.
11. My driveway washed away in the rain last night.
12. I had to go to bingo.

Source: Courtesy of Careerbuilders.com.

---

important (Singer Foust, Elicker, & Levy, 2006; Iverson & Deery, 2001), the organizational climate in which the lateness occurs is important. Blau (1995) argued that some work units develop a culture that tolerates lateness more than others. That is, in some work units, lateness becomes normative behaviour. Individual attitudes predict lateness behaviour of employees in cultures that have a tolerant view of lateness but are constrained by cultures that frown on lateness (Elicker, Singer Foust, O'Malley, & Levy, 2008). These findings suggest that lateness can be managed or reduced through organizational policies that make it clear that lateness is not acceptable and that the organizational culture is one that promotes promptness. Lateness is related to another withdrawal behaviour—absence from work (Johns, 2001; Kozlowsky, Sagie, Krausz, & Dolman Singer, 1997). Employees who are late tend to be those who take unscheduled absences from work, and tend to have more negative impressions of the organization.

Absenteeism

There are many reasons for being absent from work; some of these involve legitimate reasons related to health and family issues where the absence is taken with the employer's knowledge, if not approval, and are of a long-term nature. These types of **absence** are believed not to be under the control of the employee. The forms of absenteeism that fall under counterproductive work behaviours are those of a very short-term nature of one to three days, where the employee does not show up for work when scheduled and calls in with some excuse, including being ill. These distinctions are not always clear, as an organization's sick leave policy has an influence on the extent to which an employee takes leave due to absence (Deery, Erwin, Iverson, & Ambrose, 1995). Mercer Consulting (2008) reported that the employees in the 455 U.S. companies they surveyed averaged 5.3 days of unscheduled absence per year.

> **absence**
>
> Not showing up for scheduled work

Over the years researchers have examined many potential causes for unscheduled absences. One leading suggestion is that some individuals are predisposed or prone to be absent (Johns, 2002). This predisposition may be related to negative affectivity, the extent to which a person experiences negative emotional states across time and situations; absence is seen as a possible coping strategy to deal with the negative affectivity (Hackett & Bycio, 1996). Along these lines, coping with adverse events has been used as a possible explanation for higher absence rates among blue-collar employees; the argument is that they have fewer resources to deal with negative events other than absenteeism. Predisposition may also be related to motivation or conscientiousness, with employees who are low in conscientiousness more likely to be absent compared to those high in that variable (Conte & Jacobs, 2003). As we discussed in Chapter 4, conscientiousness is one of the Big Five personality factors. The development of that model has allowed researchers to obtain more definitive results regarding the role that personality plays in an employee's choice to be absent from work. There is no doubt that situational and organizational factors play a role in absenteeism, making it difficult to isolate the role played by personality. Two fairly recent studies have identified the Big Five factor of extroversion as being positively related to an employee's choice to be absent from work (Darviri & Woods, 2006; Furnham & Bramwell, 2006). Darviri and Woods also found that openness to experience was positively correlated with absence behaviour, while agreeableness was negatively associated with it. Darviri and Woods's results suggest that employees who are outgoing and seek new experiences while not concerned by how others view them are likely to take unscheduled absences. Unlike Conte and Jacobs, these studies did not find a correlation with conscientiousness. The results from all of these personality studies do not establish causal links; employees with exactly the same personality profiles may be the least problematic employees with respect to absence. As well, the results from these personality studies must be viewed cautiously due to the small number of participants in the studies.

Alcohol consumption is another factor that has been assumed to have an impact on employee absenteeism; however, the relationship is poorly understood, as the results from recent studies are inconsistent (Frone, 2008). Bacharach, Bamberger, and Biron (2010) identify two reasons for the inconsistency of these results. First, the relationship between alcohol consumption and absenteeism is assumed to be due to the amount of alcohol consumed and not to the way in which it is consumed. Second, the impact of alcohol consumption on absence behaviour may be moderated by workplace conditions; for example, whether the alcoholics attend work may depend on their relationships with their coworkers and supervisors. In cases where the alcoholic deems the culture to be less tolerant of absenteeism, the employee may show up at work but engage in a minimum of work. Being "present" is used as a screen of poor performance. In a longitudinal study, Bacharach et al. (2010) found that the frequency of drinking, but not the quantity of alcohol consumed, within a month predicted absence from work, but that absence was indeed moderated by perceived support from coworkers and supervisors for the employee's absences.

Another prominent suggestion is that absence is a way to cope with work-related strain; a meta-analysis by Darr and Johns (2008) found a small but significant relationship between absence and work strain. They cited reports that the strain–absence connection cost companies anywhere from $17,400 to $1.13 million a year in direct losses, depending on the size of the company, which do not include costs associated with lost productivity, health insurance claims, legal costs, and overtime wages. Darr and Johns suggested employers give workers more flexibility over the use of their work time, as flextime reduces absenteeism due to non-work factors. They also suggested that more attention be paid to organizational wellness policies as a means of reducing absenteeism. Whatever the reasons, unplanned absences have a dramatic and negative effect on organizational productivity.

Similar to the interaction between organizational culture and lateness, organizational norms play a role in absence behaviour along with individual attitudes and personality. Johns and Nicholson (1982) argued that the set of shared understandings among employees, managers, and people outside the organization about the legitimacy of choosing to be absent from work creates an "absence culture" that determines to a large extent absence behaviour of employees and management's efforts to control it. More recent research has supported Johns and Nicholson's position (Gellatley, 1995; Gellatly & Luchack, 1998; Lau, Au, & Ho, 2003; Xie & Johns, 2000).

Presenteeism

In our discussion of the relationship between alcohol and absenteeism, we mentioned that intoxicated employees might come to work to protect their jobs, that being "present" was a screen to guard against discipline even though they were not productive when physically present. In a sense, it is a complement to absenteeism. **Presenteeism** is a relatively new concept. It is defined as a measure of lost productivity that occurs when employees show up for work but are not fully engaged in their jobs because of personal health and life issues. The employees show up for work out of fear of losing their income or their jobs and may be prone to making catastrophic mistakes as well as transmitting illness among other employees (Böckerman & Laukkanen, 2010). Presenteeism may pose more of a problem than absenteeism. Robertson Cooper (2010) report that 25 percent of 39,000 workers in the U.K. reported going to work while sick. The study argued that presenteeism could have damaging and costly effects on the economy. Ivan Robertson, a managing director of Robertson Cooper, argued that

> To prevent presenteeism, managers should reward people for the work they deliver, not the hours they put in. People should not feel obliged to work long hours to show their commitment and it's desirable if genuinely sick workers feel like they should take time off for everyone's benefit. In the long-term investing in the health and well-being of workers pays dividends in terms of improved employee engagement and productivity. It delivers considerable savings over and above those caused by driving down absenteeism. Most employers focus on reducing absenteeism levels and the associated costs, but often forget that tackling presenteeism is also a significant opportunity to reduce costs and improve productivity. Get both right and the impact on the business can be profound.

presenteeism

A measure of lost productivity that occurs when employees show up for work but are not fully engaged in their jobs because of personal health and life issues

Voluntary Turnover

The most extreme form of employee withdrawal behaviour is **voluntary turnover**, where the employee withdraws completely from the organization. In some cases, the employee's withdrawal may be welcomed by the organization; however, turnover, whether voluntary or involuntary, carries with it considerable costs. The departing employee needs to be replaced, incurring recruiting, selection, and training costs for the replacement. During this period other employees may be asked to work overtime to pick up work that was to be performed by the departing employee. The departure may also lead to withdrawal on the part of the remaining employees, leading to a drop in productivity. There is also likely to be a drop-off in productivity while the replacement is brought up to speed (Sagie, Birati, & Tziner, 2002).

At one time all turnover was thought to be dysfunctional; more recent thinking accepts that turnover of some employees may have positive effects on employee morale, as well as economic benefits associated with lower costs associated with new employees. Some employee turnover may be desirable; the key issue is finding the right level of acceptable turnover. A more important issue may be not how many people are leaving but who is leaving (Dalton & Todor, 1993). Voluntary turnover may have positive effects for

voluntary turnover

Quitting a job permanently

the organization if a poor or dysfunctional employee chooses to leave and if they can be easily replaced. On the other hand, if the best performers are leaving and there is difficulty in finding replacements, then productivity will suffer. Hopefully, a good performance management system will help organizations to identify the good and poor performers and to take action to retain the former and to let the latter go, either voluntarily or involuntarily.

Absenteeism and turnover are positively related at the individual level; that is, the best predictor of turnover is an individual's degree of absenteeism. The higher the level of absenteeism, the more likely an individual will quit a job. Mitra, Jenkins, and Gupta's (1992) meta-analysis of the absence and turnover research found a positive correlation of 0.33, which supported the view that both absence and turnover are aspects of withdrawal. This view suggests that there is a progression from absence behaviour to turnover across time. The meta-analysis, however, left many unanswered questions. Mitra el al. noted that more research was needed to determine the environmental (e.g., market), organizational, and individual conditions under which absenteeism and turnover were related. That research remains unfulfilled.

Workplace Deviance

Workplace deviance generally involves the voluntary violation of significant organizational norms in a way that threatens the well-being of the organization, coworkers, or both (Robinson & Bennett, 1995). Robinson and Bennett (1995) produced a typology of deviant workplace behaviours that classified those behaviours according to whether they were directed against the organization or people and the severity of the action. Table 11.1 presents examples of the four different types of deviant workplace behaviours.

Psychological Withdrawal

production deviance
Primarily passive acts of an employee directed against the organization

psychological withdrawal
Where employees withhold effort and do not perform to their fullest capabilities

Those behaviours listed in the **production deviance** cell of Table 11.1 are typical examples of **psychological withdrawal** from the workplace. They are primarily passive acts of the employee that do not involve other workers. The acts are directed against the organization but are qualitatively different from the more serious "property deviance" behaviours such as actively sabotaging equipment or production. Withdrawal may result from frustration or dissatisfaction at work. Employees who are turned down for a pay raise or promotion may decide not to work as hard as they did in the past to compensate for the denial. Feelings of job dissatisfaction and frustration have been linked to destructive acts (Chen & Spector, 1992).

Workplace Property Deviance

workplace property deviance
Active behaviours of an employee designed to sabotage or damage an organization's property

Because of the illegal nature of **workplace property deviance** acts such as theft and sabotage, it is very difficult to do sound research on this topic. Much of what is known comes from anecdotes and case studies. For example, there is an apocryphal story about a computer programmer in a Montreal company who was responsible for developing its payroll software; he allegedly placed a worm in the program that would destroy the system should his name no longer be listed

People and Work in Canada

Table 11.1

Types of Deviant Workplace Behaviour		
	MINOR	SERIOUS
Interpersonal	*Political Deviance*	*Personal Aggression*
	Showing favouritism	Sexual harassment
	Gossiping about co-workers	Verbal and emotional abuse
	Blaming co-workers	Bullying and mobbing
	Competing nonbeneficially	Stealing from co-workers
		Endangering co-workers
		Violence and aggression
Organizational	*Production Deviance*	*Property Deviance*
	Leaving early	Sabotaging equipment
	Taking excessive breaks	Accepting kickbacks
	Intentionally working slowly	Lying about hours worked
	Wasting resources	Stealing from the company

Source: Robinson, S.L. and R.J. Bennett. 1995. A typology of deviant workplace behavior: A multidimensional scaling study. *Academy of Management Journal* 38: 555–572.

on the payroll. Acts of property deviance are intended to damage a company's reputation, products, or equipment. Ambrose, Seabright, and Schminke (2002) present five reasons why employees may perform acts of sabotage:

1. *Powerlessness or lack of autonomy*—the destructiveness provides the employee with a sense of control.
2. *Organizational frustration*—an emotional state that may lead to destruction of property. For example, an employee may become angry over a lack of resources to do the job properly and engage in the sabotage as a cathartic release.
3. *Facilitation of work*—the goal of the sabotage is to make work easier to accomplish. Employees may change a procedure or use inappropriate tools to get their job done but ignore the fact that the changes in tools or processes may lead to serious consequences.
4. *Boredom/fun*—employees may engage in sabotage to alleviate boredom or to have some fun, for example pulling the fire alarm when there is no fire to see the ensuing disruption of work.
5. *Injustice*—refers to an employee's feeling or belief of having been treated unfairly. It is an attempt to even the score, much as our computer programmer did to the payroll software. Injustice is perhaps the most frequently cited cause of sabotage.

(Source: Ambrose, M., et al. 2002. Sabotage in the workplace: The role of organizational injustice. *Organizational Behavior and Human Decision Processes* 89: 947–965. Copyright © 2002 Elsevier. Reprinted with permission of Elsevier.)

Employee theft is a form of workplace property deviance where the goal is not to destroy property but to steal the organization's property, including

employee theft
A form of workplace property deviance where the goal is not to destroy property but to steal the organization's property, including money, for oneself.

Chapter 11: Counterproductive Work Behaviour

"I've called you all here because of the alarming rise in office equipment thefts."

money, for oneself. The nature of the theft may range from small supply items such as a pack of printer paper to theft of petty cash to embezzlement of corporate or client funds. Wimbush and Dalton (1997) used different techniques to estimate the base rate for employee theft; the different techniques converged on theft rates of more than 50 percent for nontrivial theft. In many cases, organizational effectiveness may be limited by employee theft or misuse of the organization's property or proprietary information, or other forms of dishonesty. The costs associated with such counterproductive behaviour were $2.3 billion in the Canadian retail sector for 1999, an increase of 21 percent from 1997. The average amount stolen by employees, $450, is now more than triple the average amount, $116, lost through customer theft. In 1999, Dylex Ltd., a major Canadian retail chain, was forced to take a $25-million writedown, partly because of employee theft (Strauss, 2000). In the U.S., national retail surveys attribute 43 percent of inventory "shrinkage" to employee theft (Fortman, Leslie, & Cunningham, 2002). In response to this problem, many retailers have established "loss prevention" departments; they have emphasized employee training and workplace improvements as well as installing procedures for controlling inventory. Many organizations have also initiated programs designed to select people who are not only capable of doing the job but also are honest, reliable, or of high integrity.

Interpersonal Workplace Deviance

As noted in Table 11.1, these types of workplace deviance are directed against people rather than the organization and generally involve coworkers, supervisors, or clients. We will briefly examine the more serious forms of interpersonal workplace deviance.

Workplace Aggression and Violence

workplace aggression and violence

Behaviours directed toward other employees that are intended to cause either physical or psychological harm

Acts that fall into the categories of **workplace aggression and violence** involve aggression or abuse against others. These behaviours are intended to cause either physical or psychological harm. The aggression may range from shouting obscenities to actual physical assaults. Behaviours that do not involve any type of physical contact are classified as psychological aggression. Physical assaults of any type are examples of physical violence. Workplace aggression is a broader term than workplace violence, which it includes, as not all forms of aggression involve violence. Schat, Frone, and Kelloway (2006) report data on workplace deviance taken from a random, national telephone survey of more than 2,500 employed adults in the United States. They assessed the frequency of exposure to psychological aggression and to physical violence. Over 41 percent of those surveyed reported experiencing psychological aggression at least once in the last 12-month period, with 13 percent experiencing it on a weekly basis. Those figures translate into 15 million workers experiencing some form of psychological aggression on a weekly basis. The aggressive behaviours included being shouted at in anger, the target of obscenities, insulted or called names, or threatened with violence. Moreover, when survey participants were asked if they had experienced some form of physical violence in the workplace during the past year, 6 percent said they had, with 0.7 percent (785,586 workers) reporting that they were actually attacked with a knife, gun, or another weapon.

Not all workers experience the same risk of workplace aggression. Those who are most prone to aggression are workers between the ages of 18 and 30 who have been on the job between one and three years. One explanation for these results is that the knowledge and skills that workers develop over time make them better able to deal with, or avoid, potentially aggressive situations (Schat, Frone, & Kelloway, 2006). Risk of exposure to aggression also varies by occupation, with professional and service workers experiencing the greatest amount of aggression. Professional workers include social workers, therapists, and doctors, while police and security officers, health care workers, and nursing aides and orderlies are included in the service worker group. All workers who have exposure to people who are under the influence of drugs or medication or manifesting psychiatric problems are at increased risk of exposure to violence (LeBlanc & Kelloway, 2002).

The Schat, Frone, and Kelloway (2006) data are consistent with those found in surveys carried out by Statistics Canada in 2004. That survey found that 17 percent, or 365,000 of all violent incidents involving sexual assault, robbery, and physical assault, occurred at the respondent's place of work. Violence was more common in some employment sectors than in others; 33 percent of workplace violence incidents involved an employee who worked in social assistance or health care services, 14 percent of incidents involved employees working in accommodation or food services, and 11 percent of incidents were committed against those working in educational services. Physical assaults represented 71 percent of all workplace violence. Workplace incidents involving violence against men were more likely to be reported to the police than those acts against women, 57 percent versus 20 percent (de Léséleuc, 2007). In response to the growing number of incidents of workplace violence, the Ontario government adopted legislation in December 2009 that sought to provide protection to workers from violence and harassment (Ministry of Labour, 2010). The new protections will require employers to:

- Develop and communicate workplace violence and harassment prevention policies and programs to workers
- Assess the risks of workplace violence, and take reasonable precautions to protect workers from possible domestic violence in the workplace
- Allow workers to remove themselves from harmful situations if they have reason to believe that they are at risk of imminent danger due to workplace violence

Bullying at Work

Bullying can be defined as offensive, intimidating, malicious, or insulting behaviour, and is an abuse or misuse of power through means intended to undermine, humiliate, denigrate, or injure the intended victim of the bullying behaviour. Bullying can often be hard to recognize—it may not be obvious to

bullying
Offensive, intimidating, malicious, or insulting behaviour directed at another; an abuse or misuse of power through means intended to undermine, humiliate, denigrate, or injure an intended victim

others, and may be insidious. Victims may think that perhaps the behaviour is normal in the organization. They may be anxious that others will consider them weak, or not up to the job, if they find the actions of others intimidating. They may be accused of overreacting, and worry that they won't be believed if they do report incidents. People being bullied may appear to overreact to something that seems relatively trivial but which may be the "last straw" following a series of incidents. There is often fear of retribution if they do make a complaint. Colleagues may be reluctant to come forward as witnesses, as they, too, may fear the consequences. They may be so relieved not to be the subject of the bully themselves that they collude with the bully as a way of avoiding attention (Rayner & Cooper, 2006).

Bullying behaviour includes a wide range of behaviours; it may include, for example,

- spreading malicious rumours, or insulting someone by word or behaviour (particularly on the grounds of race, sex, disability, sexual orientation, and religion or belief)
- copying memos that are critical of someone to others who do not need to know
- ridiculing or demeaning someone; picking on them or setting them up to fail
- overbearing supervision or other misuse of power or position
- making threats or comments about job security without foundation
- deliberately undermining a competent worker by overloading and constant criticism
- preventing individuals progressing by intentionally blocking promotion or training opportunities

Bullying does not have to take place face-to-face. It may occur by written communications, email (often called "flame mail"), telephone, and automatic supervision methods (such as recording of telephone conversations). If unchecked or badly handled, bullying creates serious problems for an organization including:

- poor morale and poor employee relations
- loss of respect for managers and supervisors
- poor performance
- lost productivity
- absence
- resignations
- damage to company reputation
- tribunal and other court cases and payment of unlimited compensation

Workplace bullying is a significant occurrence in most organizations. Research on bullying relies on individuals to self-report whether they have been bullied, so the data may be a bit inflated. In the U.K. and Australia, 10 percent to 20 percent of employees label themselves as being bullied. In the U.S., there is a slightly higher incidence, while Sweden has about half the rate found in the U.K. In part, the lower Swedish rate may be due to the Swedish National

Board of Occupational Safety and Health passing ordinances on the actions that employers must take to prevent workplace bullying. Research has not found any reliable factor that predicts who will be bullied at work. There is more success in identifying who does the bullying. Depending on the country, 50 to 80 percent of bullying is done by someone in authority over the victim, often their boss. In the remainder of the cases, bullying is carried out by a coworker. Rarely is a person in authority, the boss, bullied by a subordinate (Rayner & Cooper, 2006).

Reasons for bullying generally fall into two classes: predatory bullying and dispute bullying (Einnarson, 1999). The former is the less frequent type and involves singling out an individual or group based on prejudice (e.g., hatred of gays, women, Jews). Dispute bullying involves interaction between the bully and victim whereby each provokes the other to ever-increasing actions directed at the other. In turn, each party becomes bully and victim. The initiation of the bullying is some dispute between the parties, with the bullying an attempt to resolve the dispute.

Many organizations and unions recognize the seriousness of bullying in the workplace and have implemented interventions designed to end bullying. The foremost successful policy is one of zero tolerance; that is, not to tolerate the mildest form of bullying and to stop it before it begins. Organizations that have clear policies for dealing with bullying and a process for dealing with bullies have been successful in preventing workplace bullying. Early action against bullying is the best means of prevention (Rayner & Cooper, 2006).

Psychological Harassment

Bullying behaviour can be thought of as one type of psychological harassment. In 2004, Quebec became the first jurisdiction in North America to prohibit psychological harassment in the workplace through the *Quebec Labour Standards Act*. The Act defines psychological harassment as "any vexatious behaviour in the form of repeated and hostile or unwanted conduct, verbal comments, actions or gestures, that affects an employee's dignity or psychological or physical integrity and that results in a harmful work environment for the employee. A single serious incidence of such behaviour that has a lasting harmful effect on an employee may also constitute psychological harassment" (*Act Respecting Labour Standards,* 2004). The Act also guarantees every employee the right to "a work environment free from psychological harassment. Employers must take reasonable action to prevent psychological harassment and, whenever they become aware of such behaviour, to put a stop to it" (*Act Respecting Labour Standards,* 2004). The Quebec Labour Standards Commission has identified a number of activities that could constitute a breach of the Act; many of these are very similar to the acts that constitute bullying behaviour:

- making rude, degrading or offensive remarks.
- making gestures that seek to intimidate, engaging in reprisals.
- discrediting the person: spreading rumours, ridicule, calling into question aspects of the person's private life, shouting abuse or sexual harassment.
- belittling the person: forcing them to perform tasks that are below their station or professional skills.

- preventing the person from expressing his or her thoughts, e.g. yelling, threatening, constant interruption, and prohibiting the person from speaking to others.
- isolating or shunning the person by not talking to them, ignoring their presence, or isolating them from others.
- destabilizing the person by making fun of their beliefs, convictions, tastes, or political choices. (Quebec Legislation, 2004)

The Act includes penalties for employers found to have violated the Act, which include:

- ordering the employer to reinstate the employee [who may have quit to avoid the harassment];
- ordering the employer to pay the employee [who may have quit to avoid the harassment] an indemnity up to a maximum equivalent to wages lost;
- ordering the employer to take reasonable action to put a stop to the harassment;
- ordering the employer to pay punitive and moral damages to the employee;
- ordering the employer to pay the employee an indemnity for loss of employment;
- ordering the employer to pay for the psychological support needed by the employee for a reasonable period of time as determined by the Commission;
- ordering the modification of the disciplinary record of the employee. (*Act Respecting Labour Standards*, 2004).

As of June 2005, one year following the coming into force of the new law, the Labour Standards Commission reported that it had received 2,500 complaints of psychological harassment, and that fewer than one percent of these complaints were considered frivolous. The Quebec Act has national importance. It squarely places the onus on the employer to prevent or stop psychological harassment from occurring in the employer's workplace. It is legislation that sets the standard for the rest of Canada. Increasingly, the Act will be used by human rights tribunals and labour arbitrators as the type of workplace behaviour that is acceptable and the standard against which employers are judged (Quebec Legislation, 2004).

Predicting Counterproductive Work Behaviours

Counterproductive behaviours are often taken into account by managers when assessing on-the-job performance (Orr, Sackett, & Mercer, 1989; Rotundo & Sackett, 2002; Viswesvaran & Ones, 2000). The more important issue is whether we can identify job applicants with a predisposition toward counterproductive work behaviours before they are hired. Normally in selection we look to screen into the organization those job applicants who posses the knowledge, skills, abilities, and other characteristics that are related to positive job performance. In the case of CWBs, the strategy is to select out those applicants who possess characteristics that have been linked to negative behaviours. When we use psychological testing and background searches to select in job applicants, we focus on verifiable information that increases their predictive validity. If these instruments are systematically developed and derived from job analyses that identified the knowledge, skills, abilities, and other characteristics related to successful task performance, they will provide reasonably good predictions of which applicants will succeed on the job. On the other hand, we have had limited success in screening out applicants who might be prone to CWBs. The reason for this is that our understanding of the causes of deviant organizational behaviour is very limited, even though these behaviours may have significant costs for individuals, the organization, and society.

Several theories have been proposed to explain deviant workplace behaviour. One theory argues that counterproductive behaviours are caused by work stress and can be triggered by negative emotions such as boredom, frustration, anxiety, and lack of self-control; others propose that differences in personality may be linked to counterproductive behaviours (Daw, 2001). In particular, different aspects of personality appear to predict violence and aggression and drug and alcohol use, along with honesty or integrity (Ones, Viswesvaran, & Dilchert, 2005). "Integrity" and "honesty" tests have been developed to predict whether a job applicant or employee is likely to engage in specific types of counterproductive behaviour, including those based on personality. When such tests are used, the employer tends to value elimination of the counterproductive behaviour over task performance on the part of the applicant, and will screen out the applicant on the basis of the honesty test regardless of how proficient the applicant might be with respect to task performance.

We next review some of these potential predictors of CWBs in greater detail. You will see that all of these predictors—even the more successful ones—have a fair degree of inaccuracy. When using different methods to screen out job applicants there is always a risk of making an error and classifying someone as prone to deviant behaviour when, in fact, they are not. There are four possible outcomes when testing for deviant behaviour. We wish to screen out job applicants who are prone to CWBs. We use one of the tools that we describe in this chapter (an honesty test), but the example applies to all predictors used to screen out applicants. In Figure 11.1, cell B represents those applicants who are truly prone to (or test positive for) deviant behaviour and have been properly rejected for the position. These applicants are called **true positives**, as the test classifies them as potentially acting in a deviant manner when they would behave that way if hired. Cell C represents those who were properly classified as not prone to deviant behaviour and were subsequently hired on the basis of other selection tools. Cells A and D represent mistakes. In the case of cell D, the honesty test identified those applicants as not prone to CWBs and they were hired only to prove the test wrong. In cell A, which tends to be the most problematic for employers, the test classified the applicants as CWB-prone when they are not. This is known as a **false positive** decision in that the test classifies applicants as those who will likely behave in a deviant manner when they will not. These are the cases that you tend to hear about in the news media, when a person has been rejected for a position on the basis of failing an honesty test. Keep in mind that when we use selection tools to "screen in" applicants, a true positive means the test indicates the person has the KSAOs needed to do the job, and those applicants are hired.

true positive

In the context of predicting counterproductive work behaviours, occurs when a test correctly classifies a job applicant as being prone to deviant workplace behaviours

false positive

In the context of predicting counterproductive work behaviours, occurs when a test classifies job applicants as being prone to deviant workplace behaviours when, in reality, they are not

FIGURE 11.1

Possible Outcomes When Using a Test to Screen Out Job Applicants Prone to Counterproductive Work Behaviours

	Non-CWB-Prone Applicants	CWB-Prone Applicants
Rejected Applicants	A False Positives	B True Positives
Hired Applicants	C True Negatives	D False Negatives

In selecting out, our goal is to maximize correct decisions (i.e., true positives and true negatives), and to minimize errors (i.e., false positives and false negatives). The best way to accomplish this is by using valid selection strategies. The more valid the selection tool, the fewer will be the misclassifications from using that tool. Selecting out someone on the basis of being prone to CWBs does not mean that those who have been screened in (cells C and D) are the best applicants to do the job. All that the test has shown is that those job applicants are not likely to exhibit CWBs in the workplace; it says nothing about their having the KSAOs needed to perform the tasks required by the position. Those applicants who survive the honesty test are not immediately hired but must be further evaluated with respect to the necessary KSAOs. In terms of a hiring strategy, selection tests related to the KSAOs required for success on the job should be given first, and then tests for deviant behaviour should be given only to those applicants who have made it through the first selection round based on the KSAOs.

Psychological Testing

Psychological testing has been used to screen out potentially deviant and aggressive employees based on an individual's predisposition to aggression or other forms of CWB. Psychological testing can take the form of both clinical assessments and non-clinical testing.

Clinical Assessments

Clinical assessments may involve interviews with a professional clinical psychologist, use of different paper and pencil assessment tools that are traditionally used with a clinical population, and statistical and actuarial

clinical assessment

Use of interviews, paper and pencil tests, and other assessment tools designed for use with clinical populations through which a clinical psychologist makes a judgment about the likelihood that a job applicant will engage in deviant workplace behaviours profiles developed with the aid of those assessment tools. These tools and methods normally lead to information on the applicant's life history, personality, history of aggression and violence, involvement in domestic disputes, propensity to undertake violent acts, and any other information that the clinical psychologist or psychiatrist feels is important in understanding deviant behaviour. This information is used to develop a global profile of the individual's propensity for violence or aggression. The determination is based on a clinical judgment on the part of the clinical psychologist or psychiatrist who has been involved in the examination of the applicant. A clinical assessment is a very time-consuming process and not suited to use with a large number of applicants. Additionally, clinical assessments fail to consider the organizational context in which the deviant behaviour might occur. Clinical assessments based on clinical judgment tend to have a high misclassification rate, particularly categorizing non-violent individuals as being prone to violent action and high risks for violence (Monahan et al., 2000). Clinical assessments, for the most part, are generally reserved for assessing applicants for high-level or sensitive positions.

Personality Characteristics

Emotions, perceptions, attitudes, and attributions influence aggressive behaviours in the workplace. Anger and frustration contribute to aggression (Fox & Spector, 1999), as does a sense of injustice that stems from an attribution of intentionally hostile behaviour on the part of others or external factors. If employees perceive some type of injustice in the workplace as being caused by external, stable, and intentionally hostile behaviours, there is an increased risk of aggression (Martinko, Gundlach, & Douglas, 2002). Other traits such as self-monitoring ability, attitudes toward revenge, negative affectivity, lack of self-control, and Type A behaviour pattern have all been linked to various forms of workplace violence, but the overall effects are very small.

Polygraph Testing

"Honesty" testing is a very controversial procedure. Honesty or integrity are personality traits and can be measured. Over the years, a number of techniques have been used in an attempt to identify these traits. **Polygraph testing,** otherwise known as using a lie detector, was once used extensively to check on employee honesty and to screen job applicants. The polygraph test is based on the assumption that measurable, physiological changes occur when people lie, and that no matter how hard they try to control their responses, changes take place in heart rate, breathing, blood pressure, and so on (Fiedler, Schmid, & Stahl, 2002). The most popular type of polygraph test is called the *control question test* (CQT), which uses a series of neutral, control, and relevant questions with the responses to the neutral and control questions used as baselines for assessing the physiologic responses to the relevant questions. Responses to the relevant questions that are different from those made in response to the neutral and control questions are taken by the polygraph operator as suggesting untruthful responses. Table 11.2 presents a series of questions used as part of a control question test.

polygraph test (lie detector)

The use of measurable, physiological changes in heart rate, breathing, and blood pressure, among other indicators, to predict if individuals are prone to workplace deviance

Table 11.2

Typical Question Series Used in a Polygraph Control Question Test (CQT)

Type of Question	Question
Introductory	Do you understand that I will ask only the questions we have discussed before?
Introductory	Regarding the theft of the rare coin, do you intend to answer all of the questions truthfully?
Neutral	Do you live in the United States?
Control	During the first 34 years of your life, did you ever take something that did not belong to you?
Relevant	Did you take the rare coin?
Neutral	Is your first name [John]?
Control	Prior to 1984, did you ever deceive someone?
Relevant	Did you take the rare coin from the desk?
Neutral	Were you born in the month of [September]?
Control	Between the ages of 18 and 34, did you ever do anything dishonest, illegal or immoral?
Relevant	Regarding the rare coin that was reported missing. Did you take it?

Source: Klaus Fiedler, Jeannette Schmid, and Teresa Stahl (2002). What is the current truth about polygraph lie detection? *Basic and Applied Social Psychology* 24(4): 313–324, reprinted by permission of the publisher (Taylor & Francis Group, http://www.informaworld.com).

Although lie detectors enjoy a reputation among the public for actually being able to detect lies, the empirical evidence shows that there are many unresolved issues about their reliability and validity. Polygraph results are mostly related to the skill of the polygraph operator, many of whom are poorly trained. Relatively few jurisdictions in either the United States or Canada have any licensing requirements for polygraph operators. Polygraph results are generally not accepted as evidence in North American courtrooms unless the test taker agrees to their admission. In Canada, the Supreme Court prohibited the use of polygraph results as evidence in trials (*R. v. Béland,* 1987); however, polygraph testing is used as part of investigations. Many legislatures, including the U.S. Congress, which passed the Employee Polygraph Protection Act (1988), have banned the use of polygraph testing as part of most pre-employment screening procedures (Jones, 1991). Employers in the U.S. may not use lie detectors as part of pre-employment testing or testing of current employees. Subject to restrictions and strict standards for their use, the act allows employers to test applicants for security service firms and of pharmaceutical-related industries. The tests can also be given to employees who are reasonably suspected of theft, embezzlement, or other economic crimes that result in economic loss or injury to an employer.

In Canada, Ontario has taken the lead in prohibiting the use of mandatory polygraph tests under its *Employment Standards Act*. This is not the case in other provinces, where polygraph testing is routinely used as part of the application process for applicants to many police or security agencies. The National Academy of Sciences (2003) reviewed the state of polygraph testing and concluded that much of the research on which polygraph testing was based was insufficient to justify the use of polygraph testing. When used as part of selection, particularly for police and security forces, the level of accuracy drops to such a level that, "Its accuracy in distinguishing actual or potential security violators from innocent test takers is insufficient to justify reliance on its use in employee security screening in federal agencies" (p. 6). The Academy concluded that there was "little basis for the expectation that a polygraph test could have extremely high accuracy" (p. 212). Nonetheless, polygraph tests are used as part of pre-employment selection by many police and security forces throughout Canada. These include the Canadian Security Intelligence Service (CSIS) and many municipal police forces.

Honesty or Integrity Testing

The restrictions placed on polygraph testing along with their questionable reliability have led to an increase in the use of paper-and-pencil **honesty or integrity tests** that can easily be incorporated into a selection system; they are inexpensive and typically inoffensive to most applicants. There are no legislative restrictions on their use; however, they must meet the same professional and scientific standards as any other type of employment test.

honesty or integrity tests

The use of paper and pencil tests, either standalone or as part of a personality inventory, to predict whether an individual is honest

There are two general types of integrity tests. *Covert tests* are included within a general personality inventory; for example, the Reliability Scale of the Hogan Personality Inventory (Hogan & Hogan, 1989) is commonly used to assess employee honesty and reliability. The Big Five personality measures of conscientiousness, agreeableness, and emotional stability have been linked to honesty in the workplace; that is, a lack of these traits predicts counterproductive workplace behaviours (Ones & Viswesvaran, 2001). *Overt honesty tests*, such as the Reid Report, ask very direct questions about the individual's attitude toward theft and other forms of dishonesty, as well as the person's prior involvement in theft or other illegal activities. Applicants may not be aware that their integrity is being assessed with a covert honesty test when they complete a personality inventory. There is no doubt about the purpose of an overt test, and this is likely the reason why overt tests are more susceptible to faking than those embedded in personality inventories (Alliger, Lilienfeld, & Mitchell, 1996).

Honesty tests are an increasingly popular method of screening out potentially dishonest employees. Dishonest applicants may be discouraged from applying for jobs when they know they will be tested for honesty. In the case of white-collar crime, personality-based integrity tests may be the best measure of psychological differences between white-collar criminals and honest employees (Collins & Schmidt, 1993). After a chain of home improvement centres in Great Britain started using an honesty test as part of its selection procedures, inventory shrinkage dropped from 4 percent to less than 2.5 percent (Temple, 1992).

Integrity tests successfully predict a wide range of dysfunctional job behaviours, including absenteeism, tardiness, violence, and substance abuse (Ones, Viswesvaran, & Schmidt, 1993). There is no evidence that integrity tests produce adverse impact. Table 11.3 presents a summary of criterion-related

Chapter 11: Counterproductive Work Behaviour

validity data for both overt and covert integrity tests (Ones & Viswesvaran, 1998b; Ones, Viswesvaran, & Schmidt, 1993). A striking aspect of Table 11.3 is that integrity tests are more successful in predicting property damage than in detecting theft. A more recent and exhaustive review came to similar conclusions, that honesty or integrity tests provide valid information about an applicant's potential to engage in certain types of dysfunctional job behaviours (Sackett & Wanek, 1996).

Nonetheless, honesty tests do have disadvantages. Test scores from honesty tests are open to misinterpretation and may constitute an invasion of the applicant's privacy. Job applicants may not hold favourable views of honesty tests, and may form a negative impression of the organization that uses these tests. The major problem with honesty tests is they result in a high number of false positives; that is, they may tend to screen out a large number of applicants who are truly honest but do poorly on the test (Camara & Schneider, 1994). An applicant who is falsely rejected may feel stigmatized and take legal action (Arnold, 1991). Organizations considering the use of integrity or honesty testing to select job applicants should weigh the benefits against the possible risks before doing so.

Background Screening

Biographical Information Blanks

One form of **background screening** involves using specific demographic or biographical data obtained from job applicants (Stokes, Mumford, & Owens,

background screening

Using biographical and life history information obtained from or about job applicants to form a prediction about their likelihood of engaging in counterproductive work behaviours; biographical information blanks, field investigations, and references are types of background screening

TABLE 11.3

Summary of Meta-Analytic Integrity Test Criterion-Related Validities[1]			
CRITERION	TYPE OF INTEGRITY TEST	MEAN OBSERVED VALIDITY COEFFICIENT, r	CORRECTED VALIDITY COEFFICIENT[2]
Detected Theft	Overt Test	0.09	0.13
Admitted Theft	Overt Test	0.30	0.42
Property Damage	Overt and Personality-Based	0.50	0.69
Accidents on Job	Overt and Personality-Based	0.37	0.52
Broad counterproductive behaviours	Overt Test	0.27	0.39
Broad counterproductive behaviours	Personality-Based Test	0.20	0.29

[1]Adapted from Table 1 of Wanek (1999).

[2]The mean observed validity coefficient, r, has been corrected for range restriction and unreliability in the criterion measure.

Source: Adapted from James E. Wanek, Integrity and honesty testing: What do we know about it?, *International Journal of Selection and Assessment* 7(4): 183–195. Copyright © 1999 John Wiley and Sons.

People and Work in Canada

1994). The applicants are asked to provide information on their personal background and life experiences by answering a series of multiple-choice or short-answer questions. This type of questionnaire is called a biographical information blank (BIB). The BIB results in a score or a series of scores that are used to make a prediction about the applicant's future work-related behaviour. The BIB is based on the premise that past behaviour is the best predictor of future behaviour. Well-developed BIBs can be very effective in predicting absenteeism, turnover, job proficiency, supervisory effectiveness, and job training in a wide range of occupations, with validity coefficients ranging from .30 to .40 (Stokes & Cooper, 1994).

Biodata information also has been used to screen out applicants who may be prone to violence (Baron, 1993; Mantell, 1994). Factors such as a history of family violence, child abuse, and substance abuse tend to be related to criminal behaviour. Past employment records, military service, credit history, criminal record, workers' compensation history, driving records, and general character and reputation have also been suggested for use in screening out violence-prone individuals (Nicoletti & Spooner, 1996). However, there has been little work to validate BIBs used for screening out potentially aggressive employees. In addition, some of the best predictive information requested on a BIB is personally sensitive and protected under provincial and federal human rights and privacy legislation. Although BIBs have good predictive validity, many organizations do not use them because of concerns over possible violations of these laws.

Field Investigations

This type of background check involves a very extensive search of an applicant's background. Applicants for sensitive government jobs or with security services such as the RCMP undergo field investigations that involve interviews with people who know the applicant, including former employers and coworkers; credit checks; and review of police files and court records, educational records, and any other available documentation. Usually, the check extends into the background for a 10-year period. Background checks of this sort are very expensive, but in most cases they provide an accurate description of the applicant and identify any problem areas that might affect counterproductive job performance. Corporations often use field investigations before they make top-level managerial appointments. Most organizations are not equipped to conduct such costly and elaborate investigations of potential new employees. Increasingly, Canadian corporations are turning to a growing number of firms such as Infocheck (http://www.infocheck.com) and AXiOM Information Checking service (http://www.axiom-int.com) that specialize in this activity.

As is the case with BIBs, there is concern over the use of field investigations into a person's background as a violation of privacy rights. In many jurisdictions, employers are not allowed to select out based on past criminal convictions, except for some high-risk occupations. Therefore, in some jurisdictions questions related to criminal convictions may not be included in the screening process (Bush & O'Shea, 1996). Arrest records may have an adverse impact on minority group members, making them ineligible for inclusion as screens (Paetzold, 1998). In addition, background checks for criminal records may not be foolproof. Background checks conducted by the FBI in the U.S. on a list of 120 convicted felons reported that only 87 (72.5 percent) had criminal records. A private security company performed worse; it identified only 56 (46.6 percent) of the people on the list as having had criminal records (Small-wood, 2004). Nonetheless, the use of security checks in Canada has risen dramatically following the events of 9/11. A Statistics Canada survey of more than 6,000 workplaces and 25,000 employees in each of three years showed that security checks remained relatively stable in the 1999 and 2001 surveys, with 9.1 percent and 8.8 percent of employees who were hired within one year of the survey reporting that they had been subject to a security check. In the 2003 survey, the percentage who reported having undergone a security check prior to being hired rose to 14.1 percent (Catano & Bissonnette, 2009).

Reference Checks

In Chapter 4 we discussed the use of reference checks as part of the screening-in process. Employers also use reference checks to obtain information that is used to screen out job applicants who have poor work behaviours or who have problematic backgrounds. References are usually checked as the last step in the selection process, and then on only the top three candidates for a position, because the process is labour-intensive.

Information in reference letters often reflects more the attributes of the person writing the reference than attributes of the applicant. The predictive validity of personal references is low. There are several reasons for the low validity of reference checks. In the case of personal references, it is highly unlikely that a job applicant will knowingly offer the name of someone who will provide a bad reference. Most applicants are fairly confident about the type of reference their referees will provide and often will ask referees whether they will provide positive comments before listing their names on an application form. It is in the applicant's best interests to do this. The result, however, is a set of uniformly positive recommendations for each applicant. The lack of variability in the references limits their use in discriminating between candidates; this is an example of range restriction, which leads to low validity coefficients. This is one reason why even the slightest negative information contained in a reference may be sufficient to eliminate an applicant from the job competition (Knouse, 1983).

While it is understandable that applicants will use the most favourable references, why are reference checks with previous employers equally ineffective as screening measures? Many Canadian employers are hesitant to make strong negative statements about current or former employees out of fear of being sued for libel or defamation. It is not uncommon for employers to have a policy of verifying only name, position, and length of service when speaking to callers about former employees (Clark & Snitzer, 2005; Hutton, 2008). Yet this could be unfair to former employees who have favourable performance records, and, in the case of problematic employees, could result in harm to the future employer, its employees, and the people it services. Also, in reality it is extremely difficult in Canada, as opposed to the U.S., for a former employer to be sued for libel or slander by a past employee as a result of a poor reference, even if that reference contains some inaccuracies. This is because Canadian courts have endowed employment references with the protection of the law of "qualified privilege." Under this law, employers cannot be sued if the comments are "honestly made"; the employee would have to prove that the referee did not believe the facts as asserted—that is, that the referee *knowingly* fabricated information, acted maliciously, or in bad faith (Hutton, 2008).

While it is unlikely that Canadian employers will be sued for honestly providing unfavourable references, employers are quite vulnerable to being sued in cases where they knowingly hold back unfavourable information, particularly where the employee is subsequently hired and causes harm to the new employer or its clientele. In this case, the new employer could sue for damages for "negligent misrepresentation" ("The legalities of...", 2007). This legal right of prospective employers seems to be well placed. For example, Charles Cullen, a nurse, was able to move from hospital to hospital, from one U.S. state to another, intentionally killing patients at each facility. This went on for 16 years, despite Cullen having been under investigation in seven of these hospitals and having been fired or forced to resign in several instances! This continued because none of these institutions was prepared to give a bad reference (Clark & Snitzer, 2005). On the other hand, failure to give a deserved favourable reference can also put an employer in a legally precarious situation, where this failure is seen by Canadian courts as having impeded a former employee's job search. For example, in a precedent-setting case, the Supreme Court of Canada ruled in 1977 that employers have an obligation to act in good faith when an employee is terminated. In this case, Jack Wallace, the plaintiff, was awarded 24 months of salary when it was found that his employer, United Grain Growers, neglected to provide a reference letter in time for him to secure a new job (Hutton, 2008). These court awards can be interpreted to suggest that employers are being encouraged to provide honest written and oral references for their former employees. Such honest letters will help to reduce the likelihood of hiring applicants who are prone to counterproductive work behaviours.

Drug and Alcohol Testing

Inevitably, societal changes find their way into the workplace. One of the most profound changes in North American society has been the increased use of drugs as a recreational activity that may carry over into the workplace. Employers often believe that workplace drug and alcohol use is an added expense through costs associated with employee accidents, absenteeism, turnover, and tardiness. Additionally, there may be costs associated with reduced product quality and productivity on the part of employees who use drugs and alcohol in the workplace. In some cases, drug or alcohol use by employees while working may result in threats to the safety of the public and coworkers. In the United States, where many workers receive health insurance through their employer, employers may face the escalating costs of health insurance due to the presence of a significant number of drug users. For these reasons, many

Chapter 11: Counterproductive Work Behaviour

employers, with support from both their employees and the public, believe that they are justified in screening job applicants for drug and alcohol use. The screening programs generally apply to all employees and job applicants and not just those in safety-sensitive positions. The intent of pre-employment alcohol and drug testing programs is to scare off any individual who may have a substance abuse problem from applying for a position with the company.

Are these concerns justified? The empirical evidence in support of alcohol and drug testing is far from clear. The relationship between drug use and turnover is relatively small, with correlations ranging from .04 to .08. However, in a longitudinal study, employees who tested positive for drug use had a 59 percent higher absenteeism rate and a 47 percent higher involuntary turnover rate than those who tested negative (Normand, Salyards, & Mahoney, 1990). While there are some links between drug and alcohol use and accidents and disciplinary measures (Parish, 1989), the magnitude of the relationship is probably smaller than people have assumed. Self-reported drug use on the job does appear to be related to how workers behave in the workplace and interact with their coworkers, including antagonistic behaviours such as arguing with coworkers. In almost every workplace there is some expression of deviant behaviour that is not related to substance abuse. When that general deviant behaviour is taken into account, the relationship between substance abuse and job performance becomes insignificant (Harris & Trusty, 1997).

Notwithstanding the empirical evidence, workplace drug and alcohol testing programs have become quite common in the United States. The Americans with Disabilities Act stipulates that pre-employment alcohol testing is a medical examination and may be required only after a conditional offer of employment has been made and in accordance with ADA regulations on pre-employment physicals. The ADA allows employers to require employees to submit to a physical only when a conditional offer of employment has been made. It allows drug tests to be made before a conditional offer is made provided that:

1. the test accurately identifies only the use of illegal drugs;
2. the test is not given in conjunction with a pre-employment physical; and
3. the test does not require the applicant to disclose information about prescription drug use, unless a positive test result may be explained by use of a prescription drug.

Drug Testing in Canadian Organizations

Random or mandatory drug testing by Canadian companies is not common. Only 1.4 percent of nearly 25,000 employees who participated in a 1999 Statistics Canada survey reported that they received a pre-employment drug test; however, this figure grew significantly to 2.4 percent in the 2003 survey (Catano & Bissonnette, 2009). Based on recent Canadian court decisions, these percentages are not likely to increase. Canadian courts have taken the position that random drug testing, on its face, is discriminatory and must meet the standards of the *Meiorin* decision to qualify as a bona fide occupational requirement (BFOR). Courts have ruled that random drug testing can meet the *Meiorin* standards for a BFOR when implemented in certain safety-sensitive positions; that is, in positions where incapacity due to drug or alcohol impairment could result in direct and significant risk of injury to the employees, others, or the environment. Court and tribunal decisions limit drug and alcohol screening to the narrowest circumstances, where a direct link can be established with respect to job performance or to the safety and health of people. Even then, the substance abuse on the part of employees is considered a disability that must be accommodated. The effect of these court decisions is to make drug and alcohol testing impractical in most work situations. Canadian workers support the limitation of drug and alcohol testing in the workplace. Seijts, Skarlicki, and Gilliland (2003) compared the reactions of Canadian and American truck drivers to workplace testing programs. The Canadian drivers perceived the testing as being less fair than their American counterparts did. Canadians were more inclined to file official protests over the implementation of drug and alcohol programs. This last finding is certainly supported by the large number of drug and alcohol–related testing cases that have gone before various courts and tribunals in Canada.

Following the *Meiorin* decision, in the limited circumstances where drug and alcohol testing may be permissible, the primary obligation of the employer is to accommodate those employees to the point of undue hardship. The accommodation procedures should include provisions for the employee to undergo treatment or rehabilitation. Policies that allow for the automatic dismissal of employees who test positive, their reassignment, or imposition of impossible or inflexible reinstatement provisions will not meet accommodation standards. However, if the health or safety risks to workers or members of the public are so serious that they outweigh the benefits of providing accommodation to an individual with a drug or alcohol problem, accommodation may be waived.

The difference in Canadian and U.S. drug and alcohol testing policies leads to problems for some industries that operate in both countries, most notably cross-border trucking and busing. In these cases, not being banned from driving in the U.S. because of testing positive for alcohol or drugs may be a bona fide occupational requirement for companies that drive exclusively or predominantly between Canada and the U.S. The company still has the obligation to show that continuing the employment of a banned driver would constitute an undue hardship. Under Canadian regulations, the company would have the obligation to accommodate the banned employee through alternate employment with the company, or by re-assigning a driver to Canada-only routes. These policies have the most impact on the truck drivers themselves.

Summary

One useful approach to understanding job performance is to recognize that job performance is a multidimensional construct composed of task, contextual, and counterproductive behaviours. This chapter focused on the latter of these three types of behaviours, with an assessment of different strategies that might be used to "select out" job applicants prone to deviant behaviour. Counterproductive work behaviours are voluntary behaviours that violate significant organizational norms and in so doing threaten the well-being of an organization, its members, or both. We examined CWBs that ranged from tardiness and absenteeism through property damage to violence and aggression toward others. We reviewed the incidence rates of these behaviours, as far as could be determined, and their costs to organizations. We also reported, where they were known, the causes for such deviance in the workplace. Finally, we reviewed attempts to predict counterproductive workplace behaviours.

Our review led to the conclusion that screening out applicants who may be prone to engaging in CWBs is problematic for the following reasons:

The different selection instruments have relatively high false positive rates; that is, they tend to predict deviance or proneness to CWB when in reality that is not the case.

We know too little about the antecedents of CWBs to allow us to develop reliable and valid predictors.

Background checks, including information on demographic, criminal and past violent behaviour, and alcohol and drug use and psychological tests, including both clinical and non-clinical tests, have all been suggested as screening tools for potential workplace violence. The use of any of these devices to screen out employees would most likely be met with legal objections.

Background checks appear to be the most promising at identifying individuals prone to CWBs, particularly those who pose a threat to security.

Organizational factors appear to interact with or set the stage for the occurrence of the more violent CWBs. Insufficient information is known about such predisposing organizational factors to allow development of complete models that examine how such factors interacted with individual characteristics.

The one bright spot is with respect to honesty or integrity testing. There are several paper and pencil measures that meet professional standards for use in identifying various CWBs. The downside is that use of these measures is controversial and may lead to negative publicity for the organization that uses them.

At present, with the exception of testing for honesty and integrity and possibly background searches, there is no acceptable way to screen potential job applicants for their propensity to commit CWBs. With the absence of such measures to screen out violent employees, employers must focus on strategies that prevent workplace aggression from occurring and, failing that, to monitor problematic workplace behaviours carefully and take immediate and decisive action when needed as part of their obligation to ensure a workplace that is free of violence while respecting the rights of all employees. These are the types of strategies that many organizations have adopted to combat bullying behaviours in the workplace. Employers should focus on organizational strategies and methods such as implementing anti-violence and anti-bullying policies, training supervisors to be alert to CWBs, creating crisis management teams to deal with violence and other forms of aggression, fostering a supportive work environment for the victims of workplace aggression, providing personal counselling, and establishing fair grievance procedures.

Key Terms

absence 301
background screening 316
bullying 307
clinical assessment 312
counterproductive work behaviours 298
employee theft 305
false positive 311
honesty or integrity tests 315
polygraph test (lie detector) 313
presenteeism 303

production deviance 304
productivity 299
psychological withdrawal 304
tardiness 300
true positive 311
voluntary turnover 303
workplace aggression and violence 306
workplace deviance 300
workplace property deviance 304

Web Links

Information on workplace violence, one form of counterproductive work behaviour, from the Workplace Violence Research Institute can be found at:

http://www.workviolence.com

The Workplace Bullying Site is a non-profit site working to provide resources to those working against bullying or harassment of any kind in the workplace. It can be found at:

http://www.workplacebullying.co.uk/

The Workplace Bullying Institute is a U.S. organization directed toward providing information about ending bullying, and offers information for those being bullied in the workplace:

http://www.workplacebullying.org/

In addition to providing information on careers and job search, the Career Builder website provides interesting information on the workplace, including the incidence of counterproductive behaviours. The website is located at:

http://www.careerbuilder.ca

Another source of information on CWBs is the surveys carried out by the Mercer Global consulting organization. These can be obtained at:

http://www.mercer.com:80/home.htm

Discussion Questions

1. Discuss the role that counterproductive work behaviours play in the productivity of an organization.
2. Discuss the difference between "selecting in" and "selecting out" job applicants.
3. What are the advantages of designing a selection system where job applicants are first "selected in" on the basis of relevant KSAOs

Chapter 11: Counterproductive Work Behaviour

and then selected out on the basis of counterproductive work behaviours?

4. Why are polygraphs still used by law enforcement and security agencies when they are banned from use in most employment situations?
5. What do we mean by "false positive" in the context of selecting out job applicants? How does this differ from "false positive" in the context of selecting *in* job applicants? Which one is more harmful to the organization? To the applicant?
6. Discuss the implications of the Quebec Act to prevent psychological harassment with respect to your province/territory. Do you have similar legislation in your jurisdiction?
7. What actions can an employer take to prevent bullying from occurring it its workplace?
8. What are the reasons that we have a poor record of predicting CWBs?
9. What are the limitations of implementing an honesty testing procedure in a workplace? What concerns should you address before implementing such a system?
10. What are the benefits, if any, of introducing a workplace drug and alcohol testing program?

Using the Internet

The Quebec Act prohibiting psychological harassment was passed in 2004. We saw that, one year later, more than 2,500 complaints that had been filed.

1. Can you determine the number of complaints that have been filed each year since then?
2. What has been the resolution of the complaints?
3. What impact has the Act had on cases of psychological harassment or bullying? To answer this question, review the different cases processed by human rights tribunals or labour arbitrators. Most human rights tribunals provide access to their cases online. The Canadian Labour Law Reporter and Lexis-Nexis report proceedings of labour arbitrations.

Exercises

1. Sample at least five organizations in your locale. Contact the human resources department and enquire whether they use techniques to assess the likelihood of job applicants engaging in deviant behaviour. What techniques do they use?
2. Survey a number of organizations to determine the incidence of various types of CWBs. Some organizations may not be willing to provide these data.

3. Determine the number of organizations that use honesty tests and background searches as part of their hiring process.
4. Interview a number of your classmates who have applied for jobs. Find out whether they have undergone any type of honesty testing. Did they try to fake the results?

Case

A large national grocery chain uses the Reid Report as part of its hiring process. One applicant who failed the test (i.e., was classified as a threat to steal based on the test results) had worked for the company for six years, but had resigned her job to stay home and take care of her children for a year. When she reapplied for a position with the company, she was required to take the Reid Report, which had been introduced during her absence. She failed the test, and her application was rejected. As an employee, she was deemed to be productive and had a spotless discipline record. The company's policy was to hire only those applicants who passed the integrity test. The failed applicant went public and the incident made local and national headlines. It was the subject of a television feature on the CBC. It also led to a great deal of discussion about the worth of integrity tests. The applicant asked how she could have been rejected for failing the integrity test when she had worked without complaint for the company for six years. The rejected applicant filed a complaint about the use of the test with the human rights commission in her province. The Civil Liberties Union became aware of the practice and publicly denounced the use of the test. It also called for legislation banning the practice as an invasion of privacy. Even successful applicants may react negatively to an integrity test and the company using it. Many find the experience to be invasive and insulting and fail to see the relevance of questions such as "I like to take chances" and "I am afraid of fire." Many claim that they lied to achieve high "honesty" ratings by denying all illegal activity and feelings of bitterness and alienation.

Discussion Questions

1. What is a better predictor of honesty, an employee's work record or the results from an honesty test?
2. Is the cost of negative publicity worth the benefit of reduced shrinkage through the use of an honesty test?
3. What can be done to minimize false positives in honesty testing?
4. Can honesty be measured quantitatively?
5. Do you think an honesty test can be faked?

CHAPTER 12

Occupational Health Psychology

This chapter provides an overview of the health and safety issues faced by workers in a variety of jobs and work environments. It reviews the types of psychosocial stressors or demands faced by workers, as well as the personal and organizational resources that may help them deal with these demands. The chapter covers several individual outcomes, including burnout and work–life conflict, as well as organizational outcomes.

Chapter Learning Outcomes

After reading this chapter you should be able to

- Define occupational health psychology, job stress, burnout, and work–life conflict
- Understand the basics of occupational health and safety (OHS) legislation in Canada
- Describe models of job stress
- Identify job demands and resources
- Recognize both negative and positive individual health indicators
- Differentiate between burnout and engagement
- Understand the major health and safety issues faced by workers across occupations
- Identify programs and interventions used to address these health and safety issues
- Describe the characteristics of a healthy workplace
- Explain the connection between occupational characteristics and employee health

What Is Occupational Health Psychology?

According to Quick (1999), "Occupational health psychology (OHP) applies psychology in organizational settings for the improvement of work life, the protection and safety of workers, and the promotion of healthy work" (p. 123).

occupational health psychology (OHP)

Uses psychology at work to improve work life, to ensure the protection and safety of workers, and to promote healthy work

Occupational health psychology (OHP) can be defined as "how workplace practices and policies, supervision, and leadership affect employees' physical and psychological well-being" (Barling & Griffiths, 2003, p. 19). OHP is not a new area of interest for organizations; in fact, how work impacts well-being and health has been of interest since the early 1900s (Barling & Griffiths, 2003). However, the primary concern of organizations at the beginning of the century was focused on "managers' best interests," whereas we are now moving toward promoting and protecting "the psychological and physical health of workers themselves, through preventions and job design" (Barling & Griffiths, 2003, p. 30). See Box 12.1 for a real-world illustration of a healthy workplace in action.

occupational health and safety (OHS)

Identifying, evaluating, and controlling both the physical and psychosocial hazards in the work environment

Occupational health and safety (OHS) involves identifying, evaluating, and controlling both the physical and psychosocial hazards in the work environment. Physical hazards may include specific physical agents, such as chemicals and biological agents, and other safety issues, such as workplace safety (e.g., loose wiring in a building, dangerous materials left lying around on a worksite). Psychosocial and interpersonal hazards involve workplace incivility, job stress, and bullying. The goal of an organization's health and safety program is to reduce occupational injuries and illnesses.

Health and Safety Legislation in Canada

Occupational health and safety is regulated under a variety of mechanisms across Canada. For example, in addition to federal regulations that apply

Box 12.1

Healthy Workplaces in Action: Secunda Marine Services

Secunda Marine Services, founded in Nova Scotia, owns and operates a fleet of offshore support vessels servicing oil and gas companies along the coasts of Eastern Canada, the North Sea, and the Gulf of Mexico. Secunda also has an international role in providing supply, anchor handling, flexible pipelay, cable lay, subsea construction, and dive support vessels.

Many Secunda employees work on their vessels for 30 days at a time, which proves a unique challenge for their health and safety. The company implemented the "Ship-Shape at Secunda" program to help improve the health and safety of its workers. Every worker received a pedometer and a personal health profile, and the company offers sessions on nutrition and disease prevention, smoking cessation, exercise, and weight loss. Secunda prides itself on being able to provide best-value solutions with a highly experienced team whose safety culture and quality of work is world-class.

So, is the "Ship-Shape" program effective? Since implementing the initiative, Secunda has had an increase in employee morale and commitment. The company boasts a 97-percent employee retention rate (very high for the industry), and its insurance premiums have been stable (unheard of in an industry facing skyrocketing premiums). Finally, Secunda has one of the lowest lost-time incident rates in the industry, with the frequency of lost-time accidents dropping from 2.68 in 1998 to 0.30 in 2005. Recordable incidents for the same period dropped from 6.56 to 1.2.

Secunda has received recognition for its achievements: The company was a 2005 recipient of the Nova Scotia Psychologically Healthy Workplace Award, and went on to win a Best Practices Award at the APA Psychologically Healthy Workplace Awards for organizations across Canada and the United States.

across Canada, each province/territory has its own regulations. Although having multiple regulations may seem confusing, the vast majority of workers and workplaces simply are regulated by provincial legislation. Therefore, employers usually have to comply with only one set of safety standards.

The *statutes* are the legal foundation with which employers must comply. The *regulations* are enacted under each statute and they establish the framework as to what the employer must do in order to comply with the law.

Who Is Responsible for Employee Health and Safety?

Several groups of people are responsible for ensuring the health and safety of workers: (1) employers, owners, and contractors; (2) supervisors; (3) workers; and (4) joint health and safety committees. Under common law, employers must take reasonable precautions to ensure the safety of their employees. In some jurisdictions, however, this common-law duty is not in effect because other compensation legislation surpasses it. The compensation legislation limits the employer's duty by proscribing civil actions between employees and their employers in exchange for awards or pensions that may be allowed following an occupational accident or illness. What are the specific responsibilities of each group?

Employers, Owners, and Contractors

Employers are responsible for understanding the administrative structure of health and safety and workers' compensation as it relates to enforcement, education, and compensation in their particular jurisdiction. Any multinational and transportation companies (whose vehicles cross jurisdictional boundaries) who operate in more than one jurisdiction must be familiar with all of the legislation in each of these jurisdictions.

Employers are responsible for providing a safe work environment. They also are required to provide supervision, education, training, and written instructions (where applicable), assist the joint health and safety committee/representative, and comply with statutes and regulations. See Box 12.2 for the specifics of employer responsibilities in Ontario.

Box 12.2

Employer Health and Safety Responsibilities for Ontario

In Ontario, the employer's responsibilities are extensive. Employers must:

- Ensure that all necessary equipment is provided and properly maintained
- Ensure the supervisor is competent
- Provide information (including confidential information) in a medical emergency

- Advise all workers and supervisors of possible work hazards
- Post the *Occupational Health and Safety Act* in the workplace
- Prepare and maintain their own health and safety policy and review it annually.

Supervisors

In the context of the *Occupational Health and Safety Act,* "supervisor" refers to any person who is in charge of a workplace and who has authority over a worker. Therefore, supervisors can be formal supervisors, general managers, union members, plant managers, school principals, or self-employed individuals. For example, in Ontario a person is considered to be a supervisor if he or she has the authority to promote or recommend promotion, discipline workers, or assign work and work schedules.

According to the *OH&S Act* and regulations, *supervisors* must:

- ensure that workers under their supervision comply with the *OH&S Act* and regulations
- ensure that their workers use or wear safety equipment, devices, or clothing as required
- advise their workers of possible work hazards
- provide written instructions to their workers, if applicable
- take every reasonable precaution to ensure the protection of all workers.

Workers

Workers' responsibilities and duties are included in the majority of statutes, although their inclusion is relatively new in health and safety legislation. Prior to the late 1970s, all responsibility for workplace health and safety rested with the employer. Although the employer still is responsible for paying for health and safety activities, the Act views everyone as being responsible for making these activities work.

According to the *OH&S Act* and regulations, *employees* must:

- comply with the *OH&S Act* and regulations
- properly use the safety equipment and clothes provided
- report hazards (e.g., defective equipment) to their supervisor
- ensure they do not use any hazardous equipment or machine in unsafe conditions or make any safety device ineffective
- act in a safe manner and avoid engaging in rough or boisterous behaviour
- report any contraventions of the Act.

Joint Health and Safety Committees

A recent addition to OHS legislation is the creation of joint health and safety committees in the workplace. These committees are required by law for certain workplaces in nine provinces. In the other four provinces, the minister responsible has the discretionary power to require the formation of committees. The primary function of these joint health and safety committees is to provide a non-adversarial atmosphere in which labour and management can work together to create a safer and healthier workplace.

Each workplace that requires a committee must train at least one management member and one worker member on topics including law, general safety, hygiene, indoor air quality, chemical safety, certified workers' rights and duties, and joint committees. These certified committee members may be involved in inspections, work refusals, and bilateral work stoppage in which there is an imminent hazard to a worker. They also may investigate critical accidents and respond to worker concerns.

These joint health and safety committees have been shown to be effective (Kelloway, 2003) in terms of reducing workplace injuries (Reilly, Paci, & Holl, 1995). Joint committees can improve health and safety through prevention, education, and training, and by providing an ongoing forum for problem resolution (Weil, 1995). See Box 12.3 for an illustration of an effective program.

Much of the preceding discussion about health and safety has implicitly or explicitly focused on the *physical* condition of the work environment and the employees. However, in defining occupational health psychology, we take a more holistic view of employee health by also including other social and psychological demands, as well as employees' psychological health and physical, psychological, and behavioural health outcomes. One of the most ubiquitous aspects of employee health involves job stress.

Job Stress

What Is Job Stress?

We use the term "stress" in our everyday language to mean external pressures, personal reactions, and outcomes. Although there is no agreement among experts as to the precise definition of job stress, in general we view job stress as a process in which we have an affective reaction to job demands.

Box 12.3

Health and Safety in Action: Northwood Inc.

Northwood Inc. was a 2005 recipient of an APA Psychologically Healthy Workplace award in Nova Scotia, demonstrating many best practices in health and safety initiatives. The company takes a holistic view of health and safety, focusing not only on physical safety at work, but also healthy lifestyle, physical health, and psychological well-being. It has created a health and wellness department to ensure the physical and psychological safety of its employees. Some of its initiatives include:

- Infection control program (e.g., influenza vaccine clinics), wellness clinics (including glucose and cholesterol screening), and blood collection services

- Occupational health/staff health nurses
- On-site fitness centre (with staff incentives to use their services)
- Employee assistance, credit counselling, and stress management programs
- SMART (the Staff Morale and Recreation Team)
- Nutrition programs and healthy living plan
- On-site massage therapy clinic
- Health fairs (including a wide range of services and practitioners, from massage therapists to financial planners to healthy eating and weight management programs).

Chapter 12: Occupational Health Psychology

Why Do We Care about Job Stress?

In 1990, the National Institute of Occupational Safety and Health (NIOSH) in the United States concluded that occupational stress was one of the leading causes of workplace death, and argued that occupational stress could be viewed as an "epidemic" (Sauter, Murphy, & Hurrell, 1990). Stress is associated with many negative physical and psychosocial outcomes. It has costs for organizations and society (in terms of absenteeism, turnover, and so on). The Conference Board of Canada has estimated that workplace stress costs the Canadian economy $12 billion annually. Although much guesswork goes into estimating the cost of work stress, workplace stress is a growing problem with negative consequences for individuals and organizations alike. See Box 12.4 for more facts about job stress.

Job Stress Models: Common Themes

As you review the various models, you will notice several similarities among them:

- They tend to identify stimuli (or demands or stressors) that may tax an individual or "damage" them in some way.
- Each stimulus has the potential to trigger a set of psychological responses, which ultimately impact on the well-being of the individual.
- Resources (otherwise known as "moderators" or "buffers") may moderate the relationship between the stimuli (demand or stressor) and the stress outcome.
- Perception and cognition play an important role in how we appraise the stimuli (demands/stressors). That is, different people react differently to stress (Lazarus & Folkman, 1984).

Typically, we can classify individual stress responses in terms of physiological, psychological, and behavioural outcomes:

- Physiological outcomes (e.g., cardiovascular; biochemical measures; gastrointestinal symptoms)
- Psychological outcomes (e.g., job dissatisfaction, depression, anxiety, frustration, hostility, incivility)

Box 12.4

Job Stress Facts

- 34 percent of working Canadians indicated that the most common source of workplace stress was too many demands or hours (Williams, 2003)
- 74 percent of employees in the U.S. indicate work is a significant source of stress (APA, 2007)
- 20 percent of employees in the U.S. report calling in sick as a result of work stress (APA, 2007)
- The annual cost in Canada of work time lost to stress is estimated at $12 billion (Statistics Canada, 1999)

- Behavioural outcomes (e.g., degradation/disruption of the work role itself in terms of job performance, accidents and errors, alcohol/drug use at work, absenteeism, and turnover).

There have been many general stress models proposed over the years, and many that pertain directly to the work environment. There are overlapping qualities among many of these models (for an overview, see Kahn & Byosiere, 1992; Sonnentag & Frese, 2003).

We review six of these models:

1. The *transactional stress model* is a general stress model that has been applied to the work context, and emphasizes the importance of individual perception in the stress process
2. The *conservation of resources model* states that stress results from losing valued resources
3. The *person–job fit model* examines how a misfit between the individual and the job can create stress
4. The *job demand–job control model* states that job stress results when workers experience high demands and a low degree of control
5. The *effort–reward imbalance model* states that an imbalance between the efforts workers put into the job and rewards earned may create individual strain
6. The *job demands–resources model* shows how demands faced by employees and the resources they have impact on employees.

Job Stress Models: Overview

Transactional Stress Model

The **transactional stress model** (Lazarus & Folkman, 1984) is one of the most prominent general stress models, and has been integral in developing other general and work-related stress and demands models (see Figure 12.1). The model differentiates among stressors, perceived stress, and strain. **Stressors** are stimuli in your environment (i.e., events, situations) that are potentially threatening to the individual. When faced with this potential stressor, you appraise it (i.e., **primary appraisal**) in terms of whether you perceive it as stressful, positive (e.g., as a challenge), or benign (no effect). If you perceive it as stressful (i.e., **perceived stress**), you then appraise your coping resources (e.g., personal resilience, coping skills, social support) through **secondary appraisal**. If you feel that you don't have the coping resources to cope with the perceived stress, strain may result. **Strain outcomes** can be in the form of psychological strain (e.g., depression, anxiety), physiological strain (e.g., increased blood pressure, high salivary cortisol levels), or behavioural strain (e.g., overeating, staying home from work, smoking).

Lazarus and Folkman (1984) identified the importance of perception and appraisal to examine how individuals cope with potentially stressful demands. That is, given the same stressor, two people may perceive it differently and thus have different personal outcomes. For example, both John and Toshi get fired from their jobs. John loved his job and doesn't have many alternatives. He perceives his firing as very stressful. He doesn't have a solid

transactional stress model

States that if you appraise external stimuli (or *stressors*) as potentially threatening, you may perceive them as stressful (i.e., *perceived stress*); if you then appraise your coping resources as inadequate, you may experience strain (negative psychological, behavioural, and physical outcomes)

stressor

Stimulus in the environment (i.e., event, situation) that is potentially threatening to you

primary appraisal

The process by which you perceive the stressor/demand to be negative (stressful), positive (e.g., a challenge), or benign (no effect)

perceived stress

An individual perception about the extent to which you perceive a demand or stressor to be stressful

secondary appraisal

The process by which you appraise your coping resources (e.g., resources, social support)

strain outcomes

Can occur in the form of psychological strain (e.g., depression, anxiety), physiological strain (e.g., increased blood pressure, high salivary cortisol levels), or behavioural strain (e.g., overeating, smoking)

Figure 12.1

The Transactional Stress Model

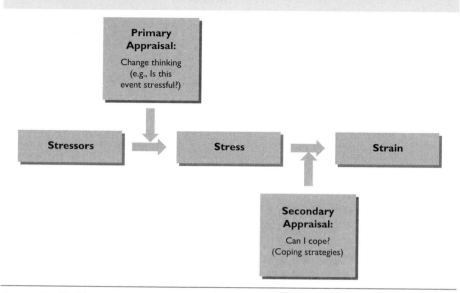

Source: Modified from Lazarus, R.S. & Folkman, S. (1984). *Stress, Appraisal,* and *Coping*. New York: Springer Publishing Company.

social network, has many expenses, and doesn't feel confident in his skills to find a new job. Conversely, Toshi didn't really like his job. Although he hadn't been looking for a new job, he views the firing as a positive event in that he is now free to find a better job that he loves. He has a great social network, who help him update his CV and provide suggestions for new jobs. Compared to John, Toshi probably will have lower strain symptoms during the aftermath of his firing.

The Conservation of Resources Theory

conservation of resources (COR) theory

States that individuals strive to obtain and maintain the resources that they value

The **conservation of resources (COR) theory** is a resource utilization theory (Hobfoll & Freedy, 1993) and is useful in understanding individual health and strain (Day, Sibley, Wentzell, Tallon, & Ackroyd-Stolarz, 2009). According to the COR model, individuals strive to obtain and maintain the resources that they value. Hobfoll (1989) defined *resources* as those "objects, personal characteristics, conditions, or energies that are valued by the individual or that serve as a means for attainment of these objects, personal characteristics, conditions, or energies" (p. 516). Resources may be individual characteristics, such as high self-esteem, or conditions such as being employed in a good job (e.g., Hobfoll, 1989). Negative outcomes (e.g., strain, burnout) can occur when individuals lose their resources and are unable to restore them (Hobfoll & Freedy, 1993). Similarly, these negative outcomes may arise if employees perceive threats to their resources due to work-related demands (e.g., a loss of work-related resources; Halbesleben & Buckley, 2004). COR theory postulates that negative health outcomes may occur not only when there is an actual loss in resources, but even when employees only perceive threats to their resources (Halbesleben & Buckley, 2004). Therefore, employees' *perceptions* of the work environment are important to our understanding of individual and organizational outcomes.

Person–Environment Fit Theory

The **person–environment fit (P–E fit) theory** identifies how negative outcomes may develop if there is incongruity between employees and their work environment. Two types of incongruity may occur: (1) incongruity between job demands and employee abilities, such that there is a mismatch between what the job requires and what the employee is able to do; and (2) incongruity between the needs of a person and what the organization gives to the person, such that the organization does not provide the benefits or resources the employee desires. See Box 12.5 and Box 12.6 for more on person–environment fit.

person–environment fit theory

Identifies how negative outcomes may develop if there is incongruity between employees and their work environment in terms of a mismatch between the job requirements and employee abilities, or between the needs of the employee and what the organization provides to them

---

Box 12.5

Person–Environment Fit

Both John and Laura work as information technology project managers. Their jobs involve planning, initiating, and managing information technology (IT) projects. They both lead and guide the work of several technical staff and serve as liaison between business and technical aspects of projects. For each new project, they monitor progress to ensure deadlines, standards, and cost targets are met. Consequently, they experience a lot of ambiguity in a constantly changing work environment. For example, their specific job tasks change depending on the project. Both John and Laura graduated from the same program in the top 10 percent of their class, both are highly skilled workers.

John is a person who loves stability, has a low tolerance for ambiguity, and prefers to have the job tasks clearly outlined. Conversely, Laura thrives on different projects and constantly changing requirements. She would get bored if she were doing the same thing every day.

Both John and Laura may be quite able to do the job effectively. However, because of the mismatch between the job requirements and his preferences, based on person–job fit theory we would expect John to experience stress and strain. Conversely, the person–job fit would be much better for Laura.

Box 12.6

P–E Fit in Action: Employee Growth and Development

So, how can we address a lack of "fit" in organizations? Obviously, the first step is to recruit and select the right type of people for our organization and for the specific job. However, we also have to ensure that we provide the right type of training for people in their current jobs, as well as development opportunities for other jobs in the organization. What kind of training can organizations offer?

The B.C. Automobile Association has been recognized for its healthy workplace initiatives focusing on employee growth and development. The company offers many opportunities for employees to increase their knowledge, skills, and abilities, and to put these new competencies into action. All employees have individual learning plans, to highlight not only the training that they *require*, but also the training that they *desire*. The company offers courses in many topics, including effective coaching, emotional intelligence, performance management, and leadership. It also provides a mentorship program for leaders and staff.

Job Demands–Job Control Model

job demands–job control model

States that high mental strain and job dissatisfaction will result if employees face high job demands yet have little control (i.e., decision latitude) over their work

The **job demands–job control model** (Karasek, 1979) is one of the best known of all models of job factors and well-being. According to this model, high mental strain and job dissatisfaction will result if employees face high job demands yet have little control (i.e., decision latitude) over their work (see Figure 12.2). That is, it is the combination of both job demands and lack of control that has the greatest negative effect on employees (Karasek, 1979). Although research tends to support the main effects of demand and control on well-being and strain, the research pertaining to an interaction between these factors is less consistent.

Effort–Reward Imbalance Model

effort–reward imbalance (ERI) model

States that psychological distress may occur if the amount of effort expended at work exceeds the amount of reward received in relation to this effort.

According to the **effort–reward imbalance (ERI) model**, if the amount of effort expended at work exceeds the amount of reward received in relation to this effort, psychological distress may occur, leading to increased risks to employee health (Siegrist, 1996). This ERI model may be viewed as a variant of the P–E fit model, such that a lack of reciprocity between the effort that individuals put into their work and the rewards they gain at work results in increased levels of stress. An imbalance between the efforts one expends and the rewards one receives has been related to health complaints, cardiovascular risk factors, and coronary heart disease (Siegrist, Peter, Junge, Cremer, & Seide, 1990).

Job Demands–Resources Model

job demands–resources (JD–R) model

Posits that employees are exposed to physical, psychological, social, and organizational aspects of the working environment that can be categorized either as demands (which can lead to health impairment) or as resources (which can lead to increased engagement)

The **job demands–resources (JD–R) model** (Demerouti, Bakker, Nachreiner, & Schaufeli, 2001) is a contemporary work stress model that can be used to explain how positive and negative health and work outcomes can be the product of various aspects of the working environment (see Figure 12.3). This model posits that employees are exposed to physical, psychological, social, and organizational aspects of the working environment that can be categorized as either

Figure 12.2

Karasek's (1979) Job Demand-Job Control Model of Job Stress

Degree of Control	Level of Demands	
	Low Demands	**High Demands**
Low Control	Low/Moderate Stress	High Stress
High Control	Low Stress	Moderate Stress

Source: Adapted from Karasek, R.A. Jr. (1979). Job demands, job decision latitude, and mental strain: Implications for job redesign. *Administrative Science Quarterly* 24(2): 285–308.

FIGURE 12.3

The Job Demands–Resources Model

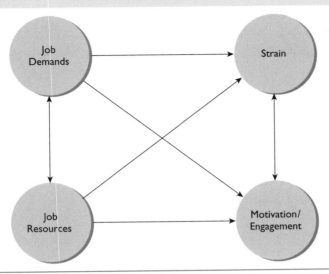

Source: Adapted from Bakker & Demerouti (2007); Demerouti, Bakker, Nachreiner, & Schaufeli (2001).

demands or resources (Bakker & Demerouti, 2007; Demerouti et al., 2001). *Job demands* refer to any aspects of the job (e.g., workload, time pressure, emotionally taxing social interactions, loud noises) that require extended physical or psychological effort on the part of the employee, and that are associated with increased physical and psychological costs (e.g., fatigue, exhaustion) (Bakker & Demerouti, 2007; Demerouti et al., 2001). Job demands are comparable to the conceptualization of job stressors within the transactional model of stress (Lazarus & Folkman, 1984), such that they may be perceived as stressful and result in negative personal outcomes.

Conversely, the work environment also includes a number of physical, psychological, social, and organizational aspects (e.g., job control, social support, task variety, and compensation) that encourage health and productive employees (i.e., *job resources*). These resources assist employees with the completion of their work, reduce the burden of job demands, and can promote personal growth and development (Bakker & Demerouti, 2007).

The JD–R model posits two psychological processes that influence employee job strain and work motivation (Demerouti et al., 2001). According to the *health impairment process,* job demands decrease an individual's physical and psychological resources, leading to burnout and other negative health outcomes (Schaufeli & Bakker, 2004). According to the *motivation process,* access to job resources can increase employee engagement and other positive outcomes (Bakker, Demerouti, De Boer, & Schaufeli, 2003). Also, even if you experience work demands (e.g., too much to do), having resources (e.g., a supportive boss) may help you cope with your work demands, thereby lessening their negative effect on your health and well-being (Bakker, Demerouti, Taris, Schaufeli, & Schreurs, 2003).

Table 12.1 provides a summary of the job stress models.

TABLE 12.1

Summary of Job Stress Models

MODEL	MAIN COMPONENTS	STRAIN RESULTS WHEN...
Transactional Stress Model (Lazarus & Folkman, 1984)	• Widely used stress model that is backed up with a lot of research • Individual perception is important: that is, strain is dependent on how individuals perceive the stressor and how they are able to cope with the stressor.	...stressors are appraised as negative (primary appraisal) and when resources are appraised as insufficient in dealing with the stressors
Conservation of Resources Model (Hobfoll & Freedy, 1993)	• Based on resource utilization theory, such that workers want to achieve and keep valuable resources. • Perceptions of resources (and their value) are predominant themes in this model.	...when resources are lost or perceived that they may be lost...
Person–Environment Fit	• Involves both person–job (P–J) fit and person–organization (P–O) fit	...there is a mismatch between job requirements and individual abilities (P–J fit) or between organizational resources and individual needs, values, and expectations (P–O fit).
Job Demand–Job Control Model Karasek (1979)	• Examines the extent to which the job demands are high or low, and the extent to which the job allows a high or low degree of control • Demand and control are dichotomized into high and low categories to produce a quadrant demonstrating the impact of these two factors on employee stress.	...when workers experience high demands and a low degree of control
Effort–Reward Imbalance Model (Siegrist, 1996)	• Is a variant of P–E fit • Emphasizes perception of worker as to how much effort expended and the value and amount of the rewards gained.	...there is a mismatch between the efforts put into the job and rewards earned
Job Demands–Resources Model (Demerouti et al., 2001)	• Defines "demands" and "resources" according to the dual processing theory • Original focus was on burnout and health care organizations, but has expanded to other areas. • Focuses both on negative outcomes (burnout, strain) and positive outcomes (engagement, motivation)	...there are high work demands and few resources (conversely high resources can lead to increased engagement)

Demands/Stressors

These models emphasize that employees face a variety of demands or stressors, not only from their work environment, but also from other areas of their lives. Demands or potential stressors are external and internal events and stimuli that may create strain in workers. So what kind of demands or stressors do people experience at work?

Work Demands

We can use Sauter, Hurrell, and Murphy's (1990) framework to summarize work "demands" (or stressors) into six categories: (a) job content and control; (b) interpersonal relationships; (c) workload and work pace; (d) role stressors; (e) career concerns; and (f) work scheduling.

Job Content and Control

The actual tasks that people perform at work (i.e., job content) can contribute to perceptions of stress and strain. For example, repetitive tasks within a job or jobs that do not make full use of the individual's skills may result in higher strain (Kelloway, Francis, & Montgomery, 2005). Conversely, having control over the predictability of work, the scheduling of work, and the amount of work (i.e., job control) is associated with lower stress and strain (Day & Jreige, 2002; Dwyer & Ganster, 1991) and increased job satisfaction, commitment, and involvement (Spector, 1986).

Interpersonal Relationships

Workplace relationships may be a source of social support or stress (Kelloway & Day, 2005a; Sauter et al., 1990). Interpersonal conflict at work is related to several negative outcomes, such as depression (Frone, 2000), whereas workplace social support tends to be associated with lower strain. Leadership issues and relationships within work units all may influence one's outcomes. Interpersonal injustice (see Chapter 8) can lead to increased stress and strain outcomes.

Workload and Work Pace

Ideally, as mentioned in the person–environment fit model, workload demands should match the abilities of the employee (Sauter et al., 1990). Being overworked is associated with both psychological and physiological strain (for a brief review, see Kelloway & Day, 2005a). Both actual and perceived workload has been commonly identified as an indicator of poor work–life balance (Adebayo, 2006; Dex & Bond, 2005; Johansson, 2002; Kodz et al., 2003).

Role Stressors

Role stressors can result in strain when employees experience conflicting demands due to ambiguous definitions of responsibilities (i.e., role ambiguity) or conflicting demands (i.e., role conflict; Day & Livingstone, 2001; Kelloway & Day, 2005a).

Career Concerns

Career concerns may arise from job insecurity, work safety, and effort–reward imbalance (Kelloway & Day, 2005a). Expending more effort in relation to the rewards gained over longer periods can lead to negative health consequences (Siegrist, 1996).

Work Scheduling

Ideally, work scheduling should allow professionals to meet the demands of their non-work life (Sauter et al., 1990). Employees who work non-standard hours tend to experience more emotional exhaustion, more job stress, a higher incidence of psychosomatic health problems (e.g., headaches, upset stomach, etc.), and higher overall burnout (Appleton, House, & Dowell, 1998; Demir, Ulusoy, & Ulusoy, 2003; Jamal, 2004).

We can organize these six demands/stressors into general categories of job-specific, interpersonal, and organization. That is, role stressors, job content, workload, and work pace are *job-specific*. Job control is a factor of the job, as well as the degree to which the leader and organization facilitate increased control. *Interpersonal* includes all relationships with coworkers, supervisors, subordinates, and clients. Finally, workload, work pace, career concerns, and work scheduling issues are addressed under both job and *organization* dimensions.

A special case of interpersonal-based work stressors is the stigma attached to mental illness and accompanying discrimination at work.

Stigma

According to the Canadian Mental Health Association, 20.6 percent of workers in Canada will suffer a bout of mental illness, and an estimated 500,000 workers are off sick each day in Canada with mental health problems. There is a growing trend to define stigmatization and discrimination as stressors (Miller & Kaiser, 2001). Using this perspective, we can use the stress models outlined above to examine the outcomes of this stressor on individual health and well-being as well as organizational outcomes. These models may also provide some guidance as to the potential role of individual and social resources, which may buffer the negative effects of the stress created by stigmatization (Miller & Major, 2000). To date, however, there has been little research in this area.

Non-Work Demands

In addition to these work demands, people can experience demands from their non-work life that may affect their health and level of job stress. We will talk about the impact of non-work demands later in the chapter, in the section on work–life balance.

Resources

As much as we focus on the types of demands that result from work, there is also evidence to show that many aspects of work can have a positive effect on worker well-being. Research has identified a number of variables that may directly impact on perception and outcomes, and also that may buffer the relationship between stressors and strain outcomes. Interestingly, some of these "resources" are simply the polar opposite of the "demands" identified above. For example, a lack of control in a work situation is associated with increased stress, whereas providing job control is considered a resource or buffer (see

Box 12.7

Healthy Workplace Best Practices

VanCity: Coping with Critical Events

Sometimes industries have specific stressors that impact their employees' physical and emotional health. VanCity is Canada's largest credit union with branches throughout British Columbia. Many are located in urban areas with high crime rates, and have experienced robberies which increased staff distress and absenteeism. In response, a Robbery Intervention Program (RIP) was implemented, including a post-robbery protocol to ensure staff and customer safety, a debriefing opportunity to help staff deal with distress, and funds and time for staff to engage in group morale activities. Compared to branches that did not have this program, the RIP intervention branches had significantly less absenteeism (10.6 versus 35.9 over a 3-month period after a robbery), and lost time was well below the industry average. Because the program was so successful, it was implemented across the organization.

Box 12.7 for an example of a program that helps employees cope with critical events). We can categorize these resources as arising from work, home and family, and personal (or individual) resources.

Work Resources

Control

Having control over *what type* of work you do in your job (e.g., getting to choose assignments), *how* you do your job (choosing the methods and tools needed to do your job), *when* you do your job (e.g., flexible work hours), and *where* you do your job (e.g., telecommuting) is associated with positive health outcomes for employees. It may also buffer the relationship between demands and individual outcomes; however, there has been mixed support for this moderating effect (Sonnentag & Frese, 2003).

Support

Support from one's coworkers and supervisors has been shown to be associated with lower strain (Rhodes & Eisenberger, 2002; Sonnentag & Frese, 2003). Similarly, higher levels of organizational support are associated with positive individual, group, and organizational outcomes (Rhodes & Eisenberger, 2002) and decreased levels of work–life conflict (Thompson, Beauvais, & Lyness, 1999). It also has been suggested as a means for reducing burnout (Duxbury & Higgins, 2003).

Social support may buffer against workplace stressors by alleviating the negative outcomes created by work stressors (Frese, 1999; Viswesvaran, Sanchez, & Fisher, 1999). Similarly, according to the job demands–job control model, more negative outcomes are expected for employees experiencing low support and higher stress. Therefore, in addition to simply resulting in more positive health outcomes, employees' experience of social support from colleagues, supervisors, and the organization overall may reduce the negative impact of workplace stressors (e.g., workload, work scheduling, role conflict) on employee health outcomes (e.g., strain, burnout, and work–life balance).

Justice

Fair treatment by the organization (procedural justice), fair outcomes (distributive justice), and fair treatment by supervisors and other organizational members (interpersonal justice) are associated with fewer strain outcomes, higher commitment, and higher job satisfaction (Colquitt, Conlon, Wesson, Porter, & Ng, 2001; Elovainio, Kivimäki, & Helkama, (2001). See Box 12.8 for organizational examples of treating employees fairly through recognition and involvement.

Family, Life, and Personal Resources

In addition to work resources, several non-work and personal resources (e.g., personality, coping styles, and social support) can enhance individual health and functioning at work. Remember that, according to the transaction model of stress, the way in which we appraise a situation or stressor influences the way we respond to it. Our initial appraisal of a situation may be a factor of our personality and coping style.

Box 12.8

Fair Treatment in Action: Canadian Healthy Workplaces

How can organizations treat employees fairly and provide them with the recognition they deserve and the open communication to help them become more involved in the organization?

Employee Recognition

Two small workplaces, Holiday Inn Express in Halifax and the Kingston and District School in rural Nova Scotia, are "recognized" for their efforts in recognizing the work of their employees. Holiday Inn Express offers its "Express Stars" program so that employees can earn points in numerous ways and redeem them for an array of rewards. The company also offers year-round formal and informal recognition—cards and movie passes on birthdays, paid holidays on service anniversaries, and family barbeques in summer. The Kingston and District School incorporates employee recognition into its motto of "Caring, courtesy, and cooperation." It has orientation-day lunches and a "welcome to the team" event for all new staff. The culture of respect underlies all efforts to recognize each others' accomplishments.

Employee Involvement: Scotiabank's Atlantic Customer Contact Centre

Scotiabank's Atlantic Customer Contact Centre in Halifax goes out of its way to ensure high involvement for all its employees. It offers an "employee voice committee" and recognition programs designed by the employees themselves. An open-door policy, coupled with employee committees, a "Coffee Talk" program, employee surveys, suggestion programs, and team meetings, ensures that their voices are heard.

But does management *really* listen? In a recent address, vice president Dave Dobrosky noted that employees were asked to rank the forms of recognition they most value. Some of employees' top choices were initiatives that were available but that had not been the focus of the recognition programs (e.g., promotions, additional training). Based on these survey results, the Atlantic Contact Centre switched its focus and started to identify ways of recognizing employees using their top choices (see Chapter 9 for more details).

Social Support

Support from one's spouse, coworkers, family, and friends has been shown to be associated with lower strain, and it may buffer the relationship between demands and strain outcomes. There is some research to show the buffering effects of community work.

Personal Characteristics

Several personal characteristics have been associated with reduced strain and higher well-being, as well as group and organizational outcomes. *Locus of control* (Rotter, 1966) has a main effect on well-being, but although cross-sectional studies support the moderating effect of locus of control, longitudinal studies are less supportive. There has been consistent evidence for a main effect of *self-esteem/efficacy* on well-being. Although there is weak evidence for the moderator effect of self-esteem, there is somewhat more support for efficacy. *Type A behaviour* can result in negative health outcomes such as cardiovascular disease. There is some support for a main effect of the impatience–irritability component of Type A behaviour on strain and job satisfaction (e.g., Day & Jreige, 2002), but findings with regard to a moderating effect are equivocal. There is evidence of a main effect of *hardiness* on strain, but the evidence for a moderating effect is conflicting (Sonnentag & Frese, 2003).

Coping Style

In the transactional model of stress, secondary appraisal involves assessing whether you have the resources to deal with a situation that you have labelled as stressful. Lazarus and Folkman (1984) distinguished between emotion-focused and problem-focused coping. Emotion-focused coping involves making yourself feel better about the situation (e.g., talking with a supportive friend). Problem-focused coping involves actively doing something to try to make the problem better (i.e., "fixing" the problem). Carver et al. (1994) included avoidance coping as a negative coping style. Avoidance coping involves mentally or physically disengaging so you don't have to address or even think about the problem. You may distract yourself by watching TV, or even by drinking and doing drugs.

Problem-focused coping style may be effective when the problem is within the control of the individual. Conversely, emotion-focused coping is more effective in situations where the individual has no or little control over the demand or stressor. It is acknowledged that *long-term* avoidance coping typically is a poor form of coping (especially when coupled with alcohol and/or drug abuse), which can lead to negative individual outcomes.

Negative and Positive Health Indicators

We can classify outcomes in terms of individual or organizational outcomes. That is, employee stress can impact one's own health, well-being, and productivity, or the overall organizational "health" and productivity.

Individual Outcomes

How does this stress affect us? Much of the research has focused on individual outcomes, in terms of behavioural outcomes, psychological outcomes, and physical outcomes.

1. *Behavioural outcomes* may include several different categories: (a) counterproductive work behaviours include aggressive behaviour, stealing, incivility; (b) flight from job involves absenteeism, turnover, and early retirement; (c) work degradation involves decreased job performance, increased work-related accidents; (d) degradation of other life roles involves a reduction in one's functioning in other roles (e.g., parent, spouse); and, finally, (e) self-damaging behaviours involve drug or alcohol abuse, smoking, and increased caffeine intake.
2. *Psychological outcomes* may involve work-related affect (e.g., increased job dissatisfaction, lowered organizational commitment) or more generalized outcomes (e.g., anger, frustration, hostility, anxiety, nervousness, and worry). It also may involve serious psychological symptoms, such as depression, burnout, and post-traumatic stress.
3. *Physical outcomes* may include more immediate symptoms, such as elevated blood pressure and cortisol levels. These types of outcomes may include more distal outcomes, such as cardiovascular heart disease (e.g., heart attacks), gastrointestinal symptoms (e.g., heartburn).

When examining these outcomes, it also is important to note that relationships among outcomes may be reciprocal. That is, psychological outcomes (depression) may then lead to further behavioural outcomes (e.g., absenteeism), which may then create more negative psychological outcomes. In effect, some of these outcomes become stressors or demands that create more negative outcomes.

Burnout

burnout

A syndrome composed of high levels of emotional exhaustion, cynicism, and a reduced sense of professional efficacy.

We've talked a lot about how stressors and stress can lead to burnout. But what exactly is burnout? **Burnout** is defined as a specific work-based psychological negative reaction or syndrome that is composed of high levels of *emotional exhaustion, cynicism,* and a reduced sense of *professional efficacy* (Maslach, Schaufeli, & Leiter, 2001; see Table 12.2). Burnout was studied initially in the context of health care or service professions (Maslach & Jackson, 1981; Maslach et al., 2001), but burnout has been studied extensively across many occupations.

Burnout may develop as a result of a lack of job–person fit; that is, employees may experience burnout if they have a chronic mismatch between their expectations and the conditions they experience in the workplace (Maslatch & Leiter, 1997; Maslach et al., 2001). Maslach et al. (2001) identified several areas of work life as the main sources of mismatch leading to burnout (i.e., values, control, reward, community). Employees or professionals who chronically experience these mismatches may be more likely to suffer from burnout (Maslach et al., 2001).

Michael Leiter

Michael P. Leiter is a Canada Research Chair of Occupational Health and Wellness, Professor of Psychology at Acadia University in Canada, and Director of the Center for Organizational Research & Development, which applies high-quality research methods to human resource issues confronting organizations. Dr. Leiter is internationally renowned for his work on job burnout and engagement. Currently his research focuses on enhancing the quality of collegial relationships to enhance work engagement and to prevent burnout.

Source: Courtesy of Michael Leiter.

Engagement

Burnout experts have argued that the opposite of burnout is engagement. **Work engagement** can be defined as "being charged with energy and fully dedicated to one's work" (Schaufeli, Salanova, Gonzalez-Roma, & Bakker, 2002, p. 119). The Utrecht Work Engagement Scale measures engagement in terms of vigour, dedication, and absorption (Schaufeli et al., 2002; see Table 12.2).

According to Schaufeli et al. (2002), therefore, we not only want employees to have a lack of burnout, but also to be engaged in that they are high in energy, are dedicated to their job, and feel absorbed by their work.

work engagement
Being charged with energy and fully dedicated to one's work; involves the components of vigour, dedication, and absorption

TABLE 12.2

Burnout vs. Engagement

BURNOUT COMPONENTS (MASLACH BURNOUT INVENTORY, GS; MASLACH ET AL., 1996)	ENGAGEMENT COMPONENTS (UTRECHT WORK ENGAGEMENT SCALE; SCHAUFELI ET AL., 2002)
(1) *Emotional exhaustion* involves feeling emotionally overextended and fatigued by one's work.	(1) *Vigour* involves high levels of energy and mental resilience while working, the willingness to invest effort in one's work, and persistence even in the face of difficulties.
(2) *Cynicism* involves having cynical attitudes and feelings about one's clients, customers, and colleagues.	(2) *Dedication* involves a sense of significance, enthusiasm, inspiration, pride, and challenge.
(3) A reduced sense of *professional efficacy* involves feeling incompetent and like a failure.	(3) *Absorption* involves concentrating on and being engrossed in one's work, where time passes quickly and one has difficulty detaching oneself from work.

Organizational Outcomes

In addition to individual health outcomes, stress may affect individual behaviours and performance that influence organizational performance. Stressors can lead to narrowed attention and decreased working memory capacity, which can impact decision making. However, there is not a lot of evidence linking stress and job performance.

However, there is evidence to suggest that workplace stressors are related to many important organizational attitudes and behaviours. For example, individuals who experience a high degree of work stressors tend to have lower organizational commitment and are more likely to think about leaving the organization (i.e., turnover intentions) as well as demonstrating actual turnover behaviour (Griffeth, Hom, & Gaertner, 2000). Individuals who report work-related strain tend to have higher rates of absenteeism.

Work–Life Conflict

Even though the focus of this book is on the work environment, we need to talk about people in their non-work environments. In the 1970s, Kanter (1977) talked about the "myth of separate worlds," such that there was a belief that what happened at home stayed at home (or at least "should" stay at home), and vice versa. She argued that people don't work (or live) in a vacuum, so we need to look at the person in all of their environments to understand work behaviour. That is, what happens at home and in other areas of our lives can impact our performance and attitudes toward work, and what happens at work can impact our home life. Individuals face demands (or gain resources) from their family members, friends, and their community, including their hobbies and volunteer work. These demands (e.g., child care and elder care responsibilities, volunteer activities) or resources (e.g., social support) can influence individual and organizational performance and attitudes.

Work–life conflict is defined as "a form of inter-role conflict in which the role pressures from the work and family domains are mutually incompatible in some respect. That is, participation in the work (family) role is made more difficult by virtue of participation in the family (work) role" (Greenhaus & Beutell, 1985, p. 77). For example, if an individual is overloaded in one particular role (i.e., work or family), they may experience decreased physical and psychological health across *both* roles (Duxbury & Higgins, 2003). Although the focus of most organizational research began with work–family conflict, there has been an expansion to include other non-family roles, so that we talk about work–life conflict.

work–life conflict

A type of inter-role conflict in which the role pressures from work and family (or other life domains) are mutually incompatible, such that participation in the one role is made more difficult by virtue of participation in another role

Causes of Work–Life Conflict

Work–life conflict is a result of conflicting demands or strain in multiple roles (e.g., work, parent, spouse) (Greenhaus & Beutell, 1985). Greenhaus and Beutell (1985) argued that conflict may arise because of incompatible time demands, strain arising from two or more roles, and/or incompatible expectations from different roles.

Time Demands

In a recent study, more than 60 percent of working Nova Scotians indicated that they have a high workload (Francis & Kelloway, 2006). This figure is similar to statistics involving other workers across Canada and the United States. Having a high workload, coupled with demands from outside of work, may result in conflict. For example, Sasha's boss frequently asks him to stay late to attend a 5:00 p.m. meeting. However, Sasha is a single father and must pick up his child at a daycare centre across town by 5:15 p.m. These incompatible time demands create conflict and stress for Sasha, as he tries to make his boss happy by attending the meeting while also fulfilling his parental responsibilities.

Role Strain

In a recent study of workers in the U.S., 74 percent of the sample reported that work was a significant source of stress. Strain experienced within either the work or family domain is likely to predict strain that occurs between the work and family relationship. Evidence suggests that stress in work or family roles (or in other life roles, such as volunteer or community member) may be associated with increased work–life conflict. The experience of work-related stress (e.g., high work demands) tends to be related to increased work–life conflict (Frone, Russell, & Cooper, 1997). For example, Carol experiences strain at work because her boss is rude and very demanding. She is so upset when she gets home each day that she frequently is withdrawn or argumentative with her family. Consequently, she begins to experience more stress at home. This spiral of stress may then create other pressures at work, affecting her overall well-being and performance.

Behaviour Expectations

Although this area has not been studied extensively, there is some research to suggest that having different expectations at work and at home can create conflict and strain. For example, Sanjay is expected to demonstrate control over crowds in his job as a police enforcement officer. He must stay calm and unemotional yet firm, and make decisions instantly and on his own. Conversely, at home his wife and family expect him to share his emotions and engage in democratic decisions, after having fully discussed the options with all family members. Sanjay finds it difficult to make the switch from home to work, and back to work. Therefore, these incompatible expectations from different roles are increasing the amount of conflict and stress that he experiences.

Outcomes of Work–Life Conflict

Similar to the research on job stress, work–life conflict can result in negative outcomes for employees. A high degree of work–life conflict contributes to perceived stress, lowered physical health, and increased alcohol use. Individuals experiencing work–life conflict tend to report reduced performance in the family role and increased absences from family events (Frone, 2003).

Despite the large amount of research on work–family and work–life conflict, there is a recent trend of researchers and practitioners to talk about work–life *balance* instead of *conflict*. So, how can we move from conflict between work and non-work roles to a more "balanced" life?

Work–Life Balance

> "Life is like riding a bicycle. To keep your balance you must keep moving" —Albert Einstein

Work–life balance (WLB) involves an absence of conflict among one's roles and being able to manage conflicting demands. However, WLB is more than simply this lack of conflict: it involves "the integration of work and family by setting personal goals and understanding personal values so that neither work nor family consumes the other" (Duda, 1998, p. 9).

There also is a "vague notion that work and family life are somehow integrated or harmonious" (Frone, 2003, p. 145). That is, it involves a degree of interrelatedness, such that being in one role can energize and improve one's performance in other roles. For example, if Kara's spouse is a computer expert, she may draw on this resource in dealing with her day-to-day technology-based hassles (such as a computer crash) at work. Similarly, conflict management classes at work may help Liam deal with interpersonal issues with his wife and children.

For more detail on work–life balance in Canada, see Box 12.9.

Reducing Conflict and Improving Balance

Similar to the resources available to reduce work stress, other variables may play an important role in alleviating work–life conflict and, conversely, improving work–life balance. Having more *job control* may help one balance work and life responsibilities. For example, workers with more control over their work schedule may have increased flexibility that allows them to balance

---

Box 12.9

Work–Life Balance in Canada

The balancing of multiple commitments, including work and family, is a reality for Canadians.

- One in four Canadians who work for medium- to large-sized organizations experience *high* levels of work–family conflict (Duxbury & Higgins, 2003).
- People are working longer hours and more shiftwork (Duxbury & Higgins, 2003). Data from the mid 1990s indicate that 32 percent of the labour force works a "non-regular" shift. That is, they work evenings, nights, or rotating shifts (Johnson, Lero, & Rooney, 2001). As of 2001, one in four Canadian employees spent more than 50 hours per week at work (Duxbury & Higgins, 2003).
- Approximately 60 percent of Canadian employees have family responsibilities (Duxbury & Higgins, 2003).
- The number of women in the workforce has increased (Statistics Canada, 2008).
- One-quarter of Canadian employees provide care and support for an elderly person (Johnson et al., 2001).

their work and life. *Social and organizational support* can have a beneficial effect by helping to eliminate workplace stressors that contribute to work–life conflict, and a supportive home environment can help reduce family and life stressors that may impede an individual's job performance and increase conflict (Frone, 2003).

There are also several *employee-friendly organizational initiatives* that may help employees reduce conflict and balance their work and life responsibilities. One of the most popular methods of improving balance is through flexible work arrangements.

Flexible Work Arrangements

Flexible work arrangements are any changes to the traditional work schedule that help employees balance their work and life responsibilities in four ways: (1) reducing the amount of time spent in the workplace; (2) increasing the amount of control over work; (3) providing support for personal and medical leave; and (4) providing support for child and elder care.

Reducing Time

One of the obvious ways of reducing the number of hours at work is by working part time. This option is used by many people who want to work, but who have other non-work demands and priorities (e.g., parents with small children). Working part-time can allow individuals to stay in the workforce while also allowing more time to spend in other areas of life.

However, some types of jobs may not be designed for part-time work. Therefore, options such as **job sharing**, in which two or more employees share the responsibilities of a single job or position, allow people to have the part-time option in a job that requires a full-time employee. With this arrangement, employees typically alternate days (e.g., Margot works Monday to Wednesday, and Ivan works Thursday and Friday) or split shifts each day (e.g., Margot works from 8:00 a.m. to 12:00 p.m. and Ivan works from 1:00 p.m. to 4:00 p.m. each day).

job sharing
A type of flexible work arrangement in which two or more employees share the responsibilities of a single position

Another option in this category doesn't actually involve fewer work hours, but simply allows employees to work the same hours in fewer days. With **compressed work weeks**, employees can choose to work a 40-hour work week as four 10-hour days instead of five 8-hours days. Although it doesn't decrease the amount of overall time at work, some employees prefer this option because they reduce their commuting time (one fewer day each week) and they feel they have an extra full day for their non-work demands and/or hobbies.

compressed work weeks
A form of flexible work arrangement in which full-time employees work longer hours each day, but fewer days per week (e.g., four 10-hour days each week)

Increasing Control

We have noted that some of the conflict between work and life roles is due to incompatible time demands; that is, people often have to be in two places at the same time. By increasing the amount of control that employees have over *when* (i.e., flextime) and *where* (i.e., telecommuting) they do their work, they may be able to avoid (or at least minimize) such conflicts.

flextime

A form of flexible work arrangement that allows employees to have some degree of control over when they start and finish their workday

Flexible work schedules, called **flextime**, allow employees to have variable start and finish times to their workday, with varying degrees of flexibility. Some organizations allow employees to choose their own start and end times, but these times are consistent every day. Other organizations may allow employees to start any time between two specified times (e.g., between 7:00 a.m. and 10:00 a.m.) and work for their prescribed work shift, allowing them to change on a daily or weekly basis. The degree of control that flextime offers allows employees to better manage time-based conflicts between their work and life roles.

Whereas flextime offers employees some control over *when* they start and end their workday, **telecommuting** provides them with some control over *where* they work. Telecommuting is a flexible work arrangement in which employees complete some or most of their job tasks away from the office (usually at home). The use of information technologies (phone, fax, BlackBerry) helps them stay connected to the work environment. There are several benefits of telecommuting to both employees and organizations: reduced commuting time for employees; more flexible work hours, such that the employee may start at a later time (once the children are off to school), or end earlier (when kids come home from school) and finish work in the evenings; and reduced overhead costs for organizations (office space, etc.). There are some drawbacks of telecommuting as well: employees may feel a loss of "connectedness" with the office and colleagues and may feel isolated; they may work longer hours (because their work is more accessible to them); and they may miss out on important information or opportunities by not being "in the loop." Therefore, some people have chosen to telecommute on a part-time basis by working at home several days a week, and working in the office the other days (NIOSH, 2002).

telecommuting

A flexible work arrangement in which employees complete some or most of their job tasks away from the office (usually at home)

Providing Leave Time

Another potential for conflict occurs when a personal illness, emergency, or family obligation arises. Therefore, providing time for people to deal with these non-work issues decreases their stress and conflict, and allows them to return to work and be fully engaged. Leave time includes maternity and parental, personal days, family leave, and sick leave. In Canada, employees are allowed to take up to one year of maternity and parental leave, while still being paid part of their salary through the Employment Insurance program. Some organizations choose to supplement this leave (up to their total salary) or extend the leave.

Providing Support for Child and Elder Care

Employers can help employees with young children balance their work and family responsibilities by providing child care–related initiatives, such as information services to help their employees find suitable daycare; financial subsidies to help offset the cost of daycare; on-site daycare (either subsidized or non-subsidized) or programs with trained caregivers who can care for sick children (when they can't attend daycare or school); and summer programs for school-aged children, which can engage children and reduce conflict and stress by providing parents with child care arrangements over the summer months.

People and Work in Canada

With the increase in numbers of employees who are considered part of the "sandwich generation" (i.e., people who are caring for both younger children and aging parents), many organizations are offering assistance or benefits pertaining to elder care. Again, some programs pertain to the provision of information about care homes, in-home care, and other elder care issues. Other organizations may offer monetary benefits to go toward child and elder care, or provide additional time off (personal leave, family leave) to help care for parents and other elderly relatives.

These initiatives help employees to balance work and life responsibilities, which may result in less stress and improved health outcomes. In addition to creating family-friendly or employee-friendly policies and practices, organizations can take a broader perspective of creating "healthy workplaces," taking into consideration both the employee's perspective and needs and the organization's need to be successful. This concept of a healthy workplace and organization (Tetrick & Quick, 2003) is gaining in popularity. Refer to Box 12.10 for real-world examples of organizations promoting work–life balance.

Healthy Workplaces

What Do We Mean by a Healthy Workplace?

Initially, the term "healthy workplace" typically referred to a safe workplace (in terms of low risks to the physical safety of workers) or the financial functioning of the organization (in terms of being able to weather economic downturns). Quick, Quick, Nelson, and Hurrell (1997) argued that the health of an organization and the health of the employees are interdependent, and therefore the definition expanded to include the physical health and lifestyle behaviours of workers (e.g., promoting exercise and introducing smoking-cessation programs). Finally, the recent trend has been to include all of these factors along with the psychological health and well-being of workers. That is, an organization or workplace is considered to be **psychologically healthy** only if it meets four criteria: (1) it has a safe and healthy environment; (2) it has a safe

psychologically healthy workplaces

Workplaces that foster employees' physical and psychosocial health, safety, and well-being, while ensuring high standards of organizational effectiveness and performance

---

Box 12.10

Work–Life Balance in Action

Both the Vancouver Airport Authority and the Westminster Savings Credit Union in British Columbia have done a lot to help employees balance their work and life responsibilities, and as such they were recipients of the APA Healthy Workplace Award. The Airport Authority emphasizes the importance of work–life balance and offers programs to help employees balance their work and life responsibilities. The company offers flexible work hours and job-sharing

options. It also offers parents up to two years' leave *on top of* the federally regulated maternity and parental leave.

Westminster Savings Credit Union has generous vacation time and work options such as job sharing, reduced work weeks, and variable hours. The company provides 12 paid days for illness in the employee's immediate family, plus three days for illness in the extended family. It also pays 100 percent of employee health care benefits.

---

and healthy psychosocial environment; (3) it supports a healthy lifestyle for employees; and (4) it has high organizational effectiveness and performance.

The World Health Organization defines health not simply as the absence of illness or disease, but rather as an overall state of mental, physical, and social health and well-being. Therefore, when creating healthy workplaces, we must focus not only on programs and practices that reduce stress and ill health, but also on ones that energize employees and promote engagement and satisfaction. That is, a healthy organization can be defined as one that promotes employees' mental and physical health and safety while demonstrating high efficiency and productivity.

Healthy Workplace Models

Several models of workplace health have been developed. The American Psychological Association defines a psychologically healthy workplace as one that fosters employee health and well-being while enhancing organizational performance (see Figure 12.4). Their model suggests that these two outcomes of well-being and performance can directly impact each other. That is, healthy employees tend to be more productive, and a thriving business may spend more time and energy ensuring healthy employees.

The focus is on five categories of workplace initiatives that influence these two outcomes: (1) *work–life balance* (i.e., promoting a healthy balance between one's work and life responsibilities); (2) *health and safety* (i.e., promoting both the physical and psychological health and safety of employees by preventing, assessing, and treating potential health risks and by supporting healthy lifestyle choices); (3) *employee recognition* (i.e., formally and informally rewarding

FIGURE 12.4

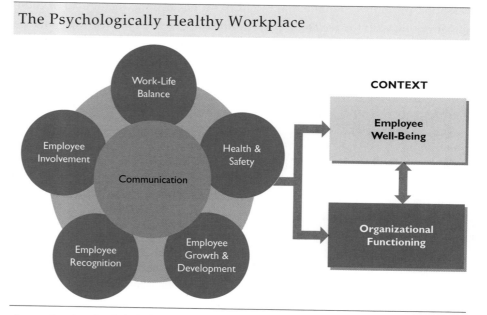

The Psychologically Healthy Workplace

Source: American Psychological Association (2008). "Psychologically Healthy Workplace Components," *Psychologically Healthy Workplace Awards and Best Practices Honors,* 2008. Washington, DC: American Psychological Association. Reprinted with permission.

employees both individually and collectively for their service to the organization); (4) *employee involvement* (i.e., involving employees in decision making and providing them with increased job autonomy); and (5) *employee growth and development* (i.e., encouraging employees to expand their knowledge, skills, and abilities and apply these competencies to new situations). For more information, see www.phwa.org.

Communication is an essential component of a healthy workplace. Open and honest channels of both bottom-up (from the employees to the top management) and top-down communication help to ensure clear communication of the healthy workplace practices across the organization and that everyone has a voice in the organization. See Box 12.11 for some facts on healthy workplace initiatives in Canada.

Based on the job stress and healthy workplace literature, Kelloway and Day (2005a) presented a general model of the contributors to the development and maintenance of healthy workplaces, as well as the outcomes (see Figure 12.5). They note that their model may not include all aspects of healthy workplaces, but may help to provide a basis for future research in the area. They included both psychosocial and physical factors as predictors of a healthy workplace: the *physical work environment*, in terms of having a safe environment and ergonomically designed workspace. A *culture of support, respect, and fairness, employee involvement*, and *interpersonal relationships* all emphasize the psychosocial aspects of how we treat people at work. *Work content* and *characteristics* involves the actual job tasks and aspects around the work (e.g., work schedule, amount of control). Finally, *work–life balance* figures prominently in their model.

Their consequences of healthy workplaces mirror those of the APA model in terms of individual outcomes (psychological, physical, and behavioural) and organizational outcomes (employee turnover and performance, organizational reputation, and customer satisfaction), and also include a broader category of societal outcomes (impact on government programs and national health care costs).

The APA and Kelloway and Day models have similarities in how they take a holistic view of healthy workplaces and how they include both physical and psychosocial indicators. Although they are intuitively appealing, more research is needed to examine their efficacy.

Box 12.11

Healthy Workplace Practices in Canada

According to a 1999 Conference Board of Canada survey of Canadian employers (Bachman, 2000):

- 88 percent offered flextime
- 50 percent had options for telecommuting
- 63 percent offered family-related leave

- 48 percent offered compressed work weeks
- 52 percent provided job-sharing options
- 15 percent provided on-site or nearby daycare (Johnson et al., 2001).

FIGURE 12.5

Antecedents and Outcomes of Healthy Workplaces

Source: K. Kelloway and A. Day. (2005a). Building Healthy Workplaces: What we know so far. *Canadian Journal of Behavioural Sciences* 37(4): 309–312.

Healthy Workplace Best Practices

We have highlighted several organizations throughout this chapter that have recognized the importance of creating aspects of a healthy workplace. They have demonstrated their excellence by promoting employee well-being and health while still demonstrating financial success. Note that many of these initiatives can encompass the APA healthy workplace model and Kelloway and Day's (2005) model of healthy workplaces.

But to what extent do organizations in general implement healthy workplace programs and policies? An estimated 90 percent of mid-sized organizations in the United States (Aldana, 2001; Riedel et al., 2001) and 64 percent of organizations in Canada (Lowe, 2003) offer some form of wellness and health-related programs. Some of this difference in program offerings of U.S. and Canadian companies may be because Canadian organizations have been slower to develop these programs because of our public health care system. See Box 12.12 for more information on Canadian initiatives.

Box 12.12

Healthy Workplace Programs

A variety of programs across Canada are designed to promote and acknowledge healthy workplace initiatives. Health Canada has partnered with the National Quality Institute to create the Healthy Workplace Awards, Healthy Workplace Week, and other initiatives designed to help organizations address the issues that impact employee health. Check it out at: http://www.nqi.ca.

Through the American Psychological Association's Psychologically Healthy Workplace Program, five provinces currently offer awards programs: B.C., Alberta, Manitoba, Ontario, and Nova Scotia (www.phwa.org; www.nshealthyworkplaces.ca).

The Halifax Chamber of Commerce offers Healthy Business Awards to recognize businesses that demonstrate leadership and commitment to workplace health. Check it out at: http://www.halifaxchamber.com/default .asp?mn=1.65.410]

In addition to programs that explicitly recognize healthy workplaces, many awards programs recognize the "best of the best" in terms of great places to work. The physical and psychological health of employees are key components. For example:

- Best Places to Work in Atlantic Canada and the Top 101 Companies (Progress Media)
- 50 Best Employers in Canada (Report on Business, Globe and Mail) report on organizational leadership, culture, and employee recognition
- Canada's Top 100 Employers (Maclean's & Mediacorp); examines eight key components: physical workplace; work atmosphere; health, financial, and family benefits; vacation and time off; employee communications; performance management; training and skills development; and community involvement (http://www. canadastop100.com)
- Financial Post's Ten Best Companies to Work For (using the same criteria as the Maclean's Top 100)

Note: To find out more about Health Canada and the National Quality Institute's healthy workplace initiatives, visit www.nqi.ca and www.hc-sc.gc.ca/whb-smt. For more information about Healthy Workplace Week in particular, visit www.nqi.ca/chww/index.htm.

Making a Business Case for Healthy Workplaces

Many organizations that have implemented healthy workplace practices report very positive employee and organizational outcomes. As noted in Box 12.1 at the beginning of this chapter, Secunda Marine has a high employee retention rate, stable insurance premiums, and one of the lowest lost-time incident rates in its industry. All these figures add up to not only a healthy and happy workforce, but also a productive and profitable organization.

After implementing healthy workplace initiatives, Vancouver Airport Authority reported a very high average attendance rate (97 percent) in 2006, with a low turnover rate. It also has a much healthier workforce with fewer injuries. For example, in 1999, it had 222 days lost due to injury for 300 employees. In 2006, there was a dramatic drop to 32 days lost due to injury.

Scotiabank's Atlantic Customer Contact Centre in Halifax and the B.C. Automobile Association both have been recognized as having psychologically healthy workplace practices. The Contact Centre experiences low turnover and absenteeism rates and improved overall productivity. B.C. Automobile Association reported double-digit growth in revenues and profits each year, part of which it attributes to improved employee engagement and morale.

Overall, the American Psychological Association reported that compared with the national average of companies in the U.S., the APA's 2009 award winners reported 28 percent less turnover, 14 percent less chronic work stress, and 27 percent lower turnover intentions. Moreover, 87 percent of employees from the "healthy workplaces" indicated they would recommend their company as a good place to work, compared to only 44 percent of the national average. Finally, employees from healthy workplaces were 24 percent more likely to be satisfied with their job than were other employees.

Despite these impressive figures, it is important to note that most are reported by organizations themselves, without rigorous standards of research. Although the extant data are positive, to date there has not been a lot of systematic, quantitative research into the impact of healthy workplace practices on employee health. However, a recent meta-analysis demonstrated that employee attitudes (i.e., job satisfaction) and employee engagement were related to organizational outcomes such as firm profitability, productivity, customer loyalty, turnover, and safety (Harter, Schmidt, & Hayes, 2002), indicating that "enhancing employee outcomes (e.g., satisfaction, well-being) translates into business success" (Kelloway & Day, 2005a, p. 230).

Individual and Organizational Interventions

Researchers have a fairly solid foundation about the sources and consequences of job stress, burnout, and work–life conflict. Organizations need to examine intervention programs aimed at reducing negative outcomes and improving health. The National Institute of Occupational Health and Safety (NIOSH) identified intervention effectiveness research as a top research priority. Experts in occupational stress interventions consistently recommend more experimental field research and more rigorous critiques of existing stress interventions at work (see Kelloway, Hurrell, & Day, 2008).

When dealing with these stressors and strains, there are three levels of intervention: primary, secondary, and tertiary (Quick et al., 1997). We can also categorize them in terms of individual versus organization-based interventions.

Primary intervention involves reducing or eliminating the amount of stressors and demands experienced by employees, and is a valuable component of stress reduction. Although it may be seen as the *ideal* form of stress management, it is not feasible as the sole solution for two reasons. First, it is impossible to eliminate all demands at work; there will always be deadlines and challenges that make up one's day-to-day work life. Second, because the same demand can be viewed differently (positively or negatively) by different people, it is impossible to identify and eliminate the demands. For example, some people thrive on the tight deadlines of the media world, whereas other people would find these demands overwhelming. Despite the evidence showing the effectiveness of engaging in primary interventions at work, primary prevention strategies are not broadly implemented in Canadian organizations, perhaps because organizational decision makers assume the cost and logistics of primary preventive strategies are excessive (Hepburn, Loughlin, & Barling, 1997).

Conversely, there has been a lot of focus on **tertiary interventions**, which involve treating health problems once they have occurred. Although

primary interventions

Interventions to reduce or eliminate the amount of stressors and demands experienced by employees

tertiary interventions

Interventions that involve treating health problems after they have occurred these types of interventions are absolutely necessary, a sole focus on them is not optimal because prevention is ignored. A focus on tertiary interventions places the burden of strain on individuals, organizations, and society. Moreover, even in the face of stressors, many illnesses, including cardiovascular concerns and diabetes, are preventable with early interventions aimed at stress management, nutrition, and exercise (Stampfer, Hu, Manson, Rimm, & Willett, 2000).

Therefore, **secondary interventions** involve minimizing negative consequences when a person is feeling stress by changing individual perceptions of stressors and increasing individual coping resources. Secondary interventions are important because they bridge the gap between primary and tertiary interventions. They acknowledge that not all stressors can be eliminated but also empower individuals to minimize their negative reactions to potential stressors, thus decreasing reliance on tertiary treatment.

secondary interventions
Interventions that involve minimizing negative consequences once a person is feeling stress by changing individual perceptions of stressors and increasing individual coping resources

Primary Interventions: Reducing Stressors

Organizations must recognize their role in creating a healthy work environment by minimizing stressors and providing supports and programs aimed at improving health, reducing stress, and improving work–life balance. However, because it is impossible to eliminate all demands in any context, and because stress and strain occur only when the individual appraises these events as being stressful and beyond their coping abilities, it is important to provide employees with these valuable appraisal techniques and coping skills. For example, although employees may not have total control over the extent of the workload in their job, they can control the demands in other areas of their life, and time management techniques may help reduce scheduling stressors.

Because poor interpersonal relations are a significant source of job stress (Sauter et al., 1990; Warr, 1987) and lead to job dissatisfaction and lower productivity (Hain & Francis, 2006; Hodson, 1997), interventions aimed at improving interactions through effective communication and conflict management techniques may reduce stressors before they result in stress and strain.

Also, as noted in the section on job stress, a lack of control is linked to decreased job and life satisfaction and increased stress (Adams & Jex, 1999; Carayon, 1995; Day & Jreige, 2002; Spector, 1986). To some degree, job control is a function of the job itself and may not be something that study participants will be able to change. However, when control can be granted in one or more areas of employees' work life (control over scheduling of work or over the workspace), employee outcomes may be more positive.

Secondary Interventions: Coping, Reappraisal, and Strain Reduction

When we can't reduce stressors or demands, secondary interventions are aimed at improving one's ability to reappraise and cope with these demands. Coping is defined as behavioural and psychological attempts to reduce the symptoms of a stressful situation (Lazarus & Folkman, 1984). *Emotion-focused coping* involves changing how one feels about a stressful situation. For instance, enacting *social support* can be beneficial and calming (Taylor et al., 2000). *Problem-focused coping* involves changing the stressful situation through problem solving (Lazarus & Folkman, 1984). *Cognitive reappraisal* involves changing the way one thinks about a stressful situation or reinterpreting the situation in a positive manner. *Disengagement* involves using food, alcohol, or drugs or other activities to "disengage" from one's problems (Carver, Scheier, & Weintraub, 1989). Both emotion-focused and problem-focused coping are associated with lower distress (Violanti, 1992). Typically, problem-focused coping is effective when stressors are within one's control, and emotion-focused coping and cognitive reappraisal are effective when the stressor is outside one's control. Conversely, disengagement is associated with negative outcomes (Day & Livingstone, 2001; Tyler & Cushway, 1995). Strain reduction techniques (e.g., yoga, meditation, progressive muscle relaxation) are aimed at minimizing the negative consequences of stress. Similar to reappraisal, these techniques tend to be most effective when employees cannot control the source of the stress. They may be able to reduce strain by invoking what control they have over their *response* to the stress.

How effective are these techniques? In general, relaxation techniques, such as progressive muscle relaxation (Jacobson, 1938), have been found to be effective, especially in improving psychophysiological outcomes. Similarly, cognitive behavioural therapy (CBT) has been shown to be very effective. Rational emotive therapy is also helpful, but it is more effective when combined with CBT. Finally, stress inoculation training (gradual exposure) can reduce performance anxiety and state anxiety and improve performance.

Tertiary Interventions: Treating Psychosocial and Physical Illness

Because we can't eliminate all demands and stressors for our employees, organizations need to include tertiary interventions in any comprehensive workplace health program (Kelloway & Day, 2005; Kelloway, Hurrell, & Day, 2008). Whereas secondary interventions focus on short-term coping, tertiary interventions focus on treating illness and minimizing future health issues and disease. For example, employee and family assistance programs (EFAPs) are a common form of tertiary intervention (Kelloway et al., 2005) and typically include services to provide information about available resources (e.g., day care and elder care services), as well as phone-based or face-to-face counselling on a wide range of employee services, such as problems with spouse and family members, substance abuse (by the employee or family members), job stress, health concerns, and legal and financial issues (Mio & Goishi, 1988). EFAPs also may include referral services to experts on various issues and/ or online and hard copy resources to help employees resolve their issues. See Table 12.3 for a summary of workplace health initiatives.

Although the benefits of individual counselling have been demonstrated (e.g., Bower, Rowland, & Hardy 2003; Lambert & Bergin, 1994), the overall value of EFAPs to organizations has been questioned because they are underutilized (especially by the employees who are in greater need of the services). Conversely, other researchers have reported significant organizational benefits of EFAPs (Landy, Quick, & Kasl, 1994).

TABLE 12.3

Examples of Workplace Health Initiatives

INITIATIVE	LEVEL OF INTERVENTION	INITIATIVE DETAILS
Job and Work Redesign	Primary	This initiative is very broad and refers to any program or change to the job or work environment that is intended to decrease demands and stressors on employees. For example, introducing a communication system that allows group members to stay more in touch with each other may be seen as positive work redesign.
Interpersonal Training	Primary	Providing training and socialization to new and existing employees about the standards of personal conduct in the workplace, and developing skills to promote civility and a culture of respect.
Employee-Friendly Programs	Primary	The programs discussed in the work–life balance section (e.g., job sharing, daycare options) tend to focus on reducing the amount of stressors experienced by employees in terms of reducing time demands, reducing strain, and providing support.
EFAPs	Secondary and tertiary	Provide resources and counselling; help identify personal and organizational resources; provide strategies and training to help deal with work and life strain.
Drug & Health Care Plans	Primary and tertiary	Provide financial resources (and access to health clinics) for primary treatment (e.g., flu shots; cholesterol screening clinics); provide resources to help treat illness (e.g., drug plan; tertiary)
Lifestyle Programs	Primary, secondary, and tertiary	Creating and improving healthy lifestyles to prevent illness (e.g., exercise to maintain health and decrease risk of heart attack; primary interventions); provide coping resources (e.g., getting eight hours of sleep, habits to give energy to deal with work demands; secondary intervention); treat illness (e.g., dietary changes to reduce high blood pressure; tertiary intervention).

Tertiary interventions also can include debriefing following exposure to a traumatic event (such as a car accident or death). Most or all Canadian emergency services offer some form of stress debriefing (Kelloway, Francis, Catano, Cameron, & Day, 2004). A program of multiple sessions, coupled with strong social support and cognitive behavioural therapy, tends to be effective (Kelloway, Hurrell, & Day, 2008; McNally, Bryant, & Ehlers, 2003).

Stress Management Programs

Stress management programs are designed to provide workers with information about the potential causes and outcomes of stress, and to provide relaxation and coping strategies for managing the physical and psychological symptoms of stress. The most common types of stress management programs are cognitive–behavioural skills training, progressive muscle relaxation, and meditation (Murphy, Hurrell, Sauter, & Keita, 1995) (see Table 12.4).

Lifestyle Programs

Another category of initiatives revolves around the behaviours and lifestyles of employees. These lifestyle programs (also known as work health promotion

TABLE 12.4

Stress Management Programs

STRESS MANAGEMENT PROGRAM	INITIATIVE DETAILS
Cognitive Behavioural Skills Training	• A type of stress management technique in which people are provided training on being aware of how they are responding to events (and why), and thinking about events in a new way that is less threatening • Provide coping strategies
Relaxation Training and Progressive Muscle Relaxation	• Activities such as progressive muscle relaxation and deep breathing techniques • Designed to physically relax the body in order to decrease the physiological aspects of stress (e.g., heart rate, blood pressure) • Also designed to identify when individuals are feeling tense so they can avoid the situation or practise their relaxation skills
Meditation	• The focus is on using some mental exercises to quiet the mind in order to temporarily disengage from a stressful situation • Many different techniques; often used in conjunction with relaxation training and yoga

programs) have typically been offered in conjunction with EFAPs. They can target the reduction of illness directly, or indirectly through prevention. Their popularity lies in the belief that a healthy lifestyle will help to promote physical and mental health on the job.

These lifestyle programs may help in three ways: (1) to prevent illness (e.g., smoking cessation and exercise may reduce chances of heart attack; primary interventions); (2) to provide people with the resources to better cope with stress (e.g., good nutrition and sleep habits to help stay energized; secondary intervention); or (3) to treat illness (e.g., dietary changes and salt restrictions to help reduce high blood pressure).

Many programs and initiatives fall under the healthy lifestyle rubric: health-promotion activities (e.g., lunchtime walking programs, healthy cafeteria options); on-site fitness facilities or gym membership subsidies; health screening opportunities (e.g., for glucose, cholesterol, blood pressure, body mass index); and clinics and programs designed to improve health through nutritional counselling, smoking cessation, and weight management. Typically, these initiatives are offered on a voluntary basis only. Organizations may provide incentives for using such resources and programs, but they can not make it mandatory.

Effectiveness of Interventions

How Effective Are Organization-Based Intervention Programs?

Similar to the research on healthy workplaces and programs addressing work–life balance, there has been very little systematic evaluation of the effectiveness of many intervention programs. Some studies suggest that employee-friendly programs may increase work–life balance (e.g., Thompson et al., 1999). Furthermore, the use of flextime may decrease rates of absenteeism but not turnover (Dalton & Mesch, 1990), and flextime and telecommuting may increase job satisfaction (Baltes, Briggs, Huff, Wright, & Neumann, 1999).

It has been suggested that these family- and employee-friendly initiatives may be integral to recruiting and retaining high-quality employees (Kossek, 2003). In fact, 85 percent of recruiters have had candidates reject a job offer because it didn't include enough work–life balance (Association of Executive Search Consultants, 2009). Moreover, 78 percent of high school students reported that they want jobs that provide good benefits, and 79 percent indicated they want jobs that allow time for personal and family activities (Galinsky, Kim, Bond, & Salmond, 2003).

How Effective Are Individual-Based Intervention Programs?

For the most part, it depends on what types of interventions are included. Typically, programs aimed at improving social support tend to be quite effective in terms of reducing stress, improving team climate, and increasing positive attitudes toward the organization.

However, there are mixed results pertaining to the effectiveness of stress management training programs. Some research has indicated that particular techniques are effective (e.g., Keyes, 1995), whereas other studies have found they may be helpful only in certain situations. For example, Thomason and Pond (1995) found that a stress management training program that involved multiple techniques, including relaxation training, cognitive training, and positive self-talk, was not effective. However, when a self-management module (which involved identifying goals and behaviours) was included, there were significant decreases in blood pressure, somatic indicators, and anxiety (Thomason & Pond, 1995).

Meta-analytic studies have found that work-related, individual stress management programs, in terms of relaxation programs, cognitive behavioural programs, and multi-model interventions (coping skills), are somewhat effective (Van der Klink, Blonk, & van Dijk, 2001). Interventions that use a combination of different approaches (e.g., relaxation and CBT) tend to be most effective. It also appears that the effectiveness of individual strategies is affected by several job factors; for example, employees who have high job control and high-status jobs have more positive outcomes.

Future Study

Despite the importance of tertiary interventions for treating physical and psychological disorders and illness, Kelloway and Day (2005b) argued that a "sole focus on treatment, however, will limit us to continually 'heal the wounded'" (p. 296). Therefore, they suggested that we also need to ensure that organizations focus on "the full range of interventions designed to enhance individual well-being" (p. 296), including EFAPs, stress management, and job redesign. Despite these suggestions, Kelloway et al. (2008) noted that they were "struck by the paucity of empirical evidence supporting the effectiveness of primary intervention" (p. 433), even though there have been many calls over the past 20 years for more research and evaluation of interventions (see, for example, Giga, Noblet, Faragher, & Cooper, 2003; Murphy & Sauter, 2003).

Some evidence has demonstrated the effectiveness of workplace programs and interventions aimed at decreasing stress and increasing well-being (for reviews, see Sonnentag & Frese, 2003; Van der Klink et al., 2001; Hurrell, 2006). However, more research must be conducted on the effectiveness of interventions, because "this research is vital to the promotion of well-being and the prevention of stress related disorders in the workplace" (Kelloway et al., 2008, p. 435).

Respite and Recovery

Given the significant impact of job stress on both individuals and organizations, it is not surprising that organizations are interested in identifying the types of workplace intervention that can help employees cope with job stress and work–life balance issues. A related area of research on work stress is devoted to understanding how *non-work activities* can improve the physical and psychological health of employees. That is, do breaks from work (respites) help people unwind, relax, and recuperate from work, and what types of activities or behaviours help people restore their energy, mood, and physical and mental health (recovery)?

respites

Using time away from work to re-energize and promote individual health and well-being; can include vacation time, weekends, and days off of work

Respites involve using time away from work to re-energize and promote individual health and well-being, and can include vacation time, weekends, and days off work (Westman & Eden, 1997). In general, the research suggests that vacations do have a substantial impact on employee well-being (in terms of decreased stress and burnout), but that these positive effects are short-lived (Eden, 2001; Westman & Eden, 1997; Westman & Etzion, 2001). Therefore, if employees take only one main vacation each year (as is typical for most workers), the positive effects of this type of respite may be minimal. Similarly, weekends and days off may have a significant effect, but are limited in duration.

Because of the short-lived effects of longer respites (in terms of vacations), researchers were curious about how one's behaviours and activities would affect health in the short term (i.e., on a daily basis). That is, what do employees do after work that may rejuvenate them and promote physical and psychological health?

recovery

The process of accumulating resources (e.g., energy, positive mood) and restoring them to help improve one's mood and physical and psychological health

Sonnentag and her colleagues (e.g., Sonnentag, 2001; Sonnentag & Bayer, 2005; Sonnentag & Fritz, 2007) conceptualized **recovery** as the process of accumulating resources (e.g., energy, positive mood) and restoring them to help improve one's mood and physical and psychological health.

According to Sonnentag and Fritz (2007), four types of recovery experiences are central to the recovery process: (1) *psychological detachment* involves avoidance of the demands or stressors (i.e., distracting oneself and not thinking about work) (Sonnentag & Bayer, 2005); (2) *relaxation* involves low-stimulation activities in which one is able to "wind down" and physically and mentally relax; (3) *mastery* is the extent to which an activity is challenging and promotes individual achievement and growth; and (4) *control* involves the extent to which one has control over their choice of activities in their non-work time (Sonnentag & Fritz, 2007).

Summary

Occupational health psychology is the application of psychology to organizational settings to protect the physical and psychological health and safety of employees and to promote healthy work (Barling & Griffiths, 2003; Quick, 1999).

Occupational health and safety legislation provides a framework for examining these issues. Employers have a responsibility to provide a safe environment for their workers, and this responsibility is also assumed by supervisors, contractors, joint OHS committees, and the employees themselves. Much of the focus of OHS legislation implicitly deals with the physical health and safety of employees. However, OHP deals with the broader health issues, including psychological well-being.

One of the most predominant OHP issues in the workplace is job stress. There are many models of job stress that focus on the external stimuli, stressors, or demands that have the potential to create stress or strain in individuals. These models also tend to highlight how individual perception or resources can result in positive outcomes or can mitigate the negative health outcomes arising from the stressors or demands.

Demands may include a lack of control; poor leadership, supervision, and interpersonal relationships at work; conflict and ambiguity within the job role; and work overload. Conversely, work can provide many resources to help employees cope. Support from peers and supervisors has been demonstrated to have positive effects on individual health and well-being. Fair procedures and outcomes at work also promote employee health. Non-work resources (such as family support) can also improve outcomes at work.

Burnout is a psychological syndrome that is composed of high levels of emotional exhaustion, cynicism, and a reduced sense of professional efficacy. Work–life conflict is a form of inter-role conflict in which the role pressures from the work and family domains are mutually incompatible in some respect. Conversely, work–life balance involves not only the absence of conflict among one's roles, but also the integration of work and life roles.

There has been a recent drive toward the promotion and creation of healthy workplaces (including "psychologically healthy" workplaces). These types of workplaces support employee health and well-being while simultaneously ensuring high organizational performance and productivity. Although they are intuitively appealing, there is little empirical evidence examining their effectiveness. However, some of the initial results are promising. Finally, recent research also has examined how time off work (either in terms of weekends and vacations or simply on a daily basis) can help workers rejuvenate or recover from the demands of a workday.

Key Terms

burnout 344

compressed work weeks 349

conservation of resources (COR) theory 334

effort–reward imbalance (ERI) model 336

flextime 350

job demands–job control model 336

job demands–resources (JD–R) model 336

job sharing 349

occupational health and safety (OHS) 328

occupational health psychology (OHP) 328

perceived stress 333

person–environment fit theory 335

primary appraisal 333

primary interventions 356

psychologically healthy workplaces 351

recovery 362

respites 362

secondary appraisal 333

secondary interventions 357

strain outcomes 333

stressor 333

telecommuting 350

tertiary interventions 356

transactional stress model 333

work engagement 345

work–life balance 348

work–life conflict 346

Web Links w(w)w

To find out more about work–life conflict and employee-friendly work policies, check out the Sloan Foundation's Work Family Network website at:

http://www.bc.edu/bc_org/avp/wfnetwork/

For more information on occupational health and safety and occupational health psychology, check out the U.S. National Institute of Occupational Safety & Health at:

www.cdc.gov/niosh

Discussion Questions

1. Think back about the various models of job stress that were presented in this chapter. Which one do you prefer? Why? What do you like about it?

2. Is there something better than work–life balance? We know that balance is a lack of work–life conflict, but can our life roles be more than simply "balanced"? Can we integrate our various work and life responsibilities to make ourselves better and/or happier somehow? Think about a situation in which knowledge or skills you have developed in one area of your life have helped you in another area of your life.

3. As we noted in this chapter, mental illness in the workplace is becoming a critical issue—as is the resultant stigma faced by people with mental illness—but there has been little research examining this topic. You have just been awarded a large grant from the Canadian Institutes of Health Research to study mental health and stigma in the workplace. Congratulations! Now you just have to decide what

questions are important and need to be examined. What are your top priorities?

4. People "unwind" or "recover" from work in various ways. What do you do when you have had a particularly stressful day at school or at work? What types of activities do you find to be most helpful? Which are least helpful?

5. Think back to a recent job you held. What was the single most stressful aspect of your job? Was it the work that you did? Your supervisor? The lack of support or control over your work? Knowing what you now know about interventions and employee stress and health, what would you do to improve your job and work environment?

Using the Internet

There has been growing discussion among researchers, managers, and employees about healthy workplaces, and more recently about *psychologically* healthy workplaces. Check out the websites for the APA's Psychologically Healthy Workplace Program (http://www.phwa.org) and the National Quality Institute's Healthy Workplace (http://www.nqi.ca/hwr/default1.aspx?name=hwr_news). How are their components similar? Which model do you think is more valid and applicable to workplaces?

Check out these varied healthy workplace sites in Canada to learn more about healthy workplaces:

http://nshealthyworkplaces.ca

http://www.phwc.ca

http://www.ohwc.ca

Exercises

1. You have decided to start up your own landscaping company. You've recently hired a number of people and must train them according to the *Occupational Health and Safety Act* and regulations.

   a. What are the regulations you must train your employees on, and how will you do so?
   b. What initiatives will you take as a supervisor and owner to ensure your company maintains proper health standards?
   c. Think of a creative way to keep your employees interested in following the regulations.

2. Selvagem Inc. is a printer company that has started laying off employees due to lack of sales. Unfortunately, the layoffs are causing the survivors (i.e., the employees who are staying with the company) to take on more tasks than they can handle. Moreover, the workers

Chapter 12: Occupational Health Psychology

perceive the supervisors to have a reduced workload because they simply delegate any extra work to the subordinates. The employees report high degrees of strain, and sick leaves and absences have increased substantially (which create even more work for the employees who do show up). The company wants to ensure that a healthy workplace is maintained despite current working conditions, and have asked for your help.

    a.   What would you do first?

    b.   Create a primary, secondary, and tertiary intervention for the company to use to help improve employee well-being. What are the pros and cons of each strategy?

    c.   If you could use only one strategy, which one would you recommend and why?

3.   Think of a previous or current job, and consider what you have learned about work demands and job stressors (e.g., role ambiguity, lack of job control, poor interpersonal relationships):

    a.   What work demands and stressors did you (or do you currently) experience? What ones did your colleagues experience?

    b.   Did you perceive these demands to be stressful? Why or why not? If they were stressful, how did you address them?

    c.   What changes could have been made to reduce the negative impact of the identified stressors? (*Hint:* Think about organizational changes, changes to the job, and individual changes.)

    d.   If these stressors and your perceived stress persisted without being addressed, what issues could arise for you?

Case

Drugs R' Us is a (fictitious) pharmaceutical company located in Ontario with approximately 400 employees in one location. The company is concerned about low morale, high rates of turnover and absenteeism, and high levels of employee strain shown in its last employee survey. Drugs R' Us has heard about psychologically healthy workplaces and is eager to start moving in that direction in order to become an "employer of choice" in the next five years. The company has hired you to create a template of what it needs to do over the next five years, and has asked you to identify some programs and policies to help it achieve its goals.

Discussion Questions

1.   What steps are you going to take to help Drugs R' Us?

2.   What will your five-year plan look like? Think back to some of the best practices presented in this chapter to help you outline your plan.

CHAPTER 13

Unionization

There are at least two reasons to consider the role of unions from the standpoint of I/O psychology. First, labour unions are organizations in their own right and create the context for unique forms of organizational behaviour. Participation in union governance, filing grievances, and other forms of union behaviour are unique in that they are voluntary and allow the individual a voice that may be denied in employing organizations. Second, unions exist in organizations and have a demonstrable effect on other behaviours, in which we are interested. To the extent that we ignore the role of unions we run the risk of the "construction and dissemination of a truncated body of knowledge" in I/O psychology (Barling, 1988, p. 103). Despite these observations, the relationship between I/O psychologists and the labour movement has been described as one of "mutual neglect."

Chapter Learning Outcomes

After reading this chapter you should be able to

- Describe the unionization process
- Identify the major influences on both general and specific union attitudes
- Explain the effect that unions have on variables of interest to I/O psychology

Unionization is a common feature of workplaces around the world. In the United States, union density in 2005 was 12.5 percent (U.S. Department of Labor, n.d.), while in Canada approximately 30 percent of the workforce belongs to a union (Perspectives on Labour and Income, 2007). In Europe the rates of labour force unionization range rather dramatically from 26.2 percent in the U.K. (Online, n.d.) to 74.1 percent and 78 percent in Finland and Sweden, respectively (Visser, 2006). Outside of the North American and European context, Australia reports union density rates of 22.9 percent, while Japan's union density rate is approximately 19.7 percent of the working population (Visser, 2006). For an explanation of some of the key terms related to unions, see Box 13.1.

Overall density rates may present a misleading picture because unionization varies by sector. For example, in Canada less than 20 percent of private-sector employees belong to unions—however, over 70 percent of the public

Box 13.1

What Is a Union?

The classic legal definition of a **union** is a combination of people who are joined together for a common cause. In the early days of unionism the primary "cause" was often the lowering of work hours and increasing work wages, although modern unions are concerned with a wide variety of issues.

Unions come in all shapes and sizes. They may represent the workers in just one organization or represent workers in several countries. Larger unions are often organized into "locals," where a **local** is a branch of the union in a particular workplace. One of the largest unions in Canada, for example, is the Canadian Union of Public Employees (CUPE). They represent a diverse group of workers right across the country. CUPE Local 30 is the branch of CUPE that represents about 2,000 outside workers for the City of Edmonton (and other municipalities).

Unions can have fewer than 10 or more than 100,000 members. Unions that represent one particular occupation (e.g., electricians) are known as **craft unions**, while organizations that represent all workers in an industry (e.g., all public employees) are known as **industrial unions**.

Whatever workers are recognized by a union, the common element is that unions bargain collectively with management. **Collective bargaining** means that the union bargains on behalf of all the members represented by the union. The agreement reached through this process (i.e., "the contract") is known as the **collective agreement**. The collective agreement is legally binding on the employer, the union, and the employees represented by the union.

union

A combination of people joined together for the purposes of bargaining collectively with an employer

local

A branch of a union

craft union

A type of union that represents only workers of a certain occupation (e.g., the nurses' union, the teachers' union)

industrial union

A union representing employees in a number of different occupations (e.g., the Public Employees' union)

collective bargaining

The process through which the union negotiates on behalf of all members

sector is unionized (Perspectives on Labour and Income, 2007). Similarly, in the United States, where overall unionization is low and declining, 47 percent of those who are unionized work in government (U.S. Department of Labor, n.d.). Unionization also varies widely by province (see Figure 13.1), with Newfoundland and Labrador being the most unionized and Alberta the least unionized province.

The Unionization Process

While unions represent individuals collectively, it is ultimately individuals who join and comprise these labour organizations. Understanding unionization, therefore, requires understanding the factors that motivate individuals to join labour unions. Barling, Fullagar, and Kelloway (1992) defined **unionization** not as a single decision, but rather as a process that begins long before the individual enters the workforce and continues throughout the span of union involvement. Key events in this process can be placed within four broad categories: pre-joining, joining the union, committing to and participating in the union, and leaving the union. We examine each of these in turn.

Pre-joining

Drawing on social learning theory (Bandura, 1977), researchers have suggested that individual attitudes toward unions may be formed through a process of socialization. That is, as children see their parents' involvement with

FIGURE 13.1

Unionization Rate by Province

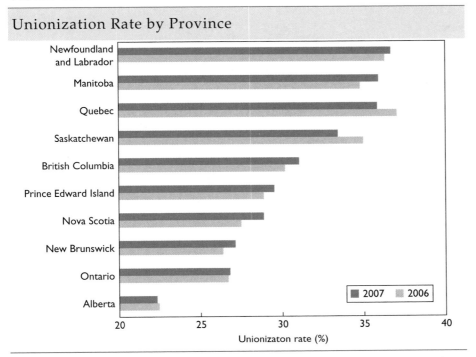

Source: Statistics Canada, http://www.statcan.gc.ca/pub/75-001-x/charts-graphiques/topics-sujets/
unionization-syndicalisation/2009/cga-eng.htm <January 2009>.

labour unions or hear their parents talk about unions, they may form their own individual attitudes toward unions that are relatively stable over time (Getman, Goldberg, & Herman, 1976). There is a wealth of data suggesting that parental work experiences affect children (e.g., Barling, 1990; Kelloway & Harvey, 1999). Finally, data consistently support the notion that even very young children can accurately report on parental job attitudes (Piotrkowski & Stark, 1987). Taken together, these observations suggest that union attitudes may develop through a socialization process.

Barling, Kelloway, and Bremmerman (1991) found that young adults' union attitudes are significantly predicted by their perceptions of their parents' attitudes toward unions. Furthermore, their degree of both Marxist and humanistic work beliefs directly affected young people's union attitudes. These results are strengthened by research illustrating that young people can indeed correctly identify and report their parents' union beliefs (Kelloway & Watts, 1994). The hypothesized role of family socialization processes on the development of union attitudes has largely been supported by a large body of empirical research (e.g., Hester & Fuller, 1999; Kelloway & Newton, 1996). Consistent with a family socialization model, the links between parental and children's attitudes are stronger when the child identifies with the parent in question (Kelloway, Barling, & Agar, 1996). Further, family socialization influences on union attitudes may affect the views of potential managers (Pesek, Raehsler, & Balough, 2006), suggesting that early family influences may impact on subsequent organizational behaviour (Kelloway & Harvey, 1999). Perhaps most interestingly, family socialization processes appear to be a more

collective agreement

The contract or agreement between union and management that is binding on management, the union, and all members of the union

unionization

The process through which an individual becomes associated with a union important influence on young workers' union attitudes than their own job attitudes and experiences (Dekker, Greenberg, & Barling, 1998).

Joining

Arguably the most researched question relating to unions is why individuals decide to join a union in the first place (Barling et al., 1992). To some extent this interest may have been misplaced, because many individuals become union members as a result of closed shop agreements. In a **closed shop agreement** (usually part of the collective agreement), the union and management agree that all employees in the bargaining unit will be union members. Thus, under such an agreement one becomes a union member simply by accepting employment in a unionized firm. Despite this, unions wishing to expand their members and employees wishing to prevent unionization are both intensely interested in why individuals would vote for (or against) a union during a **certification election**. For a summary of the certification process, see Box 13.2.

As noted in the prior discussion of pre-joining attitudes, the social context also plays a key role in unionization. Brett (1980) proposed that a belief in collective action, often operationalized as a positive general attitude toward unions (Kelloway, Barling, & Catano, 1997), is predictive of union voting. LaHuis and Mellor (2001) expanded this model, suggesting that pro-union attitudes are associated with a greater willingness to join the union and anti-union attitudes are associated with a resistance to union joining.

Finally, most of the empirical evidence supports a rational choice model (e.g., Charlwood, 2002; Visser, 2002), in which individuals evaluate the costs and benefits of joining a union. Certainly the perception that a union will be instrumental in resolving job dissatisfactions or injustice is frequently identified as a predictor of union joining (e.g., Barling et al., 1992; Buttigieg et al.,

closed shop agreement

A provision of collective agreements stating that all workers must be a member of the union

certification election

An election held to determine whether a union will be "certified" as the bargaining agent for a group of workers

---

Box 13.2

The Union Certification Process

When unions are certified, it means that they are recognized as the bargaining agent for a group of employees. When employees are trying to form a union (either on their own or by forming a new local of an established union) they conduct a certification campaign.

During a certification campaign, the union organizers will try to convince individual employees to join the union by signing a union card. Signing a card means that the individual has agreed to join a union. If the organizers are able to get at least 40 percent (the exact percentage may vary by jurisdiction) of the employees to join, they apply to the provincial or federal labour relations board to have an election held. The labour board then conducts an election,

and if a majority of employees vote to join a union then the union is certified. In some jurisdictions, the election may be waived if the union can demonstrate that more than 50 percent of employees have already joined the union.

Certification campaigns can be quite intense. Employees have the legal right to join a union and an employer cannot interfere with that right. Intimidating workers who join a union or offering benefits to those who don't are considered unfair labour practices and are illegal. Nonetheless, there is a whole industry of consultants and advisors who help employers to maintain a union-free status, and accounts of "dirty tricks" abound (see, for example, Geoghan, 1991).

2007; Charlwood, 2002; Visser, 2002). Mellor, Holzworth, and Conway (2003) found that the perceived costs and benefits of unionization, as well as contextual factors (i.e., whether individuals were asked to vote for or against a union; see also LaHuis and Mellor, 2001), were important predictors of individual voting decisions in a union representation election.

It is most likely that these models are complementary rather than competing and that there is some truth in each of the foregoing suggestions. Brett (1980), for example, proposed that unionization is the combined result of job dissatisfaction (i.e., frustration-aggression), a belief in the value of collective action (identification), and the perception that joining a union would be instrumental in resolving the dissatisfaction (rational choice). Kelloway, Francis, Catano, and Teed (2007) noted the similarity between this view and empirically supported models of participation in social protest (e.g., Klandermans, 1997, 2002; Opp, 1998).

Thus the answer to the question "why do people join unions" is a complex one. In the first instance there must be some dissatisfaction or frustration in the workplace. Union organizers recognize this with the adage "you can't organize happy workers." In Brett's (1980) model, this dissatisfaction or frustration is the "trigger" of the union-joining process. Simple dissatisfaction is not enough—the individual must also believe that the union will be helpful in resolving this dissatisfaction. This notion of the instrumentality of union joining often becomes the focus of a certification campaign, with unions attempting to show how successful they have been in similar organizations and management attempting to argue that the union will not be able to resolve any complaints that the employees have. Finally, the third necessary condition for a decision to join a union is a positive perception of unions in general. Some individuals are so anti-union that they will never willingly join a union no matter how dissatisfied they are. Without a positive or at least accepting attitude toward unions, it is unlikely that an individual would be willing to join a union.

Committing to the Union

Just because one is a member of the union (perhaps as a consequence of employment) does not mean that an individual identifies with or is involved with the union. Indeed, many members of a union may be apathetic, or openly hostile, toward the union, and it is important to understand members' attitudes toward the union. In an explicit attempt to foster research on union–member relations, Gordon, Philpot, Burt, Thompson, and Spiller (1980) developed a measure of union commitment that they defined as "the binding of an individual to an organization" (Gordon et al., 1980, p. 480). As a union-based parallel to organizational commitment (see Chapter 8), union commitment was thought to be an important predictor of union-relevant behaviours.

In their original formulation, Gordon et al. (1980) suggested that union commitment comprised four dimensions. **Union loyalty** was an affective attachment to, and recognition of, the benefits of belonging to the union and closely parallels the notion of affective commitment (see Chapter 8). **Responsibility to the union** was defined as the willingness to take on the

union loyalty

A dimension of union commitment reflecting affective commitment to the union

responsibility to the union

Willingness to undertake the day-to-day responsibilities of union members; a dimension of union commitment

Victor M. Catano

Shown here receiving the Donald Savage Award for Collective Bargaining, Dr. Victor M. Catano is both a researcher interested in issues related to unionization and an active unionist. In the latter role, he has served as chief negotiator and president for his local faculty union (SMUFU), as well as serving as a member of the executive, chair of numerous committees, and, ultimately, president of the Canadian Association of University Teachers. In his research, Dr. Catano has focused on the development and consequences of union commitment in organizations.

Dr. Catano is also a prominent I/O psychologist who has served as chair of the Canadian Society for Industrial/Organizational Psychology, editor of *Canadian Psychology*, and is a fellow of the Canadian Psychological Association and an honorary member of Canadian Forces Personnel Selection Officers Association. He was awarded the Canadian Psychology Association's Award for Distinguished Contributions to Education and Training and the Canadian Society for Industrial and Organizational Psychology's award for Distinguished Contributions to Industrial and Organizational Psychology. The Human Resources Association of Nova Scotia awarded him an honorary membership in recognition of his distinguished contributions to human resources in Canada. He is currently the chair of the Canadian Council of Human Resources Association's Independent Board of Examiners, which supervises the assessments required for the designation of Certified Human Resources Professional.

Source: Courtesy of the Canadian Association of University Teachers.

---

willingness to work for the union

A dimension of union commitment reflecting willingness to take special efforts (hold office, serve on committees) on behalf of the union

belief in unionism

A subscale of union commitment reflecting general attitudes toward unions

---

day-to-day responsibilities of union membership. An example of these responsibilities would be reporting violations of the collective agreement to the union. **Willingness to work for the union** was a willingness to go above and beyond the demands of routine membership and to take on roles such as a member of the union executive, or a member of union committees. Finally, **belief in unionism** was thought to represent a belief in the value of unions in general (as opposed to a specific union).

After the initial development of the scale, there was a flurry of research attempting to verify the measurement structure of union commitment. Researchers reported finding two, four, five, and even six different dimensions. Kelloway, Catano, & Southwell (1990) showed that these different solutions were largely a function of different researchers using different subsets of items from Gordon et al.'s initial measure. Using a common set of items across multiple samples, Kelloway et al. (1990) showed that three of the original four dimensions were stable. Most subsequent research has accepted their view that union commitment is comprised of union loyalty, willingness to work for the union, and responsibility to the union. In subsequent studies (e.g., Kelloway & Barling, 1993), union loyalty was identified as the primary dimension of union commitment, with willingness to work for the union and responsibility to the union being seen as behavioural intentions that were more properly viewed as outcomes of commitment.

Although the original intent of developing a union commitment measure was to foster more research on union–member relationships, most of the initial research focused solely on measurement issues. Nonetheless, subsequent studies have shown that union commitment is a good predictor of many union-relevant behaviours, such as participation in the union (e.g., attending meetings, holding office, serving on union committees; see Kelloway & Barling, 1993), an antecedent of **militancy** and support for industrial action (Kelloway et al., 1992; Kelloway et al., 2000), and a correlate of **strike propensity** (i.e., willingness to go on strike; Barling et al., 1992; Kelloway et al., 1992; Martin, 1986). Kelloway et al. (2002) found union shop stewards who are committed to and participate in the union are also more likely to take part in industrial action such as strike activities (e.g., picketing).

Research on the predictors of union commitment has also largely confirmed Gordon et al.'s (1980) initial suggestions. Early socialization experience in the union (e.g., Fullagar, Clark, Gallagher, & Gordon, 1994; Fullagar, Gallagher, Gordon, & Clark, 1995; Fullagar, McCoy, & Schull, 1992) and experiences with the union leadership (Fullagar et al., 1994; Kelloway & Barling, 1993) emerge as important predictors of members' commitment to the union, as do perceptions of union instrumentality and general attitudes toward unions.

Although research on union commitment has waned in recent years, the development of this measure was an important development in the relationship between I/O psychologists and the labour movement. Aside from identifying that there were I/O psychologists interested in union issues, development of the union commitment measure galvanized a great deal of research that resulted in the ability of I/O psychologists to offer very practical advice to unions as to how to build commitment to the union. Focusing on early socialization experience, such as welcoming new members to the union, inviting them to a union meeting, and helping them get involved in the union from the beginning is one such very practical strategy. Ensuring that union members have regular contact with their leaders (e.g., executive members and shop stewards), and that these leaders are trained, is another such solution. Finally, the available research has demonstrated in a practical way that building commitment to the union is a practical investment for unions—in times of labour conflict or political action, a committed member is more likely to get involved with union activities.

Dual Commitment

One question that first emerged in the 1950s and resurfaced as a result of Gordon et al.'s work is whether an individual could be committed to both the union and the employer at the same time. Known as **dual commitment**, this question had its roots in the Cold War and was especially important in the United States. During this period Americans were suspicious of "Communists," and

militancy
Willingness to take action to support the union

strike propensity
Willingness to go on strike

dual commitment
Being commitment to two entities at the same time (e.g., company and union commitment)

becoming involved in a union was seen by some as an anti-American activity. The early research focused on suggesting that one could be both an active union member and a loyal American.

The modern version of this question focused on company and union commitment. Fullagar and Barling (1992) provided the most widely accepted answer to the question when they found that the relationship between union and company commitment depended on the state of union–management relations. When union–management relationships were harmonious, positive, and respectful, then employees could be committed to both the union and the employer at the same time. However, when the union–management relationship was hostile and conflict ridden, members tended to "choose sides" and express loyalty to either the union or the company but not to both.

Stagner and Eflal (1980) provided a striking illustration of this with their quasi-experimental study of a strike in the U.S. auto industry. They compared the attitudes of union members in two union locals—one local was on strike against its employer, and the other was not. They found that members of the striking union expressed more negative attitudes toward management and more positive attitudes toward their union. This is consistent with a host of research in social psychology documenting that in-groups form during times of group conflict.

Scales, Kelloway, and Francis (2010) showed that this effect also occurred for managers. They interviewed managers of a company during a four-month strike. Managers reported many hostile confrontations with union members as they crossed the picket lines to go to work. Most strikingly, managers felt betrayed by union members, whom they had previously seen as coworkers and friends. Increasingly, they saw the strike from the company's point of view and expressed negative characterizations of union members. As Scales et al. (2010) note, these findings suggest that it may be difficult to return to normal after a strike is over—especially when the managers who are responsible for restoring normal operations in the workplace may harbour some resentment and ill feelings toward the union.

Psychological Involvement in the Union

Kelloway, Catano, & Carroll (2000) noted that research on union–member relations had been limited by reliance on union commitment as the sole focus for attitudinal research. They set out to develop a measure of **psychological involvement in the union** as the parallel to the construct of job involvement (see Chapter 8). They point to autobiographies of union leaders (e.g., White, 1988) that described becoming a union leader as a path of increasing behavioural and psychological involvement in the union. As members became more behaviourally involved in union activities, and particularly when the members took on leadership roles within the union, such activities became an increasingly important component of the individuals' lives. For many, union activity became more a vocation than a necessary task. It was this salience of union activities in one's life that they defined as members' psychological involvement in the union—the importance of union activity in the individual's life and the identification of the individual with union activity.

psychological involvement in the union

The importance of union activities in one's life

People and Work in Canada

In their analysis of data from union shop stewards, Kelloway et al. (2000) showed that psychological involvement in the union was distinct from union commitment. Involvement predicted some of the same outcomes (e.g., behavioural participation in the union and militancy) as did union commitment. However, psychological involvement emerged as a better predictor of stewards' *industrial relations stress* and work–union role conflict than did union commitment. Kelloway et al. (2000) concluded that psychological involvement in the union was a promising construct and measure to further the study of union–member relationships.

Participating in the Union

As voluntary organizations, labour unions are largely dependent on volunteers to take on the day-to-day tasks of running the union and administering the collective agreement. Thus the union's ability to attract and retain such volunteers is critical to its success (Barling et al., 1992). Aside from the practical requirement for members to participate, member involvement in union activities is often seen as a fundamental test of union democracy. Unlike most business organizations, unions explicitly advocate a democratic structure in which every member has the right to influence the affairs of the union. However, if members do not participate in union activities then the union is open to charges of being undemocratic. Not surprisingly, researchers have devoted considerable attention to the question of why some individuals choose to participate actively in the union (e.g., Kelloway & Barling, 1993).

As in the case of union commitment, early research on participation focused on the nature and measurement of this construct. McShane (1985) originally proposed a scale that purported to identify "types" of participation. However, subsequent analysis suggested that this view does not reflect the nature of unions as representative democracies.

Most of the available data paint a dismal picture of union participation. In particular, attendance at union meetings often comprises only 10 percent to 15 percent of the union membership. When the majority of members do not attend the meeting, it is difficult to argue that a democratic process was followed. Kelloway and Barling (1993) suggested that this may be a limited view of democracy, and in fact unions were representative democracies in which members elected representatives to do the work of the union. Consistent with this model, they found a pattern of participation whereby a very small number of members held union office (typically only four to five members in a local), a greater number served on committees, a still larger number attended meetings (e.g., 15 percent), a much larger number (and a clear majority of members) voted in union elections and other votes, and the vast majority of members read the union newsletter. Based on their analysis, Kelloway and Barling (1993) found that union participation is best viewed as a unidimensional and cumulative construct (i.e., a Guttman scale).

With respect to predictors of participation, we have already noted the role of union commitment. A recent longitudinal study of postal workers allows an examination of the temporal nature of the commitment/participation relationship (Fullagar, Gallagher, Clark, & Carroll, 2004). Using cross-lagged

Chapter 13: Unionization

regression techniques, the researchers demonstrated that, after controlling for the relationship between measures of union commitment across time, commitment emerges as a strong predictor of union participation even after a 10-year time span.

With the gender composition of workplaces changing over recent decades, the question of women's participation in union activities has informed a number of studies (e.g., Mellor, Mathieu, & Swim, 1994). In particular, researchers were interested in the observation that female union members typically participated in the union much less frequently than male union members. Early research attributed these differences to "barriers to participation" (Werthheimer & Nelson, 1977) for women. Such barriers included other commitments (e.g., family commitments) that were more salient for women than for men, a lack of experience with unions, and a lack of female role models in the union movement.

Mellor (1995) found that in union locals with higher female representation, female respondents reported both a higher competence level and greater opportunity to participate in local activities. This relationship was non-significant for men. Extending the work on women's union participation, Bulger and Mellor (1997) showed that union self-efficacy mediates the relationship between women's sense of union barriers and their participation in union activities. As the relationship was specific to union rather than community or family-based barriers, the researchers suggested that union barriers to participation primarily affect women with lower levels of union self-efficacy. In other words, women with a high sense of union self-efficacy participate in union activities regardless of the barriers to doing so. Given that women's participation is crucial to moving a union agenda toward greater consideration of women's needs, these findings point to the need to train women as a means to overcome low union self-efficacy. Anecdotal evidence suggests that this has been a successful strategy. Unions have frequently offered specialized courses for female members and actively encouraged women's participation in the union. In many cases, female members now are equally likely to take on leadership roles within the union.

Militancy

In the context of unions, militancy reflects the type of actions an individual is willing to take on behalf of the union. Someone who is high in union militancy is willing to take strong measures such as missing work or acting against the wishes of friends and family to show support for the union (Kelloway et al., 2002). As previously noted, commitment to the union and psychological involvement in the union have been consistently found to predict militancy.

In a recent study, Kelloway, Francis, Catano, & Teed (2007) examined the role of militancy in predicting participation in a student day of protest. The Canadian Federation of Students organized an annual Day of Protest in Nova Scotia, during which students were asked to gather at the provincial legislature for a rally to protest escalating tuition rates. Kelloway et al. (2007) collected measures of commitment to the (student) union and perceived injustice and militancy prior to the day of protest, and collected the same measures one week after the day of protest. They found that commitment and perceptions of injustice did predict militancy, which in turn predicted participation in the Day of Protest. Importantly, participating in the Day of Protest resulted in increased militancy and commitment to the union—another manifestation of the in-group effect discussed earlier in this chapter.

Leaving

Just as individuals may commit to a union, they may also choose to leave the labour organization. In most jurisdictions, the existence of closed shop agreements mean that a member cannot simply quit the union while still employed in the same job. However, in the United States and other jurisdictions, individuals can leave the union and maintain the benefits of union—which is reflected in much lower union density numbers in these jurisdictions. It makes little sense to continue to pay union dues if one can receive the same benefits without being a member of the union, and as a result a great deal of "free riding" occurs in these jurisdictions. Even where closed shop provisions exist, the members of the union may leave the union by voting to decertify in favour of another union or a lack of collective representation.

In looking at individual decisions to leave the union, Buttigieg et al. (2007) argued that leaving the union was not simply the opposite of joining. In their five-year study of union members, they found that the presence of a union representative decreased the chance of an individual leaving the union by almost 50 percent, and the more individualistic the workers were, the more likely they were to leave the labour organization. They concluded that the factors that prompt members to join unions are different than the factors that induce members to leave unions. Those who leave unions are those who are less attached to the union in the first place.

Leaving the union as a group (i.e., **decertification**) is a more involved process. Like a certification campaign, decertification requires a majority of union members to vote in favour of decertification in an election that is overseen by the provincial or federal labour relations board. The factors that prompt individuals to vote for decertification seem to deal primarily with a failure to meet expectations. That is, when individuals become dissatisfied with the union's ability to deliver on promises, or to resolve ongoing concerns in the workplace, they are most likely to vote in favour of decertification. Similarly, individuals who hold negative union attitudes are likely to vote for decertification (Barling et al., 1992).

decertification

The process through which union members decide that they no longer want to be represented by a union

Collective Bargaining

After a union is certified or recognized in a workplace, the next step is to negotiate the contract or collective agreement (in Canada, "collective agreement" is the common term for the contract between union and management) that will govern union–management relations in the workplace.

Although negotiations will occur at regular intervals periodically over the life of the relationship, the first set of negotiations is likely to be the most protracted and controversial for several reasons. First, there are fundamental issues that need to be resolved in a first contract that do not typically arise again. For example, management must agree to recognize the union as the legitimate and only bargaining agent for the unionized employees. Arrangements must be made for union dues collection and remission, the overall structure of the grievance and dispute resolution systems, and a host of other issues. Although these arrangements may be modified in subsequent negotiations, the first collective agreement does the major work of establishing the system of industrial relations in the workplace.

Second, there are some unique pressures on both parties during negotiation of a collective agreement. For the union, there is considerable pressure to deliver on the promises made during the unionization campaign and to demonstrate the value of unionization by achieving goals such as job security, better wages, and improved working conditions. On the management side, there is concern for maintaining the ability to manage effectively and to "hold the line" against increased costs and anything that would limit managerial decision making.

In general, bargaining can be characterized as distributive or integrative (Chaison, 2006). **Distributive bargaining** is characterized as win-lose or zero-sum bargaining. For example, the only way for the union to "win" higher wages is for management to "lose" some profitability (or at least to accept increased costs). In contrast, **integrative bargaining** is sometimes termed win-win or mutual gains bargaining (Chaison, 2006). For example, the union may negotiate for increased safety provisions. Although these may incur some costs for management, the costs may be offset by reductions in absenteeism or workers' compensation payments. The union "wins" increased safety and management "wins" decreased costs. Safety is frequently identified as an area for union–management cooperation (Kelloway, 2005).

distributive bargaining
Win-lose bargaining

integrative bargaining
Win-win or mutual gains bargaining

Issues in Collective Bargaining

Collective bargaining can focus on numerous issues related to the operation of the workplace, the administration of the agreement itself, wages, benefits, working conditions, and the relationship between union and management (Chaison, 2006). Arguably the most interesting—and influential—of these issues are those related to the traditional "bread and butter" issues of pay and working conditions, which have been a central focus of North American unions (Barling et al., 1992).

Perhaps the most obvious and well documented effect of unionization is the increase in wages and benefits that comes with unionization (e.g., Booth, Francesconi, & Zoega, 2004). Canadian data suggest that union members earned on average 18 percent more than their non-unionized counterparts. Part-time workers who are unionized earn almost twice the amount earned by non-unionized part-timers as a result of both increased wages and increased work hours (Anonymous, 2006).

Virtually all aspects of compensation are enhanced through unionization. Union members are more likely than are non-members to have fringe benefits, including health plans and pension plans (Marshall, 2003). The union wage effect is typically related to union power to enforce contract demands (e.g., Forth & Milward, 2002), and manifests both directly and indirectly. Direct effects emerge from simply bargaining for higher wages.

In addition to the absolute amount of wages, unions also have an effect on compensation policies in the workplace. Consistent with the emphasis placed on seniority with unions (Gordon & Johnson, 1982), they have typically advocated salary structures based on job classification and seniority (Barling et al., 1992) and opposed performance-based salary structures (e.g., Hanley & Nguyen, 2005).

Unions also directly bargain for improvements in a variety of working conditions. As previously noted, union members are more likely to receive workplace training than are non-members (Booth et al., 2004). Unions have negotiated for some forms of family-friendly policies designed to assist members to handle work and family conflict. Budd and Mumford (2004) found that unions enhanced the likelihood that members had access to parental leave, paid leave, and job sharing.

As mentioned previously, the enhancement of health and safety in the workforce has long been a primary focus of union bargaining (Kelloway, 2005). As is the case with other issues (e.g., Budd & Mumford, 2004), the union role in this area is complex. Certainly unions engage in adversarial collective bargaining around issues of health and safety (Gray, Myers, & Myers, 1998), although the data do not indicate that safety issues are used as "weapons" in bargaining (Hebdon & Hyatt, 1998). Beyond their bargaining role, unions may also collaborate with management to promote health and safety in the workplace—leading Kelloway (2003) to describe the union–management relationship around health and safety as one of conflict and cooperation.

Process Issues in Collective Bargaining

Industrial Relations Climate

The ability of management and union to deal with these issues and the manner in which union and management interact has been described as the **industrial relations climate** of the firm. A positive industrial relations climate is characterized by mutual trust and respect—although they still engage in bargaining, the union and management are able to do so with a minimum of conflict and to work out issues as they arise. A negative industrial relations climate is characterized by frequent conflicts and a lack of trust—in such a climate, bargaining is likely to result in strikes or lockouts and in general there are more conflicts between union and management.

There is some evidence that the development of a cooperative industrial relations climate has beneficial effects on firm performance (e.g., Deery & Iverson, 2005; Gittell, 2003). One means of attempting to reduce conflict in collective bargaining has been the adoption of "interest-based" (Fisher, Ury, & Patton, 1991) or integrative (e.g., Walton & McKersie, 1965) bargaining techniques. These techniques are designed to achieve collaborative solutions at the bargaining table and appear to be a key element influencing labour relations climate (Deery & Iverson, 2005). Cutcher-Gershenfeld and Kochan (2004) reported that by 1999, over 80 percent of union representatives and 65 percent

industrial relations climate

The perceived ability of management and the union to work together of management representatives were familiar with interest-based bargaining techniques. A majority of both union and management representatives had used these techniques in bargaining and both union and management representatives rated these techniques as being effective. Indeed, management representatives seem to favour these techniques, while more union members rated traditional collective bargaining higher than interest-based bargaining (Cutcher-Gershenfeld & Kochan, 2004).

Strikes

strike

The decision of workers to withdraw services from the workplace in support of bargaining demands

lockout

The decision by management to bar workers from the workplace

When collective bargaining fails, the result is often a **strike** or **lockout**. A strike occurs when the union decides to withdraw services from its employer. A lockout occurs when the employer decides to ban employees from the workplace. From the outside, these two events often look the same (in either case there is a picket line, the cessation of normal operations, and so on), and they frequently overlap. Management often institutes a lockout during a strike (to ensure that workers can return to work only when both parties agree) or in anticipation of a strike.

Although any discussion of industrial relations should consider the issues of strikes and lockouts, it should be emphasized at the outset that such events are extraordinarily rare (Bluen, 1994) and typically occur only under extreme provocation. The data presented in Table 13.1 illustrate this point; for the years 2000 to 2009, strikes and lockouts have typically involved less than 10 percent of the Canadian workforce (recall that there are approximately 17 million workers in Canada) and have typically accounted for only a very small amount of missed work time.

Most collective agreements contain a "no strike or lockout" clause. In Canada a legal strike can occur only during times of renegotiating a collective

TABLE 13.1

Work Stoppages in Canada			
YEAR	TOTAL NUMBER	NUMBER OF WORKERS	% OF WORK TIME NOT WORKED
2009	158	67,313	0.06
2008	188	41,308	0.02
2007	206	65,552	0.05
2006	151	42,314	0.02
2005	260	199,007	0.11
2004	297	259,229	0.09
2003	266	78,765	0.05
2002	294	165,590	0.09
2001	381	221,145	0.07
2000	378	142,672	0.05

Source: Adapted from Chronological Perspectives on Work Stoppages, http://srv131.services.gc.ca/dimt-wid/pcat-cpws/recherche-search.aspx?lang=eng; accessed January 30, 2009.

agreement. For example, Soya (2006) noted that between 1995 and 2005 in Canada, strikes accounted for less than 0.10 percent of work time, with a further 0.01 percent of time being lost during lockouts. Moreover, Soya (2006) notes that the significant strikes were uniformly concentrated in organizations and industries facing fundamental structural change—not the "normal" bargaining issues of wages, benefits, and working conditions. The Canadian experience is typical of other developed economies (International Labour Office, n.d.).

As implied by the use of the term "significant," strikes vary considerably in duration and intensity. Smaller unions, which are less likely to disrupt the economic activity of a firm, tend to have longer strikes than do larger unions. The use of replacement workers is associated with longer (Singh, Zinni, & Jain, 2005) and perhaps more violent (Francis et al., 2006) strikes.

In some sense a strike is a classic example of intergroup conflict in organization. One group of employees (i.e., the union members) is in direct conflict with another (i.e., managers and supervisors). Just as union members are trying to keep the organization from operating normally, managers and supervisors are often expected to keep the organization running during the strike. The results of this conflict are perfectly predictable from social psychology research. As previously noted, Stagner and Eflal (1980) found that striking workers developed more positive in-group (i.e., toward the union) attitudes and more negative out-group (e.g., toward the managers) attitudes and perceptions. The development of greater in-group cohesion may be necessary to make a strike effective—at the same time, these attitudinal shifts may make it more difficult to resolve a strike as individuals get locked into one side or another of the conflict.

One important determinant of the length of a strike is the ability of the union to garner support from members of the public. To the extent that members of the public can be persuaded to respect the picket line, or to show public support for the union such as blowing the car horn when driving by a picket, public pressure can be brought to bear and this may be especially efficacious in resolving public-sector strikes (Leung, Chieu, & Au, 1993; Mellor, Paley, & Holzworth, 1999).

Kelloway, Francis, Catano, & Dupre (2007) recently examined the predictors of third-party support for strikes in two separate Canadian public-sector strikes. Drawing on Klandermans' (1997) model of social protest, they examined the same predictors that are frequently used in studies of union joining. In both cases, they found that third-party support was predicted by perceptions the union was being treated unfairly by the employer (injustice), general union attitudes (identification), and the perception that showing support would be effective in bringing the strike to an end (instrumentality).

Grievances

While strikes emerge from a breakdown in the process of negotiating a collective agreement, a **grievance** is an allegation that one party to the agreement, most typically the employer, has violated a provision of an existing agreement (Francis & Kelloway, 2005). Most often, the collective agreement will detail

grievance

An allegation that one party to the agreement, most typically the employer, has violated a provision of an existing agreement

Chapter 13: Unionization

a grievance handling procedure that attempts to ensure a fair hearing and resolution of such complaints (Barling, Fullagar, & Kelloway, 1992). Grievance systems are typically seen as part of the workplace justice system and tied to outcomes for both unions and employers. Gordon and Fryxell (1993) spoke to the importance of grievance systems for union–member relationships when they noted "a union's relations with its constituents is tied more closely to the procedural and distributive justice afforded by its representation in the grievance system than by any other type of benefit provided in the collective bargaining agreement" (p. 251). This assertion has been empirically validated, with perceptions of organizational justice being linked to union outcomes such as citizenship and turnover intent (Aryee & Chay, 2001) as well as members' satisfaction with the union (Fryxell & Gordon, 1989).

Grievance systems also have implications for outcomes of interest to the employing organization. For example, the provision of grievance systems may predict employees' attitudinal commitment to the organization (Fiorito, Bozeman, Young, & Meurs, 2007) and intent to stay with the firm (Olson-Buchanan, 1996). Indeed, at least one set of reviewers has suggested that human resource practitioners might consider a union-grievance system as a form of high-involvement work practice (Peterson & Lewin, 2000). That is, a grievance system may result in reduced turnover and better organizational outcomes because employees can express and resolve any dissatisfactions through the grievance procedure. In recognition of these benefits, even non-union firms may institute a grievance system (this may also be a strategy to keep unions out of the workplace).

Consequences of Unionization

As noted earlier, becoming involved in union activities has widespread implications for individuals, their organizations, and third parties.

Effects of Unionization on Individuals

Industrial Relations Stress

Conflict, change (Bluen & Barling, 1987, 1988; Fried & Tiegs, 1993), and perceptions of injustice (Francis & Kelloway, 2006) are central features of industrial relations. Individual members of the union may be involved in filing grievances, work to rule campaigns, or strikes/lockouts. It is not surprising that the practice of industrial relations is inherently stressful, and adverse individual consequences have been associated with such activities.

CONFLICT   In their seminal work on industrial relations stress, Bluen and Barling (1989) pointed to the distinction between unitary and pluralistic views of industrial relations (Fox, 1973). Arguably, psychologists and human resource practitioners (Kelloway, Barling, & Harvey, 1998) subscribe to a unitary view that holds that there is a single source of loyalty and authority within an organization. In this view, all members of the organization share the same views and are working toward the same goals.

The pluralistic perspective recognizes the existence of multiple groups within an organization. In the case of industrial relations, the management and the union are the two major groups. Management seeks to maximize profits and reduce costs, while labour groups are concerned with issues such as wages, job security, and working conditions (Bluen, 1994). This view recognizes that conflict is naturally occurring and inevitable in industrial relations practice. Although it may be inevitable, virtually all models of organizational stress recognize that conflict is inherently stressful for the individuals involved (Kelloway & Day, 2005; Sauter, Murphy, & Hurrell, 1991).

CHANGE   Change is also frequently noted in models of organizational stress (Dohrenwind & Dohrenwind, 1974; Kahn & Byosiere, 1992) and is frequently associated with industrial relations. Change in industrial relations may come from external or internal forces (Francis & Kelloway, 2005). External forces such as changing government regulations, economic fluctuations, and technological development place pressure on industrial relations systems to adapt to these environmental realities. Internal factors for change include new contracts and changes among the players in a particular industrial relations unit. Industrial relations events such as strikes can create substantial changes in the day-to-day lives of those impacted by the event. For example, striking workers and their families may have to change their spending patterns and get by on substantially reduced income during a labour dispute. Similarly, management employees may be called upon to assume additional and new duties to replace striking workers during a dispute.

For example, Bluen and Jubiler-Lurie (1990) showed that individuals involved in collective bargaining (i.e., actual participants in the negotiations) experienced increased blood pressure as well as increased anxiety and decreased well-being. Union members engaged in a strike may experience stress responses such as withdrawal, exhaustion, psychological distress, decreased perceptions of health, and decreased general functioning (MacBride, Lancee, & Freeman, 1981; Milburn, Schuler, & Watman, 1983). These experiences can last for as much as six months after the strike is over (Barling & Milligan, 1987).

INJUSTICE   Some have argued that industrial relations hinge largely on issues of fairness, and there is no doubt that injustice constitutes an important organizational stressor. For example, Francis et al. (2003) found that those who perceived a high degree of distributive, procedural, or interactional injustice in their work setting also reported increased emotional strain. There is a consistent relationship between perceptions of procedural and interactional injustice and increased experience of emotional strain, increased illness-related work absences, and decreased self-reported health status (Elovainio et al., 2001, 2002; Kivimaki et al., 2003). See Box 13.3 for a description of a scale for industrial relations events.

Union Support

Although involvement in industrial relations can be stressful, there is also considerable potential for unions to help individuals deal with stress. Support from the union has been identified as an important moderator of stressor–strain

Box 13.3

Industrial Relations Event Scale

The Industrial Relations Events Scale (Bluen & Barling, 1987) is a 44-item instrument patterned on measures of life events. The scale includes such incidents as experiencing an inconsistency between industrial relations policy and practice, joining a union, being involved in negotiations, and experiencing a strike or lockout. Respondents are asked to indicate (a) whether they have experienced the event and (b) the extent to which they view such events as favourable or unfavourable. Three scores—occurrence, positive industrial relations events, and negative industrial relations events—are obtained and can offer insight about the number of industrial relations stressors to which an individual is exposed and provide information on the impact, be it positive or negative, of that stressor. Bluen and Barling (1987) provide detailed evidence for the test–retest reliability, convergent, discriminant, and known-groups validity of the scale. Generally, the psychometric properties of the scale are satisfactory. Although originally developed in South Africa, the scale has also been used in North America in various versions, including a 25-item short form (Kelloway, Barling, & Shah, 1993).

relationships (Bluen & Edelstein, 1993; Bluen & Jubiler-Lurie, 1990; Fried & Tiegs, 1993). Such support could come from shop stewards (e.g., Fried & Tiegs, 1993) or from the union itself (Shore, Tetrick, Sinclair, & Newton, 1994). Fried and Tiegs (1993) reported that strain was highest among those employees who experienced role stressors and perceived little social support from their union steward. In another study, miners who witnessed a workplace disaster and who perceived their union as supportive of their emotional responses reported less psychological distress than did those who did not see the union as supportive (Bluen & Edelstein, 1993).

Industrial Relations Violence

Although rare, strikes and lockouts are manifestations of intense industrial relations conflict that can result in various serious consequences. Picket line violence has been defined as the "non-privileged physical interference with the person or property of another, or the threat, expressed or implied, of such interference" (Thieblot & Haggard, 1983, p. 14). Thus, picket line violence includes both *physical* altercations as well as *psychologically* aggressive acts (e.g., threats and intimidation). Based on data from the National Institute for Labor Relations Research (NILRR), Thieblot et al. (1999) estimated that the annual average number of incidents of union and strike-related violence in the United States was 432 for the period from 1975 to 1995. And using data from the NILRR, Francis et al. (2006) showed that 30 percent of strike-related violence is directed at the *organization*, while 43 percent of incidents involve *interpersonal* attacks. Stennett-Brewer (1997) found that exposure to picket line violence is quite common. For example, 100 percent of picket line crossers reported that they experienced verbal assaults, 40 percent indicated that their vehicles were damaged, and 11 percent had gunshots fired at their vehicle or their property. See Box 13.4 for an expanded discussion.

The use of replacement workers (generally referred to as "scabs" by members of the labour movement) has a long and controversial history in Canadian labour relations. In most jurisdictions, the use of replacement workers is a legal strategy that employers can use during a strike.

Both Quebec and British Columbia have "anti-scab" provisions in their labour legislation. In the case of Quebec, the provisions emerged from a very turbulent time during the 1970s when Quebec strikes accounted for 40 percent of all the work stoppages in Canada. Both violence and the frequency of strikes dropped markedly after the introduction of the legislation. In B.C., anti-scab legislation was introduced in the early 1990s by the NDP government. Although Ontario's NDP government also introduced anti-scab legislation in the 1990s, it was quickly repealed when the conservative government took power.

The Canadian Labour Congress (CLC) has campaigned for Bill C-257, which would be a federal anti-scab law. Although the bill survived a second reading in the House of Parliament, it eventually was voted down as a result of strong opposition from the business community. Business owners argue that outlawing replacement workers gives too much power to the unions and makes it impossible for business to endure a strike. Unions argue that the use of replacement workers make strikes both more violent and more lengthy than they need be. Although there is empirical support for this argument, achieving a balance between the rights of unions and the rights of business remains elusive.

Source: Extracted from L. Savage and J. Butovsky, "A Federal Anti-Scab Law for Canada: The Debate Over Bill C-257", *Just Labour: A Canadian Journal of Work and Society* 13 (2009): 15–28. Reprinted by permission of the Centre for Research on Work and Society/ Just Labour.

Effects of Unionization on Organizational Behaviour

There is little doubt that unionization has been associated with a host of effects on organizational behaviour (Freeman & Medoff, 1984). Kochan (1980; see also Barling et al., 1992) proposed a model in which unions were expected to have both primary and secondary effects in the workplace. Primary effects refer to the gains at the bargaining table (e.g., increased wages, benefits, changes in working conditions) achieved by the union, while secondary effects emerge indirectly as both unions and employers respond and react to these primary changes. In particular, management has to change the way it operates in order to achieve increased productivity or increased efficiency to offset the increased costs that come with unionization.

For example, because unionized firms (a) pay better, (b) have better benefits, and (c) have better working conditions, turnover tends to be lower in unionized firms than it is in non-unionized firms. Knowing that their workers are going to be with them a long time (and recognizing that the union will also work to limit the ability to fire or lay off workers), management may develop more rigorous selection procedures and, as previously noted, spend more on training than in non-unionized firms. In turn, these primary and secondary outcomes of unionization influence organizational behaviour.

One of the most widely documented and paradoxical secondary effects of unionization is the effect of unionization on job dissatisfaction and turnover. Although increased job dissatisfaction is associated with increased turnover in the research literature (see Chapter 8), union members tend to be more dissatisfied with their jobs but less likely to quit than are non-union members (Guest & Conway, 2004; Hammer & Avgar, 2005). One explanation for this effect is that unions provide members with the potential to voice their dissatisfaction (i.e., by complaining or filing grievances) rather than to quit (Abraham, Friedman, & Thomas, 2005; Guest & Conway, 2004; Iverson & Currivan, 2003).

Unionization is also generally associated with greater absenteeism, presumably as a result of union members being more likely to have paid sick leave (Barling et al., 1992). However, this effect may appear only when union–management relationships are poor (Deery, Erwin, & Iverson, 1999; Deery & Iverson, 2005).

Effects of Unionization on Third Parties

Workers and managers are also members of communities and families, and it is not surprising that some aspects of union–management relations spill over to affect third parties who are not directly involved in the bargaining relationship. For instance, strikes and lockouts are a source of considerable stress for stakeholders who are denied valuable services during a dispute. Greenglass, Fiksenbaum, Goldstein, and Desiato (2002) found that students whose academic year was truncated by a lengthy faculty strike experienced both anger and anxiety as a result of the dispute. Day, Stinson, Catano, and Kelloway (2006) reported data from a sample of students faced with the threat of a faculty strike against the university administration. They found that students who would be more affected by the potential strike action reported higher strain and a decreased sense of control. Interestingly, having more information regarding the dispute increased perceived control among the students.

There is also considerable potential for third parties to be vicariously exposed to industrial relations stressors (Francis & Kelloway, 2005). For example, the family members of striking workers certainly experience increased stress as a result of the strike even though they are not directly involved.

Summary

We began this chapter with the observation that the relationship between I/O psychology and unions has been characterized as one of mutual neglect. We suggested that this was an inappropriate state of affairs for at least two reasons. First, unions give rise to unique forms of behaviour and there is considerable potential for I/O psychology research to address questions such as, Why do employees vote to join unions? To go on strike? To get involved in union activities? Second, unions have an effect on virtually every aspect of organizational functioning including compensation policies; human resource policies and practices including selection, training, and employee discipline; employee attitudes (e.g., job satisfaction, commitment); and employee behaviours such as absenteeism and turnover.

Key Terms

belief in unionism 372
certification election 370
closed shop agreement 370

collective agreement 369
collective bargaining 368
craft union 368

decertification 377
distributive bargaining 378
dual commitment 373
grievance 381
industrial relations climate 379
industrial union 368
integrative bargaining 378
local 368
lockout 380

militancy 373
psychological involvement in the union 374
responsibility to the union 371
strike 380
strike propensity 373
union 368
union loyalty 371
unionization 369
willingness to work for the union 372

Web Links wⓌw

The Canadian Union of Public Employees is Canada's largest union, with more than 600,000 members across the country:

http://cupe.ca/

The Canadian Labour Congress is the umbrella group for many unions (i.e., an association of unions) and often speaks on behalf of organized labour:

http://www.canadianlabour.ca/home

At the provincial level, there are often federations of labour that serve a similar function:

Alberta **http://www.afl.org/**

British Columbia **http://www.bcfed.com/**

Manitoba **http://www.mfl.mb.ca/**

New Brunswick **http://www.nbfl-fttnb.ca/index_en.php**

Newfoundland and Labrador **http://www.nlfl.nf.ca/index.html**

Nova Scotia **http://www.nsfl.ns.ca/home.htm**

Ontario **http://www.ofl.ca/**

PEI **http://www.peifl.ca/**

Quebec **http://www.ftq.qc.ca/**

Saskatchewan **http://www.sfl.sk.ca/**

Discussion Questions

1. The relationship between psychology and labour has been called one of mutual neglect. Why do I/O psychologists typically neglect labour issues or fail to consider the role of unions in the workplace?

2. Union certification campaigns are often very hotly contested, with both management and the union trying to influence the votes of employees. What role should I/O psychologists play in such campaigns?
3. I/O psychologists have developed a host of techniques for selection, performance management, training, and other aspects of human resource management. How does the presence of a union in the workplace affect these techniques? Are there specific things advocated by I/O psychologists that unions might object to?
4. If you were to provide advice to union leaders on how to build a stronger union (i.e., build member support for, and commitment to, the union), what would that advice be?

Using the Internet

Michael Gordon, an I/O psychologist who was extremely influential in promoting the study of unionization, once suggested that research in I/O psychology would be very different if we adopted a union, as opposed to a corporate agenda. He also suggested that one could develop a research agenda by looking at collective agreements to see what unions thought were the most important workplace issues.

Many unions post the full text of their collective agreement on their website. Find at least three such agreements and review them, noting what issues seem to be most important (i.e., what is mentioned in the agreements). Compare these issues with the table of contents of an I/O textbook such as this one. How are the concerns of unions reflected (or ignored) in I/O psychology? What would we do differently to address the concerns of unions?

Exercises

1. Individuals often hold strong views either in favour of or opposed to unions. Over the next week, try to assess the reactions of people you know to unions—are your family and friends pro-union? Anti-union? Do you agree with their views?
2. Interview five people who have been involved in a strike (either as a union member, a manager, or an affected third party). What were their experiences? How hard or easy was it to get back to normal after the strike was over? Were there lingering bad feelings? Did the strike affect any other aspect of the working relationship?
3. It is most likely that your instructors and perhaps your teaching assistants are members of a union. Interview them to find out (a) why they became members of the union and (b) if they had a choice would they remain a member of the union (i.e., if they could quit and keep their current job, would they?).
4. One of the most common things you will hear about unions today is that they "were needed at one time but now the need has passed."

Organize a class debate in which one side argues that unions are still needed/relevant in the workplace while the other side argues that we no longer need unions.

Case

Dr. Chuck Alksnis is an academic I/O psychologist whose research has been focused on the issue of why individuals choose to join unions. A great deal of his publications deal with the predictors of union attitudes and pro-union voting decisions.

In his home community, the major employer is Granton Tire manufacturing. The Canadian Auto Workers is trying to organize the employees of the plant into a union. The certification campaign is heating up, with both the employer and the union going all out to win the certification vote. When Dr. Alksnis came to work on Monday morning, there were two messages on his answering machine.

The first was from Rajah Das, the HR manager at Granton Tire, asking to meet with Dr. Alksnsis. "We're aware of your research," said the message, "and would like to talk to you about how we can use your findings to keep the union out of Granton Tire—we'd appreciate the chance to meet with you and get any advice you can provide."

The second message was from Debbie Frost, who introduced herself as an organizer for the CAW. "We're aware of your research," said the message, "and would like to talk to you about how we can use your findings to organize Granton Tire—we'd appreciate the chance to meet with you and get any advice you can provide."

Discussion Questions

1. If you were Chuck Alksnis, what would you do? Would you respond to either message? What would you say?
2. What is the obligation of a psychologist in this situation? Is there an ethical problem with getting involved in a certification campaign on one side or the other?
3. Both parties have indicated that they are aware of Dr. Alksnis's research and, presumably, are already in a position to use his research findings to further their own ends. What do you think about that—is there anything Dr. Alksnis could or should do about this situation?

CHAPTER 14

Positive Organizational Psychology

Seen by some as the latest development in organizational studies, the field of positive organizational scholarship is closely linked to the more general field of positive psychology. Like positive psychology, the focus of enquiry is on positive aspects of human experience.

Chapter Learning Outcomes

After reading this chapter you should be able to

- Describe the emergence of positive organizational scholarship as a field of study
- Define and discuss the organizational relevance of positive constructs such as flow, engagement, and love of the job
- Define and discuss psychological capital
- Describe the character strengths and virtues framework
- Discuss the role of the meaning of work
- Describe how positive psychology constructs are implemented in organizations

A Brief History of Positive Organizational Scholarship

The newly emerging field of positive psychology began formally in 1998 as an initiative of Martin Seligman, who was then the president of the American Psychological Association. Seligman's premise was that, since World War II, psychology had become dominated by an emphasis on pathology and the attempt to "fix" human problems (Seligman, 1999). Although not denying the benefits of this approach, Seligman argued that by exclusively focusing on pathology we ignored the positive or good aspects of life. In his own career, Seligman moved from the study of depression and learned helplessness (Seligman, 1975) to the study of optimism (Seligman, 1991), and in inaugurating a field of positive psychology he was encouraging other psychologists to consider a similar shift.

Sparked by this movement, researchers in organizational behaviour began thinking and writing about positive organizational behaviour (e.g., Luthans, 2002; Wright, 2003). Luthans, who identifies himself as one of the first generation of organizational behaviour researchers (Luthans, 2002), became inspired by the positive psychology movement and saw considerable overlap with the work he was doing as a senior researcher at the Gallup organizations (see Box 14.1). He began promoting **positive organizational behaviour**, which he defined as "the study and application of positively-oriented human resource strengths and psychological capacities that can be measured, developed, and effectively managed for performance improvement in today's workplace" (Luthans, 2002, p. 52). His work in this area was to develop into the construct of psychological capital, which is discussed in more detail later in this chapter.

Drawing on concepts from positive psychology and positive organizational behaviour (Luthans, 2002; Wright, 2002), **positive organizational scholarship** deals with the study of positive "outcomes, processes and attributes of organizations and their members" (Cameron, Dutton, & Quinn, 2003, p. 4). As such, positive organizational scholarship is a perspective that is changing the field of organizational behaviour (Nelson & Cooper, 2007).

There is no definite list of "topics" that comprise the domain of positive organizational scholarship. Indeed, many of the traditional topics of

positive organizational behaviour

The study and application of positively oriented human resource strengths and psychological capacities that can be measured, developed, and effectively managed for performance improvement in today's workplace

positive organizational scholarship

The field of enquiry that deals with positive "outcomes, processes and attributes of organizations and their members"

Box 14.1

The Gallup Studies

One prominent influence on the development of positive organizational psychology has been the work done at the Gallup organization. Gallup is of course famous for its polling work (during political campaigns one often hears of a Gallup poll showing the latest political standings). However, Gallup also does employee surveys, and based on this work single-handedly invented and popularized the notion of employee engagement.

Over many years of conducting employee attitude surveys, Gallup developed an extensive database of attitudes and organizational outcomes. Harter, Schmidt, & Hayes (2002) analyzed these data using meta-analytic techniques. They looked at the effect of employee engagement (see below) on a diverse array of organizational outcomes, including customer satisfaction, productivity, profit, turnover, and accidents. Based on data from 36 companies and almost 8,000 business units within these companies, they found evidence for the link between engagement and satisfaction. Indeed, companies whose employees were more engaged generated over $100,000 more in profit each year. Although the data do not allow us to conclude

that engagement causes profit, these findings certainly caused both researchers and businesspeople to start paying attention to notions of employee engagement.

Based on its research, the Gallup organization developed a measure of employee engagement that comprises 12 statements. When employees agree with the statements, they are thought to be engaged in work. Contrary to what some people expect (i.e., issues of compensation or financial bonuses), the items deal with having clear expectations, challenging work, positive interpersonal relationships, and regular feedback in your job (although we cannot reproduce the items here, a Google search using the keywords Gallup Q12 will turn up a host of sites where the items can be found).

Gallup also leveraged its data to develop strengths-based coaching (see later in this chapter), and in general has promoted positive approaches to organization studies. Gallup hosts summits or conferences focused on issues related to positive organizational psychology, and many of the individuals referenced in this chapter have worked with or been influenced by the work done at Gallup on positive organizational psychology.

organizational study (e.g., leadership, motivation, organizational citizenship) fit quite well with this perspective. In this chapter, we explore some of the "positive" constructs that have been applied in organizational research.

Flow: The Psychology of Peak Experience

Flow is a term first coined by Csikszentmihalyi (1975), who defined it as the "holistic sensation that people feel when they act with total involvement" (p. 4). Flow is regarded as an optimal experience that occurs when one is working at the limit of personal ability with intense engagement (Nakamura & Csikszentmihalyi, 2002).

In early definitions of the construct, Csikszentmihalyi (1975) emphasized that flow resulted from the balance of skills and challenges. Subsequent research has defined the experience of flow in more detail (Csikszentmihalyi, 1990, 1993; Jackson, 1996; Jackson & Marsh, 1996), resulting in the identification of nine features that characterize the state of "flow" (see Box 14.2).

flow

The sensation of optimal experience that people feel when they act with total involvement

Box 14.2

The Nine Dimensions of Flow

Flow is defined in terms of nine dimensions that comprise the experience. *Challenge–skill balance* is the first of these, and refers to the match between the skills required to perform the task and the challenges facing the individual. Remember learning how to drive? For most people, learning to drive can be quite frustrating because our skills are not up to the challenge—as a result, it takes all of our attention and effort to keep the car on the road. However, we soon master the task and become skilled drivers—so much so that one can be bored in driving and actually tune out from the tasks of driving, the well-known "highway hypnosis," flow only occurs when the balance between challenges and skills exceeds a level that is typical for daily experiences and the challenges are at the very limit of your skills. Neurosurgeons performing delicate brain surgery probably are acting at the limit of their skills.

A *merging of action and awareness* is also very characteristic of flow. This is the experience of being "in the zone," where your behaviour is spontaneous and you are not really thinking about what you are doing. High-performance athletes often report this experience—and, conversely, experience lowered performance when they become aware of or are "overthinking" what they are doing. This is labelled the *paradox of control* by flow researchers.

People in flow report they feel in control, but as soon as their attention shifts to trying to maintain control they lose the sense of flow. Similarly, flow is characterized by a *loss of self-consciousness*.

Flow is also more likely when the individual has a strong sense of what has to be done (*clarity of goals*) and the activity provides clear, immediate, and *unambiguous feedback* concerning how well you are doing. A high degree of *concentration on the task at hand* is also characteristic of the experience of flow. For many people the defining feature of flow is the *transformation of time* that seems to occur. Essentially, this occurs when you are so engaged in an activity that you lose all track of time and you are unaware of the passage of time. Surgeons who do extraordinarily long (e.g., 12-hour, 16-hour) surgeries often report that the time just flew by and they didn't really think that they were in the operating room for that amount of time—which suggests they had experienced flow. Computer programmers, data analysts, and even video gamers have reported this transformation of time. Finally, Csikszentmihalyi (1990) coined the term *autotelic experience* from the Greek words *auto*, meaning self, and *telos*, meaning goal. Flow experiences become enjoyable and an end in themselves. As a result, one is motivated to return to this state.

Chapter 14: Positive Organizational Psychology

Considered together, these nine dimensions of flow provide a comprehensive measure of optimal experience (Jackson & Ecklund, 2004). In practice, however, the dimensions of flow are typically highly correlated and there is a substantial proportion of shared variance (Jackson & Ecklund, 2004). Because of these intercorrelations, researchers have asked whether flow is a state (i.e., a characteristic of the situation) or a trait (a characteristic of the individual). This is an important question, as it implies very different processes and organizational responses. For example, if flow is primarily a characteristic of the situation, then organizations might endeavour to facilitate flow by ensuring that those characteristics are present. One could, for example, ensure that employees receive challenging tasks, have clear goals, and so on. However, if flow is primarily a characteristic of an individual, then changing the situation might have little effect and organizations might want to consider selecting individuals based on their capacity to experience flow.

Fullagar and Kelloway (2009) were able to address this question in their experience sampling study of architecture students engaged in lab work. Periodically during the lab periods, student were "beeped" and asked to complete various measures (including a measure of flow). By taking repeated measures over a variety of situations, Fullagar and Kelloway (2009) were able to estimate that approximately 75 percent of the variance in flow ratings was attributable to the situation. These data suggest that flow is both state and trait, but the former is the dominant influence.

Flow at Work

Flow has been studied at work but not to the same extent as it has in other forms of activity (e.g., sports, artistic pursuits). Researchers have examined both the predictors and consequences of experiencing flow. Demerouti (2006) initially reported that the motivating job characteristics identified in the job characteristics model (e.g., autonomy, variety task significance) were predictive of flow. However, that study used an overall measure of job characteristics and could not identify which characteristics of task were more likely to result in flow. Fullagar and Kelloway (2009) further elaborated on this finding by measuring individual job characteristics. They reported that flow was more likely in situations characterized by skill variety and autonomy.

hedonic well-being
Positive mood

In terms of outcomes, flow has been associated with **hedonic well-being**, or positive mood (Eisenberger et al., 2005; Fullagar & Kelloway, 2009; Nakamura & Csikszentmihalyi, 2002). This appears to be the link between flow and a variety of organizationally relevant outcomes. For example, flow has been found to be positively associated with both in-role and extra-role performance (Demerouti, 2006; Eisenberger et al., 2005). Moreover, Eisenberger et al. (2005) have shown that the relationship between flow and employee performance is partially mediated by positive mood. Earlier research has indicated that the relationship between positive mood and performance is particularly pertinent to tasks that require spontaneity and creativity (Eisenberger & Rhoades, 2001; George & Brief, 1992). Thus, flow seems to be of benefit for both individuals and organizations.

Engagement and Related Constructs

Unlike many of the concepts discussed in this chapter that are developed by researchers, the construct of employee engagement really was developed and popularized by practitioners. As a result, it is difficult to determine whether the notion of **engagement** is something "new" or whether it is simply a repackaging of well-known constructs (Macey & Schneider, 2008). For example, one provider of online engagement surveys describes its product as measuring attitudes toward

- Manager–employee relationships
- Coworker relationships
- Job responsibilities and expectations
- Job tools
- Availability of constructive feedback
- Reward and incentive programs
- Advancement opportunities
- Company communications

(Source: From http://www.infosurv.com/employee-engagement-survey.html, accessed Feb. 1, 2010. Reprinted with permission of InfoSurv.)

It is not clear how this focus on "engagement" is any different from morale surveys or organizational climate surveys that have been implemented in organizations for many years.

Nonetheless, the construct of employee engagement has become immensely popular in organizations. At least two reasons drive this concern. First, there is some evidence that engagement does predict organizational outcome of interest (refer to Box 14.1). For example, some organizations have suggested that engaged employees produce 28 percent more revenue than do non-engaged employees (*cf* Seijts & Crim, 2006). A very influential meta-analysis published in the *Journal of Applied Psychology* concluded that "employee satisfaction and engagement are related to meaningful business outcomes at a magnitude that is important to many organizations" (Harter et al., 2002, p. 267). Second, survey after survey reports that the vast majority of employees are not engaged in their work. For example, the Gallup organization reports that only 29 percent of employees are actively engaged in their work, 54 percent are disengaged and do not feel strongly about their jobs, and 17 percent actively dislike their jobs. Data from Towers-Perrin suggest that only 17 percent of Canadian workers were highly engaged in their work (*cf* Seijts & Crim, 2006). Clearly the juxtaposition of these two sets of observations has led many organizations to conclude that employee engagement is a valued commodity.

So what is employee engagement? Most of the commercially available engagement surveys actually sidestep this question by measuring the conditions thought to create a sense of employee engagement rather than measuring engagement itself. Thus, surveys often focus more on describing the employment environment than on the state of being engaged. Macey and Schneider (2008) suggested that when engagement is measured there are several common themes; engagement overlaps with constructs such as satisfaction, commitment, involvement, and empowerment. Several authors have proposed similar definitions of engagement.

engagement

Employees' attitudes toward their job

Maslach and Leiter (1997) defined engagement as a state involving energy, involvement, and efficacy. In their view, engagement is the opposite of burnout (see Chapter 12). Thus, energy is seen as the opposite of emotional exhaustion, involvement as the opposite of depersonalization, and efficacy as the opposite of lack of personal accomplishment.

Schaufelli, Bakker, & Salanova (2006) developed a popular measure of engagement known as the Utrecht Work Engagement Scale. They defined engagement as a fulfilling, positive state of mind comprising three dimensions: vigour, absorption, and dedication. By vigour they mean a high level of energy and the willingness to invest in and persist at one's work. Dedication means being involved in the work and feeling pride, enthusiasm, and inspiration. Absorption means being concentrated on and engrossed in one's work. The survey originally comprised 17 items, but a newer short form of nine items seems to give the most consistent measurement of engagement (Seppala et al., 2009).

Although not claiming to measure engagement per se, Shirom (2004) defines *vigour* as an affective state involving feelings of energy, physical strength, and cognitive liveliness. Each of these dimensions is assessed as a separate subscale. Vigour predicts health outcomes for employees (Shirom et al., 2008) and is thought to predict organizationally relevant outcomes as well, although research on the construct is still in its early stages.

Love of the Job

In giving the convocation address at Stanford University, the founder and CEO of Apple, Steve Jobs, spoke of the importance of loving what you do for a living:

> You've got to find what you love. And that is as true for your work as it is for your lovers. Your work is going to fill a large part of your life, and the only way to be truly satisfied is to do what you believe is great work. And the only way to do great work is to love what you do. (Jobs, 2005)

Jobs's views are not unique—many people seeking career advice are told to find a job that they love or are passionate about (e.g., Boyatzsis, McKee, & Goleman, 2002; Cassidy, 2000).

Despite the commonality of this advice, Kelloway, Inness, Barling, Francis, and Turner (2010) noted that there was very little development of the construct of loving one's job. Accordingly they offered a definition of the construct that was grounded in prior theoretical work on love and in the empirical literature dealing with the experience of work.

A Definition of Love

Rempel and Burris (2005) defined love as a "motivational state in which the goal is to preserve and promote the well-being of the valued object" (p. 299). Although the focus of much research is on romantic or interpersonal love, Rempel and Burris explicitly noted that their definition "allows love to be experienced toward any valued object" (p. 309). In suggesting that the job can be a focus of love, Kelloway et al. (2010) argued that paid employment (a)

Nick Turner

Shown here attending a conference in Sweden, Dr. Nick Turner is Associate Professor of Management and Associate Dean of the Asper School of Business at the University of Manitoba. Dr. Turner completed his undergraduate degree in psychology at Queen's University and his PhD in organizational psychology at the University of Sheffield in the United Kingdom. A prolific researcher, he has won several faculty awards for research and serves on the editorial boards of several I/O psychology journals.

Dr. Turner has diverse research interests, but has written extensively on topics related to transformational leadership, leadership and moral reasoning, love of the job, and positive psychology in organizations.

Source: Courtesy of Neil Walshe.

has been a central aspect of human experience throughout history (Applebaum, 1984, 1992; Kelloway, Gallagher, & Barling, 2004; Pahl, 1989), and (b) is associated with numerous manifest (e.g., pay) and latent (e.g., time structure) consequences (Jahoda, 1982) for the individual. Moreover, being without paid employment has been linked to negative consequences for individuals and society since at least the beginning of the Industrial Revolution (Burnett, 1994; Feather, 1990; Jahoda, 1982). Thus, by all accounts, a job is a valued object.

Kelloway et al. (2010) also pointed to two qualitative studies that suggested remarkably similar definitions of the experience of loving your job. First, Richie et al. (1997) explored the career experiences of high-achieving women and noted that a large number of their respondents talked about loving their work. They identified three dominant "themes" that characterized the participants' career development, namely passion for the work, persistence, and connectedness. Gordon (2006) explicitly focused on women who love their work and also identified three characteristic themes. Each woman interviewed (a) took pleasure from her job activities; (b) felt good about her reason for working, and (c) liked and at the very least respected the people with whom she worked.

Kelloway et al. (2010) suggested that these accounts paralleled the Triangular Theory of Love, in which Sternberg (1986, 1987) suggests that interpersonal love consists of passion, commitment, and intimacy. Sternberg's model has been well validated across different samples. Kelloway et al. (2010) proposed that love of one's job comprises the experiences of passion for one's work (Sagie & Koslowsky, 2000), affective commitment to the employing organization (Meyer & Allen, 1997), and a sense of intimacy with people at work (Brehm et al., 2002).

In contrast to task-focused measures such as engagement and vigour, love of the job is seen as a more encompassing measure that includes attachment to the organization and to other individuals in the workplace.

Psychological Capital

The initial interest in positive organizational behaviour of Luthans (2002) became quite specific. His definition of the field as comprising "the study and application of positively-oriented human resource strengths and psychological capacities that can be measured, developed, and effectively managed for performance improvement in today's workplace" was intended to signal both his interest in a positive orientation and his focus on strengths or capacities that could be developed. That is, Luthans was not particularly interested in personal characteristics that could not be changed—his focus was on identifying things that could be altered to improve individual and organizational well-being. He identified four such traits, which collectively became known as **psychological capital (PsyCap).**

PsyCap is defined as "an individual's positive psychological state of development and is characterized by (1) having confidence (**self-efficacy**) to take on and put in the necessary effort to succeed at challenging tasks, (2) making a positive attribution (**optimism**) about succeeding now and in the future; (3) persevering toward goals and when necessary redirecting paths to goals (**hope**) in order to succeed and (4) when beset by problems and adversity, sustaining and bouncing back and even beyond (**resiliency**) to attain success" (Luthans, 2002). In many ways, PsyCap is an integrative model that is firmly rooted in empirical research. Each of the individual elements comprising the model has been well-researched.

(Source of definition (PsyCap): Fred Luthans (2002). The need for and meaning of positive organizational behavior. *Journal of Organizational Behaviour* 23(6): 695–706. Copyright © 2002, John Wiley and Sons.)

Self-Efficacy

Bandura (1977) defined efficacy as the sense people have about the probability that they can successfully complete a given task. Perhaps not surprisingly, there is consistent evidence that self-efficacy is positively correlated with job performance (Stajkovic & Luthans, 1998). Luthans et al. (2007) note that people with a high sense of efficacy thrive on challenge, are highly self-motivated, persevere in the face of adversity, set high goals for themselves, and work hard to achieve their goals. They also suggest five key observations about efficacy in the context of PsyCap. First, they note that efficacy is domain specific—for example, you might be an excellent researcher who is very confident in your abilities but at the same time be very nervous and uncomfortable about doing public speaking. Second, even with a domain in which we are comfortable, there may be tasks in which we have less confidence. In this sense, there is always room for improvement in our sense of efficacy. Third, they note that efficacy is based on our own experiences of practice and mastery—if you have successfully done something in the past you are more likely to be confident about doing the same task in the future. Fourth, efficacy can be influenced by

psychological capital (PsyCap)

An individual's positive psychological state of development, characterized by (1) having confidence (*self-efficacy*) to take on and put in the necessary effort to succeed at challenging tasks; (2) making a positive attribution (*optimism*) about succeeding now and in the future; (3) persevering toward goals and when necessary redirecting paths to goals (*hope*) in order to succeed; and (4) when beset by problems and adversity, sustaining and bouncing back and even beyond (*resiliency*) to attain success.

self-efficacy

The sense people have about the probability that they can successfully complete a given task

optimism

An attributional style in which success is attributed to permanent, personal, and pervasive causes

hope

A positive emotional state that is based on an interactive sense of successful agency (goal-directed energy) and pathways (planning to meet goals)

resiliency

Capacity to rebound or bounce back from adversity, conflict, failure, or even positive events, progress, and increased responsibility others—when others tell us that we do something well (or poorly) our sense of efficacy is influenced.

Optimism

Seligman (1998) defines an optimist as someone who attributes their success to permanent, personal, and pervasive causes. A pessimist would attribute success to external (as opposed to personal), temporary (as opposed to permanent), and situation-specific causes. Optimists see negative outcomes (e.g., failures) as also being a result of temporary, external, and situation-specific factors. In his original work with insurance salespeople, Seligman (1998) showed that optimism was related to performance. In fact, optimistic salespeople who did not achieve the minimum score on a selection test actually outsold their higher scoring but less optimistic coworkers.

Hope

Snyder, Irving, and Anderson (1991) defined hope as a "positive emotional state that is based on an interactively sense of successful (1) agency (goal-directed energy) and (2) pathways (planning to meet goals)" (p. 287). Individuals with a sense of hope set realistic but challenging goals and then work with persistence and energy to achieve those goals (Luthans et al., 2007). Perhaps more importantly in the context of PsyCap, individuals with hope are capable of generating multiple plans to achieve their goals—it is this capacity to develop multiple pathways that Luthans et al. (2007) suggest is most important. Hope has been linked to a variety of outcomes including well-being, health, and performance in some domains, and Luthans et al. suggest that data are beginning to support a linkage between hope and job performance as well.

Resiliency

Resilience is defined as the "capacity to rebound or bounce back from adversity, conflict, failure, or even positive events, progress and increased responsibility" (Luthans, 2007, p. 702). Resilience has typically been studied within the context of stress (see Chapter 12) and particularly with exposure to traumatic stressors. However, Luthans et al. (2007) argue that resiliency has a wider role to play in the workplace.

PsyCap at Work

In developing the construct of psychological capital, Luthans et al. (2007) also identified criteria by which to evaluate whether they have met their goal. Going back to Luthans' original intent in developing positive organizational behaviour, he focused on aspects of the workplace that are changeable and positively linked to performance. To what extent does PsyCap meet these criteria?

There is some evidence that PsyCap is changeable. Luthans et al. (2008) reported the results of an experimental investigation in which participants participated in a two-hour Web-based exercise designed to enhance their psychological capital. Results of the study were supportive of the intervention in that they showed positive changes in psychological capital as a result of participating in the exercise.

There is also evidence linking psychological capital to personal and organizational outcomes. For example, Avey, Luthans, Smith, and Palmer (2010) reported on a longitudinal study showing that psychological capital was related to psychological well-being over time. Psychological capital has also been found to predict performance directly and to mediate the relationship between organizational climate and performance (Luthans et al., 2008). Luthans, Avolio, Norman, & Stevens (2007) also report significant relationships between psychological capital and both performance and satisfaction. Importantly, they provided evidence that the higher-order construct of psychological capital predicted these outcomes better than the individual components comprising the model.

Positivity

One of the most interesting lines of research to come out of positive psychology is Barbara Frederickson's work on positivity. By **positivity**, Frederickson is referring to the experience of positive emotions—which in her recent work (Frederickson, 2010) she has defined as joy, gratitude, serenity, interest, hope, pride, amusement, inspiration, awe, and love. She believes that there are intrinsic benefits to experiencing these emotions and that individuals need to work on maximizing the experience of positive emotions. Note that in some ways this is the opposite to approaches to stress management advocated by occupational health psychologists (see Chapter 12). Stress management focuses on the elimination or reduction of negative experiences. Although Frederickson (2010) recognizes the necessity to reduce the negative, she would also argue that we have to increase our experience of positive emotions.

In developing her thinking in these areas, Frederickson (1998, 2001) posited the **broaden and build theory of positive emotions**. She points to the fact that negative emotions tend to narrow the focus of individuals (e.g., individuals experiencing fear often focus solely on the cause of their fear), whereas experiencing positive emotions both broadens and builds our focus. That is, individuals who are experiencing positive emotions are more open to new experiences, more aware of their surroundings, and more attuned to a wide variety of opportunities—this is the "broaden" function of positive emotions. Individuals who are experiencing positive emotions are also more likely to build resources by learning new skills, making new friendships or contacts, and acquiring new experiences. Frederickson argues that the broaden and build function of positive emotions reflects an evolutionary advancement—our primordial ancestors were able to enhance their fitness and evolutionary advancement by experiencing positive emotions that allowed them to grow and acquire resources.

Fredrickson (2010; Fredrickson & Losada, 2005) also finds support for what she calls a **positivity ratio**. The positivity ratio is the ratio of positive to negative events that one needs to experience in order to flourish as an individual. Although few psychologists would dare be so precise, Fredrickson argues that there are sufficient data to conclude that a ratio of 3:1 (i.e., three times as many positive as negative events) is necessary.

One of the first studies in this area was conducted in a boardroom setting. Researchers observed meetings of corporate teams and coded whether

positivity

The experience of positive emotions

broaden and build theory of positive emotions

Frederickson's theory holding that positive emotions convey an adaptive advantage by enabling us to broaden our outlook and build new resources

positivity ratio

The ratio of positive to negative emotions. Frederickson suggests that 3:1 is the optimal positivity ratio individuals' statements were (a) positive or negative, (b) based on inquiry or advocacy (i.e., asking questions or defending a point of view), and (c) focused on the speaker or on others in the room. They were also able to get data on team performance in terms of profitability, customer satisfaction, and supervisory ratings. High-performing teams were found to have a positivity ratio of 6:1; low-performing teams averaged a ratio of 1:1; and a group of mixed-performance teams came in at 2:1.

In her individual work, Fredrickson (2010) has substantiated this finding, showing that individuals who flourish achieve a positive ratio of 3:1 or greater while individuals who do not do so well experience ratios on the order of 2:1. In another area of inquiry, Gottman (1994) studied the interactions of married couples and found that strong marriages achieved a positivity ratio of 5:1 while failing marriages typically scored a ratio of 1:1. Other researchers have found that clinically depressed individuals score positivity ratios of 1:1 or lower and that those who were able to improve their ratios to 3:1 or more experienced remission from clinical depression (*cf* Fredrickson et al., 2010). For more on the positivity ratio, see Box 14.3.

Positivity at Work

Although work on positivity has not been directly applied in the mainstream organizational research, there are very practical and supportable conclusions that can be drawn. First, Fredrickson's broaden and build theory points to the value of organizations fostering the experience of positive emotion at work. Certainly this conclusion is consistent with a wide range of organizational research that points to the value of positive attitudes and experiences. For many years, I/O psychologists have emphasized the experience of positive levels of job satisfaction, commitment, engagement, and similar attitudes, and there is little doubt that experiencing positive attitudes results in better outcomes for both individuals and organizations.

The new implication of Fredrickson's work for organizations may be the identification of the positivity ratio. If this finding applies in organizations, then

---

Box 14.3

The Positivity Ratio

Fredrickson coined the term "positivity ratio" to refer to the ratio of positive and negative emotions one experiences. She suggests that a ratio of three (three positive for every negative) is a critical tipping point such that those above three flourish while those that score less than three experience some difficulties.

On Fredrickson's website (www.positivityratio.com) you can take her positivity quiz to calculate your own positivity ratio for today. By enrolling in her study, you can have the website keep track of your positivity ratio over time and measure the effects of your own efforts to increase positive and decrease negative experiences in order to enhance your own positivity ratio.

one could imagine considerable benefit to training organizational leaders to ensure they have at least three positive interactions with an employee for every negative reaction. Or one might teach work groups the value of enhancing the number of positive interactions they have with each other as a means of enhancing group performance and cohesion. Although we are not aware of any empirical tests of these suggestions, the emerging work on positivity suggests that such tests will start to be conducted in organizations in the very near future.

Character Strengths and Virtues

The literature in philosophy and religious studies is replete with lists of virtues that are held up as ideals for people—in fact, the notion of virtue is one of the oldest constructs known (Cameron et al., 2004). Drawing from the observation that we have a detailed classification of psychopathology but no corresponding overview of positive behaviours, two of the leading positive psychologists reviewed this extensive literature to propose a categorization of character strengths and virtues (Peterson & Seligman, 2004). Although theirs is by no means the only categorization of virtues, it is a readily accessible framework that has been influential in promoting the psychological study of virtues.

Based on their review, Peterson & Seligman proposed a taxonomy that was based on six virtues:

1. Wisdom and knowledge—the acquisition and use of knowledge
2. Courage—strengths that involve the exercise of will to accomplish goals in the face of opposition
3. Humanity—interpersonal values involving tending and befriending others
4. Transcendence—strengths that make a connection with a larger universe
5. Temperance—strengths that protect against excess
6. Justice—strengths that underpin a healthy community life

Peterson and Seligman (2004) also proposed a set of character strengths associated with each of these virtues (see Table 14.1). In their view, the character strengths are the operationalization of more vaguely defined virtues. Character strengths are thought to be trait-like in that they are characteristic of behaviour over time. They are also thought to be intrinsically valuable—that is, we encourage these behaviours in ourselves and others because we believe that it is beneficial to act in this way.

The virtues framework developed by Peterson and Seligman (2004) is operationalized with a 240-item instrument known as the Values in Action Inventory of Strengths (VIA-ITS). The instrument is available online through the Values in Action Institute on Character (http://www.viacharacter.org/Home/tabid/36/Default.aspx). To date, more than 1 million individuals have completed the measure (other shorter but not as well established measures are also available).

Virtues at Work

Virtues in the workplace have been studied at both the organizational and the individual level. At the organization level, some data link organizational virtues

TABLE 14.1

WISDOM	TRANSCENDENCE
Creativity	Beauty
Curiosity	Gratitude
Open-mindedness	Hope
Love of learning	Humour
Perspective	Spirituality
COURAGE	TEMPERANCE
Bravery	Forgiveness/mercy
Persistence	Humility/modesty
Integrity	Prudence
Vitality	Self-regulation
HUMANITY	JUSTICE
Love	Citizenship
Kindness	Fairness
Social Intelligence	Leadership

Theoretical Categorization of 6 Virtues and 24 Character Strengths (Peterson & Seligman, 2004)

Source: Peterson, C, Seligman, S. (2004). Character strengths and virtues: A handbook and classification. Oxford: Oxford University Press.

(defined as organizational forgiveness, organizational trust, organizational integrity, organizational optimism, and organizational compassion) to organization performance. Organizations that score highly on these dimensions realize better performance (Cameron, Bright, & Caza, 2004). Their analysis showed that perceived organization virtuousness predicted measures of innovation, quality, turnover, customer retention, and firm profitability. These findings are consistent with meta-analytic data showing a positive association between organizational corporate social responsibility and performance (Margolis & Walsh, 2003).

Cameron (2003) suggested that organizational virtues have two primary effects: amplification and buffering. In the first instance, virtuousness produces an amplifying effect by setting off a "positivity spiral." In essence, the suggestion is that being virtuous causes positive emotions (i.e., we feel good about ourselves). In turn, positive emotions lead to more virtuous behaviours. Virtuousness also encourages stronger high-quality relationships among coworkers. Again, stronger relationships within the organization encourage more virtuous behaviour. The buffering effect of virtuous behaviour is that such behaviours are thought to enhance resiliency, solidarity, and self-efficacy. In turn, these qualities help employees deal with stressors and the negative effects of downsizing.

At the individual level, virtuousness has also been linked to individual performance and is plausibly associated with outcomes such as leadership, trust, commitment, and ethical behaviour. In several studies, Thun (2009) showed that when leaders are perceived as behaving virtuously, employees report enhanced individual well-being, more positive organizational attitudes (i.e., affective commitment), and more likelihood of engaging in organizational citizenship behaviours. Findings such as these led Wright and Goodstein (2007) to argue that the study of character has much to offer organizational behaviour.

The Meaning of Work

Although it is clear that people work in order to earn money, it is equally clear that many of us want more from our jobs than just a paycheque (see, for example, Meaning of Work International Research Team, 1987). Pratt and Ashforth (2003) describe the meaning of work as the subjective sense that people make about their jobs. There are at least three primary orientations to work that are common in North America (Bellah, 1985).

First, work can be seen simply as a job (Category A in Box 14.4)—a means to gain material benefits. In this view, work is a means to an end. We work in order to generate an income that, in turn, funds our leisure activities. In this view, leisure time, not work time, is when interests and abilities are expressed. Second, a career orientation (Category B in Box 14.4) focuses on the rewards that

---

Box 14.4

What Is Your Orientation to Work?

Please read the three paragraphs that follow. Which of the categories is most like you?

1. Category A people work primarily to earn enough money to support their lives outside their jobs. If they were financially secure, they would no longer continue with their current line of work, but would really rather do something else instead. To these people, their jobs are basically a necessity of life, a lot like breathing and sleeping. They greatly anticipate weekends and vacations. If these people lived their lives over again they probably would not go into the same line of work. They would not encourage their friends and family to enter their line of work. Category A people are very eager to retire.

2. Category B people basically enjoy their work but do not expect to be in their current jobs five years from now. Instead, they plan to move on to better, higher-level jobs. They have several goals for their future pertaining to the positions they would eventually like to hold. Sometime their work seems a waste of time but they know that they must do sufficiently well in their current positions in order to move on. Category B people can't wait to get a promotion. For them, a promotion means recognition of their good work, and is a sign of their success in competition with coworkers.

3. For Category C people, work is one of the most important parts of life. They are very pleased that they are in their line of work. Because what they do for a living is a vital part of who they are, it is one of the first things they tell people about themselves. They tend to take their work home with them and on vacations too. The majority of their friends are from their places of employment and they belong to several organizations and clubs relating to their work. They feel good about their work because they love it and because they think it makes the world a better place. They would encourage their friends and children to enter their line of work. Category C people would be pretty upset if they were forced to stop working and they are not particularly looking forward to retirement.

---

accompany advancement and promotion. These include the pay, occupational prestige, and increase in status that accompany work advancement. Finally, those with a "calling" orientation (Bellah et al., 1985) focus on the intrinsic value of work—those with this view often see their work as contributing to the greater good and of being of value to the world (Category C in Box 14.4). Although it seems possible that individuals have all of these orientations to some degree, empirically people tended to classify themselves as unambiguously holding one of the three orientations. Moreover, those with calling orientations seemed to get more enjoyment and satisfaction out of their work than did individuals with a job or career orientation (Wrzeniewski, McCauley, Rozin, & Schwartz, 1997). This is consistent with the view that those who find a higher purpose in their work experience better individual outcomes.

Deriving meaning from events in our lives is a "fundamental human motive" (Britt, Adler, & Bartone, 2001, p. 54) that is associated with increased will to live (Frankl, 1963) and perceiving benefits in specific stressful events (Britt et al., 2001). One striking demonstration of the power of meaning comes from a study of individuals who had been diagnosed with a terminal disease (ALS or Lou Gehrig's disease). Westaby, Versenyi, and Hausmann (2005) found that individuals who had intrinsic reasons for working (i.e., found the work to be meaningful) were more likely to continue working even in the face of a terminal and progressive disease.

How do people derive meaning from work? At least three mechanisms seem plausible. First, individuals often select in to occupations that they believe they will find meaningful. For example, an individual may choose a career in early childhood education even though other occupational choices might be associated with a higher salary and/or more chances for career advancement.

Second, individuals engage in a process known as **job crafting**. Wrzeniewski and Dutton (2001) describe job crafting as "the physical and cognitive changes individuals make in the task or relational boundaries of their work" (p. 179). In essence, individuals can change or structure their jobs in order to enhance the meaning they find in the work. The maintenance person in a long term care facility who also takes on the responsibility of caring for the assorted pets (i.e., cats, rabbits, birds) has changed task boundaries in order to enhance meaning. Similarly, the hospital cleaner who thinks of the job as contributing to infection control is engaging in job crafting. In general, the three major things that one can do to "craft" the job are:

job crafting

The physical and cognitive changes individuals make in the task or relational boundaries of their work

- Changing the number, type, or scope of job tasks.
- Changing the amount and quality of interaction with others on the job, *and*
- Changing cognitive task boundaries

Another source of meaning in the workplace is the people we work with. Arnold, Tuner, Barling, McKee, and Kelloway (2007) reported that employees who worked for transformational leaders (see Chapter 10) reported a greater sense of meaning in their work. In one of the few true field experiments, McKee and Kelloway (2009) reported that a training program designed to enhance leaders' transformational leadership skills resulted in employees experiencing a greater sense of meaning in their work. In both of these studies, the enhanced

Chapter 14: Positive Organizational Psychology

sense of meaning experienced by employees directly predicted employees' psychological well-being. Again, these findings speak to the importance for individuals of finding meaning in work.

Applying Positive Psychology

Thus far we have reviewed a number of constructs in positive psychology. We now turn our attention to how these constructs might be "put to work" at work. That is, what does one do to improve the individual experience of work? Clearly this is not a new question in I/O psychology, and interventions such as leadership training (see Chapter 10) and job redesign (see Chapter 9) have been previously discussed. However, the specific question we are now considering is whether positive psychology has any "new" implications for organizational practice. Although there do seem to be some promising areas of inquiry, research regarding applications is in its infancy. Moreover, for the most part positive psychologists have tended to emphasize changing the individual rather than changing the organization—in some sense this is not a common approach in I/O psychology, but rather reflects the more individual orientation of many positive psychologists.

Two approaches to implementing positive psychology principles are evident. First, positive psychologists have focused on identifying rather short-term, individual activities designed to foster happiness. Second, drawing on their initial work on engagement, individuals associated with the Gallup organization have popularized "strength building" approaches—one of the most common of which is strength-based coaching.

Happiness Interventions

Seligman, Steen, Park, and Peterson (2005) reported on the effectiveness of several positive psychology interventions. Although their work was not specific to the workplace, their findings do have implications for the design of organizational interventions. The focus of their research was on increasing individual happiness, and to do so they designed five happiness interventions and one placebo intervention. All the interventions were Web-based (www.authentichappiness.org). Four hundred and eleven participants took part in one of the six treatment conditions. The six conditions were:

- Placebo control exercise: Early memories. Participants were asked to write about their early memories every night for one week.
- Gratitude visit: Participants were given one week to write and then deliver a letter of gratitude in person to someone who had been especially kind to them but had never been properly thanked.
- Three good things in life. Participants were asked to write down three things that went well each day and their causes every night for one week. In addition, they were asked to provide a causal explanation for each good thing.
- You at your best. Participants were asked to write about a time when they were at their best and then to reflect on the personal strengths displayed in the story. They were told to review their story

once every day for a week and to reflect on the strengths they had identified.

- Using signature strengths in a new way. Participants were asked to take our inventory of character strengths online at www.authentichappiness.org and to receive individualized feedback about their top five ("signature") strengths (Peterson et al., 2005a). They were then asked to use one of these top strengths in a new and different way every day for one week.
- Identifying signature strengths. This exercise was a truncated version of the one just described, without the instruction to use signature strengths in new ways. Participants were asked to take the survey, to note their five highest strengths, and to use them more often during the next week. (Seligman et al., 2005, p. 416)

Comparing pre-test and post-test measures of happiness, Seligman et al. (2005) report that individuals in the "gratitude" group became more happy after one week of doing the exercise and maintained that happiness at one month after. However, this group returned to their pre-test levels of happiness at three months after the exercise. The result of the gratitude visit was a large, but temporary, increase in happiness.

Participants in the "three good things" group showed increased happiness relative to pretest at the one-month follow up and sustained the higher level at both three- and six-month post-tests. "Using your signature strengths" showed the same pattern of results. Both the "identifying signature strengths" and the "you at your best" groups showed some increase in happiness immediately after completing the exercise, but there were no longer-term effects.

Seligman et al.'s (2005) data suggest that it is possible to change people's levels of happiness. Although the research was limited to a six-month follow-up, the fact that stable changes can be obtained from a minimal intervention is promising for future interventions.

Biswas-Diener and Dean (2007) point to other interventions that have been shown to increase some aspect of happiness. In addition to expressive writing (as exemplified in some of Seligman's conditions), they point to other individually focused interventions. First, physical exercise is well known as a means to increase mood, and engaging in regular physical activity benefits both physical and psychological well-being. Second, Bryant, Smart, and King (2005) found that asking individuals to take 10 minutes twice a day to sit quietly and think about a positive memory significantly enhanced participants' happiness. Third, forgiveness and gratitude have both been associated with increased happiness—when individuals are encouraged to forgive others, and to express gratitude to others, they experience greater happiness. Biswas-Diener and Dean (2007) note that gratitude-based interventions (e.g., keeping a gratitude journal in which individuals are asked to write down five things they are grateful for each day) have shown the largest effects in terms of increasing happiness. Finally, Biswas-Diener and Dean (2007) note that engaging in acts of altruism can enhance individual well-being. Simply focusing on doing "good deeds" for others is a means of increasing happiness.

See Box 14.5 for a discussion of an index for assessing happiness.

Numerous popular books and articles have recently focused on the notion of happiness. Quebec polling company L'Observateur partnered with communications consultants Chalifour to develop a measure known as the Relative Happiness Index. The measure assesses level of contentment with various aspects of life and allows for comparisons across regions, cities, provinces, and so on. In their initial report (2006), they compared the happiness of Canadians in different provinces; as shown below, residents of New Brunswick were seen as the happiest Canadians with Nova Scotians being least happy.

Relative Happiness Index (RHI) by Province (on a scale from 0 to 100)

1.	New Brunswick	78.60
2.	Newfoundland	78.40
3.	Prince Edward Island	76.60
4.	Ontario	76.10
5.	Quebec	75.30
6.	British Columbia	75.10
7.	Saskatchewan	75.00
8.	Alberta	74.00
9.	Manitoba	73.20
10.	Nova Scotia	72.80

The creators of the index note that work plays a critical role in determining happiness. The average RHI for individuals who claimed to love their work (60 percent of respondents) was 78.90. For the 7 percent of respondents who did not like their jobs, the RHI was 64.7; for the 22 percent who liked their job somewhat, the RHI was 70.7.

You can obtain your own personal RHI score and learn more about the Relative Happiness Index at http://www.indicedebonheur.com/en/articlesen/work-happiness-inseparable-pair.htm.

Strengths-Based Coaching

One of the fundamental tenets of positive psychology is the belief that it is better to build on one's strengths rather than try to improve on one's weaknesses. This belief has found expression in both the Values in Action framework discussed earlier and the development of strengths-based coaching techniques largely attributed to work done at the Gallup organization.

As described by Clifton and Harter (2003), the aim of strength-based coaching is to develop talents into strengths. In this view, a **strength** is "the ability to provide consistent near-perfect performance in a given activity" (Clifton & Harter, 2003, p. 114). The key tasks in developing talents into strengths involve identifying one's dominant talents, integrating the talents into everyday activities, and changing behaviour to take advantage of one's natural talents. The role of a coach, in this framework, is to help individuals with these three central tasks.

Identification of talents or strengths is typically through means of some form of standardized assessment. The Values in Action framework discussed earlier provides one such assessment that, in its simplest forms, identifies an individual's five dominant strengths. Buckingham and Clifton (2001) have developed the "Strengths Finder" assessment to provide a similar purpose. The Strengths Finder instrument measures 34 common themes (e.g., a tendency toward competition). This more commercial approach typically follows the initial assessment with feedback and developmental activities designed to enhance an individual's strengths (Clifton & Harter, 2003).

strength

The ability to provide consistent near-perfect performance in a given activity

Summary

Although it may be too early to conclude that positive psychology or positive organizational scholarship is fundamentally altering the way we study individual behaviour in organizations, there is no doubt that the field has had an effect on organizational psychology. New constructs (e.g., flow, psychological capital) have emerged, and longstanding areas of enquiry (e.g., happiness) are beginning to find specific organizational applications.

In some cases, such as employee engagement and strengths-based coaching, "practice" has taken the lead, with commercial consulting organizations generating the initial interest in the field. Researchers are just now turning their attention to these issues. Other areas of positive psychology (e.g., flow, psychological capital) have been driven largely by researchers with organizational applications lagging behind—again this situation is in flux and likely to be changed even by the time this text is published.

Although researchers have adapted very specific areas related to their own interests, the field of positive organizational psychology is emerging as focusing on the "best" things about work and employment. It seems likely that this will be a fruitful area of enquiry that is closely aligned with the original goals of industrial/organizational psychology (see Chapter 1), and we anticipate that "positive" research will flourish for the foreseeable future.

Key Terms

broaden and build theory of positive emotions 400
engagement 395
flow 393
hedonic well-being 394
hope 398
job crafting 405
optimism 398
positive organizational behaviour 392

positive organizational scholarship 392
positivity 400
positivity ratio 400
psychological capital (PsyCap) 398
resiliency 398
self-efficacy 398
strength 408

Web Links

Martin Seligman, arguably the founder of the positive psychology movement, discussed the emergence of positive psychology at:

http://www.ted.com/talks/martin_seligman_on_the_state_of_psychology.html

Dan Gilbert, author of the bestseller *The Pursuit of Happiness*, discusses the question "Why are we happy?" at:

http://www.ted.com/talks/dan_gilbert_asks_why_are_we_happy.html

The Relative Happiness Index is discussed at:

http://www.indicedebonheur.com/home.htm

The Gallup Q12 are discussed at:

http://www.gallup.com/consulting/52/Employee-Engagement.aspx?gclid=
CPG2vNm23p8CFQRinAod8nnkHA

The Values in Action framework is discussed (and measures are available) at:

http://www.viacharacter.org/

The Center for Positive Organizational Scholarship at the University of Michigan can be found at:

http://www.bus.umich.edu/Positive/

Various measures in positive psychology and information about the field can be accessed at:

www.authentichappiness.org

Discussion Questions

1. Seligman's development of positive psychology was largely in reaction to his perception that psychology (i.e., clinical psychology) had become too focused on "problems" and pathology. Arguably, I/O psychologists have always studied positive aspects of organizational behaviour (e.g., motivation, leadership, organizational attitudes). Is there a need for a positive organizational psychology?

2. One of the paradoxes emerging from studies of flow is that, although work provides the necessary conditions to experience flow (e.g., skill use, challenge), people report experiencing flow *less* often at work than in other aspects of their lives. What aspects of work might work against or stop individuals from experiencing flow?

3. Some have criticized positive psychology as being simply a repackaging of known material. Does studying topics such as "engagement" or "love of the job" really add anything beyond what we already know about work attitudes?

4. Interventions in IO psychology often focus on changing the situation (e.g., job redesign). Positive psychology interventions focus largely on changing the individual. Does this raise any concerns in terms of ethics? Long-term effectiveness? Should I/O psychologists focus on changing situations or on helping people adapt to/be happy in their current situation?

5. Research in positive organizational scholarship has identified some useful constructs (e.g., flow, psychological capital, love of the job), but the field is still relatively new. What are we missing? What other positive aspects of work should be examined in developing a positive organizational psychology?

Using the Internet

Is happiness a trait or a state? Are there "happy" people, or does happiness vary with the situation? To answer these questions you can use questionnaires available on the Web to track your happiness (and other positive states) over time. Register with the authentic happiness website in order to complete some of the many questionnaires developed to measure aspects of positive psychology (http://www.authentichappiness.sas.upenn.edu/questionnaires.aspx). Every couple of weeks go back to the website to complete the questionnaires again.

In *The Happiness Project*, Gretchen Rubin describes her attempts to become more happy using various approaches. The website associated with the book provides many hints and tips on how you can make your own happiness project, which you can evaluate using the questionnaires described above (http://www.happiness-project.com).

Exercises

1. Construct a chart as depicted below. Using a scale of 1 (very unhappy) to 10 (extremely happy), rate your happiness two to three times a day over a period of several weeks. Are you generally happy or unhappy? What activities make you the most happy? The most unhappy? Why?

Date	Time	Activity	Happiness Score	Comments

2. Interview people about their experience of flow at work (*Hint:* start by asking them about when they simply lost all track of time). What were they doing? What do these tasks have in common?
3. Research typically suggests that about 50 percent to 60 percent of people claim to love their job. Interview a sample of 10 people to find out (a) whether they love their job and (b) why or why not? Are there common themes in their responses?

Case

"It's not that I hate my job," said Zhen Lee, "it's just that I find it so boring. I can't get excited about reconciling purchase orders and I spend all day just pushing paper. When I get home I'm just not interested in doing anything. Don't get me wrong, I think I am really good at my job and the salary and benefits are excellent. In fact, I just got a raise based on my performance and my manager says that I am one of the best workers in the department. I guess I just don't feel fulfilled. Is there anything you can suggest? I'm still paying my student loans so quitting just isn't an option for me right now."

A 25-year-old university graduate, Zhen Lee works in the purchasing department of a large local hospital. During university he had worked in the shipping/receiving department of the hospital, and after graduating with a business degree it seemed natural to move into the office and put his business skills to work. After three years in this position, Zhen Lee decided to seek help. He has approached your firm of I/O psychologists to help him.

Discussion Questions

1. Is this an appropriate situation for an I/O psychologist to get involved in? Do I/O psychologists have the skills necessary to help people in this situation?
2. Assuming you have decided that you can help Zhen Lee, what are your recommendations? Outline at least two strategies he can try to improve his current situation.
3. If you were Zhen Lee's supervisor, what would your response be? Do companies have an interest in making employees happy?

References

Abraham, S.E., Friedman, B.A., & Thomas, R.K. (2005). The impact of unions on intent to leave: Additional evidence on the voice face of unions. *Employee Responsibilities and Rights Journal, 17*, 201–213.

Act Respecting Labour Standards. (2004). R.S.Q. c. N-1.1, ss. 81.18-81.20 and 123.6-123.16.

Adair, J.G. (1984). The Hawthorne Effect: Reconsideration of a methodological artifact. *Journal of Applied Psychology, 69*, 334–345.

Adams, G.A., & Jex, S.M. (1999). Relationships between time management, control, work–family conflict, and strain. *Journal of Occupational Health Psychology, 4*, 72–77.

Adams, J.S. (1965). Inequity in social exchange. In L. Berkowitz (Ed.), *Advances in experimental social psychology* (Vol. 2, pp. 267–299). New York: Academic Press.

Adebayo, D.O. (2006). Workload, social support, and work–school conflict among Nigerian nontraditional students. *Journal of Career Development, 33*, 125–141.

Agle, B.R., Nagarajan, N.J., Sonnenfeld, J.A., & Srinivasan, D. (2006). Does CEO charisma matter? An empirical analysis of the relationships among organizational performance, environmental uncertainty, and top management team perceptions of CEO charisma. *Academy of Management Journal, 49*, 161–174.

Ah Chong, L.M., & Thomas, D.C. (1997). Leadership perceptions in cross-cultural context: Pakeha and Pacific Islanders in New Zealand. *Leadership Quarterly, 8*, 275–293.

Ajzen, I. (1989). Perceived behavioral control, self-efficacy, locus of control, and the theory of planned behavior. *Journal of Applied Social Psychology, 32*(4), 665–683.

Aldana, S.G. (2001). Financial impact of health promotion programs: A comprehensive review of the literature. *American Journal of Health Promotion, 15*, 281–288.

Alimo-Metcalfe, B., & Alban-Metcalfe, R.J. (2001). The development of a new Transformational Leadership Questionnaire. *Journal of Occupational and Organizational Psychology, 74*, 1–27.

Allen, N.J. & Hecht, T.D. (2004). The 'romance of teams': Toward an understanding of its psychological underpinnings and implications. *Journal of Occupational and Organizational Psychology, 77*(4), 439–461.

Allen, N.J., & Meyer, J.P. (1990). The measurement and antecedents of affective, continuance and normative commitment to the organization. *Journal of Occupational Psychology, 63*, 1–18.

Alliger, G.M., Lilienfeld, S.O., & Mitchell, K.E. (1996). The susceptibility of overt and covert integrity tests to coaching and faking. *Psychological Science, 7*, 32–39.

Alliger, G.M., Tannenbaum, S.I., Bennett, W. Jr., Traver, H., & Shotland, A. (1997). A meta-analysis of the relations among training criteria. *Personnel Psychology, 50*, 341–358.

Ambrose, M.L., Seabright, M.A., & Schminke, M. (2002). Sabotage in the workplace: The role of organizational injustice. *Organizational Behavior and Human Decision Processes, 89*, 947–965.

American Educational Research Association, American Psychological Association, and National Council on Measurement in Education. (1999). *Standards for educational and psychological testing*. Washington, DC: American Educational Research Association.

American Psychological Association's Psychologically Healthy Workplace Description. Retrieved on April 22, 2006 from http://www.apapractice.org/apo/psychologically_healthy.html#.

American Psychological Association. (2007). *Stress in America 2007*. Retrieved from www.apa.org/pubs/info/reports/2007-stress.doc

Amos, E.A., & Weathington, B.L. (2008). An analysis of the relation between employee–organization value congruence and employee attitudes. *The Journal of Psychology, 142*(6), 615–631.

Anastasi, A. (1988). *Psychological Testing*, 6th ed. New York: Macmillan.

Andersen, M.B. (2009). The canon of mental skills in performance psychology. In K.F. Hays (Ed.), *Performance psychology in action*. Washington, DC: American Psychological Association.

Anonymous. (2006). Unionization. *Perspectives on Labor and Income, 18*, 64–70.

Applebaum, H. (1984). *Work in market and industrial societies*. Albany, NY: SUNY Press.

Applebaum, H. (1992). *The concept of work: Ancient, medieval and modern*. Albany, NY: SUNY Press.

Appleton, K., House, A., & Dowell, A. (1998). A survey of job satisfaction, sources of stress, and psychological symptoms among general practitioners in Leeds. *British Journal of General Practice, 48,* 1059–1063.

Argote, L., & McGrath, J.E. (1993). Group processes in organizations. Continuity and change. In C.L. Cooper & I.T. Robertson (Eds.), *International Review of industrial and organizational psychology* (Vol. 8, pp. 333–389). New York: Wiley.

Arnold, D.W. (1991). To test or not to test: Legal issues in integrity testing. *Forensic Psychology, 4,* 62–67.

Arnold, K., Turner, N., Barling, J., Kelloway, E.K., & McKee, M. (2007). Transformational leadership and psychological well-being: The mediating role of meaningful work. *Journal of Occupational Health Psychology, 12,* 193–203.

Arnold, K.A., Turner, N.A., Barling, J., Kelloway, E.K., & McKee, M. (2007). Transformational leadership and well-being: The mediating role of meaningful work. *Journal of Occupational Health Psychology, 12,* 193–203.

Arrow, H. (1998). Standing out and fitting in: Composition effects on newcomer socialization. In D.H. Gruenfeld (Ed.), *Composition: Research on managing groups and teams* (Vol. 1, pp. 59–80). Stamford, CT: JAI Press.

Arthur, W. Jr., Bennet, W. Jr., Eden, P.S., & Bell, S.T. (2003). Effectiveness of training in organizations: A meta-analysis of design and evaluation features. *Journal of Applied Psychology, 88,* 234–245.

Arvey, R.D., Landon, T.E., Nutting, S.M., & Maxwell, S.E. (1992). Development of physical ability tests for police officers: A construct validation approach. *Journal of Applied Psychology, 77,* 996–1009.

Arvey, R.D., Renz, G.L., & Watson, T.W. (1998). Emotionality and job performance: Implications for personnel selection. In G.R. Ferris (Ed.), *Research in Personnel and Human Resource Management* (Vol. 16, pp.103–147). Stamford, CT: JAI Press.

Arvey, R.D., Rotundo, M., Johnson, W., Zhang, Z., & McGue, M. (2006). The determinants of leadership role occupancy: Genetic and personality factors. *Leadership Quarterly, 17,* 1–20.

Arvey, R.D., Zhang, Z., Avolio, B.J., & Krueger, R.F. (2007). Developmental and genetic determinants of leadership role occupancy among women. *Journal of Applied Psychology, 92,* 693–705.

Aryee, S., & Chay, Y.W. (2001). Workplace justice, citizenship behavior and turnover intentions in a union context. *Journal of Applied Psychology, 86,* 154–160.

Ash, R.A. (1988). Job analysis in the world of work. In S. Gael (Ed.), *The job analysis handbook for business, industry and government* (Vol. I, pp. 3–13). New York: John Wiley & Sons.

Asher, J.J. (1972). The biographical item: Can it be improved? *Personnel Psychology, 25,* 251–269.

Asher, J.J., & Sciarrino, J.A. (1974). Realistic work samples tests: A review. *Personnel Psychology, 27,* 519–523.

Ashforth, B.E. (1997). Petty tyranny in organizations: A preliminary examination of antecedents and consequences. *Canadian Journal of Administrative Sciences, 14,* 126–140.

Association of Executive Search Consultants. (2007). *Life–work balance: The new workplace perks.* Brent Ridge, MD. Accessed October 1, 2009.

Atwater, L.E., Dionne, S.D., Camobreco, J.F., Avolio, B.J., & Lau, A. (1998). Individual attributes and leadership style: Predicting the use of punishment and its effects. *Journal of Organizational Behavior, 19,* 559–576.

Austin, J.T., & Villanova, P. (1992). The criterion problem: 1917–1992. *Journal of Applied Psychology, 77,* 836–874.

Avey, J.B., Luthans, F., Smith, R., & Palmer, N.F. (2010). Impact of positive psychological capital on employee well-being over time. *Journal of Occupational Health Psychology, 15*(1), 17–28.

Avolio, B.J. (1999). *Full leadership development: Building the vital forces in organizations.* Thousand Oaks, CA: Sage.

Avolio, B.J., Reichard, R.J., Hannah, S.T., Walumba, F.O., & Chan, A. (2009). A meta-analytic review of leadership impact research: Experimental and quasi-experimental studies. *The Leadership Quarterly.* doi:10.1016/j.leaqua.2009.06.006.

Ayman, R., Chemers, M.M., & Fiedler, F. (1995). The contingency model of leadership effectiveness: Its level of analysis. *Leadership Quarterly, 6,* 147–167.

Babiak, P., & Hare, R. (2006). *Snakes in suits: When psychopaths go to work.* New York: Harper Books.

Bacharach, S.B., Bamberger, P., & Biron, M. (2010). Alcohol consumption and workplace absenteeism: The moderating effect of social support. *Journal of Applied Psychology, 95,* 334–348.

Bachman, K. (2000). *Work–life balance: Are employers listening?* Ottawa: Conference Board of Canada.

Bailey, C., & Fletcher, C. (2002). The impact of multiple source feedback on management development: Findings from a longitudinal study. *Journal of Organizational Behavior, 23,* 853–867.

Bakker, A.B., & Demerouti, E. (2007). The job-demands resources model: State of the art. *Journal of Managerial Psychology, 22(3),* 309–328.

Bakker, A.B, Demerouti, E., de Boer, E., & Schaufeli, W.B. (2003). Job demands and job resources as predictors of absence duration and frequency. *Journal of Vocational Behavior, 62,* 341–356.

Bakker, A.B., Demerouti, E., Taris, T., Schaufeli, W.B., & Schreurs, P. (2003). A multi-group analysis of the job demands–resources model in four home-care organizations. *International Journal of Stress Management, 10,* 16–38.

Baldwin, T.T., & Ford, J.K. (1988). Transfer of training: A review and directions for future research. *Personnel Psychology, 41,* 63–105.

Baldwin, T.T., Magjuka, R.J., & Loher, B.T. (1991). The perils of participation: Effects of choice of training on trainee motivation and learning. *Personnel Psychology, 44,* 51–67.

Baltes, B.B., Briggs, T.E., Huff, J.W., Wright, J.A., & Neuman, G.A. (1999). Flexible and compressed workweek schedules: A meta-analysis of their effects on work-related criteria. *Journal of Applied Psychology, 84,* 496–513.

Balzer, W.K., Kihm, J.A., Smith, P.C., Irwin, J.L., Bachiochi, P.D., Robie, C., et al. (1997). *Users' manual for the Job Descriptive Index (JDI 1997 revision) and the Job in General (JIG) scales.* Bowling Green, OH: Bowling Green State University.

Bamberger, P.A., & Bacharach, S.B. (2006). Abusive supervision and subordinate problem drinking: Taking resistance, stress and subordinate personality into account. *Human Relations, 59(6),* 723–752.

Bamberger, P., & Biron, M. (2007). Group norms and excessive absenteeism: The role of peer referent others. *Organizational Behavior and Human Decision Processes, 103,* 179–196.

Bandura, A. (1982). Self-efficacy mechanism in human agency. *American Psychologist, 37,* 122–147.

Bandura, A. (1986). *Social functions of thought and action: A social cognitive theory.* Englewood Cliffs, NJ: Prentice Hall.

Bandura, A. (1997). *Self-efficacy: The exercise of control.* New York: W. H. Freeman.

Bandura, A., & Locke, E. (2003). Negative self-efficacy and goal effects revisited. *Journal of Applied Psychology, 88(1),* 87–99. doi:10.1037/0021-9010.88.1.87.

Barber, A.E. & Wesson, M.J. (1999). A tale of two job markets: Organizational size and its effects on hiring practices and job search behavior. *Personnel Psychology, 52,* 841–868.

Barling, A.J., Weber, T., & Kelloway, E.K. (1996). Effects of transformational leadership training on attitudinal and financial outcomes: A field experiment. *Journal of Applied Psychology, 81,* 827–832.

Barling, J. (1988). Industrial relations: A "blind spot" in the teaching, research and practice of industrial/organizational psychology. *Canadian Psychology, 29,* 103–108.

Barling, J. (1990). *Employment stress and family functioning.* Chichester, UK: John Wiley & Sons.

Barling, J., Christie, A., & Hoption, A. (2010). Leadership. In S. Zedeck et al. (Eds.) *Handbook of industrial and organizational psychology* (pp. 183–240). Washington, DC: American Psychological Association.

Barling, J., Fullagar, C., & Kelloway, E.K. (1992). *The union and its members: A psychological approach.* New York, NY: Oxford University Press.

Barling, J., Fullagar, C., Kelloway, E.K., & McElvie, L. (1992). Union loyalty and strike propensity. *Journal of Social Psychology, 132,* 581–590.

Barling, J., & Griffiths, A. (2003). A history of occupational health psychology. In J.C. Quick & L.E. Tetrick (Eds.), *Handbook of occupational health psychology* (pp. 19–33). Washington, DC: American Psychological Association.

Barling, J., Kelloway, E.K., & Bremermann, E.H. (1991). Pre-employment predictors of union attitudes: The role of family socialization and work beliefs. *Journal of Applied Psychology, 76,* 725–731.

Barling, J., Loughlin, C., & Kelloway, E.K. (2002). Development and test of a model linking safety-specific transformational leadership and occupational safety. *Journal of Applied Psychology, 87,* 488–496.

Barling, J., & Milligan, J. (1987). Some psychological consequences of striking: A six-month longitudinal study. *Journal of Occupational Behavior, 8,* 127–138.

Barnes-Farrell, J. (2006). Older worker issues. In S. Rogelberg & C. Reeves (Eds.). *The encyclopedia of industrial and organizational psychology* (Vol. 2, pp. 531–534). Thousand Oaks, CA: Sage.

Baron, S.A. (1993). *Violence in the workplace: A prevention and management guide for business.* Ventura, CA: Pathfinder Publishing.

Barrett, G.V., & Kernan, M.C. (1987). Performance appraisal and terminations: A review of court decisions since *Brito v. Zia* with implication for personnel practices. *Personnel Psychology, 40,* 489–503.

Barrick, M.R., & Mount, M.K. (1991). The Big Five personality dimensions and job performance: A meta-analysis. *Personnel Psychology, 44,* 1–26.

Barrick, M.R., & Mount, M.K. (1998). Big Five personality dimensions and job performance in army and civil occupations: A European perspective. *Human Performance, 11,* 271–288.

Barrick, M.R., Stewart, G.L., Neubert, M.J., & Mount, M.K. (1998). Relating member ability and personality to work-team processes and team effectiveness. *Journal of Applied Psychology, 83,* 377–391.

Barrick, M.R., Stewart, G.L., & Piortowski, M. (2000). *Personality and performance: Test of the mediating effects of motivation.* Presented at the 15th Annual Conference of the Society for Industrial and Organizational Psychology, New Orleans, LA.

Bartram, D. (2005). The great eight competencies: A criterion-centric approach to validation. *Journal of Applied Psychology, 90,* 1185–1203.

Baruch, Y., Fenton, M., Hind, P., & Vigoda-Gadot, E. (2004). Pro-social behavior and job performance: Do need for control and need for achievement make a difference? *Social Behavior and Personality, 32,* 399–412.

Bass, B.M. (1985). *Leadership and performance beyond expectations.* NY: Free Press.

Bass, B.M. (1997). Does the transactional-transformational leadership paradigm transcend organizational and national boundaries? *American Psychologist, 52,* 130–139.

Bass, B.M., Avolio, B.J., Jung, D.I., & Berson, Y. (2003). Predicting unit performance by assessing transformational and transactional leadership. *Journal of Applied Psychology, 88,* 207–218.

Bass, B.M., & Riggio, R.E. (2006). *Transformational leadership* (2nd ed.). NJ: Erlbaum.

Beal, D.J., Cohen, R.R., Burke, M.J., & McLendon, C.L. (2003). Cohension and performance in groups: A meta-analytic clarification of construct relations. *Journal of Applied Psychology, 88*(6), 989–1004.

Bechtoldt, M.N., Welk, C., Hartig, J., & Zapf, D. (2007). Main and moderating effects of emotional labor on counterproductive behavior at work. *European Journal of Work and Organizational Psychology, 16,* 479–500.

Becker, E.T., & Billings, S.R. (1993). Profiles of commitment: An empirical test. *Journal of Organizational Behavior, 14*(2), 177–190.

Beehr, T.A., Ivanitskaya, L., Hansen, C.P., Erofeev, D., & Gudanowski, D.M. (2000). Evaluation of 360-degree feedback ratings: Relationships with each other and with performance and selection procedures. *Journal of Organizational Behavior, 22,* 755–788.

Beekun, R.I. (1989). Assessing the effectiveness of sociotechnical interventions: Antidote or fad? *Human Relations, 42,* 877–897.

Belcourt, M., Sherman, A.W. Jr., Bohlander, G.W., & Snell, S.A. (1996). *Managing Human Resources.* Toronto: Nelson Canada.

Bell, B.S., & Kozlowski, S.W.J. (2002). A typology of virtual teams: Implications for effective leadership. *Group and Organization Management, 27,* 12–49.

Bellah, R.N., Madsen, R., Sullivan, W.M., Swideler, A., & Tipton, S.M. (1985). *Habits of the heart: Individualization and commitment in American life:* New York: Harper & Row.

Benjamin, L.T. (2006). Hugo Munsterberg's attack on the application of scientific psychology. *Journal of Applied Psychology, 91,* 414–425.

Bernardin, H.J. (1992). An 'analytic' framework for customer-based performance content development and appraisal. *Human Resources Management Review, 2,* 81–102.

Best Practices in Performance Appraisals. (2000). *HR Focus, 2,* 8.

Bettenhausen, K.L. (1991). Five years of group research: What we have learned and what needs to be addressed. *Journal of Management, 17,* 345–381.

Beugré, C.D. (2005). Reacting aggressively to injustice at work: A cognitive stage model. *Journal of Business and Psychology, 20*(2), 291–301.

Binning, J.F., & Barrett, G.V. (1989). Validity of personnel decisions: A conceptual analysis of the inferential and evidential bases. *Journal of Applied Psychology, 74,* 478–494.

Birenbaum, A., & Sagarin, E. (1976). *Norms and human behavior.* New York: Praeger.

Biswas-Diener, R., & Dean, B. (2007). *Positive psychology coaching: Putting the science of happiness to work for your clients.* Hoboken, NJ: John Wiley & Sons.

Blau, G. (1995). Influence of group lateness on individual lateness: A cross-level examination. *Academy of Management Journal, 38,* 1483–1496.

Blau, G., & Lunz, M. (1998). Testing the incremental effect of professional commitment on intent to leave one's profession beyond the effects of external, personal, and work-related variables. *Journal of Vocational Behavior, 52*(2), 260–269.

Bluen, S.D. (1994). The psychology of strikes. In C.L. Cooper & I.T. Robertson (Eds.). *International review of industrial and organizational psychology* (Vol. 9, pp. 113–135). London: John Wiley & Sons.

Bluen, S.D., & Barling, J. (1988). Psychological stressors associated with industrial relations. In C.L. Cooper and R. Payne (Eds.), *Causes, coping and consequences of stress at work* (pp. 175–205). London, England: John Wiley & Sons.

Bluen, S.D., & Edelstein, I. (1993). Trade union support following an underground explosion. *Journal of Organizational Behavior, 14,* 473–480.

Bluen, S.D., & Jubiler-Lurie, V.G. (1990). Some consequences of labor–management negotiations: Laboratory and field studies. *Journal of Organizational Behavior, 11,* 105–118.

Bluen, S.D., & Mears, B.L., Walker, G., Wills, G., Trotman, H., Atherly, T., Telphia H., and Francis, L., v. Ontario Hydro and Watson, J., Watkiss, A., Ouelette, T., and Loveness, M. (1984). Canadian Human Rights Reporter, 5, D/3433 (Ontario Human Rights Commission Board of Inquiry, December 1983).

Böckerman, P., & Laukkanen, E. (2010). What makes you work while you are sick? Evidence from a survey of workers. *European Journal of Public Health, 20,* 43–46.

Bois, J.S.A. (1949). A progress report on industrial psychology. *Canadian Journal of Psychology, 3,* 105–116.

Bonder, A. (2003). A blueprint for the future: Competency-based management in HRDC. Unpublished presentation, HRDC Canada.

Booth, A.L., Francesconi, M., & Zoega, G. (2004). Unions, work-related training and wages: Evidence for British men. *Industrial and Labor Relations Review, 57,* 68–91.

Borman, W.C. (1991). Job behavior, performance, and effectiveness. In: M.D. Dunnette and L.M. Hough (Eds.), *Handbook of industrial and organizational psychology* (Vol. 2, 2nd ed. pp. 271–326). Palo Alto, CA: Consulting Psychologists Press.

Borman, W.C., Hanson, M.A., Oppler, S.H., Pulakos, E.D., & Whilte, L.A. (1991). Job behavior, performance, and effectiveness. In M.D. Dunnette & L.M. Hough (Eds.), *Handbook of industrial and organizational psychology* (Vol. 2, 2nd ed. pp. 271–326). San Diego: Consulting Psychologists Press.

Borman, W.C., & Motowidlo, S.J. (1993). Expanding the criterion domain to include elements of contextual performance. In N. Schmitt & W.C. Borman (Eds.), *Personnel selection in organizations* (pp. 71–98). San Francisco: Jossey-Bass.

Bouchard, T.J. Jr., Lykken, D.T., McGue, M., Segal, N.L., & Tellegen, A. (1990). Sources of human psychological differences: The Minnesota Study of Twins Reared Apart. *Science 250*(4978), 223–228.

Bower, P., Rowland, N., & Hardy, R. (2003). The clinical effectiveness of counselling in primary care: A systematic review and meta-analysis. *Psychological Medicine, 33,* 203–215.

Bowman, J.S. (1999). Performance appraisal: Verisimilitude trumps veracity. *Public Personnel Management, 28,* 557–576.

Bownas, D.A., & Bernardin, H.J. (1988). Critical incident technique. In S. Gael (Ed.), *The job analysis handbook for business, industry and government* (Vol. II, pp. 1120–1137). New York: John Wiley & Sons.

Boyatzis, R., McKee, A., & Goleman, D. (2002). Reawakening your passion for work. *Harvard Business Review, 80*(4), 86–94.

Boyatzis, R.E. (1982). *The competent manager: A model of effective performance.* New York: John Wiley & Sons.

Bray, D.W., Campbell, R.J., & Grant, D.L. (1974). *Formative years in business: A long-term AT&T study of managerial lives.* New York: Wiley.

Brehm, S.S., Miller, R.W., Perlman, D., & Campbell, S.M. (2002). *Intimate relationships* (3rd ed). NY: McGraw-Hill.

Brett, J.M. (1980). Why employees want unions. *Organizational Dynamics, 8,* 47–59.

Bretz, R.D. Jr., & Judge, T.A. (1998). Realistic job previews: A test of the adverse self-selection hypothesis. *Journal of Applied Psychology, 83,* 330–337.

Brief, A.P. (1998). *Attitudes in and around organizations.* Thousand Oaks, CA: Sage.

British Columbia (Public Service Employee Relations Commission) v. BCGSEU. Supreme Court of Canada decision rendered September 9, 1999.

Britt, T.W., Adler, A.B., & Bartone, P.T. (2001). Deriving benefits from stressful events: The role of engagement in meaningful work and hardiness. *Journal of Occupational Health Psychology, 6,* 53–63.

Brogden, H.E. (1949). When testing pays off. *Personnel Psychology, 2,* 171–183.

Brondolo, E., Rieppi, R., Erickson, S.A., Bagiella, E., Shapiro, P.A., McKinley, P., & Sloan, R.P. (2003). Hostility, interpersonal interactions, and ambulatory blood pressure. *Psychosom Med, 65*(6), 1003–1011.

Brown, K.G. (2005). An examination of the structure and nomological network of trainee reactions: A closer look at "smile sheets." *Journal of Applied Psychology, 90*(5), 991–1001.

Brown, S.P. (1996). A meta-analysis and review of organizational research on job involvement. *Psychological Bulletin, 120*(2), 235–255.

Brutus, S., & Derayeh, M. (2002). Multisource assessment programs in organizations: An insider's perspective. *Human Resource Development Quarterly, 13,* 187–202.

Bryant, F.B., Smart, C.M., & King, S.O. (2005). Using the past to enhance the present: Boosting happiness through positive reminiscence. *Journal of Happiness Studies, 6,* 227–260.

Buckingham, M., & Clifton, D.O. (2001). *Now, discover your strengths.* New York: Free Press.

Buckley, M.R., Fedor, D.B., & Marvin, D.S. (1994). Ethical considerations in the recruiting process: A preliminary investigation and identification of research opportunities. *Human Resource Management Review, 4,* 35–50.

Buckley, M.R., Fedor, D.B., Marvin, D.S., Veres, J.G., Wise, D.S., & Carraher, S.M. (1998). Investigating newcomer expectations and job-related outcomes. *Journal of Applied Psychology, 83,* 452–461.

Budd, J.W., & Mumford, K. (2004). Trade unions and family friendly policies in Britain. *Industrial and Labor Relations Review, 57,* 204–222.

Buhler, P. (2007, November). Managing in the new millennium: Ten keys to better hiring. *SuperVision, 68,* 17–20.

Bulger, C.A., & Mellor, S. (1997). Self-efficacy as a mediator of the relationship between perceived union barriers and women's participation in union activities. *Journal of Applied Psychology, 82*(6), 935–944.

Burke, C.S., Sims, D.E., Lazzara, E.H., & Salas, E. (2007). Trust in leadership: A multi-level review and integration. *The Leadership Quarterly*, 606–632.

Burke, L.A., & Hutchins, H.M. (2007). Training transfer: An integrative literature review. *Human Resource Development Review, 6*, 263–296.

Burke, L.A. & Miller, M.K. (1999). Taking the mystery out of intuitive decision-making. *The Academy of Management Executive, 13*, 91–99.

Burke, M.L., & Sarpy, S.A. (2003). Improving worker safety and health through interventions. In D.A. Hofmann & L.E. Tetrick (Eds.). *Health and safety in organizations.* San Francisco, CA: Jossey-Bass.

Burnett, J. (1994). *Idle hands: The experience of unemployment, 1790–1990.* New York: Routledge.

Burns, J.M. (1978). *Leadership.* New York: Harper & Row.

Bush, D.F., & O'Shea, P.G. (1996). Workplace violence: Comparative use of prevention practices and policies. In G.R. VandenBos & E.Q. Bulatao (Eds.). *Violence on the job: Identifying risks and developing solutions.* Washington, DC: American Psychological Association.

BusinessWeek. (2006). http://www.businessweek.com/smallbiz/tips/archives/2006/11/what_employees.html.

Buttigieg, D.M., Deery, S.J., & Iverson, R.D. (2007). An event history analysis of union joining and leaving. *Journal of Applied Psychology, 92*, 829–839.

Bycio, P., Hackett, R.D., & Allen, J.S. (1995). Further assessments of Bass's (1985) conceptualization of transactional and transformational leadership. *Journal of Applied Psychology, 80*, 468–478.

Byrne, J.A. (1998, June). How Jack Welch runs GE. *BusinessWeek, 358*, 90.

Cable, D., & DeRue, D.S. (2002). The convergent and discriminant validity of subject fit perceptions. *Journal of Applied Psychology, 87*, 875–884.

Camara, W.J., & Schneider, D.L. (1994). Integrity tests: Facts and unresolved issues. *American Psychologist, 49*, 112–119.

Cameron, K.S., Bright, D., & Caza, A. (2004). Exploring the relationships between virtuousness and performance. *American Behavioral Scientist, 47*, 766–790.

Cameron, K.S., Dutton, J.E., & Quinn, R.E. (Eds.). (2003). *Positive organizational scholarship.* San Francisco, CA: Berrett-Koehler, Ltd.

Campbell, J.P., Gasser, M.B., & Oswald, F.L. (1996). The substantive nature of job performance variability. In K.R. Murphy (Ed.). *Individual differences and behavior in organizations* (pp. 258–299). San Francisco: Jossey-Bass.

Campion, M.A. (1983). Personnel selection for physically demanding jobs: Review and recommendation. *Personnel Psychology, 36*, 527–550.

Campion, M.A., Medsker, G.J., & Higgs, A.C. (1993). Relations between work group characteristics and effectiveness: Implications for designing effective work groups. *Personnel Psychology, 46*, 823–850.

Canadian Federation of Independent Business. (2008). *Training in your business survey.* Ottawa: Author.

Canadian Human Rights Commission. (2007). *Bona fide occupational requirement and bona fide justification under the Canadian Human Rights Act: Implications of Meiorin and Grissmer.* Ottawa: Minister of Pubic Works and Government Services.

Cannon, M., & Kelloway, E.K. (2009). Regaining customers after a product recall: The role of organizational apologies. Manuscript submitted for publication.

Cannon-Bowers, J.A., & Salas, E. (Eds.). (1998). *Making decisions under stress: Implications for individual and team training.* Washington, DC: American Psychological Association.

Carayon, P. (1995). Chronic effect of job control, supervisory social support, and work pressure on office-worker stress. In S.L. Sauter & L.R. Murphy (Eds.), *Organizational risk factors for job stress* (pp. 357–370). Washington, DC: American Psychological Association.

Carless, S.A. (2000). The validity of scores on the Multidimensional Aptitude Battery. *Educational and Psychological Measurement, 60*, 592–603.

Carless, S.A. (2005). Person-job fit versus person-organization fit as predictors of organizational attraction and job acceptance intentions: A longitudinal study. *Journal of Occupational and Organizational Psychology, 78*, 411–429.

Carter, D.D., England, G., Etherington, D., & Trudeau, G. (2002). *Labour law in Canada* (5th ed.). Markham, ON: Butterworths.

Carver, C.S., Scheier, M.F., & Weintraub, J.K. (1989). Assessing coping strategies: A theoretically based approach. *Journal of Personality and Social Psychology, 56*(2), 267–283.

Carver, C.S., & White, T.L. (1994). Behavioral inhibition, behavioral activation, and affective responses to impending reward and punishment: The BIS/BAS scales. *Journal of Personality and Social Psychology, 67*(23), 319–333.

Cascio, W.F. (1998). *Applied psychology in human resources management* (5th ed.). Toronto: Prentice Hall Canada.

Cassidy, G.A. (2000). *Discover your passion: An intuitive search to find your purpose in life*. Westfield, NJ: Tomlyn.

Catano, V.M. (2002). Competency-based selection and performance systems: Are they defensible? [Summary]. *Canadian Psychology, 43*(2a), 145.

Catano, V.M., & Bissonnette, A. (2003). *Selection practices and organizational performance*. Paper presented at the annual meeting of the Administrative Sciences Association of Canada, Halifax, NS.

Catano, V.M., & Bissonnette, A. (2009). *The evolution of recruitment and selection practices in Canada*. Paper presented at the biennial meeting of the European Association of Work and Organizational Psychology, Santiago de Compostela, Spain.

Catano, V.M., Darr, W., & Campbell, C.A. (2007). Performance appraisal of behavior-based competencies: A reliable and valid procedure. *Personnel Psychology, 60*, 199–228.

Catano, V.M., Wiesner, W.H., Hackett, R.D., & Methot, L. (2009). *Recruitment and selection in Canada* (4th ed.). Toronto: Nelson.

Cawley, B.D., Keeping, L.M., & Levy, P.E. (1998). Participation in the performance appraisal process and employee reactions: A meta-analytic review of field investigations. *Journal of Applied Psychology, 83*, 615–633.

Chaison, G. (2006). *Unions in America*. Thousand Oaks, CA: Sage.

Chan, D., & Schmitt, N. (2002). Situational judgment and job performance. *Human Performance, 15*, 233–254.

Chang, H., Chi, N., & Miao, M. (2007). Testing the relationship between three-component organizational/occupational commitment and organizational/occupational turnover intention using a non-recursive model. *Journal of Vocational Behavior, 70*(2), 352–368.

Charlwood, A. (2002). Why do non-union employees want to unionize? Evidence from Britain. *British Journal of Industrial Relations, 40*(3), 463–491.

Chatman, J.A., & Flynn, F.J. (2001). The influence of demographic heterogeneity on the emergence and consequences of cooperative norms in work teams. *Academy of Management Journal, 44*(5), 956–974.

Chen, G., Thomas, B.A., & Wallace, J.C. (2005). A multilevel examination of the relationships among training outcomes, mediating regulatory processes, and adaptive performance. *Journal of Applied Psychology, 90*, 827–841.

Chen, P.Y., & Spector, P.E. (1992). Relationship of work stressors with aggression, withdrawal, theft and substance abuse. *Journal of Occupational and Organizational Psychology, 65*, 177–184.

Cheng, E.W.L., & Ho, D.C.K. (2001). A review of transfer of training studies in the past decade. *Personnel Review, 30*, 102–118.

Cheung, G.W. (1999). Multifaceted conceptions of self–other ratings disagreement. *Personnel Psychology, 52*, 1–36.

Christal, R.E., & Weissmuller, J.J. (1988). Job-task inventory analysis. In S. Gael (Ed.), *The job analysis handbook for business, industry and government* (Vol. II, pp. 1036–1050). New York: John Wiley & Sons.

Clark, L., & Snitzer, P. (2005). "Speak no evil" is a risky policy: Reference checks on former workers can be tricky for healthcare employers. *Modern Healthcare, 35,* 49.

Clarke, C.S., Dobbins, G.H., Ladd, R.T. (1993). Exploratory field study of training motivation: Influence of involvement, credibility, and transfer climate. *Group and Organization Management, 18,* 292–307.

Clifton, D.O., & Harter, J.K. (2003). Strengths investment. In K.S. Cameron, J.E. Dutton, & R.E. Quinn (Eds.), *Positive organizational scholarship.* San Francisco, Berrett-Koehler.

Coastal Contacts Inc. (n.d.). The media kit. Retrieved January 26, 2010, from http://www.coastalcontacts.com/about-us.ep.

Cohen, H.H., & Jenson, R.C. (1984). Measuring the effectiveness of an industrial lift truck safety training program. *Journal of Safety Research, 15,* 125–135.

Cohen, S.G., & Bailey, D.E. (1997). What makes teams work: Group effectiveness research from the shop floor to the executive suite. *Journal of Management, 23*(3), 239–290.

Cohen, S.G., & Ledford, G.E. Jr. (1994). The effectiveness of self-managing teams: A quasi-experiment. *Human Relations, 47,* 13–43.

Cohen, S.G., Ledford, G.E., & Spreitzer, G.M. (1996). A predictive model of self-managing work team effectiveness. *Human Relations, 49*(5), 643–676.

Coleman, V.I., & Borman, W.C. (2000). Investigating the underlying structure of the citizenship performance domain. *Human Resource Management Review, 10,* 25–44.

Colligan, M.J., & Cohen, A. (2004). The role of training in promoting workplace safety and health. In J. Barling & M. Frone (Eds.), *Handbook of workplace safety* (pp. 223–248). Washington, DC: American Psychological Association.

Collins, J.D., & Schmidt, F.L. (1993). Personality, integrity, and white collar crime: A construct validity study. *Personnel Psychology, 46,* 295–311.

Colquitt, J.A., Conlon, D.E., Wesson. M.J., Porter, C.O.L.H., & Ng, K.Y. (2001). Justice at the millennium: A meta-analytic review of 25 years of organizational justice research. *Journal of Applied Psychology, 86,* 425–445.

Colquitt, J.A., LaPine, J.A., & Noe, R.A. (2000). Toward an integrative theory of training motivation: Meta-analytic path analysis of 20 years of research. *Journal of Applied Psychology, 85,* 678–707.

Comer, D.R. (1995). A model of social loafing in real work groups. *Human Relations, 48*(6), 647–667.

Conger, J.A., & Kanungo, R.N. (1994). Charismatic leadership in organizations: Perceived behavioural attributes and their measurement. *Journal of Organizational Behavior, 15,* 439–452.

Conger, J.A., & Kanungo, R.N. (1998). *Charismatic leadership in organizations.* Thousand Oaks, CA: Sage.

Conte, J.M. & Jacobs, R.R. (2003). Validity evidence linking polychronicity and Big Five personality dimensions to absence, lateness, and supervisory performance ratings. *Human Performance, 16,* 107–129.

Conway, J.M. (1999). Distinguishing contextual performance from task performance for managerial jobs. *Journal of Applied Psychology, 84,* 3–13.

Conway, J.M., Jako, R.A., & Goodman, D.F. (1995). A meta-analysis of inter-rater and internal consistency reliability of selection interviews. *Journal of Applied Psychology, 80,* 565–579.

Cox, C.J., & Cooper, C.L. (1989). The making of the British CEO: Childhood, work experience, personality, and management style. *Academy of Management Executive, 3,* 353–358.

Cronbach, L.J. (1971). Test validation. In R.L. Thorndike (Ed.). *Educational measurement* (2nd ed.). Washington, DC: American Council of Education.

Cronbach, L.J. & Gleser, G. (1965). *Psychological tests and personnel decisions.* Urbana, IL: University of Illinois Press.

Cronshaw, S.F. (1986). The status of employment testing in Canada: A review and evaluation of theory and professional practice. *Canadian Psychology, 27,* 183–195.

Cronshaw, S.F. (1988). Future directions for industrial psychology in Canada. *Canadian Psychology, 29,* 30–43.

Cropanzano, R., & Wright, T.A. (2001). When a happy worker is really a productive worker: A review and further refinement of the happy-productive worker thesis. *Consulting Psychology Journal: Practice and Research, 53*(3), 182–199.

Cropanzano, R., & Ambrose, M.L. (2001). Procedural and distributive justice are more similar than you think: A monistic perspective and a research agenda. In J. Greenberg & R. Cropanzano (Eds.), *Advances in organizational justice* (pp. 119–151). Stanford, CA: Stanford University Press.

Cropanzano, R., Byrne, Z.S., Bobocel, D.R., & Rupp, D.R. (2001). Moral virtues, fairness heuristics, social entities, and other denizens of organizational justice. *Journal of Vocational Behavior, 58,* 164–209.

Csikszentmihalyi, M. (1975). *Beyond boredom and anxiety: Experiencing flow in work and play.* San Francisco: Jossey-Bass.

Csikszentmihalyi, M. (1990). *Flow: The psychology of optimal experience.* New York: Harper & Row.

Cutcher-Gershenfeld, J., & Kochan, T. (2004). Taking stock: Collective bargaining at the turn of the century. *Industrial and Labor Relations Review, 58*(1), 3–26.

Dailey, R.C., & Kirk, D.J. (1992). Distributive and procedural justice as antecedents of job dissatisfaction and intent to turnover. *Human Relations, 45*(3), 305–318.

Dale, K., & Fox, M. (2008). Leadership style and organizational commitment: Mediating effect of role stress. *Journal of Managerial Issues, 20*(1), 109–130.

Dalton, D., & Mesch, D. (1990). The impact of flexible scheduling on employee attendance and turnover. *Administrative Science Quarterly, 35,* 370–387.

Dalton, D.R., & Todor, W.D. (1993). Turnover, transfer, absenteeism: An interdependent perspective. *Journal of Management, 19,* 193–219.

Dansereau, F. Jr, Graen, G., & Haga, W.J. (1975). A vertical dyad linkage approach to leadership within formal organizations: A longitudinal investigation of the role making process. *Organizational Behavior and Human Performance, 13,* 46–78.

Darr, W., & Catano, V.M. (2008). Multisource assessments of behavioral competencies and selection interview performance. *International Journal of Selection and Assessment, 16,* 68–72.

Darr, W. & Johns, G. (2008). Work strain, health, and absenteeism: A meta-analysis. *Journal of Occupational Health Psychology, 13,* 293–318.

Darviri, S.V., & Woods, S.A. (2006). Uncertified absence from work and the Big Five: An examination of absence records and future absence intentions. *Personality and Individual Differences, 41,* 359–369.

Davies, P.G., Spencer, S.J., & Steele, C.M. (2005). Clearing the air: Identity safety moderates the effects of stereotype threat on women's leadership aspirations. *Journal of Personality and Social Psychology, 88*(2), 276–287.

Daw, J. (2001). Road rage, air rage and now 'desk rage.' *APA Monitor, 32,* July–August. Online: http://www.apa.org/monitor/julaug01/deskrage.html.

Day, A.L., & Jreige, S. (2002). Examining type A behavior pattern to explain the relationship between job stressors and psychosocial outcomes. *Journal of Occupational Health Psychology, 7*(2), 109–120.

Day, A.L., & Livingstone, H. (2001). Chronic and acute stressors among military personnel: Do coping styles buffer their negative impact on health? *Journal of Occupational Health Psychology, 6,* 348–360.

Day, A.L., Scott, N., & Kelloway, E.K. (2010). Information and communication technology: Implications for job stress and employee well-being. In P.L. Perrewe & D.C. Ganster (Eds.), *New developments in theoretical and conceptual approaches to job stress, research in occupational stress and well-being* (Vol. 8, pp. 317–350). Bingley, UK: Emerald.

Day, A.L., Sibley, A., Wentzell, N., Tallon, J.M., Ackroyd-Stolarz, S. (2009). Using job control and training to reduce the negative impact of work anxieties, health problems, and injuries on burnout. *Canadian Journal of Administrative Sciences, Special Issues in Health & Safety in Organizations.*

Day, A.L., Stinson, V., Catano, V.M., & Kelloway, E.K. (2006). Third party reactions to the threat of a labor strike. *Journal of Occupational Health Psychology, 11*(1), 3–12.

Day, D.V., & Sulsky, L.M. (1995). Effects of frame-of-reference training and ratee information configuration on memory organization and rater accuracy. *Journal of Applied Psychology, 80,* 156–167.

De Cuyper, N., & De Witte, H. (2006). Autonomy and workload among temporary workers: Their effects on job satisfaction, organizational commitment, life satisfaction, and self-rated performance. *International Journal of Stress Management, 13*(4), 441–459.

De Dreu, C.K.W., Harinck, F., & Van Vianen, A.E.M. (1999). Conflict and performance in groups and organizations. In C.L. Cooper & I.T. Robertson (Eds.), *International review of industrial and organizational psychology* (Vol. 14, pp. 369–414). Chichester, United Kingdom: Wiley.

De Dreu, C.K.W., & Weingart, L. (2003). Task versus relationship conflict, team performance, and team member satisfaction: A meta-analysis. *Journal of Applied Psychology, 88*(4), 741–749.

De Dreu, C.K.W., & West, M.A. (2001). Minority dissent and team innovation: The importance of participation in decision making. *Journal of Applied Psychology, 86,* 1191–1201.

de Léséleuc, S. (2007). Criminal victimization in the workplace. Ottawa, Statistics Canada, catalogue no. 85F0033MIE No. 013. Available online: http://www.statcan.gc.ca/pub/85f0033m/85f0033m2007013-eng.pdf.

Deadrick, D.L., & Madigan, R.M. (1990). Dynamic criteria revisited: A longitudinal study of performance stability and predictive validity. *Personnel Psychology, 43,* 717–744.

Deci, E.L. (1975). *Intrinsic motivation.* New York: Plenum.

Deci, E.L., Koestner, R., & Ryan, R. (1999). A meta-analytic review of experiments examining the effects of extrinsic rewards on intrinsic motivation. *Psychological Bulletin, 125,* 627–688.

Deci, E.L., Koestner, R., & Ryan, R.M. (2001). Extrinsic rewards and intrinsic motivation in education: Reconsidered once again. *Review of Educational Research, 71,* 1–27.

Deci, E.L., & Ryan, R.M. (1985). *Intrinsic motivation and self-determination in human behavior.* New York: Plenum.

Deci, E.L., & Ryan, R.M. (2008). Self-determination theory: A macrotheory of human motivation, development, and health. *Canadian Psychology, 49*(3), 182–185.

Deery S.J., Erwin, P.J., & Iverson, R.D. (1999). Industrial relations climate, attendance behaviour and the role of trade unions. *British Journal of Industrial Relations, 37,* 533–558.

Deery, S.J., Erwin, P.J., Iverson, R.D., & Ambrose, M.L. (1995). The determinants of absenteeism: Evidence from Australian blue-collar employees. *International Journal of Human Resource Management, 6,* 825–848.

Deery, S.J., & Iverson, R.D. (2005). Labor-management cooperation: Antecedents and impact on organizational performance. *Industrial and Labor Relations Review, 58,* 588.

DeGroot, T., & Motowidlo, S.J. (1999). Why visual and vocal interview cues can affect interviewers' judgments and predict job performance. *Journal of Applied Psychology 84*(6), 986–993.

Dekker, I., Greenberg, L., & Barling, J. (1998). Predicting union attitudes in student part-time workers. *Canadian Journal of Behavioural Science, 30,* 49–55.

DeLonzor, D. (2005). Running late. *HR Magazine.* Retrieved April 25, 2010, from http://www.allbusiness.com/human-resources/616852-1.html.

Demerouti, E. (2006). Job characteristics, flow, and performance: The moderating role of conscientiousness. *Journal of Occupational Health Psychology, 11,* 266–280.

Demerouti, E., Bakker, A., Nachreiner, F., & Schaufeli, W. (2001). The job demands-resources model of burnout. *Journal of Applied Psychology, 86,* 499–512.

Demir, A., Ulusoy, M., & Ulusoy, M.F. (2003). Investigations of factors influencing burnout levels in the professional and private lives of nurses. *International Journal of Nursing Studies, 40,* 807–827.

Den Hartog, D.N., House, R.J., Hanges, P.J., Ruiz-Quintanilla, S.A., Dorfman, P.W., Abdalla, A., et al. (1999). Culturally-specific and cross-culturally generalizable implicit leadership theories: Are attributes of charismatic leadership theories universally endorsed? *Leadership Quarterly, 10,* 219–256.

Deutsch, M. (1975). Equity, equality, and need: What determines which value will be used as the basis of distributive justice? *Journal of Social Issues, 31*(5).

Dex, S., & Bond, S. (2005). Measuring work-life balance and its covariates. *Work Employment Society, 19*, 627–637.

Diehl, M., & Stroebe, W. (1987). Productivity loss in brainstorming groups: Toward the solution of a riddle. *Journal of Personality and Social Psychology, 53*(3), 497–509.

Digman, J.M. (1990). Personality structure: Emergence of the Five Factor Model. In M. Rosenzweig & L.W. Porter (Eds.), *Annual review of psychology.* Palo Alto, CA: Annual Reviews.

Dionne, S.D., Yammarino, F.J., Atwater, L.E., & James, L.R. (2002). Neutralizing substitutes for leadership theory: Leadership effects and common-source bias. *Journal of Applied Psychology, 87*, 454–464.

Dipboye, R.L. (1992). *Selection interviews: Process perspectives.* Cincinnati, OH: South-Western Publishing.

Dobbelaere, A.G., & Goeppinger, K.H. (1993). The right way and the wrong way to set up a self-directed work team. *Human Resources Professional, 5*, 31–35.

Dohrenwend, B.S., & Dohrenwend, B.P. (Eds.) (1974). *Stressful life events.* New York: John Wiley & Sons.

Dolan, S.L., & Schuler, R.S. (1994). *Human resource management: The Canadian dynamic.* Toronto: Nelson Canada.

Dougherty, T.W., Turban, D.B., & Callender, J.C. (1994). Confirming first impressions in the employment interview: A field study of interviewer behavior. *Journal of Applied Psychology, 79*, 659–665.

Dreher, G.F., & Sackett, P.R. (1983). *Perspectives on selection and staffing.* Homewood, IL: Irwin.

Dubnicki, C., & Limburg, W.J. (1991). How do healthcare teams measure up? *The Healthcare Forum Journal, 34*(5), 10–11.

Duda, J.L. (1998). *Advances in Sport and Exercise Psychology Measurement.* Morgantown, WV: Fitness Information Technology.

Dupré, K., Inness, M., Connelly, C., Barling, J., and Hoption, C. (2006). Adolescent antagonism: Predicting workplace aggression in part-time teenage employees. *Journal of Applied Psychology, 91*, 987–997.

Duxbury, L., & Higgins, C. (2003). *Work-life conflict in Canada in the new millennium: A status report (final report).* Public Health Agency of Canada. Retrieved from http://www.phac-aspc.gc.ca/publicat/work-travail/index.html, February 16, 2007.

Dvir, T., Eden, D., Avolio, B.J., & Shamir, B. (2002). Impact of transformational leadership on follower development and performance: A field experiment. *Academy of Management Journal, 45*, 735–744.

Dwyer, D., & Ganster, D. (1991). The effects of job demands and control on employee attendance and satisfaction. *Journal of Organizational Behavior, 12*(7), 595–608.

Dyer, D.J. (1984). Team research and team training: A state-of-the-art review. In F.A. Muckler (Ed.), *Human factors review: 1984* (pp. 285– 323). Santa Monica: Human Factors Society.

Eagly, A.H., Johannesen-Schmidt, M.C., & van Engen, M.L. (2003). Transformational, transactional, and laissez-faire leadership styles: A meta-analysis comparing women and men. *Psychological Bulletin, 129*, 569–591.

Eagly, A.H., & Johnson, B.T. (1990). Gender and leadership style: A meta-analysis. *Psychological Bulletin, 108*, 233–256.

Eagly, A.H., Karau, S.J., & Makhijani, M.G. (1995). Gender and the effectiveness of leaders: A meta-analysis. *Psychological Bulletin, 117*, 125–145.

Eden, D. (1992). Leadership expectations: Pygmalion effects and other self-fulfilling prophecies in organizations. *Leadership Quarterly, 3*(4), 271–305.

Eden, D. (2001). Vacations and other respites: Studying stress on and off the job. In C.L. Cooper & I.T. Robertson (Eds.), *International review of industrial and organizational psychology* (pp. 121–146). Chichester, England: Wiley.

Edwards, B., Bell, S., Arthur, W., & Decuir, A. (2008). Relationships between facets of job satisfaction and task and contextual performance. *Applied Psychology: An International Review, 57*(3), 441–465.

Edwards, J.R. (1991). Person-job fit: A conceptual integration, literature review and methodological critique. *International Review of Industrial and Organizational Psychology, 6*, 283–357.

Edwards, J.R., & Cable, D.M. (2009). The value of value congruence. *Journal of Applied Psychology, 94*(3), 654–667.

Einnarson, S. (1999). The nature and causes of bullying at work. *International Journal of Manpower, 20*, 16–27.

Eisenberger, R., Jones, J.R., Stinglhamber, F., Shanock, L., & Randall, A.T. (2005). Flow experiences at work: For high need achievers alone? *Journal of Organizational Behavior, 26*, 755–775.

Eisenberger, R., & Rhoades, L. (2001). Incremental effects of reward on creativity. *Journal of Personality and Social Psychology, 81*, 728–741.

Elicker, J.D., Singer Foust, M., O'Malley, S., & Levy, P.E. (2008). Employee lateness behavior: The role of lateness climate and individual lateness attitude. *Human Performance, 21*, 427–441.

Ellington, J.E., Sackett, P.R., & Hough, L.M. (1999). Social desirability corrections in personality measurement: Issues of applicant comparison and construct validity. *Journal of Applied Psychology, 84*, 155–166.

Elovainio, M., Kivimäki, M., & Helkama, K. (2001). Organizational justice evaluations, job control, and occupational strain. *Journal of Applied Psychology, 86*(3), 418–424.

Elovainio, M., Kivimaki, M., Puttonen, S., Lindholm, H., Pohjonen, T., & Sinervo, T. (2006). Organizational injustice and impaired cardiac regulation among female employees. *Occupational and Environmental Medicine, 63*, 141–144.

Elovainio, M., Leino-Arjas, P., Vahtera, J. & Kivimäki, M. (2006). Justice at work and cardiovascular mortality: A prospective cohort study. *Journal of Psychosomatic Research, 61*, 271–274.

Employee Polygraph Protection Act. (1988). [29 USC §2001 et seq.; 29 CFR 801].

Erez, A., & Judge, T.A. (2001). Relationship of core self-evaluations to goal-setting, motivation, and performance. *Journal of Applied Psychology, 86*, 1270–1279.

Erez, M. (1977). Feedback: A necessary condition for the goal setting-performance relationship. *Journal of Applied Psychology, 62*, 624–627.

Evans C.R., & Dion, K.L. (1991). Group cohesion and performance: A meta analysis. *Small Group Research, 22*(7), 175–186.

Evers, W.J.G., Brouwers, A., & Tomic, W. (2006). A quasi-experimental study on management coaching effectiveness. *Consulting Psychology Journal: Practice and Research, 58*(3), 174–182.

Feather, N.T. (1990). *The psychological impact of unemployment.* New York: Springer-Verlag.

Ferrie, J.E., Head, J.A., Shipley, M.J., Vahtera, J., Marmot, M.G., & Kivimäki, M. (2006). Injustice at work and incidence of psychiatric morbidity: The Whitehall II study. *Occupational and Environmental Medicine, 63*, 443–450.

Ferrie, J.E., Head, J.A., Shipley, M.J., Vahtera, J., Marmot, M.G., & Kivimäki, M. (2007). Injustice at work and health: Cause, correlation or cause for action? *Occupational and Environmental Medicine, 64*, 428.

Festinger, L. (1950). Informal social communication. *Psychological Review, 57*, 271–282.

Fiedler, F.E. (1967). *A theory of leadership effectiveness.* New York: McGraw-Hill.

Fiedler, K., Schmid, J., & Stahl, T. (2002). What is the current truth about polygraph lie detection? *Basic and Applied Social Psychology, 24*(4), 313–324.

Fine, S.A. (1988). Functional job analysis. In S. Gael (Ed.), *The job analysis handbook for business, industry and government* (Vol. II, pp. 1019–1035). New York: John Wiley & Sons.

Fine, S.A. (1989). *Functional job analysis scales: A desk aid.* Milwaukee, WI: Sidney A. Fine Associates.

Fine, S.A., & Cronshaw, S.F. (1999). *Functional job analysis: A foundation for human reources management.* Mahwah, NJ: Lawrence Erlbaum and Associates.

Finkle, R.B. (1976). Managerial assessment centers. In M.D. Dunnette (Ed.), *Handbook of industrial and organizational psychology.* Chicago: Rand McNally

Fiorito, J., Bozeman, D.P., Young, A., & Meurs, J.A. (2007). Organizational commitment, human resource practices, and organizational characteristics. *Journal of Managerial Issues, 19*(2), 186–207.

Fischer, R., & Smith, P.B. (2006). Who cares about justice? The moderating effect of values on the link between organisational justice and work behaviour. *Applied Psychology: International Review, 55*(4), 541–562

Fishbein, M., & Ajzen, I. (1975). *Belief, attitude, intention, and behavior: An introduction to theory and research.* Reading, MA: Addison-Wesley.

Fisher, R., Ury, W., & Patton, B. (1991). *Getting to YES!* (2nd ed.). New York: Penguin.

Fitzpatrick, R. (2001). The strange case of the transfer of training estimate. *Industrial-Organizational Psychologist, 39,* 18–19.

Flanagan, J.C. (1954). The critical incident technique. *Psychological Bulletin, 51,* 327–358.

Fleishman, E.A. (1992). *The Fleishman job analysis system.* Palo Alto, CA: Consulting Psychologists Press.

Fleishman, E.A., & Mumford, M.D. (1988). Ability requirement scales. In S. Gael (Ed.), *The job analysis handbook for business, industry and government* (Vol. I, pp. 917–935). New York: John Wiley & Sons.

Fleishman, E.A., & Quaintance, M.K. (1984). *Taxonomies of human performance: The description of human tasks.* Orlando, FL: Academic Press.

Fleishman, E.A., & Reilly, M.E. (1992). *Handbook of human abilities.* Palo Alto, CA: Consulting Psychologists Press.

Folger, R., & Konovsky, M.A. (1989). Effects of procedural and distributive justice on reactions to pay raise decisions. *Academy of Management Journal, 32,* 115–130.

Foot, D. (2001). *Boom, bust & echo: Profiting from the demographic shift in the 21st century.* Toronto: Stoddart.

Forest, J. (2006, April). I-O psychology in the French-speaking province of Québec: An energetic North American community. *The Industrial Organizational Psychologist.* Downloaded October 21, 2009 from http://www.siop.org/tip/April07/18thompson.aspx.

Forth, J., & Millward, N. (2002). Union effects on pay levels in Britain. *Labour Economics, 9,* 547–561.

Fortman, K., Leslie, C., & Cunningham, M. (2002). Cross-cultural comparisons of the Reid Integrity Scales in Latin America and South Africa. *International Journal of Selection and Assessment, 10,* 98–108.

Fox, A. (1973). Industrial relations: A social critique of pluralist ideology. In J. Child (Ed.), *Man and organization.* London: Allen and Unwin.

Fox, S., & Spector, P.E. (1999). A model of work frustration-aggression. *Journal of Organizational Behavior, 20,* 915–931.

Fox, S., Spector, P.E., & Miles, D. (2001). Counterproductive work behaviour (CWB) in response to job stressors and organizational justice: Some mediator and moderator tests for autonomy and emotions. *Journal of Vocational Behaviour, 59,* 291–309.

Francis, L., Cameron, J.E., & Kelloway, E.K. (2006). Crossing the line: Violence on the picket line. In E.K. Kelloway, J. Barling, & J.J. Hurrell, Jr. (Eds.), *Handbook of workplace violence* (pp. 231–260). Thousand Oaks, CA: Sage.

Francis, L., & Kelloway, E.K. (2005). Industrial relations. In J. Barling, E.K. Kelloway, & M.R. Frone (Eds.), *Handbook of work stress* (pp. 325–352). Thousand Oaks, CA: Sage.

Francis, L., & Kelloway, E.K. (2008). *The experience and management of work stress: A focus on employees and organizations in Nova Scotia.* Halifax: Saint Mary's University, CN Centre for Occupational Health & Safety.

Frankl, V.E. (1963). *Man's search for meaning.* New York: Washington Square Press.

Fredrickson, B.L. (1998). What good are positive emotions? *Review of General Psychology, 2,* 300–319.

Fredrickson, B.L. (2001). The role of positive emotions in positive psychology: The broaden and build theory. *American Psychologist, 56,* 218–226.

Fredrickson, B.L. (2010). *Positivity: Top notch research reveals the 3 to 1 ratio that will change your life.* New York: Crown Publishing.

Fredrickson, B.L., & Losada, M.F. (2005). Positive affect and the complex dynamics of human flourishing. *American Psychologist, 60,* 678–686.

Freeman, R.B., & Medoff, J.L. (1984). *What do unions do?* New York, NY: Basic Books.

Frese, M. (1999). Social support as a moderator between work stressors and psychological dysfunctioning: A longitudinal study with objective measures. *Journal of Occupational Health Psychology, 4,* 179–192.

Fried, Y., & Ferris, G. R. (1987). The validity of the job characteristics model: A review and meta-analysis. *Personnel Psychology, 40*(2), 287–322.

Fried, Y., & Tiegs, R.B. (1993). The main effect model versus the buffering model of shop steward social support: A study of rank-and-file auto workers in the U.S.A. *Journal of Organizational Behavior, 14,* 481–493.

Frisch, M.H. (2001). The emerging role of the internal coach. *Consulting Psychology Journal: Practice & Research, 53*(4), 240–250.

Frone, M.R. (2000). Interpersonal conflict at work and psychological outcomes: Testing a model among young workers. *Journal of Occupational Health Psychology, 5,* 246–255.

Frone, M.R. (2003). Work-family balance. In J.C. Quick & L.E. Tetrick (Eds.), *Handbook of occupational health psychology* (pp. 143–162). Washington, DC: American Psychological Association.

Frone, M.R. (2008). Employee alcohol and illicit drug use: Scope, causes, and organizational consequences. In C.L. Cooper & J. Barling (Eds.), *Handbook of organizational behavior* (pp. 519–540). Thousand Oaks, CA: Sage.

Frone, M.R., Russell, M., & Cooper, M.L. (1997). Relation of work-family conflict to health outcomes: A four-year longitudinal study of employed parents. *Journal of Occupational and Organizational Psychology, 70,* 325–335.

Fryxell, G.E., & Gordon, M.E. (1989). Workplace justice and job satisfaction as predictors of satisfaction with union and management. *Academy of Management Journal, 32,* 851–866.

Fukushige, A., & Spicer, D.P. (2007). Leadership preferences in Japan: An exploratory study. *Leadership & Organization Development Journal, 28,* 508–530.

Fullagar, C., & Barling, J. (1991). Predictors and outcomes of different patterns of organizational and union loyalty. *Journal of Occupational Psychology, 64,* 129–143.

Fullagar, C., Clark, P., Gallagher, D., & Gordon, M.E. (1994). A model of the antecedents of early union commitment: The role of socialization experiences and steward characteristics. *Journal of Organizational Behavior, 15*(6), 517–533.

Fullagar, C., & Kelloway, E.K. (2009). "Flow" at work: An experience sampling approach. *Journal of Occupational and Organizational Psychology, 82,* 595–615.

Fullagar, C., McCoy, D., & Shull, C. (1992). The socialization of union loyalty. *Journal of Organizational Behavior, 13*(1), 13–26.

Fullagar, C.J., Gallagher, D.G., Clark, P.F., & Carroll, A.E. (2004). Union commitment and participation: A 10-year longitudinal study. *Journal of Applied Psychology, 89*(4), 730–737.

Fullagar, C.J.A., Gallagher, D.G., Gordon, M.E.E., & Clark, P.F. (1995). Impact of early socialization on union commitment and participation: A longitudinal study. *Journal of Applied Psychology, 80*(1), 147–157.

Furnham, A., & Bramwell, M. (2006). Personality factors predict absenteeism in the workplace. *Individual Differences Research, 4*(2), 68–77.

Furnham A., & Stringfield, P. (1998). Congruence in job-performance ratings: A study of 360-degree feedback examining self, manager, peers, and consultant ratings. *Human Relations, 51,* 517–530.

Gael, S. (1983). *Job analysis: A guide to assessing work activities.* San Francisco, CA: Jossey-Bass Limited.

Gael, S. (1988). Interviews, questionnaires, and checklists. In S. Gael (Ed.), *The job analysis handbook for business, industry and government* (Vol. I, pp. 391–418). New York: John Wiley & Sons.

Gagné, M., & Deci, E.L. (2005). Self-determination theory and work motivation. *Journal of Organizational Behaviour, 26*(4), 331–362.

Gagné, M., & Forest, J. (2008). The study of compensation systems through the lens of self-determination theory: Reconciling 35 years of debate. *Canadian Psychology, 49*, 225–232.

Galinsky, E., Kim, S.S., Bond, J.T., & Salmond, K. (2003). *Youth & employment: Today's students tomorrow's workforce: Summary and discussion guide.* New York: Families and Work Institute.

Garcia, M.F., Posthuma, R.A., & Colella, A. (2008). Fit perceptions in the employment interview: The role of similarity, liking, and expectations. *Journal of Occupational and Organizational Psychology, 81*, 173–189.

Gatewood, R.D., Feild, H.S., & Barrick, M.R. (2008). *Human resource selection* (6th ed.). Mason, OH: Thomson/South-Western.

Gati, I. (1989). Person–environment fit research: Problems and prospects. *Journal of Vocational Behavior, 35*, 181–193

Gaudine, A.P., & Saks, A.M. (2004). A longitudinal quasi-experiment on the effects of post-training transfer interventions. *Human Resource Development Quarterly, 15*, 567–576.

Gaugler, B.B., Rosenthal, D.B., Thornton, G.C., & Bentson, C. (1987). Meta-analysis of assessment center validity. *Journal of Applied Psychology, 72*, 493–511.

Gellatly, I.R. (1995). Individual and group determinants of employee absenteeism: Test of a causal model. *Journal of Organizational Behavior, 16*, 469–485.

Gellatly, I.R., & Luchak, A.A. (1998). Personal and organizational determinants of perceived absence norms. *Human Relations, 51*(8), 1085–1102.

Geoghegan, T. (1991). *Which side are you on?* New York: Farrar, Straus & Giroux.

George, J.M., & Brief, A.P. (1992). Feeling good-doing good: A conceptual analysis of positive mood at work-organizational spontaneity relationship. *Psychological Bulletin, 112*, 310–329.

Gerstner, C.R., & Day, D.V. (1994). Cross-cultural comparison of leadership prototypes. *Leadership Quarterly, 5*, 121–134.

Gerstner, C.R., & Day, D.V. (1997). Meta-analytic review of leader-member exchange theory: Correlates and construct issues. *Journal of Applied Psychology, 82*, 827–844.

Getman, J.G., Goldberg, S.B., & Herman, J.B. (1976). *Union representation elections: Law and reality.* New York: Russell Sage.

Ghiselli, E.E. (1966). *The validity of occupational aptitude tests.* New York: Wiley.

Ghorpade, J. (2000). Managing five paradoxes of 360-degree feedback. *Academy of Management Executive, 14*, 140–150.

Ghorpade, J.V. (1988). *Job analysis: A handbook for the human resource director.* Englewood Cliffs, NJ: Prentice Hall.

Gialacone, R.A., & Greenberg, J. (1997). *Antisocial behavior in organizations.* Thousand Oaks, CA: Sage.

Gibson, C.B., Porath, C.L., Benson, G.S., & Lawler, E.E. (2007). What results when firms implement practices: The differential relationship between specific practices, firm financial performance, customer service, and quality. *Journal of Applied Psychology, 92*(6), 1467–1480.

Giga, S., Noblet, A., Faragher, B., & Cooper, C. (2003). Organisational stress management interventions: A review of UK-based research. *Australian Psychologist, 38*, 158–164.

Gist, M.E., & Stevens, C.K. (1998). Effects of practice conditions and supplemental training method on cognitive learning and interpersonal skill generalization. *Organizational Behavior and Human Decision Processes, 25*(2), 142–169.

Gittell, J.H. (2003). The Southwest Airlines way: Using the power of relationships to achieve high performance. New York: McGraw-Hill.

Godard, J. (2001). High performance and the transformation of work? The implications of alternative work practices for the experience and outcomes of work. *Industrial and Labor Relations Review, 54*(4), 776–805.

Goffin, R.D., & Boyd, A.C. (2009). Faking and personality assessment in personnel selection: Advancing models of faking. *Canadian Psychology, 50*, 151–160.

Goffin, R.D., Gellatly, I.R., Paunonen, S.V., Jackson, D.N., & Meyer, J.P. (1996). Criterion validation of two approaches to performance appraisal: The behavioral observation scale and the relative percentile method. *Journal of Business and Psychology, 11*, 23–33.

Goffin, R.D., Jelly, B., Powell, D.M., & Johnston, N.G. (2009). Taking advantage of social comparisons in performance appraisal: The relative percentile method. *Human Resource Management, 48,* 251–268.

Goldsmith, M., Lyons, L., & Feras, A. (Eds.). (2000). *Coaching for leadership.* San Francisco, CA: Jossey-Bass, Pfeiffer.

Goldstein, I.L. (1993). *Training in organizations: Needs assessment, development and evaluation* (3rd ed.). Pacific Grove, CA: Brooks/Cole Publishing.

Gordon, J. (2006). *Be happy at work: 100 women who love their jobs and why.* New York: Ballantine Books.

Gordon, M.E., & Fryxell, G. (1993). The role of interpersonal justice in organizational grievance systems. In R. Cropanzano (Ed.), *Justice in the workplace: Approaching fairness in human resource management* (pp. 231–256). Hillsdale, NJ: Lawrence Erlbaum Associates.

Gordon, M.E., & Johnson, W.A. (1982). Seniority: A review of its legal and scientific standing, *Personnel Psychology, 35,* 255–280.

Gordon, M.E., Philpot, J.W., Burt, R.E., Thompson, C.A., & Spiller, W.E. (1980). Commitment to the union: Development of a measure and an examination of its correlates. *Journal of Applied Psychology, 64*(4), 479–499.

Gottfredson, L.S. (1986). Societal consequences of the *g* factor in employment. *Journal of Vocational Behavior, 29,* 379–411.

Gottfredson, L.S. (1994). The science and politics of race-norming. *American Psychologist, 49,* 955–963.

Gottfredson, L.S. (1997) Why *g* matters: The complexity of everyday life. *Intelligence, 24,* 79–132.

Gottman, J.M. (1994). *What predicts divorce? The relationship between marital process and marital outcomes.* Hillsdale, NJ: Erlbaum

Grant, A.M. (2009). Putting self-interest out of business? Contributions and unanswered questions from use-inspired research on prosocial motivation. *Industrial and Organizational Psychology: Perspectives on Science and Practice, 2,* 94–98.

Grau, R., Salanova, M., & Peiró, J.M. (2001). Moderator effects of self-efficacy on occupational stress. *Psychology in Spain, 5*(1), 63–74.

Gray, G.R., Myers, D.W., & Myers, P.S. (1998). Collective bargaining agreements: Safety and health provisions. *Monthly Labor Review, 121*(5), 13–35.

Greenbaum, P.J. 1996. Canada's Hiring Trends: Where Will Canadian Jobs Come From in the Next Millennium? *HR Today* (July). Ottawa: Canadian Institute of Professional Management.

Greenberg, J. (1982). Approaching equity and avoiding inequity in groups and organizations. In J. Greenberg & R.L. Cohen (Eds.), Equity and justice in social behavior (pp. 389–435). San Diego, CA: Academic Press.

Greenberg, J. (1990). Organizational justice: Yesterday, today, and tomorrow. *Journal of Management, 16,* 399–432.

Greenberg, J. (1994). Using socially fair treatment to promote acceptance of a work site smoking ban. *Journal of Applied Psychology, 79*(2), 288–297.

Greenberg, J. (2006). Losing sleep over organizational injustice: Attenuating insomniac reactions to underpayment inequity with supervisory training in interactional justice. *Journal of Applied Psychology, 91*(1), 58–69.

Greenglass, E.R., Fiksenbaum, L., Goldstein, L., & Desiato, C. (2002). Stressful effects of a university faculty strike on students: Implications for coping. *Interchange, 33,* 261–279.

Greenhaus, J.H., & Beutell, N.J. (1985). Sources of conflict between work and family roles. *Academy of Management Review, 10,* 76–88.

Griffeth, R.W., Hom, P.W., & Gaertner, S. (2000). A meta-analysis of antecedents and correlates of employee turnover: Update, moderator tests, and research implications for the next millennium. *Journal of Management, 26*(3), 463–488.

Griffin, M.A., Neal, A., & Neal, M. (2000). The contribution of task performance and contextual performance to effectiveness: Investigating the role of situational constraints. *Applied Psychology: An International Review, 49,* 517–533.

Griggs v. Duke Power. (1971). 401 U.S. 424

Guest, D.E., & Conway, N. (2004). Exploring the paradox of unionized workers' dissatisfaction. *Industrial Relations Journal, 35,* 102–121.

Guion, R.M. (1965). *Personnel testing*. New York: McGraw-Hill.

Guion, R.M. (1967). Personnel selection. *Annual Review of Psychology, 18,* 105–216.

Guion, R.M. (1987). Changing views for personnel selection research. *Personnel Psychology, 40,* 199–213.

Guion, R.M. (1998). *Assessment, measurement and prediction for personnel decisions*. London: Lawrence Erlbaum Associates.

Guion, R.M., & Gottier, R.F. (1965). Validity of personality measures in personnel selection. *Personnel Psychology, 18,* 135–164.

Gully, S.M., Devine, D.J., & Whitney, D.J (1995). A meta-analysis of cohesiveness and performance: Effects of level of analysis and task interdependence. *Small Group Research, 26*(4), 497–520.

Guzzo, R.A., & Dickson, M.W. (1996). Teams in organizations: Recent research on performance and effectiveness. *Annual Review of Psychology, 47,* 307–338.

Hackett, R.D., & Bycio, P. (1996). An evaluation of employee absenteeism as a coping mechanism among hospital nurses. *Journal of Occupational and Organizational Psychology, 69,* 327–338.

Hackett, R.D., Bycio, P., & Hausdorf, P.A. (1994). Further assessments of Meyer and Allen's three-component model of organizational commitment. *Journal of Applied Psychology, 79,* 15–23.

Hackman, J.R. (1986). The psychology of self-management in organizations. In M.S. Pollock & R.O. Perlogg (Eds.), *Psychology and work: Productivity change and employment* (pp. 85–136). Washington, DC: American Psychological Association.

Hackman, J.R. (1987). The design of work teams. In J. Lorsch (Ed.), *Handbook of organizational behaviour* (pp. 315–342). New York: Prentice Hall.

Hackman, J.R. (1992). Group influences on individuals in organizations. In M.D. Dunnette & L.M. Hough (Eds.), *Handbook of industrial and organizational psychology* (Vol. 3). Palo Alto: Consulting Psychologists Press.

Hackman, J.R. (1998). Why teams don't work: Applications of theory and research on groups to social issues, *Leader to Leader, 7,* 24–31.

Hackman, J. R., & Oldham, G.R. (1976). Motivation through the design of work: Test of a theory. *Journal of Organizational Behavior and Human Performance, 15,* 250–279.

Haggbloom S.J. (2002). The 100 most eminent psychologists of the 20th century. *Review of General Psychology, 6*(2), 139–152.

Hain, C., & Francis, L. (2006, March). Coworker relationships: Using a new measure to predict health related outcomes. Paper presented at Work, Stress, and Health Conference: Making a Difference in the Workplace. Miami, FL.

Halbesleben, J.R.B., & Buckley, M.R. (2004). Burnout in organizational life. *Journal of Management, 30*(6), 859–879.

Hall, C.S., & Lindzey, G. (1970). *Theories of personality*. New York: Wiley.

Hall, D., Otazo, K., & Hollenbeck, G. (1999). Behind closed doors: What really happens in executive coaching. *Organizational Dynamics 27*(3), 39–53.

Hambley, L., O'Neill, A.T., & Kline, T.J.B. (2007). Virtual team leadership: The effects of leadership style and communication medium on team interaction styles and outcomes. *Organizational Behavior and Human Decision Processes, 103,* 1–20.

Hambrick, D.C. (1995). Fragmentation and other problems CEOs have with their top management teams. *California Management Review, 37,* 110–127.

Hamilton, D. (2000). Resumés: Fact or fiction. *CA Magazine, 133,* 16.

Hammer, T.H. & Avgar, A. (2005). The impact of unions on job satisfaction, organizational commitment and turnover. *Journal of Labor Research, 26,* 241–266.

Hanisch, K.A., Hulin, C.L., & Roznowski, M. (1998). The importance of individuals' repertoires of behaviors: The scientific appropriateness of studying multiple behaviors and general attitudes. *Journal of Organizational Behavior, 19,* 463–480.

Hanish, K.A. (1995). Behavioral families and multiple causes: Matching the complexity of responses to the complexity of antecedents. *Current Directions in Psychological Science, 4*, 156–162.

Hanley, G., & Nguyen, L. (2005). Right on the money: What do Australian unions think of performance-related pay? *Employee Relations, 27*, 141–160.

Harley, B. (2001). Team membership and the experience of work in Britain: An analysis of the WERS98 data. *Work, Employment and Society, 15*(4), 721–742.

Harris, M.M. (1989). Reconstructing the employment interview: A review of recent literature and suggestions for future research. *Personnel Psychology, 42*, 691–726.

Harris, M.M., & Schaubroeck, J. (1988). A meta-analysis of self–supervisor, self–peer, and peer–supervisor ratings. *Personnel Psychology, 41*, 43–62.

Harris, M.M., & Trusty, M.L. (1997). Drug and alcohol programs in the workplace: A review of recent literature. In C.L. Cooper & I.T. Robertson (Eds.), *International Review of industrial and organizational psychology* (Vol. 12, pp. 289–315). London: John Wiley & Sons.

Harrison, D.A., Price, K.H., & Bell, M.P. (1998). Beyond relational demography: Time and the effects of surface- and deep-level diversity on work group cohesion. *Academy of Management Journal, 41*(1), 96–107.

Harter, J.K., Schmidt, F.L., & Hayes, T.L. (2002). Business-unit-level relationship between employee satisfaction, employee engagement, and business outcomes: A meta-analysis. *Journal of Applied Psychology, 87*(2), 268–279.

Hartman, S.J., & Harris, O.J. (1992). The role of parental influence on leadership. *Journal of Social Psychology, 132*, 153–167.

Harvey, R.J. (1991). Job analysis. In M.D. Dunnette & L.M. Hough (Eds.), *Handbook of industrial and organizational psychology* (Vol. I, pp. 71–163). Palo Alto, CA: Consulting Psychologists Press, Inc.

Harvey, R.J. (1993). *Research monograph: The development of the CMQ.* Monograph describing the development and field-testing of the Common Metric Questionnaire (CMQ). [Online]. Available: http://www.pstc.com/documents/monograph.pdf

Hausknecht, J.P., Hiller, N.J., & Vance, R.J. (2008). Work-unit absenteeism: Effects of satisfaction, commitment, labor market conditions, and time. *Academy of Management Journal, 51*(6), 1223–1245.

Heaphy, E.D., & Dutton, J. (2008). Positive social interactions and the human body at work: Linking organizations and physiology. *The Academy of Management Review, 33*(1), 137.

Hebdon, R., & Hyatt, D. (1998). The effects of industrial relations factors on health and safety conflict. *Industrial and Labor Relations Review, 51*, 579–593.

Hedge, J.W., & Teachout, M.S. (2000). Exploring the concept of acceptability as a criterion for evaluating performance measures. *Group & Organizational Management, 25*, 22–44.

Hepburn, C.G., Loughlin, C.A., & Barling, J. (1997). Coping with chronic work stress. In B.H. Gottleib (Ed.), *Coping with chronic work stress.* New York: Plenum Press.

Hermelin, E., Lievens, F., & Robertson, I.T. (2007). The validity of assessment centers for the prediction of supervisory performance ratings: A meta-analysis. *International Journal of Selection and Assessment, 15*, 405–411.

Herold, D., Fedor, D., Caldwell, S., & Liu, Y. (2008). The effects of transformational and change leadership on employees' commitment to a change: A multilevel study. *Journal of Applied Psychology, 93*(2), 346–357.

Herscovitch, L., & Meyer, J.P. (2002). Commitment to organizational change: Extension of a three-component model. *Journal of Applied Psychology, 87*(3), 474–487.

Hershcovis, M.S., Turner, N., Barling, J., Arnold, K.A., Dupre, K.E., Inness, M., LeBlanc, M.M., & Sivanathan, N. (2007). Predicting workplace aggression: A meta-analysis. *Journal of Applied Psychology, 92*(1), 228–238.

Hertel, G., Konradt, U., & Orlikowski, B. (2004). Managing distance by interdependence: goal setting, task interdependence, and team-based rewards in virtual teams. *European Journal of Work and Organizational Psychology, 13*, 1–28.

Hester, K., & Fuller, J.B. (1999). An extension of the family socialization model of union attitudes. *Journal of Social Psychology, 139*, 396–398.

Highhouse, S. (2007). Applications of organizational psychology: Learning through failure or failure to learn. In L.L. Koppes (Ed), *Historical perspectives in industrial organizational psychology* (pp. 331–352). Mahwah, NJ: Lawrence Erlbaum & Associates.

Hinkle, R.K., & Choi, N. (2009). Measuring person-environment fit: A further validation of the perceived fit scale. *International Journal of Selection and Assessment, 17*(3), 324–328.

Hobfoll, S.E. (1989). Conservation of resources: A new attempt at conceptualizing stress. *American Psychologist, 44*, 513–524.

Hobfoll, S.E., & Freedy, J. (1993). Conservation of resources: A general stress theory applied to burnout. In W.B. Schafeli, C. Maslach, & T. Marek (Eds.). *Professional burnout: Recent developments in theory and research* (pp. 115–129). London: Taylor and Francis.

Hodson, R. (1997). Group relations at work: Solidarity, conflict, and relations with management. *Work and Occupations, 24*, 426–452.

Hoel, H., Rayner, C., & Cooper, C.L. (1999). Workplace bullying. In C.L. Cooper & I.T. Robertson (Eds.). *International review of industrial and organizational psychology* (Vol. 14). Chichester, UK: Wiley & Sons.

Hofstede, G. (2001). *Culture's consequences: Comparing values, behaviours, institutions, and organizations across nations.* Thousand Oaks CA: Sage.

Hogan, J. (1991). Structure of physical performance in occupational tasks. *Journal of Applied Psychology, 76*, 495–507.

Hogan, J., Barrett, P., & Hogan, R. (2007). Personality measurement, faking, and employment selection. *Journal of Applied Psychology, 92*, 1270–1285.

Hogan, J., & Hogan, R. (1989). How to measure employee reliability. *Journal of Applied Psychology, 74*, 273–279.

Hollenbeck, J.R., Williams, C.R., & Klein, H.J. (1989). An empirical examination of the antecedents of commitment to difficult goals. *Journal of Applied Psychology, 74*(1), 18–23.

Hom, P.W., Griffeth, R.W., Palich, L.E., & Bracker, J.S. (1999). Revisiting met expectations as a reason why realistic job previews work. *Personnel Psychology, 52*, 97–112.

Hooijberg, R., & Choi, J. (2000). Which leadership roles matter to whom? An examination of rater effects on perceptions of effectiveness. *Leadership Quarterly, 11*(3), 341–364.

Hough, L.M. (1998). Effects of intentional distortion in personality measurement and evaluation of suggested palliatives. *Human Performance, 11*, 209–244.

Hough, L.M., Eaton, N.K., Dunnette, M.D., Kamp, J.D., & McCloy, R.A. (1990). Criterion-related validities of personality constructs and the effect of response distortion on those validities. [Monograph]. *Journal of Applied Psychology, 75*, 581–595.

Hough, L.M., & Furnham, A. (2003). Use of personality variables in work settings. In W.C. Borman, D.R. Ilgen, & R. Klimoski (Eds.). *Handbook of psychology: Industrial and organizational psychology* (Vol. 12, pp. 131–169). New York: John Wiley & Sons.

House, R.J. (1971). A path–goal theory of leader effectiveness. *Administrative Science Quarterly, 16*, 321–339.

House, R.J. (1977). A 1976 theory of charismatic leadership. In J.G. Hunt & L.L. Larson (Eds.), *Leadership: The cutting edge.* Carbondale: Southern Illinois University Press.

House, R.J., & Aditja, R.N. (1997). The social scientific study of leadership. Quo vadis? *Journal of Management, 23*(3), 407–473.

House, R.J., & Mitchell, T.R. (1974). Path-goal theory of leadership. *Contemporary Business, 3*, 81–98.

House, R.J., & Podsakoff, P.M. (1994). Leadership effectiveness: Past perspectives and future directions for research. In J. Greenberg (Ed.), *Organizational behavior: The state of the science* (pp. 45–82). Hillsdale, NJ: Erlbaum.

Howard, A. (1997). A reassessment of assessment centers: Challenges for the 21st century. *Journal of Social Behavior and Personality, 12*, 13–52.

HR-Guide.com. (2000). *Classification systems used as basis for or resulting from job analyses.* [Online]. Available: http://www.hr-guide.com/data/G012.htm.

Huffcutt, A.I., & Arthur, W. Jr. (1994). Hunter and Hunter (1984) revisited: Interview validity for entry-level jobs. *Journal of Applied Psychology, 79*, 184–190.

Hughes, P.D., & Grant, M. (2007). *Learning and development outlook, 2007.* Ottawa: The Conference Board of Canada.

Hunter, J.E., & Hunter, R.F. (1984). Validity and utility of alternative predictors of job performance. *Psychological Bulletin, 96*, 72–98.

Hurrell, J.J. (2006). Critical incident stress debriefing and workplace violence. In E.K. Kelloway, J. Barling, & J.J. Hurrell (Eds.), *Handbook of workplace violence* (pp. 535–548). Thousand Oaks, CA: Sage.

Huseman, R.C., Hatfield, J.D., & Miles, E.W. (1987). A new perspective on equity theory: The equity sensitive construct. *Academy of Management Review, 12*, 222–234.

Hutton, D. (2008, June 18). Job reference chill grows icier: Employers' growing reluctance to talk about former employees frustrates both those doing the hiring and those trying to get hired. *The Globe and Mail*, C1.

Iaffaldano, M.T., & Muchinsky, P.M. (1985). Job satisfaction and job performance: A meta-analysis. *Psychological Bulletin, 97*, 251–273.

Ilgen, D.R., Hollenbeck, J.R., Johnson, M., & Jundt, D. (2005). Teams in organizations: From input-process-output models to IMOI models. *Annual Review of Psychology, 56*, 517–543.

Ilies, R., Spitzmuller, M., Fulmer, I. S., & Johnson, M. D. (2009). Personality and citizenship behavior: The mediating role of job satisfaction. *Journal of Applied Psychology, 94*(4), 945–959.

International Labour Office. (n.d.). Yearbook of labor statistics. In Statistics Canada (2003). *Strikes and lockouts, workers involved and workdays not worked.* Retrieved July 25, 2003, from http://www.statscan.ca/english/Pgdb/labour30a.htm.

Ironson, G.H., Smith, P.C., Brannick, M.T., Gibson, W.M., & Paul, K.B. (1989). Construction of a job in general scale: A comparison of global, composite, and specific measures. *Journal of Applied Psychology, 74*(2), 193–200.

Irving, P.G., & Meyer, J.P. (1994). Reexamination of the met-expectations hypothesis: A longitudinal analysis. *Journal of Applied Psychology, 79*, 937–949.

Iverson, R.D., & Currivan, D.B. (2003). Union participation, job satisfaction, and employee turnover: An event history analysis of the exit-voice hypothesis. *Industrial Relations, 42*, 101–105.

Iverson, R.D. & Deery, S.J. (2001). Understanding the "personological" basis of employee withdrawal: The influence of affective disposition on employee tardiness, early departure, and absenteeism. *Journal of Applied Psychology, 86*, 856–866.

Jackson, S.A. (1996). Toward a conceptual understanding of the flow experience in elite athletes. *Research Quarterly for Exercise and Sport, 67*(1), 76–90.

Jackson, S.A., & Eklund, R.C. (2002). Assessing flow in physical activity: The Flow State Scale-2 and Dispositional Flow Scale-2. *Journal of Sport and Exercise Psychology, 24*, 133–150.

Jackson, S.A., & Marsh, H.W. (1996). Development and validation of a scale to measure optimal experience: The Flow State Scale. *Journal of Sport & Exercise Psychology, 18*, 17–35.

Jackson, S.E., Brett, J.F., Sessa, V.I., Cooper, D.M., Julin, J.A., & Peyronnin, K. (1991). Some differences make a difference: Individual dissimilarity and group heterogeneity as correlates of recruitment, promotion, and turnover. *Journal of Applied Psychology, 76*, 675–89.

Jackson, S.E., May, K.E., & Whitney, K. (1995). Understanding the dynamics of diversity in decision-making teams. In R.A. Guzzo & E. Salas (Eds.), *Team effectiveness and decision making in organizations* (pp. 204–261). San Francisco: Jossey-Bass.

Jacobson, E. (1938). *Progressive relaxation: A physiological and clinical investigation and their significance in psychology and medical practice.* Chicago: University of Chicago Press.

Jahoda, M. (1982). *Employment and unemployment: A social psychological approach.* New York: Cambridge University Press.

Jamal, M. (2004). Burnout, stress and health of employees on non-standard work schedules: A study of Canadian workers. *Stress and Health, 20*, 113–119.

Janis, I.L. (1972). *Victims of groupthink: A psychological study of foreign policy decisions and fiascos.* Boston: Houghton Mifflin.

Janis, L.J. (1982). *Groupthink: Psychological studies of policy decisions and fiascos.* Boston: Houghton Mifflin.

Janz, T. (1982). Initial comparisons of patterned behavior description interviews versus unstructured interviews. *Journal of Applied Psychology, 67,* 577–580.

Janz, T. (1989). The patterned behavior description interview: The best prophet of the future is the past. In R.W. Eder & G.R. Ferris (Eds.), *The employment interview: theory, research, and practice.* Newbury Park, CA: Sage.

Jarvenpaa, S.L., Shaw, T.R., & Staples, D.S. (2004). Toward contextualized theories of trust: The role of trust in global virtual teams. *Information Systems Research, 15*(3), 250–267.

Jehn, K. (1994). Enhancing effectiveness: An investigation of advantages and disadvantages of value-based intragroup conflict. *International Journal of Conflict Management, 5,* 223–238.

Jehn, K. (1995). A multimethod examination of the benefits and detriments of intragroup conflict. *Administrative Science Quarterly, 40,* 256–282.

Jehn, K. (1997). Affective and cognitive conflict in work groups: Increasing performance through value-based intragroup conflict. In C.K.W. De Dreu & E. Van de Vliert (Eds.), *Using conflict in organizations* (pp. 87–100). London: Sage.

Jelf, G.S. (1999). A narrative review of post-1989 employment interview research. *Journal of Business and Psychology, 14,* 25–58.

Jex, S.M., & Bliese, P.D. (1999). Efficacy beliefs as a moderator of the impact of work-related stressors: A multilevel study. *Journal of Applied Psychology, 84,* 349–361.

Jobs, S. (2005, June 12). Convocation address. Stanford University Convocation.

Johansson, G. (2002). Work-life balance: The case of Sweden in the 1990s. *Social Science Information, 41,* 303–317.

Johns, G. (2001). The psychology of lateness, absenteeism, and turnover. In N. Anderson, D. Ones, & C. Viswesvarian. (Eds.), *Handbook of industrial, work, and organizational psychology* (Vol. 2, pp. 232–252). London: Sage.

Johns, G. (2002). Absenteeism and mental health. In J.C. Thomas & M. Hersen (Eds.), *Handbook of mental health in the workplace* (pp. 437–455). Thousand Oaks, CA: Sage.

Johns, G. (2009). Presenteeism in the workplace: A review and workplace agenda. *Journal of Organizational Behaviour.* Published online in Wiley InterScience (www.interscience.wiley.com). doi:10.1002/job.630.

Johns, G., & Nicholson, N. (1982). The meanings of absence: New strategies for theory and research. *Research in Organizational Behavior, 12,* 115–173.

Johnson, K.L., Lero, D.S., & Rooney, J.A. (2001). Work-life compendium 2001: 150 Canadian statistics on work, family and well-being. Guelph, ON: Centre for Families, Work, and Well-Being. *Journal of Developmental and Behavioural Pediatrics, 20,* 9–16.

Johnson, S., Bettenhausen, K., & Gibbons, E. (2009). Realities of working in virtual teams: Affective and attitudinal outcomes of using computer-mediated communication. *Small Group Research, 40*(6), 623–649.

Johnson, S.D., Suriya, C., Won Yoon, S., Berrett, J.V., & La Fleur, J. (2002). Team development and group processes of virtual learning teams. *Computers and Education, 39*(4), 379–393.

Jones, J. (Ed.). (1991). *Pre-employment honesty testing: Current research and future directions.* New York: Quorum Books.

Judge, T.A., & Bono, J.E. (2000). Five-factor model of personality and transformational leadership. *Journal of Applied Psychology, 85,* 751–765.

Judge, T.A., Bono, J.E., Ilies, R., & Gerhardt, M.W. (2002). Personality and leadership: A qualitative and quantitative review. *Journal of Applied Psychology, 87,* 765–780.

Judge, T.A., & Cable, D.M. (2004). The effect of physical height on workplace success and income: Preliminary test of a theoretical model. *Journal of Applied Psychology, 89,* 428–441.

Judge, T.A., Colbert, A.E., & Ilies, R. (2004). Intelligence and leadership: A quantitative review and test of theoretical propositions. *Journal of Applied Psychology, 89,* 542–552.

Judge, T.A., Heller, D., & Mount, M.K. (2002). Five-factor model of personality and job satisfaction: A meta-analysis. *Journal of Applied Psychology, 87*(3), 530–541.

Judge, T.A., & Piccolo, R.F. (2004). Transformational and transactional leadership: A metaanalytic test of their relative validity. *Journal of Applied Psychology, 89*, 755–768.

Judge, T.A., Piccolo, R.F., & Ilies, R. (2004). The forgotten ones? The validity of consideration and initiating structure in leadership research. *Journal of Applied Psychology, 89*, 36–51.

Judge, T.A., Thoresen, C.J., Bono, J.E., & Patton, G.K. (2001). The job satisfaction–job performance relationship: A qualitative and quantitative review. *Psychological Bulletin, 127*, 376–407.

Kabanoff, B. (1991). Equity, equality, power, and conflict. *Academy of Management Review, 16*(2), 416–441.

Kahn, R.L., & Byosiere, P.B. (1992). Stress in organizations. In M.D. Dunnette & L.M. Hough (Eds.), *Handbook of industrial and organizational psychology* (Vol. 3, pp. 571–650). Palo Alto: Consulting Psychologists Press.

Kahn, W. (1990). Psychological conditions of personal engagement and disengagement at work. *Academy of Management Journal, 33*, 692–724.

Kamdar, D., McAllister, D.J., & Turban, D.B. (2006). 'All in a day's work': How follower individual differences and justice perceptions predict OCB role definitions and behavior. *Journal of Applied Psychology, 91*, 841–855.

Kanfer, R. (2009a). Work motivation: Advancing theory and impact. *Industrial and Organizational Psychology: Perspectives on Science and Practice, 2*, 118–127.

Kanfer, R. (2009b). Work motivation: Identifying use-inspired research directions. *Industrial and Organizational Psychology: Perspectives on Science and Practice, 2*, 77–93.

Kanfer, R., & Heggestad, E.D. (1997). Motivational traits and skills: A person-centred approach to work motivation. *Research in Organizational Behaviour, 19*, 1–56.

Kanter, R.M. (1977). *Men and women of the corporation*. New York: Basic Books Inc.

Kantrowitz, T.M. (2005). Development and construct validation of a measure of soft skills performance (Doctoral dissertation, George Institute of Technology, 2005). Retrieved from http://smartech.gatech.edu/handle/1853/6861.

Kaplan, R.S., & Norton, D.P. (1996). *The balanced scorecard: Translating strategy into action*. Boston: The Harvard Business School Press.

Karasek, R.A. (1979). Job demands, job decision latitude, and mental strain: Implications for job redesign. *Administrative Science Quarterly, 24*(2), 285–308.

Katz, R. (1982). The effects of group longevity on project communication and performance. *Administrative Science Quarterly, 27*(1), 81–104.

Katzell, R.A., & Austin, J.T. (1992). From then to now: The development of Industrial organizational psychology in the United States. *Journal of Applied Psychology, 77*, 803–835.

Katzenbach, J.R., & Smith, D.K. (1993). *The wisdom of teams: Creating a high-performance organization*. Boston: Harvard Business School Press.

Keller, R.T. (2006). Transformational leadership, initiating structure, and substitutes for leadership: A longitudinal study of R&D project team performance. *Journal of Applied Psychology, 91*, 202–210.

Kelley, E., & Kelloway, E.K. (2008). Remote leadership. In C. Wankel (Ed). *Handbook of 21st century management*. Thousand Oaks, CA: Sage.

Kelloway, E.K. (2003). Labor unions and occupational safety: Conflict and cooperation. In J. Barling & M. Frone (Eds.). *The psychology of workplace safety* (pp. 249–264). Washington, DC: American Psychological Association.

Kelloway, E.K., & Barling, J. (1993). Members' participation in local union activities: Measurement, prediction and replication. *Journal of Applied Psychology, 78*, 262–279.

Kelloway, E.K., & Barling, J. (2000). What we have learned about developing transformational leaders. *Leadership and Organization Development Journal, 21*, 355–363.

Kelloway, E.K., Barling, J., & Agar, S. (1996). Pre-employment predictors of children's union attitudes: The moderating role of identification with parents. *Journal of Social Psychology, 136*, 413–415.

Kelloway, E.K., Barling, J., & Helleur, J. (2000). Enhancing transformational leadership: The roles of training and feedback. *The Leadership and Organizational Development Journal, 21,* 145–149.

Kelloway, E.K., Barling, J., & Hurrell, J.J. (2006). *Handbook of workplace violence.* Thousand Oaks, CA: Sage.

Kelloway, E.K., Barling, J., Kelley, E., Comtois, J., & Gatien, B. (2003). Remote transformational leadership. *The Leadership and Organizational Development Journal, 24,* 163–171.

Kelloway, E.K., Catano, V.M., & Carroll, A. (2000). Psychological involvement in the union. *Canadian Journal of Behavioral Science, 32,* 163–167.

Kelloway, E.K., Catano, V.M., & Southwell, R.E. (1992). The construct validity of union commitment: Development and dimensionality of a shorter scale. *Journal of Occupational Psychology, 65,* 197–211.

Kelloway, E.K., & Day, A.L. (2005a). Building healthy organizations: What we know so far. *Canadian Journal of Behavioural Science, 37*(4), 223–236.

Kelloway, E.K., & Day, A.L. (2005b). Building healthy workplaces: Where we need to be. *Canadian Journal of Behavioural Sciences, 37*(4), 309–312.

Kelloway, E.K., Francis, L., Catano, V.M., Cameron, J.E., & Day, A.L. (2004). *Psychological disorders in the CF: Legal and social issues.* Report Prepared for the Director Human Resources Research and Evaluation. Ottawa, ON: Department of National Defence, Canada.

Kelloway, E.K., Francis, L., Catano, V.M., & Teed, M. (2007). Predicting protest. *Basic and Applied Social Psychology, 29,* 13–22.

Kelloway, E.K., Francis, L., & Montgomery, J. (2005). *Management of occupational health and safety* (3rd ed.). Scarborough, ON: Nelson.

Kelloway, E.K., Gallagher, D., & Barling, J. (2004). Work, employment, and the individual. In B. Kaufman (Ed). *Theoretical advances in industrial relations.* Madison, WI: IRRA.

Kelloway, E.K., & Harvey, S. (1999). Learning to work. In J. Barling & E.K. Kelloway (Eds.). *Young workers: Varieties of experience* (pp. 37–57). Washington, DC: APA Books.

Kelloway, E.K., Hurrell, J.J., & Day, A.L. (2008). Workplace interventions for occupational stress. In K. Näswell, M. Sverke, & J. Hellgren (Eds.). *The individual in the changing working life.* Cambridge: Cambridge University Press.

Kelloway, E.K., Inness, M., Barling, J., Francis, L., & Turner, N. (2010). Loving one's job: Construct development and implications for individual well-being. In D. Ganster & P. L. Perrewe (Eds.), *Research in organizational stress and well-being* (pp. 109–136). Greenwich, CT: JAI.

Kelloway, E.K., Mullen, J., & Francis, L. (2006). Divergent effects of transformational and passive leadership on employee safety. *Journal of Occupational Health Psychology, 11,* 76–86.

Kelloway, E.K., & Newton, T. (1996). Family socialization of union attitudes: The role of parental union and work experiences. *Canadian Journal of Behavioral Science, 28,* 113–120.

Kelloway, E.K., Sivanathan, N., Francis, L., & Barling, J. (2005). Poor leadership. In J. Barling & E.K. Kelloway (Eds.), *Handbook of work stress* (pp. 89–112). Thousand Oaks, CA: Sage.

Kelloway, E.K., Teed, M., & Prosser, M. (2008). Leading to a healthy workplace. In A. Kinder, R. Hughes, & C.L. Cooper (Eds.). *Employee well-being support: A workplace resource* (pp. 25–38). Chichester: John Wiley & Sons.

Kelloway, E.K., & Watts, L. (1994). Pre-employment predictors of union attitudes: Replication and extension. *Journal of Applied Psychology, 79,* 631–634.

Kemery, E.R., Bedeian, A.G., & Rawson Zacur, S. (1996). Expectancy-based job cognitions and job affect as predictors of organizational citizenship behaviours. *Journal of Applied Social Psychology, 26*(7), 635–651.

Kerlinger, F.N. (1986). *Foundations of behavioral research* (3rd ed.). New York: Holt, Rinehart and Winston.

Kerr, S. (1995). On the folly of rewarding A, while hoping for B. *Academy of Management Executive (1993–2005), 9*(1), 7–14.

Kerr, S., & Jermier, J.M. (1978). Substitutes for leadership: Their meaning and measurement. *Organizational Behavior and Human Performance, 22,* 375–403.

Kerr, S., Schriesheim, C.A., Murphy, C.J., & Stogdill, R.M. (1974). Toward a contingency theory of leadership based upon the consideration and initiating structure literature. *Organizational Behavior and Human Performance, 12,* 62–82.

Keyes, J.B. (1995). Stress inoculation training for staff working with persons with mental retardation: A model program. In L.R. Murphy, J.J. Hurrell Jr., S.L. Sauter, & G.P. Keita (Eds.), *Job stress interventions* (pp. 45–56). Washington, DC: American Psychological Association.

Kiecolt-Glaser, J.K., McGuire, L., Robles, T., & Glaser, R. (2002). Psychoneuroimmunology: Psychological influences on immune function and health. *Journal of Consulting and Clinical Psychology, 70*(3), 537–547.

Kilburg, R.R. (1996). Towards a conceptual understanding and definition of executive coaching. *Consulting Psychology Journal, 48*(2), 134–144.

Kilburg, R.R. (2000). *Executive coaching: Developing managerial wisdom in a world of chaos.* Washington, DC: APA Books.

Kilburg, R.R. (2001). Facilitating intervention adherence in executive coaching: A model and methods. *Consulting Psychology Journal: Practice and Research, 53*(4), 251–266.

King, W.C., Miles, E.W., & Day, D.D. (1993). A test and refinement of the equity sensitivity construct. *Journal of Organizational Behaviour, 14,* 301–317.

Kirkpatick, D.L. (1967). Evaluation of training. In R.L. Craig & L.R. Bittel (Eds.), *Training and development handbook* (pp. 87–112). New York: McGraw-Hill.

Kirkpatrick, S.A., & Locke, E.A. (1996). Direct and indirect effects of three core charismatic leadership components on performance and attitudes. *Journal of Applied Psychology, 81,* 36–51.

Kivimäki, M., Elovainio, M., Vahtera, J., & Ferrie, J.E. (2003). Organisational justice and health of employees: Prospective cohort study. *Occupational and Environmental Medicine, 60,* 27–34.

Kivimäki, M., Ferrie, J.E., Brunner. E., Head. J., Shipley, M.J., Vahtera, K., & Marmot, M. (2005). Justice at work and reduced risk of coronary heart disease among employees: The Whitehall II study. *Archives of Internal Medicine, 165,* 2245–2251.

Klandermans, B. (1997). *The social psychology of protest.* Oxford: Blackwell.

Klandermans, B. (2002). How group identification helps to overcome the dilemma of collective action. *The American Behavioral Scientist, 45,* 887–900.

Kleinmuntz, B. (1990). Why we still use our heads instead of formulas: Toward an integrative approach. *Psychological Bulletin, 107,* 296–310.

Kline, T.J.B. (1989). *Guidelines for graduate training.* Canadian Society of Industrial/Organizational Psychology.

Kline, T.J.B. (1996). Defining the field of industrial-organizational psychology. *Canadian Psychology, 37*(4), 205–209.

Kline, T.J.B. (1999). *Remaking teams: the revolutionary research-based guide that puts theory into practice.* San Francisco, CA: Jossey-Bass.

Knouse, S.B. (1983). The letter of recommendation: Specificity and favorability of information. *Personnel Psychology, 36,* 331–342.

Kochan, T.A. (1980). *Collective bargaining and industrial relations: From theory to policy and practice.* Homewood, IL: Richard D. Irwin.

Kodz, J., Davis, S., Lain, D., Strebler, M., Rick, J., Bates, P., et al. (2003). Working long hours: A review of the evidence. *The Institute for Employment Studies.* London, UK: Department of Trade and Industry.

Komaki, J., Coombs, T., & Schepman, S. (1991). Motivational implications of reinforcement theory. In R.M. Steers & L.W. Porter (Eds.), *Motivation and work behaviour* (pp. 87–107). New York: McGraw-Hill.

Komaki, J., Heinzmann, A.T., & Lawson, L. (1980). Effect of training and feedback: Component analysis of a behavioural safety program. *Journal of Applied Psychology, 65,* 261–270.

Kombarakaran, F.A., Yang, J.A., Baker. M.N., & Fernandes, P.B. (2008). Executive coaching: It works! *Consulting Psychology Journal: Practice & Research, 60*, 78–90.

Konovsky, M. (2000). Understanding procedural justice and its impact on business organizations. *Journal of Management, 26*, 489–511.

Konovsky, M.A., & Cropanzano, R. (1991). Perceived fairness of employee drug testing as a predictor of employee attitudes and job performance. *Journal of Applied Psychology, 76*(5), 698–707.

Koppes, L.L. (2007). *Historical perspectives in industrial and organizational psychology.* Mahwah, NJ: Lawrence Erlbaum & Associates

Koppes, L.L., & Pickren, W. (2007). Industrial and organizational psychology: An evolving science and practice. In L.L. Koppes (Ed). *Historical perspectives in industrial organizational psychology* (pp. 3–36). Mahwah, NJ: Lawrence Erlbaum & Associates.

Kornhauser, A. (1965). *Mental health of the industrial worker.* New York: Wiley

Koslowsky, M. (1990). Staff/line distinctions in job and organizational commitment. *Journal of Occupational Psychology, 63*(2), 167–173.

Kossek, E.E. (2003, June). Workplace policies and practices to support work and family: Gaps in implementation and linkages to individuals and organizational effectiveness. Paper presented at Workforce/Workplace Mismatch: Work, Family, Health and Well-Being. Washington, DC.

Kouvonen, A., Kivimäki, M., Elovainio, M., Vaananen, A., DeVogli,. R., Heponiemi, T., Linna, A., Pentti, J., & Vahtera, J. (2008). Low organizational justice and heavy drinking: A prospective cohort study. *Occupational and Environmental Medicine, 65*, 44–50.

Kozlowski, S., & Bell, B.S. (2003). Work groups and teams in organizations. In W.C. Borman, D.R. Ilgen, and R.J. Klimosky (Eds.), *Handbook of psychology. Industrial and organizational psychology* (Vol. 12, pp. 333–376). Hoboken, NJ: Wiley.

Kozlowski, S., & Ilgen, D.R. (2006). Enhancing the effectiveness of work groups and teams. *Psychological Science in the Public Interest, 7*(3), 77–124.

Kozlowski, S.W.J., Brown, K.G., Weissbein, D.A., Cannon-Bowers, J.A., & Salas, E. (2000). A multilevel approach to training effectiveness. In K.J. Klein & S.W.J. Kozlowski (Eds.), *Multilevel theory, research, and methods in organizations: Foundations, extensions, and new directions* (pp. 57–210). San Francisco, CA: Jossey-Bass.

Kozlowski, S.W.J., & Klein, K.J. (2000). A multilevel approach to theory and research in organizations: Contextual, temporal, and emergent processes. In K.J. Klein & S.W.J. Kozlowski (Eds.), *Multilevel theory, research and methods in organizations: Foundations, extensions, and new directions* (pp. 3–90). San Francisco, CA: Jossey-Bass.

Kozlowsky, M., Sagie, A., Krausz, M., & Dolman Singer, A. (1997). Correlates of employee lateness: Some theoretical consideration. *Journal of Applied Psychology, 82*(1), 79–88.

Kraeplin, E. (1896). A measure of mental capacity. *Appleton's Popular Science Monthly, 49*, 192–229.

Kristof, A.L. (1996). Person-organization fit: An integrative review of its conceptualizations, measurement, and implications. *Personnel Psychology, 49*, 1–49.

Kristof-Brown, A.L. (2000). Perceived applicant fit: Distinguishing between recruiters' perceptions of person-job fit and person-organization fit. *Personnel Psychology 53*, 643–671.

Kristof-Brown, A.L., Zimmerman, R.D., & Johnson, E.C. (2005). Consequences of individuals' fit at work: A meta-analysis of person-job, person-organization, person-group, and person-supervisor fit. *Personnel Psychology, 58*, 281–342.

Kuo, F., & Yu, C. (2009). An exploratory study of trust dynamics in work-oriented virtual teams. *Journal of Computer-Mediated Communication, 14*, 823–854.

Lahti, R.K. (1999). Identifying and integrating individual level and organizational level core competencies. *Journal of Business and Psychology, 14*, 59–75.

LaHuis, D.M., & Mellor, S. (2001). Anti-union and pro-union attitudes as predictors of college students' willingness to join a union. *Journal of Psychology, 135*(6), 661–681.

Lambert, M.J., & Bergin, A.E. (1994). The effectiveness of psychotherapy. In A.E. Bergin & S.L. Garfield (Eds.), *Handbook of psychotherapy and behavior change* (4th ed., pp. 143–189). Oxford, England: John Wiley & Sons.

Lamerson, C.D., & Kelloway, E.K. (1996). Towards a model of peacekeeping stress. *Canadian Psychology, 37,* 195–204.

Landy, F., Quick, J.C., & Kasl, S. (1997). Work, stress, and well-being. *International Journal of Stress Management, 1*(1), 33–73.

Landy, F.J. (1992). Hugo Munsterberg: Victim or visionary. *Journal of Applied Psychology, 77,* 787–202.

Landy, F.J. (1997). Early influences on the development of industrial and organizational psychology. *Journal of Applied Psychology, 82,* 467–477.

Landy, F.L. (1992). *Psychology of work behavior* (4th ed.). Pacific Grove, CA: Brooks/Cole.

Latham, G.P. (1988). The influence of Canadian researchers on organizational psychology. *Canadian Psychology, 2*(1), 11–17.

Latham, G.P., & Locke, E.A. (2006). Enhancing the benefits and overcoming the pitfalls of goal setting. *Organizational Dynamics, 35*(4), 332–340.

Latham, G.P., & Mann, S. (2006). Advances in the science of performance appraisal: implications for practice. *International Review of Industrial and Organizational Psychology, 21,* 295–337.

Latham, G.P., & Saari, L.M. (1984). Do people do what they say? Further studies on the situational interview. *Journal of Applied Psychology, 69,* 569–573.

Latham, G.P., Saari, L.M., Pursell, E.D., & Campion, M.A. (1980). The situational interview. *Journal of Applied Psychology, 65,* 422–427.

Latham, G.P., & Seijts, G.H. (1997). The effect of appraisal instrument on managerial perceptions of fairness and satisfaction with appraisals from peers. *Canadian Journal of Behavioural Science, 29,* 278–282.

Latham, G.P., & Wexley, K.N. (1981). *Increasing productivity through performance appraisal.* Reading, MA: Addison-Wesley.

Latham, G.P., & Yukl, G. (1975). Assigned versus participative goal setting with educated and uneducated woods workers. *Journal of Applied Psychology, 60*(3), 299–302.

Lau, V.C.S., Au, W.T., & Ho, J.M.C. (2003). A qualitative and quantitative review of antecedents of counterproductive behaviors in organizations. *Journal of Business and Psychology, 18,* 73–99.

Laughlin, P.R., Bonner, B.L., & Miner, A.G. (2002). Groups perform better than the best individuals on letters-to-numbers problems. *Organizational Behaviour and Human Decision Processes, 88,* 605–620.

Lawler, E.E. (1986). *High involvement management.* San Francisco, CA: Jossey-Bass.

Lazarus, R.S., & Folkman, S. (1984). *Stress, appraisal, and coping.* New York: Springer Publishing Company.

Le Pine, J.A., Erez, A., & Johnson, D.E. (2002). The nature and dimensionality of organizational citizenship behavior: A critical review and meta-analysis. *Journal of Applied Psychology, 87,* 52–65.

LeBlanc, M.M., & Kelloway, E.K. (2002). Predictors and outcomes of workplace violence and aggression. *Journal of Applied Psychology, 87,* 444–453.

Lee, K., & Allen, N.J. (2002). Organizational citizenship behaviour and workplace deviance: The role of affect and cognitions. *Journal of Applied Psychology, 87*(1), 131–142.

LeRouge, C., Nelson, A., Blanton, J.E. (2006). The impact of role stress fit and self-esteem on the job attitudes of IT professionals. *Information and Management, 43*(8), 928–938.

Leung, K., Chiu, W., & Au, Y. (1993). Sympathy and support for industrial actions: A justice analysis. *Journal of Applied Psychology, 78,* 781–787.

Leventhal, G.S. (1980). What should be done with equity theory? New approaches to the study of fairness in social relationships. In K. Gergen, M. Greenberg, & R. Willis (Eds.), *Social exchange: Advances in theory and research* (pp. 27–55). New York: Plenum Press.

Levine, E.L. (1983). *Everything you always wanted to know about job analysis.* Tampa, FL: Mariner Publishing Company, Inc.

Levine, E.L., Ash, R.A. & Bennett, N. (1980). Exploratory comparative study of four job analysis methods. *Journal of Applied Psychology, 65,* 524–535.

Levine, E.L., Ash, R.A., Hall, H., & Sistrunk, F. (1983). Evaluation of job analysis methods by experienced job analysts. *Academy of Management Journal, 26,* 339–348.

Levine, E.L., Maye, D.M., Ulm, A., & Gordon, T.R. (1997). A methodology for developing and validating minimum qualifications (MQs). *Personnel Psychology, 50*, 1009–1023.

Li, J., & Lambert, V.A. (2008). Job satisfaction among intensive care nurses from the People's Republic of China. *International Nursing Review, 55*, 34–39.

Lim, B., & Ployhart, R.E. (2004). Transformational leadership: Relations to the five-factor model & team performance in typical and maximum contexts. *Journal of Applied Psychology, 89*(4), 610–621.

Lim, D.H., & Morris, M.L. (2006). Influence of trainee characteristics, instructional satisfaction, and organizational climate on perceived learning and training transfer. *Human Resource Development Quarterly, 17*, 85–115.

Lindsley, D.H., Brass, D.J., & Thomas, J.B. (1995). Efficacy-performance spirals: A multilevel perspective. *Academy of Management Review, 20*, 645–678.

Locke, E.A. (1976). The nature and causes of job satisfaction. In M.D. Dunnette (Ed.), *Handbook of industrial and organizational psychology* (pp. 1297–1349). Chicago: Rand McNally.

Locke, E.A. (1997). The motivation to work: What we know. *Advances in Motivation and Achievement, 10*, 375–412.

Locke, E.A., & Latham, G.P. (1990). *A theory of goal setting and task performance.* Englewood Cliffs, NJ: Prentice Hall.

Locke, E.A., Shaw, K.N., Saari, L.M., & Latham, G.P. (1981). Goal setting and task performance: 1969–1980. *Psychological Bulletin, 90*, 125–152.

Lodahl, T.M., & Kejner, M. (1965). The definition and measurement of job involvement. *Journal of Applied Psychology, 49*, 24–33.

Lopez, A. (2009, October 21). Best companies to work for. *Financial Post.* Retrieved January 14, 2010, from http://www.financialpost.com/story.html?id=2125964.

Lowe, G.S. (2003). Healthy workplaces and productivity: A discussion paper. Ottawa, ON: Minister of Public Works and Government Services.

Lowe, K.B., Kroeck, K.G., & Sivasubramaniam, N. (1996). Effectiveness correlates of transformation and transactional leadership: A meta-analytic review of the MLQ literature. *Leadership Quarterly, 7*, 385–425.

Luthans, F. (2002). The need and meaning of positive organizational behavior. *Journal of Organizational Behavior, 23*, 695–706

Luthans, F., Avey, J.B., & Patera, J.L. (2008). Experimental analysis of a web-based training intervention to develop positive psychological capital. *Academy of Management Learning and Education, 7*(2) 209–221.

Luthans, F., & Peterson, F.J. (2003). 360-degree feedback with systematic coaching: Empirical analysis suggests a winning combination. *Human Resource Management, 42*, 243–256.

Luthans, F., & Stajkovic, A.D. (1999). Reinforce for performance: The need to go beyond pay and even rewards. *Academy of Management Executive, 13*(2), 49–57.

Luthans, F.B., Avolio, B.J., Avey, J.B., & Norman, S.M. (2007). Positive psychological capital: Measurement and relationship with performance and satisfaction. *Personnel Psychology, 60*(3), 541–572.

Luthans, F.B., Norman, S.M., Avolio, B.J., & Avey, J.B. (2008). The mediating role of psychological capital in the supportive organizational climate-employee performance relationship. *Journal of Organizational Behavior, 29*(2), 219–238.

Macan, T.H., & Dipboye, R.L. (1990). The relationship of pre-interview impressions to selection and recruitment outcomes. *Personnel Psychology, 43*, 745–768.

Macan, T.H., & Foster, J. (2004). Managers' reactions to utility analysis and perceptions of what influences their decisions. *Journal of Business and Psychology, 19*, 241–253.

MacBride, A., Lancee, W., & Freeman, S.J.J. (1981). The psychosocial impact of a labor dispute. *Journal of Occupational Psychology, 54*, 125–133.

Macey, W.M., & Schneider, B. (2008). The meaning of employee engagement. *Industrial and Organizational Psychology, 1*, 3–30.

MacMillan, S.K., Stevens, S., & Kelloway, E.K. (2009). History and development of I/O psychology in the Canadian Forces personnel selection branch: 1938–2008. *Canadian Psychology, 50*, 283–291.

Macy, B.A., & Izumi, H. (1993). Organizational change, design, and work innovation: A metaanalysis of 131 North American field studies 1961–1991. In W. Passimore & R. Woodman (Eds.), *Research in organizational change and development.* Greenwich, CT: JAI.

Mael, F.A., & Hirsch, A.C. (1993). Rainforest empiricism and quasi-rationality: Two approaches to objective biodata. *Personnel Psychology, 44,* 719–738.

Maertz, C.P., Jr. (1999). Biographical predictors of turnover among Mexican workers: An empirical study. *International Journal of Management, 16,* 112–119.

Mannix, E., & Neale, M.A. (2005). What difference makes a difference? The promise and reality of diverse teams in organizations. *Psychological Science in the Public Interest, 6*(2), 31–55.

Mansfield, R.S. (1996). Building competency models. *Human Resource Management, 35,* 7–18.

Mantell, M.R. (1994). *Ticking bombs: Defusing violence in the workplace.* Burr Ridge, IL: Irwin.

Manz, C.C. (1992). Self-leading work teams: Moving beyond self-management myths. *Human Relations, 45,* 1119–1140.

Manz, C.C., & Sims, H.P. Jr. (1987). Leading workers to lead themselves: The external leadership of self-managing work teams. *Administrative Science Quarterly, 32,* 106–128.

Mardanov, I.T., Heischmidt, K., & Henson, A. (2008). Leader-member exchange and job satisfaction bond and predicted employee turnover. *Journal of Leadership and Organizational Studies, 15,* 159–175.

Margolis, J.D., & Walsh, J.P. (2003). Misery loves companies: Rethinking social initiatives by business. *Administrative Science Quarterly, 48,* 268–305.

Marshall, K. (2003). Benefits of the job. *Perspectives on Labour and Income, 15,* n.p.

Martel, L., & Caron-Malenfant, E. (2009). 2006 census: Portrait of the Canadian population in 2006: Findings. Ottawa: Statistics Canada. Downloaded on October 21, 2009 from http://www12.statcan.ca/census- recensement/2006/as-sa/97-550/index-eng.cfm?CFID=252932&CFTOKEN=70984358.

Martin, D.C., Bartol, K.M., & Kehoe, P.E. (2000). The legal ramifications of performance appraisal: The growing significance. *Public Personnel Management, 29,* 379–406.

Martin, J.E. (1986). Predictors of individual propensity to strike. *Industrial and Labor Relations Review, 39,* 214–227.

Martinko, M.J. (1988). Observing the work. In S. Gael (Ed.), *The job analysis handbook for business, industry and government* (Vol. I, pp. 419–431). New York: John Wiley & Sons.

Martinko, M.J., Gundlach, M.J., & Douglas, S.C. (2002). Toward an integrative theory of counterproductive workplace behavior: A causal reasoning perspective. *International Journal of Selection and Assessment, 10*(1/2), 36–50.

Martocchio, J.J., & Judge, T.A. (1997). Relationship between conscientiousness and learning in employee training: Mediating influences of self-deception and self-efficacy. *Journal of Applied Psychology, 82,* 764–773.

Martz, W.B. Jr., Vogel, R.R., & Nunamaker, J.F. Jr. (1992). Electronic meeting systems: Results from the field. *Decision Support Systems, 8,* 141–158.

Maslach, C., & Jackson, S.E. (1981). The measurement of experienced burnout. *Journal of Occupational Behaviour, 2,* 99–113.

Maslach, C., Jackson, S.E., & Leiter, M.P. (1996). *Maslach burnout inventory.* (3rd ed.). Palo Alto, CA: Consulting Psychologists Press.

Maslach, C., & Leiter, M.P. (1997). *The truth about burnout.* San Francisco: Jossey Bass.

Maslach, C., Schaufeli, W.B., & Leiter, M.P. (2001). Job burnout. *Annual Review of Psychology, 52,* 397–422.

Maslow, A.H. (1943). A theory of human motivation. *Psychological Review, 50,* 370–396.

Mathieu, J.E., & Zajac, D.M. (1990). A review and meta-analysis of the antecedents, correlates, and consequences of organizational commitment. *Psychological Bulletin, 108*(2), 171–194.

Maume, D.J., Jr. (1999). Glass ceilings and glass escalators: Occupational segregation and race and sex differences in managerial promotions. *Work and Occupations, 26,* 483–509.

Mayer, J.D., Salovey, P., & Caruso, D.R. (2000). Emotional intelligence as zeitgeist, as personality, as a mental ability. In R. Bar-On & J. Parker (Eds.), *The handbook of emotional intelligence: Theory, development, assessment, application at homes, school, in the workplace.* San Francisco: Jossey-Bass.

McClelland, D.C. (1961). *The achieving society.* Princeton, NJ: Van Nostrand.

McClelland, D.C., & Boyatzis, R.E. (1982). Leadership motive pattern and long-term success in management. *Journal of Applied Psychology, 67*(6), 737–743.

McClelland, D.C., & Watson, R.I. (1973). Power motivation and risk-taking behaviour. *Journal of Personality, 41*(1), 121–139.

McCormick, E.J. (1979). *Job analysis: Methods and applications.* New York: AMACOM.

McCormick, E.J., & Jeanneret, P.R. (1991). Position Analysis Questionnaire (PAQ). In S. Gael (Ed.), *The job analysis handbook for business, industry and government* (Vol. II, pp. 825–842). New York: John Wiley & Sons.

McCormick, E.J., Jeanneret, P.R., & Mecham, R.C. (1972). A study of job characteristics and job dimensions as based on the Position Analysis Questionnaire (PAQ). *Journal of Applied Psychology, 56*, 347–367.

McCormick, E.J., Jeanneret, P.R., & Mecham, R.C. (1989). *Position Analysis Questionnaire.* Palo Alto, CA: Consulting Psychologists Press, Inc.

McCurry, P. (1999). New angle on 360-degree feedback. *Director, 53*, 36.

McDaniel, M.A., Morgeson, F.P., Finnegan, E.B., Campion, M.A., & Braverman, E.P. (2001). Use of situational judgment tests to predict job performance: A clarification of the literature. *Journal of Applied Psychology, 86*, 730–740.

McDaniel, M.A., Schmidt, F.L., & Hunter, J.E. (1988). Job experience correlates of job performance. *Journal of Applied Psychology, 73*, 327–330.

McDaniel, M.A., Whetzel, D.L., Schmidt, F.L., & Maurer, S.D. (1994). The validity of employment interviews: A comprehensive review and meta-analysis. *Journal of Applied Psychology, 79*, 599–616.

McGinn, D. (2008, November 14). Beyond the salary, there's perks. *Financial Post.* Retrieved January 14, 2010, from http://www.financialpost.com/personal-finance/family-finance/story.html?id=959175.

McGrath, J.E. (1984). *Groups: Interaction and performance.* Englewood Cliffs, NJ: Prentice Hall.

McHenry, J.J., Hough, L.M., Toquam, J.L., Hanson, M.A., & Ashworth, S. (1990). Project A validity results: The relationship between predictor and criterion domains. *Personnel Psychology, 43*, 335–354.

McKee, M., & Kelloway, E.K. (2009). *Leading to wellbeing.* Paper presented at the annual meeting of the European Academy of Work and Organizational Psychology, Santiago de Compostella, Spain.

McManus, M.A., & Kelly, M.L. (1999). Personality measures and biodata: Evidence regarding their incremental predictive value in the life insurance industry. *Personnel Psychology, 52*, 137–148.

McNally, R.J., Bryant, R.A., & Ehlers, A. (2003). Does early psychological intervention promote recovery from posttraumatic stress? *Psychological Science in the Public Interest, 4*(2), 45–79.

McPhail, S.M., Jeanneret, P.R., McCormick, E.J., & Mecham, R.C. (1991). *Position Analysis Questionnaire: Job analysis manual* (Rev. ed.). Palo Alto, CA: Consulting Psychologists Press, Inc.

McShane, S.L. (1986). The multidimensionality of union participation. *Journal of Occupational Psychology, 59*, 177–187.

Meaning of Working International Research Team. (1987). *The meaning of working.* New York: Academic Press.

Mears, B.L., et al. (1984). *Canadian Human Rights Reporter, 5*, D/3433 (Ontario Human Rights Commission Board of Inquiry, December 1983).

Meglino, B.M., DeNisi, A.S., & Ravlin, E.C. (1993). Effects of previous job exposure and subsequent job status on the functioning of a realistic job preview. *Personnel Psychology, 46*, 803–822.

Meglino, B.M., Ravlin, E.C., & DeNisi, A.S. (1997). When does it hurt to tell the truth? The effect of realistic job reviews on employee recruiting. *Public Personnel Management, 26*, 413–22.

Meindl, J.R. (1995). The romance of leadership as a follower-centric theory: A social constructionist approach. *Leadership Quarterly, 6*, 329–341.

Mellor, S., Holzworth, R.J., & Conway, J.M. (2003). Individual unionization decisions: A multilevel model of cost–benefit influences. *Experimental Psychology, 50(2)*, 142–154.

Mellor, S., Mathieu, J.E., & Swim, J.K. (1994). Cross-level analysis of the influence of local union structure on women's and men's union commitment. *Journal of Applied Psychology, 79*(2), 203–210.

Mellor, S., Paley, M.J., & Holzworth, R.J. (1999). Fans' judgments about the 1994–95 Major League Baseball players' strike. *Multivariate Behavioral Research, 34*(1) 59–87.

Mercer Consulting. (2008, October). *The total financial impact of employee absences: survey highlights*. Retrieved October 9, 2009 from http://www.kronos.com/AbsenceAnonymous/.

Mero, N.P., Guidice, R.M., & Brownie, A.L. (2007). Accountability in a performance appraisal context: The effect of audience and form of accountability on rater response and behavior. *Journal of Management, 33*, 223–252.

Methot, L.L., & Phillips-Grant, K. (1998). Technological advances in the Canadian workplace: An I-O perspective. *Canadian Psychology, 39*, 133–141.

Meyer, C. (1994). How the right measures help teams excel. Harvard Business Review, May-June, 99–122.

Meyer, J.P. (1997). Organizational commitment. In C.L. Cooper & I.T. Robertson (Eds.). *International Review of Industrial and Organizational Psychology* (Vol. 12, pp. 175–228). London: Wiley.

Meyer, J.P., & Allen, N.J. (1991). A three-component model conceptualization of organizational commitment. *Human Resource Management Review, 1*, 61–89.

Meyer, J.P., & Allen, N. (1997). *Commitment in the workplace: Theory, research, and application*. Thousand Oaks, CA: Sage.

Meyer, J.P., Allen, N.J., & Smith, C.A. (1993). Commitment to organizations and occupations: Extension and test of a three-component conceptualization. *Journal of Applied Psychology, 78*(4), 538–551.

Milburn, T.W., Schuler, R.S., & Watman, K.H. (1983). Organizational crisis. Part I: Definition and conceptualization. *Human Relations, 36*(12), 1141–1160.

Miller, C.T., & Kaiser, C.R. (2001). A theoretical perspective on coping with stigma. *Journal of Social Issues, 57*, 73–92.

Miller, C.T., & Major, B. (2000). Coping with prejudice and stigma. In T. Heatherton, R. Kleck, & J.G. Hull (Eds.), *The social psychology of stigma* (pp. 243–272). New York: Guilford.

Milliken, F.J., & Martins, L.L. (1996). Searching for common threads: Understanding the multiple effects of diversity in organizational groups. *Academy of Management Review, 2*(21), 402–433.

Milliman, J., Nason, S., Zhu, C., & DeCieri, H. (2002). An exploratory assessment of the purposes of performance appraisals in North and Central America and the Pacific Rim. *Human Resource Management, 41*, 87–102.

Ministry of Labour. (2010). Protecting workers from workplace violence and workplace harassment. Fact Sheet #2. Toronto: Ontario Ministry of Labour. Available online from: http://www.labour.gov.on.ca/english/hs/pdf/fs_workplaceviolence.pdf.

Mio, J.S., & Goishi, C.K. (1988). The Employee Assistance Program: Raising productivity by lifting constraints. In P. Whitney & R.B. Ochsman (Eds.), *Psychology and productivity* (pp. 105–25). New York: Plenum Press.

Mitchell, T.R., & Daniels, D. (2003). Motivation. In W.C. Borman, D.R. Ilgen, & R.J. Klimosky (Eds.), *Handbook of psychology: Industrial and organizational psychology* (Vol. 12, pp. 225–254). Hoboken, NJ: Wiley.

Mitchell, T.W., & Klimoski, R.J. (1982). Is it rational to be empirical? A test of methods for scoring biographical data. *Journal of Applied Psychology, 67*, 411–418.

Mitra, A., Jenkins, G.D., Jr., & Gupta, N. (1992). A meta-analytic review of the relationship between absence and turnover. *Journal of Applied Psychology, 77*, 879–889.

Monahan, J., Steadman, H. J., Appelbaum, P.S., Robbins, P.C., Mulvey, E.P., Silver, E. et al. (2000). Developing a clinically useful actuarial tool for assessing violence risk. *British Journal of Psychiatry, 176*, 312–319.

Motowidlo, S.J., Borman, W.C., & Schmit, M.J. (1997). A theory of individual differences in task and contextual performance. *Human Performance, 10*, 71–83.

Motowidlo, S.J., & Schmit, M.J. (1999). Performance assessment in unique jobs. In D.R. Ilgen & E.D. Pulakos (Eds.), *The changing nature of performance* (pp. 56–86). San Francisco: Jossey-Bass.

Mount, M.K., & Barrick, M.R. (1995). The Big Five personality dimensions: Implications for research and practice in human resources management. In G.R. Ferris (Ed.), *Research in personnel and human resources management* (Vol. 13, pp. 153–200). Greenwich, CT: JAI Press.

Mount, M.K., Barrick, M.R., & Stewart, G.L. (1998). Five-factor model of personality and performance in jobs involving interpersonal interactions. *Human Performance, 11,* 145–165.

Mount, M.K., Witt, L.W., & Barrick, M.R. (2000). Incremental validity of empirically keyed biodata scales over GMA and the Five Factor personality constructs. *Personnel Psychology, 53,* 299–323.

Mowday, R.T., Porter, L.W., & Steers, R.M. (1982). *Employee-organizational linkages: The psychology of commitment, absenteeism, and turnover.* New York: Academic Press.

Mowday, R.T., Steers, R.M., & Porter, L.W. (1979). The measurement of organizational commitment. *Journal of Vocational Behavior, 14,* 224–247.

Mullen, B., & Cooper, C. (1994). The relationship between group cohesiveness and performance: An integration. *Psychological Bulletin, 115*(2), 210–227.

Mullen, B., Johnson, C., & Salas, E. (1991). Productivity loss in brainstorming groups: A meta-analytic integration. *Basic and Applied Social Psychology, 12*(1), 3–23.

Mullen, J., & Kelloway, E.K. (2010). Occupational health and safety leadership. To appear in L. Tetrick & J. Campbell-Quick (Eds.), *Handbook of occupational health psychology* (2nd ed.). Washington: APA Books.

Mullen, J.E., & Kelloway, E.K. (2009). Safety leadership: A longitudinal study of the effects of transformational leadership on safety outcomes. *Journal of Occupational and Organizational Psychology, 82,* 253–272.

Multi-Health Systems. (2001). *Emotional intelligence: A collection of new measures and industry-leading solutions.* Toronto: Author.

Mulvey, P.W., & Klein, H.J. (1998). The impact of perceived loafing and collective efficacy on group goal processes and group performance. *Organizational Behavior and Human Decision Processes, 74*(1), 62–87.

Münsterberg, H. (1913). *Psychology and industrial efficiency.* Boston: Houghton Mifflin.

Murphy, K.R. (1989). Dimensions of job performance. In R.F. Dillon & J.W. Pelligrino (Eds.), *Testing: Theoretical and applied perspectives* (pp. 218–247). New York: Praeger.

Murphy, K.R., & Balzer, W.K. (1989). Rater errors and rating accuracy. *Journal of Applied Psychology, 74,* 619–624.

Murphy, K.R., & Cleveland, J.N. (1995). *Understanding performance appraisal: Social organizational, and goal-based perspectives.* Thousand Oaks, CA: Sage.

Murphy, L.R., Hurrell, J.J., Jr., Sauter, S.L., & Keita, G.P. (1995). Introduction. In L.R. Murphy, J.J. Hurrell, Jr., S.L. Sauter, & G.P. Keita (Eds.), *Job stress interventions* (pp. xi–xiii). Washington, DC: American Psychological Association.

Murphy, L.R., & Sauter, S.L. (2003). The USA perspective: Current issues and trends in the management of work stress. *Australian Psychologist, 38,* 151–157.

Nakamura, J., & Csikszentmihalyi, M. (2002). The concept of flow. In C.R. Snyder & J.S. Lopez (Eds.), *Handbook of positive psychology* (pp. 89–105). New York: Oxford University Press.

National Academy of Sciences.(2003). *The polygraph and lie detection.* Washington, DC: National Academies Press. Retrieved April 26 online from: http://www.nap.edu/openbook. php?isbn=0309084369.

Nelson, D., & Cooper, C.L. (2007). *Positive organizational behavior.* Thousand Oaks, CA: Sage.

Neuman, G.A., & Wright, J. (1999). Team effectiveness: Beyond skills and cognitive ability. *Journal of Applied Psychology, 84,* 376–389.

Newswire. (2009). http://www.newswire.ca/en/releases/archive/August2009/12/c4455.html.

Nicoletti, J., & Spooner, K. (1996). Violence in the workplace: Response and intervention strategies. In G.R. VandenBos & E.Q. Bulatao (Eds.), *Violence on the job: Identifying risks and developing solutions.* Washington, DC: American Psychological Association.

NIOSH. (2002). *The changing organization of work and the safety and health of working people.* DHHS [NIOSH] Publication No. 2002-16.

NIOSH National Occupational Research Agenda. (20017). Retrieved on April 10, 2007 from www2a.cdc.gov/nora/noratopictemp.asp?rscharea=ier.

Noe, R.A. (1986). Trainees' attributes and attitudes: Neglected influences on training effectiveness. *Academy of Management Review, 11,* 736–749.

Normand, J., Salyards, S.D., & Mahoney, J.J. (1990). An evaluation of pre-employment drug testing. *Journal of Applied Psychology, 75,* 629–639.

Nunnally, J.C., & Bernstein, I.H. (1994). *Psychometric theory* (3rd ed.). New York: McGraw-Hill.

O'Reilly, C.A., Chatman, J.A., & Caldwell, M.M. (1991). People and organizational culture: A Q-sort approach to assessing person-organization fit. *Academy of Management Journal, 34,* 487–516.

Offermann, L.R., & Hellmann, P.S. (1996). Leadership behavior and subordinate stress: A 360° view. *Journal of Occupational Health Psychology, 1,* 382–390.

Oldham, G. R., & Hackman, J. R. (2010). Not what it was and not what it will be: The future of job design research. *Journal of Organizational Behavior, 31,* 463–479.

Olson-Buchanan, J.B. (1996). Voicing discontent: What happens to the grievance filer after the grievance? *Journal of Applied Psychology, 81*(1), 52–63.

Ones, D., & Viswesvaran, C. (1998a). The effects of social desirability and faking on personality and integrity testing for personnel selection. *Human Performance, 11,* 245–269.

Ones, D.S., & Viswesvaran, C. (1998b). Integrity testing in organizations. In R.W. Griffin, A. O'Leary, & J.M. Collins (Eds.), *Dysfunctional behavior in organizations: Vol. 2, Nonviolent Behaviors in Organizations.* Greenwich, CT: JAI Press.

Ones, D.S., & Viswesvaran, C. (2001). Integrity tests and other criterion-focused occupational personality scales (COPS) used in personnel selection. *International Journal of Selection and Assessment, 9,* 31–39.

Ones, D.S., Viswesvaran, C., & Dilchert, S. (2005). Personality at work: Raising awareness and correcting misconceptions. *Human Performance, 18,* 389–404.

Ones, D.S., Viswesvaran, C., & Schmidt, F.L. (1993). Comprehensive meta-analysis of integrity test validities: Findings and implications for personnel selection and theories of job performance. *Journal of Applied Psychology, 78,* 679–703.

Online, N.S. (n.d.). Union membership: Up slightly in 2005. Retrieved December 13, 2006.

Opp, K.D. (1998). Does antiregime action under communist rule affect political protest after the fall? Results of a panel study in East Germany. *The Sociological Quarterly, 39,* 189–213.

Organ, D. (1997). Organizational citizenship behavior: It's construct clean-up time. *Human Performance, 10,* 85–97.

Organ, D.W., & Ryan, K. (1995). A meta-analytic review of attitudinal and dispositional predictors of organizational citizenship behavior. *Personnel Psychology, 48,* 775–802.

Orr, J.M., Sackett, P.R., & Mercer, M. (1989). The role of prescribed and nonprescribed behaviors in estimating the dollar value of performance. *Journal of Applied Psychology, 74,* 34–40.

Ostroff, C., & Kozlowski, S.W. (1992). Organizational socialization as a learning process: The role of information acquisition. *Personnel Psychology, 45,* 849–874.

Owens, W.A. (1976). Biographical data. In M.D. Dunnette (Ed.), *Handbook of industrial and organizational psychology* (pp. 609–50). Chicago: Rand-McNally.

Owens, W.A., & Schoenfeldt, L.F. (1979). Toward a classification of persons. *Journal of Applied Psychology, 65,* 569–607.

Paetzold, R.L. (1998). Workplace violence and employer liability: Implications for organizations. In R.W. Griffin, A. O'Leary-Kelly, & J.M. Collins (Eds.), *Dysfunctional behavior in organizations: Violent and deviant behavior* (pp. 1–42). Stamford, CT: JAI Press.

Pahl, Raymond E. (1988). On work: Historical, comparative, and theoretical approaches. Oxford: Basil-Blackwell.

Parish, D.C. (1989). Relation of the pre-employment drug testing result to employment status: A one-year follow-up. *Journal of General Internal Medicine, 4,* 44–47.

Pelled, L.H. (1996). Demographic diversity, conflict, and work group outcomes: An intervening process theory. *Organization Science, 7,* 615–631.

Personnel Systems and Technologies Corporation. (2000). *The common-metric system.* [Online]. Available: http://cmqonline.com/.

Pesek, J.G., Raehsler, R.D., & Balough, R.S. (2006). Future professionals and managers: Their attitudes toward unions, organizational beliefs, and work ethic. *Journal of Applied Social Psychology, 36*(6), 1569–1594.

Peters, L., & Karren, R.J. (2009). An examination of the roles of trust and functional diversity on virtual team performance ratings. *Group and Organization Management, 34*(4), 479–504.

Peters, L.H., Hartke, D.D., & Pohlmann, J.T. (1985). Fiedler's contingency theory of leadership: An application of the meta-analysis procedures of Schmidt and Hunter. *Psychological Bulletin, 97,* 274–285.

Peterson, C., Park, N., & Seligman, M.E.P. (2005). Assessment of character strengths. In G.P. Koocher, J.C. Norcross, & S.S. Hill II (Eds.), *Psychologists' desk reference* (2nd ed., pp. 93–98). New York: Oxford University Press.

Peterson, C., & Seligman, S. (2004) *Character strengths and virtues: A handbook and classification.* Oxford: Oxford University Press.

Peterson, N.G., & Jeanneret, P.R. (2007). Job analysis: An overview and description of deductive methods. In D.L. Whetzel & G.R. Wheaton (Eds.), *Applied measurement: Industrial psychology in human resources management* (pp. 13–56). Mahwah, NJ: Lawrence Erlbaum Associates.

Peterson, R.B., & Lewin, D. (2000). Research on unionized grievance procedures: Management Issues and Recommendations. *Human Resource Management, 39,* 395–406.

Phillips, J.M. (1998). Effects of realistic job previews on multiple organizational outcomes: A meta-analysis. *Academy of Management Journal, 41,* 673–690.

Piccolo, R.F., & Colquitt, J.A. (2006). Transformational leadership and job behaviors: The mediating role of core job characteristics. *Academy of Management Journal, 49,* 327–340.

Pinder, C.G. (1998). *Work motivation in organizational behaviour.* Upper Saddle River, NJ: Prentice-Hall.

Piotrkowski, C.S., & Stark, E. (1987). Children and adolescents look at their parents' jobs. In J.H. Lewko (Ed.), *How children and adolescents view the world of work* (pp. 3–19). San Francisco: Jossey-Bass.

Ployhart, R.E., & Holtz, B.C. (2008). The diversity-validity dilemma: Strategies for reducing racioethnic and sex subgroup differences and adverse impact in selection. *Personnel Psychology, 6,* 153–172.

Porter, L.W., & Lawler, E.E. (1968). *Managerial attitudes and performance.* Homewood, IL: Irwin.

Posthuma, R.A., Morgeson, F.P., & Campion, M.A. (2002). Beyond employment interview validity: A comprehensive narrative review of recent research and trends over time. *Personnel Psychology, 55,* 1–81.

Prahalad, C., & Hamel, G. (1990, May-June). The core competence of the corporation. *Harvard Business Review,* 79–91.

Pratt, M.G., & Ashforth, B.E. (2003). Fostering meaningfulness in working and at work. In K.S. Cameron, J.E. Dutton, & R.E. Quinn (Eds), *Positive organizational scholarship: Foundations of a new discipline.* San Francisco, CA: Berrett-Koehler Publishers.

Quebec legislation against psychological harassment has nationwide implications. (2004). *HRM Guide,* Retrieved December 28, 2009 from: http://www.hrmguide.net/canada/law/psychological-harassment.htm.

Quick, J.C. (1999). Occupational health psychology: The convergence of health and clinical psychology with public health and preventive medicine in an organizational context. *Professional Psychology, 30,* 123–128.

Quick, J.C., Quick, J.D., Nelson, D.L., & Hurrell, J.J. (Eds.). (1997). *Preventive stress management in organizations.* Washington, DC: American Psychological Association.

Quinn, R.P., & Staines, G.L. (1978). *The 1977 quality of employment survey.* Ann Arbor, MI: Institute for Social Research.

Quinones, M.A., Ford, J.K., & Teachout, M.S. (1995). The experience between work experience and job performance: A conceptual and meta-analytic review. *Personnel Psychology, 48,* 887–910.

R. v. Béland, [1987] 2 S.C.R. 398.

Rafferty, A.E., & Griffin, M.A. (2004). Dimensions of transformational leadership: Conceptual and empirical extensions. *The Leadership Quarterly, 15*(3), 329–354.

Rayner, C., & Cooper, C.L. (2006). Workplace bullying. In E.K. Kelloway, J. Barling, & J.J. Hurrell, Jr. (Eds.), *Handbook of workplace violence.* Thousand Oaks, CA: Sage.

Ree, M.J., and T.R. Carretta. (1998). General cognitive ability and occupational performance. In C.L. Cooper & I.T. Robertson (Eds.), *International review of industrial and organizational psychology* (Vol. 13, pp. 159–184). London: John Wiley & Sons.

Reilly, B., Paci, P., & Holl, P. (1995). Unions, safety committees, and workplace injuries. *British Journal of Industrial Relations, 33,* 275–288.

Reilly, R.R., & Chao, G.T. (1982). Validity and fairness of some alternative employee selection procedures. *Personnel Psychology, 35,* 1–62.

Reitsma, S.J. (1993). *The Canadian corporate response to globalization.* Report No. 10693. Ottawa: Conference Board of Canada.

Rempel, J.K., & Burris, C.T. (2005). Let me count the ways: An integrative theory of love and hate. *Personal Relationships, 12,* 297–313.

Résumé inflation seen on the rise. (1999). *The Globe and Mail* (December 13).

Rhodes, L., & Eisenberger, R. (2002). Perceived organizational support: A review of the literature. *Journal of Applied Psychology, 87,* 698–714.

Richie, B.S., Fassinger, R.E., Linn, S.G., Johnson, J., et al. (1997). Persistence, connection, and passion: A qualitative study of the career development of highly achieving African American-Black and White women. *Journal of Counseling Psychology, 44,* 133–148.

Richman, J.A., Flaherty, J.A., Rospenda, K.M., & Christensen, M. (1992). Mental health consequences and correlates of medical student abuse. *Journal of the American Medical Association, 267,* 692–694.

Riedel, J.E., Baase, C., Hymel, P., Lynch, W., McCabe, M., Mercer, W.R., Peterson, K. (2001). The effect of disease prevention and health promotion on workplace productivity: A literature review. *American Journal of Health Promotion, 15,* 167–190.

Roberts, G. (2002). Employee performance appraisal system participation: A technique that works. *Public Personnel Management, 31,* 333–342.

Robertson Cooper. (2010). "Presenteeism" on the rise as an estimated quarter of UK employees admit to working when ill. Retrieved April 26 online from: http://www.robertsoncooper.com/news/presenteeism.aspx.

Robinson, S.L., & Bennett, R.J. (1995). A typology of deviant workplace behavior: A multidimensional scaling study. *Academy of Management Journal, 38,* 555–572.

Roch, S.G., & McNall, L.A. (2007). An investigation of factors influencing accountability and performance ratings. *The Journal of Psychology, 141,* 499–523.

Rogelberg, S.G., & Brooks-Laber, M.E. (2002). Securing our collective future: Challenges facing those designing and doing research in industrial/organizational psychology. In S.G. Rogelberg (Ed.), *Handbook of research methods in industrial and organizational psychology* (pp. 479–485). Malden, MA: Blackwell Publishers Ltd.

Rolland, J.P. (1999). Construct validity of in-basket dimensions. *European Revue of Applied Psychology, 49,* 251–259.

Rosse, J.G., Steecher, M.D., Miller, J.L., & Levin, R.A. (1998). The impact of response distortion on preemployment personality testing and hiring decisions. *Journal of Applied Psychology, 83,* 634–644.

Roth, P.L., BeVier, C.A., Switzer, F.S., III, & Schippmann, J.S. (1996). Meta-analyzing the relationship between grades and job performance. *Journal of Applied Psychology, 81,* 548–556.

Rothstein, H.R., Schmidt, F.L., Erwin, F.W., Owens, W.A., & Sparks, C.P. (1990). Biographical data in employment selection: Can validities be made generalizable? *Journal of Applied Psychology, 75,* 175–184.

Rotter, J. (1966). Generalized expectations for internal versus external control of reinforcement. *Psychological Monographs, 1* (609).

Rotundo, M., & Sackett, P.R. (2002). The relative importance of task, citizenship and counter productive performance to global ratings of job performance: A policy-capturing approach. *Journal of Applied Psychology, 87,* 66–80.

Rowe, P. (1990). Obituary. Edward C. Webster 1909–1989. *Canadian Psychology, 31,* 181–182.

Rowe, P.M., Williams, M.C., & Day, A.L. (1994). Selection procedures in North America. *International Journal of Selection and Assessment, 2,* 74–79.

Russell, J.A. (1980). A circumplex model of affect. *Journal of Personality and Social Psychology, 39,* 1161–1178.

Ryan, M.K., & Haslam, S.A. (2007). The glass cliff: Exploring the dynamics surrounding the appointment of women to precarious leadership positions. *Academy of Management Review, 32*(2), 549–572.

Ryan, R.M. (1982). Control and information in the interpersonal sphere: An extension of cognitive evaluation theory. *Journal of Personality and Social Psychology, 43,* 450–461.

Ryan, R.M., & Deci, E.L. (2000). Intrinsic and extrinsic motivations: Classic definitions and new directions. *Contemporary Educational Psychology, 25,* 54–67.

Rynes, S.L. (1991). Recruitment, job choice, and post-hire consequences. In M.D. Dunnette & L.M. Hough (Eds.), *Handbook of industrial and organizational psychology* (Vol. 2, pp. 399–444), 2nd ed. Palo Alto, CA: Consulting Psychologists Press.

Rynes, S.L. (1993). Who's selecting whom? Effects of selection practices on applicant attitudes and behaviour. In N. Schmitt, W.C. Borman et al. (Eds.), *Personnel Selection in Organizations* (pp. 240–270). San Francisco: Jossey-Bass.

Rynes, S.L., & Cable, D.M. (2003). Recruitment research in the twenty-first century. In W.C Borman, D.R. Ilgen, & R. Klimoski (Eds.), *Handbook of psychology: Industrial and organizational psychology* (Vol. 12, pp. 55–76). New York: John Wiley & Sons.

Rynes, S.L., Colbert, A.E., & Brown, K.G. (2003). HR professionals' beliefs about effective human resource practices: Correspondence between research and practice. *Human Resource Management, 41,* 149–174.

Saavedra, R., & Kwin, S. (1993). Peer evaluation in self-managing work groups. *Journal of Applied Psychology, 78,* 450–462.

Sackett, P.R. (2007). Revisiting the origins of the typical-maximum performance distinction. *Human Performance, 20,* 179–185.

Sackett, P.R., & Arvey, R.D. (1993). Selection in small N settings. In N. Schmitt, W.C. Borman, & Associates (Eds.), *Personnel selection in organizations* (pp. 418–447). San Francisco: Jossey-Bass.

Sackett, P.R., Burris, L.R., & Callahan, C. (1989). Integrity testing for personnel selection: An update. *Personnel Psychology, 42,* 491–529.

Sackett, P.R., & Larson, J.R., Jr. (1990). Research strategies and tactics in industrial and organizational psychology. In M.D. Dunnette & L.M. Hough (Eds.), *Handbook of industrial and organizational psychology* (Vol. 1, 2nd ed.). Palo Alto: Consulting Psychologists Press, 419–490.

Sackett, P.R., & Wanek, J.E. (1996). New developments in the use of measures of honesty, integrity, conscientiousness, dependability, trustworthiness, and reliability for personnel selection. *Personnel Psychology, 49,* 787–827.

Sackett, P.R., & Wilk, S.L. (1994). Within-group norming and other forms of score adjustment in pre-employment testing. *American Psychologist, 49,* 929–954.

Sackett, P.R., Zedeck, S., & Fogli, L. (1988). Relations between measures of typical and maximum job performance. *Journal of Applied Psychology, 73,* 482–486.

Sagie, A., Birati, A., & Tziner, A. (2002). Assessing the costs of behavioral and psychological withdrawal: A new model and an empirical illustration. *Applied Psychology: An International Review, 51,* 67–89.

Sagie, A., & Koslowsky, M. (2000). *Participation and empowerment in organizations.* Thousand Oaks, CA: Sage.

Saks, A.M., & Belcourt, M. (2006). An investigation of training activities and transfer of training in organizations. *Human Resource Management, 45,* 629–648.

Saks, A.M., & Haccoun, R.R. (2004). *Managing performance through training and development* (3rd ed.). Toronto: Nelson Canada.

Saks, A.M., Leck, J.D., & Saunders, D.M. (1995). Effects of application blanks and employment equity on applicant reactions and job pursuit intentions. *Journal of Organizational Behavior, 16,* 415–430.

Saks, A.M., Schmitt, N., & Klimoski, R.J. (2000). *Research, measurement, and evaluation of human resources.* Scarborough, ON: Nelson.

Saks, A.M., Wiesner, W.H., & Summers, R.J. (1996). Effects of job previews and compensation policy on applicant attraction and job choice. *Journal of Vocational Behavior, 49,* 68–85.

Salas, E., De Rouin, R.E., & Gade, P.A. (2007). The military's contribution to our science and practice: People, places and findings. In L.L. Koppes (Ed.), *Historical perspectives in industrial organizational psychology* (pp. 169–192). Mahwah, NJ: Lawrence Erlbaum & Associates

Salgado, J.F. (1997). The five factor model of personality and job performance in the European Community. *Journal of Applied Psychology, 82,* 30–43.

Salovey, P., & Mayer, J.D. (1990). Emotional intelligence. *Imagination, Cognition, and Personality, 9,* 185–211.

Sauter, S.L., Hurrell, J.J., & Murphy, L.R. (1990). Prevention of work-related psychological disorders: A national strategy proposed by the National Institute for Occupational Safety and Health (NIOSH). *American Psychologist, 45*(10), 1146–1158.

Sauter, S.L, & Hurrell Jr., J.J. (1999). Occupational health psychology: Origins, content, and direction. *Professional Psychology: Research and Practice, 30*(2), 117–122.

Scales, A., Kelloway, E.K., & Francis, L. (2010). *Crossing the line: Managers' experiences during a strike.* Manauscript under review.

Scharf, A. (1989). How to change seven rowdy people. *Industrial Management, 31,* 20–22.

Schat, A.C.H., Frone, M.R., & Kelloway, E.K. (2006). Prevalence of workplace aggression in the U.S. workforce. In E.K. Kelloway, J. Barling, & J.J. Hurrell, Jr. *Handbook of workplace violence* (pp. 47–89). Thousand Oaks, CA: Sage.

Schaufeli, W., & Bakker, A. (2004). Job demands, job resources, and their relationship with burnout and engagement: A multi-sample study. *Journal of Organizational Behaviour, 25,* 293–315.

Schaufeli, W.B., Bakker, A.B., & Salanova, M. (2006). The measurement of work engagement with a short questionnaire: A cross-national study. *Educational and Psychological Measurement, 66*(4), 701–716.

Schaufeli, W.B., Salanova, M., Gonzalez-Roma, V., & Bakker, A. (2002). The measurement of engagement and burnout: A two-sample confirmatory factor analytic approach. *Journal of Happiness Studies, 3*(1), 71–92.

Schippman, J.S., Prien, E.P., & Katz, J.A. (1990). Reliability and validity of in-basket performance. *Personnel Psychology, 43,* 837–859.

Schmidt, F.L. (2002). The role of general cognitive ability and job performance: Why there cannot be a debate. *Human Performance, 15,* 187–210.

Schmidt, F.L., & Hunter, J.E. (1977). Development of a general solution to the problem of validity generalization. *Journal of Applied Psychology, 62,* 529–540.

Schmidt, F.L., & Hunter, J.E. (1998). The validity and utility of selection methods in personnel psychology: Practical and theoretical implications of 85 years of research findings. *Psychological Bulletin, 124,* 262–274.

Schmidt, F.L., Hunter, J.E., & Outerbridge, A.N. (1986). Impact of job experience and ability on job knowledge, work sample performance, and supervisory ratings of job performance. *Journal of Applied Psychology, 71,* 432–439.

Schmitt, N.A., Gooding, R.Z., Noe, R.A., & Kirsch, M. (1984). Meta-analysis of validity studies published between 1964 and 1982 and the investigation of study characteristics. *Personnel Psychology, 37,* 407–422.

Schmitt, N.A., Schneider, J.R., & Cohen, S.A. (1990). Factors affecting validity of a regionally administered assessment center. *Personnel Psychology, 43*, 2–11.

Schnake, M.E. (1991). Organizational citizenship: A review, proposed model, and research agenda. *Human Relations, 44*, 735–759.

Schriesheim, C.A., Castro, S.L., & Cogliser, C.C. (1999). Leader-member exchange (LMX) research: A comprehensive review of theory, measurement, and data-analytic practices. *Leadership Quarterly, 10*, 63–113.

Schriesheim, C.A., Tepper, B.J., & Tetrault, L.A. (1994). Least preferred co-worker score, situational control and leadership effectiveness: A meta-analysis of contingency model performance predictions. *Journal of Applied Psychology, 79*(4), 561–573.

Schulz-Hardt, S., Jochims, M., & Frey, D. (2002). Productive conflict in group decision making: Genuine and contrived dissent as strategies to counteract biased information seeking. *Organizational Behavior and Human Decision Processes, 88*, 563–586.

Schwenk, C.R. (1990). Effects of devil's advocacy and dialectical inquiry on decision making: A meta-analysis. *Organizational Behavior and Human Decision Processes, 47*, 161–176.

Scott, W.D. (1911). *Increasing human efficiency in business.* New York: MacMillan.

Seijts, G.H., & Crim, D. (2006, March/April). What engages employees most or the Ten C's of employee engagement. *Ivey Business Journal,* 1–5.

Seijts, G.H., Skarlicki, D.P., & Gilliland, S.W. (2003). Canadian and American reactions to drug and alcohol testing programs in the workplace. *Employee Responsibilities and Rights Journal, 15*, 191–208.

Seligman, M.E.P. (1975). *Helplessness: On Depression, development, and death.* San Francisco: W.H. Freeman.

Seligman, M.E.P. (1991). *Learned optimism.* New York: Kopf.

Seligman, M.E.P. (1999). The president's address. *American Psychology, 54*, 559–562.

Seligman, M.E.P., Steen, T., Park, N., & Peterson, C. (2005). Positive psychology progress: Empirical validation of interventions. *American Psychologist, 60*(5), 410–421.

Senge, P. (1990). *The fifth discipline.* London: Century Business.

Seppala, P., Mauno, S., Feldt, T. Hakanen, J., Kinnunen, U., Tolvanen, A., & Schaufeli, W. (2005). The construct validity of the Utrecht work engagement scale: Multisample and longitudinal evidence. *Journal of Happiness Studies, 10*(4), 459–481.

Sewell, G. (1998). The discipline of teams: The control of team-based industrial work through electronic and peer surveillance. *Administrative Science Quarterly, 43*(2), 397–428.

Shao, L., & Webber, S. (2006). A cross-cultural test of the five-factor model of personality and transformational leadership. *Journal of Business Research, 59*, 936–944.

Shields, M. (October, 2006). Unhappy on the job. *Health Reports, 17*(4), 33–37. Statistics Canada, Catalogue 82-003.

Shin, S.J., & Zhou, J. (2003). Transformational leadership, conservation, and creativity: Evidence from Korea. *Academy of Management Journal, 46*, 703–714.

Shippmann, J.S., Ash, R.A., Battista, M., Carr, L., Eyde, L.D., Hesketh, B., Kehoe, J., Pearlman, K., & Prien, E.P. (2000). The practice of competency modeling. *Personnel Psychology, 53*, 703–740.

Shirom, A. (2004). Feeling vigorous at work? The construct of vigor and the study of positive affect in organizations. In D. Ganster & P.L. Perrewe (Eds.), *Research in organizational stress and well-being* (Vol. 3, pp. 135–165). Greenwich, CT: JAI.

Shirom, A., Toker, S., Berliner, S., Shapira, I., & Melamed, S. (2008). The effects of physical fitness and feeling vigorous on self-rated health. *Health Psychology, 27*, 567–575.

Shore, L.M., Newton, L.A., & Thornton, G.C. (1990). Job and organizational attitudes in relation to employee behavioural intentions. *Journal of Organizational Behaviour, 11*(1), 57–67.

Shore, L.M., Tetrick, L.E., Sinclair, R.R., & Newton, L.A. (1994). Validation of a measure of perceived union support. *Journal of Applied Psychology, 79*(6), 971–977.

Siegrist, J. (1996). Adverse health effects of high-effort/low-reward conditions. *Journal of Occupational Health Psychology, 1*(1), 27–41.

Siegrist, J., Peter, R., Junge, A., Cremer, P., & Seidel, D. (1990). Low status control, high effort at work and ischemic heart disease: Prospective evidence from blue-collar men. *Social Science and Medicine, 31*(10), 1127–1134.

Singer Foust, M.S., Elicker, J.D., & Levy, P.E. (2006). Development and validation of a measure of an individual's lateness attitude. *Journal of Vocational Behavior, 69*, 119–133.

Singh, P., Zinni, D., & Jain, H. (2005). The effects of the use of striker replacement workers in Canada: An analysis of four cases. *Labour Studies Journal, 30*(2), 61.

Sjöberg, A., & Sverke M. (2000). The interactive effect of job involvement and organizational commitment on job turnover revisited: A note on the mediating role of turnover intention. *Scandinavian Journal of Psychology, 41*(3), 247–252.

Skarlicki, D.P., & Latham, G.P. (1996), Increasing citizenship within a union: a test of organizational justice theory, *Journal of Applied Psychology, 81*(2), 161–169.

Skarlicki, D.P., & Latham, G.P. (1997). Leadership training in organizational justice to increase citizenship behavior within a labor union: A replication. *Personnel Psychology, 50*(3), 617–633.

Skinner, B.F. (1969). *Contingencies of reinforcement.* New York: Appleton-Century-Crofts.

Smallwood, S. (2004). No surprises please. *Chronicle of Higher Education*, July 30, A8–A9.

Smith, K.G., Smith, K.A., Olian, J.D., Sims, H.P. Jr., O'Bannon, D.P., & Scully, J.A. (1994). Top-management team demography and process: The role of social integration and communication. *Administrative Science Quarterly, 39*, 412–438.

Smith, P.C. (1976). Behaviours, results, and organizational effectiveness: The problem of criteria. In M.D. Dunnette (Ed.), *Handbook of industrial and organizational psychology* (pp. 745–776). Chicago: Rand McNally.

Smith, P.C., & Kendall, L.M. (1963). Retranslation of expectations: An approach to the construction of unambiguous anchors for rating scales. *Journal of Applied Psychology, 47*, 149–155.

Smith, P.C., Kendall, L.M., & Hulin, C.L. (1969). *Measurement of satisfaction in work and retirement.* Chicago: Rand-McNally.

Smith-Jentsch, K.A., Salas, E., & Brannick, M.T. (2001). To transfer or not to transfer? Investigating the combined effects of trainee characteristics, team leader support, and team climate. *Journal of Applied Psychology, 86*, 279–292.

Smither, J.W. (1998). Lessons learned: Research implications for performance appraisal and management practice. In J.W. Smither (Ed.), *Performance appraisal: State of the art in practice.* San Francisco: Jossey Bass.

Smither, J.W., & Reilly, S.P. (2001). Coaching in organizations: A social psychological perspective. In M. London (Ed.), *How people evaluate others in organizations.* Mahwah, NJ: Erlbaum.

Snyder, C.R., Irving, L.M., & Anderson, J.R. (1991). Hope and health. In C.R. Snyder & D.R. Forsyth (Eds.), *Handbook of social and clinical psychology: The health perspective* (pp. 285–305). Elmsford, NY: Pergamon Press.

Society for Industrial and Organizational Psychology, Inc. (2003). *Principles for the validation and use of personnel selection procedures* (4th ed.). College Park, MD: Author.

Somers, M.J. (1995). Organizational commitment, turnover and absenteeism: An examination of direct and interaction effects. *Journal of Organizational Behavior, 16*(1), 49–58.

Sonnentag, S. (2001). Work, recovery activities, and individual well-being: A diary study. *Journal of Occupational Health Psychology, 6*, 196–210.

Sonnentag, S., & Bayer, U. (2005). Switching off mentally: Predictors and consequences of psychological detachment from work during off-job time. *Journal of Occupational Health Psychology, 10*, 393–414.

Sonnentag, S., & Frese, M. (2003). Stress in organizations. In W.C. Borman, D.R. Ilgen, & R.J. Klimoski (Eds.), *Handbook of psychology: Industrial and organizational psychology* (Vol. 12, pp. 453–491). Hoboken, NJ: John Wiley & Sons.

Sonnentag, S., & Fritz, C. (2007). The recovery experience questionnaire: Development and validation of a measure for assessing recuperation and unwinding from work. *Journal of Occupational Health Psychology, 12*, 204–221.

Soya, G. (2006). Industrial relations: Strikes and lockouts: What do the data tell us? *Canadian HR Reporter, 9,* 27.

Sparks, C.P. (1988). Legal basis for job analysis. In S. Gael (Ed.), *The job analysis handbook for business, industry and government* (Vol. I, pp. 37–47). New York: John Wiley & Sons.

Spector, P., Fox, S., & Domagalski, T. (2006). Emotions, violence, and counterproductive work behaviors. In E.K. Kelloway, J. Barling, & J.J. Hurrell, Jr. *Handbook of workplace violence* (pp. 29–46). Thousand Oaks, CA: Sage.

Spector, P.E. (1986). Perceived control by employees: A meta-analysis of studies concerning autonomy and participation at work. *Human Relations, 39*(11), 1005–1016.

Spector, P.E., & Fox, S. (2002). An emotion-centred model of voluntary work behaviour: Some parallels between counterproductive work behaviour and organizational citizenship behaviour. *Human Resource Management Review, 12,* 269–292.

Spector, P.E., Fox, S., Penney, L.M., Bruursema, K., Goh, A., & Kessler, S. (2006). The dimensionality of counterproductivity: Are all counterproductive behaviors created equal? *Journal of Vocational Behavior, 68,* 446–460.

Spence, R. (2007, June). Bright ideas! Electrify your employees and supercharge your sales with the management tactics of Canada's fastest growing companies. *Profit.* Retrieved on January 26, 2010, from http://www.canadianbusiness.com/entrepreneur/managing/article.jsp?content=2007 0601_102910_5560&page=1.

Spreitzer, G.M., & Quinn, R.E. (1996). Empowering middle managers to be transformational leaders. *Journal of Applied Behavioural Science, 32*(3), 237–261.

Srivastava, A., Bartol, K.M., & Locke, E.A. (2006). Empowering leadership in management teams: Effects on knowledge sharing, efficacy, and performance. *Academy of Management Journal, 49*(6), 1239–1251.

Stagner, R., & Eflal, B. (1982). Internal union dynamic during a strike: A quasi-experimental study. *Journal of Applied Psychology, 67,* 37–44.

Stajkovic, A.D., & Luthans, F. (1998). Self-efficacy and work-related performance: A meta analysis. *Psychological Bulletin, 24,* 240–261.

Stampfer, M.J., Hu, F.B., Manson, J.E., Rimm, E.B., & Willett, W.C. (2000). Primary prevention of coronary heart disease in women through diet and lifestyle. *The New England Journal of Medicine, 343,* 16.

Stansfeld, S.A., Fuhrer, R., Shipley, M.J., & Marmot, M.G. (2002). Psychological distress as a risk factor for coronary heart disease in the Whitehall II Study. *International Journal of Epidemiology, 31*(1), 248–255.

Statistics Canada. (2009). *Labour force information, Sept 13-19, Catalog # 71-001-X* Ottawa, ON: Author. Downloaded from http://www.statcan.gc.ca/pub/71-001-x/71-001-x2009009- eng.pdf, October 17, 2009.

Staw, B.M., & Barsade, S.G. (1993). Affect and managerial performance: A test of the sadder-but-wiser vs. happier-and-smarter hypotheses. *Administrative Science Quarterly, 38,* 304–331.

Sternberg, R.J. (1986). A triangular theory of love. *Psychological Review, 93,* 119–135.

Sternberg, R.J. (1987). Liking versus loving: A comparative evaluation of theories. *Psychological Bulletin, 102,* 331–345.

Stokes, G.S., & Cooper, L.A. (1994). Selection using biodata: Old notions revisited. In G.S. Stokes, M.D. Mumford, & W.A. Owens (Eds.). *Biodata Handbook* (pp. 103–138). Mahwah, NJ: Erlbaum.

Stokes, G.S., Mumford, M.D., & Owens, W.A. (Eds.). (1994). *Biodata handbook.* Mahwah, NJ: Erlbaum.

Stouffer, S.A. (1949). *The American soldier: Vol. 1 Adjustment during Army life.* Princeton, NJ: Princeton University Press.

Strauss, M. (2000, March 28). Retailers plagued by thieving employees. *The Globe and Mail,* A1.

Sulsky, L.M., & Keown, J.L. (1998). Performance appraisal in the changing world of work: Implications for the meaning and measurement of work performance. *Canadian Psychology, 39,* 52–59.

Sundstrom, E., DeMeuse, K.P. & Futrell, D. (1990). Work teams: Applications and effectiveness. *American Psychologist, 45,* 120–133.

Sundstrom, E., McIntyre, M., Halfhill, T., & Richards, H. (2000). Work groups: From the Hawthorne Studies to the work teams of the 1990s. *Group Dynamics, 4,* 44–67.

Sweeney, P.D., & McFarlin, D.B. (1993). Workers' evaluations of the "ends" and the "means": An examination of four models of distributive and procedural justice. *Organizational Behavior and Human Decision Processes, 55*(1), 23–40.

Taggar, S., & Ellis, R. (2007). The role of leaders in shaping formal team norms. *The Leadership Quarterly, 18*(2), 105–120.

Tannenbaum, S.I., Matthieu, J.E., Salas, E., Cannon-Bowers, J.A. (1991). Meeting trainees' expectations: The influence of training fulfillment on the development of commitment, self-efficacy, and motivation. *Journal of Applied Psychology, 76,* 759–769.

Tasa, K., Taggar, S., & Seijts, G.H. (2007). The development of collective efficacy in teams: A multilevel and longitudinal perspective. *Journal of Applied Psychology, 92*(1), 17–27.

Taylor, H.C., & Russell, J.F. (1939). The relationship of validity coefficients to the practical effectiveness of tests in selection: Discussion and tables. *Journal of Applied Psychology, 23,* 565–578.

Taylor, P.J., & Small, B. (2002). Asking applicants what they would do versus what they did do: A meta-analytic comparison of situational and past behaviour employment interview questions. *Journal of Occupational and Organizational Psychology, 75,* 277–294.

Taylor, S.E., Klein, L.C., Lewis, B.P., Gruenewald, T.L., Gurung, R.A.R., & Updegraff, J.A. (2000). Behavioral responses to stress in females: Tend-and-befriend, not fight-or-flight. *Psychology Review, 107*(3), 411–429.

Temple, W. (1992, April/May). Counterproductive behaviour costs millions. *British Journal of Administrative Management,* 20–21.

Tepper, B.J. (2000). Consequences of abusive supervision. *Academy of Management Journal, 43,* 178–190.

Tepper, B.J. (2007). Abusive supervision in work organizations: Review synthesis, and research agenda. *Journal of Management, 33,* 261–289.

Tepper, B.J., & Percy, P.M. (1994). Structural validity of the Multifactor Leadership Questionnaire. *Educational and Psychological Measurement, 54*(3), 734–744.

Tetrick, L.E., & Quick, J.C. (2003). Prevention at work: Public health in occupational settings. In J.C. Quick & L.E. Tetrick (Eds.), *Handbook of occupational health psychology* (pp. 3–17). Washington, DC: American Psychological Association.

Tett, R.P., Jackson, D.N., & Rothstein, M. (1991). Personality measures as predictors of job performance: A meta-analytic review. *Personnel Psychology, 44,* 703–742.

"The legalities of providing a reference check on a former employee." (2007). *AXIOM International Reference Checking Service.* Online: http://www.axiom-int.com/survey_legalities.htm.

Thibaut, J., & Walker, L. (1975). *Procedural justice: A psychological analysis.* Hillsdale, NJ: Erlbaum.

Thieblot, A.J., & Haggard, T.R. (1983). *Union violence: The record and the response by the courts, legislatures, and the NLRB.* Philadelphia: Industrial Research Unit, Wharton School, University of Pennsylvania.

Thomason, J.A., & Pond, S.B. (1995). Effects of instruction on stress management skills and self-management skills among blue-collar employees. In L.R. Murphy, J.J. Hurrell, Jr., S.L. Sauter, & G.P. Keita (Eds.), *Job stress interventions* (pp. 7–20). Washington, DC: American Psychological Association.

Thompson, C.A., Beauvais, L.L., & Lyness, K.S. (1999). When work-family benefits are not enough: The influence of work-family culture on benefit utilization, organizational attachment, and work family conflict. *Journal of Vocational Behavior, 54,* 392–415.

Thompson, D.E., & Thompson, T.A. (1982). Court standards for job analysis in test validation. *Personnel Psychology, 35,* 872–873.

Thompson, L.F., & Coovert, M.D. (2003). Teamwork online: The effects of computer conferencing on perceived confusion, satisfaction, and post-discussion accuracy. *Group Dynamics: Theory, Research, and Practice, 7*(3), 135–151.

Thun, B.N. (2009). Leadership: A Matter of Character. Unpublished PhD Dissertation, Saint Mary's University, Halifax, NS.

Tinsley, H.E. (2000). The congruency myth. *Journal of Vocational Behaviour, 56,* 147–179.

Tobias, L.L. (1990). *Psychological consulting to management: A clinician's perspective.* New York: Brunner Mazel.

Tobias, L.L. (1996). Coaching executives. *Consulting Psychology Journal: Practice & Research, 48,* 87–95.

Townsend, J., Phillips, J., & Elkins, T. (2000). Employee retaliation: The neglected consequence of poor leader-member exchange relations. *Journal of Occupational Health Psychology, 5,* 457–463.

Travagline, A.M. (2002). Online recruiting: Implementing Internet-based realistic job previews. *Dissertation Abstracts International: Section B: The Sciences and Engineering, 63(1-b),* 579.

Trembley, M.A., Blanchard, C.M., Taylor, S., Pelletier, L.G., & Villeneuve, M. (2008). Work extrinsic and intrinsic motivation scale: Its value for organizational psychology research. *Canadian Journal of Behavioural Sciences, 41*(4), 213–226.

Tubbs, M.E. (1994). Commitment and the role of ability in motivation: Comment on Wright, O'Leary-Kelly, Cortina, Klein, and Hollenbeck. *Journal of Applied Psychology, 79,* 804–811.

Tucker, D., & Rowe, P.M. (1976). Consulting the application form prior to the interview: An essential step in the selection process. *Journal of Applied Psychology, 62,* 283–287.

Tuckman, B.W. (1965). Developmental sequence in small groups. *Psychological Bulletin, 63,* 384–399.

Turban, D.B., Campion, J.E., & Eyrung, A.R. (1995). Factors related to job acceptance decisions of college recruits. *Journal of Vocational Behavior, 47,* 193–213.

Tyler, K. (2000). Scoring big in the workplace. *HR Magazine, 45*(6), 96–106.

Tyler, P., & Cushway, D. (1995). Stress in nurses: The effects of coping and social support. *Stress Medicine, 11,* 243–251.

Tziner, A., Murphy, K.R., & Cleveland, J.N. (2005). Contextual and rater factors affecting rating behavior. *Group & Organizational Management, 30,* 89–98.

Uggerslev, K., & Sulsky, L. (2008). Using frame-of-reference training to understand the implications of rater idiosyncrasy for rating accuracy. *Journal of Applied Psychology, 93,* 711–719.

Van Den Broeck, A., Vansteenkiste, M., & De Witte, H. (2008). Self-determination theory: A theoretical and empirical overview in occupational health psychology. In J. Houdmont & S. Leka (Eds.), *Occupational health psychology: European perspectives on research, education, and practice* (pp. 63–88). Nottingham: Nottingham University Press.

van der Klink, J.J., Blonk, R.W., & van Dijk, F.J. (2001). The benefits of interventions for work-related stress. *American Journal of Public Health, 91*(2), 270–276.

Van der Vegt, G.S., & Janssen, O. (2003). Joint impact of interdependence and group diversity on innovation. *Journal of Management, 29*(5), 729–751.

Van Katwyk, P.T., Fox, S., Spector, P.E., & Kelloway, E.K. (2000). Using the Job Related Affective Well-Being Scale (JAWS) to investigate affective responses to work stressors. *Journal of Occupational Health Psychology, 5*(2), 219–230.

Vance, R.L., Coovert, M.D., MacCallum, R.C., & Hedge, J.W. (1989). Construct models of task performance. *Journal of Applied Psychology, 74,* 447–455.

Vandenberghe, C., & Tremblay, M. (2008). The role of pay satisfaction and organizational commitment in turnover intentions: A two-sample study. *Journal of Business and Psychology, 22*(3), 275–286.

VanScotter, J.R., & Motowidlo, S.J. (1996). Interpersonal facilitation and job dedication as separate facets of contextual performance. *Journal of Applied Psychology, 81,* 525–531.

Vinchur, A.J., & Koppes, L.L. (2007). Early contributors to the science and practice of industrial psychology. In L.L. Koppes (Ed.), *Historical perspectives in industrial organizational psychology* (pp. 37–60). Mahwah, NJ: Lawrence Erlbaum & Associates.

Vinchur, A.J., Schippmann, J.S., Switzer, F.S., III, & Roth, P.L. (1998). A meta-analytic review of predictors of job performance for salespeople. *Journal of Applied Psychology, 83,* 586–597.

Violanti, J.M. (1992). Coping strategies among police recruits in a high stress training environment. *Journal of Social Psychology, 132,* 717–729.

Visser, J. (2002). Why fewer workers join unions in Europe: A social custom explanation of membership trends. *British Journal of Industrial Relations, 40,* 403–430.

Visser, J. (2006). Union membership statistics in 24 countries. *Monthly Labor Review.*

Viswesvaran, C., & Ones, D.S. (2000). Perspectives on models of job performance. *International Journal of Selection and Assessment, 8,* 216–226.

Viswesvaran, C., Sanchez, J.I., & Fisher, J. (1999). The role of social support in the process of work stress: A meta-analysis. *Journal of Vocational Behavior, 54,* 314–334.

Viteles, M.S. (1932). *Industrial psychology.* New York: Norton.

Vroom, V.H. (1964). *Work and motivation.* New York: Wiley.

Wager, N., Feldman, G., & Hussey, T. (2003). The effect on ambulatory blood pressure of working under favourably and unfavourably perceived supervisors. *Occupational and Environmental Medicine, 60,* 468–474.

Wagner, C. (2007). Organizational commitment as a predictor variable in nursing turnover research: Literature review. *Journal of Advanced Nursing, 60*(3), 235–247.

Wagner, S.H., & Goffin, R.D. (1997). Differences in accuracy of individual and comparative performance appraisal methods. *Organizational Behavior and Human Decision Processes, 70,* 95–103.

Wall, T., Kemp, N., Jackson, P., & Clegg, C. (1986). Outcomes of autonomous work groups: A long-term field experiment. *Academy of Management Journal, 29*(2), 280–304.

Wallin, L., & Wright, I. (1986). Psychosocial aspects of the work environment: A group approach. *Journal of Occupational Medicine, 28*(5), 384–393.

Walton, R., & McKersie, R. (1965). *A behavioral theory of labor negotiations.* Ithaca: ILR Press.

Wanek, J.E. (1999). Integrity and honesty testing: What do we know? How do we use it? *International Journal of Selection and Assessment, 7,* 183–195.

Wang, M. (2007). Profiling retirees in the retirement transition and adjustment process: Examining the longitudinal change patterns of retirees' psychological well-being. *Journal of Applied Psychology, 92,* 455–474.

Wang, M., & Russell, S.S. (2005). Measurement equivalence of the Job Descriptive Index across Chinese and American workers: Results for confirmatory factor analysis and item response theory. *Educational and Psychological Measurement, 65,* 709–732.

Wanous, J.P. (1980). *Organizational entry: Recruitment, selection, and socialization of newcomers.* Reading, MA: Addison-Wesley.

Wanous, J.P., Poland, T.D., Premack, S.L., & Davis, K.S. (1992). The effects of met expectations on newcomer attitudes and behaviors: A review and meta-analysis. *Journal of Applied Psychology, 77*(3), 288–297.

Wanous, J.P., Reichers, A.E., & Hudy, M.J. (1997). Overall job satisfaction: How good are single-item measures? *Journal of Applied Psychology, 82,* 247–252.

Warr, P.B. (1987). *Work, unemployment and mental health.* Oxford: Clarendon Press.

Warren, A., & Kelloway, E.K. (2010). Retirement timing in the context of the decision to abolish mandatory retirement. *International Journal of Manpower Planning, 31,* 281–305.

Wasylyshyn, K.M. (2003). Executive coaching: An outcome study. *Consulting Psychology Journal: Practice and Research, 55*(2), 94–106.

Weatherbee, T., & Kelloway, E.K. (2006). Cyber-aggression. In E.K. Kelloway, J. Barling, & J.J. Hurrell (Eds.), *Handbook of workplace violence.* Thousand Oaks, CA: Sage.

Webber, S., & Donahue, L. (2001). Impact of highly and less job-related diversity on work group cohesion and performance: A meta-analysis. *Journal of Management, 27,* 141–162.

Weber, M. (1905/2002). *The Protestant ethic and "the spirit of capitalism."* New York: Penguin.

Weber, M. (1947). *The theory of social and economic organizations* (translated by T. Parsons). NY: Free Press.

Webster, E.C. (1964). *Decision-making in the employment interview.* Montreal: McGill University Industrial Relations Center.

Webster, E.C. (1982). *The employment interview: A social judgment process.* Schomberg, ON: S.I.P. Publications.

Webster, E.C. (1988). I/O psychology in Canada from birth to Couchiching. *Canadian Psychology, 29*(1), 4–11.

Weekley, J., & Ployhart, R. (Eds.). (2006). *Situational judgment tests: Theory, measurement, and application.* Mahwah, NJ: Lawrence Erlbaum Associates.

Wegge, J., Schmidt, K., Parkes, C., & van Dick, R. (2007). 'Taking a sickie': Job satisfaction and job involvement as interactive predictors of absenteeism in a public organization. *Journal of Occupational and Organizational Psychology, 80,* 77–89.

Weil, D. (1995). Mandating safety and health committees: Lessons from the United States. Proceedings of the 47th annual meeting of the Industrial Relations Research.

Weiner, B.J., Hobgood, C., & Lewis, M.A. (2008). The meaning of justice in incident reporting. *Social Science and Medicine, 66*(2), 403–413.

Weiss, D.J., Dawis, R.V., England, G.W., & Lofquist, L.H. (1967). *Manual for the Minnesota Satisfaction Questionnaire.* Minneapolis: University of Minnesota.

Weiss, H.M., & Brief, A.P. (2001). Affect at work: An historical perspective. In R.L. Payne & C.L. Cooper (Eds.), *The psychology of work: Theoretically based empirical research.* Hillsdale, NJ: Lawrence Erlbaum.

Weiss, H.M., Nicholas, J.P., & Daus, C.S. (1999). An examination of the joint effects of affective experiences and job beliefs on job satisfaction and variations in affective experiences over time. *Organizational Behavior and Human Decision Processes, 78,* 1–24.

Welch, J., & Byrne, J.A. (2003). *Jack: Straight from the gut.* New York: Business Plus.

Werner, J.M., & Bolino, M.C. (1997). Explaining U.S. courts of appeals decisions involving performance appraisal: Accuracy, fairness, and validation. *Personnel Psychology, 50,* 1–24.

Wertheimer, B.M., & Nelson, A.H. (1980). Trade union women: A study of their participation in New York City locals. NY: Praeger Publications.

Westaby, J.D., Versenyi, A., & Hausmann, R.C. (2005). Intentions to work during terminal illness: An exploratory study of antecedent conditions. *Journal of Applied Psychology, 90,* 1297–1305.

Westman, M., & Eden, D. (1997). Effects of a respite from work on burnout: Vacation relief and fade-out. *Journal of Applied Psychology, 82,* 516–527.

Westman, M., & Etzion, D. (2001). The impact of vacation and job stress on burnout and absenteeism. *Psychology & Health, 16,* 595–606.

Wheelan, S.A. (2009). Group size, group development, and group productivity. *Small Group Research, 40*(2), 247–262.

Whetten, D.A., & Cameron, K.S. (1995). *Developing management skills* (3rd ed.). New York: HarperCollins.

White, B. (1988). *Hard bargains: My life on the line.* Toronto: McLelland & Stewart.

Whitehead, A.N. (1967). *Science and the modern world.* New York: Free Press.

Whyte, G., & Latham, G.P. (1997). The futility of utility analysis revisited: When even an expert fails. *Personnel Psychology, 50,* 601–610.

Wiersema, M.F., & Bird, A. (1993). Organizational demography in Japanese firms: Group heterogeneity, individual dissimilarity, and top management team turnover. *Academy of Management Journal, 36,* 996–1025.

Wiesner, W.H., & Cronshaw, S.R. (1988). A meta-analytic investigation of the impact of interview format and degree of structure on the validity of the employment interview. *Journal of Occupational Psychology, 61,* 275–290.

Williams, C. (2003). Sources of workplace stress. *Perspectives on Labour and Income, 4,* 5–12.

Williams, H., & Allen, N. (2008). Teams at work. *The SAGE handbook of organizational behavior, 1,* 124–141.

Wimbush J.C., & Dalton, D.R. (1997). Employee theft: Convergence of multiple methods. *Journal of Applied Psychology, 82,* 756–763.

Wittig-Berman, U., & Lang, D. (1990). Organizational commitment and its outcomes: Differing effects of value commitment and continuance commitment on stress reactions, alienation, and organization-serving behaviours. *Work and Stress, 4*(2), 167–177.

Wofford, J.C., & Liska, L.Z. (1993). Path-goal theories of leadership: A meta-analysis. *Journal of Management, 19,* 857–876.

Work in America (A report of a special task force to the Secretary of Health, Education, and Welfare). (1974). Cambridge, MA: MIT Press.

Wright, M.A. (1974). CPA: The first 10 years. *The Canadian Psychologist, 15,* 112–131.

Wright, T.A. (2003). Positive organizational behavior: An idea whose time has truly come. *Journal of Organizational Psychology, 24,* 437–442.

Wright, T.A., Cropanzano, R., Denney, P.J., Moline, G.L. (2002). When a happy worker is a productive worker: A preliminary examination of three models. *Canadian Journal of Behavioural Science, 34*(3), 146–150.

Wright, T.A., & Goodstein, J. (2007). Character is not "dead" in management research: A review of individual character and organizational-level virtue. *Journal of Management, 33*(6), 928–958.

Wrzesniewski, A., & Dutton, J.E. (2001). Crafting a job: Revisioning employees as active crafters of their work. *Academy of Management Review, 26,* 179–201.

Wrzesniewski. A., McCauley, C.R., Rozin, P., & Schwartz, B. (1997). Jobs careers and callings: Peoples' relations to their work. *Journal of Research in Personality, 31,* 21–33.

Xie, J.L., & Johns, G. (2000). Interactive effects of absence culture salience and group cohesiveness: A multi-level and cross-level analysis of work absenteeism in the Chinese context. *Journal of Occupational and Organizational Psychology, 73,* 31–52.

Yerema, R., & Caballero, R. (2009, November 2). Employer review: Research In Motion Limited. Retrieved January 14, 2010, from http://www.eluta.ca/top-employer-rim.

Yerkes, R.M. (1921). Psychological examining in the United States Army: Memoirs of the National Academy of Sciences (Vol XV). Washington, DC: US Government Printing office.

Zacarro, S.J., Ardison, S.D., & Orvis, K.L. (2004). Leadership in virtual teams. In D.V. Day, S.J. Zaccaro, & S.M. Halpin (Eds.), *Leader development for transforming organizations: Growing leaders for tomorrow.* New Jersey: Lawrence Erlbaum Associates.

Zacharatos, A., Barling, J., & Kelloway, E.K. (2000). Development and effects of transformational leadership in adolescents. *Leadership Quarterly, 11,* 211–226.

Zazanis, M.M., Zaccaro, S.J., & Kilcullen, R.N. (2001). Identifying motivation and interpersonal performance using peer evaluations. *Military Psychology, 13,* 73–88.

Zeller, K.L., Perrewe, P.L., & Hochwarter, W.A. (1999). Mitigating burnout among high-NA employees in health care: What can organizations do? *Journal of Applied Social Psychology, 29*(11), 2250–2271.

Zickar, M.J., & Drasgow, F. (1996). Detecting faking on a personality instrument using appropriateness measurement. *Applied Psychological Measurement, 20,* 71–87.

Ziegler, R., Diehl, M., & Zijlstra, G. (2000). Idea production in nominal and virtual groups: Does computer-mediated communication improve group brainstorming? *Group Processes and Intergroup Relations, 3*(2), 141–158.

Zohar, D. (2002a). Modifying supervisory practices to improve submit safety: A leadership-based intervention model. *Journal of Applied Psychology, 87*(1), 156–163.

Zohar, D. (2002b). The effects of leadership dimensions, safety climate, and assigned priorities on minor injuries in work groups. *Journal of Organizational Behavior, 23,* 75–92.

Zottoli, M.A., & Wanous, J.P. (2000). Recruitment source research: Current status and future directions. *Human Resource Management Review, 10,* 353–382.

Zupek, R. (2009). 12 funny excuses for being late for work. Retrieved October 9, 2009 from http://www.careerbuilder.ca/Article/CB-479-Workplace-Issues-12-Funny-Excuses-for-Being-Late-to-Work/?sc_extcmp=cbca_9479&cblang=CAEnglish&SiteId=cbca_9479.

Name Index

Subject Index

Note: Figures and tables are indicated by "f" or "t," respectively, following the page number.